The Politics of Authenticity

COLUMBIA STUDIES IN CONTEMPORARY
AMERICAN HISTORY SERIES

The Politics of Authenticity

Liberalism, Christianity, and the New Left in America

Doug Rossinow

Columbia University Press

NEW YORK

Columbia University Press
Publishers Since 1893
New York   Chichester, West Sussex

Copyright © 1998 Douglas C. Rossinow
Library of Congress Cataloging-in-Publication Data

Rossinow, Douglas C. (Douglas Charles)
The politics of authenticity : liberalism, Christianity, and the New Left
in America / Doug Rossinow.
p.   cm. — (Columbia studies in contemporary American history series)
Includes bibliographical references (p.   ) and index.
ISBN 0-231-11056-1 (acid-free paper)
1. New Left—United States. 2. Christianity and politics—United States.
I. Title. II. Series.
HN90.R3R64   1998
306.2'0973—dc21   97-42950

Casebound editions of Columbia University Press books are printed on
permanent and durable acid-free paper.
Printed in the United States of America
c 10 9 8 7 6 5 4 3 2 1

CONTENTS

PREFACE   *vii*

INTRODUCTION: *From the Age of Anxiety to the Politics of Authenticity*   *1*

Part One

1. *This Once Fearless Land: Secular Liberals Under Right-Wing Rule*   *23*
2. *Breakthrough: The Relevance of Christian Existentialism*   *53*
3. *The Issues of Life: The University YMCA–YWCA and Christian Liberalism*   *85*
4. *To Be Radical Now: Civil Rights Protest and Leftward Movement*   *115*

Part Two

5. *These People Were from America: The New Left Revisited*   *159*
6. *Against Rome: The New Left and the Vietnam War*   *209*
7. *This Whole Screwy Alliance: The New Left and the Counterculture*   *247*
8. *The Revolution Is Yet to Come: The Feminist Left*   *297*

EPILOGUE: *From the Politics of Authenticity to the Politics of Identity*   *335*

NOTES   *347*

BIBLIOGRAPHY   *453*

INDEX   *481*

UNLIKE MOST PREVIOUS historians of the 1960s, the origin of my scholarship does not lie in a personal involvement with the events and movements about which I write. I am not old enough, by many years, to have been involved in the new left, much less the civil rights movement of the cold war era; I am not a Christian believer; I am not very countercultural (in the usual sense of the term); and I am not a Texan. As an undergraduate in the 1980s, I simply stumbled on the new left as a historical topic, never having heard of this movement before.

Although I did not witness the movements chronicled here (save as an infant and, at that, only on television), this in no way furnishes me with an objective viewpoint. Rather, my own experiences give me a particular perspective on the events I discuss. In the late 1980s, my political outlook underwent significant changes, and learning that there had been a "new left" in the United States during the 1960s, I was eager to see what I might learn from its experience. Early on, I was occupied not only with the expository question of what these people had said and done but also with the question of why their movement had "failed," that is, why it had lost its bid to transform American politics and why it had collapsed around 1970. The reflection of my own situation is clear. Why did there seem to be so little guidance available to those who were only then coming to a critical outlook on their society? Why were the connections to the past severed so cleanly?

These questions are flawed, but that is somewhat beside the point, since they no longer guide my analysis. I have come to think that the new left's greatest historical significance lies not in its impact but in its meaning, including its meaning for the larger political world from which it emerged. To neglect the vociferous opposition that the new left directed toward the political and cultural order in which new left radicals lived would be foolish and misleading. I intend no such neglect when I state that possibly the single comment most consistent with my own perspective on this movement is Raymond Williams's remark that "the dominant culture . . . at once produces and limits its own forms of counter-culture." The civil rights movement, the cold war, and the cultural experience of certain social groups in the twentieth-century United States converged to produce the new left of the 1960s. This was a movement of opposition, but opposition on the most intimate of terms. In an effort either to validate or to indict this opposition, however, sometimes the intimacy gets lost.

It is clear to me that my perspective on the new left is a product of the politically conservative times in which I have researched and written this book. Once, around 1960, historians interested in the history of American radicalism—likewise shaped by a young adulthood in conservative times—came to discern deep affinities between American dissent and the American mainstream. They were inclined to look at the larger structures of political expression and action, and disinclined to romanticize rebels of the past, sympathy notwithstanding. I have gradually come to feel a certain kinship with this group of historians. They sometimes are termed an "in-between" generation, since they were too young to have been deeply involved in the "old left" of the 1930s and 1940s and too old to be part of the new left (although they have been labeled the first "new left" historians). I feel a strong and sometimes partisan sympathy for the people about whom I write. However, my purpose here is neither praise nor burial. In the future, this book may seem like the product of another "in-between" time. One can always hope.

Several institutions have supported this book's writing. The Johns Hopkins University history department, the Smithsonian Institution's National Museum of American History (NMAH), and the Pew Program in Religion and American History at Yale University provided generous financial support, for which I extend my gratitude. At NMAH, my sponsor, Charlie McGovern, and the doyenne of the fellows' office, Mary Dyer, offered unfailing reassurance. Lee Baker, Carolyn Goldstein, Peggy Shaffer, and I formed a postdissertation reading group at the museum, which supplied both an unsurpassed level of attention to works in progress and crucially timed camaraderie. Jon Butler, Harry Stout, and their support staff at the Pew Program, who are playing a central role in an important area of historical scholarship, enabled me to bring this project to completion sooner than otherwise would have been feasible. They also ran a splendid fellows' conference at Yale. Most recently, I have enjoyed the support of Michael Bernstein, Michael Parrish, and others at the University of California at San Diego, where I have been a visiting scholar.

I wish to thank all those who let me interview them for this book or who wrote me with their recollections. Without their cooperation, this book, as I imagined it, would have been impossible. I am grateful to Kristin Henry for helping me to locate many of my correspondents. I have not specifically cited every interview I conducted, but all the personal information I gathered helped shape my understanding of the time and place about which I have written. Casey Hayden, Al Lingo, and Jim Neyland were especially generous with their time and attention. I conducted many of the interviews in Texas, where Sally Clarke and Peter Jelavich showed me remarkable hospitality.

Many friends and colleagues graciously found the time to read and comment on all or part of this manuscript at some point in its development (even if they didn't know that was what they were reading). For this I thank Lee Baker, Brian Balogh, Alan Brinkley, Sally Clarke, Pete Daniel, Sandy Dijkstra, David Farber, Richard Flathman, Steve Fraser, Lou Galambos, Carolyn Goldstein, Steve Hahn, Casey Hayden, Lisa Cobbs Hoffman, Jonathan Holloway, Daniel Horowitz, Maurice Isserman, Cathy Kerr, Rebecca Klatch, George Lipsitz, Walter Benn Michaels, Michael Parrish, Leo Ribuffo, Dorothy Ross, Erica Schoenberger, Peggy Shaffer, Jim Sidbury, Gaddis Smith, Julian Zelizer, and Jon Zimmerman. At the NMAH library, Jim Roan and Bridget Burke performed yeoman service in tracking down obscure theological texts and rolls of microfilm. I'm sorry if I've forgotten anyone.

At the Johns Hopkins University, I learned a great deal about the practice of history, none of which I will recount here. I thank my teachers in the history department there—Lou Galambos, Dorothy Ross, Ron Walters, and JoAnne Brown—for all they taught me, and the department's support staff—Sarah Springer, Sharon Widomski, and Shirley Hipley—for answering uncounted questions. Lou and Dorothy have been avid in their support for this project since I earned my Ph.D. Dorothy gave me a rare and highly valuable teaching opportunity at Hopkins. Lou and Jane Eliot Sewell have shown me good cheer on many an occasion. As I developed my project in its initial stages, Lou provided a kind of mixed economy of dissertation advising: intellectual laissez-faire combined with material and emotional protectionism. As John Kenneth Galbraith once said, "It works." Lou and Brian Balogh have shown unstinting encouragement for many years, through thick and thin; I'm happy to count them as friends as well as teachers.

Alan Brinkley and William Leuchtenburg, editors of the Columbia Studies in Contemporary American History series, and Kate Wittenberg, editor in chief at Columbia University Press, have believed in this book since they first saw an earlier draft, and it has been a pleasure to work with them. I thank Margaret B. Yamashita for her work on the manuscript. I got my first education in twentieth-century U.S. history listening, as an undergraduate, to Alan's lectures—an advantageous start. His recent advice and support have greatly strengthened this book's finish.

My parents, Rhoda and Ed Rossinow, somewhere got the idea that I would not damage myself badly if I spent a lot of time reading books, so they let me. They have continually expressed their support for a course of action that, I know, has sometimes seemed mysterious to them. For this and for other things, I thank them. My sisters, Jill and Sharon, likewise have been consistently encouraging (as well as offering me places to crash when I've been in New York). I thank Bob Lowen, the late Joan Lowen, Sara Lowen, and Tom Omestad for their interest in this project and their friendship along the way; Bob also has offered indispensable technical support. Rebecca Lowen's belief in me and in this book has never faltered. The book has benefited from her razor-sharp skills as a reader and editor, and her high professional standards have provided me with a valuable benchmark, but her faith in me has proved most important. We married for better and for worse. Owing to circumstances outside our control, we've had some of each already, and she has been impressive throughout. Thanks, Becky; the best is yet to come.

From the Age of Anxiety to the Politics of Authenticity

THIS IS A STUDY of the political culture of the United States between the late 1940s and the early 1970s. It traces the somewhat surprising emergence of a "new" political left following the politically conservative era of the 1950s, the flowering of this left in the 1960s, and its frustration in the 1970s. This "new left" stemmed from white youth participation in civil rights activism in the late 1950s and early 1960s. It attracted considerable attention in the early 1960s by promoting a project of both formal and social democracy, the emphasis on formal or "participatory democracy" receiving the most attention from the movement's members and sympathizers. In the late 1960s the new left gained adherents rapidly, especially on college and university campuses around the United States, in step with the mounting frustration among Americans in general with the course of the Vietnam War. Yet this movement had dissipated as a coherent force for radical political change by the time the Paris Peace Accords officially ended the war in January 1973.

The new left broke sharply with the thought and activism of the "old left" of the 1930s and 1940s. By the late 1940s, hopes for a working-class-based social democracy—the dominant vision of the left in the previous century—had been severely dampened in the United States. Fewer than ten years later, small numbers of Americans, largely independent of one another, began laying the groundwork for a new left that would draw on a drastically different social and intellectual basis than had the old left. Although Students for a

Democratic Society (SDS), the main new left organization, advocated in its *Port Huron Statement* (1962) a liberal–labor–civil rights coalition, SDS nonetheless broke with what the radical sociologist C. Wright Mills called the "labor metaphysic" of the old left and promoted universities, not factories or working-class neighborhoods, as the most promising sites of left-wing insurgency.[1]

The new left was a movement of white, college-educated young people, few of whom ever had known poverty. Material deprivation provided neither their main explanation of insurgency nor their prime argument for social change. In fact, new left radicals launched what many have called a "postscarcity" radicalism, directing their basic criticism at the "affluent society" itself, which they, along with many liberals and conservatives of the 1950s and 1960s, considered an achieved fact. Under the influence of Mills's writings and the civil rights movement, the new left from its start viewed students and African Americans as the two groups most likely to stimulate radical social change in the United States. For a time, the new left viewed the poor—a category they differentiated sharply from the working class, for new left radicals endorsed the widespread belief that the U.S. working class was comfortable and conservative—as the agent of social change. Yet even here the new left saw the poor's political potential arising not from economic want but from political "alienation."[2]

The broad salience of the term *alienation* is the key to understanding the post–World War II left's shift away from a materialist strategy. Possibly no word was used more frequently in discussions of political discontent in the United States during the period considered here. *Alienation* means "estrangement," and Americans in the 1950s and 1960s applied this term to many contexts—different individuals and groups can be estranged from a variety of things and people, after all—and paradoxically, it took on both positive and negative connotations among dissidents. Black Americans and the poor of all races were alienated from the formal political system, perhaps even from the values that underlay the social system (the argument went), so they might prove willing to storm the palace gates, unlike the industrial working class, which had been "bought off," given a "seat at the table." Marginality was the key to radical agency.

The new left radicals sometimes asserted that college students likewise sat outside the political system and therefore also had insurgent potential, but more often the new left emphasized the strategic location of students in the universities, which were increasingly important components in the nation's political economy. It was not easy to argue that students—especially those who had grown up in an era of unprecedented material abundance and whose leading role in the consumer culture was increasingly recognized—were marginal. Yet many observers had noted a malaise among affluent youth as early as the 1950s and had labeled this a variety of alienation. Not surprisingly, new left activists devoted a great deal of time to pondering the sources and meaning of this middle-class alienation.[3]

Those who found the prospect of radical change less attractive than did the new left found the phenomenon of alienation politically worrisome, not cheering. Many political liberals expressed dismay, and did so for years before the new left came on the scene, at the link they discerned between alienation and depoliticization. (Levels of voter participation had been dropping since the turn of the century, with a temporary reversal during the 1930s, and they continued to do so until the century drew to a close.) Political liberals feared a listless and perhaps volatile citizenry. The sociologist Kenneth Keniston called alienated, affluent youth "the uncommitted." As early as 1949, as the cold war deepened, the influential historian, publicist, and liberal activist Arthur Schlesinger Jr. foresaw widespread political and moral alienation, and in the context of what John F. Kennedy later called the "long twilight struggle" against communism, an alienated citizenry seemed worrisome indeed.[4]

Alienation, Schlesinger argued, stemmed from an inability to cope with the cultural impact of industrialization, and he feared political tyranny would be the ultimate result. The transition to industrial modernity had "devitaliz[ed] the old religions while producing nothing new capable of controlling pride and power." Americans lived in an "age of anxiety," he explained. Anxiety meant the awareness of moral and social alienation, the feeling of floating adrift on foreign seas, a feeling that opened the way to brutal regimes offering a sense of certainty through a "totalitarian" program. "Red fascism," as some called communism, held a genuine appeal for many who were stricken with anxiety, Schlesinger believed, because it offered both new social forms and a new creed. The diplomat George Kennan feared that for this reason, communism would triumph. Schlesinger, too, doubted that the political culture of democracy, whose "thinness" he bemoaned, could win out over communism as a solution to alienation. "The spectacular reopening of these problems [of anxiety] in our time," he concluded bleakly, "finds the democratic faith lacking in the profounder emotional resources. Democracy has no defense-in-depth against the neuroses of industrialism."[5]

The new left, shaped by cold war anticommunism and by the collapse of the Stalinist left in the United States, set out to prove wrong this line of thought. It sought to chart a third way between the politics of communism and of anticommunism by showing that if invigorated and expanded, the culture of democracy could defeat the forces of alienation and anxiety.

Turning the politics of estrangement upside down, new left radicals asserted that alienation somehow could propel people out of anxiety and into social commitment—which was the polar opposite of alienation. Since these radicals favored drastic social and political change, the condition of alienation actually appeared as an opportunity, since an estrangement from society seemed like a prerequisite for recruitment into a new radical movement. Still, bringing people from alienation into commitment would not be easy. The new left argued that only a radical vision of democracy—a vision much more radical than anything Schlesinger entertained—could serve as the ideal that would bring water from the rock, commitment and wholeness from alienation and anxiety.

For all the social and political alienation that they observed among blacks or the poor, the new radicals of the 1960s agreed with scholars like Keniston that they themselves experienced a distinctive kind of alienation. But unlike Keniston, they felt that this alienation of the affluent provided the surest basis for new left recruitment. They felt their own alienation was an estrangement less from dominant social norms, or from conventional political activity, than from their own real selves. This estrangement from one's self caused subjective feelings like anxiety. The theologian Paul Tillich and other existentialists had long made this argument in a more spiritual vein. The fundamental estrangement that caused anxiety, they believed, was an alienation from God. According to existentialist thought, a state of unity with the self or the divine or, as Tillich put it in his disembodied way, "the ground of Being" furnished a kind of inner wholeness. This wholeness was the opposite of alienation in an internal sense, just as commitment was the opposite of social alienation; this inner wholeness was the state of authenticity. Adopting an existentialist outlook, the new left came to argue that social and political arrangements caused inner alienation and that only radical social change would open the path to authenticity. Thus a growing understanding among affluent youth of their own predicament would inspire this segment of the population to seek the twin goals of authenticity and democratization.

The search for authenticity lay at the heart of the new left. The new left was not simply a movement of opposition, the antithesis of the society that produced it, or merely an eccentric cousin of the Marxist left. Rather, it was a logical development of broad strains in twentieth-century politics and culture. Although the quest for authenticity stretches across industrial American history, only after World War II did it become a widespread preoccupation. T. J. Jackson Lears sees a sensation of "weightlessness"—a feeling of insubstantiality or inauthenticity—among the American upper class at the turn of the twentieth century. Christopher Lasch was the first to recognize that concern over this predicament, and a consequent desire to make contact with "real life," animated some of those on the modern political left, usually those from rather genteel backgrounds. In 1965 he termed this "the new radicalism."[6] At almost exactly the same time, the combination of the search for authenticity with leftist politics acquired a popular basis. Amid conditions of broad affluence, mass consumption, the bureaucratization of many areas of social life, and increasing disengagement from formal political participation, feelings of weightlessness migrated down the social scale, appearing among much broader strata of American society and leading to a widespread yearning for authenticity. Unlike the pessimistic upper-class yearning in earlier times for "real" experience, the young people who sought authenticity in the early cold war often believed strongly that they would achieve their personal and political goals. The triumphalism of cold war America influenced them as much as did American anxiety.[7]

The intersection of the search for authenticity and political life produced what, looking backward, we can see as a tradition of existentialist politics in these middle strata in cold war America. Not inappropriately, this politics appeared most conspicuously in the country's universities, among students whose experience in those institutions during the cold war had become the single clearest mark of "middle-class" identity. The poles of alienation and authenticity define existentialism, and existential politics spins political analysis and action between these two poles. It is not merely a historian's conceit to call this politics existentialist. The vocabulary of existentialism became widely popular in the United States in the 1950s and 1960s, and the young people considered in this book made it the means of expressing their personal and political hopes. They talked all the time about becoming "real" or "natural" or "authentic" and about transcending their generation's "alienation." Existentialism did not simply overtake the new left in its later years, displacing a rational, deliberative project aimed at cultivating participatory democracy, as some argue. Rather, existentialism was a powerful element in this movement from the start. The *Port Huron Statement* asserted that the "goal of man and society should be . . . finding a meaning in life that is personally authentic," and the new left's ultimate aim was to alter social arrangements so as to allow as many people as possible to pursue that goal.[8]

In the late 1950s and early 1960s, clusters of American youth became enamored of different variants of existentialism. While many high school and college students spent hours in coffeehouses over paperback volumes edited by Walter Kaufmann or written by Jean-Paul Sartre or Albert Camus (who was the more readable and the more read of the Frenchmen), the most organized and most politically consequential source of existentialist ideas in this era—still unknown to many today—was the student Christian movement of the nation's campuses.[9] The Student Young Men's Christian Association–Young Women's Christian Association (YMCA–YWCA), along with other, less far-flung organizations, immersed interested students in the heady intellectual currents then swirling through American and world Christianity, introducing young adults to such authors as Tillich, Rudolf Bultmann, and Dietrich Bonhoeffer. This environment offered Christian existentialism as a way of understanding both social and personal concerns and as a means of bringing the two together. The Student Y convened thousands of collegians at the end of 1958 for a national conference whose official theme was "The Search for Authentic Experience," encouraging a quest for personal meaning and authenticity, for a path out of alienation. In the world of Christian existentialism, salvation was returned to its original, therapeutic meaning: the healing of a wound, the bridging of the awful separation of the human from the divine. Sin was translated as alienation, and salvation now meant authenticity.[10]

This therapeutic quest for authenticity did not lead away from the world of politics; quite the contrary. The student Christian movement brought the legacy of the earlier social gospel movement into the cold war era and expressed an unusually spirited dissent from the prevailing conservative trend of the 1950s. The Student Y's association with an embattled liberal politics was never far from the surface. Most important was the identification of this Christian liberalism with racial egalitarianism. The student Christian movement was biracial; increasingly it was racially integrated; and in the 1950s, it facilitated an extraordinary degree of interaction between black and white youth.

In the mid-1950s, the questions of racial separation and inequality came to the fore in American public life. The U.S. Supreme Court's 1954 decision in *Brown v. Board of Education* invalidated public school segregation, and in 1956 the boycott by black residents of bus lines in Montgomery, Alabama, enjoyed success and also propelled Martin Luther King Jr. to national attention. With signs of weakness showing in the edifice of southern segregation, the minds of idealistic, socially concerned youth turned to the question of how to hasten a process of change that seemed to have begun. Many of them drew connections between inner alienation and the estrangement of the nation into racial parts; they concluded that personal authenticity was possible only if they could break through the barriers separating black from white. The Student Y conference at the close of 1958 ended with an impromptu, interracial civil rights rally, and starting at this time, many students involved in the student Christian movement, white and black, became leading civil rights activists around the country. Some ultimately went to work for the Student Nonviolent Coordinating Committee (SNCC), founded in 1960, the leading organization of the civil rights movement's youth wing. A smaller number, often leaving behind the religious framework of discussion that had nurtured their existentialist politics, found their way to SDS.

SNCC and SDS embodied the political side of a wide-ranging youth existentialist movement in 1960s America. When it appeared at this time in the world of politics, the quest for authenticity veered sharply to the left. It was associated closely with a search for change, with activism and agitation, and with a desire to break through existing social barriers. "Black and white together" and the "beloved community" were the slogans symbolizing this moment of fusion of different social groups and of cultural and political imperatives. Existentialist activists viewed not only individual minds and souls but also the whole world as broken and in need of healing. Hence the search for community occupied a central role in existentialist politics. Political communities committed to change formed the crucibles of authenticity, carrying it to the larger culture. Overcoming alienation meant individuals discovering a common human identity, working toward common purposes, and joining in collective action. Accordingly, one historian of the new left termed the largest goal of this movement "solidarity."[11] Even though the search for solidarity never dimmed, after 1965 it became more problematic to search for interracial solidarity. While the young African American militants of the civil rights movement ventured into a search for the authentically black, the young whites of the new left moved further left, coming to identify capitalism as the main culprit responsible for their alienation, edging toward a familiar Marxist orientation.

To cement the connection between the traditional left and the new left search for authenticity, many radicals of the 1960s—not just in the United States but around the world (in the countries of eastern Europe, under the moniker of "revisionism")—promoted an existentialist or "humanist" Marxism, drawing heavily on Karl Marx's 1844 manuscripts, which focused on the problem of alienation. Whereas Marx wrote of humanity's need to recover its "species essence," leftists of the 1960s spoke instead of "human potential" and authenticity. The new left refashioned the religious aspiration to bridge the gap between the secular and the divine into the secular goal of making oneself and the world more fully human. This radical humanism was recognizable in the existentialism of Camus, who asserted, "I am waiting for a grouping of those who refuse to be dogs and are resolved to pay the price that must be paid so that man can be something more than a dog." Striking a heroic pose, the young radicals of the new left resolved themselves willing to pay whatever this price might be.[12]

This concern with "human potential" was not, of course, the exclusive property of the political left, and sometimes it was not political at all. Psychologists of the cold war era, like Abraham Maslow, who was a political liberal unsympathetic to radicalism, and liberals, like Betty Friedan, did more than any others to popularize the aspiration to the fulfillment of potential. The 1960s "counterculture" of hippies, or "freaks," began a search for the authentic and expressed a desire to explore human potential that helped lead to the popular, therapeutic experimentalism that became known as the "human potential movement." (An explicit spirituality, often in the form of exploration of non-Western spiritual traditions, returned to the search for authenticity within the counterculture.)[13] The shared ground of humanism fueled the sense of kinship between the new left and cold war liberalism, on one side, and between the new left and the counterculture, on the other, although these relations were nonetheless fraught with tension, even antipathy. These links to the counterculture and to a broader "therapeutic culture" may confirm some people's skepticism about the political seriousness of 1960s radicalism and may alarm those who view this radicalism more sympathetically. Neither sympathizers nor detractors, however, should conclude that the delineation of these connections depoliticizes the new left. This movement did emerge from an intersection of personal and political concerns, but this is true of all political movements. To grasp this aspect of the new left is to understand better how it emerged from the larger fabric of American culture and what it meant for the development of American political life.

The centrality of the search for authenticity in the new left is what recent work on this movement has neglected to appreciate or explore, and this accounts in large measure for the failure to assimilate the new left fully to the main lines of historical development in twentieth-century America. In the future, rather than asking why a left-wing movement became so preoccupied with authenticity, we might do better to ask how it was that one branch of a broad-ranging youth existentialist movement, a search for authenticity, turned leftist. And we may have to let the new left stand or fall with its existentialist politics.

Deep in the Heart. . .

It hardly could be more ironic that we have no "histories from the bottom up" of the new left, the political movement that bequeathed this idea to the historical profession. The national overviews that we do have are invaluable, and they present a narrative that in many respects I endorse.[14] There remains, however, much more to learn about political radicalism in the 1960s. In this book, I move back and forth between the national and the local. In the context of national developments, I examine the important center of youth activism that emerged in Austin, Texas, showing, with a specificity that only a close scrutiny of particular people and places can yield, how various forces converged in individual people's lives to lead them in particular political directions. Existing accounts of the new left, surprisingly, neglect the campus environments where this movement flourished and focus on the national leadership of the movement to the neglect of the rank and file. A close look a campus environment illuminates the diversity and complexity of the new left. This method reveals not only how the child of a liberal family, like Alice Embree, came to the new left, but also how a Barry Goldwater supporter like Mariann Wizard, or a hill-country autodidact like Bob Speck, or an air force veteran like Paul Spencer did so as well.

Austin, Texas, was the largest center of new left activism in the American South, one of the biggest in the United States and probably the most important in all the vast spaces east of Berkeley, west of Morningside Heights, and south of Chicago. As the state capital and home of the University of Texas (UT), Austin is a regional political and intellectual center. During the period considered here, UT rose in status and reputation from a regional to a national center of research and learning, a characteristic story of the cold war, when the unprecedented expansion of the university system helped produce student activism.[15] Activists of national significance, such as Sandra "Casey" Hayden (a key civil rights activist who moved from the Student Y and the National Student Association to SNCC and SDS and who became an early feminist voice in the 1960s left) and Jeff Shero Nightbyrd (who became vice president of SDS), reached prominence in their school years at UT.

Most important, the Texas new left represents the radical constituency that emerged in conservative parts of the country. By 1965, the large Austin contingent in SDS became identified in that organization as leading representatives of the cohort that flowed into the new left in the mid-1960s: young people from the South and the Midwest, people with few ties to the old left. This new wave of young radicals, whose numbers dwarfed those of the SDS "old guard," seemed newly sympathetic to the counterculture, and their style earned them the sobriquet "anarchist." They became associated with the slogan "prairie power," although as already noted, their origins were geographically dispersed and the Texas group rode into the new left on the crest of this wave. The Austin new left first appears in the customary narrative of SDS with the arrival of Charlie Smith at an SDS National Council meeting in June 1964 on his motorcycle, declaring to the gathering of sober young radicals that he was a pacifist, an anarchist, a Marxist, and a beatnik. Several members of the Austin circle spent the summer of 1965 trying to run the SDS National Office in Chicago as a controversial experiment in participatory democracy.[16] Where such people might have come from and where they went back to after these seemingly disruptive appearances on the national stage we can hardly guess from reading the existing works on the new left.

The Texans' incomprehensibility to the SDS old guard points to a deeper problem, namely, that the history of American radicalism has been heavily "New York-ocentric," to borrow a phrase from the sociologist Richard Hamilton.[17] To be precise, the national histories of the new left have drawn mainly on the experiences of the early leaders of SDS, most of whom were active in a small number of cities forming a northern rim across the United States, running from New York and Cambridge in the East to Ann Arbor and Madison in the Midwest to Berkeley in the West. Intellectuals in these places formed a kind of national cultural elite, part of a metropolitan culture forged by a similarity of outlook and experience and maintained by strong personal and institutional links. The university towns just cited, small as they were, nonetheless were home to numerous members of this metropolitan elite, who were paid serious attention by their peers in New York and Washington.

The experiences of metropolitan student radicals, to be sure, furnish a highly important story of 1960s radicalism, and the story has been told well before. The initial elite of the new left exerted a shaping force on the development of SDS, whose national headquarters was in New York City until 1965. These young people, many of them Jewish, were the most deeply involved in the new left's complex relation to the old left; indeed, many had old left parents. These children wished to break with what they saw as the hierarchical and deceitful modus operandi of that earlier movement. For them, this was the driving force behind the emphasis on participatory democracy, the insistence on democratic means as well as ends. At the same time, these young radicals, disillusioned with the cold war's domestic and international ramifications, led the break with the fervid anticommunism of the social democratic trade unions that originally sponsored SDS. This fight with the trade unions, lasting from 1962 to 1965, helped alienate the new left from cold war liberalism. The most important contributions of this early metropolitan elite in the new left were their passionate commitment to a politics that was both effective and morally honest—which they popularized with the slogan of participatory democracy—and their insistence on the irrelevance of communism and anticommunism to the new left. In these commitments, they soon found, they were not alone. Participatory democracy and the politics of "antianticommunism" appealed also to young people from the provinces.[18]

There were great differences as well between the group that got SDS off the ground and the larger, provincial cohort that entered the new left later. A large majority of all those who at one time or another got involved in new left activism came from cultural and political backgrounds quite different, in important respects, from those of the early metropolitan elite. Most were neither red-diaper babies nor Jews, although both those groups were strongly overrepresented in the new left throughout its existence. The emergence of a new left in New York, Boston, Chicago, and the San Francisco Bay area was almost guaranteed by the strong old left presence that lingered in such cities through the 1950s, a presence that, in the larger context of American society, was quite unusual. Histories of the new left that emphasize the influence of old left connections and place the new left in a self-contained "history of the American left," for all the valuable insights they offer, simply cannot explain the new left's appearance in most of the country, yet the new left existed all over the United States.[19]

To segregate political radicalism from the mainstream of political and cultural history is to obscure the close and tangled connections between the new left and larger strands of political and cultural development in the twentieth-century United States—strands such as social gospel liberalism and Christian evangelicalism, cold war liberalism and Western libertarianism, liberal feminism and the search for authenticity. My investigation of these connections provides an alternative genealogy for the new left. Looking at the new left from the ground up and bringing it into focus as it appeared in and from the provinces, this book provides, in a sense, the first new left history of the new left.

In a place like Texas, the dissident search for authenticity and democracy took heart from sources unlike those to be found in metropolitan culture. Among those sources was more than one kind of political liberalism, none of which resembles very closely our received picture of "cold war liberalism." Here, communism existed almost solely in the right-wing imagination, but there were "homemade fascist" elements in the state's political and economic elites, according to the 1943 observation of folklorist J. Frank Dobie, one of the most eminent members of the UT faculty.[20] The perception of the political right's power and extremism exerted a profound force on Texas liberals. There one finds a distinctive breed of liberals, indebted to populist traditions and little concerned with debates over communism and fellow traveling. Such people, whose loudest voice after the mid-1950s belonged to Ronnie Dugger of the *Texas Observer*, located themselves in a south-by-southwestern tradition that mixed Jeffersonian democracy, agrarian radicalism, and New Deal liberalism.[21] An ideal of lonely heroism, and a slightly desperate irreverence that helped them cope with their isolation, flavored their dissent.

Just as overlooked as these secular liberals have been individuals and institutions in the dissident Christian tradition (which itself encompassed more than one strand), which communicated to young cold war idealists the ambition to find lives of meaning and authenticity even as they sought to improve society.[22] In the South and in other relatively conservative areas, Christian liberals became mentors of young Americans who ultimately took the search for community and faith well beyond the confines of liberalism. Dissident Christianity led young white people toward a stance of severe dissatisfaction with their contemporary culture, particularly with the same aspects of American life that later drew the new left's ire. Christian thought encouraged young people searching for authenticity to intervene in the larger social world.

This sort of cultural critique and this linkage between authenticity and activism opened the path to the new left's postscarcity radicalism. Dissident Christianity did not play the catalytic role everywhere in the way that it did in Texas. Nonetheless, the search for authenticity that infused American radicalism generally in the 1960s had a notable spiritual aspect. In the 1980s and 1990s, a "search for meaning," linked to both left–liberal politics and a pluralistic religious impulse, reappeared on the American scene. Sometimes the search for authenticity has taken less political forms, as in the "new age" cultural phenomenon of recent years.[23] Examining the role of Christianity in the history of the radical search for authenticity offers a chance to understand the roots of these cultural developments, which have occurred throughout the United States in a host of cultural idioms.

The clearest political connection between Christianity and the new left was the role of Christian liberals in inspiring youth participation, black and white, in the civil rights movement. In this connection, a southern setting is an especially appropriate one in which to examine the political role of Christianity in this period. Serious attempts to understand why a small minority of white southerners became civil rights activists in this period have only recently begun, but it is clear even now that religion played a major role.[24] National leaders of cold war liberalism acknowledged the moral imperative to secure civil rights for African Americans, but race, like class, often was peripheral in their social and political analysis until events forced on them an awareness of imminent political change.[25] In this respect, the people in this story, including the secular liberals who were closest to cold war liberalism, were different. Certainly after World War II, the issue of Jim Crow stayed permanently on their agenda.

The political actors examined here are notable for their tendency to view pressing racial issues as primarily a matter of black and white. The racial structure of Texas society, which included a large Chicano minority (sometimes called Tejano), was considerably more complex than that in other parts of the country. The overall racial makeup of Texas, 15 percent Chicano and 12 percent black in 1960, is not very revealing in itself. Austin straddles the intersection of the Deep South, the southwestern United States, and the Great Plains, which stretch south through the Texas Panhandle. Humid, heavily wooded East Texas, home to most of the African Americans in the state and few Chicanos, is more like Mississippi in demographics and topography than it is like dry West Texas. In the 1960s, a Mexican American movement of great cultural power and political significance emerged in the Southwest, among farmworkers, students, and others, and one of its hotbeds was South Texas, where many counties, in a wide belt hugging the Rio Grande from Corpus Christi and Brownsville to El Paso, have had Mexican American majorities for much of the twentieth century. Yet perhaps surprisingly, this *movemiento* held nothing close to the interest to the young Anglos—who are the focus of this book—that the black civil rights movement did. Nothing better illustrates the power of a national racial discussion that focused on black–white relations, a national discussion that reached new heights of urgency in the 1950s and 1960s as a result of the civil rights movement's advances. From their geographic position in the middle of Texas, closer to Mexico City than to San Francisco or New York City, these Austinites looked eastward for the decisive political cue of their time.[26]

Nonetheless, for all their concern over developments in the Deep South, Texas liberals viewed themselves as Texans, not simply as southerners or westerners. The Texan interplay of West and South emerged as a culturally powerful statewide identity, a Texan persona that exerted a strong hold on residents of the Lone Star State. The geographer D. W. Meinig summarizes the results of various social science surveys:

> The Texan ... is ... volatile and chauvinistic, ethnocentric and provincial. . . . [He] regards government as no more than a necessary evil, distrusts even informal social action as a threat to his independence, and accepts violence as an appropriate solution to certain kinds of personal and group problems. Material wealth is much admired for its own sake but industriousness has no particular virtue.

Furthermore, says Meinig, the Anglo culture of fundamentalist East Texas is specifically "egalitarian, individualistic, aggressive, and adaptable . . . volatile and conspiratorial." It is "egalitarian" in the sense of a racist "volk" populism, a rough leveling feeling among Anglos that depends on the subordination of racial minorities. We should understand this Texas identity as a myth that many Texans believe in and even try self-consciously to fulfill. Despite this belief in Texans' peculiarity, however, the elements in this Texas persona are also exaggerated forms of character traits that observers might have noted throughout the United States. An outsized belief in the uniqueness of Texas is part of the persona.[27]

Even as secular liberals in Austin, like those gathered around the *Observer*, saw themselves resisting in crucial respects the main drift of things in their state and their country, they also absorbed some aspects of the dominant culture. They—and, later on, new left activists in Austin—refused to flee from their indigenous culture. Instead they cultivated an alternative Texan identity. They pitted their own, more thoroughgoing brand of populism against the traditional volk populism. They were great libertarians. They liked to drink beer. Not a few would have called the liberals and leftists here "egalitarian, individualistic, aggressive, volatile, and conspiratorial." These dissenters played a variation on the broader new left theme of "speaking American," seeking to oppose the dominant arrangements of society and politics with tools they found in the dominant political culture. Provincial new left radicals consciously drew on the "residual" and "traditional" cultures of their environment in an effort to build "alternative" and "oppositional" cultures. Although they felt little kinship with the old left, they did not see their politics appearing *ex nihilo*. Once again, the resources they found at their disposal, like the dominant culture they opposed, were distinctively local yet in some ways representative of the situation of radicals all over the United States. From subculture to counterculture, from libertarianism to anarchism, this commitment to "speak American" spelled both promise and hazard for their political efforts.[28]

Agency and Authenticity

In the new left radicals' understanding, "speaking American," making themselves relevant to their country's culture and society, meant that they had to address issues of race. This was not something they had to push themselves to do, given the new left's roots in the civil rights movement and the profound impact that this movement had on even new left radicals who did not take part in civil rights protests. The depth of this impact demonstrates, as clearly as anything, the centrality of the search for authenticity in 1960s radicalism. The new left search for authenticity was entangled from the start with what we today might call questions of "identity," both racial and sexual. But this became clear to the new left radicals themselves only gradually.

In the 1950s and 1960s, a fraction of white American youth felt a spontaneous sympathy for the civil rights movement, building on a private feeling of solidarity with African American culture. The young whites of the new left grew up influenced by the subversive, transgressive romanticization of black Americans in mid-twentieth-century popular culture. The appeal of jazz and rhythm-and-blues, jitterbugging, baseball and boxing, encouraged among some young whites the old idea that African American culture was a repository of authenticity, which spiritually desiccated whites might tap through a kind of racial "crossover."[29] As noted earlier, according to new left thought, political marginality or alienation connoted radical agency. Yet marginal groups also, paradoxically, seemed culturally authentic to new left radicals. This was the reverse image of their own inner alienation, the alienation of affluence, which equaled inauthenticity. In this way, the new left radicals updated the tradition of the earlier "new radicals," white intellectuals who had invested people of color, the poor, and sometimes women and children with the treasured stuff of authenticity.[30]

This deep cultural affinity was always at work beneath the tendency among young white liberals and radicals in the 1960s to look to African Americans as the vanguard of social change. New left radicals' persistent fears of their own inauthenticity gnawed at their confidence in their own ability to create change. Perhaps only those already residing in a state of authenticity could open the way to a society that afforded authentic life to all. The new left longed for "solidarity" with "others," yet this was a movement of and by college-educated white Americans. This circumstance always led back to the question of radical agency. Would black or white, poor or middle class, usher in the new society, or would they do it together? These questions plagued the new left from start to finish, until its last, tempestuous efforts to settle on the true revolutionary vanguard.

Many, perhaps most, new left radicals addressed the conundrum of agency and authenticity by embracing their movement's actual social identity. Ultimately, instead of looking for an external vanguard to lead them, they asserted that white, college-educated youth could in fact move from alienation to authenticity and help make the new society. They intensified the rejection of materialism present in their politics from its inception and elevated alienation over both exploitation and marginality as the essential sign of inclusion in the revolutionary elect. They argued that the new left should be a movement not only of and by but also *for* college-educated white youth.

Ironically, black power thought, which became hegemonic in SNCC after 1965, encouraged this turn toward a doctrine of "self-liberation." Such ideas took hold among the new left's rank and file in the late 1960s, in defiance of the new left's national elites, who instead pledged the support of SDS to "external agencies" that would lead the revolution. This presumptive national leadership has dominated previous accounts of the SDS collapse, diverting attention away from ideological developments within the new left more generally. The programmatic expression of the widespread embrace of the new left's actual social character was called the "new working-class" analysis. In effect, this analysis represented an adjustment of theory to practice.[31]

The most important such practice was the attempt, beginning in the mid-1960s, to make the new left itself into a counterculture, an avant-garde that would do the traditional work of a political vanguard. The new left took a countercultural turn in its later years, hoping to develop its own constituency's authenticity as a political strategy in itself. The new left's countercultural turn did not represent a turn away from worldly, political concerns. Rather, this turn coincided with the escalation of antiwar agitation in the late 1960s, a priority whose burning importance sometimes threatened to consume the radicals. But the countercultural turn, which continued into the early 1970s, did represent a move toward more local concerns, toward far more incremental methods of social change, and toward a more pronounced concern with alleviating the alienation of the new left's own members. In the end, the new left's cultural politics moved toward neither revolution nor privatism but, rather, toward a kind of cultural liberalism, a reformist practice that exerted a considerable impact on more traditional political liberals. The new left's quiet rapprochement with liberalism in its last years is another untold part of its history.[32]

The feminist activism that developed among white leftist women between 1967 and 1973 further extended the growing conviction that the new left should be a movement of self-liberation. Clearly, feminism complicated the task of self-liberation for white, middle-class radicals, by indicating that men and women in the new left might have divergent interests. More significant, this leftist feminism challenged the whole tradition of existential politics that had developed throughout the cold war period. The longing for an authentic masculinity was one of that tradition's pillars. Men who pursued authenticity in the realm of politics had, explicitly and repeatedly, equated a strenuous sense of self and a vigorous citizenship with masculinity, just as they equated alienation with emasculation.

Arthur Schlesinger made these connections clear in 1949. In his polemic against those liberals who would follow the Communists' lead, he derisively called such dupes "Doughface progressives." The term evoked the "softness" he discerned—a softness evidenced not least in the Doughface's ingenuous attraction to the dashing "hardness" of the Communists. Schlesinger drew out the hardly concealed gender associations of political softness and hardness, ridiculing the Doughface's "feminine fascination with the rude and muscular power of the proletariat." The historian and activist asserted that he and his sort, by contrast, had brought a "new virility" into American politics. Much as he inveighed against the Communists, he slyly indicated the similar "hardness" of liberals like himself. As Lasch observes, Schlesinger was part of the "hard-boiled" tradition in American liberalism, taking a "realistic," affirmative view of the role of power in politics. The hard-boiled liberals might keep the Doughfaces in line, winning their allegiance by a display of muscularity that equaled anything the Communists could offer. "Hardness" was the sign that one had triumphed over anxiety, as few Americans could be expected to do. In America, a liberal elite alone might shoulder the twin burdens of manhood and freedom. Others could remain soft, effeminate, anxious.[33]

This consideration of Schlesinger's early cold war ruminations raises two questions regarding the new left. How easily could this movement avoid Schlesinger's elite solution to the problem of democracy and anxiety? And how "hard" did its politics need to be? For most of its history, the new left rejected the elite aspect of Schlesinger's solution while joining in its machismo. Men in the new left, residents of the same political culture as Schlesinger was, felt the enervation of the spirit in the industrial order and the "iron cage" of bureaucracy, and they, too, called it emasculation. They affirmed the equation of virility, authenticity, and citizenship. Instead of a small elite of authentic males asserting their will on the field of politics, the new left envisioned a whole society alive with participatory democracy. Yet the young radicals still equated this invigorated citizenship with masculinity, viewing it as a triumph over effeminacy. The role that women might play in such a democratic revival was unclear, but they certainly would have difficulty qualifying for full citizenship in a regime of manliness.[34]

Small wonder, then, that women on the left, encouraged by the rhetoric of self-liberation, came to view SDS as, in left-wing feminist Robin Morgan's acid phrase, a "counterfeit Left."[35] Afforded greater political opportunities when the male-dominated institutional framework of SDS disintegrated, leftist women argued, starting in the late 1960s, that the real democratic solution to the problem of anxiety was to jettison the emphasis on masculinity. Only this could allow women, as well as men, to become authentic citizens. In a sense, the project of radical feminists was to reconstitute the new left on a feminist basis. This was a viable project as long as the new left itself cohered as a movement, even if not as a single organization; as long as this was the case, the recruiting grounds for a feminist left remained open for business. In the end, the feminist radicals were unsuccessful in their effort to remake the left, because their own activism tended toward cultural liberalism, as did that of the left overall; because the Vietnam War ended and women won the right to have abortions in the United States; and because not enough radical men wanted to join a left not built on the pursuit of masculinity. In their effort to build such a left, the feminists discovered one of the limits to the American culture of dissent.

As political history, this is not a story of triumph. In the end, the new left found more success in untying the knot of inner alienation and democracy than in pursuing large-scale social change. Many new left radicals succeeded in overcoming alienation in their own lives, and they made considerable progress in building democratic local communities, which became visible across the United States in the 1960s and 1970s and in many cases remained viable long after that. This kind of dissident, geographically specific community—often developing on the fringes of a university, drenched in the spirit of participatory democracy, and linked by the common radical itinerary of the era to similar communities around the country—became the typical center of leftist activity between, roughly, 1968 and 1973. In those years the young radicals acquired a new kind of autonomy and legitimacy by building their own institutions and by attracting a critical mass of like-minded people who lived, worked, and played in close proximity to one another.

In the 1950s and early 1960s, student dissenters leaned on the legitimacy enjoyed by universities as havens of free thought and by the few faculty sympathizers the students found there. Such teachers heavily influenced idealistic and activist students during those years, and the activists were deeply interested in the controversies occurring in the universities themselves. Despite all the building occupations and ensuing controversies on American campuses between 1968 and 1970 (starting with the events at Columbia University in the spring of 1968), by the late 1960s many new left radicals were, in an important sense, less concerned with what was occurring in the universities than with the new culture they saw germinating in their own communities.[36] By then, sympathetic professors were likely to look to these radical communities for political cues, rather than the other way around. It seemed to many that the scene of social change had shifted to such autonomous communities, and my narrative follows that movement.

In the end, however, the new radical communities did not give birth to a new political culture. At best they nurtured a small subculture; they did not take over the country. In such communities, new left radicals found a place for themselves, but this was very far from their goals of political and social transformation. New leftists' adoption of the project of self-liberation in the late 1960s represented, in part, an acknowledgment of their movement's failure to identify adequate mechanisms of social change. In later years, their silence regarding the difference between self-liberation and their earlier, large-scale aspirations bespoke the pain of their grievously mistaken political diagnosis and reflected their inability to respond politically to the rightward turn in national politics.[37]

New left radicals probably were better able to deal with such distressing developments personally than they were politically, precisely because both their thought and their social endeavors had turned to the matter of self-liberation. They did not simply give up politics and start taking care of themselves in the 1970s, as some have charged; they were already taking care of themselves. It is worth noting that the young people considered here ceased talking very much about anxiety around the time the new left started spreading rapidly, in the early 1960s. Previously, in the 1950s and in the heroic phase of the interracial civil rights movement, anxiety had been an explicit concern for the discontented young; their solution was political activism, which might propel them out of anxiety and into freedom. The subsequent ebbing of talk concerning anxiety offers good reason to think that for many, this existentialist gambit worked.

In the new left, the quest for authenticity changed. Now the search for authenticity became fully socialized, with new left radicals excoriating what they saw as the inauthenticity of American culture at large. It was a culture of death and artificiality, they said. Having gradually come to assert their own radical authenticity, new leftists came to see themselves forming an island of integrity and vitality in a debased, lifeless land. Although the shadow of inner alienation still hovered over their shoulders, new left activists now felt less alienated within themselves; at the same time, they had become far more alienated from the society that bore them. In a sense, by the early 1970s the young radicals passed over the horizon of authenticity into marginality: they exchanged the inner alienation they bemoaned for the outer alienation they always had admired.

Perhaps the cold war really has been an "age of anxiety"; perhaps the entire twentieth century has been such an age. This book interprets several phases in the history of post-1945 liberalism and left-wing politics as a series of responses to this condition. This is only one way to interpret this political history, but it is one that helps make sense of a turbulent period that still, in larger narratives of the American past, often appears as a rupture—"the Sixties"—not as an epoch that flows logically out of previous developments. Scrutinizing the cultural underpinnings and meanings of the political radicalism of the 1960s brings an enhanced sense of continuity to the larger story of twentieth-century American politics; analyzing political efforts to address cultural conditions reminds us that cultural meanings and possibilities are bounded by political realities. Whatever else it was, the new left was a response to deepening symptoms of life under advanced, bureaucratic capitalism. Political movements may rebel against social structures and political regimes, but those structures and regimes produce these very movements of opposition. The dialectics of politics and culture, structure and dissent, are the real objects of this study.

The new left belongs to the past. But the social and political problems that the new left addressed—alienation, powerlessness, racism, war, sexism—have not disappeared. New left radicals' attempts to combat these social afflictions by developing democratic and compelling forms of sociality and morality continue to merit our sympathetic, if critical, attention. Today, we may judge the new left's analysis of these problems flawed or shallow. We may deem this movement's political approach time bound or inadequate to its aims. For all this, the new left's agenda remains regrettably current.

PART ONE

CHAPTER ONE

This Once Fearless Land:
Secular Liberals Under Right-Wing Rule

THE WHITE RADICALS of the 1960s were shaped by both political and personal ideals, by the twin search for democracy and authenticity. These two ideals did not necessarily come to young people from the same sources. Furthermore, different forces bore the standard of democracy in different places during the decades preceding the 1960s, leading the forces of political dissidence in different ways. In the industrial North, labor unions harbored some of the most effective resisters against the prevailing conservatism of the early cold war. In New York City and California, vestiges of the old left lingered, rallying to outposts of outspokenness like *Dissent* magazine, founded in 1954. In the urban Southeast, African American civil rights activists drew on a unique cultural milieu to protest racial segregation. In many metropolitan areas, amid the political coerciveness of the McCarthy era, dissent turned oblique, toward expressions of dissatisfaction with American culture, the personal swallowing the political. In Texas, things looked different. There, a group of secular liberals stood at the forefront of resistance to right-wing dominance. These secular liberals imparted their distinctive brand of politics, shaped by fierce traditions of populism and individualism, to young idealists who by 1960 themselves took up the banner of democracy.

In early cold war Texas, the fault lines of political life were in some ways similar to the divisions that prevailed in the rest of the United States, in other ways especially southern, and in yet other ways Texas politics seemed distinctively Texan. As in much of the country in the 1940s and 1950s, a split between liberals and conservatives shaped the formal political life of parties and elections, with issues of economic policy at the forefront of discussion. Liberals favored progressive taxation, regulation of industry, the growth of labor unions, and increased expenditures on public education and other government services that benefited citizens of modest means. Conservatives favored less of all these things and had warmer relations with the corporate sector.[1] The New Deal and World War II had imparted momentum to liberal initiatives, and many liberals had high hopes in the late 1940s that they might push their agenda further. Beginning with strong congressional gains by the more conservative Republican Party in the 1946 elections, however, the liberals were increasingly put on the defensive, at least at the national level, and by 1950 the conservative viewpoint clearly had the upper hand.

Differences over economic policy were not the entire substance of the liberal–conservative competition, however. Always standing in back of the disagreement over economic issues were racial matters, adding intensity to the struggle for state power. Liberals were more inclined to support some form of civil rights for Americans of African descent, an issue usually framed in terms of the official segregation, encoded in state and local law, that draped the entire Southeast from Virginia to Texas. Since the issue was framed strictly in terms of altering southern laws and social conditions, it is not surprising that most liberals, at least on racial issues, were northern. Black southerners, who might have sympathized with the liberal agenda generally, were simply shut out of formal political participation. Thus the most fundamental way in which liberal–conservative competition differed in the South was that there the liberals were far fewer, far more embattled, and far less likely to win any particular dispute. The cultural significance of official white supremacy in the South sharply diminished the constituency for the liberal program.

The predominance of conservatism in the South took the specific form of conservative supremacy inside the Democratic Party in most southern states. In most northern states, strongly conservative politicians and voters were concentrated in the Republican Party, and almost all the liberals were, at least by the late 1940s, Democrats. As a consequence of two-party competition in these states, the liberals held a good share of the power in Democratic Party organizations. In the South, ironically, the Republicans had been crippled for nearly three-quarters of a century by their ever receding history as the champions of emancipation and equal rights for black Americans during and after the Civil War. In this regional one-party system, conservatives—close to big business and hostile to civil rights— held sway. Southern liberals fought many of their battles out of the public eye, led by party infighters like Frankie Randolph and Creekmore Fath, one-time ally of John Connally and "Democrat No. 1" according to Maury Maverick. They scratched and clawed for gains in the Democratic Party, often fighting over procedural rules and in state caucuses and conventions. Maverick himself fought similar battles on the national stage. At one time the mayor of San Antonio, he served two terms in the U.S. House in the 1930s as a leader of the "Young Turks" trying to push Franklin Roosevelt's administration to the left.[2]

In these respects, Texas politics in the 1940s and 1950s conformed to the southern pattern. The real elections usually were the Democratic primaries; the elected governors, senators, and congressmen were mostly conservatives. A partial exception to this pattern and a partial confirmation of it can be found in the Texas gubernatorial election of 1946. It was an unusual election in that, still flush with the political strength they had acquired in the Roosevelt years, the liberals won the Democratic nomination for one of their own, and the general election meant something. The result of the election also was unusual in that a Republican won the governorship. This result was more typical than exceptional, however, since the conservative won, as usual. The winner was indistinguishable from Democratic conservatives in Texas, and conservative voters had no qualms about supporting the GOP in this case. Furthermore, the election was normal in that even though economic issues played a major role in the explicit campaign rhetoric, largely unspoken differences on racial issues were widely acknowledged to have played a quiet role in the liberal candidate's defeat by a margin of two to one.[3]

This liberal candidate was Homer Price Rainey, who had served between 1939 and 1944 as president of the University of Texas (UT) at Austin—the same city that was home to the governor's mansion he tried to capture. For his liberalism, Rainey had been harassed and finally fired by the board of regents of the university. The regents, drawn invariably from the highest business circles of the state, had final authority over all administrative decisions at UT, and the governor of Texas appointed the regents. If he had been elected governor, Rainey undoubtedly would have liberalized the board. Rainey's tribulations at UT during World War II form the backdrop to the growth of an enclave of liberalism around the university in Austin during the following years. This enclave weathered the intensely conservative climate of the early cold war, which shaped Texas liberalism in distinctive ways. Ten to fifteen years after Rainey was cashiered, this island of liberalism would nurture a group of militant liberal students. Those students in turn helped lay the groundwork for the more radical search for democracy that animated student life in the 1960s.

The Rainey Affair

The single most important event looming in the memory of cold war liberalism at UT was the termination of the university president's employment in 1944. This was the opening shot on the academic front of the domestic cold war, although in conservative places like Texas, the severe anticommunism and antiliberalism associated with the cold war had enjoyed much success with little interruption since the late 1930s.[4]

Despite his Texas roots, Homer Rainey came to represent a kind of cosmopolitanism his enemies found threatening. In the late 1930s he served in Washington, D.C., as head of the Rockefeller-sponsored American Youth Commission. He was a New Dealer in his politics. In 1939, after a nationwide search, the Texas governor, Jimmy Allred—the closest thing to a liberal who had ever won the office—and the board of regents chose Rainey to head UT.[5] This may seem surprising given the regents' later hostility toward him. But the presence of the regents appointed by Allred softened what otherwise might have been the staunch opposition of the political establishment in Texas to Rainey's appointment.

The choice of Rainey and the search that preceded it indicated a desire among many of the Texas elite to conform to the national criterion of "quality," a desire that was rooted in the feelings of provinciality that sometimes slipped through the renowned Texas bravado and that was validated by the 1886 Charter of the University of Texas. This charter declared that the state must maintain a public university and must attempt to make it "a university of the first class." This phrase was invoked time and again to legitimate any attempt at innovation at UT, especially one that sought to bring UT in line with more prestigious schools in the North and East. It became, in many cases, a rallying cry for liberals at the university. With the hiring of Rainey in 1939, the governor nodded in the direction of this demand for a "first-class" institution and encouraged hopes in Austin for further change. Rainey himself later defended his actions at UT not by saying that his opponents were right-wing extremists (as they were) or that he wished to defend the liberal values of free expression and inquiry (which he did) but instead by obscuring the ideological dimension of the conflict, stating merely that he wanted to create a first-class university.[6]

By the 1940s there was a new governor and a more aggressively conservative board of regents, and trouble was brewing. The governor— a radio personality and conservative named Pappy "Pass-the-Biscuits" O'Daniel— treated his relations with the university as a political issue to be used to his political benefit. In 1940 he met with business leaders and lawyers to discuss how they could influence, or at least make an issue of, university appointments. At a subsequent regents' meeting, a business lobbyist who served on the board handed Rainey a list with the names of four full professors of economics whom he wanted Rainey to fire. Rainey then explained the concept of academic tenure to the regents and managed to fend off the initiative. But later the regents changed the tenure rules to make it easier to fire professors.[7]

Rainey was less successful in 1942, when the regents acted in response to a political and economic issue that stretched beyond the university, that touched the interests of the regents and their cohorts directly. A trio of liberal economics professors at the university attended a rally organized by corporate interests to protest the federal Fair Labor Standards Act, which required that workers receive overtime pay for work beyond forty hours per week. The professors asked to speak in favor of the proposal; although they were not allowed to do so, someone dutifully took down their names. A federal judge in Dallas wrote the regents that the economics department at UT was "swinging away from true economics and routing our children into the camp of state socialism."[8]

Rainey then explained to the regents the concept of academic freedom, which, as he understood it, ought to protect the jobs of these professors against any objections raised concerning their political views or statements—at least concerning such a nonrevolutionary view as the one these professors had expressed. The regents were not impressed with this concept. Weren't these professors employed by the university—and thus by the regents? the regents asked. They were. They did not have tenure. Rainey warned that the American Association of University Professors (AAUP) might "blacklist" UT if the regents fired the professors. Ultimately the regents overruled both the president and the economics department and terminated the three teachers directly.

The harassment of liberal professors continued. One regent threatened to eliminate the teaching of social work, since, he said, it only created socialists. The regents changed the tenure rules so that in any particular case, they could suspend a threatened professor's customary hearing and thus fire him with impunity. Next, Governor O'Daniel and the members of the board publicly expressed their concern over the alleged presence of homosexuals among the faculty. In the interior life of cold war politics, all forms of social deviance were linked—if only implicitly—thereby joining the pink menace and the red menace. In 1944 the regents demanded that Rainey fire a professor for assigning John Dos Passos's *The Big Money*, which they deemed obscene.[9]

Having had enough, Rainey went public. At a dramatic meeting of the faculty, he recited a long list of instances in which, he claimed, the regents had interfered with his proper authority. The ideological dimension, again, was left implicit: in fact if not in words, Rainey enlisted the faculty's support not just for the president's authority but on behalf of a liberal view of a proper and "first-class" university, in which, Rainey hoped the faculty would agree, they had a clear interest. He thought a university should be an independent intellectual center in society—not threatening that society but enriching it, perhaps challenging it but ultimately serving it, even if by providing a refuge for minority opinions.[10]

The regents fired him. In their statements they never seemed angry, expressing—as if only repeating common sense—their view that whatever the proper role of a public university, it certainly was not to be an independent intellectual center. Furthermore, in their view, the president of the university was not to serve the interests of the faculty or any higher vision. Properly understood, he had a job, not a mission, and his job was to do his bosses' bidding. The president, said one businessman-regent, "occupies the position to the board of regents as a general manager of a corporation does to its board of directors."[11]

The AAUP imposed its blacklist. The students struck, staying away from classes for a week. Eight thousand of them marched to the state capitol in protest, carrying a coffin draped in black with the words "academic freedom" written on it. The state senate agreed to hold hearings on the controversy, and various professors and regents testified to their respective views of the events. It made no difference. Rainey stayed in Texas for another couple of years, entering the ill-fated governor's race in 1946 and running on proposals to tax big corporations and expand social services. After his defeat, he left the state, but his memory lingered among liberals and freethinkers in Austin, as both an inspiration and a warning.[12]

In the late 1940s and 1950s, outspoken liberals at UT continued to risk hostile attention from powerful quarters. The regents, and occasionally members of the state legislature, identified departments or even individual professors whose statements or inclinations they found questionable or sounded questionable from what they had been told. The regents thus found and took the opportunity to fire J. Frank Dobie in 1947, four years after he made his crack about "homemade fascist" elements in the ruling circles of the state.[13] Now there was no Homer Rainey standing between the authorities and the faculty. What Willie Morris, a prominent liberal journalist in Austin during the 1950s, said generally of this time was particularly true for liberals: "Texas . . . its chronic xenophobias fed by the passions of the McCarthy period, was not an entirely pleasant place in those years. There was a venom in its politics."[14]

Liberals and Libertarians

Perhaps the political factor most brightly illuminated by the Rainey affair was the extreme and unyielding conservatism of the regents. The regents could not have been more closely linked to the large corporate interests of Texas—oil and gas, construction, real estate, finance, insurance—and they were tied almost as closely to the forces of political conservatism in the state. These ties were entirely open, never denied; the regents jeopardized no pretense of political or intellectual neutrality in their management of the university, and consequently their rule was rather bare-knuckled. Little persuasion, much coercion: This style reflected a notable frankness concerning the allocation of power. The regents felt they represented a group that owned both the state's wealth and its government—hence they owned the university. (Or, if the public theoretically owned it, then the regents were the sole legitimate representatives of the owners—the board of directors, as they said.) It was a setup whose neatness would have made a Marxist swoon. It also would have primed the intellectual pump of any college student who, in later years, picked up a copy of *The Power Elite*, a book by one of the better-known members of the UT class of 1939, C. Wright Mills.[15]

Imagine the effect of such an environment on liberals in and around the university. They might treat seriously models of institutional power that others would dismiss as "conspiracy theories." They might be unremittingly suspicious of the university administration, seeing it as an extension of corporate power and interpreting its actions always in that light. Struggles in the university could take on far broader significance. Liberals there might develop a feeling that the odds were stacked unfairly against them and that their political survival was always precarious, so powerful and unified were their enemies. Others in less difficult straits might see Texas liberals at times as afflicted by paranoia and delusions of heroism, but from the Texas point of view, it was only realism. To some extent, liberals at UT did come to display these characteristics—and considering their local political background, this was not unreasonable.

The tight spot in which they always seemed to find themselves marked Texas liberals in another, perhaps less expected way. They were irreverent; sometimes they were funny, frequently sardonic. This was a relatively safe way to express anger, and it also helped make life bearable. Speaking one's mind, giving little thought to the consequences (or at least appearing to give little thought to them), was a prized quality. To be slightly outrageous was to set a good example. These were qualities seen in numerous individuals whom liberals in Austin and in Texas admired during the 1940s and

1950s: Emma Long, the Austin City Council member who specialized in her own type of political pugilism against conservatives; Frankie Randolph, daughter of a wealthy lumber and banking family who turned her back on her class to become a statewide liberal leader in the 1950s, "a hard drinker, a hard fighter, and a courageous tactician"; John Henry Faulk, the radio commentator and folklorist who fought the media "blacklist" during the McCarthy era and won, at least in court; and Clarence Ayres, the UT economist who penned Veblenesque titles like *The Divine Right of Capital* and who thwarted the state legislature's attempts to terrorize him by hauling him into the state capitol for interrogation on the stand.[16]

This tradition also highlights a substantive political issue involved in liberal–conservative competition in Texas, one suggested by the Rainey affair. This was the issue of civil liberties. The strenuous defense of civil liberties was the third leg of the liberal triad, along with economic populism and sympathy for civil rights. Civil libertarianism was important to liberals in Texas for reasons both strategic and moral, both abstract and practical. The Rainey affair illustrated the practical importance of libertarian concepts such as academic freedom at a university that existed in a conservative environment. It had become clear that professors could not rely on independent-minded administrators to protect them, as the only one who tried to do so had been removed. Under pressure from powerful conservative forces, the concept of academic freedom seemed like an awfully thin reed on which to rest anyone's career, so liberals had an interest in shoring up both the legal and cultural supports for this idea. Furthermore, students at the university also felt the heavy hand of regental and administrative authoritarianism: in 1956, students still could not invite speakers to campus whom the administration deemed "political." ("The people of Texas are not mature enough yet," explained UT President Logan Wilson.)[17] The list of the unwelcome prominently featured liberal luminaries such as Eleanor Roosevelt and Adlai Stevenson.[18]

Beyond the political protection that civil liberties afforded, libertarian ideals took on an intrinsic value for liberals in so right-wing an environment. The liberty to say whatever one thought or felt was not simply a means to an end; for many, it expressed the essence of a free person and a free people. To put it differently, many liberals in Texas did not simply value civil liberties as an insurance policy, as a concept to be employed in the event of political trouble. In this view, liberties were not to be invoked in extraordinary circumstances; they were to be practiced in ordinary situations. The liberals echoed the republican tones of C. Wright Mills's declamation, "We are free men. Now we must take our heritage seriously. . . . We must stop defending civil liberties long enough to use them."[19] The regional new left adopted this libertarianism more fully than any other element in the Texas liberal tradition. Given the power of the conservatives, given their hostility to civil libertarianism, and given the inclination of some liberals actually to put their libertarian values into practice, the tradition of civil libertarianism, which seemed so tame and ethically empty to radicals in many other places, always seemed more genuinely radical here. Especially in conservative periods, the common emphasis on civil liberties among liberals and radicals helped blur the line between them.

In 1954, the single most important outpost of this kind of outspoken, balloon-puncturing liberalism in Texas during the cold war was established. In response to their defeat in the state Democratic Party by Governor Allan Shivers, who had supported Dwight Eisenhower in the previous presidential election and was outspoken in his support for Senator Joseph McCarthy's red hunting, Frankie Randolph and others put up the money for a political journal, which was called the *Observer*, and she handed over the small operation to the young Ronnie Dugger, only recently editor of the UT *Daily Texan*. The *Observer* provided reports and commentary on statewide and national issues. Dugger was lucky to have so staunch a benefactor as Randolph, since he quickly lost perhaps half his subscribers by reporting prominently on the murder of a teenaged African American in East Texas by carousing whites, putting a large photograph of the corpse on the front page. Dugger kept up his investigation of such cases, such as one in which an all-white jury set free the confessed white killer of a black teenager. He gleefully welcomed the harassment that he sometimes received from official sources for his alleged interference in such cases.[20]

At first a line from Thoreau, "The One Great Rule of Composition Is to Speak the Truth," appeared on the *Observer*'s masthead, along with the proclamation that this was "An Independent–Liberal Weekly Journal." Explaining what he meant by "liberal," Dugger insisted, "This is a newspaper of principle, not of party." Eventually he called the *Observer* simply "A Journal of Free Voices."

These dramatic words invoked traditions of western bigtalking and American freethinking, filtered through a southern populist rhetoric. Although the ghost of William Brann, editor of the eponymous *Iconoclast*—shot dead in the streets of Waco by an irate Baptist—haunted the *Observer*'s pages, Dugger strained for a cosmopolitan identification, citing Jefferson, Woodrow Wilson, John Dewey, Thorstein Veblen, Franklin Roosevelt, and Harry Truman as his political forebears. What they shared, he asserted, was both a willingness to adapt to changing historical circumstances and an embrace of liberty. He approvingly quoted another magazine's explanation that "liberty, far from being an ethereal thing, is always identified with and related to specific and present situations."[21]

Liberals here sought a usable past of their own, linking their dissident creed, as Brann had done, to individualist elements in the dominant, right-ward-leaning political culture of their time and place. Henry Nash Smith, a prominent scholar of American culture who had left the flagship univer-sity of his native Texas because of Homer Rainey's firing, noted acerbically that the American myth of frontier independence had, "by some accident or alchemy of public-relations engineering . . . become linked in the public mind with the economic individualism of big business and the hatred of the federal government that is the one unifying emotion of right-wing rad-icals."[22] Texas liberals like Dugger wanted to wrest this myth of liberty from the political right and to update it, giving it new meaning in a world profoundly different from that of the old Southwest. But despite this polit-ical modernism, Dugger still appealed to the myth of a fiercely indepen-dent frontier culture, now supposedly eclipsed by fear and cowardice. He averred that liberalism must triumph "if fear of the consequences of honest opinions honestly expressed is to be banished from this once fearless land."[23]

The way in which libertarianism cut across conventional political cate-gories, appealing over the years to centrist liberals and leftist activists in Texas, to professional newspaper reporters and revolutionaries, indicates that in addition to the liberal–conservative axis, political life here was orga-nized along a libertarian–authoritarian axis, that this division, too, was vitally important to people's political orientation. Frequently the two axes lined up with each other, the liberals tending toward libertarianism and the conservatives almost always embracing an authoritarian creed. But it was not always so neat. People who pursued liberal political and economic goals might sanction authoritarian methods. After he and his associates rose to state and national power in the 1960s, Lyndon Johnson became the classic example of this type. Leftists might be more libertarian than liberals.

These complications may be characteristically southern; the radicalism of civil libertarianism may be simply a corollary of right-wing power and of a violent and authoritarian regional culture. But even if this pattern is dis-tinctively southern, it may not be the result of such a culture. After all, vio-lence and authoritarianism abounded in various northern local cultures in the 1960s, yet leftists there still had far less attachment to a civil libertarian agenda than their southern counterparts did. The relative weakness in the South of traditions of political dissent, such as Marxism, that criticize liberty as a "bourgeois" value allowed greater influence here for competing traditions of libertarian dissent.

Dissenters

During the late 1940s and the 1950s, there were a few notable outposts of recalcitrant liberalism at the university in Austin, voices that simply would not get with the current program. Frequently they were characterized by the irreverence and truculence discussed earlier. These liberals, such as they were, had the capacity to inspire young people, both to secure their allegiance to a liberal viewpoint and to encourage them to go further. To understand the politicization of those students who helped lay the groundwork for the new left—students who attended college roughly between 1958 and 1963—one needs to consider their exposure to these voices.

One such voice, at least intermittently, was the UT undergraduate newspaper, the *Daily Texan*. Under Ronnie Dugger and other editors like Horace Busby, the *Texan* developed a reputation for muckraking and outspokenness, a reputation that was occasionally justified, at least since the war years, when the regents asked Homer Rainey to do something to curb the allegedly socialistic sympathies of Busby's editorial page. Dugger made a name for himself, at UT and then at the *Observer*, for unmasking corporate power and wrongdoing.[24]

Starting with Dugger, there was considerable traffic between the *Texan* and the *Observer*. In 1956 Willie Morris, as editor of the *Texan*, incurred the regents' anger by writing an editorial in favor of public regulation and taxation of the oil and gas industries. When the in-house censor at the *Texan* refused to approve some of Morris's editorials, Morris sometimes ran a blank space instead, informing his readers, "This Editorial Censored."[25] In response, the regents removed him, as well as the editors of two other UT student publications, from the governing board of Texas Student Publications (TSP), the corporation that owned and had final authority over the paper. Instead of the editors sitting on the board, as had been traditional, now students from the UT student government body, the more pliant Student Assembly (SA), would take their places.[26]

After graduating, Morris went to work for the *Observer*. Others followed in subsequent years. Dugger and the *Observer* were celebrities on campus and around town. Austin was not a huge place, and editors from the *Observer* like Dugger, Morris, and Lawrence Goodwyn, who later departed for North Carolina and become a leading academic authority on the nineteenth-century Populist movement, mingled with *Texan* editors, as well as liberal state legislators, at popular watering holes like Scholz's Beer Garden, an indoor–outdoor spot just a few blocks from either the campus or the state capitol.[27] The *Observer* editors took the younger liberals at the *Texan* under their collective wing, bringing them into the circle of the well known, encouraging their self-confidence.

By the late 1950s the *Texan* had become one of the most prominent pro–civil rights voices on the UT campus. In a celebrated case in 1957, President Logan Wilson intervened to prevent the female lead in a campus production of the opera *Dido and Aeneas* from going to one of the few black students on campus, Barbara Smith.[28] There was much heated discussion of the Smith case in Austin, and the *Texan* editorial page came out against Wilson's decision. In 1958 Bud Mims, then the *Texan* editor, wrote in the paper that the South needed to go further on the racial front than even most liberals wanted to go. He insisted that it was not enough merely to strike down Jim Crow laws that formally ensured segregation—the South needed to take positive steps toward actual racial integration.[29] This prointegration position put the *Texan* a sizable step to the left of much "progressive" opinion and helped earn the paper the avid praise of U.S. Senator Ralph Yarborough, hero of Texas liberals, who, in a speech to the UT Young Democrats in 1958, called the *Texan* "the only free college paper in Texas today."[30]

More consistently feisty than the *Texan* were a few highly visible on-campus voices of outspokenly liberal professors at the university, whose iconoclastic teachings left their mark on many a student. The most notable seedbed of critical thinking in the university was the economics department, the immediate source of Homer Rainey's troubles. In the 1940s and 1950s, marginalist theory and abstract econometric models were not the pervasive dogma among economics departments that they became in later years. Instead, the UT economics department in this period followed a different path. Edward Everett Hale Jr., the department chair for much of the period between 1920 and 1950, was a Marxist scholar who kept his politics to himself in the classroom. Others followed Thorstein Veblen, studying economic institutions rather than developing abstract economic models.[31]

The most Veblenian was Clarence Ayres, who adopted not only the Norwegian American troublemaker's method but also his acerbic perspective on American industrial capitalism. Ayres criticized the American economy less for its injustices than for its wastefulness. His prescriptions for economic planning were unfashionable in the 1950s, when the United States witnessed a fresh burst of enthusiasm for the idea of (if not the practice of) economic laissez-faire. Like Veblen, Ayres depicted the cherished ideological underpinnings of the American social system as a set of curious folkways, and he conveyed his sharp views to his students, C. Wright Mills among them. For a time a board member at the *New Republic*, Ayres remained engaged throughout his career in the wider world, and he was noticed beyond his immediate environment. He testified in hearings before the state legislature many times throughout the 1930s and 1940s on behalf of liberal positions on various issues. But by 1951 chillier winds were blowing for those of his ilk, and the state house of representatives voted, 130 to 1, to denounce him for favoring "the destruction of free enterprise." One delegate said that if UT did not investigate and quiet Ayres, "we ought to knock out appropriations for the economics department."[32]

Besides Ayres, the most politically outspoken liberal member of the economics department from the 1930s through the 1950s was Robert Montgomery, known alternately around UT as "Dr. Bob" and "Bushy Bob" (because of his perpetually tousled hair). He preached the religion of southern Populism, telling his students that the South had been colonized after the Civil War by the capitalist North (thus employing a long-lived strategy among southern liberals and leftists, seeking to transcend racial divisions in their region by focusing on a sense of common economic oppression and capitalizing, to boot, on the pervasive hostility toward the North). Like some of his colleagues at UT, Montgomery had not exactly been bred for the academy. The son of "a frontier circuit-riding Methodist minister," he grew up picking cotton and punching cows for wages, attending school in the countryside only a couple of months a year. A person from a class background like Montgomery's could be represented only in a university faculty whose demographic sources had not been narrowed and calcified by the advance of academic professionalization. As a professor in the 1930s, he occasionally took students along for private conversations with Governor Allred, for whom Montgomery wrote a utilities regulation bill. During the New Deal and World War II, Montgomery served in the federal government in Washington. When the United States dropped two atomic bombs on Japan, he resigned from the government, and every year he delivered what became a famous lecture on the bombings, which some students attended over and over.[33]

One student at UT who was influenced by the atmosphere in the economics department, as well as the *Texan*, was Robb Burlage. Later he became a prominent member of Students for a Democratic Society (SDS), one of the provincials who mingled with the new left's early metropolitan elite. His experiences were both similar to and different from those of early SDS leaders like Tom Hayden and Todd Gitlin. Gitlin went from New York City's prestigious (and public) Bronx School of Science to Harvard, where at one point he and some fellow student peace activists found themselves in the White House basement gaining the attention of a Kennedy administration aide for their concerns. The impresario of SDS, Alan Haber, picked out Hayden, a newspaper editor at the University of Michigan who had come to college on an athletic scholarship, as a prime recruit for a new left. Burlage, too, was editor of the student paper at a big public university—he achieved this long-held ambition at the *Texan* in 1958/1959—and he went on to Harvard for graduate work in economics. His parents were political liberals who expressed a disdain of racism; his father became dean of the School of Pharmacy at UT. He differed from other early new left activists less in his status or social background than in the specific emphases that his upbringing as an idealistic Texan lent to his politics.

While the left-wing activists that Burlage met around Boston in the early 1960s—influenced by either the concerns of the old left or John Kennedy's priorities—held forth on international relations, Burlage—his thought shaped by the southern realities of Jim Crow and economic oligarchy—felt more comfortable "talking about democracy in the U.S."[34] As an economics major under the tutelage of professors like Ayres and Montgomery, Burlage came to favor an activist government that could forge economic order and equity. At the same time, he was touched by the antistatist currents running through dissent in Texas. An older reporter at the paper, Edd C. Clark, one of the Korean War veterans who leavened college life in the mid-1950s, introduced him to the writings of the anarchist theoretician Piotr Kropotkin. Burlage had not served on active duty in the armed forces, but he had been in the reserves since high school. The military presence in Texas seemed pervasive, he remembers; in the experience of many Texans, the military establishment *was* the state, and antimilitarism, in the 1960s, led easily to antistatism.

While still in high school, in the summer of 1955 Burlage attended the National Student Association (NSA) Congress in Chicago, and he remained involved in the NSA for several years. His participation in the Liberal Study Group, the SDS brain trust in the NSA that Haber started in 1961, led directly to Burlage's attendance at the SDS Port Huron Conference in 1962. Another UT student who went from the NSA to Port Huron was Dorothy Burlage, who married Robb after they graduated from college. Although both of them were involved in civil rights activism in Austin, Dorothy's political involvement was based more in a spiritually oriented, local activist outlook. She introduced Robb to the works of Albert Camus and other existentialist writers.

Ayres and Montgomery had been the "liberal heroes" on the UT faculty since the 1930s. But in the imagination of liberal students at UT, they were superseded in the mid-1950s by a new assistant professor of philosophy named John Silber. Starting with the *Brown* decision in 1954, race became the leading, emotionally motivating issue for young white liberals on college campuses, and on this issue Silber was far more outspoken. He was a San Antonio native who received his doctorate from Yale University. UT Vice President Harry Ransom, a scholar of philosophy and English literature, wooed Silber, who began teaching in Austin in 1954.[35] The older liberals on the faculty were less willing to disagree openly with the UT administration, and on the key issue of civil rights, they were more inclined toward gradualism. As noted earlier, their liberalism was defined primarily by economic concerns.

The racial gradualism of these older liberals was demonstrated during the Barbara Smith case in 1957, when Logan Wilson appointed a faculty committee, which included Clarence Ayres, Walter Webb, and Page Keeton of the Law School, all known as liberals, to review the controversy. The committee endorsed Wilson's decision to prevent Smith from appearing in the campus production, saying that it would be "offensive" to many whites if Smith, a black woman, played the romantic lead opposite a white man. Although they expressed hope for movement toward integration at the university, they wished to support their president, who preferred to move with caution. Silber, at this time a young assistant professor with neither standing nor security in the university, protested loudly. He peppered members of the committee with questions at a special faculty meeting, and he gave a speech at the campus Y denouncing Wilson's decision. (This open dissent may have cost him a $1,000 raise the following year.)[36]

Silber's hiring was part of an intellectual buildup that Ransom engineered in these years. Ransom had a vision of UT as the leading research university in the entire South and Southwest—"Yale on the Colorado," as one professor quipped—and to pursue his goals, he began to tap the almost inexhaustible funds that lay accreted beneath the oil fields that the university owned in the Permian Basin in West Texas. (The university had been given the land in 1875, before the oil was discovered. The regents sold drilling leases on it, as well as mineral leases and grazing rights, and the returns were invested in bonds. The university was allowed to spend only the interest from these investments, not the principle; hence it was called the Permanent Fund.)[37] Ransom acquired fancy collections of papers as well as fancy young faculty. A trio of young professors he brought to Austin in the mid-1950s who became particularly close to one another, were Roger Shattuck, a scholar of French literature and culture, William Arrowsmith, a prominent translator of the classics, and Silber. They were known as "Harry's Boys." They saw themselves as a young intellectual elite, and some students saw them that way, too. All three men were political liberals.[38]

Silber was a dynamic presence in and out of the classroom. A teacher of Kantian ethics, he pushed students to apply abstract ethical rules to real-world situations. He assigned them to research the ownership of specified areas of real estate in their hometowns. A lot of wealthy Texas families sent their children to UT, and the students not infrequently discovered that people they knew, perhaps people they knew quite well, were slumlords. Silber was the kind of teacher who believed that to do his job well, he had to unsettle his students. Furthermore, he seemed argumentative by inclination. When he thought he was right about something, as in the Barbara Smith case, he could become adamant.

Silber was as outspoken in his opposition to the death penalty as he was in his opposition to segregation, and on this issue, he was in perhaps an even smaller minority. He was president of the Texas Society to Abolish Capital Punishment, and he testified before state legislative committees concerning what he saw as the racial bias in the application of the death penalty. To many idealistic students who knew him in the late 1950s, his uncompromising, stubborn personality made him seem ethically pure, but sometimes, either inside or outside the classroom, he seemed like a bully. Many liberal students at that time viewed him as the professor on campus most sympathetic to their efforts.[39]

For many such students, Texas was a sea of conformity, and the university was, in general, simply an extension of that culture—the "football, beer-drinking culture," as Dorothy Burlage, who graduated from UT in 1959, calls it. A social class division between the fraternity and sorority members, often from elite or affluent backgrounds, who dominated organizational activity in general, and all other students, pervaded campus life.[40] Willie Morris describes his initiation rite in a fraternity, evoking his estrangement from what he considered the dominant campus culture's banality:

> It was full of such garbled mumbo-jumboes and high-flown adolescent sputterings, all thrown together in some uneasy overlay of illiteracy, that I was reminded of the way Huck Finn and Tom Sawyer had negotiated their own private blood-oaths as pirates. It was so juvenile that the Ku Klux Klan, in contrast, might have resembled the American Association of University Professors. But when the new brothers were lined up and presented with fraternity pins, I noticed that several of my fellow novitiates were crying, apparently from the impressiveness of it all.[41]

Despite her involvement in elite campus circles, Dorothy Burlage, like Morris, was determined to escape this atmosphere, and cosmopolitan teachers like Silber and Harry Ransom helped her do so. She graduated from high school in San Antonio; her family hailed from East Texas and, before that, from the slave country of the Southeast. Raised in this conservative Southern Baptist environment, her religious parents taught her to believe in the brotherhood of man, and she did not fail to notice that this principle conflicted with the white supremacy of the South. The contradictions of her upbringing were just as intense where the role of women was concerned. She was raised to be tough and self-reliant but also felt pressured to conform to the conservative values of her region. Inheriting a self-conscious tradition of "frontier women," as she puts it, she learned how to fix a flat tire and shoot a gun. Her mother, who had more formal education than most of her female contemporaries, held a bachelor's degree in journalism from UT (her father had a master's degree in geology). At UT, Dorothy was able to fulfill many of her intellectual aspirations, and she collected awards and honors. At the same time, because of the conventions of time and place, Dorothy's opportunities were sharply bounded. Young white women from middle-class families in Texas might attend college, but after that they were expected to settle down to a wifely role. In many ways, the excitement and freedom they experienced in college then ended. As a friend of hers, Celia Morris (a star in the social scene at UT), sums up the lot of women of their race and class in that setting, "It wasn't until after we got married that we got shat upon."[42]

Dorothy Burlage became involved in the desegregation activism of the late 1950s. This was the basic context for her political development, and it remained so for many years. When she graduated from college, however, an additional experience broadened her horizons beyond anything she had known before, informing her subsequent politicization. She was one of only two American students chosen by the State Department to visit the Soviet Union, which she did in the summer of 1959. It "had a major impact on me," Burlage recalls. She "could see different ways of addressing social problems." Not many people from her environment had ever seen a system of socialized health care and day care. Although the experience did not convert her to socialism, it certainly did nothing to discourage her growing criticisms of American society. The pervasive celebration of the American status quo during the 1950s was anchored in the demonization of socialism. With her picture of socialism now humanized, Burlage was more open to critical views of her own society than were most of her contemporaries.[43]

In a sense, the broadest possible social consciousness that any students developed during these years was the internationalist consciousness that a small group acquired. An internationalist consciousness was maintained on those campuses around the country where there was a significant "red diaper" presence—that is, where the children of families involved in left-wing politics were concentrated—or that were in close proximity to those few enclaves of left-wing activity that existed in the United States in the 1950s. In such circles, internationalism tended to have a leftist slant. The colleges congenial to these circles often were private schools, usually in the North— Swarthmore, Harvard, the University of Wisconsin, City College of New York, as well as the University of California at Berkeley. The University of Texas was not among such campuses.

Internationalism did extend to the provinces, however. Austin's proximity to Latin America (it is closer to Mexico City than to either New York City or San Francisco) colored the internationalism that developed at UT throughout the period considered here. In the summer of 1959, UT inaugurated an annual month-long student exchange program with a Chilean university. The Chilean students who came to UT often were further to the left than were any students from Texas. Accordingly, the UT students who went to Chile brought back a bit of the wider world. Those who went that first summer met with, among others, the youth leaders of the Chilean Communist Party, who told the North Americans, to their dismay, that capitalism was doomed.[44]

Even more politically charged were trips to the newly revolutionized Cuba. News of Fidel Castro's victory and descriptions of the changes he might make in Cuban society appeared continually in Texas newspapers, including the *Texan*, between 1958 and 1960. In August 1959 the Cuban government sponsored "Operation Friendship," an invitation for U.S. students to visit Cuba, including a promised visit with Fidel himself. The NSA also sponsored a Cuban expedition. The sixteen Texans who went to Cuba that summer on these trips got a firsthand glimpse of agrarian reform and collectivization, and indeed, they got a short lecture from a tired Castro, who promised that Cuba would always be open to them. Professor G. W. Ayer, who participated in Operation Friendship, reported that there was "freedom of expression" in Cuba, although he added, "The question of academic freedom is yet to be decided." Cuban students seemed strongly supportive of Castro. He had, after all, reopened the University of Havana, which had been closed for two years by the now deposed Fulgencio Batista.[45]

Through such contacts, students at UT in the late 1950s and early 1960s were exposed to the view that socialism was inevitable, that it represented the coming era of world history, especially in the former colonies of the Third World. This view was certainly not popular in the United States, but it had many adherents around the world. In April 1960, UT students heard it from Dr. Julian Hochfeld, a professor of sociology at the University of Warsaw. His position was distinctly evolutionary, not revolutionary: he stated that socialism would grow gradually out of the welfare states of western Europe rather than resulting abruptly from anticolonial revolts in Latin America, and he asserted, "Socialism is not a system based on opposition to capitalism and separated from capitalism by a clear line of distinction, but a method for steady improvement and progress in a democratic, industrial nation." This might not have sat well with Fidel, but it seemed calculated to appeal to North American college students. Through contacts like this, college students in the United States at this time were encouraged to feel they could enter into a dialogue with socialism without subverting the American political or social system.[46]

Of course, most of the authoritative voices that students heard were staunchly anticommunist and antisocialist. Characteristic was that of Paul Geren, executive director of the Dallas Council on World Affairs, who spoke at the Y in February 1959. He contrasted Christianity with communism, charging that communism ignored the spiritual dimension of life. Furthermore, he said, while Christianity valued the human individual, "Communism regards the individual as a fragment of society with no importance other than that of a cog in a machine." Despite the social critics who lambasted American society during this period for what they perceived as its conformist tendencies, the defenders of that society resolutely portrayed it as the fortress of individualism.[47]

The liberal role models on campus at this time maintained a position regarding communism and anticommunism that was critical of both. Clarence Ayres criticized "America-firsters" who "stomp" on traditional American freedoms in the process of fighting communism. John Silber, in a veiled reference to red-scare guilt-by-association tactics, argued that one should evaluate the logic and "sense" of what people have to say rather than judging them by their motives. The scrutiny of "motives" was perhaps one basis for judging people on their organizational associations, rather than by what they said and did. None of these liberals gave any indication that they would have any truck with communism (though Ayres, arguably, was a socialist of some stripe).[48]

In the 1950s, however, the furthest that student activists at UT went in deviating from the conventional wisdom on international affairs was to advocate an open-minded internationalism. Some student leaders discussed the

U.S. role in the world at the Y in 1959. Dorothy Burlage observed that Americans knew little about international affairs and needed to learn more—although she cautioned her fellow student activists that their political involvement should be rooted in local affairs and institutions close to home (as hers would be). One student, born in Italy, suggested that Americans should show more sympathy for nationalist movements around the world, opining that nationalism results from "having been slapped in the face" and that the United States did not know what that was like. Don Mathis, who had been a delegate to the NSA Congress during the past summer, took the opposite tack, asserting that nationalism in the United States was "so much a part of the American people that it [is] hard to talk about it objectively." He noted that without a "revolution" in the United States—a peaceful revolution, one of "ideas and awareness"—the world would be headed for another great war.[49]

These students were not radicals. Contrary to the charges often made by conservatives in the 1950s, the internationalism of such young liberals did not betoken secret socialist leanings. Instead, it expressed a dissatisfaction with the intellectually constricting nature of anticommunism and jingoism in the United States, of the way in which these tendencies shrank the spectrum of legitimate discussion. These ambitious young intellectuals wanted to broaden their horizons, and they saw conservative anticommunism as an obstacle to this goal. Their growing awareness that their fellow students in other countries stood in the vanguard of social change made the ignorance of many North Americans concerning world affairs all the more galling and further whetted their appetite for international contacts. At this time, the liberal internationalism of provincial activists was less a reflection of a capitalism-versus-communism debate than it was a variation on the larger theme of liberal cosmopolitanism versus conservative anti-intellectualism.

Rising Controversy

The pulse of conflict quickened amid the controversies between liberals and conservatives that marked the campus scene in the late 1950s, a fluid period in American politics generally, witnessing such politically disparate events as the passage, in 1957, of the first federal civil rights legislation since the Reconstruction era, and the 1958 founding of the rightist John Birch Society. Both liberals and conservatives among American youth were on the rise at this time. In 1960 not only the leading new left organization, SDS, but also the foremost "new right" group, Young Americans for Freedom (YAF), were established.

At UT, students on the right and left squared off over the issue of membership in the NSA. This was the major national collegiate organization in the United States. UT, like many other schools, paid annual dues and sent a delegation to the annual NSA Congress, which was held in the summer, usually on a midwestern campus and usually somewhere in the North. Students in Austin continually questioned the value of their school's involvement in this national organization, even after one UT student, Ray Farabee, became president of the NSA during the 1950s. The organization seemed irrelevant to many students' concerns.

Just as important, many viewed the NSA as a stronghold of student liberalism. Indeed, the UT delegations to the summer congresses were stocked with liberal activists. Many of the NSA's defenders at UT were involved with either the Y or the *Texan*. Robb Burlage and his successor as the *Texan*'s editor, Kay Voetmann, successfully argued before the SA that they should keep their membership in the NSA. The student government thus decided to put the NSA on a kind of informal probation, appointing a committee to keep its eye on the organization for the coming year.[50]

The NSA's liberal cosmopolitanism generally did not stray far from typical American views of the world at this time. Anthony Henry, an early black student at UT and a YMCA activist, was one of only fifteen students who attended a seven-week NSA seminar on International Student Relations in the summer of 1958. When arguing at UT that the school should maintain its membership in the NSA, he used an anticommunist gambit, allaying concern that internationalism was a little pink. This was the only American organization, Henry contended, that matched the Soviet Union's attempt to study the international scene and influence students around the world.[51] Indeed, in 1967, journalists at *Ramparts* magazine revealed that the CIA had funded the NSA so that the student organization could compete with Soviet student groups—just as Henry suggested—in the area of "outreach."[52] This was a double irony, for although the connection between anticommunist efforts and the NSA eluded American conservatives, the CIA's manipulation achieved mixed results, since the NSA's internationalism helped lay the groundwork for the anti-imperialist perspective that some of its members later developed. As noted earlier, many of the students who planned the 1962 SDS Port Huron Conference came together in the Liberal Study Group.

Other conflicts of the late 1950s concerned civil liberties, another issue dear to both cosmopolitan aspirations and the libertarian tradition of Texas dissent. On public university campuses, heated discussions were held concerning the anticommunist "loyalty" oaths that some state governments required of professors. The 1949 loyalty oath controversy in California is well known. In 1949 the Texas state legislature passed House Bill 837, which mandated that a question concerning national loyalty be asked of all applicants for faculty or staff positions at public universities in the state, as well as of students when they registered. Ten years later, a move was afoot to eliminate the oath. Many criticized it as both offensive and ineffective: it would have a "chilling effect" on political life, they said, and besides, a real subversive would have no compunctions about simply lying in his answer to any loyalty question. (Significantly, the arguments against such oaths generally were not based on an absolute opposition to government regulation of political beliefs—this would have involved a defense of Communists' civil liberties, a defense that even the most avid civil libertarians in Texas were not eager to make.) The *Texan* applauded the administration at the University of North Carolina, which asked its own board of regents to remove the anticommunist loyalty oath from university job applications, and urged that the Texas legislature learn from this example. This law was "freedom-assaulting" and "legally ineffective," it said.[53]

Around this same time, opposition among student leaders and faculty members—and by national political figures as well—crystallized against the loyalty affidavit required of anyone accepting one of the student loans that had been provided by the National Defense Education Act (NDEA). Passed in 1958 in reaction to the Soviet Union's launching of the *Sputnik* satellite, the NDEA pumped large sums of money for myriad purposes into American higher education, all ostensibly to improve the national cold war effort. The affidavit stated that one was not a member of any organization dedicated to the illegal or violent overthrow of the U.S. government. The objections to this oath were the same as those to the Texas state government's oath. Between early 1959 and the spring of 1960, the *Texan*, the SA, and the UT faculty all took stands against the NDEA oath. So did the NSA, as well as other student bodies and faculties around the country. In June 1960 the U.S. Senate passed a bill that removed this affidavit from the NDEA loan application procedure. Conservatives in Texas criticized opponents of the oath as soft on communism, but on this civil liberties issue, as the 1960s began, the liberals were in step with the national trend.[54]

Another oath controversy flared at UT at exactly the same time. In early 1959 three members of the Texas house of representatives proposed a bill that would have required all teachers in public colleges and universities to sign an annual statement declaring their belief in "a supreme being." University administrators were timorous in their response. A vice president of UT asserted that the administration "has no knowledge of atheism being taught" at their school. Bishop Frank Smith, the chairman of the board of regents at Southern Methodist University, a private school, commented, "It is beyond comprehension that any person who is a professed atheist would ever be employed as a teacher."[55] But students, faculty, and local clergy in Austin rallied against what they considered a gross intrusion into religious freedom, and after the testimony of clergymen before the legislature, the proposal went down to defeat. In a state where conservative Protestantism prevailed, the doctrine of religious freedom provided some of the strongest liberal ground, especially because advocates of religious liberty could appeal to the dominant Baptist tradition, which strongly favored separation of church and state.[56]

Some students worried most of all about the impact of conservative harassment on the faculty. Robb Burlage opined that the greatest threat to political freedom in the university came from within, from the administration. He cited a professor at Rice University in Houston who claimed that schools kept secret dossiers on politically outspoken professors. Burlage located the cause of this pressure in the corporate control of the university system: The American university, he wrote with a Millsian flourish, had fallen "victim to the cult of combinationism" and was controlled by the same people who controlled the wealth of the society. The "Academic Corporation," he said, had institutionalized conservatism and conformism.[57]

Arguably, the conformism of university life in the 1950s was merely one aspect of a more general spirit of caution governing American society. By the end of the decade, however, controversies over civil rights began to dispel the cloud cover that lay over American politics, largely through the work of black activists in the South. In the 1957/1958 school year, the civil rights issue that attracted the most attention in Austin was school integration. Newspaper headlines gave a day-by-day account of the events at Central High School in Little Rock, the capital of Arkansas, bordering Texas on the northeast. President Dwight Eisenhower felt constrained to send the army to Little Rock to overcome Governor Orval Faubus's obstruction of the city school board's integration plan. Such developments were not foreign to Texas; white mob violence had prevented the integration of schools in the town of Mansfield, prompting Governor Shivers to dispatch the Texas Rangers—to keep the peace, not to enforce the Supreme Court's desegregation order.[58]

The black residents of Austin had been segregated on the east side of town since the town fathers had shunted them there in the 1930s, and Jim Crow prevailed in public places and business establishments in town, but black Austinites continually pushed at the sealed envelope of segregation.[59] Even students at the virtually all white university were beginning to push.

The first African American had been admitted to UT in 1950 under court order, when Heman Sweatt was allowed to attend the Law School. In the mid-1950s a trickle of black undergraduates started to flow in. They were a small group, perhaps sixty in number, kept apart from their fellow students by segregation in both university housing and off-campus establishments.[60]

In the late 1950s, a few black students and a small group of white students started to work to change the situation for black students in the campus area. The major target of activity in the university itself was student housing. Many students lived in either fraternities or sororities or in privately owned buildings that were on a university list of approved housing. Others lived in dormitories. Finally there were cooperatives, owned by the university and supervised by UT employees. A few dorms and co-ops were available for black students. The black student housing was, by all reports, inferior to what was available to whites. In the summer of 1958 the university built a new dorm for white women, which the *Texan* said looked like a "luxury hotel" complete with modern air-conditioning. The black housing facilities, on the other hand, were marked by "sagging windows" and "aged kitchen facilities."[61] Student activists in the SA Grievance Committee wrote a report in the fall of 1959 highlighting these inequities and demanding that the black students, especially the women, be provided with decent housing. The report was adopted by the Austin Human Relations Commission (AHRC), a euphemistically named body that had been established by the city government to try to deal with racial controversies in the least explosive way. Pro–civil rights clergy and students were continually involved in the AHRC. In November 1959 the board of regents agreed to build the new housing but did not set a timetable. At this time, it seems, no one on campus called for racially integrated student housing.[62]

The other front on the student desegregation fight at this time formed along the retail establishments on Guadalupe Avenue, "the Drag," on the west border of the campus. The shops, restaurants, and movie theaters there were for whites only. In November 1958, students from the SA Student Welfare Committee scheduled a meeting, through the AHRC, with businessmen from the area to discuss the issue. The SA voted overwhelmingly to urge area businesses to desegregate. Furthermore, the SA, which regularly recommended to students a list of area establishments by issuing seals that read "Steer Here" (playing on the Texas Longhorn mascot, symbol of UT's "football and beer-drinking culture"), resolved to exclude those businesses that would not serve all university students. Despite these actions, in the 1950s, student activists had no luck in pressuring Drag businesses to desegregate.[63]

While race relations were merely simmering in Austin in the late 1950s, they were boiling over elsewhere. The contrast between Little Rock's school controversy and events in Austin is instructive. In 1955 the Austin Independent School District had technically desegregated its public schools by quietly allowing thirty-eight black students to begin attending the city's three previously all-white high schools, thus insulating itself against legal challenges (for the time being). Local white leaders, if conservative, had little taste for Faubus's style of grandstanding. Governor Price Daniel, a conservative politician who apparently wanted to avoid unnecessary trouble, held the situation steady, allowing localities to decide for themselves whether they would integrate their schools (certainly not a stance that would lead to much integration).[64]

Kay Voetmann of the *Texan*, an Arkansan, asserted that Austin's culture was less "Old Southern" than Little Rock's. This was why, she thought, the Texas legislature had been less intransigent than their Razorback counterparts. Political scientist V. O. Key speculated that in a state like Texas, where in 1940 less than 10 percent of whites had lived in counties where at least three of ten residents were black (compared with almost 70 percent of whites in Mississippi), white citizens would "have little cause to be obsessed about the Negro." Surely Key was engaging in wishful thinking. Texas could lay claim to a long history of racist violence against African Americans; in the 1950s, white Texans were generally conservative and did not appear ready to give up racial segregation. Nonetheless, Key was right in recognizing that by this time, the racial fear of the Deep South was not similarly consuming Texas political life, making the white resistance to civil rights agitation potentially less formidable than it was to the east. As the 1950s ended, change was indeed soon to come. Dugger put the matter provocatively to his fellow Texans in 1957: "We might as well join the battle early. Texas is half South, half Not South. Are you one or the other? You may put off deciding for a few years, but decide you must."[65]

Moral Individualism

Following the big Democratic Party victories in the 1958 congressional elections and John Kennedy's election to the White House two years later, liberal youth felt that the tide was turning in their direction, and their political horizons quickly outgrew the modest changes planned by political figures like Kennedy. The expansion of political discussion in the 1960s created a sharp sense of discontinuity with the politics of the preceding years. Nonetheless, the political involvement of young white activists around 1960 grew primarily out of the liberal traditions they inherited, including the tradition of secular southern liberalism. To understand how insurgency emerged from a period of rightist dominance, one needs to see the changes occurring in secular liberalism in the 1950s. Laboring in obscurity and extremity, suffering one defeat after another, liberalism mutated. In the lean years, the truest believers acquired greater influence in the liberal camp, and the "summer soldiers" of earlier, better days departed the scene. Younger people with new ideas, such as Ronnie Dugger, were able to rise fast and far within the political opposition. In sometimes subtle ways, the dissident, secular liberalism of this period broached the issues that the new left would pursue as grassroots activists and framed political issues in ways that younger radicals would absorb, if unknowingly.

The clearest shift in the white liberal agenda was the increased emphasis on issues of racial justice. Although racial liberals in the 1930s and 1940s were likely to be Roosevelt loyalists and New Dealers, they were vastly outnumbered in this coalition by white citizens, of the South and North, who evinced a reflexive and unchallenged racism. Partly in order to negotiate this alliance, liberals in that period focused their policy proposals almost exclusively on economic matters. Civil rights were relegated to an obscure place on the agenda. Only the more radical members of the New Deal coalition spoke out against racist violence, and on the issue of Jim Crow segregation, blacks stood almost entirely alone in their opposition.[66]

Lawrence Goodwyn put the matter squarely in 1958, asserting that southern Democratic power was built on a devil's compact between the different economic classes of the white race. This arrangement allowed wealthy whites to rule the South and made poorer whites their junior partners. Southern liberals, he said, had failed to break away from these relationships. Their failure to challenge the force of race baiting in southern politics had prevented the emergence of "a progressive southern movement—whether it be called Populism, Progressivism, New Dealism, or simply Liberalism."[67] The most notable aspect of the liberalism that Goodwyn, Dugger, and the *Observer* championed starting in the mid-1950s was its new outspokenness about racial inequality and violence. That Goodwyn's challenge to white southern liberals on "the Negro issue" would figure so prominently in the leading journal of Texas liberalism indicated that in one of the bleaker hours of that political creed, something new was afoot.

Dugger himself complained that it was hard for whites and blacks to be "natural" around each other, to step outside the games they had learned to play so well when encountering each other, "because our normal social life is so corrupt." Here a yearning for authenticity peeked through the nuts-

and-bolts agenda of secular liberalism.[68] If Dugger cried out in a wilderness of white southern conservatism, he found the balm for his pain in the civil rights movement. Beginning as an all-black movement, by the early 1960s it brought together the most idealistic of the black and white young, offering a vision of a "beloved community," of an end to estrangement and an emergence of authenticity. This movement furnished young white liberals with the most concerted example of political protest they had ever witnessed, and the movement became the catalyst for the subsequent escalation of youth activism, white and black. For many younger whites, as for Dugger, the interracialism of the civil rights movement at its high tide seemed to offer a possibility of "natural" and equal interaction between the races.

In more philosophical terms, a change occurred in these years in the way young white liberal activists viewed political issues in general. Just as they felt personally challenged to respond to the civil rights movement in a moral fashion, they began to view politics in general as a matter of personal responsibility and decision. Conceptually, the new emphasis was on the moral individual; only a grouping of morally courageous persons who made individual decisions to take public action would lead to social good. In the 1930s and 1940s, liberals had controlled the reins of national government and had stressed government as the main instrumentality of collective action. When liberals returned again to state power after 1960, this emphasis on government action received fresh impetus, and a fissure opened between older liberals in positions of power and younger activists who fixed their moral gaze on the character and actions of individuals.

The emphasis on personal integrity among young activists was a way of protesting the culture of conformism. Seeking to justify political dissent, activists played on the theme of individualism, to which Americans often paid lip service. In the 1950s, "individualism," as Henry Nash Smith observed, often signified a defense of "the free enterprise system," meaning economic conservatism.[69] However, political liberals found they could put this kind of rhetoric to their own uses. They were not alone in plucking out a dissident variation on the theme of individualism. After all, despite the celebration of conformity in the corporate sector and the exaltation of "togetherness" in social life generally, as well as the chilling effect of the red scare on political life, the frostiest years of the cold war produced critiques of conformist culture far more biting than most of what has been seen since, and several of these critiques found a large and enthusiastic audience. As a study of Vance Packard, the author of some of these critiques, makes clear, individual autonomy, sometimes caricatured in antigovernment polemics, remained a genuine and deeply held ideal in American culture, and dissenters could call on its authority in their indictments of a society that sometimes seemed as though it was squeezing the individual within an ever tighter compass.[70]

The ideal of individualism found many supporters, including some who were highly placed. After he became chancellor of the UT campus in 1961, Harry Ransom asserted that the belief in the uniqueness and freedom of the individual student, a belief he associated with the "progressive" movement in American education, was threatened by the growth of educational institutions, in which it was easy to view students as an impersonal "mass." Jo Eickmann, editor of the *Texan* in 1960/1961, expressed the same anxiety, writing, "As that campus has become a massive conglomerate of glass and brick, so we have become a mass." This feeling of "massification" among the "baby boomers" as they began to enter college in the 1960s frustrated them and fueled campus rebellions like the Berkeley Free Speech Movement in 1964, in which student leaders like Mario Savio condemned "the machine" that housed them. But whereas Clark Kerr, the chancellor of the Berkeley campus, stubbornly resisted the students' complaints—celebrating the same trends that the students protested—Ransom's sympathetic view indicated the cultural power of the ideal of autonomy. He himself warned against viewing students as interchangeable cogs in a "machine" or as "herds that move like driven cattle."[71]

Shades of Savio—or C. Wright Mills, who urged a distinctly individualistic, heroic role on dissident intellectuals. A native of Waco and, like Ronnie Dugger, a lapsed Catholic, Mills transferred to UT from Texas A&M as a college student in the 1930s. In the following decades, he compiled an impressive body of sociological writings. Indeed, he became the single most influential thinker in the formation of the new left in the United States. Part of this influence lay in the cold war appeal of the outlaw persona he cultivated, a kind of renegade John Wayne figure, squaring off against vast, immoral forces. He was "decisive and outspoken in speech, independent in thought, and frequently flamboyant and unorthodox in dress," wrote a clearly impressed student reporter when Mills returned to his alma mater in 1960 to give a talk. At UT, this prodigal son told students that they were entering an age of giant bureaucracies in which no one seemed to make the crucial decisions, an era "dominated by rational organization and rational moral insensibility." He challenged them to find a way to transcend this moral debauch, to raise their individual voices in dissent. In his writings Mills conjured what one scholar calls a "pastoral of autonomy," and he spoke for a tradition of individual responsibility.[72]

One student who found himself deeply affected by Mills's writings, Chandler Davidson, started writing a column in the *Texan* in the fall of 1959.

Davidson thought that plenty of students wanted to rebel against something but that, he said, they often had trouble figuring out what to rebel against. Like others at this moment, he saw students caught between caution and dissent, attracted to the prospect of involvement but still plagued by paralysis. Vance Packard, a Methodist whose characteristic style of criticism was the jeremiad, visited UT in 1960 and lamented the wayward course of contemporary students, going so far as to say that they seemed more conservative than they had been "10, 20, 30, 40 years ago."[73] In fact, several political issues had aroused the concern of young people during the second Eisenhower administration, and despite Davidson's comments, student activists were not motivated merely by an attraction to rebellion for its own sake. By the decade's close, young observers like Davidson and older commentators like Packard and Mills, as well as countless others, saw student political and cultural concerns focus sharply on the issue of race.

CHAPTER TWO

Breakthrough:
The Relevance of Christian Existentialism

THE CONSERVATIVE PRECINCTS of American life witnessed more than one kind of dissent in the 1950s. While secular liberals fought to keep the spirit of democracy alive, others confronted the second aspect of the problem that Arthur Schlesinger had limned in the late 1940s: the challenge of finding stable values and social forms appropriate to a democratic culture in the "age of anxiety." To take up this challenge would mean engaging in a kind of cultural dissent, experimenting with new ways of living and thinking. Some young people in 1950s America, fearing anxiety but determined to overcome it, explored in great detail the existentialist outlook that Schlesinger had found attractive but took it in directions that he had not foreseen. By the early 1960s, some of the young existentialists concluded that the way out of anxiety was through disruptive, challenging political activism. This vision of authenticity through dissent led them into the civil rights movement and the new left.

Some of the most politically effective young existentialists offered a relatively acceptable and appealing dissent because they grounded their experimentalism in the legitimacy of Protestant evangelicalism. The early cold war was a time of "religious revival," as some called it, of rising church attendance rates and the ascendancy of evangelical celebrities like the young Billy Graham. Outpourings of the "old-time religion" were noted on college campuses, starting with the upheaval at Wheaton College, outside Chicago, at the conclusion of World War II. In the 1950s, evangelical groups like the Campus Crusade for Christ won many converts among students. At the University of Texas, conservative Protestantism was the rule, fundamentalism alive and well.[1] Buried deep in the social conservatism of evangelical Protestantism was a latent dissidence, a radical version of this creed's sharp dissatisfaction with contemporary culture. To a minority of young people in the 1950s and 1960s, this latent radicalism came through loud and clear in the highly contemporary form of Christian existentialism.

In the 1950s, students in Austin and elsewhere immersed themselves in the currents of existentialist thought emanating from Europe and circulating throughout the Western world. What emerged from this process by the start of the 1960s was a politicized, seemingly de-Christianized dissident evangelism, a kind of "religionless Christianity," to use the pregnant phrase of Dietrich Bonhoeffer. The teachings and example of Bonhoeffer, a German theologian who was executed by the Nazis in 1945 for his involvement in an antigovernment conspiracy, were introduced to young Texans searching for authenticity by Joseph Wesley Mathews, a one-time fundamentalist preacher, at an influential place called the Christian Faith-and-Life Community (CFLC). The CFLC was a residential religious study and training center affiliated with UT. Ronnie Dugger had difficulty making up his mind about Mathews and named him an "inspired merlin . . . genuine, fraud."[2] Others committed to more familiar forms of religiosity and social concern, such as Frank Wright, head of the University Young Men's Christian Association (YMCA) in Austin, always doubted that Mathews and his teachings contributed much to the political ferment of the 1960s.[3] But contribute they did.

Many connections linked the Faith-and-Life Community, "one of those robust experiments in community intellectual living that was in such stark contrast to the comfortable campus life of the 1950s," to the political rebellion of the 1960s. Dick Simpson, a liberal activist, agreed that there was "no place else in conservative Texas" quite like "the Community," as its members commonly called it. Simpson was only one of many students who, between 1956 and 1962, resided for some period of time at the Faith-and-Life Community and later became active in civil rights protest and other liberal and radical political activity. Tom Hayden, one of the leading lights of Students for a Democratic Society (SDS) in its early phase, called the Faith-and-Life Community "*the* liberated spot on the silent campus" in the early 1960s.[4]

Members of the Community who became active dissidents invariably traveled in the larger orbit of political liberalism around the university. Had it not been for the presence in this environment of secular liberals like

Dugger and Christian liberals like Wright, young people would have been less likely to draw politically dissident inferences from Mathews's existentialism. Existentialism, like the philosophical strains of vitalism and pragmatism that it resembled in some respects, did not in itself imply political engagement of any kind. Yet at this conjuncture of historical circumstances, amid the synthesis of diverse elements in the political culture of the United States, existentialism fed a radical humanism that infused the dissident search for democracy and authenticity.

The crux of the matter was the conviction that one could turn away from anxiety and toward authenticity if one made oneself open to risk; this was the existentialist faith. Although the Community residents spent countless hours discussing the problem of anxiety, in the end they chose a bold stance of freedom, even of mastery, in a changing world. To the combustible chemistry of this historical moment Christian existentialism contributed the hope of breaking through to a new world where young people might find a new, authentic life. Joe Mathews preached a new evangel, drawing on the Protestant tradition of personal regeneration, as fundamentalists did, transforming it into a newly relevant message of rebirth into authenticity. He helped fashion "a message of love, of understanding, of compassion . . . of courage, of gameness."[5] Ultimately, the spirit of "courage" and "gameness" led to political controversy.

Dugger wondered, "Could it be that Joe knew god but just wasn't introducing him around?"[6] Mathews's theology was unorthodox, but its brash rebellion was calculated to appeal to young people as unmoved by traditional religion as he had become. (This approach found no small success in selling religion: one-tenth of the students who came through the Community reportedly went on to join the clergy.)[7] As existentialist theologians like Rudolf Bultmann had urged, Mathews sought to wrench Christianity out of its ancient trappings and recast it in modern language, symbols, myths, and hopes. Worship, and life itself, became drama. In what the French Catholic thinker Gabriel Marcel called a "broken world," salvation reemerged as therapy.[8] Jesus Christ was a symbol of openness to risk and extremity. Believers sought new selves, not as saints transported to the clouds, but in a "New Being" here on earth. One of Mathews's disciples in the early 1960s remarked, "I think the Community is more like the early Church than other groups are today, because the early Church didn't give a goddamn about life after death. Neither do we."[9] Such heterodox adherents sought to fulfill Bonhoeffer's promise of "a new language, perhaps quite non-religious, but liberating and redeeming—as was Jesus' language; it will be a new language of righteousness and truth."[10]

Building Community

In the beginning, the Faith-and-Life Community seemed like a thoughtful, conservative venture in Protestant campus ministry. The institution's founder was a genial campus Presbyterian minister named W. Jack Lewis. Steeped in local culture as an undergraduate at UT in the 1930s, Lewis had been head cheerleader, or "yeller." He served as a navy chaplain during World War II and returned home to minister to students at Texas Tech College and then at UT. In 1950/1951 he undertook further theological studies in Britain and Europe and encountered the Iona experiment, an intentional Christian community in Scotland. He thought this kind of experiment might speak to contemporary students in a way that conventional campus ministry did not, and he resolved to begin a similar community in Austin.

In 1952 Lewis assembled a prestigious board of directors that provided the CFLC with both official sanction and a springboard into fund-raising. The board included Harry Ransom, as well as Texas businessmen evidently glad to support this kind of Christian endeavor. But the board was mainly composed of prominent theologians at schools across the country, the most illustrious of whom was James I. McCord, who at this time was moving from the Presbyterian Seminary in Austin to the presidency of Princeton Theological Seminary. McCord had been with Lewis in Scotland, and their conversations had urged Lewis on.

Lewis saw the Faith-and-Life Community as part of the movement for "lay renewal" that had spread across western Europe after World War II. This movement, echoing one of the original themes of the Protestant Reformation, emphasized the religious leadership of the laity. It sought to engage laypersons in continuing theological study and to encourage them to relate theology to society. At the CFLC, the "layman" who was to be engaged in religious dialogue was the university student, "that he might be more informed and articulate in his beliefs, with a view toward his becoming a responsible churchman, parent, and citizen in his life and work." The CFLC undertook this lay training, it explained in a communication to other ministers, "for the sake of the renewal of the Church." The CFLC became a model for lay education and campus ministry known around the country and even the world. McCord averred that by the early 1960s, the CFLC had "become known throughout the nation and around the world as a symbol of how Christians might respond to the demands of a new time." Clergy at many other schools, like Duke and Brown Universities and the Universities of Montana and Wisconsin, modeled their own experiments on the CFLC.[11]

According to its charter, the CFLC was open to members of any "Evangelical Christian Communion" or church, thus placing limits on its ecumenism. In its first year it admitted only men, who numbered thirty. They lived together in what was called the "College House," with university approval. In 1953 the Community opened a "Women's Branch," also numbering thirty women, and the "Men's Branch" expanded to forty-five; each branch totaled about fifty in the later years of the experiment. Mildred Hudgins, the CFLC's "den mother," administered the Women's Branch. The women and men lived separately but had joint classes. Judy Schleyer Blanton, a student who lived in the Community around 1960, remembered students there sneaking in and out of bedroom windows, but there is little reason to believe that more sex went on at the CFLC than elsewhere on campus. Women and men ate Friday evening dinner together at the Men's Branch and participated in unified prayer services. All students who chose to join the Community knew they would have to fulfill the normal undergraduate course requirements in addition to their studies at the CFLC. The curriculum here was likely more challenging than what students encountered in most regular classes at the university.[12]

The Community's members persistently described their activities as "corporate." This reflects the cold war concern that people in advanced industrial societies were faced, in this age of anxiety, with the twin dangers of individual isolation and social conformity—conditions that amounted to a recipe for totalitarianism, according to the social thought of the day. Communal experiments like the CFLC, with its written "covenant" enunciating the social commitments of its members, underscored the need to invest social forms with meaning and intentionality in order to prevent them from becoming mindless or oppressive. Claire J. Breihan and O. R. Schmidt, undergraduates who lived at the Women's Branch in the mid-1950s, recall that the corporate discipline of the CFLC was one of its most attractive aspects to them.[13] The Faith-and-Life Community held that it was difficult for individuals to confront a changing world effectively "without the *discipline and sustenance* of corporate structures." Navigating a new world required the development of "new and creative modes of corporate existence," and the Community's members intended to play a part in this work. Where "the struggle" to create such "creative modes" occurs, they said, "there is the breakthrough. There is the future alive in the present." The CFLC searched "toward the development of the new forms that will, God willing, bring meaning into the midst of meaninglessness for countless persons who are trapped between an old world passing away and a new world being born."[14]

The Community officially stated that its experiment in intentional community was both compatible and interdependent with the pursuit of fully developed individuality, or autonomous "personality," to use the term promoted by Paul Tillich, one of the Community's favored theologians.[15] "Authentic, self-consciously disciplined community does not swallow the individual; it rather creates the very possibility of personhood by pushing the individual against the necessity to decide for himself," the CFLC's covenant read. "Genuine participation in the structures of community and authentic individuality are two poles of the same reality." The higher freedom of the gemeinschaft was not supposed to mean conformity. At least some students reported that in practice, life in the Community was animated by a bias "against accommodation for harmony's sake." (Others felt differently, as I discuss later.) The capacity to disagree was a mark of the really close relationships that bound a true community. "Let us never forget," the participants agreed, "that though we are utterly bound by our covenant, we remain free at any time and in any circumstance to break the covenant; never, to be sure, by default in decision but by a self-conscious free resolve made in light of other claims."[16]

Yet for all the innovation of its formal aspect, between 1952 and 1955, the curriculum at the Community took a "conventional approach," focusing on Bible and theological studies. Lewis grew disenchanted with this curriculum. "There was no existential 'bite' to awaken the student to the relevance of Christian faith to life as he experienced it daily," he reflected later. The study materials had been "presented from the orthodox and/or dogmatic viewpoint" and therefore "seemed often to demand the acceptance of some constituted authority for their validity." That Lewis found this problematic indicates the antiauthoritarian direction in which his religious thought already was headed.[17]

Lewis sought new students and new teachers. The criteria for admittance to the Community were radically relaxed: No longer did students need to belong to a church, either Protestant or even Christian. Starting in the fall of 1955, any "inquirer" could apply. Previously, most students, like Claire Breihan, had come from conservative Protestant backgrounds, often fundamentalist. Furthermore, university administrators, professors, and clergy had steered toward the Community many students perceived as campus leaders. Al Lingo, a CFLC undergraduate in the mid-1950s who later returned as a teacher, was a member of the Cowboys, a prestigious UT fraternal organization, as well as a Greek fraternity member in good standing. Fred Buss, another Community member from the late 1950s, was a member of the Deacons, another elite campus men's group. Now "the door was open to Catholics, Jews, agnostics, atheists, Buddhists, Hindus, and others."[18]

Ultimately, "national, racial, religious, economic, and academic barriers were eliminated" to varying degrees. Most dramatically, the Women's Branch became the first racially integrated housing on the UT campus in 1954 when it admitted a lone black woman. Residents from the time remember this as a conscious political decision by the group, and it cost the Community some sorely needed financial support. In subsequent years, other black students lived in the Community; one recalls it as "a real enjoyable place to live ... people were real friendly." A large number of foreign students lived at the CFLC between 1955 and 1962, one of its most distinguishing features on campus.[19]

Just as important to the Community's subsequent direction was the appointment in 1956 of Joseph Wesley Mathews as the director of the curriculum. Until he departed for Chicago in 1962, Mathews's teachings and personality were an omnipresent influence on the character of life and study at the CFLC. McCord recommended Mathews, who was a professor at the Perkins School of Theology at Southern Methodist University in Dallas, and the CFLC's board unanimously agreed. Although Mathews alienated and hurt at least some of the students he taught, he enraptured others. He acquired disciples and enemies, who found him, respectively, inspirational and authoritarian. He brought the "existential 'bite' " that Lewis wanted. But Mathews went beyond Lewis—eventually beyond what Lewis could stomach—taking the Community, as one of Mathews's protégés said, "in a revolutionary direction."[20]

Joe Mathews started his career as an evangelical preacher with fundamentalist leanings. The son of an Ohio Methodist minister, he went to Hollywood in the 1930s to break into the movies and got saved instead in a Los Angeles revival. He maintained a dramatic flair; his heavy silences, poetic outbursts, and fake stammer in the classroom became legend among his students. With his faith intact, he entered the army as a chaplain during World War II. His experiences in the Pacific theater of war "destroyed him" when he found that his religious verities were useless to dying men. "He could offer somebody a cigarette as they died, but he didn't have anything to say to them. They had to die themselves," as Lingo puts it.

In a state of intellectual and spiritual crisis, after the war Mathews began studies with H. Richard Niebuhr at Yale Divinity School, where he became immersed in existentialism. The younger Niebuhr's austere teachings are usually seen as quite conservative, emphasizing human sinfulness and limitations and steering attention away from broader social questions. But Mathews combined this intellectual material with both the evangelis-

tic zeal of his American Protestant tradition and his own dramatic inclinations. He became a local celebrity at Perkins, known for iconoclastic sermons during which he might rip pages out of a church's Bible to illustrate
his disdain of the traditional symbols of belief.[21] The contemporary relevance of Mathews's theatrics was indicated by Joe Slicker, Mathews's assistant at the Community, when he remarked, "The gospels are not talking
about a guy named Jesus. They are talking about a drama about a guy
named Jesus."[22]

Mathews drew students' attention to the questions that had been sweeping through European Protestant circles for decades and in particular to the
German theology of Tillich, Bultmann, and Bonhoeffer. Many classified all
these thinkers as theological existentialists; Tillich and Bultmann adopted
the term themselves. Tillich and Bonhoeffer also were associated with the
"neoorthodox" movement in theology, which historians have viewed as a
conservative reaction against theological liberalism. Existentialism, however, served as the pathway between theological conservatism and radical
humanism. Historically, existentialist philosophy had emerged from
Protestantism, particularly in the thought of Sören Kierkegaard (whose
writings the students at the CFLC also read). Small wonder, then, that in
the cold war United States, existentialism took root most securely in a
Protestant religious context. It ended by helping young people reach a place
that many of the Faith-and-Life Community's initial establishment supporters could have neither predicted nor wanted.

Anxiety and Mastery

Walter Kaufmann, the editor of an influential English-language anthology
on existentialism published in 1956, despaired of producing a definition of
existentialism, saying that it "is not a school of thought nor reducible to any
set of tenets." He asserted, in fact, that existentialism "is not a philosophy
but a label for several widely different revolts against traditional philosophy" and concluded that "revolt" and "individualism" were perhaps the
most stable characteristics of this odd anticreed. "The heart of existentialism," he wrote, was "the repudiation of the adequacy of any body of beliefs
whatever, and especially of systems" of thought, based on the belief that
such systematic thinking was "remote from life." It is possible, however, to
identify some consistent themes of those thinkers usually classified as existentialist. Kaufmann's remarks hint at a couple of those themes: first, a
belief that thought about life should take the experience of life, rather than
abstract principles, as its starting point and, second, an affirmation of the

capacity for self-conscious revolt against authority, intellectual or social, as a basic component of human identity.[23]

Kaufmann failed to consider in any detail the Christian existentialists.[24] These thinkers, studied by students at the CFLC, focused on the paired danger and promise of modern life. The danger was anxiety, and Tillich was its major expositor. Anxiety was a feeling of looking into an abyss, produced by a permanent state of estrangement from God or simply from "the ultimate," or the "ground of Being," as Tillich liked to put it, psychologizing religion for the sake of secular readers.[25] Anxiety was an existential condition, that is, a condition of human life itself, according to Tillich, but it had gotten worse in the age of modernity and industrialization. For all this, Tillich urged his readers to say " 'yes' to life," to embrace life despite the spiritual and psychological threat of anxiety, to embrace the risk of nonbeing in the way that Jesus did on the cross. The real prophet of mastery over modernity for students at the Community, however, was Dietrich Bonhoeffer, a less anxious and more politicized figure. A martyr for his political activity, Bonhoeffer became the exemplar of authentic religion in the modern world.

According to midcentury theologians, people of previous eras could get through their lives either without experiencing too much acute anxiety or they could find relief from it in the unchallenged certainties of both this world and the next. The precapitalist, certainly the pre-Reformation European, past was supposedly a time of psychological and spiritual security, the meaning of life anchored in divinely ordained patterns, social and cosmic. But, the narrative went, increasing human control over the physical world disturbed the sense that the world was a perfect and completed structure of divine making. "Only after the victory of humanism and Enlightenment as the religious foundation of western society could anxiety about spiritual nonbeing become dominant," wrote Tillich. More recently, the awareness of other cultures damaged the authority of the Western worldview. Secular humanists celebrated both human power over nature and the human freedom to consciously choose values. Liberal Protestantism was, in a sense, born of these challenges to cultural and theological certainty and of the desire to accept the lessons of the Enlightenment.[26]

Many of the existentialists could not rest easy with this accommodation, and this joined them to the neoorthodox thinkers who rebelled against an easy theological modernism. They did not think the loss of the old certainties could be absorbed so painlessly. They recognized the degree of freedom from necessity that the human species had won in its battle against the natural world, but they feared that spiritually, this physical freedom was sending them toward the abyss. In the 1930s, Tillich wrote that "the man of today. . . . is the autonomous man who has become insecure in his autonomy." Human control over the world, by itself, might be anything but a comforting prospect. "The spiritual disintegration of our day consists in the loss of an ultimate meaning of life by the people of Western civilization." As so secular a thinker as Arthur Schlesinger Jr. agreed, "progress"—science, capitalism, and culture—stripped the inherited meanings away from life, and anxiety enveloped humanity. Schlesinger prescribed a dose of neoorthodoxy for what ailed the masses. Tillich viewed fascism as a response to this spiritual crisis, an attempt to manufacture a new set of cultural symbols that would provide Europeans with a vision of social order grounded in something transcendent ("blood and soil").[27] The Faith-and-Life Community would make another, less noxious try at this symbol building.

The neoorthodox prescription of traditional Christian faith—and its assertion that God was "wholly other"—convenient though this formula might have proved as a bulwark against anxiety, was not widely convincing. It seemed to fly in the face of decades of accumulating cultural relativism among liberal Christian theologians, both European and American, who had pioneered the comparative study of world religions and who had progressively diluted the specific Christian content of what they considered legitimate belief, in search of the core religious "spirit" that was manifested differently in different cultures.[28] Traditionalists could wish these cultural developments away, but wish was not reality. It was left to others to answer the difficulties of modernity.

No theologian strode more briskly headlong into the future than Dietrich Bonhoeffer. Personally he expressed a rather orthodox obeisance before his Christian God, yet his admirers could take from him his modernism and leave behind his traditionalist aspect. Unlike Tillich, the epitome of scholarship, Bonhoeffer was better known for his life than his work, and his death was the best-known fact of his life. A young German who adamantly opposed the Nazi regime from its start in 1933, he fought the Nazification of the German Lutheran Church, eventually becoming involved in the small, indigenous anti-Nazi resistance. For his knowledge and approval of the failed plot to kill Adolf Hitler in 1944, he was imprisoned and in 1945 he was hanged. His most widely read work was a volume of fragments he wrote near his life's end, published posthumously as *Letters and Papers from Prison*. The Faith-and-Life Community was established only seven years after Bonhoeffer's death, and the moral lessons of World War II—lessons focusing on collaboration and resistance—were much in discussion throughout its lifetime.[29]

In the 1960s Bonhoeffer became, posthumously, a major player in the theological controversies associated with the phrase "the death of God."

In 1963, John A. T. Robinson portrayed Bonhoeffer as the most radical of the "new" theologians. Similarly, the American Harvey Cox, in his 1965 book *The Secular City*, positioned the dead German as the harbinger of secularism. Bonhoeffer's cryptic call for a "religionless Christianity" was congenial to Cox and to many young people of the 1960s. Bonhoeffer proposed to do away with many of the trappings of modern religion and to combine a primitive church with a sense of human control over the world. His "religionless Christianity" would be simultaneously archaic and modern. It would mean a "breakthrough," as Bonhoeffer put it, in beliefs, values, personal life, social life, and politics—a "breakthrough" to a new life.[30]

Bonhoeffer used the phrase the "world come-of-age" to describe the autonomy and mastery over the natural world that humankind had developed in the modern era. In "questions of science, art, and ethics," human understanding and control had supplanted any mythological notion of supernatural control. This was a breakthrough in the history of humankind, and Bonhoeffer celebrated it. He stated bluntly, "Man has learnt to deal with himself in all questions of importance without recourse to the 'working hypothesis' called 'God.'..it is becoming evident that everything gets along without 'God'—and, in fact, just as well as before." He thought liberal theology was correct in that "it did not try to put the clock back."[31] Unlike Tillich and most other existentialists, Bonhoeffer did not view this freedom from "God" as a source of angst. Rather, he celebrated the "world come-of-age" with no sense of unease. This meant that he saw no reason to naturalize or disembody God into "the ground of Being"; to him, human autonomy need not mean an estrangement from God. He asserted that humans' very freedom meant that they could make a radically free decision to accept God. He urged a breakthrough to God that would coexist with, not contradict, the breakthrough to autonomy.

Reflecting a modernist conviction that religion had to change with the changing times, the young participants in the Faith-and-Life Community frequently commented on the "New World" they saw emerging in the mid-twentieth century. They felt they lived in "an acutely dynamic world of flux," "an intensely technological world of automation," a world of both "space conquest and nuclear powers" and "technical psychology and inwardness." The new world of science simply "eliminates traditional other-worldly metaphysics," they insisted. Expressing a characteristic concern of their era, they worried that automation was creating "a whole new problem of leisure time," as well as the need to make this time worthwhile. Modern psychology was "transfiguring the whole meaning of personal freedom." This world "is being thrust upon us."

Like Bonhoeffer, the Community's members resolved to embrace the future confidently. Above all, they expressed the view that the people of their time could not go back to a comforting, naive past. "The question of our age," they said, "is not how to return to a static universe but how to respond to the given scene of perpetual change." The challenge, they observed, "is not how to return to naive unawareness, but how to participate authentically in this era of radical self-consciousness." They lived in "the time of experiment."[32]

They mused particularly over the character of human psychology in the world come-of-age. Like Tillich, they thought the development of depth psychology was part of a growing human self-consciousness that any thoughtful person had to confront. "With the new world has come a break-through in the human spirit," they explained. The "post-modern man is emerging," characterized by "intensive and extensive consciousness of his situation in an utterly new world. He is the man of awareness." This introspective personality acquired a new awareness of human autonomy, powers from which one could not flee. Community members thought that modern psychological self-awareness had far-reaching implications for human conduct. People know that "another can never finally determine [their] style of life for [them]," that there are "no predetermined patterns for [their] life." Such "new" personalities needed to find their own meaning and direction in life.[33]

This was the paradox of anxiety. Humans carried both the chance and the burden of creating meaning in life. This was their freedom, and it distinguished them from all other creatures. They had to wrestle meaning from the void of nothingness, despite the threat of meaninglessness that was always hovering over their shoulder. If they resisted this challenge, then they refused to be human. The young Christian existentialists of the CFLC shared this conviction with Camus and Sartre. Humans created possibilities for meaning but were never rid of "anxiety, the rubbing together of nothingness and possibility." Anxiety and freedom thus became the two sides of the human coin, both existential conditions. This is why Kierkegaard, after characterizing anxiety as the "sickness unto death," declared that the sickness was "man's advantage over the beast."[34]

The Ethics of Authenticity

Reinhold Niebuhr secured an appointment for Paul Tillich at Union Theological Seminary during the 1930s, as he had done for Bonhoeffer. But whereas Bonhoeffer, guilt stricken for escaping the Nazi regime, returned to his homeland and met his death, Tillich left Germany to remain in the United States for the rest of his life. Tillich's writings in English exerted great influence in academic circles, as with his three-volume *Systematic Theology*, and more broadly with books like *The Shaking of the Foundations* and *The Courage to Be*. Tillich moved from an early association with Christian socialism to a less clearly political theology that stressed life and love. As much as anyone, he integrated modern psychology with theology. Some have seen him, especially in his later and most influential work, as the purveyor of a therapeutic, amoral theology that avoided politics and banished any genuine religious sensibility. Indeed, he was a theorist of therapy, urging his readers to say " 'yes' to life." Young people who read his work in the 1950s, however, took from it not an affirmation of dominant values and ways of life but a critique. Although by the 1950s Tillich seldom engaged in explicit political discussion, his cultural critique helped fuel an impulse toward rebellion.[35]

Tillich reconciled allegiance to God with human freedom by refiguring God as "the ultimate," "the unconditional," or "the ground of Being." This diffuse concept of God made Tillich attractive to theological liberals (even if it remained unclear exactly what Tillich meant). He simply asserted that if one was seized by an "ultimate concern," then one was in a religious state. Thus he reconciled God with human inclinations.

The unconditional is a dimension of all things in this world, their "inner infinity." At particular moments in our lives, the unconditional "break[s] through a given form of individual existence, bringing it into union with the ultimate ground of meaning. It is the experience of being grasped by the essential power and meaning of reality, 'the really real.' "[36] Generally, however, we are out of touch with this ultimate realm, according to Tillich: "The sense of the immediacy of the origin, of the creative sources of man's life, [has been] lost." He lamented, "Under the conditions of human finitude and estrangement that which is essentially united becomes existentially split."[37]

Wholeness, or authenticity, was the goal for existentialists, and it displaced the more traditional objectives of salvation and even goodness. To the Christian existentialists, alienation and sin were one and the same; thus authenticity acquired moral freight as the opposite of sin. Overcoming sin was a matter of ending spiritual estrangement. It was not a matter of good works. Here Tillich found common ground with the neoorthodox rejection of good works as the heart of faith and with the "realist" view of human nature as inherently flawed, a view popularized and put to various political uses by Reinhold Niebuhr.[38] The concept of existential sin, for others, encouraged not a complacency regarding human fallenness but, rather, a striving toward unity—and a promise of redemption.

Nonetheless, existentialist thinkers sometimes suggested a wholesale demolition of conventional codes of morality in search of authenticity, a kind of antinomianism. Carl Michalson, for example, asserted, "Life and desire and the quest for authenticity, better known to religious tradition as faith or salvation—these supersede the restrictions of mere correctness." Authenticity was the new morality.[39]

In practice, the pursuit of wholeness meant a situational ethics, which the Faith-and-Life Community preached with little reservation. "Emphasis was placed on contextual or situational ethics" in the curriculum, Jack Lewis noted, because "in the end . . . faith is a decision, not a proof-text. It is commitment rather than dogma; risk, not certainty." This seemed a doctrine appropriate to a new and changing world. In unprecedented circumstances, a personal feel for the authentic action might be all one had to go on. Dietrich Bonhoeffer redefined responsibility thus:

> The responsible man acts in the freedom of his own self, without the
> support of men, circumstances or principles . . . nothing can answer for
> him, nothing can exonerate him, except his own deed and his own self.
> It is he himself who must observe, judge, weigh up, decide and act.

"Decide and act," uncertainty be damned: this was the existentialist credo. This was the way out of brokenness.[40]

The wholeness that Tillich promised would overcome psychological, spiritual, and social alienation, all at once. To Tillich, the achievement of an integrated and forceful "personality" would flow from our reunion with God, and it would go hand in hand with the achievement of community. Tillich agreed with Erich Fromm, a more expressly political and more dissident thinker, that "the right self-love and the right love of others are interdependent, and that selfishness and the abuse of others are equally interdependent." Tillich's insistence on a spiritual dimension to the achievement of community and personality, on the need to gain contact with the "really real," distanced him from the secular humanist ideal of autonomous personality which, he said, "tends to cut the individual off from his existential roots."[41]

The bond that joined individual persons to God was essentially the same as what bound humans together in a true community, according to Tillich: This bond was love. He wrote specifically of *agape*, one of several varieties of love, different from *eros* or *libido* or *philia*. It was the love that judged and forgave and took doubt and anxiety into itself. *Agape* was the same kind of love that in the 1950s and 1960s, Martin Luther King Jr. (who wrote his doctoral dissertation on Tillich) spoke of as the force that could judge America and overcome its divisions. It was the courageous love that judged in humility and in the knowledge of identity with the accused. It was the kind of love that would heal what was separated. The overcoming of existential alienation would be a "union-in-love with the ground of our being."[42]

According to Tillich and King, we experience this powerful love from God in moments of crisis when we exhaust our capacity to cope with our situation. This was what Tillich called the "human boundary-situation." It is the time when we experience the inadequacy of our freedom, in the proverbial "long dark night of the soul." The paradigm of the boundary-situation is Jesus' abandonment on the cross. God's love arrives when we are most bereft and vulnerable. This means that we must take risks, expose ourselves to vulnerability, be willing to experience the terror of our freedom; this is the way to make contact with the unconditional. In this way Tillich provided a religious parallel to the broader existentialist premium on risk taking. We are free to put ourselves in situations in which we are "radically threatened"; here we will find authenticity.[43]

Love is both redeeming and transcendent. It is the point of view from which we can render prophetic judgment on the world; again, *agape* is the love that forgives and reconciles while judging. Love is the source of "the transmoral conscience," the only sure guide to "ethics in a changing world," wrote Tillich. It is the only force that "can transform itself according to the concrete demands of every individual and social situation without losing its eternity and dignity and unconditional validity." These are the moral and political implications of Tillich's doctrine of love, which seemed amoral and apolitical to his critics. Love not only is the basis for spiritual and social integration but also provides the ground for criticism of the present and the guide for behavior toward other persons in uncertain, changing times. Tillich wrote that the social consequence of love as a guide to action is justice.[44]

Only by drawing these social consequences from God's love for us can we maintain a sense of connection with the unconditional. Spiritual integration cannot be achieved successfully without applying the rule of love to others. Tillich asserted what he saw as the political implication: "Without the collaboration of individuals within the movements for social justice, no spiritual reconstruction can be conceived of." Without a corollary concern for social justice, in Tillich's view, the ideal of personality can never be more than the secular humanist ideal of individual liberty—entailing the loss of meaning that he thought follows that ideal.[45]

If we experience God's love and spread it outward, living in a community of love, we will exist no longer in a state of meaninglessness, said Tillich, but in "the New Being." The New Being is a life "that overcomes the frustrations, the *fragmentariness*, and the *perversions* of human existence, *bringing together that which is separated.*" It is an authentic state of existence. Provocatively, Tillich called it the "Protestant Gestalt of grace," a healing process. "The grace of God in Christ is a therapy," said Michalson. It "is the medicine of salvation; it heals the sickness of freedom." This promise of the New Being, Tillich declared, was what the Protestant churches should preach to the people of the twentieth century. The gospel of therapy and authenticity, not the promise of a heavenly afterlife, would prove meaningful to them.[46]

Indeed, the search for wholeness and authenticity seemed by far the most salient aspect of the new theology for its student audience. Young people in the 1950s often couched the questions of "being" and authenticity in terms of a search for "identity." The staff of the Faith-and-Life Community reported that they and other campus ministers had found the question "Who am I?" was the one with which students had been "consumed" over the entire period since the end of World War II.[47] Students expressed feelings of alienation from their authentic selves and confusion about who they were or who they were supposed to be. The CFLC staff reported that many students were "acutely aware within themselves of a deep, uneasy, lonely emptiness . . . sick of the illusions, pretensions, fake roles and masks by which they hide from life as it is." One young woman said this was "an age of despair." Keith Stanford, another Community member, thought this problem was related to sexual confusion and repression. He observed a "widespread common necessity felt that one must again and again play out these masculinity or femininity pageants" and thought this compulsion pointed to "a deeper dislocation" or anxiety. "That we do not clearly know who we are as sexual beings is eloquent testimony that we do not know ourselves as *selves*," he thought.[48]

Students absorbed from Christian existentialism therapeutic concerns, as the preceding comments indicate, and they sometimes discussed this desire for personal knowledge and integrity in terms of becoming authentic or human. The "problem of ourselves," thought student Meg Godbold, was "the problem of what perspective, vision, effort, and courage we can call forth to embody competence and authentic style." In her view, to live as a human meant learning "how to live vitally and authentically." It was crucial to "know and embody very fully what it is to be human."[49] There was little theology in these complaints and ambitions. To many young people, the ideals of authenticity and humanism were the most powerful elements in the radical religion they encountered.

Breaking Through

A cataclysmic break had to be made if one wished to enter the New Being. In a sense, this was the most important message of the Faith-and-Life

Community. The existentialist message of breakthrough updated the long North American Protestant tradition of regeneration and revival into a search for authenticity. The theologian Edward Hobbs declared that one had to "die to everything he ever has been, good intentions and all." To live for the sake of the things of this world was to exist in death, he asserted. "By abandoning our old understanding of ourselves—our false, death-dealing understanding—resolutely, honestly, responsibly," we could find new life. Emil Brunner wrote that God's grace meant "reconciliation," which amounted to a "complete reversal of the direction of man's life." If we could make this break, we might discover "the new life," in which "God has really come to man." The "new life" was "the New Birth, the Divine establishment of the 'new man.' "[50]

But this New Being required a dual breakthrough: to the "really real" and to other human beings. Only in community was the New Being possible. Dietrich Bonhoeffer agreed, and he offered a concrete model for the "break-through to community" and to the New Being: the discipleship of the New Testament. Writing about the early Christian church out of his own resistance to unjust authority, Bonhoeffer's modern discipleship was a conspiratorial community of resistance.

Bonhoeffer left an account of his experience running a renegade seminary in Germany in the 1930s, *Life Together*, which became a model for the Christian Faith-and-Life Community's "common life together." Here he specified the method by which the members of a spiritual community could simultaneously strengthen their bonds and affirm one another's individual personhood. This method was confession. "In confession the break-through to community takes place." In confession, we greeted one another as sinners: "The basis on which Christians can speak to one another is that each knows the other as a sinner," Bonhoeffer wrote. Confession was humiliating. Christ was humiliated on the cross, and those who followed him needed to embrace this, to admit the experience of humiliation as equally essential as risk as a landmark on the way to the new life. "In the deep mental and physical pain of humiliation," he wrote, "before a brother—which means, before God—we experience the Cross of Jesus as our rescue and salvation." As in Tillich's human boundary-situation, in confession, we chose to make ourselves vulnerable and thereby found God. "In confession the break-through to new life occurs," Bonhoeffer declared.[51]

The CFLC covenant's discussion of guilt and community reflected a desire for transparency, leading to breakthrough, strongly reminiscent of Bonhoeffer's account. In recognition of common guiltiness, the students affirmed, each would open herself or himself to "the gaze of another." The participants in the Community affirmed their intention of "exposing ourselves to our fellows" and pledged to accept one another in their guilt. "The releasing of hidden guilt and the possibility of embracing the same, is that without which we cannot and do not have life." Participants felt that one of the most notable aspects of their experience at the Community was the "intensity of relationships" they developed. Many who came to the Community wanted "to enter into an open dialogue with other awakened people about what it means to live genuinely as human beings before one another."[52]

Joe Mathews encouraged such hopes for a breakthrough to community and for individual regeneration. Both his followers and his detractors saw him trying to induce the same kind of crisis he himself had known, a crisis of belief and identity. He had known his own boundary-situation, and his young charges would know theirs if he had anything to say about it. "Breaking people down" was important to him, as one of his protégés, Casey Hayden, later remembered. The idea that breakdown might lead to breakthrough was firmly rooted in both modern psychological theory and Protestant theology, and the Community echoed this idea clearly. Even Jack Lewis, a more conventional thinker than Mathews, saw crisis leading to salvation. "A breakthrough is a gift that we acknowledge when we have been broken through. Ask those who have returned from the valley of the shadow in mental illness, alcoholism, family disruption, business failure and other personal or social crises."

For some, breakdown did not lead to breakthrough. At least a couple of students from the Community ended up in mental hospitals, and some blamed Mathews, at least in part.[53] Foreshadowing the criticisms of new religious groups which, in the 1970s, were labeled cults, some former Community members criticized what they termed the "brainwashing" techniques that Mathews used on students. In 1964, several people complained that "a little 'cult'" had grown around a certain staff member, who went unnamed but who undoubtedly was Mathews. He "spent several weeks destroying every belief, every shred of self-confidence, every competence, and every anything else that composed our persons," one recalled. "This was a stated goal—so he could help bring us to the light." One might encounter "*ridicule* and *sarcasm* . . . if one did not accept the Community line." To some, this treatment seemed to violate the themes of openness, love, and honesty that the group championed. "This was the real paradox! The teachers emphasized openness, honesty, permissiveness, freedom of thought, etc.—and yet I found I had to vomit back the 'party-line' or I was tabbed a person who really didn't understand myself or was simply afraid to be honest with myself and others."[54]

Others were more measured in their criticism. "You could accept or reject the ideas of others, but you were pressured to say why," said one former participant in the Community, who then added, in a candid afterthought, "This pressure for responsibility is something I often resented." Doubtless by the early 1960s, the more conservative Christians felt embattled here in the face of the Community's increasingly radical theology. Casey Hayden offers a more favorable assessment, however. She moved into the Community after a short time in a women's dormitory at the university and found in Mathews a congenial ear for her dissatisfaction with mainstream campus life, as well as a kindness that others do not note. Some of Mathews's detractors saw him as domineering, even obnoxious, but not dangerous. Dorothy Burlage, far from unreserved in her enthusiasm for him, found Mathews "extreme, doctrinaire, zealous," though "brilliant." In his pursuit of breakdown and breakthrough, "nothing was sacred."[55]

When describing the experience of breakthrough, Bonhoeffer used an image of childbirth to invoke the ancient Christian tradition of spiritual rebirth. Why not simply begin again? One could be reborn in Christ as the "new man of the future." If others felt despair, the attitude of the child was the adequate response. Here, he wrote, the existential "echoless crying out from solitude into the solitude of self, the protest against all kinds of duress, has unexpectedly received an answer. . . . He who has grown to the man in exile and wretchedness grows to be the child as he finds his home." Whoever could make this leap back toward openness and simplicity could make the leap into the future. Bonhoeffer disdained "equivocation and pretence," and he hoped to find the way "back to simplicity and straightforwardness," evoking an Adamic hope for cultural and personal rebirth.[56]

Some participants in the Community reported just this kind of rebirth, evoking a modernist conversion experience. Lois Boyd, a student from the University of Oklahoma who came to the CFLC for a retreat in 1962, described how the Austin students communicated to her the themes of rebirth and freedom.

> "Come on," they shouted at us, "You can LIVE." They shouted this at us in a lot of ways—poems, a movie, and those noisy pictures that came alive in that room and spoke to us. . . . They were calling out the same message . . . over and over. . . . "Come on—You can do it—You have Cosmic Permission to LIVE!" . . . The air was sweet—Life was good—and—I KNEW IT WAS SO!

This "cosmic permission to live" echoed Tillich's " 'yes' to life." It also stood as an implicit rebuke to the conservative church culture native to the region. The students were asserting that knowing God did not mean giving up one's freedom or life's pleasures. "There was room for freedom—room to LIVE!" Boyd exulted. She compared her experience at this retreat to a butterfly emerging from a chrysalis and a child emerging from a womb. As she explained, "Our Lives were so very new . . . and birth is such a delicate, fragile thing—and violent—and personal. But good! Only the newly Alive can know how good!" Now everything appeared in a new light. "Everything was so *full of meaning*," she said. "Oh God! Can LIFE be so wonderful?"[57]

The Appeal of Avant-Gardism

Many members of the Community saw political implications in the breakthrough to community, to authenticity, and to new life. One contemporary observer noted that "debate among students [at the Faith-and-Life Community] is likely to center very rarely on whether a person should be baptised [*sic*], and very commonly on such problems as militarism, racism, and poverty."[58] In the 1960s and 1970s, Dietrich Bonhoeffer's life and work inspired the social revolutionary liberation theology of Latin America. Working in a less polarized time and place when political radicalism was far less legitimate—the United States in the 1950s—Joe Mathews drew on Bonhoeffer's example to put across the view that political rebellion was part and parcel of the search for authenticity. The CFLC stated its goals thus: "To Recover that kind of genuine dialogue among contemporary men which will issue in creative social structures capable of mediating authentic personal existence and new possibilities for justice for all men who must respond in one fashion or another to this world."[59]

Dialogue, community, and authenticity, it seems, were bound up with the pursuit of justice. This surprised some because the young people participating in this discussion came to their dissident conclusions by an oblique route; it was the personal desire for a breakthrough to authenticity that led them down this path.

If community was a necessary part of the breakthrough to authenticity, then, as suggested earlier, the question of who might belong to the community quickly arose. To Bonhoeffer, the inclusion of the weak and suffering in the community was a particular message of the gospels. "The exclusion of the weak and insignificant, the seemingly useless people, from a Christian community may actually mean the exclusion of Christ; in the poor brother Christ is knocking at the door."[60] If love was the cement of community, then the question became whom one should love. In the Sermon on the Mount,

Jesus urged love of one's neighbor. Some interpreted this conservatively, taking it to mean that we should love those near us or those like us. Bonhoeffer, internationalist and enemy of anti-Semitism, showed little patience with discriminations between neighbors and nonneighbors. "Who is my neighbour?" he asked mockingly. "Is it my kinsman, my compatriot, my brother Christian, or my enemy? . . . We have literally no time to sit down and ask ourselves whether so-and-so is our neighbour or not. We must get into action." Written in the Germany of the 1930s by an anti-Nazi preacher, the original subversive meaning of these words was clear. In the American South of the 1950s and 1960s, the words might disclose a similar meaning, suggesting the parallel, which partisans of the civil rights movement frequently drew, between the Nazis' treatment of Jews and the southern white treatment of African Americans.[61]

"Getting into action" meant political action. Instead of looking for a God of strength, the point was to accept a God of weakness and to accept responsibility oneself for doing what needed to be done. Merely bearing witness to evil events was not sufficient, Bonhoeffer decided, nor was empathy with the victims of injustice. The better response was political action intended to stop evil. If this meant becoming guilty oneself, then so be it. "I believe that God can and will bring good out of evil, even out of the greatest evil," Bonhoeffer wrote. "For that purpose he needs men who make the best use of everything," and he included the careful use of violence, as his approval of the plot against Hitler indicates.[62]

Years later, Marxist-influenced liberation theologians sought to form "base communities" that worked for social justice.[63] As noted earlier, these radicals drew on Bonhoeffer's example. Even though Bonhoeffer was no leftist, he offered a prophetic critique of a complacent, comfortable church. "To make a start, it should give away all its property to those in need," he wrote nonchalantly.[64] He envisioned a politically powerless church, an outpost of Christian spirit, what Harvey Cox, borrowing from Bonhoeffer, later called a *kerygmatic* church, announcing the "good news" of the gospels in a way that was relevant to the world, "not in the form of general propositions but in the language of specific announcements about where the work of liberation is now proceeding and concrete invitations to join in the struggle." Cox called such a church "God's *avant-garde.*"[65]

Students in the Community looked beyond their individual selves for authenticity, and ultimately many of them embraced the role of cultural and political avant-garde. They confessed to "participation in the widespread estrangement and alienation in all social structures of our day" and issued a call "to face the breakdown of authentic human relations in [our] marriages and homes." They looked to social causes to explain personal difficulties and also to social solutions.[66] To "know yourself as a whole being," Keith Stanford said, one needed to be a part of something bigger. Don Warren affirmed the sociality of personal identity, remarking, "We discover who we are[,] not in silent and lonely meditation, but in the midst of the world given to us."[67] Participation in the wider world was the only possible antidote to personal malaise, the path to a personal breakthrough. Both men thought that not just community but "being freed for community *in mission* is to discover the meaning of personal freedom."[68]

Participants in the Community grew disgusted with what they considered excessive introspection. They enthusiastically read a great deal of psychoanalytic literature, including Freud, Fromm, Rollo May, and Viktor Frankl, but they thought it was possible to be too psychologically oriented.[69] Dottie Adams derided the person who "is always prepared to pull the psychological tools out of his little black bag and start dissecting." This type reveled in the analysis of his "sick, sick society," Carol Darrell pointed out; he "delights in being told how sick he is" himself, which left him "paralyzed." Like the "cultured men" whom Kierkegaard despised, he killed everything with too much thought and avoided making decisions. "He has pushed *life* out of him," said Darrell, and "has assumed the posture of a mere spectator." He was afraid of decision and commitment.[70]

Such a person was afraid of life itself. Like many who would follow them in the coming years, the students here posed their alternatives in the rhetoric of life against death. Darrell characterized the navel gazer almost as a vampire: "He has all sorts of expressions for describing the world as one vast graveyard and he sees his job as constantly reminding people that they are dead." Unfortunately, she thought, "this fad is so much a part of our entire way of living in the mid-twentieth century" that college students could not escape it.[71]

Don Warren agreed that the time for strictly personal rumination was past. "No longer silence, no longer inwardness unaccompanied, but life, full life, historical life . . . this is the demand and the possibility in our day."[72] In the Community's rhetoric, a world of life was a world in which the "brokenness" of which Marcel wrote was reversed. Excessive introspection only prolonged the state of alienation. "We have forgotten who it is that we are," one prayer service read. "We have fragmented the world." The participants intoned, "We have come to remember our life/for we are dead men." They thanked God for giving them new life, which occurred, they said, "only in the world."[73]

They spoke of a holistic "life of commitment" that extended to both personal relationships and public behavior; this was the slogan proclaimed on the cover of the Community's main publication in 1962.[74] Mentors like Lewis and Mathews may have had in mind a social agenda from their earliest involvement with the CFLC. But for reasons of both principle and practicality, the Community's literature often discussed social commitment in a relativist fashion, urging students to commit themselves to something. The members of the Community prayed for strength "to be responsible" in "politics . . . the social order . . . education . . . vocation." When studying " 'Applied Christianity,' " said Jack Lewis, they discussed in their classes how they could lead a "responsible life in the world," in the realms of family, culture, politics, and economics.[75]

The Community's sense of worldly responsibility sometimes displayed a sharper political edge. In a prayer service in 1961, after many words about death and fragmentation, those assembled recited a section on "The Life," characterizing their new life in highly political terms.

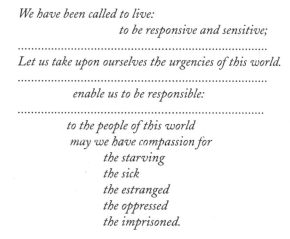

> *We have been called to live:*
>   *to be responsive and sensitive;*
>
> . . . .
>
> *Let us take upon ourselves the urgencies of this world.*
>
> . . . .
>
>   *enable us to be responsible:*
>
> . . . .
>
>   *to the people of this world*
>   *may we have compassion for*
>   *the starving*
>   *the sick*
>   *the estranged*
>   *the oppressed*
>   *the imprisoned.*

These were sympathies that resonated with Bonhoeffer's experience and thought. Committing themselves along these lines was the way, the prayer suggested, to overcome fragmentation. This was the path to a new life.[76]

Some of these Bonhoefferian sympathies were similar to those that Camus expressed. Students at the Community, like Dorothy Burlage and Casey Hayden, also read Camus.[77] Even though he was a declared atheist, there were many points of contact between him and the Christian existentialists, particularly the emphasis on individual decision and resistance against injustice as keys to human identity. Many politically minded Christians were attracted to his work, and Camus himself wrote that there was something of value in Christianity. In an essay quoted in the *Letter to Laymen*, entitled "The Unbeliever and Christians," Camus stated that "the world of today needs Christians who remain Christians." He declared that true Christians must

> voice their condemnation . . . they should get away from abstraction and confront the blood-stained face history has taken on today . . . I am waiting for a grouping of those who refuse to be dogs and are resolved to pay the price that must be paid so that man can be something more than a dog.[78]

A weekend seminar for laypersons at the Faith-and-Life Community included many readings from Camus, including this essay, as well as another entitled "No Bystanders." All existentialist thinkers believed that people should "get away from abstraction." Influenced by thinkers like Camus and Bonhoeffer, students at the Community thought that political engagement and commitment was the way to accomplish this. The way to be human was to refuse to be complicit.[79]

The Faith-and-Life Community's leaders viewed the Community as a model for a new, avant-garde church that would "get away from abstraction" and "voice its condemnation." Their mission was to announce the "good news," the *kerygma*, in a more socially involved way than the conventional churches did: "The Church's only reason for being is to declare this good news to man by living in the very midst of the world as the embodiment of her Gospel." They would be a living example of the Christian message, but not in a monastic way.[80] The Community's members often spoke of being on the "edge," of "finding the edge." The Community's ideal, Al Lingo remembers, was

> to be at the edge, between the no longer and the not yet. Most people lived in the no longer. Those things that were okay, that were ordinary institutions. But what was coming as the not yet was being forged like somebody who was laying track before the train came. . . . To point the way. The pioneer, the social pioneer.

He explains what this idea meant in practice in Texas in the late 1950s and early 1960s: "There was a cutting edge in race relations, to be on. And if you weren't on the cutting edge, then where were you?"[81] God's avant-garde could not avoid taking political risks.

This, finally, was what Community member Meg Godbold meant when she said that "we at the College House talk about responsible action, being historical people, and creating culture." This meant acting as the social pioneer, entering into unknown territory, despite the "uncertainty of fulfillment." It was "as a point of authenticity" that people should "engage ourselves this way," she wrote. Casey Hayden recalls the importance of the "tragic hero or heroine" image to her and her friends at the Community, something they derived partly from Camus's writings. This meant that it was meaningful to take political action not only when "fulfillment" was likely but also when the risks were great and the promise of success small. Political action was taken not just for instrumental purposes but because this was the path to authenticity.[82]

In their desire to be "in the world," Community members cast their gaze far and wide. They seemed hungry for knowledge of the world distant from Texas, for as much knowledge as they could get. They wanted to feel connected to what seemed like the most exciting developments in the world— "the edge." Starting in the late 1950s, CFLC staff members took summer trips to different parts of the world, making contact with clergy embarked on experiments that had something in common with theirs, and they returned to Austin to give exhaustive reports on what they had learned. Community members were assigned different parts of the world to research—economically, politically, culturally—and reported back to their fellows. They studied the political movements that at this time were sweeping both Europe and the Third World—particularly the nationalist movements in the Third World, which these American students found exhilarating, in part because of the role played by other students in those movements. As noted earlier, after 1956, many foreign students at UT lived in the Community, and no doubt this contributed to this interest in world events. Students here were sympathetic to the nonaligned movement among Third World countries. They maintained the same interest in the worldwide ecumenical movement that Bonhoeffer and his colleagues had shown in the 1930s. They also sympathized with Third World nationalism, seeing it as inevitable and healthy, and they thought an enlightened ecumenical Christianity could play a role in abetting that movement.[83]

Although the Community's staff had national and worldwide contacts and although they saw their experiment as a model for other churches, the students were most concerned with fulfilling their role as avant-garde in their more immediate environment, especially the university. Wesley Poorman, a seminary intern who worked on the CFLC staff in 1961, wrote that the campus minister should "gather a residual body of committed Christians who will be a leavening force, not only within the community of faith, but also within the community of learning." According to Lingo, among Community members, "the commonality ... was that people knew they were doing something on behalf of the university. That our mission was to somehow be a light in the midst of the university."[84]

If the Community's members were interested in resisting oppressive authority, in the South the challenge of racial oppression was presented to them more clearly than any other, especially after the advent of the civil rights movement in the mid-1950s. On several occasions, Community members expressed solidarity with African Americans. As noted earlier, the Women's Branch admitted a black woman in 1954. As an undergraduate member of the Community in the mid-1950s, Lingo, after some prodding by a fellow Community member, went to the black students' small dormitory on campus to ask the students there why they were bothered that the Cowboys, an honorary society of UT undergraduate men of which Lingo was a member, were preparing once again to stage their annual charity minstrel show. After spending several hours there on a couple of evenings, he thought he had learned a few things, and he proceeded to organize a petition against the minstrelsy, to argue at Cowboys meetings that this tradition should be terminated, and to communicate the African American students' concerns to a dean at the university. He did not succeed in stopping the show. (The minstrel shows continued until the early 1960s.) But, Lingo reflects, "It was a breakthrough for me—you know? . . . No one necessarily would have raised that for me at the student dining hall or the fraternity, you know? But the Christian Faith-and-Life Community was made up of people who—who were sensitive and aware and responsive to things." Later, as a member of the Community staff, he traveled to small-town, all-white churches outside Austin to preach sermons against segregation and in support of civil rights demonstrations.[85]

Most visibly, many Community members participated in the civil rights protests that were held near the campus in 1960/1961 (discussed in detail in chapter 4), possibly accounting for more participants than any other single source. Other students took different actions. Several of the leaders of these protests and other insurgent liberal activities, such as Casey Hayden, Anthony Henry, Jim Neyland, Vivien Franklin, and Brad Blanton, lived at the Faith-and-Life Community for some time while at UT. The Faith-and-Life Community did not undertake this civil rights protest as a "community in mission." Rather, a group of people who spent time together at several places and who felt a sense of community as a subset of the larger student population were encouraged in this political action by the Community.[86]

Such political interventions were appropriate to the "time of experiment." Political risk taking was one facet of a more general experimentalism that infused the Faith-and-Life Community, an improvisational attitude whose theatricality was part of the Community's avant-gardism. This dramatic view of life, including political life, was important throughout the dissident culture of the 1960s. Community members did not shrink from the aestheticist connotations of the avant-garde role; on the contrary, they frankly spoke of their abiding concern with style, their desire to cultivate an appealing "life image." This emphasis on style accounted for a good deal of the mystique that the Community acquired around the UT campus. The search for a "life image" was an attempt to generate a contemporary substitute for something that had always been culturally important. The Community suggested that people always had given their lives meaning and had found guidance for their actions in central images or symbols. But the old images were no longer plausible, and a self-conscious search for new images was urgent.[87]

As noted earlier, Mathews had little use for the familiar symbols of faith, but he was an apostle of symbolism, of drama; indeed, his own destruction of the old symbols gave him the opportunity to enact his own drama of rebellion. He encouraged Community members to experiment with new images from the worlds of poetry, film, and drama that were meaningful to them. Mathews viewed worship as an important site of symbolism, "the self-conscious symbolic activity of the faithful community." Members of the staff took turns leading prayer services and were encouraged to design their own formats. The script for the daily service was called the "choreography."[88] In these efforts, the Community echoed Tillich's view that we could find in all things and acts a dimension of depth and meaning that was often missing, as well as Erich Fromm's call to recover "the forgotten language" of symbolic life.[89] Casey Hayden says she took from her experience in the Community the desire to "make of one's life a sacrament."[90] Yet the Community aestheticized worship, affirming the need for symbolic richness in its rituals; thus to make life into a sacrament was, perhaps, also to make one's life into art.

No one registered the effect of the Community's dramatic mystique more sharply than did Ronnie Dugger, who was fascinated with Mathews's persona. "Joe Mathews, the inspired merlin, the mystifying poet of prayer to one's own privacy, genuine, fraud, the leader of the Community," Dugger mused. "Could it be that Joe knew god but just wasn't introducing him around? Joe wouldn't exactly say, but he wouldn't with transfixing grace." Dugger's own abandonment of his inherited faith may have fostered the ambivalence he felt about Mathews's sincerity. It is remarkable that despite his own apostasy, Dugger still found in Mathews the intoxicating, elusive promise of hidden wisdom, the mystic implication of knowledge deeper than what we see routinely on the surface of life. This was the promise of the "really real," the sense of which anthropologist Clifford Geertz, echoing Tillich, asserts is the kernel of genuine religious experience.[91]

Some found the intense group of staff and students gathered at the Community a little intimidating, even weird. "They knew it wasn't fundamentalism, but they weren't sure what it was," says Lingo. John Silber took a particular interest in students from the Community, but he also disagreed vehemently with its intellectual and ethical approach. Shortly after Mathews arrived at UT, in a timely, microcosmic clash of perspectives, he and Silber held a series of debates in the University Y. Each presented his own response to the question "What is the most important thing in life?" Mathews represented the call for individual decision, based on authentic feeling and the concrete situation; Silber stood for the rational application of clear principle.

Each night the crowd grew bigger, hundreds eventually overflowing the room. Samuel Beckett's minimalist play *Waiting for Godot* had recently been staged at UT, and it became a point of contention between Silber and Mathews, each shouldering an ego of no small mass, competing for the mantle of intellectual mentor to the brightest students on campus. Some said the play reflected an existentialist outlook and spoke to the present age of anxiety, despair, and isolation, an era that perhaps, some young people suggested, was passing. Mathews expressed the view that Beckett's work remained quite meaningful, and Silber contended that on the contrary, *Godot* was "empty" of meaning. He viewed it as an expression of hopelessness, not at all useful to young people's attempts to grapple with the world around them. Despite Silber's considerable forensic skills, it was to be the existentialist outlook, far more than the rationalist one, that enlivened young people in the years ahead.[92]

The Contribution of Christian Existentialism

This one institution illustrates, in a particularly vivid and direct way, the broader influence of existentialist ideas on the emerging dissident youth culture of the 1960s. Students who spent time at the Christian Faith-and-Life Community in the years between 1952 and 1962 subsequently moved toward diverse efforts at self-fashioning and social change, and the ideas they absorbed at the Community continued to shape these activities for many years.

Strong personal links connected the Community to the early new left. After college, Casey Hayden worked for the YWCA and became an important member of the Student Nonviolent Coordinating Committee (SNCC), laboring in the civil rights movement of the Deep South. She also served on the national executive committee of Students for a Democratic Society and was an influential presence at that group's 1962 Port Huron Conference, whence came the highly popular *Port Huron Statement*. In the mid-1960s Hayden helped spur the formation of the women's liberation movement with her writings, widely circulated among the American left, on the position of women in American society. Later on, she became deeply engaged with the counterculture of the era. Dorothy Burlage at first followed a similar path after graduation. She worked for the Y, in SDS, and with various civil rights and antipoverty groups; in addition to this activism, she was able to attend Harvard Divinity School for a time. In 1970 she returned to school and became a child psychotherapist. Tom Hayden was the main author of the *Port Huron Statement*, approved a year after his marriage to Casey, which took place at the Faith-and-Life Community. The similarity between certain ideas at work in the Community and those expressed at Port Huron may be due to the distinct influence of the Austin experiment as well as to the general currency of these ideas at the time.[93]

Others who "graduated" from the Community went elsewhere. Claire Johnson Breihan worked for more than two decades in the Austin Independent School District as a specialist in racial integration. In the 1960s and 1970s, Al Lingo worked with Joe Mathews to build a dissident, even revolutionary, church along the radical lines that the Faith-and-Life Community had laid out. Afterward, Lingo continued his involvement in countercultural, new age, and civil rights activity. Dick Simpson became a scholar of African politics, a prominent activist in Chicago city politics, and finally an ordained minister. Joann Thompson also worked with Mathews, later becoming an activist on health care issues, based at New York City's Riverside Church. For all these people and many of their contemporaries, the quest for authenticity and the sense of social mission were thoroughly intertwined.[94]

Nonetheless, the Community split in 1962 over the issue of how to balance the two. Mathews's goal, in Judy Schleyer Blanton's view, was to "infiltrate" the mainline Protestant churches and to use them as a base for the pursuit of a "social justice agenda." Jack Lewis thought Mathews was scaring away the financial donations that the Community needed and still sought from well-heeled Texans. He resolved to steer the CFLC back to a more conventional religious education curriculum. But rather than be fired, Mathews quit, and a majority of the staff members left with him. They went to Chicago where they started the Ecumenical Institute, which undertook organizing projects in localities around the world. This broke the creative tension between personal and political concerns that the Community had cultivated. By the mid-1960s, the CFLC was no longer a religious study center but, rather, a human potential workshop experimenting with various therapeutic techniques that arrived from the West Coast. This was not a therapeutics of political opposition. Lewis, no longer in control, left soon after Mathews did to become a campus minister at Cornell University, where he took part in peace protests during the Vietnam War and antinuclear demonstrations into the 1980s. In Austin, the Faith-and-Life Community moved fully into a search for personal breakthrough that was unconnected to social and political activism.[95]

Until 1962, the Faith-and-Life Community served as a medium for communicating existentialist themes that were becoming attractive to many young people in the late 1950s and early 1960s. The sense of anxiety and the need to confront it, the preference for the concrete over the abstract, the importance of decision and personal responsibility, the attractiveness of situational ethics, the desire for a sense of vital life, and, above all, the search for a life of authenticity in touch with the "really real": all these ideas were circulating with increasing velocity on the nation's campuses and not always in a religious context. But especially in the conservative provinces, Christian institutions and a Christian intellectual framework enjoyed a cultural legitimacy that left students particularly open to the power of these ideas, when those ideas were encountered in this religious context. The Protestant content and evangelical undertone of the Community helped it channel these currents of spiritual and cultural ferment into the dominant spiritual culture of cold war America.

In addition to providing cover for new ways of thinking, Christian existentialism also contributed distinct elements to the broader existentialist vocabulary. First, it grafted a strong sense of moral and social responsibility onto the search for a vital life. Christian theology certainly had no lock on morality; even among existentialists, the Christian theologians were not the only ones who articulated a strong moral dimension, as Camus's writing demonstrates. Other secular existentialists, however, whether philosophers or novelists, had only a tenuous grasp on a moral imperative. Observers like John Silber could claim some justification if they experienced trepidation when pondering the moral and political stability of the existentialist perspective. In secular existentialism, a moral dimension seemed to be optional; in Christian existentialism, it was not. (Even for Camus, one might argue, the moral dimension was a residue of the Christian tradition from which he was estranged.)

Community was another theme more characteristic of Christian existentialism than of existentialism in general. This became an important emphasis for the new left, in both thought and action, from the *Port Huron Statement* to the agricultural communes and cooperative stores of the 1970s. Where did this idea, in such a self-conscious form, come from? The idea of a community of close relationships as the solution to a culture of alienation and as the incubator of truly strong and autonomous persons—in short, as a solution to the problems that Arthur Schlesinger thought the "age of anxiety" posed for a democracy—descended perhaps most of all from religious sources.

Although nonreligious communitarian traditions existed in American life, they were not so deeply embedded in the cultural mainstream of American life as was religious communitarianism, and they could not speak powerfully to so many Americans.[96] Instead, the civil rights movement did more than anything else to spread the communitarian approach to the conundrum of democracy and alienation, with its religious idea of a "beloved community" that sustained struggles for justice, that bred vigorous citizenship, and that served as a utopian ideal for all of society. The idea of the beloved community resonated with some young white people, because it answered the unarticulated needs that emerged from the historical experiences in which their lives were rooted and because it echoed other messages they had heard. Among the most important cultural sources of those other messages, which combined with the message of the civil rights movement to create a powerful political momentum behind the ideal of a community of political opposition, was Christian existentialism.

Love was the most distinctly Christian theme of all. This was a crucial theme of both the civil rights movement and, later on, the new left and the counterculture. For all their emphasis on the need for reasoned deliberation in political life, the young radicals who approved the *Port Huron Statement* announced to the world their conviction that humans possessed an "unfulfilled" potential for "love" as well as for reason.[97] More significant than their concern with the human desire for love was their belief that this desire was politically relevant. Love was viewed as a key ingredient in the attainment of human dignity, the fulfillment of the human spirit, and the achievement of authenticity. It was the fount of creative response to the challenging world around them and the tie that bound the beloved community. It is difficult to see where this emphasis on love might have come from, directly or indirectly, except from a religious context. Love was not always a theme in existentialism; even for a secular existentialist who was deeply moral, like Camus, love did not occupy the place of importance that it did for religious thinkers, and especially for Christian thinkers.[98] According to Christian theology, love came from God to human beings and thence from humans to one another. For the civil rights movement of the 1960s, closely linked to an institutional base in African American churches, these connections remained salient. Young white activists in later years were far less likely to recall the religious roots of this still powerful element in their own outlook. They were left with a vision of a society and a community suffused with love that was in effect the residue of a Christian perspective.

Finally, there was the mystic search for something deeper in life, for the "really real." As noted earlier, some thinkers call knowledge of the "really real" the essence of religious experience. In Tillich's terms, it was a search for "the ground of Being," for "the ultimate." Existentialism, in any form, expressed a desire for a life of meaning. But this meaning was not necessarily something transcendent; it might be something created entirely out of the materials of this world. Alongside the Faith-and-Life Community's worldliness, however, there lay the suspicion that in the world they might find something more exhilarating and vital than what they had seen before, something more than most people knew. To locate them on the theological terrain that they studied, they combined Bonhoeffer's command to go to the public place with Tillich's challenge to confront the boundary-situation. They wanted to be both on the edge and in the world. They sought to find, somehow, the extraordinary in the ordinary, the margin in the center. This mystic quest, stemming originally from a religious context and continuing to reflect a spiritual desire, shimmered around the borders of the postmaterialist, postscarcity sensibility of radical politics in the 1960s.

The discussion in the Faith-and-Life Community encoded and validated the link between personal and political concerns, a link that became increasingly important to the emerging youth radicalism of the era. One student noted that the Community gave him the "freedom to talk about my questions"—questions of self, of God, of life, and of the larger world—and it encouraged students to look for connections among these concerns. Geertz writes that the "watchword" of the religious perspective is "rather than detachment . . . commitment; rather than analysis, encounter." If this is true, then the search for authenticity that the young existentialists of this era pioneered was religious indeed. According to the *Port Huron Statement*, the spirit of "encounter" characterized the participatory democracy that the new left envisioned.[99] In the coming years, the quest for authenticity took young people through a path of commitment and encounter that only the most ambitious among them might have expected.

CHAPTER THREE

The Issues of Life:
The University YMCA–YWCA
and Christian Liberalism

ONLY AMID THE PITCH and personal upheaval of social change did existentialism and the search for authentic life appear as signposts pointing to political engagement. The civil rights movement ultimately provided that context of upheaval. Yet by the time the interracial youth wing of the civil rights movement took institutional shape, with the formation of the Student Nonviolent Coordinating Committee (SNCC) in 1960 on the heels of that year's sweeping tide of black student sit-ins at retail establishments across the South, the search for authenticity had already become part of a political consciousness of a sector of white youth who favored activism, even protest. In the late 1950s, groupings of white youth in the South and around the country crystallized into nodes of liberal political dissidence, able and willing to break out into insurgency, almost seeming to wait for opportunities to do so. The civil rights movement gave them their greatest opportunity and pushed many of them toward the left.

These young people, influenced by existentialism, came to believe that activism was the path to authenticity. A more direct influence on them, however, was the social gospel tradition of Christian liberalism, descended from the early twentieth century, which provided them with a straightforward defense of political liberalism, with adult models of responsible dissidence, and with an institutional base for protest activity.[1] Christian liberalism communicated to young people the message that they could live a life of meaning only if they decided on, and acted on, their values. It also upheld an interracialist ideal and provided for an extraordinary degree of contact between black and white youth in the 1940s and 1950s, paving the way for white youth sympathy with the civil rights movement.

The stronghold of Christian liberalism in Austin, as in many other college towns and cities, was the University YMCA–YWCA (Young Men's Christian Association–Young Women's Christian Association), which was housed in its own building across the street from the university campus on "the Drag," Guadalupe Avenue. From the 1930s to the early 1960s, the University Y was where the action was, politically, for students. The adults there, like Block Smith, Frank Wright, Rosalie Oakes, and Anne Appenzellar, ensured that students and teachers alike viewed the Y as the center of dissent, controversy, and open discussion of the most urgent, worldly issues. As Frank Wright said, "We start with the issues of life—no holds barred—and work toward the issues of faith."[2] The worldliness of Christian liberalism made it the real home of the secular Christianity that Harvey Cox preached. Although these adults did not foment political protest, they did help lead students to a stance of dissent, and they tacitly approved of the student protest activity that emanated from the Y building starting in the late 1950s. For this approval they would pay a price.

For some, the intersection of existentialism and liberalism ended in the rejection of liberalism. This is ironic because it was the indigenous American tradition of political liberalism, firmly rooted in the political culture even if embattled, that gave political impetus to existentialism. But civil rights was the issue on which liberalism seemed to run its course in the late 1950s and early 1960s, illustrating both the potential and the shortcomings of liberal politics. The watershed of white student involvement in civil rights protest in Austin occurred in the year between the fall of 1960 and the fall of 1961, when activists from the University Y and the Christian Faith-and-Life Community organized a series of desegregation protests at local cinemas. The story of the Student Y movement and its role in civil rights protest demonstrates the flexibility and continuing vitality of liberal Christianity as a politically oppositional force in the American South in the middle decades of the twentieth century. After these protests, many of the participants moved on to other places and other politics, some becoming more radical and some withdrawing from activism. Eventually some of the young existentialists exhausted liberalism and cast it aside like an empty can. This determination that liberal politics was insufficient to make a broken world whole, to achieve both authenticity and social justice, opened the way for the emergence of the new left.

The Social Gospel Legacy

To understand how either liberalism or existentialism could have attracted teenagers from politically mainstream backgrounds in a conservative environment, one has to recognize that both these traditions, in this setting, were filtered through a lens of Christian religion. This religion lent great legitimacy to what otherwise seemed dangerous and alien to many Texans. Liberalism appeared in Christian tones on the campus to a much greater extent than in Texas in general, or even in Austin. Although student liberals here took inspiration and encouragement from the secular liberals gathered around the *Observer* and in the state legislature, their own activism was based more in the social gospel tradition of the University Y.

The Y fit into a subculture of Christian liberalism, both theological and political, evident in the cluster of Christian churches on the west side of the campus area. A handful of pastors nearby were known as liberals, and they saw it as their duty to prod the consciences of their usually more conservative congregations: Blake Smith, the pastor of the University Baptist Church, Ed Heinsohn at University Methodist, and Lawrence Bash at University Christian.[3] Students who attended services at these churches often had come from more conservative congregations, and perhaps the Sunday sermons of these pastors awakened the latent moral and political content that lay in the familiar religious precepts the students had learned. In the mid-1950s Chandler Davidson, who later became involved in civil rights agitation in the campus area, was impressed by the tenacious morality of Laurie Hildreth, the pastor at the off-campus church that Davidson was attending. The church had always been for whites only, and even though Hildreth wanted to integrate it, he said he would respect the wishes of the congregation. Although some right-wing members of the congregation did organize resistance to the initiative, Hildreth persisted and prevailed.[4]

Throughout the 1940s and 1950s, these ministers were "right up there on the front edge" of liberalism, says Bob Breihan, who came to Austin in 1951 to work in the Methodist Student Center, which he headed throughout the 1960s. Ed Heinsohn was prointegration, and sympathetic to pacifism—he was vice chairman of the National Methodist Church's Commission on World Peace. Breihan recalls that there had been quite a bit of pacifist feeling around UT during World War II and the Korean War, and in fact Breihan came to UT after his predecessor at the Methodist Student Center, Paul Dietz, was forced to resign because of his own pacifism. Dietz had jointly sponsored a meeting at the University Y in 1950 at which he prayed that God would forgive the United States for resorting to the use of force;

Lynn Landrum, editor and columnist at the *Dallas Morning News*, devoted a week's worth of columns to Dietz, whom he called "a pinko."

When he started in Austin, Breihan also had to contend with some negative feedback that the university ministry was getting from a pastor in East Texas, who had come into possession of a piece of their educational material, printed when Dietz was in charge, that depicted black and white hands clasping. The off-campus pastors were better protected than Dietz, as some of them were tightly connected to the secular liberals in Austin. Heinsohn and Blake Smith, who was known to be especially "outspoken" on political matters, openly supported Homer Rainey in his fight against the regents and then in his gubernatorial race. Indeed, they maintained their loud presence in the UT environment for decades.[5]

The Y was the religious institution by far the closest to the students at the university. Physically it was hard to miss, as it occupied the building on the corner of Guadalupe and Twenty-second Street, directly across the street from the West Mall of the campus, which was the most frequently used entrance to the university. Students could not help but walk past the Y building all the time, and they often went inside because so many of the events held in the Y were nonreligious. The staff at the Y saw as their task the preservation of a space in the campus environment for free discussion, and they repeatedly asserted that their rooms were open for the airing of any issue, and to anyone. As many guest speakers may have appeared there as in the Student Union. When invited to UT, George Washington Carver spoke at the Y after being barred from university buildings because of his race. During the 1950s, at both UT and Southern Methodist University (SMU), the Y invited the one-time Communist Party USA leader John Gates to speak. (Logan Wilson said he would not let Gates speak at UT, and a disappointed Y staff canceled the visit when Gates refused to guarantee that he would provide a Marxist viewpoint—he had come a long way since his salad days in the 1930s.) The commitment to free speech was the issue on which Christian and secular liberalism shared the most ground in Texas.[6]

The University Y's liberalism overlapped with secular liberalism on other issues as well, but it had different origins. When young people arrived at UT fresh from fundamentalist Baptist congregations all over the state, they encountered people at the Y who carried with them the most radical edge of the social gospel tradition, people who for decades had been using this tradition to push against the limits of southern politics and culture. Like the secular liberals of the 1950s, the Christian liberals who stuck to their beliefs during this period of rightist dominance tended to be those who leaned a bit to the left, and they gained influence in the Christian liberal camp because of their persistence, waiting for the political wheel to turn once more.

The University Y was separate from the downtown Austin YMCA, which was not politically active. The salient institutional framework for the University Y was the Student YMCA–YWCA, at both its national and its Southwest Regional levels. Even in the Student Y structure, individual branches had a great deal of autonomy, and the University of Texas Y took advantage of theirs. While the permanent staff at some Y branches cultivated close relationships with their campus administrations—to some extent depending on those administrations for money—the UT-Y staff always sought to maintain a rigid independence from the UT administration. Although they depended on money from a yearly, campus-based, student-conducted funding drive, called the Campus Chest, the Y did not take money from the administration. This was a sign of the staff's intention to make the University Y a haven for the expression of unpopular views. They made it clear to the campus administration, as well as to others, that the wishes of the administration would be paid little attention in the development of Y programs. In this intention they were successful. Partly because of their commitment to make the Y a place where free speech was not only given lip service but also practiced, by the 1950s, the UT-Y acquired the reputation as the most radical Student Y in the South, perhaps in the whole country.[7]

To a great extent, its reputation was the result of one person's efforts. Block Smith was the executive secretary of the University Y, the chief administrative post there, from 1921 to 1956. He seemed like "a primitive Christian," noted one student in the mid-1950s, in the crystalline simplicity of his egalitarian outlook: a "spare man" who displayed a "clarity of soul." From a rural Texas background, Smith started school at UT in 1908 and spent little time elsewhere until his retirement. His major sojourn outside Texas was a tour of duty with the YMCA serving the American troops who were sent by President Woodrow Wilson as part of the multilateral Expeditionary Force to Siberia in 1917 to try to crush the Soviet Revolution. Anticommunism not only was compatible with even the most ardent belief in the social gospel but also defined its outer limit. Although in the future, the UT-Y staff was intermittently red-baited, just as American rightists consistently attempted to link liberalism with socialism, the Y staff could deny any such affiliations, with their commitments intact.[8]

Within the limits of these commitments, the University Y played a challenging, questioning role. Block Smith preached a message also heard at the Faith-and-Life Community, that religion should not be walled off in the church, separate from the rest of life. As he put it, "We've tried to show that

Christianity isn't just something for Sunday exercise, that Christianity is something that has to do with living seven days a week if it's worth a hoot, that it has something to do with your treatment of people." For Smith, Christianity meant Christian behavior, and this meant, in the tradition of Christian liberalism, deriving ethics from religion and applying them to life. "I think making a theological statement isn't necessarily Christianity. It's standing up when the going's rough." He cited the Supreme Court's 1954 *Brown* decision as an example of a truly Christian act.[9]

When Block Smith retired, he was replaced by Frank Wright. Raised in the social gospel tradition of midwestern Protestant clergy, Wright was a pacifist early in life, as well as an active participant in the student peace movement of the 1930s, and he became part of what Casey Hayden calls "the old-line radical religious left."[10] He went to prison in World War II as a conscientious objector (CO). Then he was one of the group of COs who, after the war, founded the National Mental Health Association, many of them having been revolted by the conditions they witnessed in mental hospitals where they had served in lieu of military duty. Wright wrote a book on these conditions in 1947, entitled *Out of Sight, Out of Mind*. After the war he went to work for the Y, serving at Johns Hopkins and the University of Washington in Seattle. After eight years in Seattle, in 1956 he was assigned to the Austin campus.[11]

In 1954 Rosalie Oakes arrived to serve as executive secretary of the campus YWCA. She had spent virtually her whole life in the South. A single career woman at a time when social approval for such a role was to be found in only a few environments, she had worked full time for the YWCA since finishing her work at Crozer Seminary in Chester, Pennsylvania (a liberal seminary that was experimenting with an interracial student body; Martin Luther King Jr. numbered among its later alumni). Oakes had first become involved with the Y in college, at the University of Richmond, in the late 1930s, "raising the questions" of peace and racial politics. During the later years of World War II, she worked at the University of Kentucky Y, doing the same for the many armed services personnel and Ivy League students who were in Lexington, which was designated during the war as a center for training engineers.[12]

Starting in wartime and throughout her years afterward traveling around all the campus Y branches in the Southeast Region, Oakes was part of the contingent in the Y that pushed the regional and national structure toward a more militant stand on racial equality. Historically the Y had had separate black and white structures, and racial egalitarianism in the white Y was far from widespread. But starting in the 1930s and 1940s, younger Y members of different races, many of them influenced by the leftist radicalism of the Great Depression, started demanding that the Y movement both integrate itself racially and place greater emphasis on pursuing racial equality in American society.[13]

In 1943 Oakes was in an interracial group of fifty, mainly students, who left their Y encampment in Hendersonville, North Carolina, just in time to miss the arrival of three hundred Klansmen who were outraged by the spectacle of coed interracial swimming at the camp. In the late 1940s and early 1950s, she traveled around the Southeast with a black woman, who represented the separate black YWCA region, and experienced firsthand the harassment and exclusion that Jim Crow entailed. In 1946 the racial liberals prevailed in the National Y, passing resolutions that required branches of the Y to merge their black and white organizations. (Individual branches complied haltingly and unevenly.) Throughout the late 1940s and 1950s, Y activists stood at the forefront of the cause of integration and racial equality in the South.[14]

In the mid-1950s, these staff members at the University of Texas Y— personally mild mannered but determined, their principles laid bare for all to see—held out an alternative, both politically and personally, to students there. They demonstrated by their example that one did not have to blow with the prevailing winds. Furthermore, they grounded their liberal—in some ways, radical—politics in a liberal Christian theology of long standing in the United States.

Theologically, theirs was the kind of "applied Christianity" that made not only fundamentalists but also the more trendy neoorthodox thinkers shudder. To such thinkers, translating Christianity into a doctrine of brotherly love and political liberalism seemed like a corruption of the specifically Christian message of the gospels. These critics of liberal theology influenced the curriculum at the Christian Faith-and-Life Community. But while noting the gulf between neoorthodox and liberal theologies, it is important not to exaggerate the distance between the outlooks represented at the Community and the University Y. The Community was far more concerned with theology, whereas the Y focused directly on contemporary social, political, and international issues in its committee meetings and study groups. Yet students involved in both institutions arrived at the same activist conclusions. In fact, in the late 1950s and early 1960s, there was considerable overlap between the membership of the CFLC and the Y student leadership. Casey Hayden, Dorothy Burlage, Mary Gay Maxwell, Anthony Henry, Judy Schleyer, Brad Blanton, Vivien Franklin, Jim Neyland, Dick Simpson, Charlie Laughlin, and others were leading University Y activists who also lived at the Faith-and-Life Community at some point between

1958 and 1963. For these students, the Y and the Community were simply two pieces of a larger political–intellectual environment at the UT campus that nurtured their growing activism, an environment that included other student religious organizations like the Methodist Student Center, as well as campus leadership institutions such as the Student Assembly (SA) and honorary societies like Mortar Board, the Orange Jackets, and the Friars.[15]

This overlap was so great that a student journalist in 1962, reporting the popularity on campus of theologians like Tillich, Barth, Bonhoeffer, Bultmann, and the Niebuhrs—in other words, the CFLC roster—mistakenly referred to all this theology as "liberal." But the students who were drawn to this existentialist literature, which was quite critical of liberal *theology*, were among the best-known *political* liberals in the student body. Furthermore, they enacted their existentialist beliefs through the vehicle of the University Y's Christian liberalism. This is confusing only if we reify the intellectual distinction between existentialist and liberal theologies. Although tensions among various strands of religious thought were present, to students immersed in intellectual discussion and political action around the beginning of the 1960s, existentialism and liberalism seemed to meld together. The imperative to engage in activism provided the common ground for these traditions. These students showed how people can, in practice, borrow freely from intellectual traditions that some might see as hopelessly opposed to one another.

The University Y stood as a vindication of Christian liberalism. Some scholars have portrayed this tradition as a complacent creed, socially conservative, unable to speak to people's inner longings; it has been caricatured as a cloistered, reassuring pablum religion.[16] The Y showed that this was not necessarily so. Liberal Christianity could be militant and activist, bringing people face-to-face with the most charged of social issues, and it could answer the call for meaning in life that many young people were starting to hear in the late 1950s. As the Y's student officers expressed the organization's purpose in 1962, it sought "the development of people of faith in the world rather than the transmission of faith by creed or sacrament." The Y shared with the Community a commitment to living "in the world," but the Y left aside the Community's search for ritual and symbolism. To the Y leaders, Christian meaning was to be found more strictly in worldly action. "In contrast to the 'Silent Generation' of the Fifties," they wrote, "the student of the Sixties sees that he must be concerned to act responsibly in society. Only in the enactment of his values in concrete life experiences does he divulge his faith to himself or others."[17] Y activists would meet with those "concrete life experiences" in the cauldron of civil rights activism.

"The Search for Authentic Experience"

The preoccupation with action and behavior in no way precluded concerns over personal identity and the quality of personal experience, concerns that were often expressed as the search for meaning and authenticity in life. These concerns reached their full expression in the 1958/1959 National Student Assembly of the Y (NSAY), the quadrennial gathering of Student Y representatives from all over the country, which was held at the University of Illinois in Champaign-Urbana over the 1958 Christmas holiday. The official theme of this assembly was "The Search for Authentic Experience." Both personal and political concerns received expression here. These two kinds of concern—psychological and social, inner and outer—were thoroughly intertwined for Y activists. In the same figurative breath, the Y officers posed questions such as "Who am I? Why am I here?" and more worldly questions like "To what causes will I commit myself?" By the early 1960s, to Y activists, these questions seemed to flow into one another.[18]

This was not always clear to outsiders. In the 1950s, some observers saw a concern with personal identity and authentic life as necessarily apolitical, as a withdrawal from controversy and activism. In anticipation of the 1958/1959 NSAY, a student reporter noted that since the 1930s and 1940s, the assemblies had moved "away from social problems toward personal ones." In the 1950s the assemblies had begun "'looking inward,'" marking a "return to religion."[19] This fit with the widespread view that the 1950s witnessed a culturally conservative "religious revival" of sorts in the United States, with rates of church attendance rising after years of decline and church construction booming.[20] In this observer's view, the upcoming collective search for authenticity seemed to promise only further movement into interior terrain and away from politics. But this turned out not to be the case.

As far back as 1955, discussion in the national Student Y had, in fact, linked the search for meaning and identity with a call for political commitment. In that year, A. L. Kershaw addressed the annual National Student Council of the YMCA and YWCA, and the Student Y printed the transcript of his talks and distributed them to Ys around the country, including the University of Texas Y. Kershaw lamented the "intellectual anarchy" that he saw on the nation's campuses, complaining that no one was forcing students to ask themselves what they really believed in. This, he thought, should be the Student Y's role. The Y should confront students with the questions "Who am I as a whole person?" and "What is most important?" Just as Tillich presented a "centered" person as the norm toward which persons should strive, Kershaw advocated a holistic view of human nature, upholding a norm of spiritual and psychological integration. Confronting the "question of personal identity," he asserted, would replace "anarchy" with a centering, and this would open the way to "freedom," to the "openness and spontaneity" that characterized Tillich's New Being—a concept to which Kershaw enthusiastically referred in order to explain his views.[21]

But the "intellectual anarchy" that Kershaw saw on the campuses was characterized not only by incomplete, dis-integrated conceptions of identity but also by the "hesitancy to give ourselves to anything." He was alarmed at the lack of commitment to anything in particular among the youth of the mid-1950s. Without supreme values to which one was committed, life had no meaning, he worried, and he saw a human need, as did the psychiatric theorist Viktor Frankl, "to determine meaning for our lives." To satisfy that need, "idealism" was required. To be centered, Kershaw argued, one had to be centered on something other than oneself. In a version of the old Protestant paradox, one had to "lose oneself" in order to "find oneself," to develop an integrated personality. In the most extreme neoorthodox rendering, the external object of commitment was simply God. Like other liberal theologians, Kershaw spent little time discussing God. Instead, he emphasized the "innovation" that would mark the New Being, and he expressed the hope that by preaching the New Being, "a new heart"—a new center, figuratively—"for social action" would emerge on the campuses. Values, applied socially, might indeed form the core of the integrated person.[22]

Harvey Cox, who exerted a great influence on American religious thought through his writings in the 1960s, pressed these buttons even harder. Cox spoke frequently to Student Y gatherings, including the 1958/1959 NSAY—where he made a bigger impression than did anyone else on one delegate, Jim Neyland, who became president of the University of Texas Y in 1960/1961—and the Christmas 1960 Southwest Regional Conference, an annual retreat in which the UT contingent always figured prominently. In August 1959 Cox gave a talk to the National Student Council of the Y entitled "Radical Renewal: The Response of the Student YMCA and YWCA in a World 'Come-of-Age,'" in which he brought Dietrich Bonhoeffer's ideas to an American audience, as he did more broadly in his book *The Secular City*, published six years later. Cox thus charted a path for the Student Y that was both more politicized and more theistic than Kershaw's. Unlike Kershaw, Cox urged students to turn away from introspection, away from the question of identity. One should not ask "Who am I?" he instructed, but instead, "What is God doing?" Citing H. Richard Niebuhr, he emphasized that it is God's work in the world that is "making us who are less than human fully human." This was the same humanist theme that appeared in the Faith-and-Life

Community. One's less-than-fully-human state was to be overcome not by fleeing the world to find God but by joining in God's worldly work. Although Cox was theistic and this-worldly, he was antireligious. "We are not called to 'bring religion to the campus,'" he wrote. "The campus has too much religion, most of it bad."[23]

Cox made it unambiguously clear that he wanted students in the Y to take a more political path, but just how "radical" he thought their politics should be he left ambiguous indeed. He called for "radicalism in its true etymological sense," which meant an imperative "to attack the social roots of the sickness of our time." Cox derided intellectual conformism. "To be radical now," he wrote, "means to refuse to accept at face value the standard interpretations of what is happening in the world." He went further still, encouraging students to reconsider the "largely bourgeois, negative and individualistic notion of freedom" that in his view dominated American culture. But he added the customary criticism of leftist radicalism, calling the American left of 1959 a "so-called 'radical' cult," "imprisoned in its own ideology." Radicalism today required a spirit of "experimentalism," he observed, and this was not possible for those who remained straitjacketed by a rigid doctrinal viewpoint. Ultimately Cox recommended that the Student Y function as a "loyal opposition" in the university, a "gadfly." If radicalism meant "asking questions which have stopped being asked," this questioning was meant simply to help restore, by example, "the traditional function of the scholar, 'to think otherwise.'" He urged the Y to remain an "indigenous" part of the university environment, for "the Student Y exists not for itself. It exists for the university," just as "the Christian community . . . exists not for its own sake but solely and uniquely to bring life and light to the world." When the Y criticized the university, he said, "we must be very sure it is a criticism from within and not from outside."[24]

This was the kind of radicalism that a lot of student activists could live with. In a brochure explaining the purpose and activities of the University of Texas Y in the 1959/1960 school year, Frank Wright and Anne Appenzellar, the executive secretaries of the YMCA and YWCA, stressed "our witness on the campus," asserting both the Y's "independence of" and its integral relation to the "institutions to which we relate ourselves freely and responsibly." Mary Gay Maxwell, student president of the YWCA that year, wrote that the University Y was used to "taking stands" on political issues but that the ultimate goal of such activity was to promote an "exchange of ideas which takes place in an atmosphere of freedom" and thus to serve the campus intellectually. Indeed, she made sure to say that the Y's major activity was "providing programs for the campus," and so it was. Although many of the Y's committees dealt with political issues, many others did not. In addition to their "Race Relations" and "Pacifism and Disarmament" committees, they offered "Psychology and Religion" and "Contemporary Literature." A campus reporter calculated in December 1961 that each month an average of 1,142 students at UT participated in Y committees. The Y ran twenty-eight study and program groups in all, serving a wide range of students on the campus.[25]

In late 1961 the president of the YMCA who had been so impressed with Cox's speech at the 1958/1959 NSAY, Jim Neyland, an artistically inclined young man from the conservative East Texas town of Palestine, made it clear that in his view, the Y was a liberal institution, not a radical one, in the conventional political sense. He did not even mean liberal, however, in the conventional political sense, writing in the *Daily Texan* that "the 'Y' is not a group devoted to liberal social, political, or economic ideas." The liberalism that the Y embraced, he explained, was a kind of philosophical pragmatism that echoed Cox's prescription for "radicalism." "To be liberal in the way the 'Y' is liberal," Neyland said, "is to be willing to hear all sides of an issue and to refuse to accept at face value the 'standard' interpretations of what is happening in the world. It means to refuse to accept any value without . . . testing and applying it to life." Neyland's version of Christian liberalism focused on the individual, on the individual's "capacity to move toward Truth," and it affirmed the "sovereign unity" of the individual.[26]

The way toward "Truth" and "sovereign unity" for the individual, Neyland stated, was to search for values and thus meaning. This connection echoed Kershaw's ideas; "unity," like "wholeness" or centering, would be achieved when one became committed to a set of values; this would give life meaning. "Real personal commitment is the goal of the 'Y,' " Neyland wrote, "as it encourages a free and open search for meaning." The centrality of this search for meaning was affirmed continually in Student Y literature. The program for the 1958/1959 NSAY in Champaign-Urbana cited "a serious desire to find out what gives meaning to one's life" among contemporary students. The 1959/1960 brochure for the UT-Y was headed by the phrase "Students search for meaning," and it then asked, "What does it mean to be a person?" "What will I value?" and "To whom or what am I responsible?" suggesting that the "search for meaning" was the master theme that encompassed these quests for humanity, values, and commitment.[27]

The existentialist image of wholeness versus fragmentation, integration versus disintegration, was a persistent one in this student religious culture, from the mid-1950s onward into the 1960s. Moreover, it is a theme that extended beyond this particular environment, passing into more general usage by the late 1960s in dissident youth circles. As explained earlier, this image had existentialist origins, for wholeness or integration is the opposite of the existentialist bugbear, alienation. Most often, the image of fragmentation versus wholeness was applied to individual psychology. The program for the same NSAY asserted that as part of "the quest for authentic personal existence"—again, the theme of the entire assembly—students were searching for "wholeness," trying to overcome "fragmentation" at a personal level. In the existentialist argot that pervaded this youth religious network, authenticity, wholeness, and meaning were inseparable goals for individuals and ultimately for communities.[28]

If the desire for feelings of wholeness was one aspect of the search for "authentic personal existence," another was what they called the search for the real and in fact is comparable to the yearning for the "really real" that was prominent in existentialist discussion. We "must decide what it means to live in that which is real," the brochure for the June 1959 Southwest Conference asserted. At one level, this search for the real simply meant a longing for honesty and sincerity and a disapproval of pretense. The NSAY program for 1958/1959 stated that students sought to do away with "fronts and disguises," which, it implied, accompanied "loneliness and alienation." Students longed for "reality and integrity," the program read, not "artificiality and 'phoniness.'" These same students ostensibly wanted an atmosphere of honest relationships and dialogue. "If it [dialogue] is authentic, and not pretentious," the program read, "both persons *listen* and both persons *speak*."[29]

But beneath this *Catcher in the Rye* type of disdain for "phoniness," this search for the real contended with something more troubling than simple insincerity. It referred to feelings of self-alienation, to a distinction within oneself and in the world, between honesty and dishonesty and also between what was "really real" and what seemed to be real but turned out to be insubstantial. This same NSAY program related an anecdote about a college student who awoke one morning and was unable to recognize himself in his bathroom mirror. "Unable to sift the real from the superficial, the pain gave way to a sense of alienation and lostness." Instead of just behaving honestly, in the everyday sense of the term, he is forced to ask himself, "What is genuine honesty . . . ? Who will tell me?" If he doesn't know, then it is safe to infer that by "honesty," he means something beyond not telling lies. The student is making a distinction between those aspects of his self that are real and authentic and those that somehow are not. "How can I be my true self?" he wonders—"the real me?" According to the existentialist outlook, inside our apparent selves there are truer selves, and the process of overcoming self-alienation is the process of finding that truer self and "sifting" out the rest. Or perhaps it is more precise to say, as the NSAY program stated, that "the real answers will not be in/the finding/but in/the *becoming*." This passage from inauthenticity to authenticity could only be a long journey, perhaps never ending.[30]

This distinction between the real and the unreal was not made just with reference to the individual self. At the annual Installation Banquet of the UT-Y in May 1962, where the presidencies of the YWCA and YMCA were passed, respectively, from Susan Reed to Susan Ford and from Jim Neyland to Dick Simpson, a "Prayer of Dedication" was recited that stated as one of the Y's goals, "To strip away from our religion all that is unreal and underneath the outer form to find a living God within a living universe, and to find ourselves more living in the living world of God." This radically expanded the search for the real beyond the self. Or else it radically expanded the traditional Western concept of the self, as in Tillich's theology, in which God and the "ground of our Being" are one and the same and are the source of authentic life. Here the students at the Y joined God, self, and authentic life and merged them all into the slightly pantheistic image of "a living universe."[31]

Student Y activists sought authenticity within themselves and between themselves and the universe and also in interpersonal relations. When they asked themselves what kind of personal relationships they wanted to have, they, perhaps inevitably, touched on the question of relationships between women and men. These young people displayed more sensitivity in their discussion of gender relations than did most of their peers, and they expressed an unusual degree of criticism concerning dominant attitudes and modes of behavior on campus. To many of them, dealings with the opposite sex were another area of life in which they longed for authenticity and in which they rejected "phoniness" and "de-personalization." Authentic selfhood could be achieved in relationships only if both partners treated each other as full human beings and not as sexual objects. In a written dialogue between a man and a woman handed out at the 1958/1959 NSAY, the man wonders why the young woman feels "she has to act so dumb" and thinks to himself, "I'm really not so strong and brave," and wonders, "Why can't we be ourselves!" In Jim Neyland's view, traditional definitions of maleness and femaleness were a barrier to "the seeking of authentic selfhood." In response, the University Y set up committees on "Man–Woman Relations" and "The Nature of Love" to explore these quandaries further.[32]

This critical perspective on contemporary culture emerged more clearly in the criticism of "the American creed of success" that surfaced among Y activists. At the 1960 Kerrville conference, students read Arthur Miller's play *Death of a Salesman*, which attacked the hollowness of this materialistic and careerist "creed." The NSAY program cited perhaps the best-known critique of American business culture when it inveighed against "the new slavery of the group culture in which we live with its suburban conformity, its 'inconspicuous consumption' to quote *The Organization Man*." There was a strong dose of individualism in this critique of conformism and status climbing. But in the context of the Student Y, this cultural critique also conveyed a spiritual and moral judgment on materialism. Jim Neyland worried that a materialistic culture would stand in the way of authentic selfhood.

> The materialistic values, the values of security have been followed with such intensity and zeal that the values of freedom have been overshadowed. It is the omission of the "spiritual," the philosophical, the aesthetic or the cultural that has made possible the dehumanization and, perhaps more important, the depersonalization of our society.

People couldn't be valued as human beings, Neyland insisted, so long as they were valued only according to how much they made or what they owned or their position in an organization.[33]

Y activists looked to the education system as a place where people might be treated as human beings. They thought universities should not merely prepare students to become parts in a corporate machine. Myra Nicol, a University of Oklahoma student active in the Southwest Region of the Student Y, asserted in 1962 that the universities should provide "education, as opposed to training." Nicol used the old ideal of liberal education to criticize the utilitarian view of education, which she linked to that "organization man" world whose pull the Y activists sought to resist. "Far too many universities serve only as massive personnel offices," she wrote. Her criticism both echoed the elite liberal humanism of Harry Ransom and anticipated the left humanist critique of the American higher education system that the new left would articulate in the coming years. As far as she and other college Y activists were concerned, the search for a more humanistic way of life should begin at home.[34]

This way of life, as Neyland's earlier comments indicated, would have many aspects in which its values would be realized—including aesthetic aspects. Art was an important part of the alternative culture that student activists were developing on college campuses in the early 1960s. To them, it "gave relevance to things around us which often seem remote. . . . [Art makes] us conscious of the necessity of a larger scope of critical participation in the world," Susan Reed pointed out.[35] Art seemed to offer a view of the world different from the materialistic or the scholarly perspective and, in some ways, a richer view. Plays and films, often newly imported from

Europe, added considerably to the air of excitement on many American college campuses in these years. This certainly was the case at UT, and the Y joined in these explorations. At the 1960/1961 Kerrville retreat, students discussed stories by Sartre, poems by Lawrence Ferlinghetti, and paintings by Picasso. At the Southwest Y Conference held more than a year before that, in June 1959, when Casey Hayden was the conference cochair, the gathered participants witnessed "dramatic presentations" of "reality as seen by contemporary artists such as Sartre, Beckett, Faulkner." In the early 1960s, the UT-Y presented on one occasion a reading of the Albert Camus play *The Misunderstanding*, whose "message" was the "inability of men to reveal themselves to each other." The Y even presented an original play by Jim Neyland in the spring of 1961, *A Memory of People.*[36]

These artistic efforts at the Y blended imperceptibly into the larger campus environment. Professors on campus sometimes assigned classes to view movies directed by Federico Fellini or Ingmar Bergman—whose work was all the rage in the United States at the time—at the Texas, the "arts" cinema on the Drag. At the Methodist Student Center in the fall of 1960, Bob Breihan opened a coffeehouse called Ichthus—the Greek word for "fish," which had been used by early Christians as a secret symbol for Christ. In early 1961 Ichthus featured a rendition of *Waiting for Godot*, which had led to the spat, mentioned earlier, between Joe Mathews and John Silber, who now were on hand to provide commentary. Mathews spoke at Ichthus on its first night in operation on the topic of "Conversation," on the same bill as a jazz group led by a UT student. Wesley Seeliger, a UT senior who was active in the Y and lived for a time at the CFLC, was Ichthus's first manager. The Ichthus also presented readings from *Catcher in the Rye*, as well as improvisational performances. Much of this artistic material dealt precisely with the issues of alienation and authenticity that concerned students in the Y and the Community and dealt with them perhaps more directly and powerfully than did any other available material.[37]

Y activists were developing an alternative culture on college campuses. By the early 1960s this cultural milieu flowed smoothly into liberal political activities. The 1958/1959 NSAY, which in prospect appeared apolitical to some, turned into a civil rights rally, the assembled black and white delegates joining hands to sing "We Shall Overcome" and "Kumbaya." By the next NSAY, in 1962/1963—also held at the University of Illinois—the Y's political concerns had become more explicit and prominent. The sit-in movement had swept the South; SNCC had been formed; and the Freedom Riders had been viciously attacked in Alabama and had desegregated southern bus lines. The civil rights movement seemed to put into practice the ideas that Y activists had been talking about for years. In a gesture of recognition to the political upheaval, the theme of this next NSAY was "Revolution and Response." The slate of speakers and discussions put politics front and center: sessions on "Social Injustice," "A World in Revolution," "The Dilemma of Atomic Power in a Divided World," and "Challenges to the Democratic Ideal" were planned, and Harvey Cox, William Sloane Coffin (the Yale chaplain who later became deeply involved in the movement against the war in Vietnam), *Nation* editor Carey McWilliams, and Carl Rowan, assistant secretary of state for public affairs and a civil rights advocate, all were scheduled to appear.[38]

In October 1962, Jim Neyland and Myra Nicol wrote a skit that they distributed to Southwest Conference Ys, suggesting that their fellow Y activists perform the skit on campus as a way to promote the upcoming NSAY. The skit was simply a series of words and phrases uttered by two "boys" and two "girls." It reflects the way in which political consciousness, existentialist literature, and humanist cultural critique were mixed together in the minds of young white activists at that time.

"We've been apathetic"
"A silent generation"
"But the world is in revolution"
"And we are in the world"
. . . "Freedom without equality"
"Equality without freedom"
"Inequality"
"Social Injustice"
. . . "Affluent Society"
. . . "Mass Culture"
"Sex"
"Masculine"
"Feminine"
"Changing roles"
. . . "Faith, Sex and Love"
"The Art of Loving"
"SNCC"
"Martin Luther King"
"CORE"
"Between Man and Man"
"The Beat Generation"
"The Lonely Crowd"
"Growing Up Absurd"
. . . "Irrational Man"

... "Response"
"Action"
"Response"
"Demonstration"
"Response"
"Responsible"
"Revolution"
"Response"
[all together:] "REVOLUTION AND RESPONSE"[39]

Some thought that nothing very political could come from the search for meaning and authenticity, but the civil rights movement pulled all the potential political consequences out of that search. Without the stimulus of that movement, this potential might never have been realized. But it was there all along.

"What are you *doing out* there?"

When young people got involved in the Student Y, they encountered a long-standing tradition of political discussion and activism. The Y's activism in the 1950s largely consisted of learning about and "taking stands" on social issues. To understand the confidence and organizational skill that these students displayed in the direct action in which they eventually engaged, one needs to appreciate the preparation and training they had earlier received in the expressly political activities of the Student Y.

The binary structure of the Y held consequences that ramified through all its activities, local, regional, and national. From the University Y in Austin to the NSAYs, all activities were organized into joint YMCA–YWCA committees, each of which had a woman and a man as cochairs. (They were called "cochairmen.") As a result of this institutionalization of gender equality, many young women found opportunities to rise to positions of leadership. As of December 1961, the student membership at the University of Texas Y was nearly two-thirds women. Women who got involved at the Y found themselves anything but stifled.[40]

Casey Cason, later Casey Hayden, was the most important Y activist helping move a group of white UT students into civil rights action between 1958 and 1961. Joe Mathews was her mentor, and she engaged in more directly political activity with Frank Wright and the students at the Y. Her fellow Y activists from Austin universally remember her as a dynamic, independent figure, intellectually and tactically aggressive, one of the real "movers" of the group.[41] Hayden found at the Y on Guadalupe a place where women were respected and shouldered responsibility as a matter of course. She goes so far as to call this a "woman-centered" atmosphere, in which people emphasized the nuts and bolts of planning activities, not the pompous oratory that she associated with more male-dominated environments. She became cochair of the University Y's Race Relations Committee. In addition to local activities, Hayden went to the regional retreats and the National Assembly in 1958/1959, along with Neyland, Wright, and Appenzellar, which inspired them all to get more involved in civil rights activity. In the summer of 1959, now as a college graduate, she had what was in some ways an even more worldly experience. While other Y activists traveled abroad, she worked in a church school in East Harlem, in New York City, sharing an apartment with a few other young women and making money by working in a department store. From this experience she brought back a determination to begin working directly for social change.[42]

Hayden grew up in the southeast Texas town of Victoria, raised by her mother and her aunt in what she remembers as a female-dominated environment, fostering in her a sense of competence and equality with men that determined many of her political choices and actions. Her mother and her father, an accountant who worked in the Allred administration and organized the Texas public employees union, both held college degrees, and the Victoria household was a place where learning was honored. They divorced when Casey was six months old. (Her mother's brief second marriage was marked by abuse at the hands of Casey's stepfather.) When she was twelve, Casey was baptized in the Presbyterian Church at her own request, becoming religious as an adolescent. Without substantial means, after two years at a local junior college she transferred to UT. In Austin she gravitated to the University Y, as well as the Christian Faith-and-Life Community.[43] Highly articulate and confident, as well as tall and blond, she had many admirers. Tom Hayden, who married her in 1961, saw in her "the image of a sought-after 'goddess,'" and she confesses that at the time she warmed to the role of "southern belle," apparently holding at some remove the men, Ronnie Dugger among them, who buzzed about her during evenings at Scholz's Biergarten.[44]

Casey also became drawn into the National Student Association (NSA), where she met Al Haber and Tom Hayden, from the University of Michigan, and many other militant student activists. This in turn led her into SDS, which proved to be the kind of male-dominated political environment that she recalls finding so different from the Y. She coauthored NSA pamphlets, *Civil Rights in the South* and *Civil Rights in the North*, which SDS distributed. In 1960 she took part in NSA's Southern Student Leaders Seminar at the University of Minnesota and stayed for the annual NSA Congress that took place there in August.[45]

Here Casey Hayden first spoke to a national audience, challenging the assembled student delegates to endorse the growing civil disobedience of young African Americans in the South in defiance of segregation laws. Another white southern liberal in the NSA, Connie Curry, placed Hayden on a panel of whites who, it was generally expected, would try to rebut the arguments that black students had made the previous evening in favor of civil rights protests. The audience was in for a surprise. Accomplished student of existentialism that Hayden was, she spoke on the need to rebel against injustice and to decide in favor of action if one was to be truly human.

> When an individual human being is not allowed by the legal system and the social mores of his community to *be* a human being.... Perhaps in this situation protest is the only way to maintain his humanity....
>
> I cannot say to a person who suffers injustice, "Wait." Perhaps you can, I can't. And having decided that I cannot urge caution I must stand with him. If I had known that not a single lunch counter would open as a result of my action I could not have done differently than I did. I am thankful for the sit-ins if for no other reason than that they provided me with an opportunity for making a slogan into a reality by making a decision into an action. It seems to me that this is what life is all about. While I would hope that the NSA Congress will pass a strong sit-in resolution, I am more concerned that all of us, Negro and white, realize the possibility of becoming less inhuman humans through commitment and action.

Finally she pulled out all the stops, recounting the story of Henry David Thoreau's jailing for his protest against slavery and the Mexican War. His friend Ralph Waldo Emerson came to see him and asked Thoreau, "Henry David, what are you doing in there?" Hayden continued, "Thoreau looked at him and replied, 'Ralph Waldo, what are *you* doing out *there?*'" Then, to end her presentation, she turned to her audience and repeated the question: "What are you doing out there?" The speech was a hit, and Hayden soon became widely known as a leading activist in the as-yet-unnamed movement of militant liberal young white Americans, a movement that attentive observers could see coalescing.[46]

Another woman who became a leader of political activity at the UT-Y was Vivien Franklin (later Rasjidah Franklin-Alley), who entered UT in 1959. She was from the nearby town of Wimberley, and she grew up steeped in the history and politics of the region. Her mother's family was one of the original land-grant families that Stephen Austin brought to the area with the permission of the Mexican government in the 1830s. Her father was a quite impressively connected rancher: He played baseball as a teenager with his contemporary Lyndon Johnson, and his ranching partner was Leon Jaworski, another of Johnson's intimates. Jaworski was Vivien's "mentor." Thus her proximity to power was such that not only did she work as a page at the 1960 Democratic National Convention in Los Angeles (at the behest of another family friend, Abe Fortas, the future U.S. Supreme Court Justice), but Johnson, as the Democratic vice presidential candidate that year, chose her as his female youth representative during the campaign. This meant she took trips with his entourage on his official plane and sat on the dais, along with Jim Neyland, with whom she was involved romantically, at Johnson's victory celebration on election night.

Early in her life Franklin imbibed from this Democratic activist environment a basic belief in social justice and a "feeling for the underdog." These feelings found a focus in race relations. Franklin attended one of only a handful of racially integrated high schools in Texas, and while a student there, she circulated a petition to integrate the whites-only basketball team. There was little doubt she would attend UT, and her political development continued there along the same lines, virtually without a pause. Her family attended an interdenominational Protestant church in Wimberley, and she attended a University of Texas Y retreat in Wimberley the summer before she started college. In her recollection, the Y staff and Jim Neyland, who was a counselor at the retreat, picked her out there, perhaps recognizing her as someone who had been groomed for leadership. Indeed, this was a role she easily assumed in the Y's political activities. In the spring of 1961 she was elected chair of the YWCA Southwest Regional Council. After Casey Hayden's departure in 1961, Franklin and Neyland were the two most important leaders of civil rights action around the Y.[47]

From Franklin's perspective, it was the relatively nontheistic, nonphilosophical environment of the University Y that crystallized the civil rights activism among students on campus. She lived for a semester at the Faith-and-Life Community, and although she found it a comfortable, somewhat offbeat living environment, she had little time for or interest in their curricular pursuits, which she found "bothersome." The Community was not important to her political development, as it was to that of many others. To her, the Y was the place where she could exercise and extend the worldly interests of her youth and where she was treated as the equal of any male student.[48]

Even if Franklin did not find attractive the intellectual discussion at the Community, one element of the Community she enjoyed was the presence of a large contingent of foreign students. Activists in the NSA also sought contacts with students from other countries. As discussed earlier, internationalism was a way for students in the provinces to make a statement about their own cosmopolitanism. The Student Y displayed an even stronger internationalism, offering students in the United States extensive exposure to other countries, in addition to its long-standing tradition of providing support services for foreign students visiting the United States. Through these contacts, by the late 1950s, Student Y activists developed an awareness of a global youth movement, a movement perhaps strongest in the Third World, as part of a larger nonaligned movement of nations recently emerged from colonialism.[49] Admiration for and identification with this global movement corroded the loyalty of young Y activists to cold war orthodoxy, which virtually denied the possibility of a "third camp" between the U.S. and Soviet blocs. Because of this pronounced internationalism in the late 1950s and early 1960s, it was through the Y, more than anywhere else in a conservative state like Texas, that students expressed a clear political dissent from the common wisdom on foreign affairs in the United States.[50]

Since the Y was a worldwide organization, an international perspective was built into it, so to speak. The National Student Y expressed the imperative to learn about the world and to pursue a nonbelligerent approach to world affairs, in the discussion section entitled "In Search of World Community" that was part of the 1958/1959 NSAY. Casey Hayden was the YWCA's cochair for this section. As preparation for the assembly, the National Y recommended a book on the 1955 Bandung Conference of nonaligned nations. They also planned a "Folk-lore evening" at which students from Y branches around the world would offer stories or songs from their cultures. While maintaining a "Christian witness," the Y program asked, how could Y activists "show respect and appreciation for other interpretations of the meaning of life?" They thought Americans were generally ignorant of other countries, and they recommended "increased direct contact of American students with the peoples of other countries," stating specifically that they wanted the National Y to continue a U.S.–USSR student exchange program. While careful not to say anything that might suggest an endorsement of Soviet thinking on any issue, the students made it clear that they disagreed with cold war thinking, pointing out that the present course of events dehumanized the peoples of much of the world, turning them into pawns in a power game. Rather, their stated aims were to appreciate the humanity of these peoples and to listen to their voices.[51]

The Y's liberal internationalism extended to the regional and local levels as well. The Christmas 1960 Southwest Regional Conference, at which

Harvey Cox appeared, was entitled "You, Me and the World." The theme of the next regional conference, held one year later (after the Bay of Pigs invasion but before the Cuban missile crisis), was "World Crisis Confronts College Students." International students, as well as "student travelers" who had been to foreign lands, discussed their experiences abroad.[52] A Y activist from SMU wrote in 1962 that it was vital that citizen of the United States try to view the situation of "the 'non Western' world" from "their perspective."[53] The regional assembly in 1961 urged the National Student Council of the Ys to reassert the 1950/1951 NSAY's recommendation that the United States recognize the People's Republic of China. The same regional assembly enthusiastically endorsed the Peace Corps and recommended that local Ys do what they could to inform Y members about the program. These Y activists could be critical of cold war policies, but they also were open to the appeal of liberal initiatives, like the Peace Corps, that assumed a fundamentally benign role for the United States in the world.[54]

College students active in the Y could learn firsthand about how the United States interacted with the rest of the world and, more generally, what the world looked like from alternative perspectives, through the extraordinary opportunities the Y arranged for travel abroad. These trips usually were taken during the summer. For example, in July 1960, Bill Fielder, who had been president of the UT-YMCA in 1959/1960, attended the World Y Seminar in Geneva, Switzerland, on the topic of "The Role of a Christian Movement in the International Community." This was the summer after the student sit-in movement began, and Fielder reported that the assembled delegates saw this North American phenomenon as the vanguard of the world Christian student movement. In the summer of 1961, Dick Simpson and Larry Manire of UT joined other YMCA members from the United States and Europe at a "building for brotherhood" work project in Liberia, helping construct school buildings. Simpson came back and told his fellow students that he had met Liberians who really didn't trust white governments and who wanted to know why the United States, despite its democratic rhetoric, did not support anticolonial movements in the Third World.[55]

In addition to gaining knowledge of Third World perspectives and joining in world youth meetings, some Y activists were more daring in their travels, going into the ostensible belly of the beast—the Soviet bloc. As noted earlier, the National Student Councils of the Y ran a sometimes controversial U.S.–USSR student exchange tour. As part of the tour, students from the United States spent six weeks in the Soviet Union, followed by visits to various East European countries. There were other programs that enabled students to go to East bloc countries as well. As it did for Dorothy Burlage (who did not go to Russia under Y auspices), such travel inevitably humanized the peoples of socialist countries for American students and furthermore gave socialism itself a human face. One UT student who visited the Soviet Union in the summer of 1961 reported that the Russian people, their memories of World War II still fresh, "want peace more than any people in the world." This was not the standard line that U.S. citizens usually heard from their government and media. That same summer, Vivien Franklin and Susan Reed also visited the Warsaw Pact countries: Reed visited Poland, and Franklin went on a tour of ten European countries, both East and West, followed by a month-long stay in Berlin, where she attended an International Student Peace Seminar. Upon her return to Texas, Franklin gave an unusual series of talks at local "luncheon clubs." She reported that the United States had sabotaged a nuclear inspection agreement with the Soviets in the early 1950s, that "business interests" in the United States were "blocking disarmament for economic reasons," and that Communists posed a far smaller threat to freedom and democracy in America than did the "ultraright." Susan Reed was less incendiary. She professed her own "violent" anticommunism but said she favored socialized medicine and prounion legislation in the United States and was now "leaning" toward pacifism. "I think the philosophical aims of communism sound good," she conceded and remarked that socialism had helped the Polish people. But she was careful to add, "I'm not saying that socialism would help the United States."[56] Nonetheless, Reed's approval of communist goals even in theory and her rather relativist stance regarding different ways of organizing society were vastly different from prevailing views in the United States, which held that an irreconcilable conflict existed between libertarian capitalism and authoritarian communism. How different her view was from that of a national liberal spokesperson like Arthur Schlesinger Jr.

By sharing their experiences abroad with their fellow students back home, these travelers helped bring a consciousness of the wider world to their campus. Indeed, the Y's function on the UT campus was not only to provide worldly experiences for a handful of students but also to maintain a center of discussion about world affairs in Austin. Experts and visitors frequently gave talks on such issues. Rosalie Oakes left the UT-Y in 1958 to work with the YWCA in South Africa, but in 1960 she visited Austin and filled in the students and staff on the situation there.[57] In September 1961, Joseph Jones of the English department talked about his time teaching in South Africa, and Mel Zuck, peace education secretary of the local American Friends Service Committee (AFSC), gave a critical perspective on U.S. military policy. Three

African students who were studying at nearby Huston-Tillotson College spoke at the Y soon afterward about the Congolese independence movement.[58] Also in 1961, representatives of the National Student Christian Federation and the Student Christian Movement of Cuba discussed the issue of relations between the student Christian movements in the two countries, now that one was socialist.[59] The Y was the acknowledged center of internationalist discussion on campus, and so when three representatives of the International Student Conference (one of whom was from Uganda) came to the UT campus for a day in May 1961, they met with those student leaders whom they saw as enlightened—namely, representatives of groups involved in civil rights activity—and also met with Frank Wright of the Y. Students from other countries made it clear that in their view, liberal internationalism and support for civil rights in the United States went hand in hand. Student activists at UT seemed to see it in the same way.[60]

Indeed, the same Y activists who expressed global concerns consistently discussed domestic, regional, and local issues. The domestic issues on which they concentrated bore a strong resemblance to the secular liberal agenda in Texas. This kind of secular liberalism and the Y's Christian liberalism, with its search for meaning and its global consciousness, did not exist in separate universes. Liberal students were immersed in a local political culture in which these different traditions bled into and reinforced one another. Some concerns that Y activists at UT shared with local secular liberals were, for example, the House Un-American Activities Committee (HUAC), capital punishment, and, most important, civil rights.

Starting in late 1960, Vivien Franklin pushed the Y's cabinet to pass a resolution advocating the abolition of the House Un-American Activities Committee, and she circulated a petition around campus calling for the same. She based her opposition on the civil libertarian and due process concerns that were typical of political liberals in Texas. HUAC, she said, was "incompatible with free intellectual inquiry and expression." The Y formed a civil liberties study group in early 1961 that showed the HUAC film *Operation Abolition*, about the mass arrests of college students who protested at HUAC hearings in San Francisco in 1960. As it did on many campuses, the footage of police brutality directed against peacefully protesting students had an effect directly contrary to what the filmmakers intended. That is, the narration seemed so much at odds with the images that it provoked laughter, the only applause coming when a student in the film grabbed a policeman's leg. In April 1960, the Southwest Regional Assembly of the Student Ys resolved to "support the reconsideration of the duties and methods" of HUAC (this was when Vivien Franklin became chair of the Regional Student YWCA).[61]

Opposition to capital punishment was perhaps a less popular cause, but it attracted some of the same liberal student activists. This was a cause championed in great measure by older liberals. John Silber, it was noted earlier, was the most prominent foe of capital punishment in the area, serving as president of the Texas Society for the Abolition of Capital Punishment. Ronnie Dugger and the *Observer* also strongly opposed executions, giving ample coverage to cases that involved extenuating circumstances or doubts about the prisoner's guilt. Dugger expressed his views on the issue emotionally in a poem he printed in the *Observer* in 1961.

> *I accuse you, Texans. I accuse you of murder. . . .*
> *You are all murderers.*
> *We, we, we are the murderers. . . .*
> *We stuff the gag in the boy's mouth.*
> *We give the signal.*
> *We pull the switch.*
> *You. I. . . .*
> *Smell his burning flesh, Texans.*

Some students indeed felt a collective responsibility to do something to stop capital punishment, which to Texas liberals epitomized a violent regional culture. On the door to the off-campus apartment of Chett Briggs and Charlie Laughlin, UT students who were prominent Y members and liberal activists, was a card that designated their abode as the headquarters of the University Society for the Abolition of Capital Punishment. In May 1961, several students took an interest in the case of a black man on death row after a conviction for raping a white woman in an East Texas town. He had been retried four times, and the case was then before the U.S. Supreme Court. A group of five students, including Vivien Franklin, Dick Simpson, and Brad Blanton, met with the chairman of the Texas Board of Pardons and Paroles to protest the impending execution. For these students, active opposition to state executions was an important element of the liberal humanist conscience with which they increasingly identified.[62]

Although many concerns moved the white Y activists, race overshadowed all other issues. This was the heart and soul of the Student Y movement from the 1930s through the 1950s, the organization's most consistent and consistently radical emphasis. Indeed, it would have been surprising if, when a small number of white students started taking direct action in support of civil rights in the South in the early 1960s, they had not had connections to the Student Y movement. During the 1950s, as mentioned earlier, Y activists directed much of their energy on this front to the cause of integration inside the Student Y itself. The 1958/1959 NSAY went further,

resolving to denounce discriminatory clauses in fraternity and sorority con-
stitutions, and urging college administrations and state legislatures to bar
discriminatory Greek societies from state-supported schools. Despite this
strong protest against racism, at this time Student Y activists, at least at the
level of national policy, observed certain limits when attacking racial discrimination (just as they did in their dissent from cold war foreign policy).
When it came to the national scene, they merely recommended "better
understanding between the races," a typical moderate formulation. They
recommended "understanding," not justice.[63]

It was right after this NSAY that activists at the University of Texas Y
began more militant civil rights activities. In February 1959, inspired by their
experience in Illinois, an interracial group of Y members attempted a sit-in
at a coffee shop down the street from the Y building. The staff of the restaurant ignored them, and they were not a big enough group to interfere seriously with the shop's operation. Later, Jim Neyland first took part in a sit-
in during that spring semester at a downtown Austin bus station café, along
with Jennie Franklin and Gwen Jordan, two black UT students. They sat at
the counter for fifteen or twenty minutes until the angry manager closed the
café rather than serve them. Because the students had acted peacefully and
with dignity, Neyland remembers, and because they hadn't gotten hurt by
any hostile bystanders, they were left with a feeling of "liberation and exhilaration." "It was a victory for us, because we now knew that 'Christian nonviolence' could work; we did not know how long it would take, but we were
certain our rectitude would eventually wear down the opposition."[64]

The students started calling themselves the "fellowship of sitters." By
April 1959 they had visited several Austin restaurants. The University Y
cabinet, the University Religious Council, and the Religious Workers'
Association all went on record supporting their efforts. The UT-Y cabinet
expressed its approval in the classic terms of liberal Christianity: "The Y
sees value in this project as one in which a student can take action 'in behalf
of' the values he is beginning to affirm," it stated. The "becoming" that
would make one whole was impossible unless one put one's chosen values
into practice. The cabinet cited the recent "State-of-the-Association message," which asserted, "Action is necessary for a person to be whole in his
convictions. . . . The greatest need of both education and religion today is
to have more ways in which we can put our muscles into support of our
thoughts, emotions, and our convictions." The students saw civil rights
activism answering the spiritual and philosophical queries posed in the Y's
long-developing internal discussion.[65]

As time passed, this circle of Y activists became increasingly involved in civil rights activity. Groups from Austin traveled fairly often to black schools such as Texas Southern University in Houston, Wiley College in Marshall, Texas, and Prairie View A&M in Arkansas. The most dramatic such trip occurred in March 1960, when Frank Wright drove a group of students—including Vivien Franklin, Jennie Franklin, and Jim Neyland—to Tougaloo Southern Christian College, a black school with a Y chapter near Jackson, Mississippi; they also visited Millsaps College, a white school in the area where some students were interested in forming a Y. A Louisiana state patrolman flagged them down as soon as they crossed the Texas state line and told them they wouldn't be allowed to stop anywhere in Louisiana, not even for gas, then followed them all the way across the state. It was late by the time they arrived at the Tougaloo campus, and the cafeteria was closed, so a couple of the students there agreed to go with the visitors to a convenience store, run by whites, for some food. This "pretty naive" group, as Neyland recalls them, attracted some unwanted attention.

> As we went through the aisles, picking up what we needed, we noticed some large tough-looking white men arriving, one or two at a time, following us around. At least one was carrying a hefty sized piece of wood, club-sized. The black students came to me and whispered, "We've got to get out of here."

They dropped their food and made for the car, and a "terrifying chase" ensued, a few cars tailing them until they made it into the apparently safe confines of the Tougaloo gates.[66]

On the following morning, Neyland was to address the Tougaloo students in their chapel, the first time a white student had ever done so. But once at the podium, he forgot what he had planned to say,

> something filled with platitudes and pretentious intellectual ideas. . . . I was too frightened to speak for a moment; tears welled up in my eyes because facing them was a revelation, and all I could do was tell them what I was experiencing. It was a realization of what they must feel most of the time trying to live in a white world by the white man's rules. If other whites could experience this, they would realize that things had to change.

This analogy between a black person in a white-ruled society and a white person at black college is less than convincing. Yet the feeling of identification that Neyland experienced, curious as it is, remains highly noteworthy. Such feelings fueled whatever degree of direct white support for the rights and dignity of black Americans emerged in the South. In situations like these, white activists felt, race ceased to matter; it simply disappeared as a barrier to human interaction. On the trip back to Austin, the group stopped at the Vicksburg Civil War battle site, and Neyland and Jennie Franklin both ran up the hill to the monument there, he yelling "Charge!" and she yelling, "Kill those damn yankees!" Neyland remembers them as two southerners, joking about their past in order to release nervous energy yet genuinely feeling that they shared a heritage of which both were proud. One doubts whether Jennie Franklin, or the students at Tougaloo, saw these incidents in the same way that he did. Yet despite Neyland's naïveté, the black students responded positively to their visitors' sincere intentions and proved willing to interact with them in a casual social setting (a willingness that white students at schools like UT generally did not extend in kind). The UT students spent their day at Tougaloo getting to know the students there better, and that night their hosts held a dance, where the Austinites learned new dances like the "slop" and the "Madison."[67]

By September 1960, the experiences of students from UT in this and other situations had moved them well past the pleas for "understanding" that had been the standard Y line in early 1959. By this time, Suzy Young, the cochair of the UT-Y's Race Relations Committee, was willing to assert that her committee's purpose was "to aid all students in gaining their just rights in the University community." Now they talked the language of justice and rights. The bonds of empathy forged in interracial political action upheld a commitment to racial justice, not merely to improved race relations. This was a crucial difference between traditional white racial liberalism and the new, pro–civil rights liberalism. This new commitment formed the bedrock of white youth activism, first liberal and then leftist, for more than a decade to come.[68]

To be sure, around 1960, these differences remained safely within the bounds of the liberal camp; nothing in this civil rights activity was in any way leftist. When acting through the Y, these students trod in the tradition of militant Christian liberalism that the Student Y had upheld for decades. By taking their politics out of the Y building on Guadalupe, they demonstrated the activist potential of this tradition. They sought both to make themselves whole and to heal the wounds of the world by putting their values into practice. By the late 1950s, the searches for authenticity and social change, simmering among white youth in a liberal framework, found their most welcoming institutional structure in the Y movement.

It was only when some who were active in the Y, along with other young people, began to act in behalf of civil rights outside the Y's institutional framework that their activity began to offer hints of a more politically radical perspective. It was then that tensions began to emerge between those student activists who maintained a liberal perspective and hoped to work for change through the mainstream institutions of society and those who developed a more politically alienated and radical point of view. The relations between this second type of activism, which first appeared in Austin in 1960, and the activity officially organized through the University Y itself, were complex. Both types of activity occurred simultaneously; the participants in both overlapped greatly; and those involved in each used the Y as a base of planning and operations. The extra-Y activity grew out of the local political and intellectual environment that the Y did so much to foster, and perhaps it would not have been possible had not the Y opened a "free space" for discussion, extracurricular education, and liberal political activism on the edge of the UT campus.[69]

CHAPTER FOUR

To Be Radical Now:
Civil Rights Protest and Leftward Movement

BETWEEN 1960 AND 1963, a new political consciousness emerged among American youth. In retrospect, this orientation seems distinctly to the left of the liberalism of the 1950s, yet those who embraced this new consciousness eschewed the category of "the left." Sometimes they called themselves liberals. In any case, this civil rights–oriented, "postliberal" stance crucially abetted the emergence of a national new left in the 1960s. In a few metropolitan areas of the Northeast, handfuls of young radicals clustered around SDS, formerly the Student League for Industrial Democracy (SLID), avowing an explicit left-wing politics from 1960 onward. Yet the new left became a significant factor in national political life only after winning the loyalty of the much larger and more geographically dispersed cadres of young white civil rights agitators who did not previously embrace a leftist identity. These militant liberal or postliberal activists could be found in places like Austin.

After 1963, the new left bore little direct connection to the Christian-influenced activism of the 1958–1963 period and virtually no institutional connection. Yet the continuities between the two phases of activism are notable: the emphasis on direct action, the elevation of racism to the forefront of social concern, and the infusion of this political outlook with the existentialist search for authenticity. In the early 1960s, student militants acted on their belief that political action would dissipate anxiety. Their activism exhilarated them and succeeded in marginalizing the fear of anxiety, which had been a prominent component of youth existentialism until this time. In these years, a bolder search for authenticity and democracy went forward among American youth, pointing confidently toward ever greater social change.

The Christian-oriented civil rights protest of the early 1960s, which at the University of Texas was mainly white, certainly did not develop in a political or social vacuum. It was supported by the long-developing network of liberal Protestant institutions on American campuses and was based specifically in the University Y (it received support from campus clergy of all faiths, although Catholic and Jewish clergy were generally not so directly involved as Protestant ministers). Most directly important, white activism emerged in the context of the political mobilization of African American students in the Southeast in the early 1960s, at both historically black and formerly segregated colleges and universities.

Although the focus in this book is on white participation in civil rights protest and what it portended for the development of white youth radicalism, it is difficult to understand the trajectory of this white participation without a brief examination of the regional black youth mobilization. The experience of interracial activism was of the utmost importance to the political development of white activism. The environment and ideas of the student Christian movement already inclined some white students toward sympathy with civil rights activism, and the 1958/1959 NSAY instigated some desegregation activity among Student Y activists, both white and black, before 1960. But the black student activism that surged ahead in 1960, beginning with the famous Woolworth's lunch counter sit-in by four students from North Carolina A&T College in February and culminating in the formation of SNCC, precipitated the escalation of civil rights agitation all around. It was this agitation that opened the way to a wholesale reconsideration of American politics and culture that spread like wildfire in the following years.

First in Their Class

In 1946 Heman Marion Sweatt, a Houston mailman, applied for admission to the Law School of the University of Texas at Austin. He was not admitted, as he was black and citizens of African descent had never been admitted to any part of the university. UT was the alma mater of the state's Anglo elites, a school adorned with palatial fraternity and sorority houses inhabited by the children of the wealthy. Black and Mexican American students might attend other, far more poorly endowed public universities in the state, like Texas Southern University in Houston, Texas Western in El Paso, or Prairie View A&M in East Texas, or private historically black and Chicano schools like Wiley College in Marshall or St. Mary's in San Antonio. (Mexican American students were not officially barred from entering UT, as blacks were, but few were admitted. Fewer than 200 enrolled in the 1958/1959 school year, and perhaps 550 did so in 1966/1967.)[1] There certainly were no law schools open to black students in Texas that could rival UT's for prestige.

Sweatt pressed his case in court, and in 1949 the United States Supreme Court declared that UT must admit him to its Law School, where he began his studies in 1950. After this, with more Supreme Court decisions slamming like cannonballs against the edifice of southern educational segregation and with black students and parents constantly knocking, the doors to UT were opened to black students, a crack at a time. In June 1950 two African American students were admitted to the graduate school. But in September 1954, UT refused to consider applications from black students for admission to the college. Then, two years later, UT allowed the first black undergraduates ever to matriculate.[2]

In the late 1950s the black presence at UT was tiny and elite. In 1960, the *Texan* estimated there were about 200 black students at the campus of 19,000; two years later the Religious Workers' Association could only identify 135. Although UT was reserved for the social and educational elite of the eligible student body from Texas overall, the early black students there were a particularly select group: 90 percent of them came from the top quartile of their high school classes, as compared with 51.5 percent of white incoming students, and the black students came mainly from the "higher educational–occupational grouping" of the African American population in Texas. They came mainly from urban settings, many of them from Austin, and one-quarter were transfer students. They came to UT in pursuit of education, credentials, and upward mobility.[3]

A small amount of inferior, segregated university housing was open to black students. A few lived in the Faith-and-Life Community or the Y. Many black students preferred to find housing in East Austin. After complaints surfaced concerning the construction of the comfortable Kinsolving Dormitory for white women while black students still lived in dilapidated housing, the administration agreed to build a new facility for black women. Some white students then complained that this new housing was too good, and administration officials expressed concern about offending "public opinion" by appearing too solicitous of the black students. Casey Hayden and Mary Simpson wrote to the *Texan* in response, "It may well be true that integration concerns 'public opinion and social and economic mores.' It also concerns human beings who may be demanding the right to be human beings with the fulness [*sic*] of human dignity and human interchange which this involves." They felt that the real issue was segregation on campus, as did the folklorist John Henry Faulk, who asserted, "The nightmarish conduct of . . . segregationists in New Orleans, apartheid in South Africa, the Warsaw ghetto and the dormitory at 2500 Whitis [an existing black student facility] all have more in common than any of us would like to think." Dormitory segregation remained a point of controversy on campus until the spring of 1964, when the regents officially ended it.[4]

Heavy collective hopes rested on these black students' shoulders, and they risked a great deal if they violated any of the norms of their new environment. The vanguard of the black student civil rights movement emerged on the historically black campuses, where the main threat to politically active students came from conservative black administrators. At UT, the Religious Workers' Association (RWA) report concluded, "The image of the Negro student as a 'trouble maker' . . . coming to the University to obtain his rights is pretty well exploded." The RWA may have been trying to do the black students a favor by playing down their involvement in civil rights activity, however, for the same report found in late 1962 that nearly two-thirds of the black students on campus had, in fact, been involved in integration efforts at UT since arriving there. Nonetheless, the number of African Americans on campus was so small that even a majority of them were sometimes outnumbered by the white participants in civil rights actions on campus, even though the white activists were themselves a minute fraction of the white student body. Robert Bell, a graduate student in psychology at UT in the late 1950s and early 1960s who took part in civil rights protests, risked more than most, since by 1960 he was on the verge of gaining his doctorate, but he participated anyway. He remembered that starting in early 1960, most of the black students on campus were involved somehow with these political efforts, although perhaps they were less outspoken or militant than the students at historically black schools. They understood their situation all too well.[5]

The Spring of Discontent: 1960

In February 1960, the black student sit-in movement accelerated, starting with the Woolworth's in Greensboro, North Carolina, and spread rapidly, lighting kindling that had been waiting for a match.[6] Black students at UT decided to take action in Austin. Unlike the students at historically black schools, who directed their protests against retail establishments, the UT students first called attention to segregation in the university. In addition to dormitory segregation, many UT activities, including athletics and drama, remained closed to black students. A group of about thirty students, about twenty-five black and five white, met at the Y on a Sunday evening in March, with Anthony Henry presiding, to decide what action to take. They decided to work on the on-campus situation, and they asked President Logan Wilson to consider making changes. He released a statement saying simply that UT was making progress in coping with a "difficult situation." So the group of thirty picketed silently on the edge of campus one afternoon, the men in suits, carrying signs protesting unequal treatment on campus. Henry said he thought most white students on campus simply didn't know that these vestiges of segregation persisted at UT and that one purpose of the picket was to educate the white campus majority.[7]

One of the white students taking part in the picket explained his presence by saying, "Well, to me, I'm just following Christ's teaching." Ronnie Dugger, noting with excitement the new developments, declared,

> Now, suddenly, the hesitant liberals are irrelevant. They do not matter. The students are saying, "This is wrong. We do not care what anybody says. . . . *I* know this is wrong . . . !" And so the plain, confronting force of a moral idea: the dignity of a person: sweeps all else before it.

The *Texan* supported the action. A sports reporter expressed the common student opinion that it was absurd to bar black students from intercollegiate athletics (this, of course, was the easiest part of integration to support, given the racist stereotypes about black athletic ability—many white students saw no reason to deprive their school of an extraordinary talent pool). "Let's face it!" he said. "Integration is here to stay."[8]

But as it turned out, the small group of black students was not able to sweep the UT administration before its determination. Four of them, including Henry and Mary Simpson, met with Wilson but made no headway. The group—which called itself simply "The Group"—had now grown to about forty-five. After just three days of picketing against the university, they decided to seek other means of raising student awareness of racial discrimination on campus and called off their protest efforts in mid-March.[9]

Integration activists at UT had their greatest success with efforts directed against businesses in Austin. Integrationists in the Student Assembly (SA) were already trying to make progress on this front before the black student sit-in movement began. Traditionally, the SA gave "Steer Here" seals of approval to restaurants on the Drag that met certain sanitary qualifications. As noted earlier, activists intermittently tried to apply an integration requirement as well. In January 1960 the Steer Here Committee announced that it would use a scale of one hundred points to decide who made the grade: a restaurant would need eighty-one points to pass, and integration would count for twenty. A list of approved restaurants would be posted on the West Mall, and, the chair of the committee stated, "to serve Negro students at the back door or in a separate, closed off room" would not be sufficient. Restaurants had to serve all UT students equally. The *Texan* endorsed the idea.[10]

In late March, the black student sit-in movement arrived in Texas. Students at Bishop College and Wiley College in Marshall in northeast Texas—known as "one of the capitals of the Old South"—engaged in a series of sit-ins at local lunch counters. They received training from emissaries of the Southern Christian Leadership Conference, Martin Luther King Jr.'s group, in Gandhian nonviolence. One of their adult advisers was Doxey Wilkerson, a professor of education at Bishop, who was fired by the college president for his role (he had been a rather prominent member of the Communist Party in the 1930s, so he made an inviting target). The local police arrested the demonstrators in large numbers and dealt with them roughly. The protests escalated beyond lunch counters and ended when the fire department turned their water hoses on a crowd of seven hundred protesters—half of whom were white—who had gathered on the town's courthouse lawn, in a violent preview of the more notorious incident that occurred in Birmingham, Alabama, in 1963. Governor Price Daniel ordered an investigation—not of the behavior of law enforcement authorities, but of the subversive sit-in activities. (More than a year later, the investigating committee concluded that the protests had been "communist-type.")[11]

Meanwhile, in March, black students from Texas Southern University in Houston conducted a series of sit-ins at downtown Houston eateries. Two white men kidnapped and attacked a black man in Houston, hanging him from a tree by his heels and carving the letters "KKK" on his stomach and chest, they told him, in retaliation for the sit-ins. Attempted sit-ins also occurred in Waco, near Paul Quinn Negro College. Sit-ins and pickets at restaurants in San Antonio resulted in the integration of six lunch counters and shutdowns by others. The protest movement, and the various forms of white response to it, had moved to the western edge of the Deep South.[12]

Activists in Austin started to move, and the city authorities sought to head off trouble. Mayor Tom Miller vowed, "As long as I am able, I am not going to have any Marshall, Texas," in Austin and cited "the receptivity of the Austin community to change."[13] In early April the Austin Human Relations Commission (AHRC) arranged a meeting with local business leaders and student activists, but the businessmen would not agree to make any changes. That night, more than 150 people met at the University Y and issued an ultimatum: They wanted local restaurants to start integrating within a week, or else unspecified action would take place. More than 80 percent of those at this meeting were black; they included students from UT, from Huston-Tillotson, and from the Presbyterian and Episcopal seminaries in Austin. William Clebsch, a white professor of history at the Episcopal Seminary who became a public spokesperson for the group, stated, "This is not a Negro movement, it is a student inter-racial movement," and in fact, at the sit-ins and pickets that followed, the activists were careful always to assemble racially mixed groups of protesters, both to protect the black students from harassment and to practice the interracialism that they preached.[14]

The businessmen ignored the ultimatum, but not the protests. Groups ranging in size from nine to thirty picketed along Congress Avenue, the main retail street running south to the river from the state capitol, and sat in at lunch counters in bus stations and department stores throughout April and May, including on one occasion a blitz by 150 protesters at twelve lunch counters simultaneously. The Austin Human Relations Commission, stocked with integrationists and frustrated at the business community's stubbornness, openly supported the pickets, as did the SA and a "rump" convention of the Texas Young Democrats.[15] By mid-May, thirty-two lunch counters and restaurants in Austin had integrated voluntarily. (Black leaders and businessmen in Dallas struck a deal to integrate downtown lunch counters in that city around the same time.)[16] The accumulated pressure that began with the "fellowship of sitters" a year before had worn down local business resistance. The businesses that changed wanted their troubles to end. After a fairly brief period of concerted pushing, a substantial amount of restaurant segregation in Austin gave way. Locally, it was the easiest of civil rights victories.

The most successful student agitation in the spring of 1960 was interracial, but mainly black. It was directed against local businesses, not the university. It took inspiration from Christian nonviolence, but it was not explicitly Christian activism. This black-led activism, pragmatic and politically savvy, showed how a well-organized campaign of nonviolent protests could generate broad-ranging support and could meet with substantial success in Austin. Over the following summer, a group of more explicitly Christian activists at UT, mainly white, used some of these same tactics, taking more direct guidance from the Marshall protests and planning what would become a more spectacular integration campaign in Austin during the following school year.

Students for Direct Action

The Marshall protests had a direct impact on Student Y activists at UT. The students at Bishop and Wiley, with their Christian orientation, were in continual contact with the Southwest Regional Student Y office in Dallas, which related to the Student Y in Austin the "truly existential" moments of decision and commitment that the Marshall protesters had experienced.[17] The Bishop students themselves sent a statement "to their supporters," including the UT-Y, which affirmed their activism as an enactment of both democratic and Christian ideals. "As American citizens we have a responsibility to make democracy practical and real," they wrote. To them, the idea of democracy was "based on the worth, dignity and equality of all human beings," and they had acted in defense of these ideas. They could "no longer stand silently by and see our democratic ideals and ideas exploited and our Christian principles remain simply a theory." A black woman from Bishop also came to the UT-Y and gave personal testimony on the events in Marshall that Casey Hayden, for one, found inspiring. Here was activism justified: the Bishop students showed the UT students how they could "put our muscles into support of our thoughts, emotions, and convictions."[18]

During the summer of 1960, white activists from UT, some of them associated with the University Y, began planning action for the fall. This was the summer when Hayden attended the NSA Southern Student Leaders Seminar, where she met civil rights activists like Charles McDew, who later became the chairman of SNCC, finally making her dramatic speech urging support for civil disobedience at the NSA Congress in August. This was a broadening and energizing time for her, as she came into contact with wider circles of activists than ever before, including some who were clearly involved with the left. In addition to Al Haber and Tom Hayden, who numbered among the few members of SLID/SDS, while she was in New York she met students like Robert Stone, soon to graduate from Yale and later a graduate student at UT, who was associated with the famous socialist Norman Thomas (a SLID board member) and who was working to keep American attitudes toward the revolutionary regime in Cuba from hardening. Casey Hayden, standing at the intersection of the New York–centered world of hardheaded secular activism and the Y movement's Christian influence, came home from the NSA Congress with a renewed determination to organize political action among her peers.[19]

Back in Austin in the fall and now a teaching assistant in the English department, Casey Hayden chaired the Student Assembly's Human Relations Committee. By the end of November, a group of activists had decided to form a new, completely independent organization, specifically for the purpose of organizing political activity in behalf of racial integration. Such an organization would circumvent the "jungle of bureaucratic procedures" involved in taking action through the SA, said the new group's chair. Furthermore, this strategy might insulate from criticism the SA, or any other organization that the integration activists tried to work through. Making their intentions clear, they called themselves Students for Direct Action (SDA).[20]

There was more than one piece to the effort. Although many who were in on the planning, like Hayden, Neyland, Jenny Franklin, and Mary Simpson, were Y activists, others were not. The chair of the group was not Hayden, which would have reflected her leadership, but Chandler Davidson, who was writing a column for the *Texan* entitled "The Jabberwock." He found himself involved in SDA through no design of his own.

Davidson was finishing his second stint as a student at UT. He had led a somewhat itinerant childhood as the son of a U.S. Border Patrol officer in the Southwest. His parents each had had one year of college education, and his mother at one time had been a schoolteacher. There was little political discussion in the household. Davidson's studies at the university, in the mid-1950s, interested him little, so he left school and did a hitch in the navy, which he liked better. When he came back to Texas, he worked for a year in the oil fields and then reenrolled at UT in 1958. He attended the University Baptist Church where, as noted earlier, he was impressed by the pastor's determination to integrate the historically whites-only church. Davidson then started working on the *Texan*, eventually writing columns that struck a tone of slightly cynical humor but that also touched on political issues. He penned columns ridiculing segregation, asserting that the advances that had been made locally toward integration were the result of political agitation, not the enlightenment of those in power. If integration were to progress further, he said, "constant publicized pressure upon those who resist" change was required. People started calling him a "liberal." Previously he had not thought in these terms, he reflects, but he figured the label probably fit. He caught the eye of Willie Morris, now working at the *Observer*, who told Davidson that if the official censors at the *Texan* ever suppressed something Davidson wrote, which they sometimes did, the *Observer* would print it. Davidson started spending time at Scholz's with Morris, Ronnie Dugger, and prominent liberals from the state legislature like Maury Maverick Jr. and Bob Eckhart. This was a "colorful" group, full of "vibrant" personalities, Davidson remembers. This coterie of outspoken, hard-drinking male liberals was also rather macho. Belonging to this circle of local celebrities gave the undergraduate a feeling of elevation.[21]

Those who wanted to bring precisely the kind of "constant publicized pressure" to bear on segregated establishments that Davidson advocated decided to recruit him. The approach was made by a graduate student, later a physician, named Houston Wade, who along with Casey Hayden was one of the "movers" of SDA. Davidson calls him "one of the evangels of the new left." Associated with neither the Y movement nor the NSA, Wade was perhaps the only member of the white civil rights circle at UT with personal connections to the "old left" of the 1930s and 1940s. He reportedly had an uncle who had been a cartoonist for the *Daily Worker*, the Communist Party newspaper, but he himself evinced no warm feelings for communism. On one occasion, he and Davidson met a group of Soviet students who were visiting UT, including the editor of the youth version of *Pravda*. Davidson was frustrated with the visitors' unwillingness to concede that there was discrimination of any kind in their home country. Wade, it turned out, knew quite a bit about Soviet history, and he ended up embarrassing the foreign students. Wade was "a horse of a different color," as far as Davidson is concerned.[22]

Wade first introduced Davidson to the writings of C. Wright Mills, which other activists encountered through the SLID–SDS circle. Davidson had no clear ideological conception of his own support for integration; he simply saw it as a moral issue. He and others he knew were, so to speak, in the market for a political analysis. They found Mills's thinking attractive because it seemed to go "beyond the pragmatic" type of liberalism to which they were accustomed. Conventional liberalism, it seemed to them, dealt with social issues in a piecemeal way, without an overarching perspective on how American society worked and without a philosophical grounding from which positions on all issues flowed. Mills, by contrast, "seemed to have everything figured out." His focus on power and who wielded it seemed to be a key that could unlock the mysteries of society. Reading Mills's *The Power Elite* was "a transforming experience" for Davidson. Mills's passion for both individual autonomy and tightly bound communities (he called them "primary publics") offered both a picture of political action and a social ideal with a strong appeal. As noted earlier, Mills's persona as a modern-day Texas cowboy, loose in the groves of academe, underlined his emphasis on individual freedom and responsibility and certainly would have held a special appeal for younger Texans raised on the Lone Star State's preoccupation with individual liberty. Houston Wade, for one, was a fiercely independent person, Davidson recalls, and it seemed to Davidson that his new friend took support for his own iconoclasm from Mills's image. Wade, this "short, rather squat fellow" with a "high-pitched voice," was "a dreamer" with no use at all for anything that seemed like "politics-as-usual."[23]

But Wade subordinated himself to a collective political effort in the case of SDA, and after an initial refusal, Davidson also came on board, becoming one of the public articulators of the SDA viewpoint in the months to come. SDA had a twenty-five-person central committee, which included representatives from several campus organizations that were sympathetic to the group's integrationist goals, including the Young Democrats and the University Religious Council. At one of their early planning meetings in the basement of the Y, they were the object of an amateurish bombing, in which no one was hurt and no serious damage was done except to a window. Nevertheless, it gave them a fright. They resolved to target the two movie theaters on the Drag. (Robert Bell, who took part in SDA's protests, recalls that the white students were perhaps more timid than the black students about protesting university policies.)[24]

The tactic the SDA chose became known as the "stand-in." Demonstrators lined up at the ticket windows; the whites asked to buy tickets and also whether the theater admitted all citizens, and when they were told no, they went to the back of the line and waited to come to the window again. Black demonstrators simply asked to buy tickets for themselves, and when they were refused, they too returned to the back of the line. This succeeded in both clogging up the ticket line with people who ended up not buying tickets and attracting a great deal of attention from both passersby and the local population. From the businessmen's point of view, the publicity was perhaps the worse part. At the end of each evening's activities, the demonstrators adjourned to the University Y for a meeting to regroup and plan their next move.

These tactics clearly were a variation on the sit-in movement, as were SDA's methods. They were not doctrinaire Gandhians, and they did not practice nonviolent resistance to authority, as the demonstrators in Marshall had, but they wanted to behave nonviolently. In late November, the University Y received a visit from Glenn Smiley, a Texan and a former Methodist minister, who at that time was the national field secretary for the pacifist organization the Fellowship of Reconciliation, which had become heavily involved in civil rights activism. Smiley gave a talk on the doctrine and practice of nonviolence that several people involved in the stand-ins attended. He told them that Jesus "meant [us] to do the imaginative thing, the unexpected thing, the thing that catches your enemy off balance—moral judo." He warned them they might be accused of being communists but told them not to be deterred. "The charge of communism is a verbal tourniquet to stop the flow of new ideas," he asserted.[25]

The students who led the stand-ins took these lessons to heart. SDA's "Statement of Purpose" announced that they were a group of "mature students who desire to effect an organized peaceful protest.... We are strongly opposed to mob action, to poorly-planned or poorly-coordinated programs, and to emotionalism." To short-circuit the potential charge that the demonstrators were "outside agitators" trying to instigate dissent among a normally satisfied African American population, Chandler Davidson added, "We are not wide-eyed visionaries who are doing this without consulting Negroes at all. Most of us are average students, many with scholarships and families of our own . . . we have joined Negro student leaders in acting."[26]

Echoing the Marshall protesters, SDA also justified its actions in a most legitimate political language, that of democracy. The petition it circulated pledging that one would only attend integrated theaters read, "I do this because I am convinced that in a democracy each person should be received as an individual and judged on the basis of his own talents, accomplishments and behavior." Democracy as meritocracy: this was probably the least treacherous, least radical formulation of their goals that the activists could present. At this point, to these activists, the languages of democracy and individualism were one and the same. "We . . . firmly believe," SDA stated, "that a person's race is a totally invalid criterion of his worth." At least as SDA expressed it publicly, the idea was to get rid of racial discrimination so that the true worth of individuals could be ascertained.[27]

The students also stressed democracy and individual action in justifying their own activism. Houston Wade noted, "Democracy should be able to have a feed-back from society so that the laws may keep up with the people and progress," and this feedback was the ability of citizens to protest existing conditions and press for social change. The willingness and freedom of citizens to do so, he said, was "the saving grace of democracy." SDA's official statement also emphasized the role of citizen mobilization in effecting social change. "Social injustice never 'takes care of itself,'" it said. "It is corrected only by concerned, active citizens." The young integrationists did not trust established authority, including the government, to take the lead in bringing progressive social change.[28]

The students gave this familiar theme of individual political action a new existentialist twist. Casey Hayden averred that "the real issue" of the stand-ins was "whether an individual has the capability and the right of making a decision and acting on the basis of this decision."[29] Those taking part in the protests had shown they were capable of making such a decision, and they put to shame those who only stood and watched, she suggested. In her view, civil rights protest was momentous not only because it promised to secure rights for black Americans but also because it challenged a slumbering, complacent citizenry to break out of their political torpor. To the SDA activists, collective action consisted of an accumulation of individual decisions. Wade spoke in this existentialist vein when he told a group of 125 protesters at a demonstration just before Christmas vacation that they should spread the word about the stand-ins wherever they went for the holiday: "*Take it upon yourself* to get things going into action," he exhorted. Dugger, once again, was enthralled by the young protesters' emphasis on action, by their unwillingness to wait for permission from any authority before acting. "Do it yourself; your self," he wrote admiringly. "This is [the] idea that moves them now. Whether they got it from 'existentialism,' Sartre, Camus, or Martin Luther King, they have it." He paid them his highest compliment, saying that Thoreau would have joined their effort. "We have simply seen the need for action," Chandler Davidson said. Here was existentialism made concrete.[30]

Consistent with this existentialist articulation of the SDA viewpoint was the involvement in the stand-ins of a large number of students from the Christian Faith-and-Life Community. Of course, Casey Hayden had lived in the Community and knew many of the people there. Dick Simpson, who was living in the Community at this time, remembered that when news of the stand-in activity reached the Community one evening in late 1960, practically everyone there spontaneously decided to walk to the Drag and join the effort, "en masse." It became de rigeur for those who lived at the CFLC to take part in the stand-ins; Charles Erickson, for one, took part in the protests, even acting as SDA coordinator on certain evenings, mainly because everyone else at the Community was involved.[31]

In his column Davidson joked, in a parody of red-baiting rhetoric, "I have uncontestable, documentary, notarized evidence that Students for Direct Action is a front organization for the Christian Faith and Life Community. I have personally seen Christian Existentialists in the stand-in line."[32] At the Faith-and-Life Community, as at the Y, they liked to talk about enacting their values in the world, and this seemed like the perfect opportunity to do so. "We talk about ideals all the time and never do anything about them," one student in line at a stand-in told a reporter. "You get sick of that." To those like Simpson, Jim Neyland, Brad Blanton, Judy Schleyer, and others who were involved in both the CFLC and the Y, the stand-ins integrated the different parts of their college lives as did no other event or activity.[33]

The distinction between empty talk and real life that characterized existentialist thought now was applied to existentialism itself. Talk was cheap, the activists thought; something more was required if one was to act responsibly, if one was to respond to the imperatives of the new world. Indeed, something more was required if one was to fulfill one's potential as a human.

Talking about social change or democracy or civil rights was even somehow unreal; it fell short of authenticity. The young demonstrators were going beyond just watching and talking, Ronnie Dugger pointed out. By making individual commitments and involving themselves physically, they were "doing something real."[34]

They certainly were doing something effective. SDA succeeded in regularly putting between 40 and 200 people on the sidewalk for this evening activity—usually they had somewhere between 100 and 150—for more than six months. They usually stood in for two or three nights a week. The students involved were about 70 or 80 percent white, according to Davidson; one night early in the protests, 4 December, 80 whites and 20 blacks were present. To the protesters, Rasjidah Franklin-Alley recalled later, it was "mandatory that it be interracial or else it made no sense."[35] The leaders of SDA made good use of the social contacts and organizational skills they had developed in their varied campus activities. Y activists like Hayden had a wide, and interracial, network of concerned students they could contact. The Civil Rights Committee of the Young Democrats (which included Franklin-Alley) could call a list of 150 members of their organization and urge them to attend the stand-ins, as they sometimes did.[36] Although SDA was not officially affiliated with any other organization, other groups undertook actions that they coordinated with the stand-ins. For example, in late November the Social Action Committee of the University Religious Council (URC), a group closely associated with the Y, started passing out cards on the Drag in front of segregated restaurants, asking patrons to sign them and give them to the restaurant management. The cards stated that if the restaurant were integrated, the patron would continue to frequent it. (By late December they had passed out 3,800 cards; in a poll of first-year students at the university taken at the time, 81 percent said they would continue to eat in integrated restaurants.)[37] The combination of these integrationist activities in close proximity to one another created an atmosphere charged with political electricity.

The leaders of SDA certainly were not orchestrating all the support for their activities, in the sense that many people got involved in the stand-ins by means that SDA did not design. Someone at the Faith-and-Life Community told Brad Blanton about a meeting being held at the Student Union, and he went to see what it was about. It was led by Booker T. Bonner (or B. T., as he was known), an African American part-time student in his mid-thirties who became a close friend of Blanton's and a highly visible presence among civil rights activists in Austin in the next few years. Bonner apparently was exhorting a group of students to get involved in direct action on behalf of civil rights. In the spring of 1961, during a lull in the stand-ins, Bonner staged a one-man fast and vigil at one of the Drag theaters, and he remained something of a lone wolf in Austin politics. He and his wife Florence were, however, in the middle of the local activists' social scene. Judy Schleyer Blanton recalls parties at the Bonners' house where activists, liberal faculty couples from the university, and *Observer* reporters would drink beer and dance until early in the morning. (She remembers that all the white professors' wives wanted to dance with B. T. Bonner to show how liberal they were.) The Bonners and the Blantons became frequent companions, partners in both political efforts and less serious escapades. The Bonners had several children, and they worked various part-time jobs, some of which B. T. Bonner lost because of his political activities. He was known around Austin in the early 1960s as the most militant local black activist.[38]

Bonner, alone in front of the theater at night, was periodically harassed. Sometimes his friends, like Blanton, stayed with him to help ward off potential attackers. In general, however, the large stand-ins endured little harassment, although cars periodically swung by, the passengers shouting "nigger lover." But when in addition to the stand-ins, SDA started pickets in January 1961, consisting of just two people in front of each of the two theaters in two-hour shifts, they did attract some physical attacks. Three young men came by to push, shove, and spit at the picketers. They ripped up one picketer's sign; one of them was apprehended and pled guilty. Thus the police hostility toward civil rights demonstrators, including collaboration with vigilantes, that characterized the situation in the Southeast where the demonstrators were mainly black, was absent in Austin. As Brad Blanton notes, there was no community sanction for violence against the protesters in Austin.[39]

Beyond this, the stand-ins generated substantial support among the local population, both from local ministers and most emphatically from the faculty at the university. Blake Smith opened the doors of his church to the protesters. Louis Buck, a local white minister with a mainly black congregation, appeared on the stand-in line, as did Lee Freeman of the University Baptist Church.[40] Starting on 9 December with a letter from twelve members of the classical languages department, a cascade of encomiums to the stand-ins from the members of various departments appeared in the letters section of the *Daily Texan*, including one signed by sixty-six members of the English department, headed by the chair, the well-known folklorist Mody Boatright. This letter called segregation a "fundamental violation of human dignity" and viewed SDA's actions as a welcome blow struck against inequality.[41] In May, SDA ran an advertisement in the *Austin American-Statesman* with the names of 260 UT faculty members attached. The signers paid for the ad by donating the price of a movie ticket each. On occasion, a few faculty members even joined the stand-ins; John Silber, Roger Shattuck, and Irwin Spear, a botanist, were spotted in line. Perhaps the professor most closely involved with SDA was Ernie Goldstein, a professor at the Law School who gave the group legal advice. At one point, Spear addressed the protesters at one of the stand-ins, saying, "I want you people to know the faculty of the University is proud of you. I haven't heard any faculty member express anything but pride in this movement. . . . I don't think the faculty has lived up to your idealism." Some of them were trying, though. A relatively liberal group in a conservative environment, many of them (like Spear) from the North, many of the faculty saw this as an opportunity to go on record not only as integrationists but also as supporters of nonviolent civil rights protest.[42] This faculty support for SDA was crucial to legitimating it on campus, just as the support from clergy helped legitimate it in Austin more generally.

The activists received support from more distant quarters as well. Most sensationally, Eleanor Roosevelt devoted one of her daily "My Day" columns to the Austin demonstrations. Roosevelt applauded the students and wrote (in a perhaps, or perhaps not, inadvertent paraphrase of Bob Dylan), "This should serve to point up the fact to our older generation that times are changing and that the young are closer to the future."[43] In April, the *New Republic* also ran a story on the stand-ins. In the spring, SDA planned to send eight hundred letters to college newspapers around the country, complete with the signatures of UT professors and local clergy, asking people to contribute the price of a movie ticket to SDA so that they could buy a full-page advertisement making their case in the *New York Times*.[44]

Over the Christmas vacation, Hayden and others in SDA also made contact with student activists outside Austin. She traveled to Ann Arbor to confer with the NSA Steering Committee and then went to California to talk to activists there. Davidson and Wade talked with students around the country during the holidays as well and went to San Antonio early in the calendar year to make plans with students there. As noted earlier, Wade had urged all the demonstrators in Austin to talk up the stand-ins when they left town. All these contacts were directed toward a nationwide set of stand-ins that SDA wanted to coordinate for one day in February, to spread the protests among both white and black students and also to bring pressure on the nationwide theater chains. February 1961 was the one-year anniversary of the Greensboro sit-in. SDA chose 12 February, Lincoln's birthday, and NSA, SNCC, and CORE (Congress of Racial Equality) officially endorsed the idea.[45]

In anticipation, the stand-ins in Austin grew in size, with more than two hundred demonstrators appearing on the lines at the Varsity and Texas Theaters on Saturday, 14 January and picketing as well. Large numbers of black students from Huston-Tillotson and members of the Canterbury Association, an Episcopal student group, took part. On Lincoln's birthday, more than four hundred demonstrators stood in at four Austin theaters, the two on the Drag, and two others downtown. Demonstrations also were held in San Antonio, Dallas, Houston, Shreveport, New York, Chicago, and perhaps elsewhere. Some of these demonstrations were composed mainly of black students, some were largely white, and others were mixed.[46]

This was the climax of SDA's campaign. They continued the stand-ins as well as other activities in the spring 1961 semester. In late February, SDA members met at the UT-Y with students from Southern Methodist University, Texas Christian University, Wiley College, and Trinity and St. Mary's Universities in San Antonio to coordinate a statewide campaign against segregated movie houses.[47] In March the group started sending racially mixed groups to segregated area restaurants, getting served at a couple of them. They also participated in a food drive for a group of four hundred black sharecroppers who had been evicted from their land in Tennessee for voting in November 1960 and who now were living in a tent city. Casey Hayden went to the encampment, called "Freedom Village," where she met up with Tom Hayden once again. B. T. Bonner's uncoordinated vigils were held throughout the semester as well.[48] SDA's stand-ins had peaked, but no one could be sure of that at the time. The protest organization had been fully accepted, it seemed, into the mainstream of university life and politics. The support and acceptance that SDA's activities received contributed to the camaraderie and good humor that the demonstrators displayed during their protests, humor that evokes the mood of this political moment and opens a window onto the protesting students' thoughts.

One student who took part in the stand-ins noted the "air of warmth and congeniality" at the theater protest, the first demonstration he had ever attended. "They are a long and cheerful cry from the grim picket lines of the thirties," Dugger observed. "A minister from a Methodist church across the street (from where they were served coffee one especially cold and drizzly night) said they seemed, in spirits, like a cross between a varsity parade and a panty raid." Student couples came to the stand-ins as a cheap date. Even couples with small children appeared.[49]

Amid this almost carnival atmosphere, the management at one of the theaters had a photographer take pictures of the protesters in line and asked them for their names, hoping to frighten them away. The students posed for the camera, some "slipping in line ahead of others to be sure they had their pictures taken." Andy Schouvaloff, vice president of the UT Young Democrats and an enthusiastic stand-in participant, showed up with an empty camera, clicking it in front of the theater employees.[50] On one occasion, a trio of black UT students pointed up the absurdity of segregation with an elaborate joke, which they played at a downtown theater. Robert Bell and another student wore some African clothes they had and posed as Egyptians, and the other, a young man of middling complexion, claimed he was from Hong Kong. The theater sold them tickets and admitted them and then threw them out when they revealed that they were in fact African Americans.[51] Recognizing that they were attacking a system rather than individuals, the demonstrators strove, however, to avoid alienating the staff of the theaters. In December 1960, shortly after the stand-ins began, SDA presented the woman at the Texas Theater ticket window with an orchid and a card that read, "With kindest regard for your long suffering patience." The manager of the Varsity said that the pickets "had become a matter of routine and are being carried on in a sensible manner." SDA was careful to determine the legality of their actions, figuring out how close to the entrance of the theater they could picket and how far apart from one another the picketers had to stand.[52]

The most obvious example of the protesters' good humor was their tendency to sing. They sang some of the "freedom songs" of the civil rights movement such as "We Shall Overcome" (originally an old labor movement song) and labor anthems like "Solidarity Forever" and "I Dreamed I Saw Joe Hill Last Night." During Yuletide they sang Christmas carols. Sometimes they sang "The Star-Spangled Banner" on the steps of the Y after an evening's stand-in before going inside for their wrap-up meeting. The theme song of the University of Texas, and the official song of the state, was "The Eyes of Texas Are upon You," but the demonstrators sang instead, "The Eyes of Asia Are upon You," referring to the integrationist argument, common at a time of high tension in the cold war, that the United States could never win the hearts and minds of the Third World unless Jim Crow were abolished. At the Lincoln's birthday stand-ins, Schouvaloff, displaying a sharper edge, made up lines for a new version of "The Battle Hymn of the Republic" using the names of prominent segregationist politicians; he sang, "We'll hang Orval Faubus from a sour apple tree," and "We will send Bill Blakey COD to Stanleyville." Most imaginatively, a graduate student in economics sang the following words to the tune of "God Bless America":

> *God bless free enterprise,*
> *System divine,*

Stand beside her
And guide her
Just so long as the profits are mine,
God bless Wall Street,
May she flourish,
Corporations,
May they grow,
God bless free enterprise,
The sta-tus quo.[53]

This humor had serious implications. "Patriotism" and "free enterprise" were slogans typically used, respectively, to impugn integrationist agitators and to defend segregation in places of business. Such use of these slogans, ironically, made them a little suspect to young people who were committed to racial integration. When "free enterprise" was posed by segregationist politicians as the opposite of integration, young civil rights activists, even those who did not see themselves as at all radical, might come to regard this slogan as nothing but a cover for a reactionary political agenda. Thus was a sharp skepticism about conventional political rhetoric insinuated into the basically liberal perspective of young idealists, perhaps corroding their admiration for the very social ideals that this rhetoric celebrated.

The summer of 1961 found Jim Neyland in New York City. Having been elected president of the UT-YMCA in the spring, he soon left for an experiment in "shock therapy" at the Judson Church's Urban Life Project in Greenwich Village. He was one of nineteen students there, many from the South, who were working at summer jobs of all kinds, observing life in the big city, and engaging in group discussions about how the church could become more relevant to contemporary society. While he was there, he tried to visit Leonard Goldenson, the president of ABC–Paramount, which owned one of the Austin cinemas under siege, but to his dismay Neyland found himself shut out. He was unhappy, losing weight, losing his job. In mid-August he received a letter from Anne Appenzellar, the executive secretary for the YWCA on Guadalupe—or "Appy," as everyone called her and as she signed her letter. She had heard he was having trouble, and so she sent him a check to tide him over and reminded him that he was loved unconditionally by both God and his friends at the Y like her. "It's precisely when you get thoroughly put out with yourself—maybe even disgusted with your own tendency to self-criticism and to despair—that you learn that you are loved, in the ultimate sense, and accepted and forgiven by God as you are." His personal nadir could lead to a breakthrough, to real personal "growth," she assured him, "if you assume this posture." She encouraged him to think that things were looking up with some "Great News: Theaters on the Drag integrated last night. Negotiations carried on two weeks ago. All done quietly. No publicity to be given for now."[54]

Indeed, the news that must have been so welcome to Neyland remained known to only a small circle until early September when the new school year started. As the story emerged publicly, it seemed that additional pressures on the parent companies of the two theaters in the early summer finally had pushed them into negotiations. In June, Jewish organizations in Austin planned to buy nine hundred tickets for a showing at the Varsity of the movie *Exodus*, about the founding of the nation of Israel, and then to sell some of these tickets to local blacks as a way of circumventing the ticket window at the theater. But they canceled the ticket order when they learned that black ticket holders would not be admitted to the theater. Then a large number of Jewish Austinites received letters from the Varsity's management urging them to see the film and from the local chapter of the Anti-Defamation League of B'nai B'rith saying they "should think twice" before doing so. Some prominent Jews started to contact Goldenson, who was Jewish, pressuring him to order ABC–Paramount's Interstate Theaters (of which the Varsity was one) to integrate. Next, some SDA representatives managed to get Edward P. Morgan, a news commentator for ABC, to present "sympathetically" the case for theater integration on his program. Finally, a meeting between representatives of both theater chains involved and other interested parties was set for 4 August.[55]

Houston Wade attended for SDA. Claude Allen, a teaching assistant in English who had gotten deeply involved in the stand-ins, represented the UT faculty. Rabbi Charles Mintz, then the president of the AHRC, also attended, as did a couple of local businessmen. (No black Austinites, so far as I know, were present.) The theaters agreed that for an interim period of sixty days, all UT students could buy tickets with proper identification and that black UT students could buy tickets for other African Americans. After that, the theaters would be open to all. In return, SDA agreed that all demonstrations would cease at the theaters, and everyone agreed to say nothing to the press until the theaters had finally been integrated. The issue of downtown Austin theaters was left to the fall, with the understanding that they would integrate shortly "and without incident." Indeed, as of 1 September, the Drag theaters were admitting all UT students. Dugger, for one, thought that the primary impetus behind the agreement was the protests. Business at the Texas and the Varsity clearly had been hurt by the stand-ins, he noted.[56]

Private businesses in cities all over Texas were integrating. In light of the concerted, well-organized, and persistent civil rights protests that had emerged in the last one-and-a-half years, it no longer seemed rational for businessmen to hold the line for the white supremacist cause.[57] With this impressive local victory under their belts, the members of SDA now faced weighty choices about what to do next if they wished to continue their activism. They could extend their civil rights efforts beyond their local environment. They could work toward a broader vision of social change. Or they could turn their attention to the institution that now appeared as the most stubborn practitioner of segregation in their immediate environment, the University of Texas. "Where SDA will go from here it cannot be determined," Houston Wade wrote in the *Intercollegian*, the magazine of the National Student Y. "However, the meaningless honor of 'respectability' without responsibility has been struck a blow. There are things to be done in a democracy and many college students are eager to get on with the task."[58]

Meeting Up and Spreading Out

In the fall of 1961, in the aftermath of the victory over the movie theaters, a notable proportion of the "movers" of the early new left gathered for a celebration, far from Ann Arbor. They met at the Christian Faith-and-Life Community to witness a scene of commitment. The marriage of Casey and Tom Hayden symbolized the connections between the SDA circle in Austin and the emerging new left. Dorothy and Robb Burlage were in the wedding party, and Ronnie Dugger, Houston Wade, Claude Allen, and Al Haber, Hayden's confederate from Ann Arbor, also attended, as well as Michael Harrington, an older Catholic leftist soon to criticize SDS for what he perceived as its insufficient vigilance against Communist infiltration. SDA was "plugged into the nascent radical movement," remembers Chandler Davidson, who was not at the wedding because he had left UT during the summer and gone to France on a Fulbright Fellowship.[59]

Joe Mathews performed the ceremony, and Vivien Franklin and Jim Neyland acted as legal witnesses. On their wedding program, the Haydens included passages from Camus, to whose writings the bride had introduced the groom, and Ecclesiastes. "Vanity of vanities, says the Preacher, vanity of vanities! All is vanity." They conferred with Mathews about their vows before the ceremony, agreeing that there would be no pledge of fidelity. Subtle but significant differences separate the two principals' accounts of this point. Casey Hayden says she did not trust her betrothed to keep such a promise, and she was disinclined to force him into a lie. Tom Hayden writes, "Casey wondered aloud how we, so young and free, could take a vow of permanent sexual fidelity," implying she was at least equally as unsure as he about the value of fidelity, which she disputes. In any case, Mathews turned the tables on the couple, reneging on the agreement and asking them during the ceremony to swear their fidelity to each other—in effect, daring them to make a public decision about what kind of commitment they really wished to make. They both backed down and swore. (Before long, however, the groom showed that doubts about his fidelity were justified.)[60]

After the wedding there was a celebration, complete with political discussion, late into the night. Some later claimed that the idea of the Port Huron Conference, at which SDS put its views before the nation's students, leading to terrific growth in the organization, grew out of that evening. Tom Hayden argued with Neyland, contending that social change could come only from "outside the system," whereas Neyland wanted to continue working inside mainstream institutions. "Most of us in the civil rights movement had fundamental disagreements with Tom," Neyland remembers; "we believed in Christian non-violence," and Neyland intuited that SDS represented a break with that tradition. After the wedding, the new couple left town, on their way to greater adventures.[61]

Casey Hayden now began a peripatetic phase of devoted political activism that lasted for years. When Al Haber formed a national executive committee for SDS in the coming winter, she was on it (as was Houston Wade); she was an important force at the Port Huron Conference in the summer of 1962. She was employed for a while by the National Y, taking the job Dorothy Burlage had left at the University of Illinois. Then she worked for SNCC, both in its Atlanta office and in the field in the most hazardous parts of Mississippi before, during, and after the "Freedom Summer" of 1964. Brad Blanton traveled to Mississippi to visit her once during this period but did not see her because the building where she was staying was virtually under siege. This brought home to him the difference at that time between Mississippi and Texas.[62] Hayden then worked among poor women in Chicago, an experience that renewed and expanded her contacts with white female radicals, who became the major audience for her criticism of the subordination of women in American society, which she aired in 1965. Hayden's political work never brought her back to her native Texas to live again.

Franklin and Neyland were becoming increasingly involved in regional civil rights activism. Franklin attended a SNCC conference in Atlanta in May 1962 as a voting delegate. She and Neyland set up a regional civil rights group of their own, the Southwest Student Action Coordinating Committee

(SSACC), whose name recalled both SDA and SNCC. It was an interracial group; at a conference the group held, delegates from ten black schools, nine white schools, and sixteen schools that were at least minimally integrated attended. They even got Pete Seeger to come to Austin to do a fund-raising concert for them, and he stayed at the garret apartment behind the CFLC's College House that Neyland was renting at the time. In early 1963 the SSACC organized stand-ins at downtown Austin movie theaters, coordinated with stand-ins in Dallas, Houston, Fort Worth, and Denton.[63]

During this time, Franklin was traveling abroad, coming in contact with socialist countries and international perspectives. This, combined with the resistance she encountered in her continued civil rights work, was moving her leftward. Indeed, she found the *Port Huron Statement* so exciting that she organized a civil rights conference for SDS in Dallas. Possibly the most harrowing experience she had in her political work during this period was her imprisonment for two days in Tyler, a town in East Texas, in April 1963. She, Charlie Laughlin (another member of the Y-SDA circle), and Robert Morrison, all white UT students, went to Tyler to find George Goss, a coworker of theirs, who had called them from jail. Goss had been awakened by the Tyler police in a black dormitory room at Tyler College, where he was doing political work, and thrown in jail. The three white students arrived in town and started talking with a couple of local blacks in a café, and a group of white men gathered outside. The visitors were advised to get out of town, and they left, but a sheriff's car stopped them several miles outside the city limits anyway and arrested them for vagrancy. After a couple of days incommunicado, all four prisoners were released after posting bond, and they were told to get out of town for good. This was not the only time Franklin was arrested for her civil rights activism.[64]

Franklin and Neyland were drifting apart. She was moving in wider circles of activism and was becoming increasingly alienated from mainstream political institutions. Neyland did not become as radicalized and continued to work closer to home in the UT environment. In the 1961/1962 school year, when he was president of the YMCA, he lived in a cottage that the CFLC owned, and he directed the drama program for the College House. Over the summer, SDA circulated a petition calling for the integration of athletic activities, eventually gathering 6,159 names—maybe the biggest petition that had ever been generated at the university. That fall, he, Franklin, and Houston Wade organized what they called "read-ins" to protest the continuing dormitory segregation and exclusion of black students from athletics at UT. A group gathered every day at noon in front of the Main Building of the university, the tower on whose front was inscribed

"Ye Shall Know the Truth and the Truth Shall Make You Free," and simply read the phrase. This sardonic comment on the university's official high ideals continued the stand-ins' use of parody against power.[65]

The most concerted effort by Neyland and other SDA veterans to effect change on campus was through the Student Party (SP), a reform party they organized in the spring of 1961 that both foreshadowed later "student power" initiatives and paralleled other student liberal political parties that were forming around this same time, such as SLATE at Berkeley and VOICE at the University of Michigan. At the time there was only one organized political party on campus, the conservative Representative Party, dominated by the fraternities and sororities. Neyland, Franklin, Susan Reed, and Dick Simpson, all involved in starting the Student Party, wanted to salvage student government as an independent political force and use it as a base for liberal advocacy and activism.[66]

The SP supported full integration at the university and officially endorsed SDA's actions; it opposed either political pressure from the board of regents on the university or any political considerations in the selection of regents; it called for an end to outside censorship of student publications and criticized restrictions on women students; it opposed increases in tuition and expressed concern for financially strapped students; and it wanted teachers' names to be listed along with course titles before registration, to eliminate attendance as a factor in grades, and to institute student evaluations of teachers. It wrapped all these demands, many of them popular ones, in a language of public responsibility. "In past years," the SP platform read, "the commitment of the University of Texas student has been to the private, to the immediately controllable, to that which fails to elevate the conduct of public affairs.... He has shirked his responsibility to himself and to his fellow man." But the new generation, they said, "is developing a deep confidence in its ability to understand and improve the conditions of its society." The rhetoric of public commitment versus private apathy was appearing among young people around the country and foreshadowed the *Port Huron Statement*, adopted a year later.[67]

In the spring 1961 elections, the SP ran or supported eight candidates for seats in the SA, and seven of them won. They included Mo Olian, who became president of the SA.[68] In the fall elections, four more SP candidates won seats, including Gwen Jordan, who became the first African American member of the UT student government. ("In the euphoria of that victory," Jim Neyland and Jordan attended a dance at the Student Union together, which made her the first African American to attend this kind of official social affair on campus and where they also became the first black–white couple to dance at an official UT party, according to Neyland.)[69]

The liberal forces in the assembly quickly went to work on the issue of integration. In May the SA voted unanimously in favor of integrating all athletic programs and voted strongly for the integration of a men's dorm that was split into white and black sections. Furthermore, they conducted their own poll of the student body and found that large majorities favored both athletic and dormitory integration. That summer Olian publicly criticized the board of regents for their official statement that no further university integration would be forthcoming, since it would offend a "majority of Texans"; he called their conservatism on this issue "narrow-minded, backward and hypocritical." This provoked a demand by Thornton Hardie, chairman of the regents, for an apology from Olian, who said he was sorry if he had offended the board members but expressly refused to retract the substance of his comments. This incident seemed to cost both Olian and the liberals in general support in the SA. By the fall, resolutions by SA member Susan Reed (also chair of the YWCA at this time) to commend Olian's actions and to advocate the abolition of the loyalty oath for UT students were defeated. Although Dick Simpson, president of the SP, kept the Student Party going throughout the 1961/1962 school year, the Greeks regrouped and took control of the SA once again by the fall elections of 1962, in which none of the SP's five candidates won a seat. The SP disappeared after this.[70]

Between 1960 and 1962, liberal campus activism did not depend on sustaining new institutions. Those who had gotten politicized in the Y, even though they had officially separated the stand-in activity from the Y, continued their political work there. In addition to continuing civil rights work, a group of students, along with Frank Wright, formed a peace group called Austin for Peaceful Alternatives (APA) in early 1962. APA combined the traditional peace orientation and internationalism of the Y with the newly activist stance that the stand-ins had inspired. In addition, a movement for disarmament, with substantial socialist participation but critical of both major players in the cold war, had grown stronger since 1957 in both the United States and Britain, and the peace activists in Austin saw themselves as part of this movement.[71] In February 1962, APA gathered 120 people at the state capitol to demonstrate for the nonresumption of nuclear testing by the United States, for the withdrawal of U.S. troops from central Europe and elsewhere, and for a diversion of government funds away from the military and into "the struggle against poverty, hunger, and disease throughout the world." This demonstration coincided with a gathering of four thousand in Washington, organized by the national group Turn toward Peace. APA was also associated with the Student Peace Union (SPU), a nationwide group, and by the 1962/1963 school year, the peace activists at UT were simply functioning as an SPU chapter. They were a small group on a big campus, and they habitually endured petty harassment and accusations of communism. The Reverend W. S. Arms, at an Austin City Council meeting, called APA a "far-left group" and protested the council's decision to grant the group a permit for a "Picnic for Peace."[72]

This March 1962 gathering was the single biggest event the APA pulled off. Held in an outdoor amphitheater in Zilker Park, the rally included a speech by Norman Thomas, who declared that "a military–industrial complex opposes disarmament," the same conclusion that Vivien Franklin had made after her trip to Europe. Bob Stone, now a graduate student in philosophy at UT and active in APA, had gotten Thomas to come to Austin. Other speakers included the ubiquitous Ronnie Dugger, Mel Zuck of the American Friends Service Committee, Margret Hofmann—a German emigrant who was now a peace activist in Austin, writing a column in the *Daily Texan* entitled "Satyagraha"—and Helen Spear, married to faculty activist Irwin Spear; attendees also were treated to folk singing by UT notables like Americo Parades and Roger Abrahams. Ralph Person, minister of University Presbyterian Church, asserted that four "truths" needed to be spoken: "That the American people are not the chosen people of God"; "That nuclear warfare is evil"; "About who is making money off the war machine today"; and about the real damage that a nuclear war would do.[73]

The small but determined group continued their peace activism in the 1962/1963 school year. In October 1962 the Cuban missile crisis began, and the SPU activists were some of the very few on campus who dissented from the general approval of President John Kennedy's brinkmanship. (At the Faith-and-Life Community, Brad Blanton remembers, the approval for Kennedy's actions was unanimous.)[74] A group of only fourteen—which included B. T. Bonner and Dee Brown, one of the SPU leaders along with her husband, Desta—picketed at the Texas capitol during the crisis in favor of a peaceful resolution. Virtually alone in their local environment, they suggested the Cuban buildup might be attributable "in part, to our past invasion and hostility toward Cuba." After the crisis passed, Albert Bigelow, a former navy officer and radical pacifist who had gained notoriety when he sailed his ship into a nuclear testing zone in the Pacific, spoke at the Y, and his words reflected the newly reinforced sense of distrust that peace activists directed toward their government. "Hypocrisy is one of the characteristics of a warfare state," he claimed, sounding quite a bit like the antiwar orators of the late 1960s. "In a warfare state people cannot afford to know what is going on."[75]

Subsequently SPU opposed the establishment of fallout shelters on campus (part of a massive program the Kennedy administration initiated), and got three hundred signatures on a petition calling for an end to the peace-time draft as a militarily unnecessary practice that, in Charlie Laughlin's view, "tends to promote militarism."[76] To most people in Texas in the early 1960s, *militarism* was a new word. The peace activists on campus had moved beyond the confines of conventional politics in Texas. The alienation from the government reflected in the peace movement—an alienation that stemmed, to a great degree, from young people's experiences in the civil rights movement—and the critical discussion of American society's overall priorities in which the participants in this movement engaged mark the peace activity between 1961 and 1963 as a bridge between civil rights liberalism and a more radical and wide-ranging political perspective.

Integrating the University

In the early 1960s, as some veterans of the stand-ins shifted their activism to issues other than desegregation, other students continued to work on issues of race and integration. All this activity occurred simultaneously; while white students, for the most part, were pursuing peace agitation and changes in student government, a group of mainly black UT students pushed the university administration to eliminate the remaining elements of racial segregation on campus.

In October 1961, shortly after the victory over the movie houses was secured, about fifty African American students staged a protest against dormitory segregation. Like their counterparts in the Student Party, they brought the issue of integration home to the campus. According to unwritten rules, black men were forbidden even to set foot in a white dorm unless they were delivering food or messages, and black women were allowed to visit the dormitory rooms of white women friends only if they walked straight to and from their hosts' rooms and only if the door remained shut during their visit. After this policy was reiterated to white dormitory residents and related in a *Daily Texan* article, the black students gathered and went to Kinsolving Dormitory, where for one hour they sat, read, and played the piano in the forbidden "public area." One of them told a reporter, "We are not backed by Students for Direct Action, the NAACP, Nikita Khrushchev, or anybody like that. I would say we were all incensed by that article" in the paper.[77]

After trying and failing to intimidate individual students into acknowledging they had done something wrong, the administration placed several of the sit-in participants on disciplinary probation. This prompted a mobilization of support among liberal student activists, including many who had been involved in the stand-ins. Students like Stephen Oates, Don Tillerson, and Charles Erickson, all involved with the Faith-and-Life Community and SDA, felt that a racist fear of "mongrelization" lay beneath the dormitory restrictions—that the regents secretly feared sexual liaisons between black men and white women.[78]

With such expressions of outrage surfacing, Olian arranged a meeting of student groups, the SA, and the administration, using the threat of student protests to get the administration to agree. Olian, Mary Simpson—who was now a student at the Law School and reportedly had been one of the leaders of the Kinsolving protest—Houston Wade, Claude Allen, and John Silber attended the meeting, at which all agreed to a one-week "cooling-off" period. The supporters of the protesters held a rally afterward at the University Y. It was at this rally that the most significant result of the dormitory protest was announced: Two black students planned to bring a lawsuit against the board of regents, pressing for full integration of all university facilities and activities. Houston Wade said SDA would help raise funds and find a lawyer for the suit. Two and a half years later, this lawsuit succeeded in bringing about the final integration of the university.[79]

Not student protest but faculty action, most of all, signaled the administration's embarrassment and increasing isolation on the issue of integration. In the spring of 1961, the faculty adopted a resolution calling for the integration of all university facilities. After the administration punished the black students for venturing into white territory on campus, Ernie Goldstein circulated a resolution calling for an end to racial restrictions on living and eating facilities, stating that such regulations "degrade the dignity of the individual, subvert the academic community and interfere with the educational process." At an emotional meeting of the full faculty on Halloween, the teachers voted, 308 to 34, to adopt the resolution. The regents, all appointed by segregationist governors, were out of step with their faculty and had been ham-handed in their response to the student action. The liberal faction in the administration, personified by Harry Ransom—who by now had been kicked upstairs to the chancellorship of the UT campus—had remained silent throughout the controversy and, as Dugger observed, had lost a great deal of credibility with the faculty, including the prominent teachers that Ransom had brought to Austin himself. Although Ransom trumpeted the cause of individual growth in education, he would not take a stand for the civil rights of individual students at his university. Not since Homer Rainey's dispatch had the UT faculty shown so much independence from their higher-ups.[80]

The faculty were greeted by a line of applauding students as they left the meeting. A crowd of 250 gathered at the Y once again for a rally. Goldstein, introduced to "thunderous applause," declared that the integrationists would win in the end—"The stupid thing is that it has to be done by students and faculty pressure rather than by leadership." Houston Wade announced that Sam Houston Clinton Jr., counsel for the Texas AFL-CIO, would represent the integration lawsuit against the regents, which now involved three students, including Leroy Sanders, a black student who had been chair of SDA during the previous summer. SDA had raised from faculty couples a thousand dollars so far for the court costs, Wade announced, and Ralph Person of University Presbyterian Church would also try to raise funds. Wade told the crowd, "I saw a very gallant and scholarly faculty go way out on a very tiny limb and hack away on our behalf as well as theirs, and I am inclined to follow suit."[81] Robb Burlage, hearing about the faculty vote, was moved to write back to Texas that "those who love the University . . . for its dynamic potential for rightness and truth, for leadership on the frontier that is the New South, must have been heartened" by the professors' behavior.[82] For the moment, the faculty gave student activists hope that their university might yet play a leading role in a process of progressive social change. Indeed, those gathered in the Y after the vote may have felt like a "beloved community" on that evening. On the rare occasions when a university's faculty broke ranks with their administration and openly sided with students against the university authorities, the faculty action gave inestimable encouragement to student activists. But the UT faculty would never do so again with such virtual unanimity.

By the end of 1964, the edifice of segregation in higher education in Texas had crumbled, at least in formal terms. After 1960, word of change appeared frequently in the news. In 1961, Texas Tech, in Lubbock, announced it would admit black students for the first time. Later that year, the students and faculty at Rice University voted strongly in favor of integrating all its facilities. In early 1962 the Student Congress at Baylor voted to admit black students to that school. The student body presidents of seven schools in the Southwest Athletic Conference together called for racial integration of all conference events. In early 1964 Texas Christian University announced it would integrate its athletic programs and dormitories.[83]

At UT, student groups continued to apply pressure for full integration. The Y cabinet in late 1963 passed a resolution asking for the integration not only of student activities but also of the faculty and staff. In the fall of 1963, a new integration group on campus, the Campus Interracial Committee (CIC), brought an integration resolution before a regents meeting. In an unprecedented (and unexplained) move, the board put aside protocol to hear the petition from the group's chair, a black student named William

Spearman. After the meeting, the regents announced they would allow the integration of athletics and arts, leaving university-owned housing as the only outpost of racial segregation on campus.[84] Finally, at the end of the 1963/1964 school year, when Texas's native son, President Lyndon Johnson, arrived at UT to give the commencement address, the regents announced that this last vestige would be eliminated. The university's lawyers, led by Vivien Franklin's mentor, Leon Jaworski, had dragged out the legal proceedings over the lawsuit brought by the three black students (two of them now ex-students) as long as they could; now they got the plaintiffs to agree to drop the suit in exchange for a promise of full university integration.[85] The most recent appointments to the board of regents had been made by Governor John Connally. Connally, a close friend of Johnson's, was a conservative politician but not one to hold the fort when others had fled and not one to embarrass his friends.

Backlash

While the *cause* of integration was meeting with gradual success, the activists who stood in the vanguard of the movement for integration in Austin were not all faring so well. White liberal activists suffered rejection and dejection in the years after the stand-ins, leading to their estrangement from mainstream political institutions. The arguments for integration were accepted, but an ongoing liberal activist presence on campus was not, which contributed to the movement toward a more radical orientation by some.

As should be clear by now, the University Y was the rock of liberal activism at the University of Texas into the early 1960s. It was logical, then, for conservatives to target the University Y for attack. They first did so during the stand-ins. In February 1961, at the height of SDA's protests, Dean of Student Life Arno Nowotny, an officer of the Y, proposed to the Y's board of directors that nonstudent groups not be allowed to meet in the Y building. He mentioned, none too subtly, that he had heard reports that the University Y was "losing prestige because of the lack of a balanced program." This meant SDA, for of the twenty-six groups that met regularly at the Y, it was the only one without university approval (which it had not sought). Suggestions were afloat about northern or Communist influences on SDA. But in March, the Y's board affirmed the present policy, saying that nonstudent groups could in fact meet there.[86]

The following year, when Jim Neyland and Susan Reed were presidents of the YMCA and YWCA, the political criticisms of the Y continued. Neyland took to the pages of the *Texan* to defend the Y's "policy of freedom to all," as he called it. He was at pains to put some distance between the Y and SDA, to portray the University Y as a general student service institution with a variety of functions, most of them nonpolitical. He explained that any student group could meet in the Y, including conservative groups if they wished. And some conservative organizations did in fact use the Y, for example, the Campus Crusade for Christ and Young Americans for Freedom. The Y's information showed that about two-thirds of the members of all Y study groups identified themselves as Republicans, and half the Y membership in the previous year were members of sororities or fraternities, known as solidly conservative groups. At least forty-six groups used the Y building in an average week, Neyland reported, including twenty-eight Y study and program groups that in no way engaged in political activity. Neyland also spoke directly to the real cause of the criticisms, explaining that although "there is rather full agreement in the Cabinet with the SDA objectives, any proposal to co-sponsor SDA action has always been defeated in Cabinet." Political groups could use the Y building, but the Y officially allied itself with no political group.[87]

This just was not good enough. Everything Neyland said was true, but it also was true that the Y's program of discussion and study nurtured liberal activism and that liberal activists were welcome nowhere else on campus as they were at the Y. The Y's opponents did not wish simply to sever an alleged institutional connection between a religious organization and a political group; they were political conservatives who wanted to repress liberal activism. The Christian Anti-Communist League, based in Dallas, criticized Neyland personally for proposing a resolution at a recent Southwest Regional Student Y meeting condemning the House Un-American Activities Committee (HUAC). Some people reportedly stopped making donations to the Y because of the growing publicity, and there was word that some local Ys were even being cut off from the United Fund, on which many Y branches depended heavily. In March 1962 the conservative *Dallas Morning News* struck the most public blow against the Y, running an eight-part series about the University Y in Austin. The series, by Jimmy Banks, was entitled "University YM(?)A," questioning how Christian the Y's activities really were and suggesting that the "C" on the building stood for something else. Banks focused on the leaders of the Y, implying that they were leading astray a traditionally sound institution. He specifically targeted Vivien Franklin, Susan Reed, Charlie Laughlin, Chett Briggs, and Frank Wright, in addition to Neyland—"Wright Exerts Influence on Thinking of Students," read one headline. Banks focused on the pacifism, the critical attitude toward the arms race, and the travels abroad to socialist countries. The reaction came swiftly. The downtown Austin YMCA and YWCA issued statements disclaiming any connections to the University Y. The Southwest Area Council of the YMCA, meeting in Oklahoma, asked the University Y's board of directors "to evaluate and investigate the nature and type of program and leadership" of the Y on Guadalupe. The board included many establishmentarian figures from the UT environment; the chair at the time was Ed Price, a former football coach at the university (there was hardly a more highly respected position in the entire Lone Star State).[88]

"Belated congratulations. I've just seen the DMN articles and it's good to know at least one Y in the country is deserving of such right-wing reaction.

"Seriously, I hope the series wasn't too damaging. Things are getting tighter all over, I fear." Casey Hayden's note to Jim Neyland and Susan Reed was on target.[89] Things certainly were getting tighter for the activists at the UT-Y, but their friends and colleagues rallied to their defense. More than forty-five members of the Faith-and-Life Community sent a letter to the *Morning News* specifically protesting the article on Franklin, who lived in the College House at the time. "Miss Franklin advocated in the article nothing which has not been advocated many times before by well-known, thoughtful Americans," they said. The University Y received letters of support from the SMU-Y cabinet and from its president. The Regional Council's cochair of the YMCA wrote that "there are many people here who respect and support you as you endeavor to present a vital and challenging program to your school." The National Student Committee of the YMCA in New York City resolved to express their support for the UT-Y's program as well, as they informed both Ed Price and Frank Wright.[90]

The student leadership on Guadalupe Avenue knew, however, that support from other student Y activists might not be of much help, and so they struck a conciliatory note. Reed and Neyland issued a statement to the press suggesting that the bad feelings were rooted in misunderstanding. They invited "all who are interested to visit us at any time and talk with the students and staff about" the Y and its program. Dick Simpson and Susan Ford, who were elected to succeed Neyland and Reed as presidents of the YMCA and YWCA in early April 1962, went even further, expressing the view that perhaps "the 'Y' lacked in tact in dealing with conservative viewpoints" and admitting that they had to make conservative students feel they were heard at the Y. Perhaps the diplomatic approach would work.[91]

But the criticism did not stop. In the spring of 1962, Neyland was "inundated with nasty letters and vicious phone calls." Someone broke into the cottage where he was living and "ransacked" the place. General Edwin Walker, a right-wing political figure, began a campaign for the governorship, running on an anticommunist, segregationist platform, and he accused Neyland and Vivien Franklin of running a Communist Party cell at UT. Reflecting the hardening attitudes toward religious liberals in Texas, during the summer the chair of the Texas Student Ecumenical Council wrote an associate at the UT-Y that his group had wanted to have their convention at Baylor but that the president of this flagship Baptist university wouldn't allow it, because he already was having trouble with the Southern Baptist Convention. "Both the college chaplain and president McCall said that if we had asked them just one year ago, everything would have been fine." Franklin felt that the immensely wealthy Hunt family of Dallas, the largest source of funding for far-right political activity in Texas, was responsible for at least some of this escalated hostility, some of which she felt was directed not only at her but also at her family. Both she and Neyland took it all very hard.[92]

Finally, the Y's opponents went after its funding. In 1962, the downtown Austin banks withdrew their customary contributions to the University Y. More important, the Y depended on the student-run Campus Chest fund-raising drive for its operating budget. The Y, such an important part of the intellectual and social milieu on campus, traditionally received more of the Campus Chest funds than did any other organization. But in the fall of 1961, the SA's Campus Chest Committee turned down the Y's customary request, in this case for $3,000, for a contribution to the World University Service, a larger pool of money that was used to fund various Student Y activities around the world. In the following fall, in October 1962, the real blow came: the Campus Chest Committee voted to remove the Y from its fund-raising drive. The Y would get no money. At the committee's meeting, the Y's critics expressed their concerns about the entanglement of SDA with the Y, about an anti-HUAC petition that was available at the Y, and about the presence in the Y's basement of some signs supporting the gubernatorial bid of Don Yarborough, a young liberal candidate who was running against John Connally.[93] (Brad Blanton, recently elected vice president of the Texas Young Democrats, headed the publicity for Yarborough's shoestring campaign. The election of a liberal slate to the statewide student organization brought a walkout by a conservative rump group; Blanton's car was burned during the campaign, which the upstart liberal Yarborough lost narrowly.)[94]

The Y's defenders made the standard responses: the Y did not endorse any of these groups or activities, and students who favored other causes could also use the Y if they wanted to. Flexing their political muscle, the conservatives announced that if the Y was a beneficiary of the drive, "10 Greek groups" would refuse to support it. A former head of the campus Young Republicans threatened to organize pickets against Campus Chest activities if the Y were included. The committee's decision stood. The *Texan* expressed tepid disapproval of the exclusion but still encouraged students to support the Campus Chest. Consequently, the Y had to mount its own fund-raising effort, which hardly could match what it had lost.[95]

The conservative offensive against liberalism on campus between 1961 and 1963 was directed against the Y as well as the NSA, the other local symbol of liberal cosmopolitanism and pro–civil rights sentiment. In October 1961, Tom Hayden and Paul Potter, two of the SDS–Liberal Study Group circle, received widespread attention when they were beaten in McComb, Alabama, where they were reporting on the civil rights conflict for campus newspapers. Because they identified themselves as NSA representatives and clearly were sympathetic to the civil rights movement, they were accused of acting as outside agitators and of committing NSA to one side in what conservative students portrayed as a local conflict in which NSA should remain neutral. Furthermore, NSA voted for the abolition of HUAC. The critics also claimed that NSA was a northern-dominated organization, though Don Richard Smith, a UT graduate who had been a vice president of NSA in 1960/1961, noted that UT could have had one of the three biggest delegations to NSA if only UT would send its allotted fourteen representatives, which it usually did not.[96]

NSA's apparent preoccupation with international affairs, which was suspect in itself to the right, earned additional ire from conservatives. Specifically, conservatives were angered that NSA voted to express "regret" over the United States–sponsored invasion of Cuba in 1961, that they had condemned the Guatemalan government after hearing of its repressive policies from the former head of that country's student association, and that the organization provided the bibliography for a course taught at UT's Institute for Latin American Studies on "the revolutionary left in Latin America."[97] NSA's defenders on campus protested that they were not reds. Ed Garvey, NSA's president, visited UT in early 1962 and protested that NSA was helping in the fight against communism. Liberals on campus claimed that NSA was far more effective in disseminating an anticommunist viewpoint to Latin America students than the U.S. government could be, and that, said one, "if NSA were to fall apart, it would [leave] a void which the Communists would fill up."[98]

The Universities of Oklahoma, Nebraska, Iowa, and Missouri, as well as Kansas State and Ohio State, withdrew their memberships in NSA in the early 1960s, and conservatives at UT urged the SA to follow suit. They asserted that "there is no 'national student viewpoint' on political issues" for

NSA to represent and that NSA simply promoted an ideological agenda under the cover of such a claim. Those who favored staying in the organization trotted out the standard UT defense of liberal cosmopolitanism: the need to maintain a "university of the first class." "If the University is to maintain any significance on the national student scene, it must keep its membership in NSA," the *Texan* editorialized. "If the University is to maintain its reputation as a college campus in intellectual ferment, it must identify with the only organization which acts as a sounding board for ideas."[99] But it didn't wash this time. After some nighttime hearings on the issue, in March 1963 the SA held a student referendum on membership in NSA, and 59 percent voted to leave. The SA promptly followed this cue, voting for withdrawal, 20 to 7. Ellen Shockley, the campus coordinator for NSA at the time, commented sarcastically, "Now we can get down to really important, pressing issues such as parking problems, dance committees, and flash cards. Now we can concentrate on provincialism."[100]

Such biting remarks were the main consolation left to campus liberals who wanted to work through mainstream, official organizations like student government. With the defeat of the Student Party, the cutoff of the Y, and the withdrawal from NSA, it became clear that at present, in such mainstream groups, either official or dependent on the approval of official university structures, liberals were no match for the Greek system and the conservatives. One group of activists, including Vivien Franklin, as well as Faith-and-Life Community members like Carol Darrell and Dorothy Adams, was so disgusted with the Student Assembly by March 1963 that they urged it to disband. They called the SA "a farce," a "puerile and absurd extravaganza." No such reorganization was forthcoming, though, so at this point many liberal or radical students simply gave up on student government at UT. Even though they had succeeded in winning institutional victories for the cause of civil rights on campus and in Austin, they had failed to secure a permanent place for themselves in the official campus political structure. From this point on, the most militant liberal activists acted outside such an official structure. This estrangement from local mainstream institutions fed upon itself, contributing mightily to the emergence of a student left.[101]

Houston Wade expressed with bitter humor this alienation from the official institutions of the UT environment. At almost the same time as the Student Assembly was withdrawing from NSA, the university administration was infringing on the independence of the *Daily Texan*, changing the editorship from a popularly elected position to an appointed one and changing the makeup of the board that would appoint the editor and oversee the paper. Wade evoked a general sense of disappointment. Never mentioning the university, he wrote in the *Texan* all about the circus, which he said he formerly had viewed as "certainly the greatest of man's achievements, a collection of the best of culture and science. Now, alas, the glitter is largely lost for me . . . the runny makeup and the toothless old lion on a stool regrettably dim the spangle and glitter." Wade warned that heavy-handed attempts to treat university students like children would bring a reaction that neither the administration nor the faculty had bargained for. A system of control in which "the animals are allowed a maximum of freedom and kindness and are trained by reward" would be far more effective, he advised sardonically. Clearly, the hope that Wade had expressed in late 1961 about the faculty as a force for progressive change had faded. Moreover, his tone suggested that he did not truly expect the student rebellion of which he warned.[102]

Tears of Victory

It was only in the following school year, 1963/1964, in the aftermath of this backlash against liberal activism, that an explicitly leftist presence appeared at UT. Despite charges of left-wing sympathies from the right, the campus activists in the Y, the Student Party, and NSA saw themselves as civil rights liberals, not as leftists. Even those who trafficked with the Liberal Study Group, which was clearly intent on establishing a new student left, and Bob Stone, who was associated with SLID/SDS and Norman Thomas, did not identify themselves with "the left."[103]

No doubt the political climate of the cold war, then at perhaps its chilliest, fueled this reluctance. Looking back, we today might see more radicalism in these student activists' politics than they were willing to admit, even to themselves, in the early 1960s. Still, there is no reason to doubt the sincerity of these students' political identification. Those active in the Y sought a community and a society based on love and a society in which people would feel that their lives had meaning and authenticity. Before 1964, they did not believe that a comprehensive process of social change was required to achieve these goals. Most of the few in this cohort who became involved in SDS worked as members of that group after leaving Austin. With the exception of those who had moved into peace activism by 1962, the only institutional changes that the UT activists of this time desired, and the only inequalities they sought to remedy, pertained to civil rights for African Americans. Nonetheless, closely linked though these young people were to political liberals, the goals of love, peace, and authenticity were not the typical stuff of establishment liberalism in the United States as it was embodied, for example, in John Kennedy's administration. The social changes required to achieve these goals were substantial indeed. These young activists in the early 1960s hovered somewhere between liberalism and the left. Even many who followed them and were more estranged from liberalism preferred to call themselves "radicals," not leftists, insisting that something new had appeared under the sun.

White students' involvement in civil rights protest, which brought them feelings of exhilaration and purpose and which approached an apogee of success in the early 1960s, carried the seeds of radicalization. The civil rights movement relegitimized the issue of social equality, which had lain dormant in American political life during the early cold war. If inequality existed, why not do something to change it? And if attacking one form of inequality was the right thing to do, then what about other forms? Furthermore, the experience of civil rights activism legitimized direct action outside mainstream political institutions and without the approval of established authorities. Civil rights activists of the early 1960s thus bequeathed to the students who followed them a legacy of direct action that they would carry forward in a process of rising militancy in the years to come.

Nothing about civil rights activism affected the white participants more deeply than the experience of interracial contact and cooperation. Robb Burlage reflected years later that this was "the annealing experience" in which the new left was formed. The continuing prominence of racial inequality among the concerns of white leftists in the next ten years, as well as their consistent support for militant action on the part of subordinated racial groups both domestically and abroad, suggests that the civil rights experience indeed lay at the root of the new left.[104] All that came before it—Christian liberalism, secular liberalism, libertarianism, existentialism—might have come to very little, politically, in the 1960s had it not been for the moral challenge that the civil rights movement presented and the deeply personal meaning it held for young white activists. This experience told them that although they were implicated in a rotten society, they could be redeemed. It told them they could feel love and acceptance and that they could spread these things outward. This message was conveyed to them not only by their white mentors but also by black Americans, who might have scorned them but who instead accepted them as partners in political action, and this made the message incalculably powerful. The promise and practice of political reconciliation made the idea of a new and authentic life seem real for both these young whites and their society. It also helped push the 1950s quest for authenticity out of the realm of the individual self. Instead, in the 1960s this quest became a search for a "whole" and democratic society.

At UT, these developments depended on the institutional and intellectual roles that the University Y played. The Y provided a place where students—black and white, women and men—who were critical of the society they saw around them or who were merely venturesome could come together to discuss whatever was on their mind. The University Y was a particularly open space for women. The structure of gender equality that shaped the activities there planted seeds that sprouted years later, when some women in SNCC who had been involved in the Student Y movement, most notably Casey Hayden and her friend Mary King, began to protest the lack of gender equality in the ostensibly more radical movements of the 1960s and in American society generally.[105] There was no other place on campus like this, save perhaps the Faith-and-Life Community. Intellectually, the message of love and meaning that Christian liberalism offered was similar to Christian existentialism, but the Y grounded this message in a more familiar tradition of Protestant social concern, thus making it more approachable to many. This social gospel tradition always had harbored a set of radical criticisms of industrial capitalist society and of racism, even if that radicalism often lay dormant. Given a particular set of circumstances and the right caretakers, Christian liberalism disclosed a radical message to those who were inclined to hear it.

Whether the University Y and Christian liberalism could have continued to influence a student movement in Austin that was moving leftward is difficult to say. The political damage that the Y sustained between 1961 and 1963 all but ended its substantive role in the development of the white radical movement on campus. After the 1962/1963 school year, the Y organization and Christian liberalism lost their position as the vanguard of political activism on campus, although radicals continued to use the Y's rooms throughout the next ten years for various activities. The most direct political involvement of campus clergy later in the 1960s was the support of liberal Catholic priests and nuns of the Mexican American farmworkers' movement that emerged in South Texas after 1965, but these Catholic activists did not become closely linked to the developing campus left.[106]

The leaders of the stand-in activity also did not participate in the Austin left that first appeared in 1963. Houston Wade went to medical school in Canada and returned years later to his native San Antonio where he, always independent, maintained his political commitments by running a clinic for the poor of that city. The Burlages remained active in SDS, but not in Austin. Casey Hayden sometimes visited Texas, but her activism continued elsewhere. Chandler Davidson returned to Texas years later as a professor of sociology. Charlie Laughlin left for California, having joined Folksingers for Peace, a touring trio that had tramped through Austin after being deported from Mexico. Dick Simpson, as mentioned earlier, went on to become a scholar of African politics, became active in Chicago politics in the 1970s, and eventually returned to the religion of his youth after a lapse of many years, becoming an ordained minister. Claude Allen, the Blantons, and the Bonners stayed in Austin for a few years, remaining politically active together, but they never connected politically with the emerging campus left. The most radical members of the Faith-and-Life Community went to Chicago with Joe Mathews. Like many participants in student movements, they all made their marks and moved on, leaving behind a legacy and an influence on subsequent waves of students that is difficult to evaluate precisely.

In late 1963, Bruce Maxwell, a leading civil rights activist at UT who joined in the Freedom Summer efforts to bring change to Mississippi in 1964, lamented the racial inequality he saw every day in East Austin. In light of the continuing poverty and degradation he saw here, the integration of university dormitories amounted to little in his eyes. A believer in a society of love, he pondered the superficiality of racial progress and declared, "I am filled with hate, and I am filled with despair, and I cry bitter, bitter tears."[107] The sweetness of integration victories proved fleeting, as hopes for social change escalated among civil rights activists.

After 1963 there was no one left in Austin who had been a leader in SDA, although some younger students had taken part in the stand-ins. More important, the civil rights movement, either directly or through the mediation of newsprint and television, shaped the political consciousness of vast numbers of young people who began college in the 1960s. The impact of this movement and the lessons it taught were inescapable in these years. For those who favored social change, chief among these lessons was the apparent unreliability of mainstream political institutions as vehicles for militant protest or engines of change. This conclusion became part of a widespread, largely unquestioned folk wisdom that 1960s radicals of all races absorbed in their youth.

The young people who learned this lesson early sought to avoid Maxwell's disillusionment and bitterness by never investing much hope in mainstream institutions. African American activists maintained feelings of security and hope in a movement defined by racial commitment above all. Some young whites established beachheads for the new left in Texas and elsewhere in places relatively untouched by the old left but deeply affected by the civil rights movement. Those whites who moved left, like the Haydens and the Burlages, maintained their sense of participation in the upward sweep of history, their feeling that they were looking ahead to a more just society and a more authentic life, avoiding Maxwell's tears for many years more. Each component of youth activism preserved its precious sense of a "beloved community" in its own way, and sometimes they even did so together.

For some young white civil rights activists who could not negotiate the transition to the new left, however, the lessons of these years were crushing. Again, this may seem surprising in light of their political victories; one might think that the losers in the civil rights battles of these years, the white segregationists of the South, should have been the ones to despair. Yet the changes occurring in the racial regime of the United States paled next to the expansive personal and political hopes of those like Vivien Franklin and Jim Neyland. Of all the players in the drama recounted here, they made perhaps the most serious breaks with their previous lives. Franklin was caught between loyalty to her politically establishmentarian family and her increasingly radical leanings. In 1963 she graduated from college and escaped to Europe. She did not return to the United States for several years, and when she did, she went straight to California, which she had visited in the early 1960s. She became involved in various strands of the late 1960s counterculture, and later she converted to Islam. She never lived in Texas again.[108]

"It was difficult for both of us to make the break from the intense purpose of student activism into 'real life,' " Jim Neyland writes of himself and Franklin. "Those of us who were most intensely involved, those who were at the Community, the Y, and participating in SDA . . . were 'living on the edge,' " and psychologically, Neyland could not sustain it. In the spring of 1962, the art department, in which he was enrolled, discovered that he was color blind and prevented him from taking the courses he needed to graduate. Faced with this, with the political attacks and harassment he had suffered, and with crises in his personal life, he tried to kill himself with gas from his apartment stove. Fortunately, a phone call from Franklin interrupted him and ended the attempt. He tried to make a go of it at school in the fall of 1962, withdrawing somewhat from political activities, but could not. He never graduated from UT, leaving school for New York, where he started a new life as a husband and father, a commercial writer and editor, and a liberal who favored "pragmatism" in politics. He left activism almost entirely behind.

When Neyland left UT, he and his friends had a big farewell party in the adjacent apartments that he and Franklin occupied behind the Faith-and-Life Community. "There was one wall of my place that I had painted a mural on; and during the party, I opened up my paintbox and asked everybody to contribute toward turning it into an abstract 'community' painting, which they did." For him, and perhaps for others like Franklin, it was a final enactment and celebration of a "beloved community." For them, this was an ephemeral experience. It would be left to others, younger than they, to carry forward the search for authenticity and democracy, confidently leaving behind the sense of anxiety that for years had been so prominent a part of the discussion among socially concerned young Americans. The new generation of activists still spoke of alienation, but they located it and its causes more clearly in the larger society around them rather than in themselves. They felt that they had achieved authenticity in their own radical communities. For those like Neyland, in contrast, the life of love and community that they had sought proved elusive, and their experience of "living on the edge" left them, perhaps unavoidably, with an irrepressible feeling of loss.[109]

PART TWO

CHAPTER FIVE

These People Were from America:
The New Left Revisited

In June 1964, Charlie Smith, a heavyset young man known to his friends as "the mad pamphleteer," formerly a one-man independent leftist band at the University of Texas at Austin, addressed the national convention of Students for a Democratic Society (SDS). In the two years since its adoption of the *Port Huron Statement*, SDS had become the leading student leftist organization in the United States. Smith announced himself a pacifist, an anarchist, and a Marxist, and "no one could classify" him. Those assembled at Camp Gulliver in Pine Hill, just north of New York City, nonetheless put this odd bird on the group's national council.[1]

A few other Texans had traveled to the meeting, among them Jeff Shero Nightbyrd (also elected to the council) and Robert Pardun, both of whom played important roles in the new left of the 1960s. Nightbyrd and Pardun attempted to speak on behalf of a large constituency that flooded the new left after 1965 and shattered what one member of the SDS "old guard" candidly called "the we-happy-few mystique" of the early new left.[2] The old guard moved in a northern Ann Arbor–New York–Cambridge circuit, and the cadres that reported for duty in the mid-1960s hailed from different places and brought different experiences with them. "They kidded about standing for 'prairie power'" in the radical movement, as against the cosmopolitan old guard; "they tended to come from the Midwest and Southwest, they were not Jewish, they were more likely to come from working-class families, and they were less intellectual, less articulate. . . . They were instinctive anarchists, principled and practiced antiauthoritarians." The new crowd had few connections to the old left.[3]

One year after the Texans' appearance in Pine Hill, the newcomers were present in full force, and at the June 1966 national convention, recently arrived midwesterners won all the national offices of SDS. The appearance of this cohort had profound consequences for the new left, as these new recruits broadened the new left into something like a mass movement. The Texas contingent was widely seen as the advance guard of the "prairie power" group. In the name of far-flung SDS chapters, the UT radicals argued for organizational decentralization in the new left. In the summer of 1965 they went to the national office in Chicago and attempted to institute a controversial regime of "office democracy," adding to their reputation in the movement as naive anarchists from the countryside.[4] The Texans were content with these perceptions, even though their Wobbly image concealed a more complicated reality. Charlie Smith, for example, came from a fairly elite background; his father was a pioneer in the field of medical law. On one occasion in 1965, when a group of Texas SDS members protested what they saw as the high-handed behavior of the organization's national officers, the Austinites simultaneously embraced and satirized this image, calling themselves "brethren of the pineywoods."[5]

Despite its shaky basis in fact, this Texas mystique points up the continuing significance of the search for authenticity in the youth politics of the 1960s, a search that became both socialized and politically radicalized in the new left. Both the first and second waves of the new left were self-conscious about one variant of this search, namely, the search for an authentically "American" radicalism. Aware of the hazards of anticommunism in the United States, the SDS old guard were determined to "speak American" and hence to give themselves a chance of building a mass movement.[6] But they still worried that their old left connections would mark them as "un-American," and their disproportionate Jewish representation added to this anxiety. So to the old guard, the prairie power cohort seemed threatening not only because of its lack of discipline and experience but also because the newcomers threatened to trump the old guard's carefully cultivated "nativist" authenticity. This apprehension was mixed with excitement, as indicated by the reaction of Richard Flacks, a Jewish old guard member with a Communist background in his youth. Flacks enthused that "these people were from America."[7]

The Texans in particular evoked a volatile response because of their subliminal connection to the "prophet" of early SDS, C. Wright Mills

(University of Texas, class of 1939). An early SDS member recalls that in this organization, " 'you had to know C. Wright Mills'—to know not just the major texts and concepts, but the personal anecdotes, the rhetorical style."[8] Mills's influence drew on both his writings and his persona: both contributed to the nativist radical heritage that the new left constructed for itself. Mills offered a leftist social analysis that was non-Marxist, which was all that "American" radicalism really meant in theoretical terms.[9] A lapsed Catholic from the Baptist citadel (Waco), Mills also played the authenticity card skillfully if not subtly. His cultivated outlaw image, which he raised to the level of self-parody on the faculty of Columbia University—carrying his papers in a surplus army duffel bag, sporting a bomber jacket and boots, goading his students with his knowledge of firearms, and, according to rumor, carrying on sexual affairs with female students—appealed powerfully to the young men in the new left who carried with them the fears of devitalization that always had been central to the search for authenticity. Mills's machismo, accentuated at the end of his life by his championship of the era's foremost symbol of the manly left, Fidel Castro, was the mark of his authenticity.[10]

The visible sign of the Texas new left's kinship with Mills was Charlie Smith's Honda 250 motorcycle, which he rode from Texas to New York, evoking Mills's well-known love of his BMW.[11] The old guard from New York and Ann Arbor could scarcely imagine appealing to their multitudinous contemporaries who had thrilled to Marlon Brando in *The Wild One*, but a sneaking suspicion arose that the newcomers might prove able to forge such a link with the larger youth culture. Perhaps this simply was the kind of radical they grew in Texas.

The new left wrote a new, turbulent chapter in the tradition of existentialist politics in the twentieth-century United States, socializing the search for authenticity and taking it toward radical conclusions. The poles of alienation and authenticity structured the discussion taking place among the most thoughtful of the young in the 1960s, as in the previous decade. SDS cast both the formal and social democracy that it called for as means toward the existentialist objective of "finding a meaning in life that is personally authentic."[12] As Arthur Schlesinger Jr. had argued was necessary, new left activists sought to advance values and social forms that could stave off the forces of alienation that industrial society bred. In the 1950s, both apolitical "rebels without a cause" and earnest religious liberals had struggled to experience authenticity, to keep anxiety at bay. The latter group had found their answer to anxiety in activism on behalf of democracy. In the 1960s, in a world of constant political protest and escalating conflict, the new left seemed to shake off the fear of anxiety. Although the young radicals feared that their society might rob them of the sense of community and authenticity that they had found through struggle, increasingly they emphasized that others inhabited the world of alienation they themselves had escaped. The causes of weightlessness, of deadening alienation, they felt, lay not within but without. Overturning those malign forces, it seemed, required an ever more radical realization of democracy.

In the 1960s, the critique of the consumer society that had lain dormant in the search for authenticity came clear, and the Marxist interpretation of weightlessness—as the alienation symptomatic of life's spiritual emptiness under "late capitalism"—ultimately found adherents in the land of "roast beef and apple pie."[13] The initial encouragement in this direction came from mainstream sources. The cultural criticism of the 1950s did its bit to damage for the baby boomers the attractiveness of the economistic "growth liberalism" championed by the Democratic Party, a program that held more appeal for those who had endured the Great Depression. The postscarcity aspiration to cultural refinement—initially a new frontier for liberals who styled themselves aesthetes and idealists—helped spawn a growing rejection of the materialist world in the 1960s.[14]

But nothing did more to shape the new left's variant on the search for authenticity than the civil rights movement. The southern black movement shifted all of American politics leftward and pulled along with it the search for authenticity, whose politics—indeed, whose very status as political— had previously been uncertain. Despite the continuing political instability of that quest, during the 1960s this search maintained a leftist image. With the ascent of the Student Nonviolent Coordinating Committee into mythic status, both Norman Mailer's nihilistic black "hipster" and Albert Camus's moral "rebel" enjoyed a decade as symbols of radical insurgency for young whites.[15] Rebellion, social justice, and authenticity were bound together in the minds of many young Americans.

The linchpin of these associations was a rejection of racism and racial separation. Under the influence of the civil rights movement's vision of "black and white together," the quest for personal solidity—largely the province of the comfortable and hence the white—was joined, analogically and logically, to a search for "solidarity" with those perceived as "other," as different. The "beloved community" of differences harmonized in equality was the crucible for the newly complete and fully human individual. Both socially and psychologically, what was wrong would be put right; what was essentially one but existentially split—both a nation and the individuals in the movement—

would be united in time and space. Between 1955 and 1965, a vision of social justice converged with the vision of authentic human existence. In a sense, the message of the civil rights movement to white Americans was that not only civil peace but also the attainment of authenticity, the security of spiritual ease, carried the price of social justice.

If the achievement of social justice was now imperative, for political as well as personal reasons, the problem of social change became paramount and remained so for as long as a new left existed. With the Marxian vision of structural failure and revolutionary transformation safely banished from the national imagination by wartime prosperity and postwar economic growth, the question of social changed flowed into the familiar channels of American interest-group pluralism. The question became, Who could, who would, be the agents of social change? Where was the "key sector," to use the terminology of the old left, that would exert the necessary pressure on the political system?[16]

From its inception, the new left puzzled over this question, announcing a variety of answers. Partly because the civil rights movement showed that people of modest means would take the risks necessary to build an insurgent politics, from 1963 through 1965 the answer seemed to be that an "interracial movement of the poor" formed the key sector and that such a movement likely would work in coalition with "intellectuals" based in the university system on a project of social democracy and a downward dispersal of political power. In the later 1960s, when the quickening sense of crisis in the United States and the world led the new left to make revolution its avowed objective, the movement splintered into several factions, each of which located the key sector differently. Some, influenced by both the rise of black power doctrine and the United States's poor showing in Indochina, thought that an "internal colony" of African Americans, in concert with the formerly colonized peoples of the Third World, would overthrow North Atlantic power essentially on their own. Others in the white left returned fully to an old left vision, seeing the manufacturing working class as the only possible agent of social revolution in capitalist America. Yet others viewed the new left's own constituency—white, college-educated youth—as a revolutionary sector in its own right, though one that would likely combine with others to overthrow "the system." This third position was perhaps the most influential in the middle and late new left, yet it has received the least attention in retrospect. This view of relatively privileged baby boomers as a revolutionary force owed much to the developing idea of a cultural revolution, which became a cliché before the era of turbulence came to a close.

More than a new existentialist departure in a continuous history of leftist agitation, the new left was a newly insurgent departure in a continuous and multifaceted history of existentialist hopes for authenticity. This observation helps explain much of the complicated history of the new left, its impulses and internal conflicts. From the new left's viewpoint, revolutionary agency and authenticity were yoked together so that those who possessed one of these automatically possessed both. Was it black people, or the poor, or young people, or workers, or women, or some combination of these? Previously, the process of transcending alienation and achieving authenticity had been imagined in an abstract way, as a process that might occur in any individual and any community; the action and commitment that were required to achieve authenticity could and should be made by anyone and everyone.

New left activists continued to believe in this kind of universal vision, but at the same time, both the centrality of racial difference in the crucial events of the era and the familiar interest-group pluralism of American political culture worked to project the search for authenticity onto a social map. The previous generation of young activists had asked how the individual became authentic and had provided answers that remained satisfactory for the new left. Community, commitment, and a decision to take action formed the individual's path to authenticity. But the new left came to view authenticity not only as a goal in a process of personal development but also as a state in which certain social groups already resided. Some of the more fiercely burning questions for the new left were, Where is authenticity located? and Who possesses it? Those who lived in authenticity might make the revolution.

Race, Rebellion, and Radicalization

"If there hadn't been a civil rights movement, there wouldn't have been an SDS." So says Jeff Nightbyrd, the leader of the early SDS chapter at the University of Texas (UT).[17] Other political concerns, such as opposition to the nuclear arms race and atomic testing, and enthusiasm for the Cuban revolution also contributed to the emergence of a white left in the early 1960s.[18] James Miller locates the *Port Huron Statement*'s Deweyan, highly formal vision of participatory democracy, rather than any more historically specific political issues, at the center of early new left politics.[19] Not the ban-the-bomb effort, *fidelismo*, or the search for participatory democracy was so important to shaping the emerging new left's spirit and political concerns as was the civil rights struggle. In particular, the youth wing of the civil rights movement, its ethos and news of its doings, permeated the political world inhabited by those who started SDS.

Todd Gitlin chose Christian metaphors when evoking the psychological attachment of white student leftists to SNCC. "In northern movement circles, the names of SNCC leaders became legendary, along with the sites of SNCC's passion, the Delta, Parchman Penitentiary, and the rest. The southern martyrs became our saints; cherishing them, we crossed the Mason–Dixon line of imagination, transubstantiated."[20] To early SDS leaders, the southern African American movement as exemplified in SNCC was both a political model and a moral exemplar.

Tom Hayden and his comrades hoped that SDS could become "a counterpart to SNCC" outside the South.[21] For the Liberal Study Group, which included not only northerners like Hayden and Al Haber, leaders of the SDS nucleus at the University of Michigan, but also Texans Casey Hayden, Robb Burlage, and Dorothy Burlage, and a few black members like Charles McDew of SNCC, the civil rights conflict was clearly the salient context. When Tom Hayden and Haber wanted to goad white collegians into political action in 1961, the year that the "Freedom Riders" risked life and limb trying to integrate southern bus lines, they asserted, "While the Negro student has been struggling to gain his own and this people's civil rights, Northern students [read whites] have failed to meet their responsibility."[22] Nightbyrd felt that the political force of anticommunism was so great in the 1950s that there was, as Irving Howe said, a kind of "missing generation" of white leftists who might have been mentors to people like himself.[23] "That whole generation had been cut off by fear. And so blacks, in the Deep South, gave us models, of how to be."[24] The discussion of participatory democracy and "publics" versus "masses" in early SDS seemed meaningful because the civil rights conflict created an opening for a full-scale reconsideration of American political life. To young, left-leaning activists, this was the dominant political factor of the early 1960s.[25]

The most common political experience shared by early SDS members from around the country was participation in civil rights protest, and in fact, some of the early SDS chapters emerged from such activity. This was not just true in the South. One case in point was the SDS chapter at Swarthmore College, in a sense the archetype of the SDS old guard, a "fantastically influential" chapter whose members included a disproportionate number of "red-diaper babies" from old left families.[26] One widely known precursor to the 1964 Freedom Summer project and to SDS's later urban organizing efforts was the involvement of the Swarthmore Political Action Committee (SPAC) in the civil rights battles between 1961 and 1963 in Cambridge, a city on Maryland's Eastern Shore.[27] These northern activists had a variety of political concerns, but it was civil rights activism that galvanized them, convincing them that insurgent political organization was indeed possible in a society in which "ideology" supposedly had ended. SPAC contributed some of the key participants in the Port Huron Conference of 1962, and it thereafter functioned in fact as an SDS chapter. Leading the trend that developed nationally in SDS between 1963 and 1965, SPAC moved from strictly racial civil rights protest to an organizing project in the city of Chester, Pennsylvania, devoted to building an "interracial movement of the poor."[28]

The University of Texas chapter of SDS, which was perhaps the second biggest in the country as early as late 1964, seemed the antithesis of the Swarthmore contingent.[29] Robb and Dorothy Burlage, members of the old guard who hailed from Austin, had blended in rather well and didn't prepare their comrades for what was heading north. The Texans were whimsical, sardonic, often angry, and slightly paranoid, whereas the northerners affected a high seriousness. They "didn't have much of an Old Left bumping around to react to."[30] Along with their "decentralist," even anarchist, bent, the Texas group became known for a culturally libertarian streak, the men among them likely to sport facial hair, an important distinction at the time, and all of them more open to psychedelic drug use than the old guard, who were leery of such substances until their complete criminalization in 1966.[31] In this sense, too, the new Lone Star cadres anticipated the coming trend in the new left. What the Texas activists and the old guard had in common—and what provided the initial basis for political sympathy between them—was their political baptism in civil rights agitation.

As a UT student, Jeff Nightbyrd was involved in civil rights agitation in Austin in 1963 and decided to join SDS, although he knew little about the organization. He was by this time a fairly accomplished troublemaker. Raised with "basically a right-wing anticommunist outlook on the world," he simply found Jim Crow segregation morally repugnant in a visceral way; he did not see himself as a liberal. Perhaps at the insistence of his stepfather, a "bomb-em'-back-to-the-Stone-Age" air force colonel, Nightbyrd started college at Texas A&M in Bryan, where he had attended high school; A&M kicked him out. He also attended the University of North Dakota, where he took part in protests by local Sioux, and Sam Houston State Teachers' College in Huntsville, in East Texas, where he was drawn into integration efforts, organized secretly for fear of violent retribution, in the back of a local black-owned barber shop. That black southerners would take such risks impressed him deeply. "East Texas at that time was a little bit like a Nazi operation," he half-jokes years later. Occasionally he made long car drives into Alabama or Mississippi if he caught word of explosive civil rights conflicts in cities and towns there, adding to the growing legion of activists who, on short notice, would converge where needed. After the school chancellor in Huntsville told Nightbyrd he "really wasn't Sam Houston material," he enrolled at UT because he knew it was a center of civil rights activism. He joined the Campus Interracial Committee (CIC), the main activist organization at the time on the UT campus, demonstrating at whites-only retail establishments like an ice-skating rink where the university held physical education classes, and a cafeteria where he met another student who later became a local SDS leader, Alice Embree.[32]

Embree was the daughter of a UT education school professor, the child of liberal, church-going Episcopalians who had migrated south from Minneapolis, where they both had been involved in a teachers' union—an ideal new left recruit. Embree's first political act, when in high school in Austin, was to insist that she and her fellow drill squad members leave a restaurant when they discovered that the one black member of their party would not be served. Upon entering college, she was "predisposed . . . to be a Young Democrat." But the Young Democrats seemed unenthusiastic about civil rights agitation in the early 1960s, torn as they were between liberal and conservative factions, a replica of the adult political scene in this one-party state.[33] Embree then joined the CIC and helped force the final integration of UT student housing by picketing First Daughter Lynda Bird Johnson's dormitory in 1963 and 1964 in anticipation of President Johnson's visit to campus to deliver the 1964 commencement address. Primed by civil rights activism, Embree responded positively to the small group who brought their SDS sign to spring registration in early 1964, Nightbyrd among them. To her they seemed "very alive, very intense, very interesting."[34] Embree and Nightbyrd, who soon became romantically involved— one historian calls them "the ultimate movement couple"—represented two important tendencies in the new left: she, the liberal child of cold war idealists who was radicalized by her attempt to practice what she was raised to believe; and he, driven more by anger than a coherent politics, a renegade from his own past, attracted to the civil rights movement's belief in "direct action" to stop what seemed wrong. "I was a local girl gone bad," Embree remembers, rather proudly, "not an outside agitator." "I was an action guy," Nightbyrd remembers with a touch of self-mockery. "I didn't have any ideology, I just wanted to *go*—*do*—*it*. 'Let's go do it! More, bigger, let's stop 'em! Have bigger demonstrations.' "[35]

There is no single way to explain why when confronted with racism, certain young white people at this time experienced what the SDS leader Carl Oglesby called "the soul-basic explosion against injustice which is the one redemption of the damned."[36] A fierce negative reaction against the white resistance to the civil rights movement and a feeling of solidarity with civil rights activists were typically the pivotal experiences. Some, like Embree, came from politically liberal households. Some, like Judy Perez (née Schiffer), had parents with Communist Party pasts, and even if such parents concealed their old left connections from their children, as Perez's did until she was in college, these children were likely to be raised with an intense sense of "moralism" and a scorn for racism. Perez was one of the few Texas new left recruits swaddled in red diapers; she started out demonstrating in the CIC and joined SDS in 1964.[37]

Some, like Robert Pardun, a mathematics graduate student at UT who had grown up in the steel town of Pueblo, Colorado, spent their childhood in racially mixed, working-class neighborhoods and never thought much about race when they were young; Pardun's first experience with Jim Crow was in Austin in 1963.[38] Scott Pittman joined the air force to get out of West Texas (and participated in a Marxist reading group organized by the linguists at his air base in Turkey), had little contact with African Americans until his time overseas in an integrated setting, and found himself in violation of local mores when he came to Biloxi, Mississippi, for a training session. He joined in the CIC and SDS civil rights agitation when he came to UT after leaving the service.[39] Still others, like Mariann Wizard and Paul Pipkin, schoolmates during high school in Fort Worth, were attracted to African American culture for distinctly nonpolitical reasons: the jazz-based nightlife of black clubs drew them in. They cared little for mainstream white culture but found black culture exciting.[40] This cultural appeal and their consequent social interaction with African Americans predisposed them to feel a strong sympathy for the civil rights movement—even if, in Wizard's case, she was a Young Republican who canvassed for Goldwater in 1964.

For those from upwardly mobile homes, it was important that outright expressions of belief in white supremacy had acquired, over several decades, a tinge of disrespectability, a touch of the low class, in popular understanding. Many new left activists came from households with one or two parents with college educations, and such children might feel distaste for the young toughs who appeared in press photographs harassing black civil rights demonstrators. Still, distaste is not outrage.

Finally, many whites who became civil rights and new left activists had religious backgrounds that, even if religiosity in a traditional sense dropped out of their lives, shaped their early ethical commitments, making powerful the explicitly religious appeal of the civil rights movement, its call for personal and national redemption. Pardun, whose grandfather was a Methodist minister, argued in a high school essay that the church was the enemy of true religion.[41] Wizard likewise felt that religious beliefs were relevant but that church institutions had become irrelevant by refusing to take their own stated beliefs seriously enough. "You came to feel that you *couldn't* go to church, you couldn't participate in it the way it was, without accepting that hypocrisy." Wizard lived in a Methodist dormitory during her first year at UT. Although she disliked it enough to leave, Wizard gravitated toward the Methodist Student Center, where the Reverend Bob Breihan had established a religious environment she found more congenial. She feels her radical politics were consonant with the religious teachings she absorbed as a child—"what Jesus said, loving your neighbor like yourself."[42] George Vizard attended the same Episcopal church as Alice Embree did after he moved for college from San Antonio to Austin. For a time, he considered entering the Episcopal priesthood, but instead he directed his spiritual and ethical concerns into social activism, becoming a civil rights activist and another leader of the SDS group at UT.[43]

Despite their primary commitment to the issue of civil rights, if this had been the entirety of this group's politics, there would have been no reason for them to organize an SDS chapter. The CIC would have been sufficient for them. In fact, the early new left activists, here as elsewhere, had a crucial but curiously detached relation to the civil rights movement, in the sense that they never saw the civil rights movement as their home in the way that the earlier generation of white activists such as Casey Hayden did. These younger whites early on wished to push their politics into a movement for comprehensive political change, even though their political work focused on civil rights.

Charlie Smith, Jeff Nightbyrd, and Robert Pardun first went to national SDS meetings because they had heard that SDS was four-square behind civil rights. But they discovered something more. At Pine Hill, Nightbyrd found that the old guard of SDS did not conform to his image of stodgy northeastern radicals, and he felt outclassed.

> Smartest people I'd met. . . . Clear in their thinking and passionate. . . .
> And they weren't, like, classroom people. . . . They could . . . handle the
> classroom but . . . we camped by a lake, you know? They could do it all.
> They were all-stars. It's like if you're a baseball player and you've been
> playing in Class A league and all of a sudden you go up to the Bigs and,
> you say, "*Jesus*! Look at those guys hit."[44]

Ironically, both the old guard and the newcomers harbored insecurities about the other group. Nightbyrd decided he wanted to join "the Bigs." The Texas group came home determined to proselytize for the new faith.

What distinguished the SDS appeal from the civil rights liberalism already present on American campuses was what the new group's members called its "multi-issue" approach. In February 1964 Robert Pardun informed the general campus population that SDS concerned itself with "poverty, civil rights, civil liberties, and the arms race."[45] Soon they had forty members attending regular meetings and a mailing list of two hundred.[46] Talking about four issues in one breath in itself seemed new and exciting to Embree, who stopped to talk at the SDS table during the spring 1964 registration. The restlessness and moral dissatisfaction with American society that young people like her expressed crystallized into a striving for radicalism. The Marxist politics offered by sectarian groups, like the minuscule bands of Spartacists and Young People's Socialist Leaguers (YPSL) that existed in Austin at this time, held little appeal for even the angriest young people. SDS maintained its connections to the burning issues, particularly civil rights, in both its rhetoric and its activities, while "talking about connections between issues, which not too many people talked about," as Embree points out. SDS members argued that "things were fundamentally flawed and needed . . . to be fundamentally changed." They felt that violence against civil rights activists, nuclear brinkmanship, and the problem of poverty simply would not be solved by the piecemeal reforms that liberals seemed to advocate. A desire to move beyond liberalism, a yearning for radicalism, was present in Texas SDS before the group had any radical vision of a new society or of social change.

Embree thinks that many of them were "unconscious socialists." Pardun says that as early as 1964, he and his friends thought of themselves as leftists, and he would have called himself a socialist.[47] In the early and middle 1960s, though, members of SDS were more likely to call themselves "radical" than "socialist," and the former term seems the more apt description of their politics at that time. It harks back to the common use of "radical" by members of the "lyrical left" in the early twentieth century, many of whom described themselves interchangeably as radicals and "liberals."[48] The early new left, especially in a conservative environment like Texas where "liberalism" also was a sharply oppositional category, felt akin to liberals, at least of the populist Austin variety, even while moving left. This intimacy with liberalism is clear, for example, in the SDS-UT chapter's civil libertarianism, more daring here than in the Northeast.

The provincial new left's conflicted feelings about liberalism came to the fore at the time of John Kennedy's assassination in Texas in late 1963, just as students like Smith, Nightbyrd, and Pardun were getting interested in forming an SDS chapter. Drawn to the allure of his public image, many who joined the new left viewed Kennedy sympathetically and maintained an attachment to him even after he died and they became more radical. "I was a worshiper of John Kennedy" in high school, recalls Paul Pipkin. Others took a more critical view. Nightbyrd was part of a group that was busily constructing signs complaining that Kennedy's administration was not enforcing existing civil rights laws, in preparation for a picket upon the president's arrival in Austin, when word arrived that he had been shot in Dallas.[49]

Regardless of these differences, Kennedy's assassination reinforced the feeling among the most sensitive of the young in Texas that they lived in a brutal, right-wing environment, and it fueled their growing feeling that a moderate program of change, pursued within the mainstream political system, was a weak response to the violent forces of reaction in the society. Most Texans, and others as well, looked to the right-wing subculture of Texas for responsibility. Both the John Birch Society and the Minutemen, a paramilitary rightist group, were quite visible in the state, and the rightist gubernatorial candidacy of retired General Edwin Walker drew on this constituency in 1962.[50]

The SDS contingent in Texas did not find convincing the hastily produced Warren Commission report on the assassination, and in April 1964 the new SDS chapter, in its first big event on campus, packed a hall in the Student Union with students eager to hear Mark Lane, the original Kennedy assassination conspiracy theorist, tell them that their government was lying to them.[51] In Texas, the embattled position of liberals, let alone leftists, and the open collusion of business and governmental elites had long lent a conspiratorialist quality to political dissent. This strain in the political culture of rebellion now received a fresh infusion of blood, making the young radicals feel they were adrift in a sea of illegitimacy and violence.

This sense of defamiliarization, a kind of political vertigo that erupted after Kennedy's death, added to this provincial SDS group's feeling that they were leaving the familiar political world behind them and contributed to their sharp sense of isolation. Because of the regular turnover in the youth population typical of university communities and also because of an unusually complete decampment of youth activists from Austin between 1960 and 1963, the white civil rights protesters who started the SDS chapter at UT had virtually no sense of continuity with earlier local activism. The perception of political isolation decisively shaped the image of the provincial new left, due in no small measure to a single, powerful remark by Jeff Nightbyrd. Deploying the Christian imagery favored by southern radicals, Nightbyrd asserted that "in Texas, to join SDS meant breaking with your family . . . it was like in early Rome joining a Christian sect." Instead of family approval, "you couldn't go home for Christmas," as you were likely to get a response from your loved ones on the order of *"You Goddamn Communist."*[52] He exaggerated. No doubt some Texas new leftists encountered such emotionally scarring rejection from their families. One radical's parents apparently had her institutionalized and given electroshock treatment.[53] More typical, however, was the parental relationship of "strain[ed]" emotional support that activists like Embree and Wizard experienced. Parents often recognized their children's attempt to act on the values learned at home.[54] This is not to say that Texas youths pleased their families by becoming radicals and protesters. But it is unlikely that most Texas SDS members really could not go home for Christmas.

Provincial leftists did experience a sharp sense of isolation and embattlement, but this resulted not primarily from family hostility but from a right-wing regional political environment. Southern, southwestern, and midwestern leftists outside a liberal island like Austin, of course, did not enjoy even the meager protective environment that the UT group did. In 1965, Robert Pardun helped organize an SDS chapter at Texas Tech University in Lubbock and reported that it was like trying to establish a black student political organization in South Africa, so thick was the atmosphere of fear.[55] UT leftists came to view the university administration as their enemy, yet the administration's hostility to SDS here was, though sharp, not necessarily greater than that exhibited by university administrators elsewhere in the country, including those at elite universities like Harvard, Berkeley, and Columbia.

The real difference was in the vitriol that leftists in a place like Texas received from fellow students and private citizens, which shaded into the organized vigilantism that was a much-remarked-on part of the Texas political landscape in the 1960s. The line between vigilantism and official harassment was blurred. In the late 1960s, a scandal broke in Houston when the Ku Klux Klan's infiltration of that city's police force became public knowledge. Most routine was the aggression, from mere name-calling to physical assault, that conservative individuals directed at those who bore the outward marks of rebellion, especially men with long hair. The potential for violence came clear even in relatively tolerant Austin in isolated instances, as Pardun discovered in the fall of 1963. In his first semester at UT, having chosen to study math rather than join the air force, he was out to dinner at an Austin steakhouse with a couple of men he had just met and had a surprise.

> They were friendly enough, and as we talked about this and that the
> conversation drifted into politics. One of the guys said that he thought
> we should nuke the Russians with a first strike. I said something

provocative like, "The Russians are people too." To which he replied, "You're a goddamned communist, I'm going to kill you," and attacked me on the spot. I escaped with a broken finger.

Pardun realized that "as far as some people were concerned, it didn't take much to be a communist."[56]

The most likely manifestation of hostility toward Austin SDS members was the kind of mass jeering and intimidation, organized in the fraternity houses around the UT campus, that materialized in reaction to SDS-led protests at a local bar in early 1965. The protests against Roy's Lounge followed an incident in which the bar's owner (Roy) assaulted and threw out a black student, Leo Worthington—the latest confirmation of the businessman's reputation as a racist. By this time, it was expected around campus that SDS would be the group most likely to react. In its first semester on campus, one year before, the SDS chapter focused on antiracist activities, for all its "multi-issue" rhetoric. SDS worked closely with the CIC and with students from Huston-Tillotson College, jointly sponsoring protests at retail establishments that would not admit blacks (singing at one restaurant, "Until we get our dinner/We shall not be moved").[57] The SDS chapter agitated for the passage of a local antidiscrimination ordinance by the city council.[58] SDS criticized the Cowboys' annual minstrel show in 1964, which did not stop until after that year, castigating the honorary society for what Robert Pardun called its "racist antics."[59]

The young leftists arranged a public debate with the campus chapter of the rightist Young Americans for Freedom (YAF), a group founded in 1960 whose spread attracted much attention in the early 1960s, on the topic of President Lyndon Johnson's proposed civil rights bill, with SDS arguing that it didn't go far enough in outlawing discrimination and YAF contending that the desegregation provisions of the bill violated the right of free assembly. (As a result of both this and another debate over U.S. policy toward Cuba, with SDS taking a "hands off" position, Nightbyrd reported in May 1964 that his group's dogged "opposition" to the "new right" on campus had "ground their movement to a clinking halt.")[60] In the spring of 1965, Nightbyrd boasted privately that SDS ran the CIC; SDS had taken over that group's role as the leading organizer of antiracist activities on campus, and the committee soon was defunct.[61]

In Texas, as elsewhere around the country, developments in the civil rights movement accelerated the trajectory of its left flank, black and white, out of the mainstream liberal camp. The violence of the white southern resistance to the civil rights campaign and the equivocal response of the federal government to this resistance were perhaps the most important elements in this process of disaffection. In no time and place was the violence worse than in Mississippi in 1964. In the summer of that year, Charlie Smith, Judy Perez, and Robert Pardun traveled eastward to take part in the Freedom Summer effort.[62] After the summer, Pardun went on to New York, where he got SDS to hire him as a "regional traveler" for the organization in the Southwest, establishing chapters and furnishing SDS literature at campuses mainly in Texas and Oklahoma but also in Louisiana, New Mexico, and Colorado, working from a base in Austin.[63]

The group that had gone to Mississippi seemed to have changed when they came back to Austin, bearing the torch of increased militancy and radicalism. This also happened elsewhere around the country in the fall of 1964, most spectacularly in Berkeley, where white students fresh from Freedom Summer launched the Free Speech Movement after administrators in the University of California system forbade the collection on the edge of campus of contributions to political organizations, specifically civil rights groups.[64] Charlie Smith announced at an SDS meeting that fall, called to discuss events in Mississippi, that he thought African Americans should be armed and ready to defend themselves. He stated that it was "time for revolution."[65] SDS-UT raised money for the Deacons for Defense and Justice, a black group in Louisiana that also favored armed self-defense.[66] This was the same kind of sentiment that gained ground in SNCC following Freedom Summer, although a principled commitment to nonviolence had never been so important to early SDS as it was to SNCC.

By early 1965, then, the SDS chapter was primed to respond sharply to blatant instances of white racism like those at Roy's, which was a popular watering hole for students just on the edge of campus. George Vizard did the most to instigate the pickets in front of the bar. Mariann Wizard by this time had drifted out of the UT Young Republicans, who seemed awfully stiff, and had ceased her political activity. She spent a lot of time in the Chuckwagon, a ramshackle eatery in the Student Union that was a gathering place for motorcyclists, foreign students, "the quasi-beat literati, the drug community such as it existed at that time," and others who felt like misfits at the football- and fraternity-dominated campus, who styled themselves "the ragged fringe."[67] A man named Bob Speck approached her that spring in the Chuckwagon and asked her what she was doing. "Wasting my life," she said. "Good. Come with me." He instructed her to collate papers for a colloquy that campus activists had planned on the Vietnam War. This was Wizard's "first experience with shitwork."[68]

Wizard's introduction to the debate over the war was soon followed by her initiation into civil rights activism. One evening she was having a cup of coffee with her biology lab partner, an African American student, when Vizard approached her, accompanied by a black woman. He said, "I notice you are an interracial couple. This young lady was just told to leave a bar up the street, apparently because she is black, when she asked to use the phone. Will you go there with us and try to have a beer? If they won't serve us, we'll know they are discriminating against black people, and we'll throw a picket line around the place."[69] Wizard often went to Roy's and didn't want to believe this was the case, but the group of four soon found that Vizard was correct. Suddenly Wizard was involved in civil rights protest. SDS brought together perhaps between fifty and seventy-five people, a group composed of students, faculty, and Austin residents for nightly pickets in front of the bar.

The activity and postprotest meetings were based in the University Y, as they had been during the civil rights protests of 1960/1961. But now, screaming counterdemonstrators typically outnumbered the protesters by a long way. Between two hundred and four hundred "frat rats" assembled either outside the Y building when the protesters met there or on the sidewalks next to the pickets, spoiling for trouble.[70] To the SDS activists, it seemed like a signal that resistance to social and political change was not abating, that if anything, it was growing more intransigent, less temperate.

A bit more than one year later, this perception seemed to be confirmed when the violence endemic to Texas culture reached Austin in an incident that shocked people around the country, indeed the world. One of the young men who had joined the mob of counterdemonstrators at Roy's Lounge, a student with strongly racist views and apparently with ties to the Minutemen, reached a psychological breaking point on 1 August 1966. Charles Whitman, supposedly the country's youngest Eagle Scout, killed his wife and his mother, and then he took his rifle to the top of the administration tower in the middle of the UT campus and shot forty-four people—including one member of the SDS chapter—killing twelve of them. Numerous men rushed up the tower, guns drawn, hoping to bag the prize, which one of them did. Perhaps one hundred others, freshly deputized, fired uncounted volleys toward the shooter from ground level, seeming to enjoy themselves. The police had no need to distribute guns to the local menfolk.[71] The overall scene of mayhem seemed to radicals in Texas to be a symbol of the dominant culture's violent character. It confirmed their worst fears about the violence of their regional and national society, fears already stoked by the violence against civil rights activists and the escalating Vietnam War.

In political terms, the violence would get worse. By the late 1960s, rightwing violence was directed specifically against both black and white radicals in Texas, especially in Houston and the Dallas–Fort Worth area. In 1970 the

Houston police, infiltrated by the Ku Klux Klan, shot and killed from the city's rooftops a militant black activist named Carl Hampton; two other radicals wounded by police sharpshooters in this incident, one white and one black, then went on trial for attempted murder.[72] *Space City News*, a paper started by Thorne Dreyer in 1969 after he left Austin, suffered numerous raids and much property destruction by the police, and both the newspaper and a Pacifica radio station later established in Houston were bombed.[73] The White Panthers, a white group that identified strongly with the Black Panthers, had a Fort Worth contingent that was the object of beatings, arrests, and destruction of its property after it organized an antiwar rally in 1970.[74] SNCC activists in Dallas were convicted of felonies and received jail sentences of ten years on questionable evidence when ordinarily they might have gotten slapped with misdemeanors.[75] The Dallas police raided the *Dallas Notes*, a new left newspaper, at least twice, claiming to look for illegal drugs but taking the opportunity to haul off or damage the paper's vital equipment. The editor, Stoney Burns (né Brent Stein), not only got beaten up (by both private citizens and police officers) and found his car vandalized or stolen on more than one occasion but also was arrested on various charges in 1970 after he led an antiwar demonstration in a Dallas park. The charge that stuck was the alleged possession of 0.05 ounces of marijuana, and eventually Burns went to prison in Huntsville, pardoned only in 1975.[76]

More notorious in Austin was the case of Lee Otis Johnson, a militant black organizer who had moved from Houston to Austin and who in 1968 received a sentence of thirty years in prison for supposedly passing a marijuana cigarette to an undercover police officer. He served about seven years of the sentence.[77] The cumulative impact of this repression and violence on Texas radicals was severe. It drove a few to their own, largely inert, version of paramilitary politics, although most recoiled from the very thought of violence, coming to define this as a basic aspect of the political culture that they wished to overturn.[78]

As early as the mid-1960s, the threat of violence seemed to hang in the air, and not coincidentally, the middle years of the decade also were a time of rapid radicalization. This was true even for some, like Wizard, who had not been involved in liberal or radical politics in the past. In the fall of 1965 she and Vizard were married after he returned from an SDS organizing project in Cairo, Illinois, and talked her out of joining the air force. Bob Breihan officiated at the ceremony at the Methodist Student Center. Over the next two years, George Vizard was at the forefront of the SDS chapter, and they both immersed themselves in Marxist and other radical literature and inspirational materials like the prison writings of Dietrich Bonhoeffer, feeling certain that some kind of revolution, probably a working class–based one, was necessary to remedy the ills of American society. In 1966 they joined the Communist Party USA (CP) in San Antonio, signaling their commitment to enlarging the new left's political imagination and breaking down its remaining political taboos, as well as their conviction that Marxism was the most sensible general framework they had found for thinking about social change.[79] Their new affiliation did not keep others in SDS from holding the Vizards "in very high esteem," remembers Bobby Minkoff, one of the New York exiles in Austin. Minkoff came from a working-class family of New Deal Democrats and had become involved in the SDS chapter when he entered UT for graduate study in psychology.[80]

Nonetheless, the Texas left's anarchist tendencies were becoming more self-aware, and some of the Vizards' friends were alienated by their embrace of communism. Mariann found this disappointing. "He hadn't changed. He had been a Marxist before that, and they hadn't had a problem." George's politics still was fueled by his religious commitments, but he had left behind any hopes to work through church structures. The two of them also were strongly sympathetic to the hippie counterculture, which was unusual for Marxist radicals.[81]

George remained a leader in the SDS chapter, and both Vizards were fully a part of its close-knit culture. At moments of political conflict, George's character made him a focal point. He was a physically imposing figure, prone to challenge authority, who first attracted his future wife with his gentlemanly demeanor. She recalls, "George just wasn't afraid. He wasn't afraid of authority. He wasn't afraid of physical violence. He did not like it, he did not seek it. But he was not . . . intimidated by it."[82] He frequently got arrested in protests, first in front of Roy's Lounge and then at protests against the Vietnam War that SDS organized in the spring of 1967 in response to visits to Austin by Secretary of State Dean Rusk and Vice President Hubert Humphrey. In the latter protest, which took place in April 1967 at the state capitol, Vizard intervened when a counterdemonstrator grabbed a protest sign out of one woman's hands and then hit her in the face with it. He shouted at the police who stood by, "You goddamn cops!" and suggested that the dissidents might need to arm themselves for self-defense in the future if they could not expect the police to do their job properly.

The following morning Vizard was arrested in the Chuckwagon by the chief of the UT police force and several state policemen, for using "abusive language" at the protest. He "went limp" in the manner of noncooperating civil rights protesters. When the officers started to carry him away, their superiors ordered them to drag the suspect instead. He "received severe abrasions that . . . removed all the skin from his back" and was treated in a local hospital. Two others who protested his treatment also were arrested.[83] At this time, the university administration also banned the SDS chapter from campus for organizing the previous day's rally, despite Chancellor Harry Ransom's order that they not do so. In protest, a broad coalition of campus groups organized a week-long series of mass meetings and rallies, which they called the University Freedom Movement (UFM), in a conscious echo of the Berkeley Free Speech Movement more than two years earlier.

Two other young white people who underwent a similar process of radicalization around mid-decade were Becky Brenner and Dick Reavis. An active Baptist from a wealthy San Antonio family, Brenner was runner-up in the competition for Miss Youth for Christ in high school. In the fall of 1965, she was attending UT while also teaching Sunday school. In the back of a sociology classroom, she met a small, sharp-featured, overall-clad young man, who was articulate if "a little paranoid" and who had transferred to the state university from remote Texas Tech.[84] During his childhood, Reavis's family moved continually, his father publishing newspapers in one small town after another but usually living in southwest Texas—"beyond Dixie"— in areas with few African Americans, mainly populated with a mix of Anglos and Mexican Americans. When as a child, he moved to a new town, says Reavis, the first of his peers to befriend him were invariably the poor ones, and the last to do so were "the petty-bourgeoisie kids like me." He too had been raised a Baptist and still was considering a career as a minister in 1965, even after he got into trouble in Lubbock for refusing to print "racist fraternity songs" at his campus job and for leading a free speech protest. He considered himself a liberal Democrat at that time.

Reavis told Brenner about his experiences during the past summer as a civil rights activist in Demopolis, Alabama, working for the Southern Christian Leadership Conference (SCLC), by the end of which time he concluded that "most whites were racists." Reflecting his newfound militancy, he "found Austin SDS to be verbally sympathetic to the civil rights movement, but not really conscious of its issues, and almost entirely uninvolved with them by the time I came"—several months after the demonstrations at Roy's Lounge. He joined SDS anyway, as well as the DuBois Clubs, the CP's youth group.[85] (The U.S. Justice Department had just targeted the DuBois Clubs as a supposedly dangerous subversive group, and many SDS members, from Texas and elsewhere, viewing this as an "eleventh-hour attempt to resuscitate the McCarthy era," hastened to join the group as a show of solidarity. This also prompted SDS to strike from its constitution the "exclusion clause," which forbade Communists from joining the organization.)[86]

Reavis convinced Brenner that working for civil rights was her Christian duty. She was shocked to find that her "country club church" in San Antonio did not respond to her appeal for money to support such work or to her request to speak to the church about the issue. She and Reavis went to Alabama for long weekends to help black residents register to vote and cast their ballots, and they were frightened by the intimidation they encountered. Her parents remained supportive, though they hated Reavis. Nonetheless, the two of them went back to Alabama for the summer of 1966 when SNCC, led by Stokely Carmichael, was organizing the independent Black Panther Freedom Party in Lowndes County, close to Demopolis.

That summer Brenner broke decisively with her past. Reavis was convicted of a vagrancy charge he had received earlier (a common charge used against outside agitators), along with Charlie Saulsberry, a black Demopolis resident who sometimes lived in Austin and who also had joined the DuBois Clubs. Brenner was jailed for contempt of court during the proceedings, and the authorities also arrested their lawyer, who hailed from New York, for practicing without a license. The five days she spent in jail put her "on a path" toward the left. In the style of so many white civil rights activists, Brenner started to wear blue jeans, put on less makeup, and stopped curling her hair. Despite their volk-ish affectations, though, she and Reavis were not sympathetic to the "hippie lifestyle" that was becoming the preferred form of cultural rebellion for their fellow white youth. They saw no connection between psychedelic drugs, for example, and political radicalism.[87]

Reavis was drawn to anarchism after his spell in jail, and so he joined the Industrial Workers of the World (IWW); he was able to quote Bakunin, unlike many who styled themselves anarchists.[88] But at some point he brought home a copy of Mao Zedong's "little red book" and became attracted to the model of cadre organization that Maoism represented.[89] Reavis dates his conversion to Maoism from his trip to Mexico in the summer of 1967, where he met up with some Maoists who soon were arrested for blowing up a train that carried a payroll for the Mexican army. "By 1967 it was evident SDS needed a new track," he says.[90]

At this time, Reavis formed a chapter of Friends of Progressive Labor (FPL) in Austin, which he led for the next two years. He also started waving the little red book at SDS chapter meetings. FPL was a front organization for the Progressive Labor Party (PL), which in 1966 resolved to move into SDS in the form of caucuses. At that time, PL was known for its anti-imperialist politics and its vocal support of the African American movement, which was moving toward a "black power" orientation.[91] In Austin and many other localities around the country, PL became the main representative of Marxism-Leninism and, in the minds of many, of Marxism overall on the U.S. left, until the dissolution of SDS in 1969. In addition, because of its attempt to take over SDS, PL became hated by many new left radicals. Austin was no exception in this matter, either.

The event in the summer of 1967 that attracted the most attention on the Austin left was the murder of George Vizard on 23 July when he was twenty-three years old. After he left school, he held several jobs and was shot late at night in the convenience store where he worked the graveyard shift. An emotional meeting was held the next night at the University Y, at which many people expressed the view that this was a political killing, that right-wingers had assassinated perhaps the most visible leftist in town.[92] They "wanted to take to the streets." Much of this talk came "from people who had been George's dear friends, and who had differed with him in recent months, and then felt like shit, because they loved him so much . . . people were just wrecked by it."

Mariann Wizard did the city fathers a favor by talking the group out of any destructive action. She was unsure that the murder had been an assassination, and moreover, she felt that violence "would have been an embarrassment . . . to [George's] life," since he believed in nonviolent change. But his death, she feels, did leave a residue of fear and timidity among the campus left. Moreover, it created a "serious leadership vacuum," with Nightbyrd and Pardun more involved by then in national SDS than in the local scene and with others reluctant to assume leadership roles. Mariann thus found herself thrust into such a position, speaking more and taking more control in meetings than she ever had before. For her skills at listening, Alice Embree renamed her "Wizard," and she used the name for decades afterward. At this time Dick Reavis also began exercising a greater leadership role. Indeed, Wizard thinks that if George Vizard had lived, he would have challenged the version of Marxism-Leninism that Reavis and the FPL advanced.[93]

Although Wizard's increased authority marked the first time a romantically unattached woman had gained such a position in Austin SDS, it was typical of the new left that her initial path to authority lay in her relationship to her late husband. In the early years of SDS-UT, a set of couples comprised the inner circle, framing most debates and sometimes making decisions in private that had not been made in chapter meetings: Nightbyrd and Embree, Perez and Pardun, Scott and Charlotte Pittman, and, a bit later, the Vizards, Trudy and Bobby Minkoff, and Thorne Dreyer and Carol Neiman. Of the women, only Embree and Perez spoke for themselves at the rambling chapter meetings, at which anyone who wished supposedly could speak ad infinitum but at which a series of men, such as Nightbyrd or Gary Thiher, another chapter leader, typically held forth, sometimes merely to "demonstrate [their] knowledge of international working-class history for forty-five minutes." Embree was "stunned" that Perez, a "petite, feisty woman," would take the floor and hold it as she did. Yet Wizard recalls that despite this, Perez "was viewed, at least in part, as an extension of Robert's ego."[94]

Robert Pardun, however, believes that this was not "a particularly oppressive time to women."[95] It may seem that the position of women in the new left was no worse than in American culture at large, but in a movement that declaimed a radically egalitarian creed, this rationalization ultimately proved inadequate. Moreover, in the world of student activism, from the women's perspective, things had actually changed for the worse. Gender relations were surely more hierarchical in SDS than in the liberal student activism of the immediate pre–new left period, since that activism was based in the Student YMCA–YWCA, which ensured at least a minimal representation of women in leadership roles. Between 1958 and 1963, the single most important activist leader on the UT campus was a woman, Casey Hayden. Although her talents were estimable, in themselves they do not explain her ability to rise so far. Institutional differentiation by gender was considered retrograde, culturally conservative, by the radicals of the 1960s, but in practice, the institutional looseness of SDS resulted in a rule by the most aggressive and garrulous, and this turned out to mean a rule by men.[96] A loosening of cultural constraints accompanied these institutional changes, so that the decorum of the older activism, now viewed as straitlaced, gave way to an ethos of "free expression." The earlier regime of politesse afforded women greater political opportunities and recommended to men a more tempered mode of behavior than did the liberationist culture of the mid-1960s. With respect to personal relations and their reflections in political behavior, the SDS activists were far from the rebels they styled themselves.

The Power Elite Revisited

Only in April 1967 did the Texas new left do what it had wished to do all along—confront the power structure. The group had devoted most of its energy to protesting segregation, but it was not in the vanguard of that battle. When the SDS chapter was formed in Austin, President Lyndon Johnson had acted personally to integrate the UT faculty club on a visit to town, shortly after Kennedy was assassinated.[97] On the issue of Jim Crow, the "power elite" was busily capitulating, realizing that the free enterprise system, of whose beauties establishmentarian Texans never tired of singing, might be the stronger for it.

But two developments brought young white students face-to-face with sharper and more united resistance from above. First was the metamorphosis of the early new left complaint about the impersonality, even the dehumanization, of life in rapidly expanding universities—a complaint with which the more sensitive of campus administrators sympathized—into a left-wing critique of the university's functions in contemporary American society. Second was the Vietnam War.

In 1964 Mario Savio labeled the "multiversity" of Clark Kerr (the chancellor of the University of California at Berkeley) a "machine"—inhuman, productive of alienation, not authenticity.[98] Students on campuses across the country, in step with a cultural trend toward sexual liberalization, sought to do away with parietal rules that governed student life and that weighed most heavily on female students to prevent their virtue from being besmirched. The new left stood at the forefront of this move, arguing that paternalism was no way to encourage the vigorous citizenship required for participatory democracy. A demand for "student power"—for meaningful training in citizenship—ensued, and the SDS chapter in Austin offered slates for student government offices in the springs of 1966, 1967, and 1968 on this basis, calling for a student "bill of rights," the institution of a pass–fail grading system, the availability of contraceptive materials at the campus health center, and the institution of a "peace studies" program to match the ROTC program on campus. Eventually SDS advocated a student union that might call strikes, and, most radical, it argued that students and faculty should together determine the content of the curriculum and also should elect the regents. These platforms suggested that alienation and tyranny could be dealt a blow at the same time.[99]

By chance, in 1963 a new generation of business-beholden Democratic politicians from Texas installed themselves in new and finer residences, namely, Johnson in the White House and his former fund-raiser, John Connally, in the Texas governor's mansion. In his six years as governor, Connally appointed uniformly conservative regents to preside over the university. This was the golden age of university expansion, with U.S. college enrollments rising from two million to seven million between 1950 and 1968.[100] UT was becoming a "university system," absorbing and expanding formerly private schools and building new campuses, and Connally made little secret that he viewed the attendant plant construction as a patronage bonanza for his campaign contributors and cronies.[101] In a setting in which the uses of power were so open, C. Wright Mills's concept of a "power elite," an interlocking set of high-level decision makers in the tripartite bureaucracies of business, the military, and the civilian government who worked in concert for common goals, seemed far less outlandish than it did in places in which the powerful were more solicitous of liberal sensibilities.[102]

The public face that the power elite showed to students was that of the regents' chairman, Frank Erwin, a member of Phi Beta Kappa who affected a rough manner, seen on football Sundays decked out in his burnt orange Longhorn blazer, carrying a drink across San Jacinto Avenue from the pregame party in the Arts Building to the supposedly dry stadium. He also might be observed tooling around town in his orange-and-white Cadillac or in frequent consultation with state legislators, from whom he extracted unprecedented appropriations for the university. Erwin also happened to be the Texas representative on the Democratic National Committee, as well as a lawyer for Texas banks and oil companies. Sophisticated, nationalized and internationalized wealth had succeeded the "ruddy nabobs and crossroads potentates" of old in Texas, and the regents came from the ranks of its lawyers and lobbyists, including former U.S. congressmen, who invariably were conservative Democrats. Oil, construction, and banking were the most important clients. Because of his inclination toward public involvement in campus controversies, Erwin took on—for liberals as well as leftists in Texas—the role of "devil in the life of the mind, the marauder in the university."[103]

Erwin seemed almost to welcome this image of a bull in a china shop, such as when President Johnson came to UT for a birthday party for Governor Connally, held in a university building. A large antiwar demonstration was in progress outside, and Erwin ranted that "a bunch of dirty nothins" should not be able to spoil the fine time that he had arranged for these great men. The phrase became a popular tool of ridicule among students, an enterprising few of whom produced buttons seen around Austin reading "I'm a Dirty Nothin."[104]

Some of this opprobrium attached to the country's president, whose recent history did not prepare his fellow Texans for the liberalism of his presidential vision. It remains unknown to many from other parts of the United States that Johnson was never part of the liberal wing of the Democratic Party in Texas. After his New Deal period in the 1930s, he drew closer to the state's wealthy interests and walked a tightrope between the party's reactionary and liberal factions. All his close associates, however, were "conservatives," which in this context meant that they viewed government largely as a mechanism for placing public power at the disposal of big business. Chief among those intimates were Connally and Erwin, who routinely met with the president in the 1960s when he returned home on visits. Johnson was no more polished than Erwin, and liberals and leftists alike in his home state viewed him as something of an embarrassment. He revealed all the crude provincialism of their region to the world, in contrast to Kennedy's cosmopolitanism. Clear-eyed political analysis, guilt by association, and class-based derision combined in what one observer called "the permanent, irrational hatred" that the Texas left displayed toward the illustrious alumnus of Southwest Texas State Teachers' College.[105]

For all that Johnson's largesse toward higher education benefited the liberal arts, he claimed that he was most concerned that the campuses produce engineers in sufficient numbers to facilitate U.S. economic growth in the 1960s and afterward. He evoked a postscarcity politics when he envisioned a world in which "the city of man serves not only the needs of the body and the demands of commerce but the desire for beauty and hunger for community." But commerce came first, the foundation of all else. This duality of vision, this tension between crass capitalism and "the great society," mirrored the tension between the conventional wisdom and the peculiarly idealistic view of many mid-twentieth-century Americans concerning the function of the university. Ronnie Dugger expressed the same outraged disillusionment as did the new left:

> From Texas we are given a prevision of the future for mass higher education. The students become ingredients to be fit into an evolving corporation-dominated civilization as the universities cease to be free and stimulating places of learning conducted for the students' culture and development and become the new adjuncts of corporate and governmental bureaucracies.[106]

Universities once had served to provide cultural polish and a uniformity of outlook to the sons of the wealthy. The meritocratic children of the swollen midcentury middle class thought they likewise were going to college to receive "culture" and encouragement of their creativity besides. Once there, however, they began to realize that university expansion was meant not to broaden the ranks of the old upper class but to train a newly expanded middle stratum of salaried functionaries.[107] This realization took shape as the new left's theory of the "new working class," which I discuss later. Out of these frustrated middle-class dreams arose a surprisingly penetrating insight.

Then there was the Vietnam War, which Johnson took north of the seventeenth parallel in early 1965, shortly after winning a landslide election to the presidency as the peace candidate. For reasons that I enumerate in chapter 6, between 1965 and 1967, SDS became the country's leading vehicle of student protest against the war. Moreover, the Texas contingent of SDS took the lead in arguing in the national organization during this period that the new left should dive headfirst into antiwar protest. Robert Pardun, traveling to campuses around the Southwest, found that students everywhere wanted to know where SDS stood on the war. But nowhere was the agitation more fraught with tension than in the president's hometown, at what the president and his friends considered his university. It did not go unnoticed that these friends considered the war a further boon to their businesses, adding credence to the version of power elite theory that became known as the theory of the "military–industrial complex."

In the two years after an Easter 1965 demonstration that SDS organized at the LBJ Ranch outside Austin, where Johnson had gone to escape the national protest rally that SDS put together in Washington, the war escalated relentlessly and steeply, and the protests became correspondingly angry. In April 1967 Alice Embree and Dick Reavis arranged for Stokely Carmichael, avatar of black power, to speak at UT as part of a series of springtime protests. This, together with the SDS student power campaign, generated an atmosphere of controversy on campus. Soon afterward, Vice President Hubert Humphrey came to town to defend his administration's war policy to the Texas legislature.

SDS called an outdoor meeting to plan a protest rally, and Chancellor Harry Ransom, displaying uncharacteristic iron—and leading many to wonder who really was calling the shots—issued a statement proclaiming, "This meeting has been specifically and officially disapproved. Any student organization deliberately ignoring this decision will be eliminated from the list of General Student Organizations"; that is, SDS would no longer be approved as a campus group.[108] SDS considered this an arbitrary attempt to control political discussion, since Ransom cited no university rule that the meeting would be violating, and so went ahead with its plans. "We were really hell-bent on replaying the Berkeley episode, if at all possible," says Paul Pipkin, meaning the Free Speech Movement.[109] The meeting thus became a rally against the war and also for free speech.

During the rally, none other than Frank Erwin appeared, standing across from the speakers' platform, conspicuously gesturing to an aide. The next day, the capitol rally was held that prompted George Vizard's subsequent arrest, described earlier. The university administration carried out its threat, barring SDS from the campus. Erwin secured a restraining order keeping off campus the nonstudents who had been arrested, citing as one of the reasons for their exclusion their opposition to U.S. foreign policy. Furthermore, six students found themselves charged with violating campus rules and were told to await hearings before a disciplinary board. These six included Alice Embree, Gary Thiher, Dick Reavis, and David

Mahler, all members of the SDS slate running for campus offices. It was something more than a marginal opinion on campus and around town that those held responsible for the rally were carefully chosen, perhaps by Erwin himself, as a means of repressing the campus left, whose program was getting too close to arrangements concerning which the men of power would not consider capitulating.[110]

The impact on the local left was mixed. The six students put up a spirited defense with the help of some tenacious libertarians from the UT Law School and got off with probation. Embree left school and departed from Texas (as did Nightbyrd; they both went to New York, where they joined in the tumult at Columbia University one year later), not returning until 1969.[111] Reavis moved decisively to the left shortly afterward and abandoned (at least theoretically) the campus as the main site of radical agitation. The UFM mobilized several thousand students in mass meetings, day and night, for a period of a week, on behalf of political freedom.

The UFM was quite limited as a political vehicle, however, with political liberty the only basis of the coalition. Students in general at UT, united though they were on this issue, were far less militant than their counterparts in the national media spotlight at Berkeley or Columbia, and the same was true of the campus left. The Texas students did not occupy campus administration buildings, as students did with Berkeley's Sproul Hall in late 1964, Columbia's Hamilton Hall in 1968, and Harvard's University Hall in 1969, a tactic that led to arrests and violence that in turn prevented the student uprisings at those schools from sputtering out, as was the UFM's fate by the semester's end.[112]

Nonetheless, for all this, the UFM also strengthened the campus left. SDS-UT already had started to draw more than one hundred students to its meetings before these events, and the UFM doubled its size; by the fall of 1967 it numbered perhaps five hundred, becoming, by some estimates, the biggest chapter in the country. Moreover, many who didn't join SDS now looked to it for political guidance.[113] SDS was strongly positioned to agitate among students after it regained its licit status in November 1967, since its program was gaining adherents and its willingness to defy authority had created an aura of heroism that also had its following.[114] The irony is that soon thereafter, SDS—reeling from the violence it experienced, under pressure from the FPL contingent in its ranks, struggling to find political methods commensurate with its escalating political rhetoric, and moving to a new, more organizationally dispersed means of agitating among its white youth constituency—lost its place at the cutting edge of radical politics; it even lost its role as the embodiment of the new left.

"The Young Intelligentsia": Adventures of an Idea

By 1966, the new left and the African American movement concurrently reached the conclusion that the interracial civil rights movement of the early 1960s was insufficient as a means to the social change that both desired. The black power tendency that ascended in the civil rights movement between 1964 and 1966 asserted that the black movement needed to operate independent of white control, which was defined broadly, in order to allow African Americans to pursue their own interests without interference and to use the black movement as an incubator of citizenship skills (much as the new left sought to use its movement to prepare the way for participatory democracy).[115] Consequently, in 1966, SNCC excluded its few remaining white members.[116]

The new left agreed with this analysis, and it became a crucial point of division between white liberals and radicals at mid-decade. Older whites, like Casey Hayden, had made the interracial civil rights movement their "church" and felt bereft when they were told to leave, but younger new left radicals' reaction to black power was enthusiastic.[117] In the fall of 1966, the *Rag*, the new "underground" newspaper that members of the Austin SDS chapter had begun publishing, prominently featured a vigorous defense of black power doctrine, clearly aimed at a white audience.[118] In late 1965 Paul Pipkin discussed the implication of black power: a separate radical white movement. "Now, I can hear the howls already," he said. " 'What do you mean, a WHITE movement?!!' " Given recent political developments, he said, this was only realistic.[119] The doubts extended to those positioned on the border between liberalism and the left, such as the journalist Andrew Kopkind, who claimed one year later, in the wake of riots in black neighborhoods in several cities around the country, "To be white and a radical in America . . . is to see horror and feel impotence."[120]

This feeling of political "impotence" was due to the scuttling of the left–liberal dream of an independent interracial political force in the country's mainstream, the kind of force that the abortive National Conference for New Politics (NCNP) tried to develop in the fall of 1967. Many insurgent white liberals were unsure of where to take their politics outside this interracialist vision.[121] Not so the new left. In the summer of 1966, an SDS couple from Austin, the Freudigers, visited Lowndes County, and they reported, accurately, SNCC's new message to white leftists: "Go make your own revolution."[122] In the second half of the 1960s, the new left in Texas worked to find a way to make a revolution it could call its own. The first step in doing so was to embrace the idea of the new left as a white movement, in theory as well as in practice.

The new left was able to do this in part because—despite the centrality of race in the new left's social vision—from the new left's origin, its members felt that American society harbored two different sources of authenticity and agency: the colonized and the young. C. Wright Mills argued vociferously in 1960 that leftists should not look to the industrial working class for insurgent leadership, and he did his best to anoint students instead as the new vanguard. "Who is it that is getting fed up? Who is it that is getting disgusted with what Marx called 'all the old crap'? Who is it that is thinking and acting in radical ways? All over the world . . . the answer is the same: it is the young intelligentsia."[123] This shocking departure in leftist political thought found receptive ears in SDS, in which a discussion of "the intellectual and social change" ensued. It was clear that "the intellectual" stood for "the young intelligentsia," which in turn was code for the young, white, college-educated middle class that provided SDS's membership. The conflation of "youth" with white youth was the connection that opened the path to the easy acceptance of black power by the white left.

Between 1963 and 1965, the intelligentsia and the poor were seen as constituencies competing for SDS's attention. The "interracial movement of the poor" seemed to win, with most of the new left's leaders moving into collective houses in cities around the country to do local organizing work in Economic Research and Action Projects (ERAPs), shrugging off criticism from Al Haber that the ERAPs represented a "cult of the ghetto" with little radical content. But in 1965, the arrival of the prairie power cohort, representing the expanding baby boom on the campuses, gave new impetus to a "young intelligentsia" strategy.[124]

The debate between the old guard and the new activists was joined when Jeff Nightbyrd and Tom Hayden squared off at the organization's national convention in June 1965, held in Kewadin, Michigan, during a session on "Agents of Social Change," chaired by Robb Burlage. Hayden defended the ERAP strategy, which Nightbyrd saw as "these old kind[s] of lefty ideas, old ideas about the dispossessed and labor and that crap. And I said campuses, that's where it's happening. I mean, it didn't take a genius." The issue of organizational centralization versus decentralization and the brewing debate over the importance of antiwar work were conflated with the argument over the poor versus students as target constituencies. Nightbyrd argued in favor of decentralization and antiwar agitation because both these positions made sense in the context of the campus-based organizing approach he favored. He contended that social and cultural conditions had intensified the feelings of alienation in society's middle strata, making the middle class—by which he meant those who could go to college—a fertile field for radical agitation.[125]

Clearly, Nightbyrd meant that the unhappiness that students in Berkeley had expressed in recent months about life in the multiversity was only the tip of a middle-class iceberg of dissatisfaction with life in a bureaucratic society and that the radicalization of college students offered a path to an insurgency in the American social mainstream. Gitlin made the connections explicit:

> The largely unconscious intuition of 1965 was this: Suppose the New Left were only apparently small. Suppose it were actually the thoughtful, active "vanguard" of a swelling social force, one that embodied the future forming in the cocoon of the present the way Marx's proletariat was supposed to do. Suppose that SDS stood for students-as-a-whole, and students-as-a-whole stood for the young. . . . With a bit of subconscious imagination, the longhaired, dope-smoking Texans who showed up at Kewadin could be seen as the advance guard of the new generational armies.[126]

Again, the promise of a link between the new left and the larger currents of the postwar youth culture tantalized.

Actually, the Texas SDS group had earlier shown an interest in organizing the poor as an insurgent constituency, but this approach had evolved toward the campus-based strategy. Before 1965, the Texans had sought to work among poor white southerners, believing that racism among poor whites historically had helped thwart the development of class-based leftist politics in the South. They felt that in particular, the Populist movement of the late nineteenth century had been a promising effort that had fallen victim to racism, and they thought they could perform no more important task than to help southern whites become "innoculated [*sic*] against racism."[127]

One of the Austin chapter's first events in 1964 was a fund-raiser for the striking coal miners of Hazard, Kentucky—where SDS had established its only rural ERAP—held in the Ichthus coffeehouse in the Methodist Student Center, complete with folksinging from Carolyn Hester, a well-known Austin product.[128] In April the chapter sent fourteen members to the "Conference on Poverty" that SDS held in Hazard.[129] George Goss, a white Austin activist, concluded that the situation in Kentucky was economically and politically similar to that in East Texas, the area where the bulk of African American Texans lived and also the stronghold of white racism in the Lone Star State.[130]

The Freedom Summer experience, however, seemed to cast doubt on the promise of this approach. While most of the civil rights activists in Mississippi that summer worked in the black areas of the Delta region, the Texas group took on a different assignment, working in the so-called white folks' project in Mobile, Alabama. On their way to Mississippi, they visited the Highlander Folk School in Tennessee, an extremely important education center for southern radicals, which provided links between black and white activists as well as between the old and new lefts. Myles Horton and his associates at Highlander had ideas about organizing in the South that no doubt encouraged the SDS activists in their plan to cultivate support for civil rights among poor and working-class whites. The "white folks' project," however, made little headway. Robert Pardun and Judy Perez (who at that time went by Pardun, her common-law husband's name) feel this made them only more determined to pursue this line of work, and as late as the end of 1965, Pipkin averred that SDS-UT "intend[s] to build a movement of the poor and working-class whites, hoping to ally it as soon as possible with the Negro movements."[131]

Yet shortly after Freedom Summer, in a presidential election season, SDS-UT activists like Nightbyrd, Robert Pardun, and Scott Pittman moved to a different approach in terms of both constituency and political method, making overtures to the Texas Democratic Coalition, a mainstream liberal group. "We believe that the goals of Texas SDS are substantially similar to those of the Democratic Coalition," the students asserted.[132] The key liberal activist in these discussions was Lawrence Goodwyn.[133] SDS developed a proposal for a series of conferences for college students around the state "to educate students on the problems of poverty, peace, civil rights, unemployment, and civil liberties." They also hoped to send a couple of organizers, "one Negro and one white," around the state to organize students at the forty-three colleges in Texas.[134]

The SDS-UT activists hoped the Democratic Coalition would foot the bill. In return, the new left would cultivate a youth constituency that would enlarge the liberal electoral coalition in Texas, which seemed on the verge of a breakthrough. This scheme represented an abrupt turnabout from the politics of independent insurgency and a move toward the "realignment" politics that in national SDS was associated with the oldest, least militant faction—a group typically derided for its lingering attachment to the Democratic Party.[135] Yet in a conservative environment, a liberal, Democratic-led voting coalition may have seemed ambitious enough, especially when populist-inflected liberals like Goodwyn were involved. Several SDS-UT activists worked in the fall reelection campaign of Senator Ralph Yarborough, indicating that the new left group was indeed willing to make common cause for a genuine liberal candidacy. (Besides, said Gary Thiher, Yarborough's Republican opponent, George Bush, was a "reactionary.")[136]

Indeed, the lines of communication remained open between the new left and Texas liberals as long as there was a new left, because leftists could not take liberals for granted in a right-wing environment and because the populist streak in Texas liberalism made both camps take a more sanguine view of left–liberal cooperation than their northern or eastern counterparts did. For his part, *Observer* editor Greg Olds spoke for a united front, warning in 1967, "We must not presume . . . to judge our ideological allies too harshly. We need each other."[137] In 1968, the *Observer* and the *Rag* staged a "liberal–radical conference" which did not achieve the meeting of minds that the organizers had hoped for, in part because many liberals, including some of the scheduled speakers, stayed away.[138] Later that year, SDS activists and civil libertarian lawyers held a conference in the hill-country town of Wimberley to develop a legal defense network that could respond rapidly to the political indictments that were coming thick and fast.[139] Leftists continued to try to pry money out of better-heeled liberals.[140] We should not read too much into this conviviality, however. The leftists were more interested in liberal support for an independent left-wing project than they were in a political coalition. Goodwyn doubts that SDS-UT was firmly in favor of a realignment strategy even in 1964.[141] Most likely, the group's thinking on the sources and means of social change was in flux at that time.

Thus, from the SDS perspective, ambiguity was a virtue of the new Southern Student Organizing Committee (SSOC), begun in Nashville in 1964 by white civil rights activists to mirror SNCC's coordinating work among white liberal students in the South. SSOC pledged to be "multi-issue, rather than single-issue, oriented," and it had close links to SDS. But in light of the environment in which it operated, it pledged to be "virtually all-inclusive," bringing together "moderate" and "radical" southern whites.[142] Three Austin SDS activists had attended the Atlanta meeting where SSOC was planned, and Texas SDS leaders hoped they could both use SSOC as "a pool to draw talent from" and lead SSOC to the left, but within a year after its establishment, Nightbyrd complained that SSOC was developing a Young Democrat profile.[143] Although SDS hoped that SSOC could help spread the new left message to southern students, that task was left to SDS. Partly thanks to the travels of Robert Pardun and Nightbyrd throughout the Southwest, by 1965 there were SDS chapters in Houston, at Southern Methodist University in Dallas, and at the University of Oklahoma in Norman; and in the Southeast many more chapters were created, notably at Duke University and the University of Florida in Gainesville.[144]

In a horrid variation on the main theme of fratricide in the new left in the late 1960s, SSOC became a political football in the competition between PL and the SDS "national office cadre." SSOC had fulfilled its aim of becoming a coordinating body, providing links in the South between SDS and liberal groups like the Southern Conference Education Fund (SCEF) and NSA. Despite its apparent irrelevance to SDS factionalism, each of the two main SDS groups alternately wooed and attacked SSOC. PL denounced its "liberal" and "reactionary" politics and its acceptance of money from liberal foundations. At the March 1969 SDS National Council meeting held in Austin, both factions voted to dissolve SSOC, which had been damaged so badly by outside machinations that it actually disbanded on command.[145]

The SDS activists ended their mid-decade period of strategic uncertainty by tailoring their program to fit the political opportunities that seemed most promising. Instead of farming in the rocky soil of white working-class or poor southern communities, they gravitated toward the loamy ranges of the campus. The "student power" campaigns and campus antiwar work of the 1966–1968 period, addressing the hottest issues among students, proceeded in earnest. So did the efforts of the left to get involved in the mushrooming counterculture as a way of making the prized connection to the white youth masses.

It was more than mere convenience or expediency, however, that led to the new strategy. The idea of "the young intelligentsia" as a radical force received a new lease on life at mid-decade, and this updated idea answered the desire for authenticity among the new left's constituency as well as the political fix in which the movement found itself. The major contributions came from Greg Calvert and Carl Davidson, who were elected SDS national officers in June 1966, at a convention held in Iowa. Calvert, from an impoverished petit bourgeois background in Washington State by way of Iowa and the Sorbonne, and Davidson, a philosophy student in Nebraska who hailed from the steel country of western Pennsylvania and sported a handlebar moustache and a corncob pipe, seemed to epitomize prairie power. Davidson's signature slogan was "student syndicalism," indicating the victory of the decentralist perspective that the Texas group had first pushed, as well as of the emphasis on campus organizing.[146] The term *student syndicalism* also evoked the allure of "direct action" and signaled the new left's appropriation of the pre-Communist, American leftist past, especially the appeal of the Wobbly figure, which Mills had used as a favorite term of endearment. In early 1968, Calvert, disillusioned with what he viewed as the Leninist posturing and power plays in the national office of SDS and smarting from personal attacks on his bisexuality, moved to Austin at the invitation of Carol Neiman, who had started the *Rag* in Austin with Thorne Dreyer.[147] Calvert, whose grandfather actually was a

Wobbly and who was trained in economic and social history, advanced the idea of the new working class. This concept, shaped by the writings of French sociologists, was the only major insight into American social structure and social change to emerge from the new left.[148]

As discussed earlier, the new working class was the stratum of college-educated managerial and technical employees, usually salaried, who were increasingly numerous and important in the changing U.S. economy. According to Calvert, they commonly viewed themselves as middle class because they enjoyed a relatively high standard of living and because their white collars and college degrees conferred a social status at least above that of manufacturing workers with a high school education. Yet this was a false consciousness. Consumer blandishments and a sense of superiority to industrial workers blinded the new working class to their disempowerment on the job, to their true relation to the means of production—in short, to the fact that they, too, were exploited and alienated workers.[149] As Austin radical Harvey Stone put it, "We, no less than the guy in the assembly line, will be members of the working class; the extent of our salary or the color of our collar will not alter our relationship to the companies for which we will be working."[150] In Calvert's thoroughly Marxist view, it was the objective alienation of the college-educated young from their own labor and its products that produced the malaise commonly referred to as *alienation*.[151]

The theory of the new working class drew a connection between the evident discontent among college-educated youth and the new left critique of the university as a tool of economic elites, a critique that gathered force with every year that the war continued. At the beginning of the 1966/1967 school year, not only did Austin SDS activists argue that universities served merely "to produce the personnel needed to ensure the smooth functioning of an advanced capitalist society," but George Vizard contended specifically that the higher education system produced "technocrats" for the "war machine."[152] In early 1967, national SDS activists publicized the Selective Service System's (SSS) intention to use the military draft and its system of deferments to "channel" personnel toward both war-related industries and other enterprises that were deemed economically important by the government—"developing more effective human beings in the national interest," in the memorable words of General Lewis Hershey, director of the SSS—suggesting that universities and the military–industrial complex worked hand in glove to manipulate and exploit students.[153]

The concept of the new working class depicted the new left's constituency as central to a war and a social system that the new left increasingly wished to destroy and also asserted this group's exploitation, a subliminal requirement for radical authenticity. A popular idea, it attracted leftists in Austin and around the country, including the influential Robert Pardun, who preached the new gospel. Dick Howard, a student of philosophy and an Austin SDS activist who traveled to France in the late 1960s, also liked this concept and helped spread it by means of his own work.[154] In short, the theory of the new working class painted the new left as the vanguard of the new proletariat. This identification may have held a greater appeal at public universities, at which many students had working-class parents and students generally were trained for occupational niches that, if salaried, were far from exalted in either status or remuneration. At the same time, however, this theory sought to moot many common understandings of class—class as income, class as status, class as educational attainment—in favor of a grand alliance of all those who served capitalist employers.

This was the theory's great value in facilitating the new left's movement away from the possibility of a strategy based on organizing among the white poor and the working class, as traditionally defined. The theory of the new working class validated the complaints of college students by asserting that material deprivation was not the only legitimate source of unhappiness, that in fact it was not the most politically salient one. Dreyer summed up the feelings that the new left had harbored for years when he declared in early 1968 that "alienation isn't restricted to the poor."[155] There was no longer any need to feel guilty about saying so. Gone were the lingering doubts about the respectability of abandoning a traditional leftist agenda based on the search for economic equity.

In Texas, a focus on power, not wealth, was urged by Bob Speck, who really did fit the ballyhooed SDS-UT image of working-class anarchism. An autodidact from the dirt-poor "cedar-chopper" subculture of East Texas and older than the other SDS activists in town, Speck had gotten thrown out of the navy for organizing an anarchist reading group aboard a submarine. He had spent time in the Baltimore ERAP, as an SDS organizer on the West Coast, and in the SDS national office, where his "scrappy" manner did not sit well with everyone.[156] "While the resolving of the problems of poverty, automation, etc., would be nice," he blithely told his fellow Austin activists in late 1965, "the major problem of our time is the issue of powerlessness."[157] Likewise, Carl Davidson took inspiration from the tradition of labor syndicalism because, he pointed out, "in the labor struggle, the syndicalist unions worked for industrial democracy and workers' control, rather than better wages and working conditions."[158]

Speck's remark came in a presentation aptly entitled "The Mechanics of Social Change," at a retreat the Austin chapter held following their difficult experience in Chicago during the summer of 1965. Here the leading activists in the group distinguished between their local movement and national SDS. "Last year our Texas chapter was a real 'community'—we treated one another as people, with affection and respect," Judy Pardun observed; "somehow we all felt it was necessary to treat people as individuals, not things," and thus they created "a real alternative to the present American society." By contrast, the national officers of SDS had treated her like any employee, and she felt "totally alienated."[159] Her husband spoke of the "spirit of comeraderie [*sic*], honesty, and egalitarianism" that inspired him to get involved in the new left and asserted that young people came to the new left in general "because they are looking for a group which can offer a community in which they can be *real individuals* rather than the game-players of the society."[160] In other words, they wanted to transcend a condition of inauthenticity. Speck refashioned alienation as powerlessness, giving it political legitimacy and fusing the goal of participatory democracy, in which "each person has to . . . become a leader" to wield some fraction of power over her or his own life, with the movement from alienation into authenticity.[161] Whether in the political economy, in the university, or in the left itself, young people had a radical project in their search for their own liberation from alienation. This was the message.

The same message gained ground around the country. Its locus classicus was a speech Greg Calvert gave at Princeton University in February 1967, reprinted in the *National Guardian*. Here Calvert deployed one of the more rhetorically effective tools in the new left arsenal: the accusation of liberalism. Despite all the kinship that leftists and liberals may have felt, the suggestion that one was peddling a liberal line (a suggestion whose sting Calvert himself later felt) held the power to send young radicals scurrying to repudiate one another. "The liberal reformist is always engaged in 'fighting someone else's battles,'" Calvert asserted. Furthermore, liberals were motivated largely by the "guilt" they felt at their own condition of privilege and comfort and so wished to make others materially more comfortable as well. He claimed the liberal "wants everyone to be 'white, happy, and middle class.'" This was oppressive. Seeming to invite charges of political masochism, Calvert ventured, "We owe SNCC a deep debt of gratitude for having slapped us brutally in the face with the slogan of black power, a slogan which said to white radicals: 'Go home and organize in white America which is your reality and which only you are equipped to change.'" The new left had to organize a radical constituency "in white America," which became the title of the speech in print form. "If no such constituency can be developed," Calvert said, making crystal clear the new left's impasse, "then our only hope lies with external agencies."[162]

It was already well established in the new left that liberalism marked those who resisted the logic of black power; now Calvert linked such irredentist interracialism to materialist politics. He was speaking at a conference where other participants had argued that material desires formed the engine of revolutionary change, and he considered this "a perversion and vulgarization of revolutionary thought and a misreading of history." Rather than searches for comfort or enrichment, Calvert declared, "all *authentically* revolutionary movements are struggles for human freedom," attempts to erase the "contradictions between human potentiality and oppressive actuality." He joined this historical interpretation of radical politics as existential politics—as efforts to transcend alienated existence and enact a fulfilled "potentiality" or, as the young Marx put it, a "species essence"—with black power doctrine's emphasis on cultural difference.[163]

This led to Calvert's final conclusion: "No individual, no group, no class is genuinely engaged in a revolutionary movement unless their struggle is a struggle for their own liberation." He stood in favor of a multiracial, multiclass coalition for social change, but that coalition, based on a "common humanity," could emerge only from a whole range of struggles in which distinct social groups discovered this humanity through "the discovery of oneself as *one of the oppressed*."[164] Marx had thought that the proletariat would form a universal class that suffered both alienation and immiseration; the new left now separated these two forms of mortification and elevated alienation above poverty as the core of oppression. Alienation became simultaneously the polar opposite of authenticity and the sign of authentic political agency. These connections had been present, though submerged, since the new left's inception. By 1967 they became explicit and dominant, although they did not go unchallenged.

What Don't You Need?

Even as new working-class theory ascended in the new left, various tendencies in the movement continued to argue, with increasing stridency, that some group other than white, college-educated youth constituted the "key sector" that would lead the way to revolution and that the new left had to serve as either a vanguard leading or foot soldiers following the other group. This debate was the substance of the factional strife that destroyed SDS in 1968/1969, during the same span of time when most Americans were engrossed in the traumatic events of the Tet offensive, the assassination of Martin Luther King Jr., the turbulent Democratic National Convention in Chicago, and the fateful ascension of Richard Nixon to the presidency.

In Austin, SDS found a new leader in Larry Caroline, a philosophy professor who began teaching at UT in 1967 and who ultimately was fired after he called for "a revolution" at an antiwar gathering that year. (He said, referring to the American social system, "The whole bloody mess has to go" if the war was to end. The sanguinary metaphor brought him much grief, as the local headlines screamed that this "corruptor of youth" had called for bloody revolution. A great deal of the SDS chapter's energies in the next one and a half years went toward protesting Caroline's pending dismissal.)[165] He furnished intellectual authority for the local left's developing politics, offering classes on Marxism at the "free university" that Dick Howard and other activists established as an alternative to university education and articulating an existentialist or humanist Marxism, as did many other leftists at that time, which drew heavily on Marx's discussion of alienation.

Caroline reflected the state of new left thinking on racial matters, as on others. Although he offered a philosophical viewpoint that bolstered the existentialist emphasis on self-liberation, Caroline retained a very strong concern with racism, feeling, as Alice Embree did, that racial inequality in the United States could not simply be reduced to economic causes.[166] He befriended Larry Jackson, who was the leading African American militant in Austin starting in 1968, and because of his support for black militancy, Caroline became a thorn in the side of his erstwhile mentor, John Silber, who had become dean of the College of Arts and Sciences at UT. Now, outraged by black power politics and still defending the interracialism that had made him the most prominent liberal on campus since the mid-1950s, Silber started moving toward his later neoconservatism and worked to get Caroline fired.[167]

In the second half of the 1960s, the white activists of the new left had an odd relationship with African American activists and with the very issue of race. White leftists expressed a fervent political solidarity with militant black activists, but only tenuous organizational ties joined the two groups. Political coordination was infrequent and strained. In the late 1960s, the new left operated "in white America," and antiracist activism was displaced by antiwar and countercultural activism in SDS and associated groups, yet the issue of race was never far from the minds of white leftists. They endorsed the doctrine of institutional separation but still longed for the occasional interracial contact, for the political legitimacy and aura of authenticity that it conferred.

The unexpected consequences of the new thinking on race became clear in an incident that occurred fairly early in this process of estrangement, at a national SDS conference at the University of Illinois during the Christmas 1965 vacation. Accounts of the conflict vary widely. Lee Ellis, a black Mississippi civil rights activist who had moved to Cleveland and joined the new left ERAP there, was one of the few African Americans attending the conference. Dickie Magidoff, a white SDS activist who worked with Ellis in Cleveland, remembers him as a "rough" character, from a different environment than most SDS members and prone to confront white activists about what Ellis perceived as their racism. Scott Pittman, one of the SDS-UT attendees, recalls that Ellis "strutted around" the conference, perhaps acting out a stereotype of black male machismo for an audience of awestruck white radicals. One morning during the conference, Charlotte Pittman, Scott's wife, slept late at the house where the Austin delegation was staying while all her friends went to the conference sessions. She awoke to find Ellis (whom she did not know), 250 pounds strong, standing in her bedroom. Ellis said something to the effect that he desired sexual relations with her. The situation was "touch-and-go," and she was frightened, but she managed to fend off his advances. Although she told few people about what had happened, still the SDS-UT members met to discuss what action they should take in response. Reports of aggressive "come-ons" by Ellis to other women at the conference circulated.[168]

Bob Speck seemed especially angry about Ellis's behavior. He took it upon himself to tell Ellis that if another such incident occurred, Speck would punch Ellis's lights out. Speck then reportedly did hear such a story and "cold-cocked" Ellis. Someone else from Texas called the local police, which infuriated many of the conference attendees, because Ellis was on the run from the authorities in Mississippi (which the Texas activists did not know). A screaming match ensued between the Texas contingent and everyone else. The conference participants considered forbidding Speck's participation in any further sessions. Carolyn Craven, one of the few nationally prominent black SDS activists, remembers Speck calling Ellis a "nigger," which Scott Pittman thinks quite possible, since Speck was a "reformed redneck." Craven viewed the Texas contingent generally as latecomers to the new left whose politics were not very radical, basically a "bunch of draft-dodging crackers." Many of the northern SDS members accused the Texas radicals of a lingering racism. The SDS-UT group insisted that even if all white people were racists, Ellis was still a "bully" and that this, not white racism, had caused the conflict.[169]

This incident can be viewed as a symbolically important continuation of the same explosive combination of racial and sexual interaction that had caused great turbulence in SNCC. Yet perhaps what was most significant about it was the distinctive line of argument advanced by the Texas group in defense of Speck's actions. Their viewpoint reveals the new currents of thought that the Texans were among the first white radicals to embrace.

Nightbyrd, who attended the Illinois conference, acknowledges that many northern SDS members viewed his group as southern racists. "We saw them as white liberals," he retorts, "who were basically rolling over because it was a black–white confrontation." He asserts that southern white leftists had earned their antiracist bona fides on the frontlines of civil rights battles and therefore felt confident enough to disown the blame for the conflict, whereas the northern whites, feeling a greater need to demonstrate their antiracism, did so by accusing the Texans of racism. He derides the northerners as "campus kids . . . their black–white ideal was theoretical."[170]

Nightbyrd invokes the "realist" theme that was, ironically, a prominent part of black power thinking on race relations. According to Kwame Ture (Stokely Carmichael) and Charles Hamilton, writing in 1967, it was time to banish sentiment from race relations. Like them, Nightbyrd recalls a time of testing in the past that tempered a simplistic interracialism and antiracism: "If you'd marched in picket lines and gone to jail . . . you knew how to read what was going on." He defends a hardheaded pursuit of group self-interest—"we were going to protect our people."[171] The "realist" turn in radical political thought, like Calvert's doctrine of self-liberation, ridiculed the politics of "guilt," which supposedly epitomized liberalism.

To some whites, the interior search for one's own complicity in oppression had grown tiresome, what seemed like an automatic cession of moral authority from whites to blacks had become unconvincing, and they began to view efforts to prove one's moral purity in matters of race as immature, less than radical. Although perhaps few realized it, the response of the Texans to this incident in a way foreshadowed a line of thought that was to gain ground in the new left. Almost four years later, Mariann Wizard expressed this tendency, complaining that the relations between black and white radicals were "based on guilt, intimidation and servility on the part of the whites." (It is intriguing in itself that only six months after the old guard–dominated Illinois conference considered barring Bob Speck from discussions for his behavior, the 1966 SDS national convention, overwhelmed by the prairie power constituency, put Speck on the group's national council.)[172]

This "farewell to white guilt" tendency competed in the later new left with the perhaps better-known continuation of white radical solidarity with militant black activists. This latter politics of solidarity was linked with the rise of anti-imperialist politics in the new left, with African Americans specifically cast as an "internal colony" that would join with the peoples of the Third World to overturn the world system of economic and racial hierarchy over which the United States presided. Such solidarity operated largely among movement celebrities and in the realm of the imagination. This politics emanated chiefly from the national office of SDS and, after the June 1969 split between the PL and anti-PL forces at the national convention of SDS, the group that championed this viewpoint became known as Weatherman.[173]

In the national office of SDS, a small (and unelected) contingent of Marxist-Leninists rose in authority in no small part because they claimed a close relationship to James Forman, the Marxist-inclined SNCC leader. (They published an SDS pamphlet by Forman, entitled *Liberation Will Come from a Black Thing*.)[174] When Forman's star moved past its apogee, the national office cadre looked to the Black Panther Party (BPP), founded in 1966 by Huey Newton and Bobby Seale in Oakland, California, to take SNCC's place in the new left's political dreamscape. The BPP was a strong candidate for this role, for even though it embraced black power, it was far friendlier to left-wing interracial coalitions than SNCC was. The Panthers became a strong presence in Chicago, and BPP representatives were available for guest appearances at national SDS gatherings there.

Neither the Panthers nor SNCC had much of an organizational presence in Texas, where militant black organizations were established locally in Dallas and Houston. Black activists were clustered at Texas Southern University in Houston, the scene of a shoot-out between police and black students in 1967.[175] Larry Jackson and Lee Otis Johnson, who at first were loosely associated with SNCC, were the African American radicals with whom the white Austin left had the closest relations. Jackson, from a well-off landowning family in East Texas and formerly an aide to U.S. Congressman George Bush, came to Austin in early 1968, possibly because he thought that "the only thing lacking [in East Austin] is a true black leader." Over the next few years, he was centrally involved in virtually every important militant black political effort in town, the most visible of which was the Community United Front (CUF), based in East Austin, which waged a successful battle with the support of white leftists to establish a free breakfast program for impoverished Austin children in UT's student union. For about three years, between 1968 and 1971, Jackson lived with Mariann Wizard.[176]

In the spring of 1968, Jackson persuaded the SDS-UT chapter to return to its earlier antiracist protest, and they organized demonstrations against a gas station owned by Don Weedon, who was well known locally for harassing both blacks and hippies. The interrracial demonstrations culminated in more than forty arrests, and a handful of radicals were put on trial, under an old Texas antiunion statute, as the putative ringleaders.[177] They included Jackson (who was charged with assaulting a police officer), Dick Reavis, a black student named Grace Cleaver, and Greg Calvert. Jackson and Reavis sat at one table, without counsel, and the other SDS activists mounted a separate defense. Reavis read from Mao's little red book, and Jackson gave speeches. (Jackson was convicted.)[178] Calvert views the SDS chapter's decision to follow Jackson's lead as based less on clear political thinking than on a desperate desire for solidarity with black activists. "It was hard for people at that point to say no to a black activist," he contends and thinks that Jackson understood this well.[179] Despite these events, though, by early 1969 Jackson expressed disappointment with the white Austin left because he was not convinced of their commitment to the African American movement and because he found infuriating the factional debates between FPL and the anarchist–new working-class wing of the SDS chapter (and he observed that many students who were interested in SDS did, too). At one point, he said that the lack of support he saw from white activists made him feel "castrated," indicating that the tendency to express political fears in the language of male sexual anxiety knew no racial bounds.[180]

"You become a revolutionary through struggle," Jackson intoned to white leftists in early 1969, appealing to their predilection for "direct action." But this offering requires a grain of salt. In the late 1960s and early 1970s, beneath the rhetoric of revolution and militance, amid university building takeovers and "Third World student strikes," and even occasional gunplay, many African American activists were moderating their political hopes and turning to traditional liberal interest-group politics. Gloria Edwards, director of CUF's Child Care Center in East Austin, remarked that in 1968, "all radicals"—by which she meant activists from the BPP, SNCC, and the National Welfare Rights Organization—"decided to work in the system to accomplish their goals."[181]

Indeed, a breakfast program for needy children, Larry Jackson's signal initiative in Austin, bore no discernible relation to "revolutionary" politics. In 1968, Jackson also organized a new black student group at UT, Afro Americans for Black Liberation (AABL), which compiled a list of demands that was given to the university administration. Although it included extravagant items, like the demand that the LBJ Library, then under construction, be renamed for Malcolm X (this elicited outrage from John Silber), shrewd observers saw that many of the demands, such as a black studies program and increased minority faculty hiring, were reforms that the university might grant with little pain.[182] One university administrator understood the emergent meliorism of black protest activity at this time, likening the difference between black and white student activists to the gulf between the American Federation of Labor and the Knights of Labor.

Universities well might accommodate the incremental demands of black students, but they were unable or unlikely to support the "utopian" wishes of white leftists.[183]

White leftists paid more attention to the militant rhetoric of black activists than to the details of their program, and this lack of heed contributed to the false expectations of imminent revolution that afflicted white leftists after 1968. The other contributing factors included the wave of campus protests and occupations between 1968 and 1970—wrought by the effective collaboration of white leftists, militant students of color, and intransigent administrators—and the expansion and increasing militance of the antiwar movement.

In 1969, the BPP issued an appeal for a "United Front against Fascism" in the United States, for a coalition between leftists and liberals of all races around a program of civil liberties and social reform. This was a logical response to the violence that the BPP was suffering at the hands of police agencies, who had taken their cue from the "law and order" politics that had gotten Richard Nixon elected president the year before. SDS largely ignored this call, and at the group's June convention in Chicago, the proto-Weatherman forces continued to look to the BPP as the vanguard of the revolution. PL recently had done a programmatic about-face and now opposed all forms of nationalism, including the brand offered by the BPP, as reactionary forces that would divide the industrial working class—which PL argued was the real vanguard. A Panther speaker at the convention made a grossly sexist comment about what he called "pussy power," and PL took the opportunity to complain loudly of this "male chauvinism" (PL never had cared about sexism before). The BPP subsequently threatened to read SDS out of the revolution if it did not spurn PL; then the anti-PL forces of the SDS national office bolted the convention, in order to keep PL from winning control over the organization. As Gitlin remarked, "The Weathermen had no qualms about dismantling the largest . . . American organization anywhere on the Left in fifty years." Both PL and Weatherman declared themselves "the real SDS," just as each had declared themselves the real "communists" at recent conventions.[184]

But this shadow dance was about to come to an end as each side in the faction fight discovered the irrelevance of its program to new left activists around the country. Becky Reavis was put on the national interim committee of SDS-PL—taking what might have been her husband's place, since Dick had been expelled for having an affair and thus damaging the wholesome image that PL wished to project—and was sent to New York and then around the country to deliver the new line to SDS chapters, apparently in the expectation that they would toe it. But SDS never had worked in that way, and it was not about to start.[185]

The national office cadre had issued a manifesto entitled "You Don't Need a Weatherman to Know Which Way the Wind Blows," from which came the Weatherman moniker. In Austin, the prevailing sentiment reflected the satiric line soon heard around the country, "You Don't Need a Rectal Thermometer to Know Who the Assholes Are." But this feeling applied to all the organized factions. (One blunt wit conveyed his disdain of factional competition at the 1968 national convention by nominating a garbage can for office; it lost narrowly.[186]) Factionalism itself was one of the things that had estranged many in Austin from national SDS as early as 1965, one of the things that indicated the SDS national leadership were still the "game players" of the old society. The Texas group colorfully evoked their feeling of disillusionment, saying that working for national SDS was "like getting saved by a traveling preacher, who you later find out is a drunkard and beats his wife."[187]

Weatherman found no recruits in Austin (though, interestingly, the group found some in the less important new left circles in Houston and Dallas).[188] The main factional presence in Austin was FPL, and this small contingent, perhaps only five or six, wreaked such havoc with the growing SDS chapter there as to provoke a hatred that remains acute even a quarter century later. At the first chapter meeting in the fall of 1968, four hundred students appeared, many of them inexperienced in radical politics but moving to the left at a time of social crisis. What the group needed was a plan of activities that spoke to the issues that had attracted the newcomers and an inviting program of political education that could solidify their commitment to leftist politics. Neither of these materialized, however, as the FPL group took the floor to issue Leninist pronouncements at every turn, refusing to debate their line and instead only repeating it, with the clear intention of preventing any proposals or voices besides their own from getting much of a hearing. FPL pushed its "Worker–Student Alliance" but never organized students to support wage workers; their program seemed entirely rhetorical. The students fled in droves. Larry Jackson noted, "I've watched as many as 600 people congregate at local sds chapter meetings. I saw 400 of them walk away before the meeting was over, strictly because of bullshit." Within a month, only twenty-five remained.[189]

Few were as articulate in their criticism of PL as Robert Pardun. He emphasized that "you could never *argue* with the PL people, you could never *convince* them of anything."[190] Mariann Wizard, whose Communist politics might have made her sympathetic to the PL line, in fact echoes this

criticisms.[191] In SDS, the normative mode of internal operation was persuasion, but PL members were not open to persuasion when interacting
with other SDS members. PL caucused before SDS meetings and decided
on their line, and they viewed meetings simply as a place where they would
work their will by winning votes. Something like a consensus was required
to implement any program in an SDS chapter like the one in Austin, and
the PL adherents never seemed to grasp this, thus undermining their own
efforts to take power.[192] By late 1968, SDS seemed simply "dysfunctional"
to rising leaders like Jeff Jones, who was elected student body president at
UT in 1970 on a left-wing student power platform. The group was "pretty
crazy," he recalls thinking, and he simply took his concerns elsewhere.[193]

Nor was the Weatherman approach to politics on the same frequency as
that of the more pragmatic Austin left, as one anecdote concerning a Texas
appearance by Bernardine Dohrn, a lawyer who became a national officer
of SDS in 1968/1969 and then one of the Weatherman leaders, indicates.
Dohrn had declared herself a "revolutionary communist," but Calvert contends that her willingness to play the role of revolutionary pinup also contributed to her popularity in the new left, a popularity that is revealing on
the character of the "feminism" that supposedly appeared in the last years of
SDS. Here Calvert gives full vent to his anger:

> When I first met her, she . . . was clad in . . . a bright orange sweater
> with a prominent lapel button announcing that "Fellatio Is Fun." Her
> taste for black leather boots and mini-skirts . . . made her a popular fig-
> ure with a certain segment of SDS's more macho male leadership. . . .
> A purge of the gay-to-bisexual element in SDS was the first order of
> the day for [Michael] Klonsky and Dohrn.[194]

Dohrn flew down from Chicago in late 1968 to attend the Wimberley legal
defense conference, a more successful counterpart to the BPP's "United
Front" gambit. Once there, Dohrn informed the attendees that they were
"liberal sellouts," that it was "counterrevolutionary" for them to accept the
authority of "bourgeois courts." This kind of performance might have
played well at the national office, but Calvert, who had organized the meeting to seek help for the left from liberal lawyers, was aghast. Fortunately for
his plans, "the Texas lawyers were elated at what seemed to them first-rate
camp theater." Pleased with the entertainment and aware that leftists in
Texas had a keener sense of the present political climate than did their
national "leaders," the lawyers went about their business. Dohrn continued
to hone her "revolutionary gun moll" routine.[195]

None of the factional groups cared for the "anarcho-syndicalist" tendency
that grew stronger in SDS-UT's last years, fueled by newcomers like Bill

Meachem, a philosophy graduate student from a religious Presbyterian background who arrived in Austin in 1968 after some time at Columbia. He found the new working-class analysis compelling, and he allied himself with the anarchist faction in the chapter, which also was known as the "new left" faction; PL and others were distancing themselves from the very term *new left*. Weatherman and PL alike loathed this anarchist sentiment, labeling it bourgeois and reactionary. It also spelled disaster for their own ambitions, since it conveyed a radical distrust of all national leadership. The anarchists returned the favor.[196]

The last national council meeting of a united SDS was held in Austin in March 1969, four months before the fateful Chicago SDS convention. Judy Smith, on her way to becoming the most important leader of the Austin left in its post-SDS phase, lived in a group house that kicked out some national SDS figures who were camping there, because the visitors had brought guns with them. "They had a very different image of themselves than we did in Austin," she reflects. Some local SDS activists simply stayed away from the meeting, which became a "donnybrook . . . contentious and unpleasant." Meachem and others (advised by Calvert) united in a "decentralist" or "anarchist" caucus to express the derision that many radicals felt for the entire factional conflict, but to no avail, and then they walked out of the meeting. Thus the activists in one of the largest new left centers in the country signaled, before the fact, that the organization that had given them a framework for their politics was headed for oblivion.[197]

Scott Pittman, a prominent member of the chapter since its early days, wrote that he was leaving SDS, painful as this was, because it was enveloped in a "despair and frustration politics which have become as inhuman as the establishment's politics." "My basic beliefs haven't changed that much since I first joined SDS," he explained, but the organization had abandoned those beliefs. He got to the heart of his politics, alluding to the new working-class analysis, abandoned by the national leadership: " 'Other'-oriented politics builds phony solutions into the mentality of an impotent and frustrated population."[198] This preoccupation with " 'other'-oriented politics" also came in for criticism from the University of Arkansas chapter in Fayetteville, which declared itself independent of national SDS "because we do not feel that either bureaucratic Stalinistic group represents the politics of our chapter." It distanced itself from both what it aptly—if awkwardly—called "the tailism and deification of [Weatherman] toward the Panthers" and "PL's stand on the black colony." Furthermore, the Arkansas radicals felt that both factions were "objectively chauvinistic because they give Women's Liberation a back seat to all other policies and programs and use it as a political football." Both "so-called leaderships of SDS are a serious threat to the Movement and therefore," they said, "we cannot align ourselves with either 'SECT'!!!!!"[199]

Of the two sects, PL faded from the scene more quickly. Weatherman maintained the spotlight (if not many adherents), promoting "street fighting" as a way for privileged whites to build revolutionary character and to prove their toughness to the Panthers and the Young Lords. Later in 1969, Weatherman held a "war council" in Flint, Michigan, adorned by a huge cardboard cutout of a rifle as well as large posters of black and Third World heroes. They called their discussion sessions "wargasms," indicating the therapeutic value they saw in violence. One Austin radical, Michele Clark, found a recent Weatherman manifesto, which expressed similar sentiments, to be disgusting. Seeing neither intrinsic nor tactical value in violence, "there is no choice here," she said. "It's only a culture of death the bourgeoisie offer us versus a culture of death offered by the Weathermen."[200] Although at first some Austin radicals were inclined to side with Weatherman in the split, perhaps because they had closer experience with PL, the SDS-UT chapter quickly announced that it was simultaneously affiliated with both SDS leadership claimants, which indicated that in practice it was loyal to neither.[201] It stopped meeting by the end of the fall 1969 semester.

By the time of its "Days of Rage" vandalism in Chicago in the fall of 1969, Weatherman had, at most, five hundred members in the entire country, perhaps fewer. They became notorious, left-wing Bonnies and Clydes, the media and political conservatives happy to join them in exaggerating their influence and representativeness. Weatherman could lay little claim to leadership of the new left. Both they and PL had moved far from the politics that animated most participants in "their" movement. No one could claim national leadership by this time, partly because Weatherman and PL had collaborated to destroy SDS, leaving a vibrant, growing radical movement with no organizational framework on the national level. This loss, combined with the rightward shift in electoral politics, dimmed revolutionary hopes on the left.

At least, that is, revolutionary hopes of a familiar kind. New left radicals felt alienated from their own national organization by the end of the 1960s, and they felt more alienated than ever from the mainstream of American life. Yet they had gone far toward escaping the specter of personal, or inner, alienation. Increasingly, they grounded their political radicalism in their conviction of their own authenticity. It was the larger culture around them, it seemed, that manifested signs of inauthenticity. To the extent that they still felt they suffered from alienation, they located the affliction's cause in the surrounding culture. Furthermore, there were more young radicals than ever; they felt the strength of their numbers as never before. Having arrived at a confidence in their own political agency and in the social character of personal alienation, new left radicals survived the demise of SDS and sought to colonize the dominant culture of the United States with the life of authenticity that they had found. They also shifted their political agitation to follow the burning preoccupation of middle-class Americans, which changed in the late 1960s from race to the Vietnam War. Looking for a new kind of revolution, new left radicals pressed forward with the joint search for an authentic and democratic society, the fused quests for personal and social transformation. This was the politics that national SDS had spurned, cutting itself off from its roots and withering.

CHAPTER SIX

Against Rome:
The New Left and the Vietnam War

To transcend tragedy requires the nerve to fail.

WILLIAM APPLEMAN WILLIAMS

"WHERE WOULD WE be if peace were to break out tomorrow?" Some in the SDS national leadership raised this question in the spring of 1965, when that group seemed poised to take control of the protest activity then emerging in response to the escalation of the Vietnam War.[1] Democrat Lyndon Johnson had crushed Republican Barry Goldwater in the presidential election of the previous November, in part by running as the peace candidate with regard to the struggle, still obscure to most Americans, of the Saigon government and its U.S. patron to resist the nationalist revolution in Vietnam. Since 1954, when an international agreement temporarily divided Vietnam at the seventeenth parallel, the U.S. government had worked to make South Vietnam a permanent country under a friendly, anticommunist regime. By the early 1960s, however, Communist leadership had brought the revolutionary forces, both south and north of that latitude, to the brink of victory and reunification. With little that was concrete at stake for the Americans, the Vietnam War became, it would seem to many, the cold war conflict par excellence, perhaps the most purely ideological war in U.S. history.[2]

As 1965 began, Americans saw few hints of the deep division that the war would cause in the United States in the coming years. Some, like the young conservative Larry Waterhouse, considered most recent American wars to be creations of the Democratic Party and felt heartened by Goldwater's assurance during the 1964 campaign that he would withdraw the United States from Vietnam if the conflict seemed unwinnable. Arriving at UT for college in that election year, hoping to become an astronaut, Waterhouse's reflexive hostility to the war led him down an idiosyncratic path, through the 1968 presidential campaigns of Eugene McCarthy and Robert Kennedy to SDS and the fringes of the Communist Party.[3] But in early 1965, Waterhouse was extremely unusual in his distrust of Johnson's handling of the Vietnam conflict. As a candidate, Johnson had made it clear he would not use nuclear weapons against North Vietnam to keep South Vietnam alive, as Goldwater had suggested might be necessary. This was an impressive difference to most Americans. They felt that under Johnson's stewardship, communism in Southeast Asia would be overwhelmed without a large expenditure of either blood or treasure on their part.

Soon this confidence suffered a setback. In mid-February, scant weeks after Johnson's inauguration, the Texan ordered that Operation Rolling Thunder proceed, bringing extensive bombing sorties north of the seventeenth parallel. Then in March, the president dispatched the first 3,500 U.S. ground troops to South Vietnam (180,000 more would follow by the year's end). Although the Congress had passed the Gulf of Tonkin resolution with almost no dissent in August 1964, giving Johnson *carte blanche* to use military force in Southeast Asia, there had been no declaration of war. Yet by the summer of 1965 the United States' involvement in Vietnam looked very much like a war.[4]

"Overnight the campuses became active" in an unexpected negative reaction to Johnson's actions.[5] The response was especially charged at UT, which Johnson called "my own school," but it was apparent everywhere. The "teach-in" movement began in late March 1965 at the University of Michigan at Ann Arbor, bringing an unprecedented level of information about the war to the nation's students and staging debates between pro- and antiwar speakers.[6] In April, SDS organized in Washington, D.C., an antiwar rally of twenty thousand people, the biggest peace demonstration in U.S. history to that date.

To close observers, it looked as if SDS might simply assume the national leadership of a mushrooming antiwar movement. For the first time, a constituency of dissent had appeared that resembled the members of SDS. This was the first large-scale, nationwide political protest by white college students since the peace demonstrations against the United States' entry into World War II (a comparison that critics of the new antiwar activism quickly made). Yet domestic, not international, issues had brought SDS together, and some of the group's leaders worried that if they shifted their emphasis to the hottest concern of the moment, they might get caught up in a controversy that could simply disappear because of unforeseen developments, with attention diverted from their original agenda. As late as January 1966, the SDS National Council, reflecting this concern, made the following resolution:

> We should be prepared to reject activities that mobilize thousands of people but do not build constituencies. . . . We should be prepared to argue with the antiwar movement that the real lever for change in America is a domestic social movement . . . we should also say that radicals have more important priorities than working simply to end the war.

In the council's view, it would be better to continue along the lines that, in the previous five years, had attracted a growing corps of talented, highly dedicated organizers.[7]

Some on the left harbored a deeper worry as well. In the late 1950s and early 1960s, amid the debris of the Communist-led old left, some were convinced that a new left had to adopt a stance of "isolationism," in the writer Stanley Aronowitz's term. That is, it had to be based on ideas that would not be viewed by Americans at large as alien and primarily concerned with domestic issues, not international politics. The international links of the U.S. left, both real and imagined, had proved a crushing political liability.[8] These concerns about the war issue were far from idle. The distinctive aspect of the left wing of the antiwar movement—its solidarity with Third World nationalist revolutions—was, if admirably cosmopolitan, a strategic move with mixed consequences.

The new left's concern over an outbreak of peace was equally important. By the early 1970s, the U.S. war in Southeast Asia became so much the focus for the left that when the war ebbed as a pressing concern among the majority of Americans—as a result of President Richard Nixon's de-escalation of the American ground war in favor of a more exclusive, and more lethal, emphasis on aerial bombing—and ended in 1973, the American left as a cohesive political presence had lost its raison d'être. There certainly remained many other issues for leftists to press. But protest against the war was the glue keeping the new left together during the Nixon administration's first term in office, staving off the centripetal forces internal to the radical movement and countering the dispiriting impact of the rightward turn in American politics.

Larry Caroline recalled that in Austin by the late 1960s, "the war was ninety percent of everything" that SDS did, and the same could be said of virtually any place else in the country.[9] Those who had worried about peace "suddenly" breaking out probably felt foolish as the years passed, and Vietnam became America's longest war. Nonetheless, the suggestion that shifting the new left's focus to the war would damage the movement's longer-term aim of organizing a movement around a broad agenda for radical domestic change ultimately proved prescient. The Vietnam War was the best organizing tool that ever dropped into the new left's hands, but in the end it proved to be a double-edged knife.

As the SDS resolution cited earlier indicates, reservations about antiwar agitation prevailed in national SDS in 1965. Indeed, SDS organized the Washington march only after the famous journalist I. F. Stone convinced them to take dramatic action on the Vietnam issue. Activists in the new left were concerned about international affairs, but the Cuban revolution and events in South Africa had been more on their minds than had Southeast Asia. At the march itself, SDS president Paul Potter urged the crowd to look beyond the single issue of the war, to change "the system" that created the war (a "system" Potter chose not to name), and he received a warm response. That same spring, SDS declined to adopt a proposal to launch an effort (wittingly illegal) to persuade young men to resist the draft; only at the end of 1966 did SDS formally endorse a draft resistance program.[10] Several analysts argue that because SDS did not at that time view the war issue as a promising means of radicalizing people and moving them into the left, SDS "declined to take the mantle which its march had won."[11] The "abdication" of leadership by SDS supposedly left the burgeoning antiwar movement either in the control of political liberals or else (depending on who tells the story) under the sway of Communists and Trotskyists.[12]

The full story is more complicated, however. First, the national SDS leaders may have "decided" not to get the organization deeply involved in antiwar activism, but their decision had little influence on chapters around the country and served mainly to put distance between the national leadership group's perspective and that of the membership. Robert Pardun, working as a regional traveler for SDS in the South and Midwest in the mid-1960s, found himself confronted at the campuses he visited with questions about the war and his organization's position on it, regardless of the other issues he sought to raise.[13] It was harder for SDS activists on campuses to ignore the rapidly spreading concern over the war than it was for those who talked mainly among themselves at national SDS meetings. Starting in the summer of 1965, "hundreds of SDSers across the country decided to pick up and go with the war issue on their own."[14] What was true of the new left was true of the antiwar movement overall. Ordered by President Lyndon Johnson to uncover Communist direction of antiwar efforts ("I've seen it in my own school," he thundered), the Central Intelligence Agency (CIA) reported accurately and repeatedly that neither the Communist Party nor anyone else really controlled the burgeoning protest.[15] Both the new left and American liberalism were pulled by the roots toward antiwar activism.

The hesitance of the SDS national leadership on the war issue in no way deterred the strongly decentralist chapters in Austin and elsewhere from embracing this grassroots sentiment. The tension between the SDS "old guard" and the provincial activists over the war issue was illustrated in the debate between Jeff Nightbyrd and Tom Hayden at the organization's national convention in June 1965, when Nightbyrd argued for a campus-based organizing strategy. The war was the coming issue on the campuses, as Nightbyrd knew. Before the April 1965 rally, Nightbyrd had proposed, albeit finding few takers, that SDS take the legally dubious step of sending medical supplies to the National Liberation Front (or NLF, the southern wing of the Vietnamese revolution) through the U.S. mail.[16]

A few lonely souls in Texas were upset over the war even before 1965, when most Americans were scarcely aware of their government's military effort to suppress the revolution in the South Vietnamese countryside. By late 1963, the peace organizations that had mobilized opposition to atomic testing and the Cuban missile crisis, such as the Student Peace Union (SPU) and Turn toward Peace, had become moribund at both the local and national levels. But perhaps the SPU's last gasp was its early opposition to the Washington–Saigon connection. Shortly before John Kennedy's assassination, Charlie Smith and George Goss, two of the earliest Texans to get involved in SDS, circulated an SPU petition on the Austin campus calling for an end to U.S. aid to South Vietnam and for a United Nations investigation of the Saigon regime. SPU and SDS together demonstrated against Madame Nhu, sister-in-law of America's man in Saigon, Ngo Dinh Diem, when she made a stop at Vice President Johnson's hometown as part of her October 1963 public relations tour of the United States.[17]

Once dissension from Johnson's war policy began to spread rapidly in 1965, opponents of the war banded together and in general acted cooperatively. In many places, ad hoc antiwar groups sprang up to lead protest activity. Destructive competition for leadership of the antiwar movement was less marked around the country than within the national leadership of the antiwar movement. In the early and mid-1960s, the old left groups that were active on national antiwar committees were barely in evidence, if at all, in most places, diminishing the likelihood of factionalism among antiwar activists. Particularly in conservative provincial locales, liberals and leftists sensibly banded together in the face of prowar hostility. It seemed the obvious thing to do.

Liberals and Radicals

In October 1965, at the follow-up rally to the April gathering, SDS president Carl Oglesby made a famous distinction between "corporate liberals" and "humanist liberals." According to Oglesby, the humanist liberals harked back to the tradition of Wilsonian idealism and simple decency and would join the fight to remove the United States from the path of Vietnamese self-determination. The corporate liberals, like the "NATO intellectuals" whom C. Wright Mills derided, would forsake the ideals on which they were nourished and truckle before power, helping prolong an unjust war. In characteristic new left fashion, Oglesby believed that by dint of moral will, individuals could transcend the structural forces that pushed them toward a "corporate" identity. He foresaw a liberal–left alliance against the war and extended the new left's hand.[18] In Austin, as around the country, this alliance indeed took shape over the following years, touching off a momentous conflict among American liberals. Simple humanism furnished a sufficient basis for the coalition.

Between 1963 and 1967, the new SDS chapter in Austin took the lead in organizing left–liberal antiwar protests. Starting in 1964, it became customary for Austin peace activists to hold a peace vigil at the nearby LBJ Ranch on Easter weekend, following a holiday tradition started by the British anti-nuclear movement. In Texas the peace protesters were confronted with Nazi and Ku Klux Klan contingents who came spoiling for a confrontation. On the day before Easter 1965, the weekend of the SDS Washington rally, Austin SDS rallied four hundred picketers to the ranch, where President Johnson had gone to escape the protest on the National Mall. "Old and young, long and short hair, black and white"—one activist painted the assembled protesters at the ranch in motley colors.[19]

In the fall of 1964, protesting the Gulf of Tonkin resolution, Austin SDS staged a decorous parade down Congress Street, sporting ties and dresses, carrying signs saying "US Out of Vietnam," and endorsing the call by the lone Senate dissenters, Wayne Morse and Ernest Gruening, for negotiations with North Vietnam. In the fall of 1965, as part of the "International Days of Protest" instigated by national antiwar forces, the SDS chapter organized a "March of Death" on the UT campus, carrying a coffin to symbolize the war dead. (An inconclusive and distracting court battle followed when the Austin City Council denied SDS a parade permit for a downtown march.)[20] Alice Embree later recalled the somber tenor of those early protests. "In 1963, when I first learned about the war, I would read the newspaper accounts in the student union building and I would cry. Our first demonstrations always had that moralistic tone; we were some kind of noble minority who would somehow—at least in the footnotes of history—atone for the sins of our government."[21]

In those naive days, the SDS protesters encountered more disbelief than hostility, with people looking at them "as if we were the Flat Earth Society," Nightbyrd remembers. Most Texans knew less about Vietnam than the SDS members did. Even as adept a conservative rhetorician as William F. Buckley Jr. apparently was disarmed by Nightbyrd's readings on the matter when Buckley visited UT around this time and the two of them squared off during a session of "Stump Speaking," an unstructured debate forum that was held in front of the undergraduate library. In the fall of 1966, new left activists staged another protest designed to corral wide support. Taking a cue from the "motherist" politics of Women Strike for Peace (WSP), a group of six women, including Embree, Mariann Wizard, and Judy Kendall, sat down in the Austin office of the Selective Service Board and issued an antiwar and antidraft statement declaring that as women, they didn't want their husbands, boyfriends, or sons turned into killers in an unjust war. In April 1967, SDS-UT's countercultural series of events, "Flipped-out Week," incorporated antiwar agitation and was coordinated with the national Spring Mobilization of the National Mobilization Committee Against the War in Vietnam. The SDS activists were willing to try a bit of everything.[22]

The University Freedom Movement (UFM) of April 1967 became a turning point in the orientation of the local antiwar movement. As explained in chapter 5, the UFM stemmed from an attempt to stifle antiwar protest in Austin. Amid the controversy, with SDS banned from campus, a strictly antiwar group took shape in Austin, with more a liberal than a leftist flavor but nonetheless one in which liberals and leftists worked together harmoniously. This was the University of Texas Committee to End the War in Vietnam (UTCEWV), which was affiliated with the National Mobilization Committee ("the Mobe") and the 1967 "Vietnam Summer" campaign.[23] For about two years, the UTCEWV led a united Austin antiwar movement. By November 1967, after a campaign of sustained agitation by both SDS and the new CEWV, one-third of UT students voting in a referendum favored the United States' immediate withdrawal—a minority opinion, to be sure, but one that had gone from marginal to mainstream.[24]

The committee itself was an organization that started with only a dozen dues-paying members but that quickly accumulated a mailing list of one thousand. The active members spanned a broad political spectrum. The leftish professors Charles Cairns, of the linguistics and speech department, and Robert Palter, of the government department, alternately acted as faculty sponsors for the committee. Liberal faculty members at UT like Irwin Spear, no leftist but nonetheless a dissenter from the hawkishness of cold war liberalism, also found a home in the CEWV. So did liberal campus clergy like Bob Breihan, and soon the UT Religious Student Liberals (RSL) began working closely with this united-front antiwar movement. Chett Briggs, who had participated in the stand-ins on the Drag and who now extended his religiously based activism in the Quaker AFSC, became involved. He provided a link between the older religious liberalism and the newer spirit of insurgency and illustrated the haziness of the line separating the two in the world of religious pacifism. Another important UTCEWV activist was Martin Wiginton. He was an activist for the Texas Democratic Coalition and one of a small group of liberal lawyers in Austin who became increasingly estranged from both mainstream professional practice and mainstream politics in the 1960s. By 1969 Wiginton was a full-time antiwar activist identified with "the movement," which is to say he had become a committed leftist. Throughout his changes, though, he maintained warm relations with people across the entire left half of the local political spectrum, functioning as an important point of contact between liberals and radicals.

This look at Austin suggests that the waning of the new left's leadership of antiwar protest dated from a somewhat later time than the national accounts of the antiwar movement assert—after the spring of 1967 in Austin, rather than the spring of 1965. Nonetheless, wane it did. But—and this is the important point—this limitation on the new left's influence was not due to an "abdication" of leadership by SDS. Rather, it resulted from the rapid influx into antiwar protest of large numbers of people who did not share the radical, anti-imperialist analysis that SDS articulated. SDS called for a unilateral U.S. withdrawal of forces from Vietnam, but in contrast, the CEWV called for either a unilateral U.S. withdrawal or a cessation of military "escalation" and attacks on North Vietnam, which was a considerably more moderate position.[25] The University Freedom Movement entangled the issue of the war with that of political repression on campus. This linkage helped attract many new recruits to the local antiwar movement who were more civil libertarian than leftist. Liberal umbrella groups like the UTCEWV, which not only took a more flexible position than SDS but also eschewed anti-imperialist analysis and required no attachment to a multi-issue political agenda, quite logically became the main vehicles of antiwar activism.

It hardly could have been otherwise. The only way for SDS to have remained the fulcrum of the peace movement would have been to submerge its radical analysis and instead to organize a broad-based coalition around minimal antiwar demands. This was the path taken by the Trotskyist Socialist

Workers Party (SWP) through its various front groups in the late 1960s, a choice that had virtues as well as shortcomings. Perhaps the most obvious criticism of that approach is that it simply duplicated the work of antiwar liberals, and many new left activists came to view the SWP as duplicitous as well as duplicative. SDS chose instead to keep a radical analysis in the public eye and functioned after 1965 as the left wing of an antiwar coalition, albeit a left wing whose size steadily increased along with that of the entire coalition. From 1968 to the war's end, the new left continually sought to bring a multi-issue perspective to antiwar protest, adding speakers on racism, political repression, sexism, and other topics to the agendas of antiwar gatherings.[26] Speakers on these other topics generally were more tolerated than paid heed by the crowds that had massed to protest the war.

On the issue of the war itself, although SDS and the UTCEWV worked together, the divergent premises of their antiwar appeals became increasingly clear. The liberal appeal was based on a straightforward humanist moralism, on a visceral revulsion at the monumentality of the violence the United States and its allies were committing in Indochina. "Our primary concern is the concern of all human beings—life," the CEWV avowed in 1967. "We want the killing, maiming, and human degradation stopped now!"[27] Liberals focused at times on the violence being done to children. The CEWV reprinted for distribution on campus an article in which a journalist cited the testimony of diplomat George Kennan before the U.S. Congress that "considerations of prestige" alone justified a continuation of the war. The reporter then reflected, "For *considerations of prestige*. It is an interesting reason for killing children."[28] Liberals and leftists alike displayed a remarkable capacity to identify with the victims of violence on "the other side." In 1967 Sara Clark, a UT graduate student and antiwar activist, drove out into the hills southwest of Austin.

> I tried to imagine foreign soldiers in the dooryards of the small farms
> and ranches that faced the road. I tried to picture a red-faced Texan's
> reaction to having his place burned, his vegetables destroyed, and his
> stock shot, all for his own good. I tried to imagine a Texas farmer who
> would not join an underground resistance movement composed of
> other Texans against the foreign destroyers.[29]

This analogy between rural Texans and the National Liberation Front surely would have outraged most residents of the Lone Star State. Such humanism was uncommon.

One theme that antiwar liberals often sounded was that of personal, individual responsibility for one's government's actions, and they frequently articulated this theme by means of a jolting analogy to Nazi Germany. As UT student and CEWV leader David Gray asked his peers, "Will you be the Germans who allowed Hitler's rise to power?" He implored, "Speak out now! Our government must not be permitted to carry on the Vietnam War in our name any longer."[30] But Gray did not believe, as some on the left did, that "fascism" had actually come to the United States, and he distanced himself from those radicals who, he claimed, had concluded that the government was beyond the reach of the public's appeals. Gray thought an analogy to Naziism was more appropriate to the public that supported the war than it was to the leaders who prosecuted the war. "These men," he said of the decision makers, "are not the hot-heads of the right but concerned men who believe they are doing what is necessary for eventual peace. Their one mistake is in believing that military conquest is the proper means for establishing peace."

The key word here was *mistake*. This idea, that the United States had, through ignorance or poor judgment, stumbled into a "quagmire" in Vietnam, as the journalist David Halberstam put it, became a flash point for the antiwar left.[31] Leftists objected to this characterization of the war on two counts. First, it suggested that the war was exceptional, an aberration from a larger pattern of fundamentally benign U.S. activity in the world. The new left felt that the Vietnam adventure reflected an all too typical U.S. attitude toward nationalist movements in the Third World. Oglesby argued in his fall 1965 speech that the United States' intervention in Vietnam was part of a pattern of recent interventions, including those in Iran, Guatemala, and, most recently, the Dominican Republic.[32] Second, a "mistake" was something that one did not wish to do, and the new left argued that U.S. decision makers went into Vietnam eagerly. This outlook on the war pointed to an almost unbridgeable intellectual chasm between antiwar liberals and the antiwar left, no matter how much the two camps cooperated.

In late November 1967, SDS circulated a series of newsletters on the UT campus, systematically putting forward their analysis of the Vietnam War in preparation for the visit to campus of General Harold K. Johnson, the U.S. Army chief of staff. These students depicted a militaristic power elite, insulated from citizen control or even civilian governmental control, standing behind the war. Corporate power—or simply the "men of Wall Street," as Charles Cairns put it—placed irresistible demands on the U.S. government to act as its enforcer. The SDS members documented what they viewed as "the rise of military power after [World War II] and the decline of civilian controls over the military machine."[33] As to the culprits, they pointed not to militarists run amok but, rather, to a "military–industrial complex" with a huge stake in defense spending. The activists quoted a speech by General Johnson to a group of defense contractors in 1965, "reassuring" them that the Vietnam War might last another ten years and that even if it did not, defense expenditures would not necessarily drop off. The students thus implied that other wars might follow Vietnam, and they thought naive those "liberals who speculate that the $30 billion we spend annually in Vietnam might be diverted to constructive uses if only the war could end."[34] They agreed with liberals that the spending priorities of the national government were askew, but they saw those priorities as rooted deeply in a political structure that would have to go if the priorities were to change.

By 1969, this analysis had penetrated the ranks of liberals. At the 15 October 1969 Moratorium rally at the state capitol in Austin, part of the biggest day of antiwar activism yet in the United States, Ronnie Dugger conceded that protesting against the policies of the Nixon administration was insufficient. "There is something deeper wrong," the liberal avatar said. "The military–industrial–labor complex . . . is locking itself into the structure of our country."[35] There was a basis for agreement on this dire state of affairs in the muckraker's vision that Texas liberals and the new left shared. But this criticism of the military–industrial complex lingered among liberals only as long as the new left was around to provoke them.

Holding aloft another piece of the military puzzle they had cracked, the antiwar left advanced the following thesis, which became crucial to the new left view of the Vietnam War and their own political role in opposing it: *"American universities provide an essential link between the military power structure and the corporate power structure through defense research."*[36] This was a funhouse-mirror version of Clark Kerr's picture of a scholarly "knowledge industry" that played a vital and positive role in an emerging postindustrial economy.[37] The new left focused on the Department of Defense (DoD) contracts that universities around the country received for their work in developing weapons systems and other instruments of counterinsurgency. (According to figures compiled in 1968, although UT was not in the first tier of Defense money recipients overall, it ranked ninth in the country in DoD dollars devoted to research and development.)[38] If the university really was "an essential link" in the war-making chain, then antiwar students might be well placed to jam the works.

This critique of "the uses of the university" was one side of the new left's view of the higher education system. The other side was a lingering sense that the university might be the repository of "rationality and sanity," as a group of antiwar students at UT put it in 1967, not an "ivory tower" standing aloof from social controversies, but a source of social criticism somewhat insulated from external pressures.[39] This was what Dugger and liberals of his ilk thought the university should be, what they thought it sometimes had been, and still could be, if only professors and their allies could fend off the depredations of wealth. It also was the hope expressed in the *Port Huron Statement*.[40] The new left never fully decided whether the university was more a villain or a potential savior in the political drama that unfolded around them. At a provincial school like UT, with its cherished memory of conflict with the regional power elite, the idealistic hope that reason and the critical spirit might continue to emanate from the campus clung to the hearts of both liberals and leftists. The two constituencies always could join forces in defense of this ideal.

But the smell of corruption and the ideal of the university were not all there was to the new left analysis. The radicals also increasingly raised the issue of global power relations and geopolitical change, and here they and the liberals parted company, Wilsonian idealism notwithstanding. According to the new left, the power elite did not simply manufacture U.S. military interventions in order to keep themselves rolling in public monies; the threats to the system on which the elite fed were real. As Oglesby contended explicitly in a 1967 book and in a speech at an August 1967 "Hiroshima Day" peace rally in Austin, these interventions were made in order to quell the rising tide of anticolonialism around the world and thus maintain an "empire" from which U.S. elites derived concrete benefits.[41]

In this view, the United States ruled over not a formal political empire but an economic one in which U.S. elites wielded decisive power over the allocation of resources in the economies of Third World countries. But the political momentum imparted by the post–World War II dissolution of the older formal empires could not be contained, and in the framework of cold war competition between the Soviets and North Americans, the more southerly, poorer, and darker peoples of the world were asserting themselves against the "New Leviathan." By 1968, SDS-UT activists spoke of "imperialism" as the driving force behind U.S. activity around the globe.[42] Liberals viewed this as an extreme characterization, even hysterical. In America, imperialism was widely considered a foreign word.

A Choice of Heroes

In retrospect, it is not surprising that an anti-imperialist analysis of the Vietnam War became dominant in the new left. Whereas critics on the right (and in the White House) sometimes saw the hand of the Comintern in this perspective, the new left's anti-imperialism did not descend from the old left's

Soviet-inspired "line" or from any sort of allegiance to the Soviet viewpoint among new left activists. A useful contrast with the mainstream of the new left is offered by the Progressive Labor Party (PL), whose early opposition to the Vietnam War was grounded in an allegiance to Chinese Communism, a fealty that led PL to execute a turnabout in the late 1960s, condemning the Vietnamese Communists—whom PL formerly had defended—in response to renewed tensions between Beijing and Hanoi.[43]

From the movement's start to its finish, most new leftists exhibited a sharp distrust of all superpowers—the United States, the Soviet Union, and China—and instead grounded their view of world politics in an allegiance to the countries of the Third World (China was something of a special case, since it was both an ascendant superpower and a Third World society). In this sense, the new left was continuous with the youthful liberal internationalism of the late 1950s, which had viewed the emergence of the non-aligned movement with hope and sympathy. Taking a pluralistic view of social structures, those earlier internationalists had accepted the embrace of state socialism by Third World regimes in search of rapid economic development while maintaining that this acceptance implied nothing at all about social change in the United States.

The Cuban revolution was the principal event that altered this liberal internationalism among student activists, shifting it to the left.[44] Larry Caroline was a young liberal at the time, an undergraduate at the University of Rochester from 1957 to 1961. By the time he had graduated from college, he had joined the National Committee for a Sane Nuclear Policy (better known as SANE), thinking that testing atomic bombs seemed like "not a good idea," even though most of his peers thought this was a "semi-communistic" notion. Like many young liberals, he was enamored of Fidel Castro, who skillfully kept his political coloration hazy when touring the United States in 1959. "He seemed like a real folk-hero. Which he was." Even as Castro moved left, Caroline's loyalty remained intact. It seemed to the philosophy graduate student that the United States was behaving in an "incredibly stupid" manner toward the new regime, driving it into the arms of the Soviets, whom Caroline did not see as a benign force. He thought the American government shouldn't "be so uptight about [Castro's] socialism." The early new left took the position that the United States' hostility to Cuban socialism should bend to the principle of self-determination. And this was the basis on which the new Austin SDS chapter debated the right-wing Young Americans for Freedom on the topic of Cuba in early 1964.[45]

Increasingly, the new left viewed Cuban socialism as a model for change in the United States. In the last years of his life, C. Wright Mills celebrated the Cuban revolution and exhorted students in the United States to take the lead in fomenting political change in their country, warning them that if they did not, they would pale in comparison to their contemporaries in the postcolonial world.[46] Larry Caroline endorsed Cuban socialism just as he was self-consciously adopting a "Marxist or socialist outlook" himself, less because of the influence of his ethics teachers at the University of Michigan than because of his Ann Arbor friends who adopted the *Port Huron Statement* in 1962. Although Caroline did not join SDS at that time, he "loved everything about it, from the very beginning," including its open sympathy—even identification—with Third World revolutionaries.[47]

New left activists wished to model their personal experience and even their selves, more than their society, on what they saw in revolutionary Cuba. Rarely did they envision transferring Castro's social program from a poor, agrarian society to the wealthiest, most highly industrialized country in the world. By the late 1960s, some, particularly the Weatherman faction (which identified most closely with Third World revolutionaries) did speak of "expropriating" the holdings of wealthy Americans in a social revolution. More widely felt, however, was an admiration for the Cuban public services, such as education and health care, that surpassed anything available to the poor in the United States. More alluring still were the collective work enterprises of Cuba, which some *norteamericanos* (Austin leftists included) visited during trips to Cuba that SDS and the independent Venceremos Brigade organized from 1968 on.[48] What "socialism" meant most of all to the new left activists who were attracted to the concept was, perhaps, the social dominance of the highly participatory, communal or collective experience that they discerned in Cuba and tried to create in their own politics, work, and leisure.

Alienation, rather than poverty, in the collective mind of the North American new left was the affliction that the revolutionary spirit was meant most of all to cure. This was the key to the romanticization of "Fidel," "Che," and "Ho." Although not descended directly from any left-wing antecedent, the attraction of the new left to these figures echoed the old left's idealization of Lenin and the Russian Bolsheviks. New left thinkers suggested that one aspect of the cultural enervation of contemporary America was the sapping of political will, the feeling that attempts at change were hopeless, that "history" simply had ended.[49] From this point of view, the new left's very belief that it could change the United States was in itself a victory over "weightlessness." The guerrilla and political leaders of the Third World displayed an indomitable spirit in the face of apparently overweening conservative forces, and new left activists felt they could use some of that spirit in their own daunting attempts to change the United States. Just as the American left of old in desperate moments had looked to Lenin's stunning defiance of Marxist theory in creating a socialist revolution in backward Russia, the new left sometimes clung to thoughts of Castro's tiny band of men taking refuge in the Sierra Maestra after the failed Granma landing of 1956, seemingly defeated, only to return triumphant to Havana two years later.

The question of alienation was most explicit when the Cuban concept of "the New Man" arose. Philip Russell, a high school friend of Jeff Nightbyrd's who had participated in civil rights demonstrations in Austin in the early 1960s, had since moved away and become a self-educated expert on Latin American affairs, visiting Cuba along with Alice Embree on an SDS trip in 1968. He returned from Cuba a socialist, though one willing to admit he could not get past page thirty of Marx's *Das Kapital*. He came back to Austin and became a central figure in local interest in Cuban affairs. With the assistance of other Austin activists, Russell produced pamphlets on Cuban developments, including one that discussed the Cuban attempt to form a New Man out of and in service to the social revolution.[50]

The New Man would find fulfillment in collective endeavors, not in individual success and elevation. Perhaps indicating the residual power of a Christian vocabulary of revolution, the radicals said this new personality would lay the basis for "a whole society based on love."[51] Although it was the most difficult task ahead, without such a cultural change, Russell reported, the Cubans believed their revolution would be doomed. (He reported that they were on their way. Without comment, he passed on Cuban workers' stated opinion—which came in response to questions from the *norteamericanos* on tour—that their legal inability to strike was not a problem, since they perceived no difference of interests between themselves and the economic enterprises where they labored.)[52]

Since World War II, some sociologists and industrial relations experts had argued that the highly individualistic personality structure of entrepreneurial capitalism was obsolete in the contemporary U.S. economy.[53] The New Man of whom the Cubans dreamed bore a curious similarity to the team player whom corporate capitalists extolled. When focusing on American culture, the new left celebrated individualism as a rebellion against a gray world of regimentation and conformity, even against a "soft" form of totalitarianism.[54] Yet young leftists' identification with the search for a New Man among Third World revolutionaries betrayed a simultaneous desire for solidarity, for a transcendence of social alienation. Their thoughts on the matter were deeply conflicted.

The New Man also was manly in the extreme. Machismo occupied a central role in the phenomenon of *fidelismo*. Mills contrasted the existential appeal of the Cuban revolution, the promise of overcoming alienation to "make history," not simply with a failure of human potential but specifically with American intellectuals' "failure . . . as political men." Like Paul Goodman, another new left inspiration, Mills saw the achievement of manhood as the sine qua non of political revitalization in the United States.[55]

Sexism in Cuba merited at least a passing mention in Russell's pamphlet, as in Austin activist Michele Clark's reports in the *Rag* on the 1968 SDS trip to Cuba.[56] They both cast Cuban sexism as a sort of cultural lag, a vestige of the past that the revolution likely would erode in time. However, this hope rested uneasily with the foundations of *fidelismo* in the vision of a male hero who could outtalk, outthink, and outfight any rival. Men in the new left shared with other American males of their era a feeling that a new assertion of male vitality was in order amid the world of bureaucracy and mass society. The oft-expressed fear that the organization man was a eunuch united Americans of diverse political persuasions. Men as different as John F. Kennedy, for whom "balls" (that is, the possession or lack thereof) formed a major category of political and psychological analysis, and Abbie Hoffman, who lamented that the United States as a culture collectively had lost its "balls," shared this concern.[57] The heroic individualism of a Castro (which so infuriated Kennedy), breaking through apparently insurmountable obstacles seemingly by force of will, both answered and aggravated this anxiety, which was in the end but one aspect of a more general sense of weightlessness. The perception of the guerrilla-as-supermale accounts for an unquantifiable, but surely considerable, part of the figure's attraction for young American men.

Ultimately the machismo of the Cuban revolution came under attack within the U.S. left, not by feminists but by the gay liberation movement of the 1970s. In the summer of 1971, left-wing gay groups condemned the anti-gay policies promulgated at the recent First Congress on Education and Culture in Havana. As was traditional on the left, they based their argument not simply on general humanist principles but on the grounds that the behavior they sought to discredit was incompatible with "a true socialist society."[58] What marked this as a distinctly *new* left criticism was that the perceived contradiction with socialist principles did not lie in the perpetuation of inequality—in this case, along lines of sexual orientation. Rather, the gay left declared that the Cubans, ironically, were insufficiently committed to the emergence of the New Man.

In the very cultural hopes that had fueled U.S. youth's support for Castro's revolution were buried the seeds of disappointment and disillusion.

The gay liberation movement was committed to personal "transformation," and this was the paramount project of the contemporary socialist movement. The Cubans wished to repress what they saw as a disruptive cultural presence—homosexuality—in the name of revolutionary cohesion because they put social change ahead of "transformation." Yet in the view of Austin Gay Liberation, "in transformation, the principle of revolution, a straight 19th Century way, is not only contained but superceded [*sic*]." Their struggle for transformation was "a deeper one [than] radicalism and ideology."[59] The enthusiasm of the U.S. left for Cuban socialism never recovered from such criticism.

What no blemish on Castro's regime could damage was the new left critique of imperialism, specifically the radical analysis of the United States' role in the Third World. Rather than just cultural hopes for a New Man, this economic and political analysis, too, underpinned the new left's sympathy for the Havana government. The evidence was ample that Cuba, as one Austin activist put it bluntly, had long functioned as "a gigantic sugar plantation providing the U.S. with sugar . . . and the North American plantation and refinery owners with high profits from . . . cheap labor." Many young Americans concluded that the Third World goals of national self-determination and development, goals that liberal internationalists had long lauded, were blocked by U.S. corporations and their own government. "Batista represented the U.S. interests in Cuba. *There was no way to reform the situation without running into conflict with U.S. interests.* This is the situation underdeveloped countries all over the world face today."[60]

Thus reform efforts led to political revolutions because the power elite of the United States, defending their material interests in the Third World, fostered a process of escalating conflict with nationalist reformers. This insight, particularly its extension from the Cuban example to the status of a general rule regarding the role of the United States in the Third World, was a signal event in the ideological development of a new left in the United States. The argument was available in the Marxist economics journal *Monthly Review*, and it was implicit in the works of the eminent historian William A. Williams. As Williams wrote—inverting a slogan long used to justify U.S. investment and power abroad—in order to make way for the reasonable aspirations of people in the Third World, it was necessary to leave "an open door for revolutions." The view of the United States as a counterrevolutionary force in the world ran contrary to the image that many liberal Americans held of their country, that the Kennedy administration had encouraged, and to which Williams exhorted Americans to be loyal.[61]

It was not easy or painless for new left activists to break with the image of the United States as a force for democracy. The early new left professed its patriotism even as it broke with its government's foreign policy. Antiwar activists addressed the problem that this entailed in a culture in which an antiwar stance was commonly equated with treason, by arguing that they were trying to bring U.S. foreign policy into line with the "real" principles of the republic. Paul Pipkin of Austin always contended that the war's opponents were the truest patriots of all. And in his October 1965 speech, Oglesby asserted that he was against the war because of principles he viewed as fully American. The men who made the war in order to maintain the status quo in the Third World "broke my American heart," he remarked plaintively.[62] This was the representative cri de coeur of young Americans who embraced the new left analysis of the Vietnam War in the mid-1960s. The belief lingered that their country ought to be, and still could be, the keeper of liberty's flame.

Nightbyrd reflects the frame of mind of this mid-decade new left in his hesitation, even decades later, to use the term *imperialism*. The situation in Vietnam "was clearly a part of the whole—I don't like to use these words much but this is an applicable word in this case—the imperialist tradition." The best-known case of such uneasiness with one's own left-wing views was Paul Potter's disinclination to "name the system" in his April 1965 speech. This generation of activists was culturally close enough to the political mainstream as to be acutely aware of the risks of merely using terms like *capitalism* or *imperialism*, or of taking an antiwar position. If SDS became active in the antiwar movement, "we knew that . . . we would be attacked for being Communists, that we would be transformed as an organization," says Nightbyrd.[63] This awareness of risk reflected, in addition to an aversion to ugly accusations, the desire current in the new left at that time to influence the political mainstream, and the confidence that they might do so. This desire and this confidence, along with the resistance to a traditional left-wing vocabulary, eventually faded.

The responses that activists in Texas encountered were as crude as Jeff Nightbyrd anticipated. In 1965, even the "domino theory" was not yet current there—it was too nuanced a justification of U.S. military involvement in Vietnam. Instead, new left activists found themselves debating people who insisted an internationally coordinated Communist conspiracy was attempting "to take over Asia." In fact, the least indirect argument regarding the threat of Vietnamese Communism to the United States—that the National Liberation Front and the North Vietnamese army some day would land in California if the United States did not stop them in Indochina—was rather influential among prowar Americans.[64]

The domino theory did surface by 1967, though, and SDS members tried to refute it, contending that political developments in Third World countries depended on indigenous conditions, not on the fate of Vietnam.[65] Antiwar activists marshaled the facts they had gleaned from their readings. Nightbyrd rehearses their argument: "The United States created a mythology of two countries. It was supposed to be a temporary demarcation line [the seventeenth parallel, established as a cease-fire line in 1954 in the Geneva Accords, to have been rendered irrelevant in two years' time through national elections] that was turned into North Vietnam and South Vietnam. Then we said the North had attacked the South." Following the liberal internationalist tradition, the antiwar students viewed Vietnamese Communism not as an implacable foe of the "free world" whose existence the United States could not tolerate but as an understandable response to conditions in the Third World with which the United States ought to reach an accommodation. "Historically Ho Chi Minh was a great admirer of the American Constitution. . . . China was . . . a historical enemy of Vietnam, et cetera, there was plenty of room to come out with some face-saving negotiation and have a relationship with that country." But most people who spoke on the matter of Vietnam insisted on a "bipolar" view of the world, in which "everything was either under Russia's or under our orbit."[66] It seemed to antiwar activists that the prowar viewpoint they encountered existed in pristine isolation from any knowledge of recent events in Indochina, or of world events generally. In this situation, they saw themselves standing for mere rationality against narrow-minded provincialism, much as the earlier liberal internationalists did.

The campus antiwar contingent came in for a rude awakening when they encountered harsh criticism from their liberal elders. At the University of Texas, cold war liberalism was incarnate in John Silber. Silber always had been "a hawk," according to Irwin Spear.[67] A readiness to use military force, especially where communism or socialism of any kind was concerned, was in fact a hallmark of mainstream liberalism in the 1950s and 1960s. By the 1970s, if self-identified liberals were likely to harbor dovish tendencies on foreign policy matters, then this was a change wrought by renegades in the liberal camp, and Silber was one of the older breed who was left behind in the wake of this insurgency. Intensely loyal to the Johnson administration, in whose Texas election campaign he had participated, Silber no doubt saw himself defending both "freedom" and liberalism. Defenders of Johnson's Vietnam policy commonly claimed that antiwar activism damaged the administration's expansive domestic agenda (and the antiwar critics came to argue that it was the war that did the damage). Silber also was arrogant, convinced of his own superlative rationality, and he displayed little respect for those with whom he disagreed strongly, especially on important political matters. Liberal protesters on campus had previously benefited from his slashing rhetorical skills; now the shoe was on the other foot. Even a quarter century later, Jeff Nightbyrd expresses the hurt feelings of a young man who felt betrayed by a potential mentor.

> I was called "Communist" by [John] Silber. Called us "Stalinists," in fact . . . who was supposedly one of the progressives, I mean the progressive professors here denounced us as Stalinists, I mean Jesus— 'cause we were against the war, and they were seeing it all in those bipolar terms. So here I'm a twenty-three-year-old kid out of a right-wing background being called a Stalinist. I mean, talk about disillusioning [laughs], the generation that preceded me, these guys that were supposed to be [voice trails off].

They "were supposed to be" sympathetic, it seemed.[68]

The contrary realization was embittering and gave rise to the new left belief that liberals were apologists for empire, that their professed humanism was only skin deep. This partial estrangement from liberalism helped pave the way for the new left's later and fuller-throated support for Third World revolutionary socialism and nationalism. If liberals exhibited only hostility toward such movements, then they would forfeit whatever restraining influence they might have had on young Americans' Third Worldist enthusiasm. To some degree, it was a matter of the young choosing their heroes.

By the early 1970s, sympathetic reports of anticolonial and anticapitalist movements around the world, including the Tupamaros of Uruguay and the rebels in the Mexican state of Guerrero, circulated among the Austin left. The Chilean socialist government of Salvador Allende received warm support, although by 1970, when that regime appeared, there were those on the U.S. left who criticized Allende for abandoning "armed struggle." Palestinian nationalism found allies. Some extended the anticolonial analysis to Quebec's separatist movement, and the morality of the Irish Republican Army became a topic of sharp debate. Although Austin leftists virtually never condoned or advocated violence against persons in the United States, they did feel that circumstances in the Third World might require a different moral calculus. Then in 1970, the new left's concern with global politics came full circle, as Austin radicals founded the Committee on Racism and Apartheid (CORA), which publicized and agitated against investment by U.S. corporations in South Africa. This was precisely the concern that had motivated forty-one SDS members to get themselves arrested one month before the April 1965

Washington antiwar demonstration, protesting loans to South Africa at the Wall Street headquarters of the Chase Manhattan Bank.[69]

To its political and economic analysis of U.S. foreign policy, the new left added its spontaneous sense of solidarity with its opposite numbers around the world. In 1968 Austin leftists expressed support for the dissidents of the Prague Spring, trampled under the heel of Soviet dominion. Philip Russell reported in some detail on the Mexican government's violent suppression of that country's student movement in 1968.[70] The feeling that a worldwide youth movement of cultural and political renewal was afoot went back to the liberal internationalism of the 1950s. Even as it became radicalized, this global sense of solidarity with those standing against authoritarian, corrupt regimes paid little respect to the bipolar cold war framework, with most leftists refusing to choose sides in the U.S.–USSR conflict. But this mattered little in a country where empire was "a way of life."[71] The new left's internationalism brought it isolation and obloquy at home. Its concept of political solidarity stretched beyond the usual boundaries of what Oglesby might have called an "imperial culture." This extraordinary solidarity helped build the "firebreak" that separated the left wing of the antiwar movement from that movement's mainstream.[72]

Men under Fire

The new left's anti-imperialist politics mixed with the turmoil surrounding American men's sense of their masculinity. Third World revolutionaries furnished only one template for the assertion of masculine identity. Even on the left, there were alternatives, but none so fully formed. As the war wore on, antiwar activists came to think that a martial identity was normative for men in the United States and that if they wanted to make future wars less likely, it was important they find other ways for men to "grow up." The radical pacifist wing of the antiwar movement led these efforts. Clearly, the search for nonviolent masculine identities posed a problem for those inclined to identify with Third World guerrilla heroes, although this tension rarely became a topic of discussion.

One search for an alternative masculinity took place in the draft resistance movement, and it respected few ideological lines. The most frequently heard justifications for refusing to cooperate with the Selective Service System (SSS) were individualistic and libertarian. "The draft represents a gross denial of personal freedom in our 'democratic' society," said the small group of UT students, affiliated with the national group "The Resistance," who sent their draft cards back to the local SSS office in San

Antonio in October 1967. Despite the ideological ambiguity of this argument, the draft resistance movement had connections to both the civil rights movement's legacy of civil disobedience in search of social justice and the antiwar left. The liberal UTCEWV hastened to distance itself from the action.[73]

After Greg Calvert moved from Chicago to Austin with Carol Neiman in 1968, he became more involved in draft counseling than in any other protest activity, working in the busy Austin Draft Information Center that was housed, from its inception in 1967, in the University Y. He was part of a group of white men who came from the civil rights movement and the new left, who saw a deep personal meaning in militant nonviolence, and who concluded that draft resistance could be a vehicle of personal and political transformation for people like themselves who no longer could be a part of the black movement. Staughton Lynd, who strongly supported David Harris in founding The Resistance on the West Coast, stated that draft resistance could mean for young white men what the work of SNCC had meant for young people a few years earlier. Some criticize this vision on feminist grounds, noting that draft resistance relegated women to an auxiliary role in support of male heroism. Calvert, who in the late 1960s was coming to grips with his own gay sexuality, finds this characterization unfair. He counters that the antiwar movement had to address the draft, which, after all, was exclusively male and that in general the draft resistance movement did so by offering a dissident, nonauthoritarian identity to young American men. This, he contends plausibly, complemented the youth feminism then emerging.[74] At the same time, this countercultural vision of draft resistance had an intense homosocial cast that did indeed suggest a distinctly male "beloved community" in search of a new society.

A somewhat different tension between conventional machismo and an alternative male identity was evident in the resistance to the Vietnam War that emerged in the armed forces and among veterans of the war. Central Texas became one of the most important centers of this movement. By mid-1968, which antiwar activists dubbed the "Summer of Support" for GIs, in an effort to disprove the common charge that the movement was hostile toward servicemen, the antiwar movement's first "coffeehouses" were opened next to military installations around the United States. These were places run by antiwar activists where GIs could gather and discuss the war and other political issues, free from surveillance by their superiors; they also were places "where the soldiers could go, relax, bullshit, and most importantly, be treated as people, not Government Issues."[75] One of these coffeehouses was the Oleo Strut, which serviced Fort Hood, the biggest armored post in the United States and a major disembarkation point from Vietnam. This simmering cauldron was located in Killeen, less than an hour's drive from Austin.[76] Even though the Killeen City Council voted in 1968 to begin legal proceedings to shut down the Strut as a "public nuisance," the coffeehouse managed to hang on for several years.[77]

Antiwar activists first realized that they could do something useful near military bases because of early instances of GIs protesting against the war, such as the "Fort Hood Three," a multiracial group of soldiers who were court-martialed in 1966 for refusing to go to Vietnam. They became a cause célèbre, invoking the "Nuremberg doctrine" in civilian court to argue that they refused to serve in Vietnam in order to avoid committing war crimes. They lost in court, however, and received sentences of three years in military prison.[78] Once aware of the dissension brewing in the ranks, a variety of agitators, including pacifists, PL members, and unaffiliated radicals like Larry Waterhouse—whose draft board sent him to Fort Ord in California in late 1969—set out to organize antiwar GIs from within the armed forces, sometimes by volunteering for duty. Waterhouse and Mariann Wizard, who moved to California to join him, compiled a volume on the GI antiwar movement with the incendiary title *Turning the Guns Around*. Mainly through the Oleo Strut, Austin leftists developed extensive contacts with antiwar GIs at Fort Hood. GIs from Killeen began to appear regularly in antiwar rallies and marches in Austin, and they frequently camped out in the Neiman–Calvert residence on weekends when they came to the university town in search of fun as well as political support.[79]

This was hazardous duty for the soldiers. The most active found themselves on the business end of military justice, as GIs were court-martialed for speaking at antiwar gatherings.[80] Fort Hood soldiers also began to refuse riot duty, resisting their assigned role as the suppressors of domestic protest activity and unrest; one who did so was repeatedly beaten while in the stockade.[81] Pfc. Bruce "Gypsy" Peterson and Joshua Gould were the victims of the most egregious political repression. Peterson was the founding editor of the *Fatigue Press*, a GI newspaper produced "underground" in Killeen whose cover assured, "THIS IS YOUR PERSONAL PROPERTY IT CANNOT BE TAKEN FROM YOU." Gould was the civilian manager of the Oleo Strut. They both were charged with marijuana possession, as Killeen police claimed to find two-thousandths of an ounce in the interior of Gould's car after using a vacuum cleaner on it. The police told Peterson's army tribunal that their lab had destroyed the cannabis they had extracted from his pocket lint in the process of examining it. Peterson, "a very heavy GI organizer, too heavy for the Army to ignore," was found guilty and sentenced to eight years at hard labor. He appealed to the Army Court of Military Appeals and was released after serving thirteen months.[82]

The conflict reached a climax in the fall of 1971. In September, municipal, county, and state police joined forces to suppress a Killeen protest in support of the two GIs who had been blamed for a recent protest by stockade prisoners against conditions in the jail. The police beat many of the protesters and arrested 34, of whom 30 were GIs. In October, while marching on Killeen sidewalks, 118 protesters were arrested for parading without a permit. The *Fatigue Press* called the arrestees "political prisoners," and the GI antiwar movement developed a sense of solidarity with others similarly labeled by the political left.[83] The paper ran a poem, amid photographs of police and protesters, by a Vietnamese poet that included these lines:

> *Workers and farmers rise up!*
> *Intellectuals rise up!*
> *Let's raise our voices together*
> *Determined to fight and to win.*
> *We must push forward!*
> *The golden star lights our road,*
> *The path to revolution!*[84]

This was one case in which the argument that political repression brought radicalization was perhaps borne out.

The Vietnam Veterans Against the War (VVAW) chapter that Terry DuBose and Mike Lewis started in the Killeen–Austin axis in 1971 sought to bring the philosophy of nonviolence to the angry young men of Fort Hood. DuBose had served in an administrative, not a combat, post in Vietnam, and in this position he was privy to the discrepancies between the truth of the war and the public statements of the U.S. Army and the government. His antiwar stance quickly evolved into a pacifist orientation. In school at UT, he became involved in a pacifist antiwar group. VVAW became a voice not only against the Vietnam War but also against racism, for better conditions in Veterans' Administration hospitals, and against drug addiction, which it viewed as a problem that afflicted Vietnam veterans particularly. In the early 1970s, VVAW became an important stabilizing force in the Austin counterculture.[85] But the organization's most personal appeal was directed to both Vietnam veterans and Americans generally, an appeal to turn away from a violent way of life. VVAW lamented that "many of us do not understand . . . the concept of nonviolence.

> We grew up in a violent society with John Wayne movies, *Dragnet*, and all the other things. And in the Nam we saw many of our brothers die

because they thought they were John Wayne. Nonviolence does not mean nonaction. Nonviolence is a special form of action designed to point out the contradictions inherent in using violence to obtain peaceful goals.

The VVAW activists vowed to free themselves of the traditional masculine "role" that made them suitable instruments of war. They fairly pleaded with their fellow veterans to "be creative with [their] energies."

> We must maintain a sense of humor as well as a sense of urgency and determination. We must control ourselves and show the people of this nation and the world that we have had it with war—all wars. That the needless dying in Indochina must cease now. *And in order to do it we must live it. We have to be free.* And that freedom includes freedom from the role we were trained for—the role of violence.[86]

For veterans like these, the figure of the guerrilla held no existential thrill. Their war experiences had spurred grievous doubts about the intimate relations between violence and masculinity. In their search for a nonviolent "freedom," they encountered obstacles from a government that harassed and slandered them, from citizens who viewed them as traitors to both America and manhood, to others on the antiwar left who thought nonviolence was unrealistic, and from fellow veterans who could not let go of their anger. As "Winter Soldiers," they fought some of the more difficult battles.

Marxists and Radicals

By the end of the 1960s, a new breed of students was arriving on campus. These students had reached adolescence in the 1960s, not the 1950s; they had grown up with the Vietnam War. Some of them quickly embraced the new left's anti-imperialist analysis of the Vietnam War, but they felt ambivalent at best about the left-wing groups on campus. The SDS chapter's collapse in 1968/1969 meant that those students in search of an antiwar left were voices without a stable platform. Lori Hansel was part of this new trend. Attending a private high school for girls in Houston, she was politicized by what she learned about the civil rights movement, and "when I went away to college I went [with the thought] in mind that I wanted to do political things. I couldn't [have] care[d] less about college." She matriculated at the University of Wisconsin in Madison in the fall of 1969 but transferred to UT one year later, when she was eighteen. In Madison she witnessed the arrival of Weatherman representatives at an SDS chapter meeting. The meeting's participants as a whole stood and turned their backs to the schismatics, but Hansel found them "pretty interesting," perhaps because she, like them, was more concerned with race than with any other issue. She attended the moderate Moratorium in October 1969 in Washington, D.C., but soon her position on the war moved well to the left of that event's official slogan, "Bring the Troops Home." "It probably took me two months to realize that what I wanted to do was carry a National Liberation Front flag and really support the Vietnamese revolution rather than just being a pacifist and having an antiwar slant." She came to this conclusion on the basis of "gut-level feelings."[87]

By 1970, these loyalties were far less extraordinary on American campuses than they had been a few years before. But ironically, because of the SDS debacle, by this time there was no serious vehicle on most campuses for the mobilization and expression of that kind of radical sentiment. Starting in the fall of 1969, the most important leftist antiwar group in Austin—the Socialist Workers Party (SWP)—represented precisely the organization that had fought hardest for tactical moderation in the national antiwar coalitions, a moderation that students like Hansel increasingly derided. The party's campus antiwar organization was the Student Mobilization Committee to End the War in Vietnam (SMC). At the national level, an SMC had existed since 1965; in mid-1968, however, anger at the Trotskyist contingent led others to bolt from the organization, and it played a far less important role in national actions thereafter. But the SMC perceived the vacuum on the student antiwar left, and as a result, the SMC's affiliates actually increased their significance on the campuses.

The Trotskyists of the SWP[88] doggedly opposed militant tactics as well as radical rhetoric about the war. The Trotskyists called the militants "plate-glass revolutionaries," agreeing with many working-class antiwar activists that the "trashing" phenomenon—the destruction of property as a form of antiwar protest—and the insurrectionary rhetoric of groups like Weatherman represented an irresponsible "bourgeois adventurism," perhaps reflecting the frustration of privileged youth who were unused to not getting their way.[89]

In both national and local antiwar committees, the Trotskyists pressed their "line," which held that the antiwar movement's most important goal was to reach the political mainstream, especially the industrial working class, and that either militance or radicalism would impede the achievement of that goal. Therefore, peaceful, legal, mass demonstrations against the war constituted the only acceptable tactic for the movement, and there had to be an official "line" at such demonstrations, a line that would proscribe any anti-imperialist sentiments or anything else that might strike mainstream Americans as "anti-American." Hence SWP emissaries argued vociferously for official slogans such as "Out Now" or "Bring the Troops Home" at demonstrations. But most radical antiwar activists, whether new leftists or pacifists, wished to go well beyond this. Radical pacifists favored militant but nonviolent civil disobedience as one tactic, in the manner of the civil rights movement, and by 1968 both they and the new left favored draft resistance, but the Trotskyists viewed any lawbreaking as a tactical error. Moreover, the Trotskyists believed that the countercultural dimension of antiwar protest was still another barrier between the movement and the mainstream, and the "straight" appearance and lifestyle of the Trotskyist operatives contributed greatly to the enmity between them and the new left.

After 1968, both the new left and the SWP avowed "revolutionary" goals. The SWP contended that only by building a majority behind their leadership could a political revolution occur in America. The new left activists argued that the only way to build a revolutionary force was to disseminate a revolutionary viewpoint. But the new left eventually learned that even a radical analysis of the Vietnam War was not an adequate basis for building and maintaining a revolutionary movement; so much less so was a position on the war like that of the Trotskyists, which above all sought to avoid giving offense. Furthermore, the Trotskyist position on tactics lagged behind that of even many antiwar activists who did not consider themselves radicals.

As the war dragged on, increasing numbers of activists became interested in militant tactics, and the SWP found itself not only failing to reach the mainstream of the country but also increasingly out of touch with the segment of the mainstream that had joined the ranks of committed antiwar activists. Steve Russell, for example, came to school at UT in 1969 as "a [Eugene] McCarthy liberal and an anti-war veteran," and joined the SMC because it was "the only organization that seemed to be moving against the war." But he ultimately criticized them, both for their unwillingness to run the risk of arrest, or even to help bail out those who were arrested for protesting the war, and for their "systematic . . . suppress[ion]" of moral criticism of the war. Russell "wanted to argue that the lunacy of Vietnam went far beyond the number of American casualties," but the Trotskyists did not.[90] In the climate of 1969, a commitment to militant tactics and moral argument in antiwar protest sometimes was exactly what was needed to give a leftist organization credibility with young antiwar activists, even liberals, but this was just the reverse of the Trotskyist analysis.

The Trotskyists' desire to repress their Marxist-Leninist viewpoint out of public view led to a modus operandi that deeply offended many in the new left, partly because it recalled the machinations of Progressive Labor. The SWP employed a "front group" structure, a tactic that in the 1960s generally existed only in the imagination of police agencies. The national party established a youth affiliate, the Young Socialists Alliance (YSA), from which it dispatched members to central Texas in the summer and fall of 1969.[91] The head "Trot" in Austin was Melissa Singler, a nonstudent and a dedicated, full-time antiwar agitator. She and her cadres established the SMC. Its leader was Travis Burgeson, who ran as an SWP congressional candidate in 1970. Over the next three years, the YSA also set up front organizations on the UT campus relating to other political issues, such as women's liberation. Once the national SWP leadership deemed an issue promising, the Trotskyists would alternately join the existing groups already working on these issues or set up their own groups to compete for membership among the campus constituencies. Ultimately, most campus leftists came to conclude that "YSA works inside of other movements but their primary loyalty is to YSA, not the women's movement, the anti-war movement."[92]

In Austin, SDS had died and the CEWV had run aground, so the SMC picked up the slack. Students like Jim Denney, Pat Cuney, Jeff Jones, and many others—members of the post-SDS new left—joined the SMC, as did Steve Russell, because it was the only game in town. Denney rose to become SMC regional coordinator. He, Cuney, Jones, and Doyle Niemann all attended a national SMC conference in Cleveland (a major site of antiwar organization) in early 1970. But within a year, most of them had become disillusioned with what they considered the dishonest and authoritarian internal structure of the Trotskyist organizations, and they chafed at their higher-ups' tactical timidity. Russell, Betty White, Niemann, Wizard, Waterhouse, and others established "the 'independent faction' within SMC" that sought and failed to turn the SMC into "a multi-issue anti-imperialist organization that could fill the void left by SDS's demise." This faction moved from "a non-YSA position" to outright opposition.[93]

Everyone knew that the YSA ran the SMC and that the SWP ran the YSA, but the Trotskyists tried to present the groups as independent of one another. The YSA contingent apparently would caucus before a full meeting of the SMC to decide what the meeting's outcome would be; "General meetings were invariably a Trot chairman engineering the Roberts' Rules railroad," Russell reported.[94] The recruits, imbued with the antiauthoritarianism and spirit of openness that characterized the new left, thought it absurd that they should operate on the basis of party lines, orders from above, and closed caucuses. By the fall of 1972, the *Rag*—which became the main platform for new left criticism of the Trotskyists—spoke bluntly of "Trot cowardice and duplicity." It ran a picture of a tree whose roots were labeled SWP, its trunk YSA, and its branches the local Trotskyist front groups; the picture's caption read simply, "Dogmatism."[95] It seemed that the new left's early animus against "ideology" was once again strong.

The Trotskyists adroitly accused the new left of "red-baiting." Indeed, Judy Smith asserted that "Trots are a particularly dangerous group because they really do work like something out of *Masters of Deceit*," an exposé of the Communist Party authored by J. Edgar Hoover.[96] Although this may seem like a shocking charge to have come from someone in the left, it is not so uncharacteristic of the new left, a movement that always had defined itself partly in opposition to the old left. Aside from personal distaste, this distinction among varieties of the left entailed a practical problem. Some local activists, reflecting widespread sentiment in the early 1970s, explained that they sought "a libertarian socialist revolution. It ain't easy and having the Trots around doesn't help the movement much. People might think all radicals are like them!"[97]

As this stress on "libertarian socialism" indicates, the conflict over countercultural influences was a sore point between the Trotskyists and the larger radical community in Austin. In the eyes of many local radicals, the Trotskyists' antipathy to the counterculture, combined with their seemingly manipulative methods, added up to people who were living in the old society, unwilling to venture into the new. The staff of Sattva, a local, collectively run vegetarian restaurant, complained that the Trotskyists

> may be socialists, but the kind of society they want is very different from what we want; it is dull, authoritarian, and anti-democratic . . . just as we refuse to be treated by capitalist amerika as merely consumers, cannon fodder, or whatever, we refuse to be treated by the Trots as mere political converts, voters, or demonstrators.[98]

In the new left view, political form and method reflected principle, and means stemmed from ends. The "dullness" of Trotskyist politics, its resistance to the confluence of politics, art, and life that was so important to radicals in this era was thought to betoken an authoritarian personality. The playfulness that new left activists tried to bring into their politics was sometimes directed at the Trotskyists, and here the play turned rough. Radicals made up ditties, set to popular tunes, about "smashing the state"—"If yer gonna smash the state, ya gotta keep a smile on yer face and a song in yer heart!"—that also included jabs at the "Trots."[99] They took to making stabbing motions toward their ears to annoy the Trotskyists at antiwar gatherings, a reference to Leon Trotsky's murder.[100] (A calculated violation of good taste often was part of the new left's political theater.)

The difficult project—indeed, the problematic concept—of libertarian socialism also got in the way of the SWP's recruiting efforts on at least one occasion, when the party considered Jim Denney, their best Austin recruit, for membership (unlike most political parties, the SWP did not welcome just anyone who wished to join). Denney was gay, and the SWP did not knowingly admit gay members. This, too, they felt would keep them from reaching the masses. (By 1972, the party had changed this policy.)[101]

Both sides in the new left–Trotskyist dispute were guilty of errors: on one side, tactical rigidity and dishonesty and, on the other, a rigid insistence on prefigurative, countercultural politics and a confusion of militance with radicalism. The Trotskyists organized broad-based student antiwar activism in the 1969/1970 school year in particular, when no one else was doing so. The SMC organized the Austin Moratorium on 15 October 1969, which drew between 7,500 and 12,000 people—part of an enormous national day of protest, in effect an attempt at a general strike.[102] In mid-April 1970, in response to the escalation of the U.S. air war in Indochina, protests again erupted around the country, and the SMC's march down Austin's sidewalks mustered 8,000, a number that would have been lower had it not been for the city council's foolish denial of a parade permit (which would have ceded the street to the marchers), thereby bringing out the civil libertarians.[103]

The biggest antiwar demonstration ever in Austin came on 8 May 1970, twenty thousand people marching peacefully against the United States' invasion of Cambodia and the shooting deaths of students at Kent State University on 4 May 1970, the culmination of several days of mass protests.[104] On this occasion, broad ad hoc coalitions overtook the SMC, but the Trotskyists nonetheless contributed their organizational skills. The Marxist-Leninists facilitated, though they did not cause, the antiwar movement's move into the mainstream during the crucial 1969/1970 school year. But ironically, the rift with the new left that the Trotskyists did so much to create drained considerable energy from the antiwar left just as it entered a crucial period of reconstruction. Despite the efforts of other groups in the next few years, the reconstruction never fully took place.

Democracy in the Streets?

Both a worsening sense of frustration among antiwar activists as the years of war piled up and a loss of connection with the emphasis on nonviolence that earlier antiwar protesters had absorbed from the civil rights movement led to the rise of trashing, both substantial and petty. This also resulted from the loss of SDS, which could have served as a vehicle of more effective militance, and the related fall from influence of those leaders of the new left, such as Greg Calvert and Staughton Lynd, who were closer to the earlier tradition of militant nonviolence. Between 1969 and 1973, with few local organizations committed to disciplined militance in opposition to the war, radicals like Hansel ended up expressing their anger over the war in sporadic antics like spray painting (for example, spraying "Preston Pig" on the Texas governor's residence, when Democrat Preston Smith occupied it), occasional window breaking, for example, at the demonstration by three thousand protesters against the dedication of the Lyndon B. Johnson Library and School of Public Affairs on campus in May 1971, and raucous protest marches of which no one was in charge.[105]

The level of trashing at UT never approached that at many other campuses around the country; even the approbation for greater antiwar violence found elsewhere was slight on the Austin left, as Hansel learned when she encountered fierce disagreement from the staff of the *Rag* after writing an article supporting the explosion at the University of Wisconsin's Army Mathematics Research Center in 1970, the only instance of antiwar sabotage resulting in the death of someone besides an antiwar protester.[106] Militants usually directed such sabotage at targets clearly related in some way to the war effort or to the financial and political underpinnings of U.S. foreign policy. The purpose of this behavior, however, was not entirely clear. To a large extent, it was simply an expression of outrage, with little impact on the war effort expected.[107]

At the same time, many radicals argued that militance had a positive effect on those who participated in it or even witnessed it as bystanders. Militance might "fairly quickly lead to significant numbers of Americans deciding to break through their conditioning and to start taking control of their own lives," maintained Martin Wiginton, echoing the logic that the Weatherman contingent of SDS sometimes used to explain their activities.[108] On the other hand, many justified the militance as a way "to increase the domestic cost" of the war, in the hope that U.S. political and economic elites would decide the game was not worth the candle and so end the war.[109] But the war had dragged on far too long for anyone to express confidence that militance had this impact; instead, the domestic conflict of this period ended in right-wing electoral victory and political repression.[110]

Indeed, peaceful mass mobilizations such as the October 1969 Moratorium probably did more to constrain military action, even temporarily, than militance did.[111] Furthermore, the militance that appeared in the war's later years often worked to the detriment of the antiwar movement's public image and, by extension, possibly damaged the antiwar position in the public mind.[112] Even relatively minor destruction of property, such as that in Austin, became the object of disproportionate outrage, often coming from those who wished to discredit antiwar activism in general and who aimed to do so, outrageously, by suggesting a moral equivalence between the actions of the U.S. government in Southeast Asia and those of the antiwar movement in the United States.

Even on its own terms—at least as a reminder to those in power that the antiwar movement still harbored the potential to create great disorder—the militance of the antiwar movement's later period was not highly successful. The costs it imposed on the "war machine" were dubious. The loss of connection to the recent history of political protest might help account for the poor planning of even the best-organized and biggest militant protest of this period, the 1971 "Mayday" activities that brought tens of thousands of people to Washington, D.C., in an effort to immobilize the center of war-making power. Various police and military agencies took extraordinary measures against the protesters on 3–5 May, such as summary arrests without cause and mass detentions in commandeered sports facilities. But the simpler step of ordering federal employees to appear at work early on the first morning of the action did perhaps as much to stymie the planned disruptions. The organizers' failure to foresee such eventualities makes them look amateurish in comparison with the planning that went into the civil rights movement's major urban assaults, such as those on Birmingham in 1963 or Selma in 1965.

The Mayday actions were organized on a highly decentralized basis, in keeping with the antiauthoritarian tide that was then cresting on the left, further limiting the protests' effectiveness. One of the regional building blocks of the Mayday protests was Austin's "Mayday Armadillo Tribe," named for the animal that had become a local countercultural symbol and for the fanciful identification of young leftists with nomadic Native American peoples—a further token of their "anarchism," accompanied by "adventurism" and "anti-intellectualism," as one of the Armadillo Mayday Tribe's organizers recalled. Their assigned target in Washington was Scott Circle. In the months before May, the Austin group mobilized activists from dozens of towns in Texas, Oklahoma, and Arkansas, eventually prompting "more than 250 people to make the trek in Volkswagen vans, rented buses, and overstuffed automobiles."[113] The resulting protests reminded both local activists and the federal government that the number of militants who could be brought together was greater than ever—indeed, it was massive and national in its basis. But the main costs that the protesters imposed on the government were the monetary costs of a temporary police state; the war-making capacity of the state suffered no damage, in either logistical or political terms.[114] The Mayday bedlam overshadowed the innovative and thoughtful attempt by the People's Coalition for Peace and Justice (PCPJ), which had instigated the protests, to promote a "People's Peace Treaty," which the National Student Association had negotiated with Vietnamese citizens. It also tarnished the public image of the half-million-strong rally that antiwar activists pulled off in Washington a week before May Day and blunted the effectiveness of the VVAW's powerful protest on the U.S. Capitol steps.[115]

New left activists expressed frustration about their inability to harness the anger of the antiwar left during this period, to channel it into productive activity. They often made the same criticisms of militance that Trotskyists and liberals made: criticisms of the limits it could place on the antiwar movement's appeal, especially class limits. Looking back on several days of militant protests in Austin in response to Nixon's bombing of civilian areas in Hanoi and Haiphong in late April 1972, protests that involved thousands and ended in teargassing by local police, one activist lashed out at what he saw as "ego-gratification. Marching to the Federal Building [in downtown Austin] banging trash can lids may be a lot of fun, but we must realize that in addition . . . we must also reach people, like secretaries, office workers, clerks, who cannot relate to a 'bunch of weirdos making asses of themselves.'"[116] Steve Russell, who had become a leading new left critic of new left politics, noted that the *Daily Texan* had called the protest "A New Left Pep Rally," and he charged that it "was, if anything, more irrational than UT's endemic displays of football fever." He also expressed disgust for the decision by a VVAW contingent to lead a march around campus under an NLF flag. "Again, a total, egotistical, contemptuous, and I hope unthinking disregard for 'The People' in whose name some of these clowns claim to be making revolution."[117] On another occasion, one antiwar activist, sounding a commonly heard theme, worried about the enmity between protesters and the police. "Our side fucked up," this activist concluded. "We were not there to confront the cops, but to confront the warmakers."[118]

Some Austin leftists tried to mount an alternative that would navigate between the shoals of undisciplined anger and minimalist coalitions. A small group retrieved and revived the legacy of militant nonviolence. This was "Direct Action," started in 1970 by Ed and Grace Hedemann and affiliated with the War Resisters League in New York. Although focused primarily on the war, Direct Action had a broader view, founded on the belief "that human life is more important than property." It sought a new society, according to the Hedemanns, based on "trust." Thus they drew a pointed contrast with other groups on the left that local activists would have perceived easily, and with this emphasis, the group harked back to the early new left's stress on honesty and transparency as the basis for a new politics. Direct Action promoted a variety of tactics, including draft resistance, tax withholding, civil disobedience, and interference with campus recruiters "for the military–industrial complex."[119]

The effort that received the most attention was tax withholding, in which antiwar activists increasingly engaged after the imposition of an extra 7 percent federal surtax on telephone bills in 1966, a surtax explicitly intended to defray the costs of the war. Many who engaged in this form of protest acted from a religious motivation, although the Hedemanns did not. By 1972, both the Unitarian Universalist Church and the Central Conference of American Rabbis voted to withhold this tax.[120] Ed Hedemann claimed that this small act, which carried little risk of penalty, was "a simple first step to more comprehensive forms of civil disobedience in the spirit of Thoreau, who said: 'If a thousand men were not to pay their tax bills, that would not be so violent and bloody a measure, as it would be to pay them and enable the state to commit violence and shed innocent blood.' "[121]

Drawing on such a venerable pedigree, this antistatist activism might have been expected to catch fire amid the anarchistic political milieu of the Austin left. But Direct Action's marches and demonstrations remained small. They may have garnered much local respect but little enthusiasm. The common wisdom on the left at that point was that the time for inspirational, nonviolent "witnessing" against the war had long since passed (by at least three years—a whole era in the minds of young activists), that it could not stop the war, and that it was an insufficient vehicle for expressing anger at the war. Perhaps the divergence of religion and the left during the decade of the 1960s made it difficult for most on the left, by 1970, to see militant nonviolence as a compelling means of political protest.[122]

In the early 1970s, many new left activists did step back from the undisciplined politics of anger that threatened to overwhelm their movement. But instead of moving into the territory of radical nonviolence, the more notable shift was into the familiar terrain of electoral politics. This reconciliation with conventional politics marked a substantial change since 1968, when the new left loudly abstained from the presidential election. At that time, reflecting widespread sentiment on the left, Austin radicals called the elections "a hoax," claiming that all three major candidates, Richard Nixon, Hubert Humphrey, and George Wallace, were closely tied to the country's business and financial elites. "The people may pick the actual winner, but the choices are pre-selected to conform to the interests of the large capitalists. The candidates do differ on issues, but none are fundamental."[123] In 1968 Greg Calvert also proclaimed this view from a position of influence, building on the new left thesis that reform politics in modern America constituted a sophisticated attempt to save the capitalist system and that the left should not assist in this task; therefore, the Democratic Party's candidates were no more attractive than the frank rightists of the Republican Party.[124]

Of course, the issue that really soured the new left on the Democrats—with whom the new left had considered a kind of coalition early on—was the Vietnam War. It was known as "Johnson's War," and Vice President Hubert Humphrey barely distanced himself at all from Johnson's war effort in 1968, prompting an angry SDS–CEWV demonstration against the Democratic standard-bearer when he stumped in Austin.[125] Even the proposals of the peace faction at the Democratic National Convention came in for criticism from leftists like Harvey Stone, who viewed the proposed bombing halt against North Vietnam as an attempt to stop an ineffective military tactic, and the proposed coalition government in South Vietnam as a last-ditch effort at maintaining some share of power for the illegitimate United States–backed regime in Saigon. Carl Oglesby's support for Robert Kennedy's presidential candidacy made him a virtual leper in the new left's national leadership.[126] In 1968, the American left was both disillusioned with liberalism and confident that the antiwar movement could hold out for a better deal than was on the table.

After four years of a Nixon administration, however, this stance had changed. In October 1972 the *Rag* prominently featured its electoral endorsements, a conventional newspaper practice that was unthinkable in the underground press of four years earlier. Vietnam was now Nixon's war, it charged, and leftists had a duty to use all means available to stop it. The paper summarized the statistics of "death and destruction" visited on Southeast Asia since early 1969: "4.5 million Indochinese civilians killed, wounded, or made homeless," "1.5 million soldiers on all sides killed or wounded," "40,000 South Vietnamese civilians executed without trial under the Phoenix Program," "750,000 acres of crop and forest land bulldozed," and more. The paper's staff urged the election of George McGovern. "While St. George has certainly done some shuckin' and jivin' here and there, he has remained firm on one point: there is no national interest that calls for an American military presence in Indochina. . . . Under McGovern, the executive would no longer rubber stamp military spending requests."[127]

The *Rag* also found McGovern's reform stance on domestic issues preferable to Nixon's positions. No more the previous derision of reform; these radicals sounded like born-again liberals. With McGovern as president, they said, "farm workers would be guaranteed their right to organize, we would probably see a woman on the Supreme Court." The *Rag* also endorsed Ramsey Muniz, the candidate of the new Mexican American party, La Raza Unida, for governor "not because he's the Raza Unida candidate, not because he's the Chicano candidate," it said, "but because he's the best candidate."[128] The regional political system had opened up somewhat in the previous decade, thereby offering the left–liberal voter more choices.

The older rejectionist view of electoral politics did not die easily. Jim Simons, a local "movement lawyer" who had made a wrenching break with liberal politics in the late 1960s, wrote angrily in the spring of 1972, "The semiannual game is on and attracting many movement and counterculture people." His comrades seemed to have forgotten the insight that election work "drains away energy in a cause that is about as related to the objectives of our community as the Baptist Church." Perhaps one day, after substantial change had already occurred, elections would be meaningful. But, he said, "under circumstances as they now exist in this country, taking the business of elections seriously is fostering falsehood and undermining radical consciousness." The concept, even "the word 'cooptation' has faded from the scene—apparently taking with it the insight of a generation that it embodied"—his generation, as he ruefully implied.[129] He was far from alone in thinking that the project of developing "radical consciousness" was paramount and that supporting one or another capitalist-backed candidate would only impede that project.

The rejoinder to Simons came from a perhaps surprising source: Mariann Wizard, who had been a Communist Party organizer for several years. Actually, the CP traditionally supported electoral coalitions with liberals, and in line with this tactic, she and her friend Gavan Duffy supported Frances "Sissy" Farenthold, the candidate of the liberal Democrats, in the gubernatorial primary. These leftists seemed to have a domestic agenda uppermost in mind, and the Democratic Party's complicity in the war would not deter them from pursuing that agenda. Farenthold "supports increased welfare payments . . . establishment of day-care centers, adequate family planning, lower consumer taxes and a corporate profits tax, unionization, etc.," they said. Wizard and Duffy pointedly noted that these matters were meaningful to poor and working-class people in Texas, even if not to leftists from middle-class backgrounds. They poked fun at nonelectoral political activism, noting that their support for Farenthold did not "imply a belief in the electoral process any more than going to a demonstration implies [a] belief that marching around like a herd of sick cows mooing 'demands' will bring a revolution." Getting the best of this exchange, they asserted that only "the TEN COMMANDMENTS OF REVOLUTIONARY ETIQUETTE" made electoral politics seem distasteful to their fellow leftists.[130]

Some leftists moved into electoral politics as a method of grassroots political organizing. This was the attitude especially of women like Pat Cuney, Victoria Foe, and Judy Smith, who engineered a virtual takeover of their local Democratic Party precinct in Austin. These precinct meetings were a good way to meet your neighbors and spread your subversive viewpoint to them, Smith thought. This group floated two proposals in precinct meetings: one for the immediate withdrawal of all U.S. forces from Vietnam, long the demand of the antiwar left, and the other for the repeal of all abortion laws in Texas.[131] To their surprise, Cuney and Foe found themselves as delegates on the floor of the statewide party convention in Houston.[132] Without necessarily meaning to, they rode the McGovernite "new politics" wave to influence in partisan politics.

Endgame

One certainly can view the antiwar left's rapprochement with the mainstream as a sign of success. The standard narrative of the antiwar movement holds that this movement did win a secure place for its perspective in mainstream partisan politics, in effect capturing the Democratic Party, a substantial achievement despite the debacle of November 1972.[133] Some see in the McGovern campaign more than a change in the complexion of the American establishment's foreign policy debate; they depict the new blood in the Democratic Party as the vehicle of a comprehensive "movement for a new America."[134]

But this purportedly happy ending blurs important political distinctions. The "movement for a new America" was a newly inclusive politics that sought greater protections for citizens against predatory business practices as well as a less stridently martial foreign policy. Its social vision was not that of the new left, however. Many new left activists returned (or came for the first time) to the liberal fold in the waning years of antiwar protest because they simply had run out of left-wing alternatives. The left itself was in disarray. Martin Murray, a left-wing sociology graduate student at UT in the early 1970s, accurately perceived the political cul-de-sac into which the antiwar left had ventured. The tendency in the left that "demanded action, and action for its own sake," he wrote ruefully, "won the ideological battles . . . but was unable to sustain momentum after the Paris Peace Accords in 1973."[135] "Where would we be if peace were to break out tomorrow?" The question from 1965 was far more pertinent eight years later.

The new left could not escape the issue of Vietnam, and any suggestion that it might have done so would distort the history of this era badly. Both leaders and followers in the radical movement came to agree with the spirit of Ronnie Dugger's emotional appeal, offered in late 1967: "Until our nation turns back from its disastrous, uncivilized, immoral, illegal, un-American, inhumane, atrocious, undeclared war in Vietnam, no US citizen who cares about our society, our political life, can fully consider other public needs, no matter how pressing."[136] The Vietnam War assumed first priority for the left, as it did for humanist liberals such as Dugger, and the decisions of those who prosecuted the war and would not let it end ensured this.

For the left, this domestic conflict over the war held consequences that are rarely admitted. The hard truth is that the new left's entanglement with the war and the antiwar movement helped derail its initial project of developing a movement for fundamental political change, rooted in a thorough critique of American life. It is true that the new left's entry into the antiwar movement was the source of the left's explosive growth in the late 1960s, but that growth was unstable and proved ephemeral, dependent as it was on the war issue. The war could make a large and disruptive left, but it could not make a revolutionary movement, as some on the left thought it could.

In contrast, the radical movement's growth between 1960 and 1965, based on a comprehensive political critique and an alternative vision, was steady and impressive if not as dynamic. There is good reason to think that in the absence of the war's escalation, the new left would have continued to grow in the late 1960s and that the resulting movement might have become a "lasting, deeply rooted . . . phenomenon," in the anarchist Murray Bookchin's words.[137] The sense of desperate urgency produced by the war led the left away from long-term strategic thinking, toward displays of anger that got it nowhere. The course of antiwar protest encouraged the new left's conflation of militance and radicalism.[138] Anger at the war became the fuel on which the left ran, and when the fuel ran out, the movement sputtered. Furthermore, the new left's radical anti-imperialism reintroduced to North American politics the issue that the early new left worked so hard to banish: allegiance to foreign socialist governments. The early possibility of an effectively "isolationist" left was lost, for both better and worse. The young radicals' concern with the misery of people in far-away lands and their determination to trace that suffering to its roots were extraordinary in their cosmopolitanism and moral bravery. Although this focus on the experience of Third World peoples was not the only factor that did in the new left, a good share of the radical movement's blood was left splashed on the altar of imperial culture.

CHAPTER SEVEN

This Whole Screwy Alliance:
The New Left and the Counterculture

NEW LEFT RADICALS came to believe that "the revolution is about our lives."[1] In the late 1960s, reports of campus takeovers and antiwar protests made newspaper headlines across the United States, and the new left, apparently hell-bent on its revolutionary course, featured prominently in many of these dramas. These associations have led many to believe that new left radicals staged confrontations as their primary means of creating political change, of bringing about a revolutionary situation. Doubtless this is how some leftists viewed these incidents. However, the headline-grabbing conflicts, like the widely reported faction fights at national SDS meetings, have obscured the development of thought in the later new left concerning the methods of social change. The widespread belief in the new left that "the revolution is about our lives" not only indicated who the radicals thought could make the revolution—themselves—but also expressed their dominant thinking concerning the techniques of revolution during the new left's most vibrant years. The most important strategy by which new left radicals concluded that the new class, or new class fragment, of which they were a part, could actually work for a new society was what became known as "cultural" activism.[2]

In the late 1960s and early 1970s, the new left came to view itself as a part of the larger "counterculture" and as a counterculture in itself. Whereas antiwar protests and other confrontations were sporadic, if continual, activities, countercultural activism became a virtually ceaseless task for young white leftists. They set about fashioning what Lawrence Goodwyn, an insurgent Austin liberal, later called a "movement culture" in his historical discussion of the nineteenth-century Populist farmers' revolt. Just as his evocation of that culture conjures the aura of the organic or "traditional," of people whose very lives were rooted in the soil, so the new left wished to create through self-conscious effort an authentic community, which was set against the artificiality of life in "the received, hierarchical culture" and in which they could cultivate a revolution. In evaluating the new left's strategic thinking and its fate as a radical movement, no other dimension of this movement is so important.[3]

New left radicals and their sympathizers have often argued that the radicals of the 1960s redefined politics. They have contended that the attempt to change the national "culture" represented the most profound type of political radicalism that the United States had seen since the "lyrical left" of the early twentieth century, to which "the cultural revolution seemed as important as the social revolution."[4] In this view, the new left's countercultural side represented an expansion of the scope of "politics" after several decades in which political activity was understood in a constricted way, merely as the attempt to influence governmental institutions and the social allocation of material resources. New left activists loved to hear that in the old left, as the folksinger Malvina Reynolds told them, "there was an inhuman quality about radicals" that the new left had overcome.[5] The new radicals meant "to change the way we, as individuals, actually live and deal with other people"; they wished to "prefigure" the ideal society in their own social relations; and they tended to view positively anyone who was trying to do the same, such as the hippies (or "freaks").[6] Spokespersons for the counterculture made it plain that they rejected politics. The author Ken Kesey, for example, gained notoriety when he spurned protest politics at an antiwar gathering in Berkeley in 1965. "That's what *they* do," he said, and everyone knew who *they* were: the squares. Nonetheless, many new left radicals, and historians who have taken up their viewpoint, have protested that the politics of which Kesey spoke was simply the "old" politics. They, like he, were pioneers.[7]

What was the counterculture? In fact, there were many 1960s countercultures: pastoral and high-technology, rural and urban; misogynist and feminist; black, white, brown. Some say the "lower-middle-class" subculture that came to the fore as the victorious "silent majority" in 1968 rebelled against an oppressive cultural elite, and therefore perhaps these "little people" deserve the honorific of counterculture as well.[8] Since the mid-1960s, the pose of rebellion has become normative in our political culture; virtually everyone strikes it. But the counterculture to which the new left felt linked, and the one I refer to as "the counterculture," was the loosely associated set of cultural rebellions among affluent white youth in the 1960s and 1970s.

These were the young hippies or freaks who first appeared in U.S. cities by 1965, most noticeably in the San Francisco Bay area, site of the 1967 "Summer of Love." They lived in voluntary poverty, refugees from the "at least modest comfort" of their social class. By the early 1970s, they had migrated to rural settings, establishing countless experiments in intentional community. They either sought to live off the dross of a wealthy society or tried to subsist outside the consumption-driven, market-organized economy altogether. In any case, they revolted against the work discipline, the instinctual repression, and the sensory deprivation that in their view defined mainstream culture in the United States. The mantra of "sex, drugs, and rock-and-roll," superficial as it was, represented tools that freaks used to achieve their aims of escape, mystic vision, or transcendence. They evinced both an antinomian indifference to the cultural rules by which most of their fellow citizens lived and a conviction that they had to break these rules if they were to reach the "ground of Being." Like the new left, freaks believed in the power of transgression, of crossing boundaries. Like the new left, they felt that they lived in a society of alienation, and they searched, above all, for authenticity.[9]

The affinities between the new left and the counterculture are clear. Their strongest link lay in the common quest for authenticity, not in consistent political goals. This affinity was apparent during the 1960s. The counterculture helped the new left project outward its own search for personal authenticity, locating the causes of inner alienation in larger social forces and opening an avenue for all people to achieve authenticity at a societal level. The new left and the counterculture were two parts of a larger white youth existentialist movement of the cold war era—two parts of a larger historical formation with common roots, even if they were not close tactical allies. This larger existentialist movement appeared not only in the United States but also in highly industrialized European consumer societies. It sought to displace the predominant "values" of industrial society with new values that would affirm and allow the full development of human potential and would end estrangement—estrangement from the realm of the divine, from the cosmos, from one's true or higher self, from repressed dimensions of human personality, and from other living beings. The old values had developed in the context of economic scarcity, but now scarcity had been transcended, and the new values would function well in a postscarcity society. The instinctual repression of American culture in the cold war entailed "surplus repression," needlessly instilled by a social–political regime and internalized by individuals, in the words of Herbert Marcuse, the "critical theorist" whom new left radicals adopted as an intellectual eminence.[10]

Disagreements abounded concerning which values prevailed in this repressive society and which needed to ascend. Whereas many in the counterculture felt that Western culture suffered from the rule of reason and exalted emotion and creativity, leftists rarely spoke against rationality, even if they felt it important to balance reason with emotion. There also was closer agreement. Both the new left and the counterculture drew on the residual religious language of love and life, opposing these values to hatred and death, negative values that they claimed reigned supreme in America. Mariann Wizard embraced the counterculture's message: that young Americans of the 1960s had inherited "a culture of unhappiness and misery, and a culture that promulgates death and conformity. And we want a culture that's open and alive . . . where love is able to happen." She agreed with the poet Allen Ginsberg, who when he visited Austin in 1967 urged young people "to search for . . . happiness among each other at small grassroots levels."[11]

Above all, the new left and the counterculture shared the basic feeling that American culture was not "natural," that it was somehow artificial or twisted. Perhaps such a perversion once had been necessary to ensure the survival of the human race, but no longer. Ginsberg contended that the common American view of human nature as competitive was simply false and that in fact, "man's basic nature is that he's a pretty decent fellow when there's enough to go around."[12] The point was to release the natural human tendencies toward love and cooperation that politics and culture in the United States had suppressed. This opposition between the natural, or the "real," and the artificial most directly expressed the existentialist search for authenticity, forming a kind of preface to any discussion of specific practices and values that ought to change. The radicals of the 1960s reworked the 1950s search for personal integrity and wholeness into a search for a whole and natural way of life, a natural culture.

Possibly the most influential section of the *Port Huron Statement* was its discussion of "values." Although some people thought that the new left differed from the old mainly in the priority it assigned to racial justice or in its commitment to "direct action," others believed that the real difference lay in the prefigurative dimension of new left politics, the new left's determination to live by a dissident set of values. Jeff Nightbyrd puts great stock in "the difference between positions and values," recalling acidly that the "neo-Marxists had lots of positions." Bobby Minkoff says SDS activists felt that an exclusive focus on creating economic and institutional change unaccompanied by an immediate change in values might result in a society that resembled the Soviet Union, a model of socialism that they rejected. Indeed, the *Port Huron Statement* asserted that both sides in the cold war had perpetrated Orwellian distortions of language so deceitful (it cited the parallel slogans of "the free world" and "people's democracies") that "making values explicit" had become a "devalued and corrupted" activity, but one whose integrity the new left wished to restore. The need for a clear and honest statement of values was tied to the new left's "third camp" orientation.[13]

"Fraternity and honesty," as well as "love, reflectiveness, reason, and creativity," were the values the *Port Huron Statement* affirmed. These were conventional values, but in the new left's view, they were honored only in the breach in contemporary America, so that to live by them would constitute a rebellion of no mean proportions. (The new left's articulation of community as "fraternity"—a band of brothers—was consistent with this affirmation of values so traditional as to make the new left sometimes seem conservative.) In late 1965 Robert Pardun agreed that the emphasis on stating and living by such values was what made the new left really new, and he termed this prefigurative politics "social radicalism," as opposed to mere "political radicalism." Individual young people came to the new left, he explained, for the same reason they might become freaks: they were radically dissatisfied with the way of life they found in mainstream American culture, in which they could not become "real individuals." If Pardun was right, then the new left had to embrace its role as a part of the emerging alternative culture, or else it might have forfeited the loyalty of its adherents.[14]

New leftists, like hippies, came to believe that they were participating in a cultural revolution and that in this way they could circumvent the difficulties in conventional methods of political change. As one leftist put it in 1966, "I'm not worried about overthrowing the government at all—if we can just survive another ten years or so the ruling classes will no longer seem the least bit relevant or legitimate to the new generation. And it's the end of people's belief in a way of life that brings revolution."[15] Starting in 1966, countercultural activity became the new left's most important strategy for fomenting social change in America and its strongest expression of faith in the historical agency of the social stratum from which it derived. By the logic of the 1960s—according to which marginality indicated radical potential and cultural authenticity—the new left's understanding of itself as a counterculture became in itself the movement's strongest claim to both authenticity and radicalism: a counterculture was, by definition, both marginal and oppositional.

The new left's countercultural activity embraced the same hopes that the new working-class analysis expressed. Just as white leftists felt they no longer could function as a part of the black political movement, many of them began to look away from African Americans and toward themselves as guides to a new culture. Young white leftists believed that the culture of the baby boomers itself might prefigure the new society they wanted to create—a society more peaceful, cooperative, egalitarian, loving, and open to new experiences than the old one was. Larry Freudiger, reporting on the widespread dissatisfaction among white youth in California in 1967, told his Austin comrades that teenagers there had entered the market as consumers looking for new cultural models to emulate. This incipient "white revolution," as he called it, had found a template: "Us, baby—*us*."[16]

Beneath the factionalism of the late 1960s, this grounding of authenticity and the cultural method of social change seized the imagination of new left radicals. The new left's avant-gardism hollowed out the search by the factions in SDS for a more conventional political vanguard, leaving the faction leaders with few followers. The results of the new left's countercultural gambit disappointed widespread revolutionary aspirations. Still, the results were far from inconsequential, if quite different from what new left radicals expected. Ultimately the new left's efforts at cultural change had their greatest impact on political liberalism, helping turn liberals toward issues of "culture." For several years, however, the new left's counterculturalism—far from intending to chart a new path for liberalism—expressed the new left's belief that its own social milieu was where the revolutionary action was. The new left came to view the consumer society as the enemy of both authenticity and social change. Yet ironically, the consumer juggernaut of "pleasure-oriented" baby boomers signaled the cultural power of white youth, demonstrating that if the new left could persuade its peers to join in the project of prefiguring a new society, "inevitable victory" would lie ahead.[17]

A Single Movement?

Although both the new left and the counterculture were parts of a larger youth existentialist movement, they did not function together as a coordinated, harmonious enterprise during the 1960s. In this sense they were not a single "movement," despite retrospective attempts to unite them. Nightbyrd, for example, insists that this kind of unity was present at the creation of the Austin SDS chapter in the 1963/1964 school year. The rudiments of the 1960s counterculture were evident then in the "ragged fringe" at UT: the campus folksinging club, the motorcyclists, the spelunkers—cave explorers who ventured into Mexico and were known to sample psychedelic mushrooms—and others who congregated in the Chuckwagon. Nightbyrd says that he patched this motley bunch into a white constituency for civil rights agitation, under the leadership of militant political activists like himself. This picture of events suggests that political activism may even have played a crucial role in annealing the previously unstable alloy of the counterculture itself. "There was this whole screwy alliance" of perhaps two hundred people at the time SDS began meeting, a political–cultural front of the "alienated and rebel groups." The basis for this unity was ostensibly a common dissatisfaction with the mainstream campus culture. In the early 1960s, in the South, segregation seemed thoroughly entwined with the smug, starched-shirt provincialism of campus life.[18]

This is far too simple. The notion of an early united front between the new left and the counterculture is a myth, although like many myths, it has a factual basis. According to the conventional wisdom concerning insurgent politics in the 1960s, no single piece of the emerging counterculture should have been more receptive to a united front than the folksingers. The so-called folk revival—which was really not a revival but a continuation of the popularization of "folk music," a category that musicologists and folklorists invented earlier in the twentieth century—picked up steam in the early 1960s, when performers like the Kingston Trio; Peter, Paul, and Mary; and, most important, Bob Dylan achieved commercial success. In the 1940s, folk music had been a powerful propaganda instrument for the Communist-centered old left, epitomized in the songs of Woody Guthrie and the Weavers, and many of the best-known folk songs of the 1960s told tales of ongoing struggles for racial and class equality and against war.[19]

In the cold war years, college students who were unsympathetic to the main political tendencies of the day gravitated toward the folk scenes springing up on campuses around the country. Young people whose parents held leftist sympathies often grew up listening to folk records, and schools like Swarthmore College, which many such children attended, held folk festivals during the 1950s.[20] Besides its political import, those who performed and listened to folk music attempted to evoke the "aura of authenticity" that attached to the vision of "precommercialized" culture—the sepia images of rural southern white "hillbillies" and black laborers—that the music conveyed. The very idea of the "folk" captured the same explosive combination of the quest for authenticity and the vision of a downtrodden historical agent that animated the new left.[21]

Austin was one of the centers of the "revival." In previous decades, UT had been an early base for folkloric investigations, in the 1920s home to J. Frank Dobie and John Lomax, the original academic recorder of "cowboy songs." Here the "revival" boasted a direct connection with the past, an iconic emblem of authenticity, Kenneth Threadgill (called "Mr. Threadgill" by young people who supposedly did not respect anyone over thirty). Threadgill bought a filling station on the edge of town in the 1930s, and for two decades an audience of local Anglo workingmen gathered regularly to hear hillbilly musicians play there. Around 1959, four UT students who listened to blue-grass and folk records from the public library learned how to play some of the songs and started joining in the sessions. In 1960, a young folklorist named Roger Abrahams joined the English faculty at UT and began spon-soring a weekly evening "Folksing" in the Chuckwagon, where amplifiers were not forbidden, as they were among purists, and where the electrifica-tion of blues and jugband music pointed the way to 1960s rock. Student per-formers like John Clay, Powell St. John, and the one who went on to great-est fame by far, Janis Joplin, took part in both Threadgill's sessions and the Folksing in the early 1960s.

"In Austin, folksinging quickly became a way of marking one's difference from the student body represented by fraternities, sororities, and football players," says historian Barry Shank. Students from the *Ranger*, a campus humor magazine influenced in roughly equal proportions by *Mad* and *Playboy*, gravitated to the Folksing as well, taking a jaundiced view of this mainstream campus culture. The Folksing–*Ranger* group held relatively wild parties once a month, financed with the proceeds of the magazine's current issue, sometimes in the group house where Joplin lived for a time, known as "the Ghetto." This group was the nucleus of the white 1960s counterculture in Austin. This was also the group that a young Jeff Nightbyrd ostensibly found so politically promising and specifically so receptive to the message of civil rights activism.

In fact, the bloom on this particular rose has grown brighter with time. Threadgill's place did not allow blacks, and the young folksingers did not challenge this policy. On one occasion, Ed Guinn—an African American student who integrated the UT marching band in late 1963 and who in 1965, with Powell St. John, started the Conqueroo, the first well-known rock band in Austin—wanted to go to the musical gathering at the filling sta-tion, but John Clay talked him out of it. This suggests to Shank that the folk phenomenon carried an inextinguishable element of cultural conservatism, that it celebrated an "authentic" cultural milieu entangled in a history of white supremacy.[22]

Still, although Threadgill's was the fount of the local folk "revival," the young folk fans could easily behave differently in another venue. Certainly, they had a chance to express support for a political crossover to match their musical endeavors when civil rights activism accelerated in Austin in the early 1960s. The involvement of Folksing performers in civil rights agitation was minimal, however, and Roger Abrahams states flatly that they found radical politics "boring."

This view is supported by an incident in early 1964 when the folksinger Joan Baez, whose following was growing steadily and who was outspoken in her support for civil rights, came to town to sing. She visited the site of a picket outside a marathon Austin City Council meeting, and the fans she brought in tow had a tense encounter with the local SDS activists conducting the protest. A few black and white activists associated with the local NAACP were inside the meeting, conducting a filibuster and demanding the passage of a local antidiscrimination ordinance; the SDS picket was in solidarity with the filibuster. Baez approached the scene, where she expressed her support to the protesters and the media representatives who surrounded her, and then she began to sing. The SDS leaders did not seem enthusiastic about this celebrity support. "This is not a hootenany," said one, who stood angrily with his arms folded as Baez performed. His suggestion that the folkies were not serious seemed to be borne out when the star attraction left after singing and her fans followed, declining to join the picket.

Afterward, Nightbyrd, supposedly the architect of the political–cultural front, dismissively wrote of "the campus folksinger types—those who love to drink beer and sing songs of Protest and Freedom but who also limit their progressive battle against the force of [the] status quo to growing beards and wearing smelly T-shirts." With time, this derision cooled into earnest criticism. In the summer of 1966, when touring campus chapters for SDS, Nightbyrd sympathized with the growing freak counterculture but still saw it, in itself, as politically null. The new left "must deal with questions of power rather than act out our generation's alienation," he said. The distance separating the two constituencies was clear.[23]

Turning On

The counterculture mushroomed in Austin starting in the mid-1960s, fueled, as it was around the country, by the ever larger numbers of college students bearing ready cash. College enrollment nationwide grew from three million in 1960 to ten million in 1973. The percentage of the national population enrolled in colleges and universities rose from 2.5 to 3.2 in the 1950s but jumped to 7.1 during the 1960s (it continued its dramatic rise in the 1970s, reaching 12.1 by 1980).[24] For the growth of the counterculture, just as important as these aggregate numbers were the high concentrations of college students and other young people in specific cities, towns, and neighborhoods,

forming self-conscious localized "consumption communities" that channeled money into the new subculture. Conclaves of graduates and dropouts
who lingered around universities, becoming the stable consumer base for
"hip" entrepreneurs, followed the growth in student populations as morning
follows night. The UT student population was about 15,000 in 1958, moved
past the 20,000 mark in the early 1960s, and swelled to near 35,000 in the last
school year of that decade.[25] Other major public universities also doubled or
even tripled their student populations in this period as well. By 1974 there
were half a million college students in Texas, and in the Austin area alone,
students were dropping about $90 million a year as consumers.[26]

The music industry furnished the pioneers of this new market, carving
out social spaces where new cultural alternatives could take hold. Ed Guinn
persuaded Ira Littlefield, a black businessman in East Austin, to let the
Conqueroo play at his I. L. Club. Littlefield, a bit behind the times, advertised them as "Austin's best beatnik band." In 1967 the group's soundman,
Sandy Lockett, helped start the Vulcan Gas Company, a club meant specifically to bring in rock fans. Before the club opened, the Vulcan Gas Light
Show Company used strobe lights and "a kaleidoscope" of slide images—of
"love-ins," Allen Ginsberg, and civil rights protesters getting beat up, among
others—that were projected onto a two-story wall, in various venues around
town, to create an experience clearly patterned on the "acid tests" conducted
in California by Kesey and the "merry pranksters."[27] Screening silent films
and hosting bake sales, the Vulcan became a gathering place for the growing
number of freaks who grew their hair long and smoked marijuana, which was
sold openly from a van parked outside the club. Jim Franklin, an employee,
lived in the hallway, and he and Gilbert Shelton started producing posters to
advertise the club's offerings. Shelton achieved fame as the author of "The
Fabulous Furry Freak Brothers," a comic strip satirizing the drug culture that
ran in underground newspapers around the country, and Franklin's halluci-
natory drawings of armadillos engaged in various natural and unnatural acts,
such as eating a policeman's brain and copulating with the Texas state capitol, made the hard-shell critter a local countercultural icon.[28]

The growing use of psychedelics was the decisive emblem of the freak
subculture's arrival. In 1966, the 13th Floor Elevators, a new local rock band
whose name played on the metaphor of "getting high," started performing
songs celebrating drug use. In Austin, the most important rock band of the
late 1960s was Shiva's Head Band, which bathed the fiddle, harmonica, and
jug of southern folk music in electric juice and whose performances featured
"extended 'druggy' improvisational passages" designed for listeners who were
indulging. Not only was marijuana prevalent, but so was peyote, a local psy-

chedelic product that was outlawed only in 1966. Until then, one could buy peyote buds at retail on a certain street corner in town or purchase the entire plant—five for a dollar—from Hudson's Wholesale Cactus in San Antonio.[29] (One either ate the buds raw, often inducing a powerful nausea, or cooked them in a way that coaxed their psilocybin in purer form. John Clay was known to walk into the Chuckwagon openly chewing on a bud.) Because of its proximity to Mexico, Austin was "a major transit center" for psychedelics. Mariann Wizard, who first got "turned on" to marijuana in 1965 by a folksinger she met at the Methodist Student Center, saw closets filled with burlap sacks of cannabis.[30] The youth revolt against mainstream culture did not entail throwing over the old drugs for the new, however; both leftists and freaks enthusiastically affirmed the revered Texan practice of heroic beer consumption. Indeed, activists who arrived in Austin from the East and the Upper Midwest in the late 1960s remarked that they had never seen anyone drink so much beer.[31]

Austin's new left contingent gained a reputation in national SDS for its openness to the counterculture, and it worked to maintain its notoriety in this regard. Todd Gitlin recalls the relative squareness of the SDS old guard, stating that as late as 1967, "I doubt whether a single one of the Old Guard had sampled the mystery drug LSD. Most were leery even of marijuana." Many leftists with "hard-core political ideas" detested the counterculture on principle, says Robert Pardun, but "we weren't so hard-core, so we didn't care." Thorne Dreyer, the impresario of the *Rag*, the newspaper that Austin SDS activists started in 1966, averred that "Austin's a very funny scene. . . . There aren't the real ideological–philosophical splits between politicos and hippies that exist [in] many places. We probably have the most political hippies and the most hip politicos around."

As pointed out earlier, such statements exaggerate the unity of the new left and the freak counterculture in Austin. Nonetheless, a genuine, and perhaps unusual, conviviality developed over time between the two groups here. The close-knit SDS-UT circle were avid participants in all three sides of the countercultural triad, generally agreeing with the freaks that rock music, drugs, and "free love" were avenues to enlightenment. They went to the clubs, they embraced psychedelics, and they agreed that conventional sexual mores were repressive. Wizard recalls, "Basically, everybody turned on; basically everybody smoked; very few people did not smoke dope." (They were willing to distinguish between good and bad drugs, however; in the early 1970s, new left activists worked to combat the spread in the counterculture of heroin, which bore a "death karma.") They enjoyed the counterculture thoroughly, and their relations with the freaks were friendly.[32]

If there was a greater affinity between the new left and the counter-culture in Texas than elsewhere, it was perhaps because the two groups encountered greater hostility from the mainstream and instinctively banded together—"it's kind of the result of us against THEM," said Dreyer.[33] The mainstream often treated the left and the freaks as one and the same. Police and private defenders of the American way of life might harass either political or cultural rebels, seemingly at random, often on the basis of the superficial signs of rebellion they held in common, such as long hair on men. Larry Freudiger grew his hair long by mid-decade and got beat up several times as a result, just the beginning of a long trend. Freaks found themselves typically derided as "queers." On one occasion, some Dallas policemen complicated the associations of illegitimacy when, after arresting two hippies on suspicion of narcotics possession (an intriguing charge), not only called them "anti-social queers" but also asked why the young men were "dressin' up like a bunch of niggers."[34]

This sense of cultural animosity was reinforced by the official harassment and violence, discussed in chapter 5, that police agencies increasingly visited on political radicals as the years passed. The belief that political repression stemmed in part from cultural antagonism was widespread. The convergence of political and cultural polarization encouraged leftists in the sense of kinship they already felt with the freaks, the feeling that they fought "for the sake of the freedoms for which the hippies fight." The "revolt against personal repression, against dominance and exploitation felt by individuals in their own lives" in the end was "what 'the revolution' is all about."[35] The cultural revolution was perhaps what the "straight" culture would fight hardest to prevent.

But when it came to creating "the revolution," the differences between the new left and the freak counterculture were uppermost in the minds of leftists, even in Texas. The leftists here may have flocked to the counter-culture in a way that their opposite numbers elsewhere did not, but the warmth of this relationship says nothing about how these political activists viewed the counterculture in political terms. They might participate in the rituals of the counterculture, but in order to turn cultural rebellion into political change, they resolved to create their own rituals and institutions—their own leftist counterculture, which would not be merely an "alternative" subculture but a stridently "oppositional" one.[36] This was the project on which the Austin left embarked energetically starting in the fall of 1966. The two most important countercultural projects initiated there by the new leftists were the *Rag* and a public celebration known as "Gentle Thursday."

It is not coincidental that this countercultural turn in their politics was contemporaneous with the new left's vigorous embrace of black power doctrine and its turn toward the new working-class analysis. As I have stated, black power played a decisive role in turning the white left's gaze in on itself, in both racial and class terms. The most urgent task for white sympathizers, according to black power doctrine, was to temper the racism of the white "community." Black power thought held that racism was not merely a problem of individual moral failure or ignorance, instead pointing to institutional arrangements that perpetuated inequality. This political tendency also cast racism as a problem of "culture," a relationship of group inequality reproduced by a deep conviction of white supremacy among both whites and blacks, manifest among blacks in the form of self-loathing.

Two major tasks, then, that faced African Americans were institutional self-reliance and cultural revolution.[37] The tasks facing white sympathizers mirrored these. Whites had to remove themselves from the path of black self-reliance, almost as if they were a drug whose institutional presence would induce dependency, and they needed to engage in a cultural reformation of white America, to break down the culture of white supremacy. It is important to note that when, in 1966, SDS at the national level officially endorsed SNCC's turn to black power, the white leftists stressed not so much their own implication in an institutional structure of racial inequality as in an "essentially racist culture."[38] Besides directing whites to focus their energies on their own social milieu, black power thought specifically provided ideological validation for a program of cultural activism. The inclination of new left radicals to emphasize the racism of American culture suggests that their thinking already had turned toward "culture" as the salient political terrain. The need of young white leftists to explain and defend militant African American politics and to dissect the realities of white racism for a white audience quickly gave way to a wholesale program of cultural change. Black power and the burgeoning freak counterculture combined to help convince white leftists that the entire culture they had inherited was rotten but that they could make it anew.

Going It Alone

The most important of the Austin left's countercultural efforts was the *Rag*, which SDS-UT activists, especially Thorne Dreyer and Carol Neiman, along with Nightbyrd, Thiher, the Vizards, and others, planned in the summer of 1966 after the *Daily Texan*'s editorship passed to an outspokenly right-wing, pro–Vietnam War student. The *Rag* was perhaps the sixth underground or alternative newspaper in the country during this era and the first in the South. Most of the others in 1966 were located in New York City and the San Francisco Bay area. The *Rag* continued in operation for ten years, passing to subsequent cohorts of youth leadership despite continual harassment by local authorities, especially the UT administration, which banned the paper's sales staff from campus and relented only after the *Rag* sued and the case went all the way to the U.S. Supreme Court. More than once, printers were intimidated into dropping the *Rag*'s account, resulting in occasional pauses in production.[39] The *Rag* was enormously important to the local left, especially after SDS fell into disarray. In those later years of the new left, the paper and its staff—the "Ragstaff," as it was known—became the real center of the left in Austin.

Abe Peck, the leading historian of the 1960s underground press, writes that "the *Rag* was the first independent undergrounder to represent, even in a small way, the participatory democracy, community organizing, and synthesis of politics and culture that the New Left of the midsixties was trying to develop." Once again, there is truth in such bold pronouncements, but they should be taken with a grain of salt. The *Rag* supposedly operated on the basis of consensus, with anyone who worked on the paper in any capacity free to participate fully in the weekly editorial meetings. The paper also had no editor—only a "funnel" who brought letters and inquiries to the staff's attention. The paper's staff wanted to practice what the UT contingent preached to national SDS. Other new left papers soon experimented with participatory democracy as well, for example, the *bg Student Press*, at Bowling Green State University in Ohio, which in late 1966 instituted a rotating editorship and a "democratic division of labor."[40]

However, this was easier said than done. The *Rag* in its early years was effectively run by a "male graduate student triumvirate" drawn from the leadership of the SDS chapter.[41] In the first year Thorne Dreyer retained the "funnel" position, which in practice resembled that of editor. Carol Neiman and other women typed most of the articles. Commenting on the respective roles of Nightbyrd and Alice Embree on the *Rag*, Abe Peck comments, "He'd been the honcho; she'd run the Multilith."

The internal politics of the paper changed over time, though, as the staff changed. Five years after the *Rag*'s founding, its staff ran a retrospective claiming that by 1971 the paper operated in a far less hierarchical fashion than it had at first. Deploying a popular countercultural image, they wrote that "the Indians of today's anarchistic Ragstaff would never tolerate" the conditions that prevailed in 1966 (in Texas, of course, the cowboys and not the Indians were usually cast as the heroes). In 1971 there was a "political faction" and a "cultural faction," but they coexisted amicably, according to this account, airing their differences and each having its say in print.[42] The changes in the *Rag*'s operation were related to the emergence of feminism in the Austin left by 1969 and the arrival of new leaders at the *Rag*, most notably Judy Smith. Around 1969, women and men on the paper negotiated a policy of not accepting advertisements that the staff considered sexist, thus deviating from the pornographic tendency of many underground papers. Still, a running argument continued among the staff over this policy and over the question of what exactly qualified as sexist.[43]

The notion that the *Rag* effected a "synthesis of politics and culture" likewise can be oversold but also has a basis in fact. It is true that the earliest underground papers leaned heavily either, like the *East Village Other* and the *Oracle*, toward the counterculture, or, like the *Berkeley Barb*, toward political activism.[44] The *Rag* in truth was far closer to the latter than the former, filled with reports on racial politics, the Vietnam War, antiwar activism, labor conflict, and local intrigues. At the same time, the staff expressed loyalty to a synthetic vision of a single youth "movement," a movement still far more united in rhetoric than in practice. Larry Freudiger implied this vision in his laundry list of commitments, writing, "The *Rag* stands for—such basic things as free speech, black liberation, sex . . . student power, consciousness expansion, children . . . and all the other good things in life."[45] The staff of the paper was quite aware that a display of interest in the counterculture might entice readers who otherwise would not be exposed to a left-wing discussion of political matters. In sum, the *Rag* was more an appeal for unity among distinct constituencies than a real synthesis. To a limited degree, the paper succeeded in forging this unity, since the *Rag* became the primary source of information for both freaks and leftists in Austin.

In the fall of 1966, the Austin chapter of SDS made its countercultural intentions clear when it announced its agenda for the new school year. The members planned to step up their antiwar activities, forming a conscientious objection (CO) committee that would provide information to those considering filing for CO status and a committee that would organize the UT contribution to a planned national "student strike for peace" sometime during the year. But at the same time, they announced plans for "Gentle Thursday." This was a free-form festival that would take place at school and that the campus left intended to contrast with "Eeyore's Birthday Party," an annual by-invitation-only costume party run by the fraternities on campus and attended by members of the Austin power elite.[46] The leftists planned a happening that would be open instead of exclusive. They also introduced issues of democracy and hierarchy into the sphere of leisure, a hallmark of the new left's politics.

Gentle Thursday was not to be a day for protest but, rather, for a "celebration of our belief that there is nothing wrong with having fun," as the *Rag*'s announcement read. There were no planned activities: "We are asking that on this particular Thursday everybody do exactly what they want/on gentle thursday bring your dog to campus or a baby or a whole bunch of red balloons . . . maybe you would like to wade in a fountain . . . you might even take flowers to your Math Professor . . . at the very least wear brightly coloured clothing![*sic*]"[47] The activists gave a further indication of the new left's idea of fun in their promotional leaflet for events, which suggested, "SDS chicks should hug fraternity guys and sorority chicks should take emaciated beatniks out to lunch."[48]

A couple of hundred people answered these calls, gathering on a Thursday in early November on the West Mall. A crowd "five or six deep," most likely outnumbering the celebrants, stood on the sidewalk alongside the grass and gawked.[49] The participants blew bubbles, drew peace symbols in chalk on the sidewalks, and generally relaxed for the afternoon. Graffiti appeared on a warplane that was stationed permanently in front of the ROTC building: "Fly in peace, gentle plane." A group of ecstatics danced around the plane. "I swear," SDS-UT activist Susan Olan remembers, "what came to be thought of as the Austin community was born that day."[50] Indeed, perhaps it was at this time that the idea of the united front of leftists and freaks—the "community," a word of talismanic power among 1960s radicals—attained self-consciousness among the young and hip in Austin.

Gentle Thursday received much attention and proved a popular idea. Subsequently, SDS chapters in Colorado, Iowa, Kentucky, Missouri, and New Mexico, all at conservative public universities, organized imitations.[51] Despite the cultural hostility toward hippies, a countercultural venue was a relatively safe forum for advancing dissident political views. Americans were becoming used to the appearance of freaks and also freak institutions, and so a set of social boundaries emerged, enabling freaks to be safe in "their" spaces but risking harassment or even assault elsewhere. New left activists sought to create their own countercultural venues, their own safe havens, even if they were only temporary, where they could get a hearing for their politics. (With such temporary intrusions into public areas, such as open space on university campuses or municipal parks, dissidents skated on thin ice; hostile bystanders witnessing dissident gatherings in such places sometimes felt entitled to engage in disruption, in effect policing the boundaries of alternative social space.) Leftists simply might draw in disaffected young people through the promise of fun and relaxation and then deliver a more explicitly political message to their audience. In conservative locales, student activists, subject to habitual harassment, worried about such things when developing strategy, something that many of the national figures in SDS from less conservative areas understood less vividly. For the duration of the decade, Gentle Thursday was a hip institution in Austin. It was repeated at UT in the springs of 1967, 1968, and 1969, with both psychedelia and antiwar protest increasingly visible. The spring 1967 happening was part of the SDS-organized "Flipped-out Week" when Stokely Carmichael visited campus, just before the University Freedom Movement. Kazoo bands and electric rock groups appeared as well. Because by early 1969, SDS-UT was paralyzed by factionalism, a group of Ragstaffers organized the last Gentle Thursday.[52]

The leftists suggested that an upper-crust fraternity party simply was not as enjoyable as a hippie-influenced celebration. This was far from a minor issue; the promise of fun was more than just a gimmick meant to entice political innocents (though it was also that). New left radicals were eager not only to ventilate a critique of elite culture but also to offer a vision of a better, more fulfilling way of life. Glenn Jones, an organizer of Gentle Thursday turned folklorist, notes that it was a textbook example of prefigurative politics, as one SDS member indicated when he noted, "Gentle Thursday is a day when we act like we'd act if the Revolution [had] already come." Here, when they made explicit their idea of a new, better culture, new left radicals expressed most clearly their version of the search for authenticity. Gary Thiher declared that the new way of life would be more "human," more "spontaneous," and more "organic" than life in the current social system. "The bureaucratic system cannot survive if people are people," he declared. Dreyer agreed, declaring that this kind of celebration represented "open warfare against all that is dull and inhuman."[53]

The desire for a life that seemed organic and spontaneous, whole and rid of the stifling artificiality of life under bureaucratic capitalism, runs like a bright thread through the new left's prefigurative politics, connecting these young people to earlier rebels like Randolph Bourne and the lyrical left.[54] The earnest search for integrity and integration, so visible among activist youth in the 1950s and early 1960s, gave way to the old quest for the unmediated ecstasy of "real life," now contrasted to a dominant culture perceived as both repressive and unjust. The new left updated the search for real life by linking that search to the postscarcity humanism of cold war liberal culture. To be democratic, organic, and spontaneous was to approach the fulfillment of human potential.

Looking for Mr. Natural

The quest of the young in the 1960s for wholly new values did not emerge, as their rhetoric sometimes suggested, *ex nihilo*; it was borne of deep and wide strains in American culture, specifically out of the long-developing aspiration toward a way of life beyond the limitations of economic scarcity.[55] Nothing better illustrates this connection to the mainstream than the "sexual revolution" of which both freaks and new left radicals were such avid partisans. The commercial introduction of the birth control pill in the United States in 1960, of course, facilitated the enactment of relaxed sexual values, but these values had been changing for a long time. Although young men and (perhaps more ambivalently) women in the 1960s struck a pose of radical rebellion with their embrace of "free love," this was more an extension of long-term cultural trends than an overturning of dominant "Victorian" mores.

In the 1950s, *Playboy* magazine urged on American bachelors an unencumbered, adventurous sex life as part of a newly voluptuous consumer experience (and offered a fantasy of such a life to others). Soon in *Cosmopolitan*, Helen Gurley Brown offered the same to "career girls."[56] Betty Friedan argued in her 1963 classic, *The Feminine Mystique*, that women ought to reach for a life of fulfillment and noted that sexual satisfaction was both a necessary part and a likely result of this overall project. She built on the psychology of "human potential," a typical doctrine of the ascendant culture of abundance, which argued that the bottom layer of a "hierarchy of needs," economic necessity, had been satisfied and that higher, nonmaterial needs now awaited fulfillment.[57] More broadly, a process of liberalization in the courtship and sex habits of both married and unmarried people had been under way in the United States at least since the 1920s.[58]

Yet still in 1963, Jeff Nightbyrd complained of the lingering power of "myths that deprive humans of joy," myths about the evils of sex. "Americans are gripped by a search for new ethical values. Traditional values have proven unsatisfactory to the demands of our changing culture." Discussion of these matters was widespread. Friedan attracted much attention when she visited UT in February 1964. New left activists in conservative areas, where in loco parentis restrictions on the behavior of female college students often were severe, garnered broad student support by contesting those restrictions. Radicals argued that parietal rules insulted the integrity of young women who needed to participate as adults in a democracy. Women at Oberlin College "live under a dictatorship," charged SDS activists there, and University of Missouri radicals similarly spoke of "the almost military regimentation of women dorm residents." University of Kansas SDS felt that parietals prevented female students from becoming "independent, responsible human beings." A leader of the chapter there saw in this issue an example of the disempowerment pervading American society and took the opportunity to voice the standard SDS wisdom: "It's goodbye to democracy when elites deny you the right to participate in making the decisions that affect your life."[59]

But the desire to eliminate barriers to the pursuit of "joy" was never far from the student activists' minds, and college administrators and their antagonists alike saw sex at the bottom of the parietals issue. To many liberals, the point was that young adults should learn to make their own decisions about personal conduct. New left radicals not only argued that women ought to be able to choose whether to have sex but frequently suggested that they ought to make an affirmative decision, discerning a connection between the development of competent citizenship and the pursuit of human potential, one of whose principal arenas, to radicals, was sex. Despite this difference between liberal and liberationist viewpoints, the rationale that the new left offered for sexual freedom was quite close to the "need to grow" that Friedan, no leftist, asserted during her visit. She and the new left shared a social vision of relatively autonomous, empowered individuals, although for the new left, this was a necessary condition for the creation of a politically desirable society, whereas for her it was more strictly an end in itself.[60] Moreover, the consumerist *Playboy* vision of sex as a vehicle for fulfillment also resembled that of the new left. Despite these links to the mainstream, the new left chose to emphasize the embattled quality of its views on sexual rules, to portray itself as a lonely and enlightened minority, and as a result it exaggerated the radicalism of those views. On this issue the radicals invited Daniel Bell's derision of their "strident opposition to bourgeois values and to the traditional codes of American life . . . a set of codes that had been trampled long ago."[61] The rhetoric of "cultural lag," which pitted the authority of historical inevitability against the culture of the benighted masses, proved irresistible.

If the theory of sexual liberation was less innovative than its advertising suggested, the practice also was less than revolutionary. A loosened sexual ethos seems to have gradually taken hold in the Austin left. The 1960s radicals agree that both men and women, certainly by the later years of the decade, embraced "free love." What this meant is a matter of some dispute. The inner circle of SDS activists included many couples, some married, others simply long standing, but the inhibitions of monogamy were taken somewhat lightly.

Lori Hansel recalls that by 1970, "people were into, on the one hand having monogamous relationships and at the same time sleeping with everyone they could get their hands on. And I think that was true of both men and women." Nightbyrd says bluntly, "People fucked a lot, it was quite lovely. Without much guilt." Greg Calvert, arriving in Austin in 1968, reports encountering a regional culture that was "not sexually uptight" for the first time in the United States. Central Texas was "truly not a Puritan society," and the radical subculture was affected by this, he says, contrasting Austin favorably with the activist scenes elsewhere in the country. With a laugh, Paul Pipkin confides a more cynical view. "I gotta tell you the truth," he says. "I never . . . saw just a hell of a lot of free love in Austin. I did get laid a lot in Austin. . . . Y'know, people traded off partners an awful lot." Judy Smith, who, like Calvert, moved to Austin in 1968, thinks a lot of people on the left at that time were acting out "fantasies" of what they thought sexual freedom was. Judy Perez also takes a critical view of "free love," affirming that both women and men viewed sexual experimentation enthusiastically and felt that it connoted freedom but remembering as well that people encountered peer criticism for their "hang-ups" if they remained attached to conventional notions of fidelity. (Some had to be forced to be sexually free.) Jeff Jones recalls that "Are you liberated?" merely added to the university male's repertoire of pickup lines, hardly marking a revolution in youth culture.[62]

Perhaps the new left itself was caught on the horns of the dilemma that Marcuse called "repressive desublimation." This was the process in which a fundamentally repressive cultural system allowed for a small amount of instinctual indulgence, thus giving individuals an opportunity to let off steam—just enough to reconcile them to continuing to live and work in the present system.[63] The velvet glove of libidinal license might conceal the iron fist of regimentation; things were not what they seemed. As Gary Thiher acknowledged, "Modern, liberal, corporate America no longer represses sex. It capitalizes sex. Sex manufacturers use sex to sell almost anything you can think of."[64] The Marcusean analysis came in handy, for it squared this widespread use of sex in advertising with the new left's attack on America's "puritanical" culture. The vulgar objectification of women's bodies, the pandering to male fantasies of sexual omnipotence, the whole *Playboy* culture: this was not what instinctual liberation really looked like. It was a fake, fiendishly designed to reinforce the puritanism of the overall culture.

This was not merely a gimcrack argument devised to mask a contradiction in the new left view of American culture. The Marcusean analysis of sex was one variation of the new left quest for authenticity. Consistent with their entire frame of thought, new left radicals made a distinction between authentic and inauthentic sexuality. Barbara Ehrenreich remarks that rather than rejecting consumer culture entirely, the 1960s counterculture searched for the "transcendent" satisfaction that consumer culture promised but failed to disclose. "The counterculture did an end run around the commodities . . . to the true desire: real sex, not the chromium sublimation of sex; real ecstasy, not just smoke." The same was true of the new left. The sexual images beamed across the sky by television were "sterile" and "imitative," said the left, not at all the real thing. New left radicals wanted to free people's "*natural* eroticism."[65] The problem was not, the radicals suggested, that sex was unavailable; rather, it was that the sexual stimulation most easily available was not natural.

The search for natural sexuality took concrete form in 1960s radicalism most commonly as a search for an authentic, confident masculinity, once again indicating the links between the young insurgents and the cultural mainstream. Sometimes they harked back to a precommercial culture of natural manhood, suggesting that consumerism had generated the neurotic male personality of their time, as when Nightbyrd lamented that "in earlier times young men used to be sure enough of their masculinity to not be sucked in by advertising." Often the new left's picture of authentic masculinity was cruder than this, as when the *Rag*'s motorcycling columnist ("the bent spokesman") informed his readers that "cycling is a real turnon [*sic*] when you've got a chick on the back."[66] The pages of the *Rag* (in its early years) made it clear that the search for a natural sexuality in the 1960s counterculture did not imply dissent from the sexual objectification of women but, rather, turned women into "natural" sex objects rather than "artificial" ones. Any underground newspaper from that time prominently featured sketches and photographs of women naked from the waist up (at least). On one occasion, the *Rag* ran an appeal for volunteer workers, featuring a photograph of a group of women seated at typewriters, bare breasted, above the caption, "Put out for the Rag." A group of women clearly sat for the picture ("putting their bodies on the line"). Perhaps women on the left were under the sway of male radicals' viewpoint; alternatively, perhaps they would have articulated the search for a natural sexuality differently than men did had women enjoyed equal access to the media of radical expression.

The new left spoke to a pervasive feeling of disempowerment among Americans. Yet the hoary republican myth of the once-vital male citizen, the notion that modern conditions had conspired to strip men of any autonomy that they, if not women, once had enjoyed, made this feeling especially acute among male radicals. Whatever the reasons, in the new left's sexual politics, men's need to feel empowered clearly took precedence over the call for a society of equals. The objectification of women served to make young men on the left feel potent, to compensate for their perceived loss of autonomy in the larger society—just the purpose it served for other men.

Certainly in the freak counterculture, this objectification persisted into the 1970s in the "back-to-the-land" movement, in which women frequently were cast in the role of frontier Madonna: sandal-footed, braless, bread-baking, with children in tow. (Hansel saw a *Life* magazine article on communes around 1968 and had a revelation: "All these women were barefooted and had on long skirts, it was like—'I'm gonna be a radical, I am *not* gonna be a hippie.' ")[67] By 1970, many on the left at least paid lip service to feminist sentiments, and many were sincere, but feminism encountered unrestrained hostility from the freak counterculture. But in the 1960s, the tendency to make women the authentic objects of desire, to view them as helpmeets to men on a quest for liberation and empowerment, helpmeets who derived their own share of liberation from their assistance in that quest, stretched far indeed. It not only joined the new left to the counterculture (though it was a far more pronounced tendency in the latter); it could be found among white and black radicals; and it respected few class or political bounds. In this way, the swinging bachelor, the ghetto people's fighter, the domestic suburban fantasist, the modern homesteader, and the new left strategist were brothers under the skin.

The deepest problem with the new left view of sex is all too clear. How to tell the difference between the sham and the real thing? Which instances of instinctual release were authentically liberating, and which functioned to stabilize the present culture? In fact, there was no way to tell the difference. One might not find a particular example of commercial advertising stimulating, but that was beside the point. If actual arousal were sufficient evidence of erotic authenticity, then matters would have been simple indeed. The problem lay precisely in the capacity of inauthentic culture to provide instinctual relief. From the Marcusean viewpoint, the question was not how skillful the entrepreneurs of titillation were but what cause they advanced when they were successful: social stability or instability? Some forms of instinctual expression reinforced inequality between men and women, and others did not. But this political distinction does not correspond with certainty to some alleged division between inauthentic and authentic desublimation.

The rise of the natural sex object in the 1960s and the embrace of this figure by the radicals of the era throws into question the simple correspondence between the new left searches for radical democracy and ecstatic "real life." Perhaps the issue is as simple as it seems after all, despite what the new left thought. To put it bluntly, there is little reason to think that the erotic satisfaction that men derived from alternative forms of objectification was not real or "natural." The new left, like Marcuse, conflated the search for authenticity with the quest for social justice. This fusion marked a specific historical moment in the development of American political culture. Even though the new left ventured insightful criticisms of the mainstream culture, its own dreams and desires tasted of that culture. The children of the consumer society remained tantalized by the promises of ecstasy and transcendence that society made. They felt angry and disappointed, and rather than reject the promises as false, they wished the promises made good.

The American Way of Death

Sexuality was the area in which the new left pioneered its critique of inauthenticity in American life. With time, however, this critique broadened into a pervasive discussion of the artificiality that radicals saw in the cultural mainstream. One important trope that radicals used to pit their vision against the dominant culture was that of life against death (an opposition that also furnished the title for a countercultural classic of the era).[68] New left radicals came to denounce the United States as a "death culture" and their own alternative as a "life culture." They insisted that they lived in a society in which values that ended in death and destruction were institutionalized, and sometimes they even suggested that death itself was worshiped, perhaps subconsciously. This was what Larry Freudiger charged in 1966. In the funeral rituals of North Americans, he saw "attempts to sanctify death" that he found "feeble at best, macabre at worst," and he claimed that young people increasingly felt the same. "We are becoming the children of Camus," he wrote, "seeing death as meaningless, absurd, sometimes cruel, but never a religious occasion." A culture focused on death was a culture in flight from the "real life" that the new left sought; what many Americans considered "life," radicals did not think was really alive at all. The tasks before cultural revolutionaries thus were to expose the death-dealing character of American culture, to exalt life, and to create new institutions where authentic life could take root. Thorne Dreyer emphasized to his fellow radicals that just opposing death was not enough. They needed to "be affirmative, creative. It is not enough to scream no (though scream we must). We must do a love thing: show that there are alternatives to the death we are asked to become a part of. Affirm life."[69]

After 1965, the Vietnam War was the chief factor leading radicals to see in the United States a culture of death. One Austin activist celebrated Gentle Thursday as "the first widespread . . . public affirmation in Austin by white people that Love is a viable and realistic alternative to War."[70] The patriotic accoutrements of wartime, especially the celebration of military might, were pervasive. Although these activities usually did not invite revulsion in the homefront population, they did so among a minority during the Vietnam War. The exploits glorified by many U.S. citizens and by the government at all levels seemed to some not very brave and, in fact, particularly cruel, featuring as they prominently did rather indiscriminate bombing of a peasant society. As the war dragged on for several years, a growing fraction of Americans found grotesque the continued celebration of the war effort. The most vocal supporters of the Vietnam War acted as if it were, in moral terms, a replay of the war against global fascism; yet even some who supported the war found it morally uninspiring.[71]

Some opponents of the war began to search for cultural factors standing back of what seemed, to them, like irrational enthusiasm for the war. In his novel *Why Are We in Vietnam?* Norman Mailer perhaps went furthest, suggesting that the frustrations of American masculinity—which he epitomized in a mix of violent and homoerotic urges on display in a hunting expedition undertaken by a Texan father and son—produced individuals warped by a neurosis of violence and conquest.[72] By the later years of the war, such meditations on the culture of war became widespread among leftists and antiwar liberals. In addition to the war, as explained in chapter 5, the violent reactions from official and vigilante quarters that civil rights activists, antiwar protesters, and political radicals elicited compounded among these dissidents the sense of living in a violence-prone society—the sense that had floated through American culture since John Kennedy's assassination. Nowhere was this feeling stronger than among dissidents in Texas, but it was apparent throughout the country.

In liberal and leftist circles everywhere, it became something of a cliché in these years to say that North American society was distinctively violent, to suggest a tendency toward violence deep in the culture, or at least in white American culture. This was the time when many radicals started spelling America as "Amerika," an allusion to both Nazi Germany and the KKK, suggesting some elemental connections among racism, imperialism, and brutality in the hearts of American citizens. D. H. Lawrence's comment that the white American had the soul of a killer became fashionable.[73] This awareness of violence was not confined to those on the left, however. Liberal historians who had built reputations arguing that their country's culture was uniquely consensual came to acknowledge the violence of the American past.[74]

This perception of rising violence also affected the right half of the political spectrum, in which Americans were more likely to cast the problem in terms of cultural degeneracy and a breakdown in traditional moral restraints.[75] The urban rioting between 1965 and 1968 left a deep imprint on many conservative Americans, driving them further to the political right. They associated violence with black Americans, not whites. In fact, the whole post–World War II period was an era of rising crime rates in the United States, and many white Americans saw a black face on the violence and violation that crime meant to them. In the 1960s, many whites also blamed supposedly indulgent liberals for encouraging a breakdown in civil order, paving the way for Alabama Governor George Wallace's resonant criticism of liberal technocrats and intellectuals during the 1968 presidential campaign.[76] In the Chicago police force's attack on raucous antiwar demonstrators outside the Democratic National Convention in the summer of 1968, left and right each saw confirmed its diagnosis of American turmoil—incipient "fascism" or brick-throwing anarchy.[77] Concern over these events led to a cottage industry in government- and foundation-sponsored studies of violence in the United States in the late 1960s, the most famous of which was the Kerner Commission's report, whose rhetoric was often cited but whose social democratic recommendations were ignored.[78] Popular culture also reflected the discovery of violence in America, as movies not only dwelled on increasingly graphic representations of violence but also were widely viewed as "meaningful" for their supposed insight into the soul of America.

The new left agreed that American culture was in trouble and that violence was a large part of this trouble. To the radicals, however, the underlying problem was not incivility but inauthenticity. As always, they linked the problem of authenticity to what they felt was the lack of vigorous democracy in America: alienated persons could not make strong citizens. With increasing stridency, they identified corporate power as a principal force corroding the conditions for participatory democracy. Advanced capitalism, said the new left, required people who were passive consumers and nothing more— docile, fearful, and submissive people—and such people were not what human beings truly were meant to, or at least could, be. One Austin radical thought television helped shape such creatures, bombarding Americans with advertisements and encouraging them to lead an isolated and sedentary life. The United States was "a society which tries to make its citizens into unfree plastic zombies," he said. To be made docile was to become "plastic"—artificial—and to join the walking dead. To him, the ideal character was one that displayed "life, vitality, activity, enthusiasm," and he saw modern capitalist culture draining these things away from people.[79]

In drawing a connection between this metaphoric soul-death and the decline of genuine democracy, the new left echoed the liberal and conservative critics of totalitarian and "mass" societies. A vigorous and active citizenry, the only guarantee against tyranny, could be subdued by means other than terror; perhaps television might do the trick. In the 1950s, both liberals and conservatives had warned of the danger of a "soft totalitarianism" in the United States.[80] But where the new left parted company with such mainstream cultural critics was in identifying capitalism as the source and the beneficiary of creeping tyranny. To the new left, a world of consumers seemed like a world of dehumanization and death, a "comfortable concentration camp," in Friedan's harsh phrase.

The problem, of course, was how to break through these powerful forces. Some radicals felt they should address the iron fist directly, and others focused on the velvet glove. After the events of 1968, the former group gravitated toward a vision of violent insurrection. The constituency for violence in the new left has been exaggerated, but it certainly is true that political radicals in these years seriously debated the morality and wisdom of violence as a means of creating the social change they desired. Bill Meachem contended in the summer of 1969 that "we don't dig violence" but that violence had become necessary for "self-defense" in "Amerika." He thought the time had come "to fight for the freedom to love, to create, to grow, to become more free." An uprising in the conventional sense would pave the way for a cultural revolution. Pat Cuney argued in the *Rag* that radicals should become educated in the use of firearms as a precaution against all-out repression by the state. She had "a deep conviction that the history of Amerika is so rooted in violence" that only the capacity for armed self-defense would provide adequate protection against what lay ahead. She derided the "simplistic, romantic view" that "a non-violent love . . . can absorb and transform man's violent urges," especially when powerful social forces excited those urges. "The way to end violence is eliminate the system which makes it necessary," in her view. "Thus the real question is one of power, not of the abstract morality of violence or nonviolence."[81]

This was a fairly sophisticated critique of pacifism, echoing older "realist" critics like Reinhold Niebuhr.[82] Yet it missed the point, since the new left aversion to tactical violence was not based on a doctrinal pacifism but, first, on a visceral repugnance against violence, and second, on the longstanding new left understanding that the great political battles of the day took place on the field of "culture." Judy Smith, responding to Cuney, added, "To me it's not [a] question of having a right to armed self-defense. This society has already legitimized violence." Smith understood the power of "the Texas-gun-manhood cult," but the violent strain in American culture convinced her that a strategy of armed rebellion was suicidal for radicals in the United States, that they would never win such a fight. Just as important, she felt the new left's task was to prefigure an alternative to this cult, a new culture. The real question was whether violence would help the new left achieve its goals, about which Smith demanded clarity. The radical movement's project was, she asserted, to create "a non-authoritarian socialist society," and any embrace of violence would spoil that effort, since it would constitute a capitulation to the authoritarian dominant culture. By getting a new culture up and running, the new left could appeal to Americans who suffered the same alienation from their true nature of which radicals spoke. "I believe that to really change this society we must reach the mass of the U.S. people," Smith said, and without the allure of a new and different way of life, the left would hold little attraction for the masses.[83]

Even wrapped in the protective rhetoric of self-defense, violence ran contrary to deep strains in the new left's cultural vision. Years of railing against death and violence had had their effect, and the difficulty of justifying violent tactics to the radical constituency itself was immense. The increasing presence of antiwar GIs and veterans reinforced the antipathy to violence in the new left. Serviceman Louis DiEugenio spoke at an antiwar rally at UT in August 1969, where those assembled renamed a fountain on campus "Peace Fountain." "May there be a merging of peoples in Love and Peace even as these waters merge together," he said. "And may these waters wash away the filth of Hate and War." In general, radicals found this dualistic rhetoric impossible to resist. Only in love and peace would what was separated—"these waters"—become one, authentic; the old vision of social integration, of reconciliation as the solution to personal alienation lingered. "Help this poor, stinking world," pleaded another Austin activist, Judy Baker. Like other leftists, she viewed the young radicals as a saving remnant who might yet redeem a fallen culture, but only if they maintained their distinctiveness from that culture. "This country is still able to change. I am betting on it, and working for it. Maybe I still believe in flowers, children, and love."[84]

In Austin, the politics of insurrection never gained more than a toehold. The Ragstaff voted not to print an informational article on guns, instead running the debate between Cuney and Smith. The new left view of violence as the epitome of the old society contributed mightily to the widening gap between the movement's rank and file and the branch of the national SDS leadership that indulged in fantasies of guerrilla war.

Ecology

Hardly any aspect of the new left's search for a "life culture" was more long lived than its ecological activism, as it was called, which emerged in the post-

SDS phase of the new left's career. Ecological or environmental activism certainly began before that time. The call for a healthier and beautified public space had migrated out of the imagination of postwar liberals like John Kenneth Galbraith and, mingling with an older preservationist imperative, onto the agenda of suburban homeowners whose more basic desires on the hierarchy of needs—or, as the historian Samuel Hays argues, the hierarchy of consumption—had already been satisfied. Rachel Carson's *Silent Spring* was a best-seller in 1962, and the movement against the use of the pesticide DDT, the dangers of which Carson spelled out in vivid detail, was well under way by the late 1960s. But the new left and the counterculture added to the budding ecology movement a cultural and political critique far more radical than that articulated by earlier environmental activism.[85]

In Texas, there were precedents for environmentalism. Before the 1960s, outdoorsmen like Ronnie Dugger and J. Frank Dobie, southwesterners with a strong attachment to the land as they had known it, hoped, like Theodore Roosevelt, to conserve these surroundings for the future. To this conservationism they brought a populist anger at the spoilation of the non-human environment at the hands of oil companies and other new corporate wealth. According to Casey Hayden, Dugger was a strong advocate for the protection of Padre Island, the long, skinny strip of land that runs along the Texas Gulf Coast.[86] Perhaps this somewhat obscure legacy of populist environmental concern in Austin received amplification amid the anticorporate mood of 1960s radicalism. This mood combusted with the search for a natural way of life in the late 1960s to produce a seemingly abrupt outpouring of ecological concern among young people here.

This conflagration was what became known as the "Waller Creek Massacre." In the spring and summer of 1969, the UT administration planned to enlarge its already massive football stadium, located near the northern edge of campus; the stadium, of course, was the biggest symbol of the dominant campus culture and the pride of the Texas power elite. To do so, the administration planned to move the street next to the stadium, San Jacinto, so that it would pass over what at that point was a creek— Waller Creek, "one of the few 'wilderness' areas on campus," said Judy Smith. This in turn would require that the creek be moved, straightened, and narrowed, in the end simply channeled into a cement tube. The element of the plan that incited strong opposition was the proposed removal of numerous trees that grew next to the creek, including some live oaks and century-old cypresses.[87]

Students in the landscape architecture program, allied with Professor Alan Taniguchi, dean of architecture, organized in early October to alter these plans. They drew up an alternative that would both allow expansion of the stadium and preserve more of the trees and the existing landscape of the creek, and the *Daily Texan* printed these plans. The students appealed to the university to consider their alternative. An ecology group had formed at the "Critical University" (discussed later), and it joined with the architecture students to stage demonstrations against the administration's plan. On the day before the scheduled bulldozing of the trees, the administration agreed to meet with the critics and told them it was powerless to change its plans now; contracts had already been signed. That night a small group joined in "a celebration of life at Waller Creek," as one participant called it. "As one, we sang, smoked, danced, and loved. Loved each other, loved the earth, loved . . . our gypsy camp." As the morning dawned, about three hundred people gathered at the creek, and many of them climbed into the trees to prevent their removal. Frank Erwin appeared on the scene to direct the proceedings and, adding to his legend, told the police and workmen present, "Arrest as many as you need to. . . . Get those goddamn trees down. When they are gone, the students won't give a shit about them." The police dragged the protesters out of the trees, arresting twenty-seven. The defiance of the students inspired a similar action by their counterparts in Houston.[88]

The only juvenile among those arrested was seventeen-year-old Nancy Folbre, whose participation exemplifies the way in which political radicals were able to build bridges to the counterculture and draw recruits from it. Until then, Folbre, new to Austin, had not been politically active; instead, she says, "The counter-culture took care of me, sort of. I hung out on the streets, smoked dope, used to camp out at Eastwood Park or Barton Springs in order to get out of the dorms. The Chuckwagon was my second home." One morning when a woman walked into the Chuckwagon, Folbre heard about what was happening to Waller Creek, another of her favorite spots. After her foray into the trees and her arrest (and after seeing her "screaming face" on the front page of the *San Antonio Express*), she quickly became part of "a left political community." Her political views remained intact for the next quarter century, as she went on to a career as a left-wing economist.[89]

Ecological concern worked as an issue for the left at this time because criticism of corporate capitalism and its impact on the physical world coexisted in the new left with a cultural critique of pervasive attitudes toward that world, a cultural critique that echoed the counterculture's viewpoint. Certainly these different explanations for environmental degradation were not incompatible, but nonetheless the tension between them illustrates both the power and the limits of the new left's appeal. The new left's desire to restrain the institutional powers that it faced at Waller Creek and elsewhere contended with both the movement's strategic turn toward building a counterculture and its own criticism of Western culture's relation to "nature."

Showing its traditional leftist face, the new left emphasized that the power elite were the biggest polluters. Those with Vietnamese blood on their hands, those who repressed political dissent on campus, those who bulldozed the trees, those who ran the oil companies, those who contended that Americans needed more automobiles, and those who built ugly cities for their own profit: these forces were fundamentally the same, sometimes sharing top personnel, certainly holding a common view of everyone and everything but themselves as resources to be exploited for profit, and using government as a tool for their rapaciousness. Recent instances of government collusion with corporate power confirmed what new left radicals—and populist liberals like Dugger before them—always had thought. In Texas, Frank Erwin once again offered neat confirmation for the power elite analysis. One radical analogized the Waller Creek Massacre to the prosecution of the war:

> Erwin says the University (read Amerika) has commitments to contractors (read Brown & Root [the most prominent construction firm in Texas, and one of the biggest in the United States, long a leading contractor for public works projects, university expansion, and the Vietnam War, procuring fat contracts from all levels of government in no small part due to its close relationship with Lyndon Johnson, whose career it had subsidized heavily since his election to the U.S. Senate in 1948]) which it must maintain. The football stadium (read Vietnam/Amerikan imperialism) must be maintained and expanded at all costs (read death and defoliation). Those who would protest or offer intelligent alternative solutions (read War Critics) are dirty nothings (read commies, hippies, etc.). Erwin vindicates his stand with an appeal to the taxpaying people of Texas (read "the great silent majority").[90]

The comparison indicated that the new left had discovered a new realm of violence—environmental violence—that seemed like a war against the world itself, and thus against all its inhabitants.

Leftists in Austin proceeded to rake the Texas mud for evidence supporting their indictment of the corporate–government nexus. What they found demanded little reconsideration of their initial suspicions. They unmasked a plan to rearrange the state's water system in a way that would maximize both corporate profits and ecological degradation, and they publicized the destruction of the old-growth pine stand of the "Big Thicket" in East Texas. Looking farther from home, in the early 1970s they discussed the U.S. government's use of Agent Orange and other deadly chemical defoliants against the Vietnamese, spreading word of the large number of birth defects that the chemicals seemed to cause.[91]

Starting in 1972, many new left activists became involved in a long-running and ultimately losing fight against another corporate–government scheme, one endorsed by leading liberals in the area, to involve Austin in the South Texas Nuclear Project, a power-generating plan meant to fuel economic growth in the area. This marked the early phase of what became, in subsequent years, a widespread "slow-growth" political sentiment that built on the hostility of 1960s radicalism toward the impact of corporate power on both the physical world and cultural life. In Austin, and many other southwestern locales where the mantra of "growth" was most fervently preached in the 1970s and 1980s, the old conservationist sense of natural beauty ruined by wealth and greed gained a new lease on life.[92] The environmental violence was real enough, and its sources indeed lay where the new left analysis speculated they did.

The new left's ecological activism was consciously two pronged, emphasizing political reform and a change in attitudes. To radicals, this was simply sophistication, not ambivalence. In early 1970, as much of the country prepared for the government-ordained Earth Day, a liberal initiative endorsed by President Nixon, left-wing radicals in Austin began their own strategy of ecological activism. They would continue to expose corporate wrongdoing, but they also would work to change values and behavior among local citizens. A group of radicals, led by Judy Smith and others, formed a branch of Ecology Action (EA), a group started in Berkeley. In accord with the prevailing sentiment on the left, EA was organized in a highly decentralized fashion. "The basic problem," it said, was environmental exploitation undertaken "to satisfy the often-manipulated needs of a swollen population and to fill the corporate coffers of Amerikan capitalism." The only solution was ordinary citizens' "accepting responsibility for the world we live in and accepting the responsibility for changing it." Yet how could this responsibility be enacted?

Different project groups within EA established the first recycling operation in Austin, spread information about organic food, and promoted voluntary population control.[93] While the group tried to show that environmental degradation belonged on the familiar new left menu of war, inequality, and disempowerment, the means on which they fixed for reversing the environmental degradation focused on changing the behavior of citizens who, according to the power elite analysis, were hardly the worst polluters. By the late 1960s, the new left had become focused on developing tangible practices that together would comprise a politically radical counterculture.

It had become an article of faith that cultural changes in the new left's social stratum would lead to fundamental social change; as they went, so went the nation. This tendency took precedence over the more traditional political tasks of organizing to change government and corporate policies. Instead, those tasks fell more to insurgent liberals, such as consumer advocate Ralph Nader and his followers, who formed Public Interest Research Groups (PIRGs) in the 1970s and who certainly were influenced by the new left.

In the left wing of the environmentalist movement, the critique of corporate power never dimmed. Yet not only was the practical force of this critique blunted by the later new left's countercultural strategy, but it also faced an intellectual challenge from the left. Alongside the exposé of corporate malediction, the new left embraced a cultural explanation for ecological problems that cut into what would have been the traditional leftist approach to these problems. The Enlightenment tradition, from which the traditional left arose, held that humans had created the social world and so could remake it for human good by abandoning tradition in favor of reason as a guide to action. The new left, heavily influenced by the counterculture but also reaching the logical consequences of its own drive to overcome alienation, turned against this tradition, just as the leftist Dwight Macdonald had done in the 1940s. In the aftermath of the atomic bombing of Japan, he had argued that the entire "progressive" or Enlightenment tradition, with its dream of rational human control over the world, aided by technological advance, was destructive, and he called on leftists to abandon the progressive camp. In its later years, the new left, like countercultural promoters such as Theodore Rozsak, embraced Macdonald's perspective.[94] They came to chastened conclusions concerning the relations between humans and their environment that were, new left radicals conceded in their reflective moments, profoundly conservative.

The new left's emphasis on values as key factors in social change led it in this direction. Bea Vogel, a Ph.D. in biology who became a leading new left voice in Texas on these matters, asserted that creating socialism would not solve environmental problems. Rather, destructive values and attitudes stood behind environmentally destructive practices, and these values were institutionalized in both socialist and capitalist regimes. The root problem was the prevalent "notion of man's ability/need to completely control his environment," a project that united socialism and capitalism. "This idea should be critically analyzed by radicals." Vogel conceded that "a properly operating socialist government could better ensure the socially beneficial management of natural resources" than capitalism could but that "present forms of socialism and communism are applying technology in much the same fashion as the U.S."[95] The goal of controlling nature through technology represented a disastrous hubris, warned Vogel, for it attempted to scale what were in fact insurmountable biological barriers. "Human ecological understanding emerges from biological reality," she claimed. The great biological danger that ecologists in the new left cited was overpopulation, and the positive theme in their thinking that they likewise endowed with biological certitude was interdependence. They affirmed what they saw as "the fact of interconnection as a general principle." After the Waller Creek Massacre, the *Rag* printed a "Declaration of Interdependence," which proclaimed "that all species are interdependent . . . that each species is subservient to the requirements of the natural processes that sustain all life."[96] The demand that humans subordinate their desires to "natural processes," the assertion of a biological limit to human endeavor, allowed the new left to marshal great authority behind its criticism of environmentally destructive practices. This demand also partook of traditionally conservative themes and helped, as Macdonald had urged, blur the familiar division between left and right.

The new left sought an end to estrangement not merely between different social groups but also between humanity and "nature." Vogel argued, "Nature is not where the skin stops. We exist in nature, not with it." Viewing nature from the inside was what constituted an "ecological" perspective.[97] Related to this desire for a reconnection with "nature" was the countercultural drive to reverse what Max Weber called "the disenchantment of the world." Many freaks, romantics that they were, found non-Western cultures attractive because in the "East" and in Native American traditions, they saw a harmony between humans and the rest of nature and a belief in a spirit-life that connected all living things, which seemed absent from the deracinated "West." New left radicals did not generally believe in spirits in the way that some freaks did, but they did cherish dreams of solidarity that extended to relations between humanity and the planet, and they, too, saw the Western world as a barren plain of estrangement. These were the terms in which they often expressed their entirely rational desire for healthier physical surroundings. Looking for authenticity, they declared their culture full of death and artifice. One noted that "our lives and our environment have taken on such an artificial character that some of us simply want to turn on to our nature again." Another, fresh from the trees of Waller Creek, spoke of "our struggle for life, our struggle to communicate that Spark of life to a dead, empty society."[98] Whereas earlier generations of leftists had sought reconstruction, the new left sought reanimation and reconnection.

These differences can be overstated. Environmentalists, including those on the left, hardly ever hesitated to recommend the manipulation of biological processes, from birth control to the reintroduction of endangered species into their former habitats, when such manipulation aimed to create a healthier or more wholesome world. The call to reverse the effects of environmental damage was itself a call to intervene in and manipulate the physical world. New left radicals were not shamans, although in the movement's later years, some of them began to experiment with various forms of spirituality, including Buddhism and Native American beliefs, often in connection with a newfound ecological awareness. Scientists like Bea Vogel made a rational case for ecology, not a spiritual one.

Nonetheless, while the new left's environmentalism reinforced its anticorporate animus, this new concern also greatly strengthened those tendencies that took the movement away from a traditional leftist perspective. Like Macdonald, Vogel called herself a "radical," an identification whose ambiguity had had its uses since the new left's inception and that now became even more attractive to some on the left. Struggling to name her revised political identity, she endorsed the category that the new left's critique of centralized power had created already and to which the critique of technological optimism added extra luster, as counterculture heroes like the poet Gary Snyder made clear.[99] Vogel told her fellow Austin radicals that "we should be well advised to come to some understanding of what it is to be a humanist and a socialist and an *anarchist* in nature."[100] The anarchist vogue in the new left was cresting, and the anarchists of this era were more likely to create a new society within the old than they were to look for ways to overturn the power structures they confronted. No bomb throwers, they.

Better Living through Cooperation

Small Is Beautiful, announced the title of economist E. F. Schumacher's 1973 tract, expressing the search for a simple, nondestructive way of life that emerged from radical ecology.[101] The allure of the small—which some, like the anarchist (and early new left inspiration) Paul Goodman called "human scale"—had previously been based in the fear and loathing that both leftists and freaks felt for the political havoc and feelings of alienation that large, centralized, unaccountable bureaucratic systems produced.[102] The ecological argument that such systems created terrible physical damage as well only tightened the radical embrace of a vague social vision of innumerable and decentralized small units. The concrete form of this anarchist sentiment—and the new left's most earnest attempt to build a new, oppositional culture—took shape in the cooperative movement.

By 1970, "hip" neighborhoods in Austin, as in Madison, Minneapolis, Athens, Iowa City, Gainesville, and other college and university towns across the United States, were identifiable by the hip establishments that dotted them, storefronts adorned with artfully hand-painted signs and blue-jeaned worker-owners.[103] The *Rag*, which endured until 1976, was the prototypical cooperative, or co-op, in Austin. These co-ops spread like wildfire in the last years of the new left, and many of them lasted well past the new left's demise as a coherent political movement. Indeed, those who wish to defend the accomplishments of "the movement" sometimes emphasize the co-ops, among the most tangible legacies of 1960s radicalism. Gitlin, for example, celebrates the "thousands of communes, underground papers, free schools, food 'conspiracies,' auto repair and carpentry collectives, women's centers and health groups and alternative publishers" that were thriving by the early 1970s. The historian Jon Wiener sees these co-ops institutionalizing the new left's vision of participatory democracy, which leads him to call the later new left "the real '60s," playing perhaps the ultimate authenticity card in this game.[104]

There were several types of hip entrepreneurs. There were the sharpies who knew a good market when they saw it and took on the accoutrements of the counterculture with visions of dollar signs dancing in their heads. Some of these thought big, and the biggest was Jann Wenner, founder of *Rolling Stone* magazine, who made his fortune offering a venue in which record companies, making the same youth-friendly noises, could tap into the market he had targeted. (The copy on one Columbia Records advertisement, depicting jailed young protesters, reads, "The Establishment's against adventure"—"But The Man can't bust our music.")[105] The ranks of the more sincere included freaks who simply liked making things and working for themselves and leftists who likewise searched for unalienated labor but who also thought that in so doing they might change society. (Neither of these camps worried much about doing better than breaking even.) The left wing of the co-op movement offered young people places where they could work as part of a collective, participating as coequal owners and managers, and where they could shop in the knowledge that they were supporting the oppositional culture, not strengthening the lineaments of the old society.

Perhaps the best-known and longest-lived such endeavors were the food co-ops. Activists in Austin first established the Milo Minderbinder Memorial Co-operative in 1969, sardonically named after the enterprising character in Joseph Heller's novel *Catch-22*. The Wheatsville Food Co-op took hold securely, its bookkeeping benefiting from Bill Meachem's knowledge of early computers, and remained a going concern into the 1990s. Sattva, a collectively run vegetarian restaurant, began in 1970 in the University Hillel and later moved to the Methodist Student Center. The prevailing ideas in these food co-ops were to run the stores as democratically as possible, to eschew the profit motive, and to obtain and provide to the local hip population "natural" food—food that was uncontaminated by chemical additives and relatively unprocessed. The idea of selling "natural" products also appeared in a venture called Revival, a craft shop opened by Austin activists in 1969, which sold "local handmade things," the prices set by the "artists and craftsmen." An interest in craftsmanship, the attraction to products that did not remind one of or support the factory system, and the desire to work in democratically run enterprises represented attempts to combat different conceptions of industrial-era alienation, those supposedly generated by production and by consumption.[106]

Some co-ops made explicit the left view that the solution to the problem of alienation was political, avowing an explicit anarchism and anticapitalist radicalism. In the summer of 1969, a group that included Connie Lanham and Alex Calvert started the Armadillo Press, a cooperative print shop. They announced that the staff would form a local of the Industrial Workers of the World (IWW), "in keeping with that Union's tradition of workers' control." The Wobblies of the IWW had become icons of decentralist socialism for the new left. "We share some fundamental political convictions," they said, "the most fundamental being that capitalism is an economic system that creates a host of miseries for the overwhelming majority" and profits for the few. Although they identified themselves openly as socialists, they wanted to distance themselves from what they called the "Stalinist" left, code for Progressive Labor and the Trotskyists. Echoing the distinction between "political radicalism" and "social radicalism," they expressed "distrust" for "those who speak only of economic and political transformation and not of the liberation of persons." They desired "a fundamental change in personal values and in personal and group relations" as well as economic and institutional changes—bread and roses, too. The values they wished to bring to cultural dominance were "honesty," "trust," "joy," and "love." "We want to be free to fulfill our deepest longings for growth and creativity in cooperation with others." A few years later, they pursued yet further their desire for personal transformation. The women at the press staged a kind of "coup," recalls Alice Embree, taking it over and renaming it Red River Women's Press. In addition to feminist materials, they won the contract to print the national IWW's constitution.

They really did become Wobblies, fulfilling a long-held dream of many youthful radicals.[107]

Rarely did cooperative ventures express so clear and radical a political position. Leftist politics and enthusiasm for the counterculture infused the "free universities" that sprang up all over the country after 1965, for example, but these counterinstitutions, typically begun by SDS activists, straddled the line between insurgency and reform. SDS-UT member Dick Howard began the Critical University (CU) in the summer of 1965 and argued in national SDS that developing such independent bases of political education was "the only way to build a reform movement in this country which will operate with a solid foundation." Despite his desire for "reform," he sounded a radical note, asserting that political efforts "within the existing political structure" were "doomed to frustration." Furthermore, he contended, a system of free universities would operate on an entirely decentralized basis, promoting democracy within the radical movement and allowing the growth of authentic communities in local settings, unencumbered by the national SDS "bureaucracy." "The problem is community. The answer can be found in the Free University."[108] The Austin CU was one of the early free universities, and it enjoyed international recognition after Howard, as a student at the University of Nanterre in France, took part in the political debates of March 1968.[109] The Austin CU operated intermittently, periodically lapsing and then starting up again, eventually going by the name "Communiversity." The ambiguity of this initiative allowed it to appeal to diverse constituencies. Was it a vehicle mainly for the development of community among radicals, or for political agitation? Was it part of an effort to build a new society or to prod "reform" in existing educational institutions? The thesis of student agency, the feeling that by changing students' lives, the new left would change society, facilitated the deferral of these questions.

The free universities offered an intellectual and pedagogical alternative to the standard curriculum and classroom experience, and both form and substance reflected the new left perspective. Most new left radicals did not go so far as to say, with the writer Jerry Farber, that the student was a "nigger" trained by classroom experience for subservience and obsequiousness, as Farber put it in his overripe essay, first published in Los Angeles and widely reprinted around the country.[110] Nonetheless, leftists did see university education as basically authoritarian, like parietal rules ill preparing young people for vigorous citizenship, deadening their creativity in something like the way that television did. Classes at free universities were meant to be more egalitarian and interactive.

The class topics also offered something new. In the fall of 1969, the Austin Critical University advertised classes, to be held in the University Y, such as "Surrealism," "Racism," "McLuhan," "Marcuse," "Ecology," "Community Research," "Cuba," and "Women, Their Roles, Their Liberation." The Free University of Florida, in Gainesville, offered "Sexuality and Freedom," "Comparative Economic Systems," and, harking back to the heyday of the University Y, "The Young Christian Conscience and Its Problems." The free university at Bowling Green State University in Ohio sponsored a peace seminar, folk dance classes, and, getting to the heart of the matter, an "alienation workshop." Many of the topic areas pioneered by the free universities, as well as their emphasis on less hierarchical relations in the classroom, exerted a great influence on college education in the 1970s and afterward. The Free University of Florida was advertised as "a freedom-spirited community of scholars who choose to work for the renewal of the collegiate experience," and this goal of renewal was the one that the free universities achieved most fully.[111] Despite the occasional intersection of these ventures with political agitation, as when the Austin CU ecology group got involved in the Waller Creek affair, the free universities generally did not become bases for political interventions. Still, many participants would have said that the free university classes themselves constituted such interventions—interventions in the minds of young people.

More romantic, and in some ways more radical, than the free universities were the "free schools" for children that radicals started in the late 1960s. According to Gitlin, there were only about thirty of them in 1967, and perhaps eight hundred in 1973. These took inspiration from the "freedom schools" organized in Mississippi during the summer of 1964 by civil rights activists intent on imparting a politically insurgent curriculum to black youth, but A. S. Neill's *Summerhill*, with its romantic evocation of childhood as the freest and most natural stage of life, perhaps exerted a stronger influence. (Some looked to B. F. Skinner's rather authoritarian *Walden Two* and to Aldous Huxley's *Island*.) Children were "open" and "spontaneous," observed Harvey Stone. Independent educational institutions would preserve the child, who could grow into the ideal citizen. Adults, by contrast, usually had become emotionally repressed and closed minded. Stone decried the "internal codes of law and order" that, in the orthodox educational regime, "instilled self-hatred, guilt and feelings of unworth and alienation" in place of our natural "instincts." Like Dietrich Bonhoeffer, 1960s radicals like Stone hoped to make a "leap backward towards openness and simplicity."[112]

In 1969, Dave Mahler, one of the radicals who could draw on independent wealth, bought 172 acres of wooded land in Bastrop, about thirty-five miles east of Austin, where he, Larry Caroline, Bobby Minkoff, Arnie Kendall, and others started the Greenbriar School. They hoped that here their teenaged pupils "wouldn't be brainwashed into authoritarian ways of being," says Caroline. They built a bridge over a creek (and rebuilt it when a flood washed it out), cleared a space of trees, and scarred their feet by walking on the freshly poured concrete they used for the floor of their geodesic building. The school dispensed with grades, mandatory tuition payment, and as much structure as possible. Three years after it started, it was teaching between fifty and seventy students (including the child of one member of Lyndon Johnson's cabinet) and had a staff of twelve; no one had been turned away for lack of money. The *Rag* reported that all involved were "growing, evolving and struggling with each other to become an open, honest community of people who respect each other."[113] This kind of unrepressive education was a "true" education. Perhaps the adults involved in such enterprises thought they could regain some of their own inner children in the bargain. One Greenbriar enthusiast said that here he found a "community" of " 'radical' politics, and people just trying to be free of middle class baggage, the draft, marraige [*sic*] and artificial needs."[114] Of course, their embrace of this romantic critique of the educational mainstream indicates that their own cold war education had perhaps been less emotionally stifling in intent than they thought, or else less than entirely successful in assimilating them to "authoritarian ways of being."

Some of the counterinstitutions, like Greenbriar and certain food co-ops, endured for many years. So did the *Rag*, running almost entirely on the esprit de corps of its workers. Greenbriar had a benefactor, of course. The food co-ops fared best in finding a stable consumer base that gave them financial viability. Not surprisingly, however, many of the co-ops that required customers to choose between making their regular purchases in either the "straight" or the hip economy were plagued by troubles. For example, in the winter of 1968/1969, some activists started an "anticapitalist" service station, but it was short lived, a participant reported, because "it was a little too rigorous in its anti-capitalism." It lost several hundred dollars in its two months of operations. The hip entrepreneurs tried again, this time charging for labor.

Equally daunting was the problem of getting workers to do regularly the tasks they were supposed to do. The *Rag* columnist who wrote the food column "Aquarian Kitchen" (under the nom de plume Hermes Trismegistus, an Egyptian mystic of some fourteen centuries earlier) observed in late 1970 that the main Austin food co-op had started and folded three times so far, due to a lack of labor and organization. "I don't know where people's energy is going," the *Rag* editorialized around the same time, "but there doesn't seem to be much around."[115] North American radicals found on a small scale, as the Cubans had discovered on a vastly bigger one (in which the standard unit of production was a "collective," not a cooperative), that political exhortation was not always an adequate spur to laborers, the transcendence of alienation notwithstanding. It was no small challenge to develop a working alternative to capitalist enterprise.

The co-op movement also had to contend with criminal behavior in the counterculture. One food co-op found itself the target of repeated theft, most seriously of the cash it kept in a jar. The *Rag* lost $75 in December 1969, a near-crippling blow to such a shoestring operation. Perhaps some in Austin's hip population thought that stealing things that one needed, even money, was consistent with the anticapitalist views espoused by many in the co-op movement. These highly open institutions were particularly vulnerable to predators who must have been pleased to discover what easy marks some of the radicals made.[116]

"Counterinstitutions were ways of settling down for the long haul," Gitlin writes, accurately evoking the political ambiguity of these enterprises. In these projects, radicals could maintain their values and even change their lives, continuing to prefigure the future society even as they remained trapped in the present. As long as a cohesive new left still existed, leftists saw a connection between this prefiguration and their revolutionary aspirations. In 1972, Embree challenged her fellow radicals to start the process of social change "at home—where we live, where we work." Sounding like someone considering heading underground, she recommended the organization of "cells, cadres, affinity groups"—and co-ops. That same year, the radicals who were running the cooperative service station (having taken it over from its founders, such as Paul Spencer) were ousted from power in a takeover by those who wanted it to run on a sounder business footing and who proceeded to strip it of its political associations and to cultivate the student market more assiduously.[117] By this time the new left's decline was advanced. The cooperatives continued to make consumption a less alienating experience for the youth market than it otherwise would have been, and the co-ops continued to offer an alternative, less authoritarian work setting for a relative few. But the rhetorical linkage of co-ops to cells and cadres was becoming increasingly implausible.

Leftists were not entirely naive about the politics of cooperative enterprises. Indeed, one activist charged that the rural commune movement—which occupied the extreme, separatist end of the co-op tendency—constituted "cooperation with capitalism" and worked "to coopt and disaffiliate potential revolutionary cadre." These communes were, he intoned, "concentration camps where people go willingly!"[118] Leftists, though they might direct such hostility toward particular types of co-ops, virtually never treated the overall co-op trend with such disgust. Nonetheless, many worried that involvement in co-ops could turn activists toward private concerns and away from political conflict. Radicals simply distinguished between, on the one hand, co-ops that were compatible with the capitalist system and attracted " 'do-your-own-thing,' free-license individuals," and, on the other hand, those that tried to separate themselves entirely from capitalist values and institutions and displayed "an understanding of freedom and . . . responsibilities." Again, this corresponds roughly to the scholarly distinction between "alternative" and "oppositional" subcultures. Not surprisingly, activists sometimes labeled bad co-ops as "liberal," as distinct from good, "radical" co-ops. But as with other new left distinctions between gold and pyrite forms of liberation, the criteria by which one could make these distinctions were elusive. "To build community—the new phrase of the past few months," commented two concerned activists in the fall of 1970. "But what does it mean?"[119]

The People, Yes!

Some leftists were determined to resist what they feared were the solipsistic tendencies of their movement's countercultural turn. Not content merely to improve their own "heads," they hoped to plant the seeds of a cross-class white radical alliance. Alice Embree distanced herself from the vision of a white affluent youth movement, what Abbie Hoffman, the premier hip publicist, called "Woodstock Nation." As of 1971, she saw the radical youth phenomenon "disappearing like a soap bubble" and contended that only a program of social outreach could save it. Among those on the left who shared this analysis, a new cultural populism took hold in the early 1970s. Disillusioned with the attempt to fashion a subversive politics from the "emergent" culture of Woodstock Nation, some radicals looked instead to the transgressive power that seemed to lie, largely untapped, in the "residual" culture of working-class whites.[120] Certainly the authenticity of "redneck" culture seemed unassailable. Before long, this tendency came in for sharp criticism and withered, thereby vindicating Embree's fears about the evanescence of the radical youth movement.

Some attempts to cross class lines merely sought to bring the new left perspective to new audiences, rather than to borrow from working-class culture. A prominent example was the "Mother's Grits Austin Anarcho-Terrorist

New Left Beatnik Evangelical Traveling Troupe," whose geographic origin many new leftists might have guessed from the name, even had it not mentioned Austin. Martin Wiginton was the organizer of this bus tour, which set out in the summer of 1968 for college towns like Denton and Bryan, where the students were more likely to come from working-class backgrounds than were the students at UT. During a tumultuous election campaign season, with the country reeling from political assassinations and urban riots, this band of self-styled merry pranksters lit out for the territory. The troupe, including Larry Caroline and Mariann Wizard, spread the new left gospel with rock bands, artwork, drug paraphernalia, theatrical skits—any sort of fun and games they could think of, in addition to political speeches. Wizard expressed a populist sympathy with enthusiasts of George Wallace, who was cutting a figure of ominous size that summer, while also attacking Wallace from the left.[121] Caroline peddled the new left's postscarcity perspective in his talks, linking the issues of the Vietnam War and sexual freedom. Influenced by his reading of Marcuse and Wilhelm Reich, he explained to his audience that "when they repressed themselves they were also amenable to being repressed by others," that sexual repression contributed to an authoritarian personality. "My speeches were quite outrageous," he recalls.[122]

"Guerrilla theater" was the signal tactic for the Mother's Grits Troupe. The popularity of experimental theater encouraged the combination of propaganda with entertainment. Using a scenario they had tried out at UT that spring, the troupe staged a human Monopoly game, with place-names like "Vietnam" and "University" on a human-scale playing board. Participants walked around the game wearing big draft cards around their necks that hindered their movements. The itinerant activists also acted out skits, such as one depicting a workplace where people acted like "automata" and had to be turned on with a large switch; when something went wrong with the machinery, everyone screamed until the operator turned them off. Jay McGee did a "revival bit" in which he "reads a passage from Scripture which points to the truly 'Christian' spirit of the movement." This liturgy seems to have been a sincere, if tentative, attempt to revive the buried link between the new left and religious idealism. When McGee did his "bit" in Denton, a woman in the audience came forward to give him a loaf of bread, which he then used for a communion service. "All those people committed to change and revolution were asked to come partake of the bread and water," and well over half of the two hundred in attendance did so.[123]

Some, like Embree, sensed that if the new left wished to draw on the power of residual culture, it had to take seriously cultural experiences other than its own, more venerable than its own. She glimpsed the promise of the traditional in August 1971 when she attended the annual "People's Music" festival in Pipestem, West Virginia. She saw clog dancing and heard folk music that, as in bygone days, featured prominent labor themes. She contrasted this environment favorably with recent mammoth electric rock festivals. "Altamont and rock music are sexist to the core," she said, echoing a sentiment that had spread among radicals as feminism made headway. This kind of aggression seemed absent from the Pipestem gathering.[124]

Perhaps most impressive to Embree, the West Virginia event was intergenerational, bringing together long-haired, dope-smoking young people with grandmothers singing spirituals. Embree delivered a jeremiad on her contemporaries: "Youth, cut off from history and from the rest of the people in real, basic ways. Orphaned from the strength that comes from roots and experiences." The Woodstock Nation was pathetically narrow in terms of both age and class: "the youth nation is built off the fat of Amerika, the privileges of the white middle class, the rip-off opportunities which are not open to the poor." At Pipestem, however, Embree saw both a greater political possibility and a more authentic cultural experience. She wanted what she saw. To get it, she said, the new left had to commit itself

> for the long haul. Defining, consolidating, strengthening our communities. Reaching back for our lost histories of struggle and strength. And reaching out to people not impressed with our symbolic rebellions . . . stop glorifying superstars and putting energy into national media events . . . start paying attention to real, steady, serious work. Breakfast programs, working food cooperatives, community gardens, tenants unions, abortion referral services, day care centers, free clinics, communications networks. The kinds of thing[s] that can cross lines of privilege, lines of age, and that can make a real difference.[125]

Perhaps the new left's constituency could still build an authentic, revolutionary culture, in part by imitating and making contact with "the people," apotheosized here as the white folk of Appalachia.

Those in the white youth culture who felt a similar fascination for the authenticity of white working-class culture in the coming years, however, fixed on a sector of that culture rather different from the one Embree admired. In Texas, the cultural populism of hip white youth in the early 1970s emphasized a rehabilitation of the cowboy figure and even of "rednecks," converting these distinctly male and, in the conventional liberal or leftist view, politically retrograde personae into counterculture heroes. The identity that emerged from this process of experimentation in Austin, achieving national renown by mid-decade, was known as the "cosmic cowboy," an amalgam of redneck and freak male images.[126] The annealing agent that forged this alloy was popular music.

The most famous place where this recombination took place was the Armadillo World Headquarters, a music hall that hip entrepreneur Ed Wilson started in 1970, renting an empty warehouse along Barton Springs Road in Austin. The cavernous hall soon became a routine stop on tours by musicians of all sorts, ranging from Delta bluesmen like Muddy Waters and Howlin' Wolf and straight country pickers and crooners to psychedelic rock bands like Vanilla Fudge. (It also hosted a long-remembered convention of the National Lawyers Guild in 1974.)[127] Suddenly the tastes of the young, white, and hip tilted away from nationally known rock stars and toward regional "roots music." The synthesis of the Anglo elements of this music was promoted as "progressive country." Local boy Willie Nelson, who became a staple of the Armadillo's schedule, epitomized the cosmic cowboy blend of country and western with electricity and hippie accoutrements like his long, braided hair and his well-known friendliness to recreational pot smoking, both of which reflected increasingly apparent practices among young white males. His image and appeal ostensibly mirrored the conviviality between freaks and rednecks that many observers noted in the Armadillo's audiences. Here, in this "temple of the counterculture," white Texans of different classes, cultures, and politics bonded over beer and music.[128] Some on the left saw great political promise here. One group sought to control the scene of the populist coalition's formation, purchasing a honky-tonk and renaming it "Emma Joe's" after a pair of pre-Communist new left icons by the names of Goldman and Hill.[129]

Music and long hair, beer and cannabis, were not enough. Critics soon noted the weakness of the link between the cosmic cowboy identity and political dissent. The manner in which Jeff Nightbyrd—involved in the mid-1970s in the *Austin Sun*, a newspaper begun in 1973 as a more mainstream alternative media outlet than the *Rag*—deflated the vogue is revealing. At this time, he was already constructing the myth of the united front of the 1960s, and he contrasted the superficiality of the cosmic cowboy's identifying markers with the commitments of the 1960s hippie, which Nightbyrd claimed were not only deeper but also political. Becoming a cosmic cowboy "doesn't require any changes in attitude like being a hippie in the sixties did," he wrote. "You don't have to know anything about the war, give a damn about race . . . or worry about male chauvinism."[130]

Notwithstanding this distortion of the 1960s counterculture, the cowboy/redneck identity certainly did not embrace feminism or antiracist politics or pacifist sentiment. Barry Shank sees a "powerful conservative strain" in the cowboy tradition that the cultural populists of the 1970s could not expunge, and he even contends that "the effort to blend audiences from different economic classes forced the progressive country movement to emphasize the traditional racial and gender characteristics associated with the mythical identity of the Anglo-Texan cowboy." This meant affirming an "aggressive 'outlaw' masculinity" that celebrated a distinctly violent form of resistance to authority and that was implicated in deep-running cultural traditions of racism and sexism.[131] Certainly in this instance, cultural populism turned out to be a strategy fraught with difficulties for a left-wing movement that, whatever the strains of its relations with African American activists, was acutely aware of its origins in the fight against white supremacy and in which feminism had become a central factor. The cosmic cowboy identity was ominous for non-Anglos and seemed almost to erase women from the cultural vista. The new left wanted both the authenticity and the political capacity that a cross-class alliance could bring, and some radicals thought they might reap all these rewards by working in the realm of culture, but this late hope for that kind of radical agency met with frustration.

Toward Cultural Liberalism

By the early 1970s, the prominence of Austin's countercultural scene had given the city a national reputation as a kind of dissident oasis (or a cancer, depending on one's point of view) in the Southwest. "What can I tell you about Austin?" asked one local humorist. "This town, this community is so organic people will turn to compost before your very eyes."[132] A large part of the countercultural presence was due to the efforts of the new left to cultivate a left counterculture. The increasing emphasis on a cultural method of political change, although pronounced in Austin, reflected a trend at work in the left nationally.

In evaluating the cultural turn in radical politics during the 1960s and 1970s, it is best to avoid hyperbole, although unfortunately, extreme judgments abound. Too often, discussions of the new left's cultural politics are polarized into all-or-nothing choices: the counterculture was revolutionary, or it was politically meaningless. The new left's cultural initiatives, then, represent either a quantum leap in left-wing practice or an avenue of depoliticization. Either "the counterculture ended by affirming the middle-class, materialistic culture it had set out to refute," or it expressed a revolt "against *the totality of bourgeois social relations*," a rebellion undreamed of in the old left's philosophy.[133] Either the revolutionary prestige or the embarrassing memory of the hippie movement rubs off on the new left. Another interpretive response is to throw up one's hands and simply declare that the new left's cultural politics was "meaningful." To most of those touched by 1960s radicalism, culture "counts" as politics. But how much it counts and what it counts for are the important questions.

The new left's cultural politics spelled neither a new and socially transformative mode of radical politics nor an end to politics. Instead, it is best understood as a kind of reform politics, a cultural liberalism. This is not what the radicals of the 1960s and 1970s said they were up to; they viewed their cultural activities as revolutionary. Yet, despite their initial intention, reform is what they undertook.

The new left's cultural liberalism focused on making incremental advances in the direction of a less racist, less hierarchical, less bureaucratic, and less alienating everyday experience, particularly in the lives of the new left's social peers. By the early 1970s, new left activists agreed that sexism was another major evil to combat in their own lives. Amid the disintegration of a cohesive leftist movement, a group of radicals affirmed in 1972 that the urgent task was to "confront and work to overcome sexism and racism *in our immediate experience*."[134] The most tangible achievements of the new left's cultural politics lay in the changes that this radical movement prompted across the country in institutions of higher education and in the neighborhoods adjacent to those institutions. Thus, new left activists worked above all to make a better way of life for the college-educated white population. The new left thought this would ring in the birth of a new society, so firmly sewn into their consciousness was the view that this social group established the terms on which the entire culture operated. In 1970 one radical iterated the standard opinion that the job at hand was "to start creating the revolutionary organization and culture right now, among ourselves and among the people." The vague populist addendum was not clever enough to conceal the direction of this political imperative.[135]

The methods the new left used to spread its cultural vision reflect a curious confidence in the "marketplace of ideas." Political radicals planned simply to demonstrate the superiority of the egalitarian and authentic way of life to which they aspired, and they hoped that their cultural alternative would triumph as a result. "If we can relate to each other with honesty, depth, and commitment and show others a better way of life through being better people, then we'll be on our way to a society that encourages those qualities instead of stifling them."[136] Reflecting their faith in the irresistible cultural power of the baby-boom generation, new left radicals thought that they could establish a new version of the old American ideal of a city on a hill and that if they achieved perfection there, the corrupt society around them could not help but be affected. The new left evinced a belief, which has a long history among dissenters in the United States, in a voluntaristic, libertarian picture of cultural and political change. Despite the radicals' fear that American citizens had become "unfree plastic zombies," subjects of a velvet consumerist totalitarianism, this movement still believed that somehow Americans could exercise free choice. The demonstration of a more authentic cultural alternative, an alternative that answered the deep and unmet needs of the population, would eventually cause the wholesale abandonment of the existing social system.

The new left's cultural politics is vulnerable to criticism of both its method and its substance. The new left, after all, dealt severely with political incrementalism, seeing in it a failure of vision typical of political liberals. Yet in the end, the new left fixed on cultural incrementalism as its means of creating a social revolution. One sociologist echoed new left historians' merciless evaluation of traditional liberalism, arguing in a Marxist vein that the new left elaborated innovative patterns of social relations but that rather than prefiguring a new society, those social relations merely helped "rationalize" and stabilize the existing society by promoting a kind of social flexibility and "self-direction" congenial to the changing needs of advanced capitalism.[137]

There is a good deal of truth in this analysis. For example, once institutionalized in American higher education, the curricular and pedagogical reforms of the free universities may have helped universities operate more smoothly. To take another example, the cooperative movement helped unleash a wave of entrepreneurial energy in the baby-boom generation that served American capitalism well. In the 1990s, one could hear an echo of 1970s cooperative ideals in "new age" labor-relations rhetoric. A leading example is the antiunion stance of the Whole Foods supermarket chain, based in Austin, which appropriated the rhetoric of "individual freedom, voluntary community, openness, trust, and love" for its own ends.[138] Despite this conservative redirection of values such as "love," however, values like love and life were the residue of a religious framework, and if they really were taken seriously, they were not so easily harmonized with the society and culture that the new left faced. Martin Luther King Jr. argued persuasively that the principle of love implied a society of nonviolence and social justice. The political meanings of values like love and community remain hotly contested.

Not simply the antithesis of modern America, the new left was an expression of that society. As Raymond Williams observes, "The dominant culture . . . at once produces and limits its own forms of counter-culture."[139] This does not mean that the achievements of the new left's cultural politics were insignificant or that they did not mark positive changes in the dominant culture. Furthermore, this reform politics did not undermine a serious chance at political revolution, for no such opportunity existed. The partial and scattershot nature of the successes the new left enjoyed in changing American culture, as well as the functionality of some of these successes with regard to the larger social system, reflect this radical movement's deep involvement with the dominant culture against which it rebelled.

The new left wished to serve as the avant-garde of a revolutionary culture, but this was not to be. The political radicals, looking askance at the hippie rebellion even as they sympathized with it, hoped that through their own cultural activities they might lead a "hegemonic historical bloc" controlling the development of American political culture and decisively influencing the emergence of dominant values and perceptions of reality. Some think they failed to win this role because their critique of their society was "incomplete," but this view is mistaken.[140] If a countercultural vision is completely oppositional, after all, it has little chance of achieving hegemony, since it will seem alien to most participants in the culture. In fact, unsettling as it may be to realize, those elements in the new left's cultural politics that were not consistent with the movement's professed radical democratic values, such as its rather inegalitarian gender politics, may have aided the new left's hegemonic aspirations (while at the same time sowing the seeds of internal revolt), precisely because such elements furnished the new left with evident links to the broader culture.

The new left's achievements represented, in cultural terms, amelioration not transcendence and, in political terms, reform not revolution. In the end, the new left's failure to achieve its largest goals stemmed from both the social limits of its postscarcity appeal and the means that the movement used to spread its vision. The highly decentralized and localized methods that the radicals used to spread their values helped confine to their own patches of society the influence of the most sharply oppositional values they embraced. The new left's members became cultural models mainly for people culturally and socially like themselves, and it was on those people that they were able to exert a political influence through their cultural politics.

For decades before the new left appeared on the scene, cultural modernism had made inroads among the affluent middle strata of the United States. This creed looks to a loosening of outdated mores, inhibitions, and social divisions and rigidities as a process of increasing collective maturity and celebrates an openness to new and different experiences.[141] This perspective gained unprecedented acceptance at the same time the new left was both disintegrating as a cohesive political force and pressing its own cultural agenda with increased energy. Many former new left radicals joined the liberal political constituency after the organized left's collapse, and the ambitious hopes that had animated the new left's cultural politics were absorbed into the larger stream of cultural modernism, with which the new left had always had a closer relationship than the radicals seemed to realize. The new left ultimately helped forge a close and consequential association between cultural modernism and political liberalism. The new left had shaped the cold war search for authenticity into a hope for a revolutionary way of life, a natural, holistic, life-affirming culture. Yet in the end, the new left achieved instead a holistic consumer society, naturalized sexual commodities, a less bureaucratic university education, and an authenticated capitalism: a softened social experience for themselves, not a transformed society.

CHAPTER EIGHT

The Revolution Is Yet to Come:
The Feminist Left

Let me recall a scrap of conversation with the new Chancellor. He was pointing out to me that the chief obstacle to university reform was the teachers, inflexible, narrow, specialist, status-seeking. I cut him short impatiently: "Administrators have parroted this story to me verbatim at fifty colleges across the country. The fact is that for a hundred years you have cut their balls off and now you say they are impotent. Delegate power!" [Martin] Meyerson reddened. . . . A couple of days later he said to the counsel of the Regents, "Goodman is right. Administration turns them into eunuchs and then complains that they are eunuchs."

PAUL GOODMAN, "THE REVOLUTION IN BERKELEY," 1965

IT IS IMPOSSIBLE to know whether Paul Goodman understood how glaring a light he had cast on the new left in relating this anecdote about the University of California at Berkeley in the heady days after the Free Speech Movement.[1] Martin Meyerson assisted Goodman in showing that concern over emasculation was not the exclusive property of the left or of the baby boomers. Goodman, an objector to World War II, an anarchist, a gay man, a nonconformist among dissidents, had come of age in the 1930s and 1940s. Like his contemporary C. Wright Mills, Goodman looked with despair on the leviathan state, as new left radicals called it, that emerged from the world war. He anticipated the domination of this state by corporate and military interests, the absorption of dissent into a militarist program of "growth," and the soul-death of a comfortable and unified America triumphant. What seemed to most Americans a dream come true appeared to a few as a nightmare of "soft totalitarianism," a vision of "a new, repressive organicism."[2]

Goodman and Mills were a world away from Arthur Schlesinger Jr., or so it seemed. As stated earlier, a sharp unease belied Schlesinger's triumphalism in 1949. He, the cold war liberal, sensed a crisis of belief, of myth, and a failure in the capacity for vigorous citizenship required in a democracy. Whereas Schlesinger feared that "anxiety" boded ill for American democracy, Goodman and Mills worried that developments in political economy had rendered democracy and citizenship obsolete. The latter men swallowed this misgiving and declared, as the new left would, that participatory democracy was both necessary and possible. The Free Speech Movement supplied Goodman, at least, with a feeling of vindication.

If such politically disparate men maintained a common concern over the fate of democratic citizenship amid a changing world, their tendency to equate political vitality with virility also united them. In their thought, authenticity and citizenship were joined, and both were fused to potency. Anxiety was for eunuchs; authenticity meant manhood. Schlesinger thought it might be sufficient to maintain virility among a political elite. Mills, Goodman, and then the new left projected the unsettling prospect of a whole nation of he-men. Goodman made no bones about it: he saw political and cultural promise in the Free Speech Movement because there he saw "the rising of students and of professors recalled to manhood."[3] By 1969, Staughton Lynd, another mentor to leftists of the 1960s (and not exactly the embodiment of conventional machismo) echoed a widespread refrain on the left when he asserted that the Vietnam War–era draft posed the choices of "emasculation" and "manhood," exactly reversing the dominant perceptions of military service and the avoidance thereof in the United States.[4] Not coincidentally, Lynd saw the possibility of recapturing manhood particularly in resistance to the military state that had filled Goodman and Mills with dread.

To understand fully the emergence of feminism within the later new left, we need to view it against the backdrop of this prevalent concern over emasculation. The social facts of power being what they were, women in the new left found themselves in the position of responding to the expression of this concern and its effect on their political movement. Virtually until the demise of SDS, men dominated the movement's formal leadership and frequently the internal discussion over the movement's direction and meaning. These men shared in the widespread concern over the loss and recovery of manhood.[5] Like their male counterparts, new left women were searching for democracy and authenticity. Their feminism was in a sense an elaborate rejoinder to the way men like Goodman and Mills articulated that search, an attempt to reformulate it in a way that was internally consistent and that women could abide. The radical feminists of the late 1960s and early 1970s rebelled against the sexism of the new left. But they also, to an extent not always understood, attempted to form a new, feminist left.

The idea that alienation meant political impotence passed from the World War II generation into the new left. This way of posing the challenge of political rebellion formed an unbroken line in American culture during the postwar decades. A few years before Goodman's trip to Berkeley, Mills had sought to trump the authenticity of the cold war liberals revolving in the Kennedy administration's orbit by pointing to Fidel Castro and to his own support for the Cuban, unsubtly mocking the liberals, as noted earlier, for their "failure . . . as political men" when they declined to offer similar support. Van Gosse's study of *fidelismo* makes clear how compelling this formulation of authenticity and rebellion was for the earliest cohort of the new left, just as it was for those political liberals who were drawn to Castro before he ventured across the no-man's-land of the cold war.[6]

White men's fear of insufficiency often fixed on other male specimens, more typically African American than foreign. Norman Mailer brought this tendency out in the open in 1957 in his exoticist essay, *The White Negro*.[7] It is not surprising that the racial turmoil of the National Conference for New Politics (NCNP) ten years later elicited comments from white male leftists concerning their own feelings of impotence, even castration.[8] In this light, the subversion of feminist mobilization at the NCNP, which forms an important moment in the standard tale of the women's liberation movement, seems unsurprising.[9] Soon Eldridge Cleaver, in *Soul on Ice*, commended what he saw as the quest of young white Americans to recover their lost physicality, a quest expressed earlier in college-educated civil rights activists' determination to "put their bodies on the line." The search for authenticity had traditionally appeared as an upper- and middle-class search for physical sensation, often specifically for a sexual awakening, and in the experience of white participants in the civil rights movement, sexuality and danger mingled closely in the existential search for a fuller life and a just society. Although Cleaver saw both white men and white women embarked on this search, his prescription of rape as the best way for black men to claim their own manhood symbolized the preoccupation of public discourse on these matters with the perceived need of American males for empowerment, a preoccupation sometimes taken to such an extreme as to urge violence against women.[10] (It is no small irony that at the same time when young white men depicted young African American men as epitomes of masculine authenticity, young black men themselves were becoming more strident in their parallel assertion of their own emasculation.)

The fusion of authenticity with aggressive male sexuality was widespread in the postwar period, in contexts political and nonpolitical, but in the 1960s this equation not only became pervasive but also acquired a tone of urgency— even hysteria. Perhaps this is because the 1960s followed the 1950s. Alice Echols argues that the will to machismo in the new left represented a "counterhegemonic" revolt against "the domesticated, attenuated sort of masculinity critiqued by William Whyte in his book, [*The*] *Organization Man*." This formulation neatly joins men in the new left to the new left women who became feminists in the late 1960s and 1970s, since those women "were rebelling against the domesticated femininity of their mothers."[11] In this view, women and men in the new left fought the same battle because despite their well-documented conflicts over feminism, they respectively took up cudgels against June and Ward Cleaver.

The broad historical sweep of the male complaint, however, makes it unsatisfying to interpret the new left's sexual politics as simply a revolt against 1950s domesticity. When complaining of their emasculation in the 1960s, American men became newly plangent in their articulation of a rather old viewpoint. In the 1930s, the Frankfurt school theorists (who found in C. Wright Mills a close student) speculated that the rise of industrial bureaucracies a few decades into the twentieth century already had robbed men in the world's richer countries of their sense of masculinity. Fears of feminization were heard in the United States before the century even began.[12] The search for authenticity historically had received expression among men as a desire for authentic manhood. Since the onset of heavy industrialization, many observers had associated the supposed loss of manhood with the rise of white-collar employment. It therefore was appropriate that Mills, the new left's apostle of radical masculinity, should do so much to publicize the eclipse of manual labor by the ranks of paper pushers in his 1951 book, *White Collar*.[13]

It may be true that many of the "children of domesticity" in the 1960s disliked the roles that their parents offered them, and it may be that some of these children became convinced that their parents virtually invented these unfulfilling gender roles. Some argue that daughters in the 1950s saw their mothers' domestic labor devalued, even in the home: a mark of disempowerment.[14] But there is little basis for thinking that the renewed cult of domesticity actually brought sons less liberty, happiness, or status than family life had afforded their counterparts in the immediately preceding decades. It remains unclear whether domestic relations between middle-class adult women and men in the 1950s conformed to any simple pattern. Overall, the available evidence gives us little reason to conclude that 1950s domesticity produced the search for authentic masculinity visible in the 1960s. To say that it did is, in fact, to endorse the poisonous "Momism" analysis of the 1940s (as Betty Friedan did), which depicted pathological mothers crippling their sons' psyches, keeping them from attaining manhood.[15] This is but another version of the discredited generational interpretation of the new left, which sees the young radicals of the 1960s as rebels mainly against their parents. In this respect, as in political terms more generally, young people in the new left did not simply see themselves rejecting the figures their parents cut. What changed was the more general ethos of restraint in American culture, giving way to an ethos of free expression, itself seen as a necessary part of the search for authenticity in the 1960s. Men began to ventilate more easily long-simmering sentiments and resentments and to express them in new ways.

As Friedan demonstrated, in the 1950s the "feminine mystique" was celebrated, and alternative lives for women were ridiculed.[16] Yet this mystique was simultaneously savaged not by radicals but by voices in the cultural mainstream, who alleged that devouring mothers were creating she-men, not he-men. The very same domestic arrangements were simultaneously presented to women as their only path to normal womanhood and to men as threats to their manhood. The attack on "Momism" was an attack on homemakers who were not content with that role, and as Barbara Ehrenreich shows, it initiated a male rebellion against domesticity that flowed beneath the exaltation of the feminine mystique in the 1950s.[17]

To take one prominent example from popular culture, James Dean's father in *Rebel without a Cause* was the archetypal eunuch neutered by his domestic wife (not by a careerist wife). Although Dean's character wanted to reconstitute a new family in which he could be a man, he also sensed that domesticity might be a trap. (The Natalie Wood character's home life was likewise a minefield of dangerous sexual identities, not at all a haven of secure and satisfying gender roles; this film offered a troubled conservatism.)[18] In sum, the attack on "Momism" simply added to a long tradition of encouraging men to chalk up their sense of disempowerment and unhappiness to the denial of their manhood and to express their search for authenticity as a quest to retrieve this grail. Although this tradition migrated to the new suburbs in 1950s America, it was not at all new.

To see the new left's rebellion against the gray flannel suit as "counterhegemonic" is to take too much at face value. As shown in earlier chapters, men in the new left were not the rebels they took themselves to be in their search for an unbuttoned male identity. As Sara Evans notes, "Although the new left was engaged in a cultural revolt . . . it reflected more than it challenged the underlying sexual stereotypes" of its day.[19] In fact, one can even say that the new left's political program garnered what support it did among American men in no small measure because this movement tethered its counterhegemonic political perspective to a gender politics that was thoroughly mainstream, in step with broad strains of popular culture. Those women who also sought authenticity and social change had to contend with this legion of men in search of their manhood.

The National Scene

Organized feminist dissent first emerged in the new left at the national SDS meeting at the University of Illinois in late 1965 where the controversial fight occurred between Bob Speck and Lee Ellis. During the preceding summer, Casey Hayden and her friend from SNCC, Mary King, had prepared a memo concerning the problem of women's positions in both American society and the black and white youth movements. They asserted, boldly for the time, that relations between women and men constituted a "caste" system of institutionalized, material inequality, similar to systems of race and class. The two white women's experience gave them little reason to think this criticism would receive a warm response from African American women in SNCC, and they distributed the document that fall not only within that organization but also to many women they knew in SDS, the Southern Student Organizing Committee (SSOC), and the budding antiwar movement.[20]

Indeed, the white left proved to be the most fertile ground for their seeds of criticism. Hayden insisted years later that her and King's internal criticism of the "peace and freedom movements" was "not a rebellion" but, rather, an attempt "to make more firm and then expand the community of vision" in those movements. As whites, she and King were on their way out of SNCC in accordance with the new thinking in that group; one year earlier they had helped initiate a discussion of sexism within the civil rights movement.[21] Now they viewed gender as a way to stem the fragmentation of both SNCC and the larger "movement." "Women's issues were something to 'organize around,' a means to organize people into the redemptive community," Hayden said frankly.[22] This suggests that more than seeking to spur discontent among activist women, King and especially Hayden, who because of her wide travels and the unusual fluidity in her relations to both SNCC and SDS had a better sense than most of the state of mind of such women, meant to get out in front of an inevitable wave of discontent, making the case that "the movement" (broadly defined to include both SNCC and SDS) could resolve the problem of internal sexism and even that the movement was the best vehicle for attacking sexism in the larger society.

Despite Hayden's attachment to the idea of a larger confederated movement, SNCC and SDS were not the same, as she well knew. Although SNCC's concept of a "redemptive community" had fed the search for authenticity that nourished the new left's growth, and although new left radicals always saw that search occurring in a communal context, the vision of community was honored in the breach more characteristically in SDS than in SNCC. (By 1966, SNCC, too, had abandoned this vision of itself, as

Vivien Franklin, back from Europe, discovered when she and Hayden took a car trip south to a SNCC conference. The level of tension they experienced as white women had taken a quantum leap forward in three years.)[23] Hayden felt from her first involvement with SDS at the Port Huron Conference in 1962 that its atmosphere was less hospitable to women than that of either the Student Y movement or SNCC, that men in SDS were more intent on dominating the organization, and that they were relatively untrammeled in this desire. She recreates a typical evening among the SDS crowd in Ann Arbor: "The guys would discuss C. Wright Mills and I'd go upstairs and discuss the women's lives with them."[24] This kind of experience doubtless helped her views on the "sex-caste" system find a receptive audience among women in SDS.

As explained earlier, the gendered organization of the Student Y, which prevented this kind of domination, was alien to the new left in its heyday, for ironically, the new left, like the liberals of its time, viewed institutional distinctions of race and gender as vestiges of a benighted past. By the summer of 1965, pushed out of SNCC, her marriage to Tom Hayden surviving only in a legal sense, Casey Hayden moved north to Chicago, looking in the ERAP projects for a new activist community and a fresh venue where she could pursue her sense of mission. She had worked several summers earlier among poor women in Harlem, and now she became the leading figure in plotting a predominantly female welfare recipients' union. As is well known, the greatest organizing successes the ERAPs enjoyed were those that women in SDS directed toward poor women, and here Hayden hoed the same row, helping pave the way for the later work of the National Welfare Rights Organization and, more to the point, having her perceptions of new left women's frustrations amplified.

The formal and informal dominance of men in the early years of SDS grated against the evident skill and accomplishment of women as organizers, creating possibly a greater contradiction than existed in SNCC. In the mid-1960s, the women's situation in SDS got worse. Among the old guard, although women had never held national office, there were many women who were respected, but the prairie power cohort seemed more thoroughly male dominated. Evans contends that had the 1965 Illinois gathering been the "rethinking conference" that the old guard had wanted and had the prairie power group not streamed into SDS—and had the war issue and the counterculture not also intervened to encourage sexism in the left— SDS might have had a better chance than it did of dealing constructively with the women's workshop that convened at this meeting to discuss the Hayden–King memo and other items.[25]

Although some men in the old guard viewed the workshop as a salutary development, others offered resistance.[26] The workshop prompted a national council resolution calling on SDS members to recognize the legitimacy of sexism as an issue within and for the left.[27] Six months later, Jane Adams, a former SNCC activist and a prominent SDS regional traveler, was elected national secretary of the organization, the second woman to hold national office in SDS.[28] Despite this symbolic gesture toward equality, however, it seems clear that the rising urgency of the war issue and the changing demographics and culture of SDS snuffed out the initial bid for a feminist left in the 1960s.

By 1967, women in the new left managed to get a hearing once again for their concerns in the organization at large, even though many men, and women, on the left insisted that other matters, particularly the war, were more pressing. Adams wrote an article for *New Left Notes*, then edited by Cathy Wilkerson, a veteran of the Swarthmore SDS organizing efforts in Chester, Pennsylvania, criticizing "male chauvinism" (the designated term for sexist behavior in the old left) in SDS.[29] In December 1967 a "Women's Liberation Workshop" met at the SDS national convention and excited possibly more hostility than had been engendered two years earlier. *New Left Notes* printed a derisive—soon to be infamous—graphic of a woman in a baby-doll minidress along with the workshop's statement, which had received the convention's approval against vigorous opposition. The statement's authors couched their critique of sexism in boilerplate language about the larger struggle and strenuously pressed their analogy between feminism and Third World nationalism, in effect conceding that gender issues did not enjoy freestanding legitimacy in the left in the way that racial issues did.[30]

Although the need to argue from analogy in this way demonstrated the weakness of the feminist camp in the new left—indeed indicated the very unfamiliarity of the feminist case to most men in the movement—the analogy to African American and Third World nationalism (by this time, the former was routinely cast as one instance of the latter) also reveals the new feminism's solid roots in the substratum of the new left. The most salient justification for the formation of women's workshops and discussion groups between 1965 and 1967—that it was every group's right and duty to seek its own liberation by overturning its own oppression—was of a piece with the new working-class analysis and the new left's countercultural turn. I have described how the rise of black power doctrine sanctioned these developments in the new left; early women's liberationists looked to the same source of legitimacy.[31]

There probably had been discussions in the SDS national office over the relation between the new thinking and the situation of women in the left. Greg Calvert, who became the leading exponent of new working-class theory in the U.S. left, first served in the national office as assistant national secretary under Jane Adams, and Calvert assumed her post when she left it in August 1966.[32] By the beginning of 1968, however, Calvert left the national office for Austin, and with his departure, the national leadership of SDS began an unremitting campaign of hostility toward the idea that the new left should create social change primarily by organizing around the experiences of its major constituency, college-educated white youth. This hostility was misleading to outside observers (as it has been to historians), for it masked the continuing appeal to the new left of the sentiments expressed in both the new working-class analysis and the countercultural turn.

It is no mere coincidence, then, that the last years of SDS, when the competition between PL and the "national office collective" dominated the organization's national image, were also the years when the new left's resistance to feminism in its ranks reached its fiercest pitch. The 1968–1969 period witnessed the rapid organization of women's liberation groups among both women in SDS and those in other walks of activism: in Chicago, in New York, in Washington, in Gainesville, in New Orleans, in Durham, in Boston, in Palo Alto, and in Canada as well. The dam had broken, to cite Evans's metaphor, and the waters rushed forward.[33] Continuing anger over the war, campus confrontations, and the sharpening racial confrontations in American cities in the late 1960s all affirmed the view in some quarters of the left that gender issues could wait for another time and encouraged the "street-fighting man" tendency among white male leftists who saw a heroic opportunity to reclaim a manhood they thought had been denied them.[34] Still more notorious incidents followed, probably none worse than the grotesque behavior of some male attendees at the January 1969 "Counter-Inaugural" protest in Washington. When a woman was delivering one more careful call for the left to deal with its sexism, from the audience came catcalls like those heard at a striptease and suggestions of rape to boot. The event's moderator nervously told the women speakers to cut short their presentations.[35]

An equally important event was the national office group's elevation of Bernardine Dohrn. As explained earlier, Dohrn symbolized the substitution of sexual liberalism for gender equality; now SDS had its very own Vargas Girl. This token adoption of a woman was the national office group's tactical response to feminism in the left. Even on those terms, it is highly revealing that instead of looking to a woman with long experience and credibility in SDS, such as Jane Adams or Cathy Wilkerson, this faction propelled forward a relative unknown, who could not become a rival for supremacy in her own right because she lacked an independent base of support.[36] Calvert claims that Dohrn and Adams teamed up in 1967 to push him out of influence in Chicago, using his bisexuality against him.[37] Both his personal inclinations and his political thought expressed an ideal of "self-liberation" that found little favor in the late SDS national leadership; the Chicago group suggested that activists channel their desire for liberation into a conventional sexuality, which partook of the same sexual commodification that Dohrn and Naomi Jaffe criticized in a 1968 article.[38]

The greatest challenge to the prevailing view in the SDS enclaves of Chicago and Morningside Heights—that there was fighting to do, that "men of steel" were needed, and that self-liberation was a "bourgeois" indulgence—came not from gay men or bisexuals and not from the new working-class analysis but from the burgeoning women's liberation movement.[39] Expecting an eschatalogical battle for the nation's future that never came, certain that someone else would lead them to the promised land, the national officers of SDS sought to suppress anything that might block their expected path. To see the true development of feminism in the left at this time, as with the other significant contemporary trends in radical politics, one has to look beyond those who believed themselves to be leaders of brigades but who could muster only handfuls of stragglers and who never found the battle they sought.

A Local "Matriarchy"

One leftist and women's liberation activist in Austin, Pat Cuney, remarked around 1970 that a "matriarchy" had come to preside over the local left. She exaggerated, but her comment accurately reflected a redistribution of power in the Austin left during and after the collapse of Students for a Democratic Society. In 1966 or 1967, Bobby Minkoff recalls, a group of men who ran the *Rag* sat around talking about the women's meetings that were starting to be held in SDS. This could change everything, he realized. But it did not change for a couple of years; the appearance of feminism in Austin lagged a bit behind developments elsewhere. Some women in the local left spoke with Becky Brenner around this same time about her evidently subservient role in her relationship with Dick Reavis. Women raised the issue of sexism in the SDS chapter, but "they were put down hard and fast," says Paul Spencer, causing some women, like Trudy Minkoff, to move away from the group. Men generally responded with "a lot of snorting."[40]

When Alice Embree returned to Austin in 1969 from New York, where she had contributed an essay to the widely read anthology *Sisterhood Is Powerful*, she found herself "somewhat seen as a feminist," a well-traveled and widely known woman radical. She had undergone her own political changes, shaped by her broadening political experience. Just before leaving school, she traveled to Chile in 1967 as part of a UT exchange program (despite the U.S. State Department's attempt to stop her), and she went on the first SDS trip to Cuba in 1968. In New York, Jeff Nightbyrd raised enough money to start a left-wing publication called *Rat*, and Embree, living "in desperate circumstances" near the Port Authority in lower Manhattan, worked with the North American Congress on Latin America (NACLA), where feminist sentiment was bubbling up. She recalls a woman ripping a much-seen poster of Che Guevara off the NACLA office wall and replacing it with a likeness of Rosa Luxemburg; Embree herself got "dressed down" in a meeting there for addressing Marge Piercy, who became a prominent left-wing feminist writer, by her husband's name, Shapiro (Embree had never before heard of a woman not using her husband's name). After taking part in the tumultuous events at Columbia University in the spring of 1968—Nightbyrd was inside the occupied president's office, and Embree stood beyond the police barricade where she caught the university documents he tossed to her, which NACLA then published, verifying accusations leveled by SDS at Columbia—events forced the "ultimate movement couple" to contend with the personal implications of feminism.[41]

Nightbyrd went to Mississippi to work on a book about working-class white southerners, hoping to promote the populist vision of an insurgent biracial South that the southern new left had nurtured for years, and soon a group of women on the left, fed up with the pornographic aspect of *Rat*, insisted that the paper allow them to produce a women's issue. This featured Robin Morgan's celebrated essay "Goodbye to All That," in which she denounced the new left as a "counterfeit Left" and called for the release of numerous women, including Embree, as if they were political prisoners of the men in their lives. A fight between women and men for control of the paper ensued, with Nightbyrd, from Mississippi, first assenting to the women's claim and then reversing himself after a friend from SNCC insisted to him that the insurgents were "a bunch of rich bitches, dilettantes." Nightbyrd also strongly sympathized with his friend Gary Thiher, whom he had gotten to take over as editor during his absence and who, from a modest background in the Texas Panhandle, seemed both a bit at sea in the world of New York radical politics and, to Nightbyrd, an inappropriate target for feminist ire.

The involvement of Thiher and, on the other side, the child television star Morgan and other well-heeled women, allowed Nightbyrd to view the conflict as "a class fight," and he told Thiher on the phone, "Don't give in." As it happened, Embree was visiting him when he urged this hard line on Thiher, but she did not stay after this. It was the end of their life together.[42]

Although Embree became quite involved in feminist activities after her return to Austin, it remained for others—younger, not rooted in SDS, and not faced with such traumatic breakups as the price of feminism—to take the lead in women's liberation activities. Some discussions like those around the country may have taken place in 1968 in Austin, but more certain involvement in the national wave of left-wing women's meetings, meetings linking personal "problems" to political "issues," began only in the aftermath of the March 1969 SDS National Council meeting in Austin. An outlandish sexism seemed like part of the "heaviness" of the national SDS members who made such a negative impression on the locals. Women on the left here held regular discussion meetings during the subsequent months, including Judy and Linda Smith, Victoria Foe, Barbara Hines, and Barbara Wuensch Merritt, all relative newcomers to radicalism, as well as Becky Brenner, Mariann Wizard, and other familiar faces.[43]

Both the decay of SDS and generational changes in the left contributed to this development. Women in the later cohort of the new left grew up in a changed political atmosphere in which a vibrant left and antiwar protest were established facts of life. The very prospect of a political left was not thrilling enough to reconcile them to "internal contradictions" like sexism. Furthermore, most of the younger women were aware of the debate over Betty Friedan's work—many of them had read *The Feminine Mystique*— and even if their brand of feminism ultimately differed from Friedan's, she and other liberal feminists, who started the National Organization for Women (NOW) in 1966, had established the legitimacy of gender inequality as a public, political issue by the mid-1960s, and this encouraged young women to speak their minds on such matters. Because of this and because SDS was paralyzed by factionalism, the major new left organization exercised only a tepid hold on radical women looking for political outlets after 1968. Linda Smith, for example, was never "drawn" to SDS. Judy Smith tried it out but became disillusioned with the preference of many members for endless discussions over activism and with the authoritarian streak that was becoming prominent in the organization. Like most new left radicals, Judy Smith had little patience with doctrinaire politics. "When someone would come in and say, 'Oh, Mao did it this way in China, let's do it this way here,' we'd all say, 'Oh poo.'"[44] They and others found a political home at the *Rag*, which displayed a greater capacity for change than did SDS, partly because it was not targeted by groups like PL.

No woman became more prominent in the Austin women's liberation movement, and no individual was more important in the last years of the Austin left, than Judy Smith—whose background had much in common with Embree's, including Protestant liberalism and a father who was a professional educator of high status. Raised in Oak Park, Illinois, where their father was the superintendent of schools, Linda and Judy Smith grew up in a cosmopolitan household that often hosted international students. Their father died young, and before going to college, they spent their last few years near Dallas, where their mother, a trained classical singer, found work as a librarian at Southern Methodist University. Their parents were practicing Methodists. But by the time she was in high school, Judy had fallen away from religious observance, although she still participated in a church youth group which, by the time she graduated in 1962, was more inclined to discuss J. D. Salinger than Scripture. Linda returned to the Midwest for college while Judy transferred a couple of years later to Brandeis University, where she took philosophy classes from Herbert Marcuse. Judy, the younger sister, had always been "antiauthoritarian," joining the junior NAACP in high school and contacting the local ACLU when school authorities forced students to watch a HUAC-produced film. In college her liberal activism deepened. She joined the Congress of Racial Equality (CORE) and participated in organizing efforts in black neighborhoods, her early, rather instinctive opposition to the Vietnam War becoming stronger. She was part of a group of students who protested Secretary of Labor Arthur Goldberg's visit to Brandeis in 1966, over the government's war policy. Both sisters joined the Peace Corps.

Linda Smith spent two and a half years in Ecuador working on an irrigation project; Judy spent a year in Biafra, returning to the United States after civil war forced the evacuation of Peace Corps workers in the summer of 1967. Linda gradually came to have misgivings about some aspects of the corps's work abroad, but she knew fairly little about geopolitics before she came back home in 1966, the conflict in Southeast Asia included. In Ecuador she became used to living simply and found herself repulsed by the "opulence" of Dallas, where she returned to be with her mother. After trying and not liking some graduate courses at SMU, she moved to Austin, which she found more congenial, and began studying anthropology at UT. Judy, for whom the sight of people getting killed in Biafra had been "pretty determinative" in fixing her attitudes toward war generally, worked on the Vietnam Summer antiwar project in 1967 and then went to the San Francisco Bay area, participating in the shutdown of the Oakland Draft Induction Center. She thought San Francisco was "fun" but found it filled with hostility as well as political ferment. "I don't like cities," she comments simply in retrospect.[45]

Linda sent some copies of the *Rag* to Judy, who sent Linda some feminist literature she was reading. In the summer of 1968, the sisters hitchhiked together in Europe (catching the end of the Prague Spring, leaving Czechoslovakia just before the Soviet invasion), and in the fall they returned to Austin together. Judy enrolled in graduate courses in molecular biology. Here life seemed more "integrated," as the left and the counterculture overlapped more than in San Francisco. There was a great deal of green space, and the two sisters spent a lot of time outdoors. Although the pastoral dimension of the freak counterculture appealed to them, other elements did not. By this time there was a group of "Motherfuckers" in Austin, angry motorcyclists and antiwar anarchists of a sort, who helped police the hippie precincts of town. Typically they were paired off with much younger women and, like the national SDS heavies, they were "into total macho bullshit."[46]

Judy Smith started working at the *Rag*, where she continued to pursue her earlier political concerns. At first she reported mainly on the continuing struggle in Austin over the city government's slowness in integrating the schools (a goal to which it had officially committed itself more than a decade earlier). The U.S. Department of Health, Education and Welfare (HEW) supplied proposals for racial integration, gave the school board deadlines, and relented when Senator John Tower and Representative Jake Pickle intervened. The board ventured a one-way busing proposal that involved shipping African American students to the historically white schools and shutting historically black Anderson High in East Austin, but local pressures staved off this gambit, and Austin inched toward a plan that everyone could live with, years after supposedly less liberal cities in Texas and around the South had been compelled, as a result of their initial intransigence, to integrate their schools.[47]

Smith also investigated the ongoing "urban renewal" of low-cost rental housing areas in Austin, which put the squeeze on both working-class residents and young radicals with little income. (Late in 1968, the SDS Housing Committee floated a proposal to cap rents at 20 percent of the renter's income.) Alterations in the landscape of Austin proceeded apace, with the university playing a major role, buying land north of the campus and tearing down cheap housing to build the Johnson Library and other structures, and taking down the old college houses and shifting the undergraduate population to new high-rise dormitories far from the main campus.[48] This last decision presaged a great change in the university culture. In the 1950s, students and teachers alike had gathered in the evenings on campus to hear speakers and debates, contributing to an atmosphere of intellectual and political ferment. But starting in the 1970s, students rode shuttle buses back to their homes after a day of classes. The campus was no longer the intellectual community it once had been. Not only the organized left but also the local intellectual environment that had nurtured it was fragmenting.

It did not take long after her arrival in Austin for Judy Smith to become a leading figure on the left. A high school debater, a tall woman, described by her sister as "a very powerful person . . . very verbal," she always "seemed like the person who had the information" as well as an "analysis" to offer, says Jeff Jones, one of the men in the post-1968 new left who also looked beyond SDS. Despite the reaction of radical feminists against the existence of a hierarchy in the new left, it is clear that there were leaders and followers among the left-wing feminists. Nancy Folbre, whose political involvement focused more on Latin American issues than on concerns about gender, lived in a group house on Twelfth Street in Austin where Vic Foe, a prominent member of the feminist circle, was "queen." Jim Denney, a left-wing antiwar and civil rights activist who by 1971 became a gay liberation leader in Austin, found Judy Smith "dominant," calling her "a hard woman." Such comments simply indicate (in addition to anything else) that the burgeoning women's liberation movement, operating in the same structureless mode as did SDS, striving for consensus, similarly did not escape the power relations involved in any collective endeavor.[49]

The Smith sisters, Wizard, Brenner, Susan Olan, Judy Walther, Barbara Hines, and Barbara Merritt all took a philosophy class taught in the spring of 1969 by Larry Caroline, shortly before he departed the local scene. During the first week of the semester, someone made an announcement in class that a women's liberation meeting would take place at the Student Y, and they all went.[50] Merritt, a recent arrival from Virginia whose father was a top-ranking officer in the U.S. Coast Guard, had cut her political teeth by simply stating her antiwar views, which was enough to elicit continual, combative arguments at Mary Washington College. "The first meeting; nothing but women," she wrote in the *Rag* in September 1969. She found it "amazing," empowering; it was a "very incredible experience" for Hines. Members of the women's liberation circle in Austin repeatedly commented on their realization that they had been trained to value and compete for the company of men and to devalue their female friendships. Women's meetings brought many to this realization and represented an attempt to change the way they viewed themselves and other women. " 'We'—you're referring to sisters, rather than chicks" now, said Merritt. Although some of them possessed a commanding sense of competence, to others, acquiring feelings of self-worth in a specifically political context was no small matter.[51]

Feminists in Austin tried to maintain this kind of all-women's environment, although most of their political activity involved both women and men. In the fall of 1970 they held a Women's Liberation Conference at the university that brought together feminists from around Texas and elsewhere. In 1970, Austin Women's Liberation (now an official campus organization) started the Women's Center in a house near the university, which they called Everywoman's Center, to provide a "liberated space." This lasted perhaps a year. In 1972 other feminists, not affiliated with the left, started another Austin Women's Center, which was still in existence more than two decades later. Austin Women's Liberation planned a Women's Festival over the Halloween 1971 weekend. This was not "a conference to determine policies"; it was more countercultural. "What we want is a festival of living together, and together discovering new ways to live." They would gather "out in the country to make music, life and love." They planned seminars on automobile mechanics, printing, gardening, and cooking, continuing the broader counterculture's emphasis on self-sufficiency.[52]

These activities represent what historians of feminism call "cultural feminism." Contrary to the impression that some historians convey, however, this tendency was present in Austin Women's Liberation consistently and virtually from its beginning, stemming from the preexisting countercultural tendencies of the left. Moreover, whereas some analysts view this kind of cultural feminism as antagonistic toward more conventional political activism, in fact, feminists in the late 1960s and early 1970s viewed cultural feminism as conducive to their protest activities, not as a retreat from political agitation. Before 1973, many feminists combined "cultural" and "radical" brands of feminism.[53] It marked an important change in Alice Embree's life, for example, that in 1969 after she moved back to Austin, for the first time most of her friends were women. Spending time with other women in itself was an important goal, not as an opening toward separatism, but as a means toward a more empowered position in relation to men.[54] The maintenance of all-women's environments, it seemed clear, helped women build the confidence required to confront the sexism they encountered both in the world at large and from their male comrades.

The end of SDS did not mean, at least not immediately, the end of the new left. In fact, only the death of SDS opened the possibility, for the first time in this era of activism, of a feminist left.[55] Virtually all the leading women's liberation activists here remained deeply committed to and involved in leftist and antiwar activities. This, more than anything else, is what existing accounts of the women's liberation movement obscure, just as histories of the new left omit discussion of the feminist left in the post-SDS years. Years later, many people might be surprised to hear a visitor to the first Austin Women's Center recollect seeing "the poster that hung in the front room there. It was yellow, black, and red, with half the picture showing a Caucasian woman putting on lipstick and half a Vietnamese woman with blood streaming from her nose."[56] These feminist radicals already had been pulling away from SDS when SDS immolated itself in the fire of its own factionalism, yet it is not true to say that they "broke away from the left."[57] Judy Smith was first arrested at an all-women's antiwar action, distributing leaflets at Fort Hood in Killeen, an action certainly infused with a stronger feminist consciousness than the women's sit-in at the Austin draft board in 1966.[58] The participating women were radical feminists, but in the years between 1969 and 1973, they devoted as much time to antiwar, anti-imperialist, environmentalist, antiracist, prolabor, and general leftist activities as to specifically gender-related issues. They were determined to form a new, feminist left.

Speaking Bitterness

Lori Hansel remarks that after becoming a committed leftist, what she really wanted was what she had read about in *Fanshen*, William Hinton's popular account of the Chinese Revolution in one village: "to . . . turn everything upside-down."[59] Although the revolution did not come, left-wing feminists in the United States, more than any other manifestation of the new left, echoed (albeit in a far milder form) the Chinese practice of "speaking bitterness" and "struggling" against members of the privileged classes. The feminists, sometimes including sympathetic male radicals, did not just discuss the sexism of the larger culture among themselves; they confronted men with their criticism. One of the basic activities the radical feminists undertook, starting soon after their initial meetings, was finding venues where they could tell others what they had been telling themselves. They got themselves invited to appear before groups of all kinds—college and high school classes and church congregations, for example—and aired their views. They encountered much hostility, perhaps in equal measures from women and men. But they kept it up, on a "proselytizing mission."[60]

Guerrilla theater was a favored method of communicating feminist social criticism, as when Bill Meachem joined a group of women in a parody of the "slave auction" that campus fraternities and sororities held annually to raise money for charitable causes (reminiscent of the minstrel show, ended years before). The radical women cowered on the administration tower's steps, where women usually were "sold" in the show, and Meachem acted the part of slave master, whip and all. Alice Embree got involved with a "crazy bunch of women" when she moved back to Austin, participating in many guerrilla theater actions, including a witches' hex of the Johnson Library at its dedication and similar actions at a Catholic school and a bank, echoing the activities of the socialist feminist group WITCH (Women's International Terrorist Conspiracy from Hell) at the New York Stock Exchange. They also performed a "women's history of the world," with narration read from a long scroll, at locations like the Oleo Strut and the Chuckwagon. Other actions were less scripted. Cuney, Hansel, and others organized a "Make a Man Feel Like a Sex Object Day," whistling and catcalling at men as they walked by, "just to kind of make them feel like we were made to feel every day, and they didn't like it a bit." At one point, a man picked Hansel up, slung her over his shoulder, and disappeared with her into a university building, bringing things to an end. Women defaced a large placard hung on a fraternity building one football weekend, which featured a drawing of a scantily clad woman with enormous breasts and the UT Longhorns slogan "Bust 'Em Bevo." The activists spray-painted "This Exploits Women" over the sign, prompting a debate over private property. Late in the SDS chapter's lifetime, a man made a sexist comment in a meeting, and the next day women continually walked up to him and fingered his crotch. "He was totally shook up by it," Meachem remembers.[61] Neither men's sensitivities nor general rules of decorum were uppermost in the women's minds. Although those who took part in guerrilla theater were having great fun, they also were angry.

As this last incident indicates, men on the left were hardly exempt from criticism. Quite the contrary; their sexism was the most relevant of all, since it blocked the formation of a feminist left. When the Weatherman faction of SDS admonished white youth not to "wimp out" by failing to show up for the big battles, Michele Clark of Austin derided them. "Why don't they just say 'limp out' and get it over with?" she asked. "You can either be hard or limp, right? Just like a cock, right? We can all grow them if we try? Yeah."[62] By 1969, women on the left had developed a critical consciousness of the language of masculinity that for so long had gone unquestioned, a staple of American radicalism. They had listened to this kind of thing for as long as they had been involved in the left, and now when individual women discovered that others also found the rendition of authenticity as manhood odd, to say the least, they did not hesitate to air the responses that they had perhaps rehearsed to themselves already. A critique of sexist language thus became a central part of the feminist criticism that women's liberation activists turned on radical men.

One of the fatter targets for criticism was the terminology that men (and women) in "hip" circles used to refer to women. Sue Hester and Steve Russell had an exchange in 1971 over the term *chick*. He knew the term was sexist, he said, but it was part of his culture; the use of this word was merely the result of his socialization, so he was morally blameless. Cleverly enough turning around the rhetoric of self-liberation, he said he needed to be freed, too—freed from his sexist upbringing. Another man agreed that personal judgments directed against men who used such terms were not constructive. "The key to salvaging some of the magic of Peace," he stated, was trying "to *Know Each Other*." Besides, he said, tossing oil on the flames, "chick" had some positive connotations. It came from the counterculture, not from the repressive straight culture.[63]

He was not alone in thinking that personal judgments had no place in a true counterculture. "This is supposed to be an alternative community," said one man in the pages of the *Rag*. "When we start telling each other what to say and what we can't, what kind of community is that? It puts you right back with the society we are trying to get away from." The Ragstaff responded collectively, "Do you use the words 'nigger,' 'spic,' 'wop,' 'kike,' etc. when speaking of Blacks, Chicanos, Italians, Jews, etc.???" reminding their readers that on some issues, judgments were considered not only legitimate but necessary in hip circles. "A chick is fluffy, cute, stupid and in need of protection. . . . Now if that don' fit the ol' PATERNALISTIC image of a woman who stays in her place, I don't know what does." Things had changed at the *Rag*. It was clear that different participants in the counterculture had differing ideas about what, fundamentally, the counterculture was meant to oppose—hierarchy or moralism. Which of these was the greater source of hatred, the greater threat to an authentic, natural life?[64]

For some, living in the counterculture meant escaping the rules that governed behavior in the straight society. Obviously, many who reveled in the counterculture were in no way committed to leftist ideals, and for them, sexist behavior entailed no contradiction. Jayne Loader, an Austin radical, noted the continual sexist come-ons that she and other women endured from the *Rag*'s sales staff around campus. She felt a "depressing and almost totally sexist atmosphere here—freaks included and emphasized." Some suggested that freak men were especially likely to prey on young women in violent fashion. In 1971 the *Rag* reported recent instances of rape or assault of women in the local hippie subculture, bringing to mind Chester Anderson's declamation four years earlier that "rape is as common as bullshit on Haight Street" in San Francisco. One of the Austin victims concluded that the rhetoric of "sexual liberation" was just a cover for new forms of male exploitation of women.[65]

This suspicion grew stronger among radical women in the early 1970s. Usually it was not a matter of sexual assault, but more generally a question of whether the elimination of sexual inhibitions was truly oppositional with respect to the dominant culture. The orthodox view on the left still answered in the affirmative. As discussed in chapter 7, women as well as men in the new left experimented with "open" sexual relationships and casual liaisons. After 1968, feminist leftists saw themselves involved in a project of "libertarian socialism," and with the emergence of both feminist and gay activism, it was almost an article of faith in the post-SDS left that in a sense, consensual sexual behavior and sexual expression "should be considered an inalienable human right."[66] Women's liberation activists also criticized the nuclear family structure, which they associated with sexual monogamy. "We have no reason to believe," Judy Smith declared, that "the monogamous, nuclear family is a good form for structuring human relationships—look what kind of human it produces." Both women and men associated traditional monogamy with sexual repression.[67] "Traditional" family life—meaning the kind of life with which young people of this time had grown up—was perhaps not natural, the conventional wisdom be damned.

Indeed, harsh criticism of monogamy remained fashionable among left-wing feminists. After all, one could argue that this tradition reduced women's bargaining power with men as long as men held themselves to a less stringent standard of fidelity. When Barbara Merritt returned to Austin from a trip to India that had led to a spiritual awakening for her, some of her fellow feminists greeted with hostility her announcement that she wanted a long-term relationship with a man. To some, this seemed like retrogression: how she had slipped backward while out of their company! Furthermore, many radicals, feminist or not, viewed the pursuit of such personal goals as a drain on political commitment. When another woman in the circle told her comrades she wanted to have a child, a group led by Judy Smith reportedly confronted her and told her this would amount to selling out the movement (also noting, in line with ecological criticism circa 1970, that the world was crowded already). To Merritt, this all seemed hypocritical, especially the criticism of her vocal heterosexual monogamy, since most of the leaders of the Austin women's liberation group, Smith included, were themselves involved in serious monogamous relationships with men.[68] The feminist radicals were divided within themselves on these matters.

Despite the lingering legitimacy of sexual bohemianism, those on the left now more readily acknowledged the link between the dominant culture and hip sexuality. One man advertised in the *Rag* in 1969, "Gentle man needs live-in girl while wife and kids are gone for a month," and a woman responded, "It seems that sexual exploitation is justified if it is dressed in the trappings of 'peace, love, or freedom.' And it seems like you are revolutionary like Hugh Hefner is revolutionary." Another woman cut to the quick a man who had complained about "prudes" on the left. "You sound like a little kid in a candy store," she said; "ah, now that the revolution is here and everyone is 'liberated,' you can get all the pieces of ass you want." She warned him, "The revolution is yet to come."[69]

Perhaps these comments were simply directed at a double standard. By 1970, however, the very experience of sexual experimentation, even if egalitarian, was beginning to seem stale to some radicals. One Austin feminist advised, "Try [having] sex . . . whenever possible and you'll probably find that it's an emotionally sterile experience and not even physically very satisfying." Ultimately, feminism did much to restore prestige to monogamy in the left. Although many women's liberation activists continued to criticize familiar sexual practices, for other feminists, the next debate over sexuality centered on the question of heterosexuality and lesbianism.

Once they asserted themselves openly as a distinct presence in the women's liberation movement, lesbian feminists were as critical as any concerning the "sexual revolution." Reportedly, the prevailing view in Gay Women's Liberation (GWL) in Austin was that the conventional definition of sexual liberation was "only 'free to be screwed,' maybe free to panhandle."[70] Feminists continued to question the institution of monogamy, but generally they looked askance at compulsory monogamy, just as they did at compulsory heterosexuality, rather than monogamy per se, thus settling on a stance of liberal toleration. The 1960s witnessed the second romance of bohemianism in the twentieth-century American left (the first had occurred in the "lyrical left" of the 1910s). By the mid-1970s, though, this second interlude had passed. This further weakened the already unsteady new left strategy of creating political change through cultural revolt, perhaps more than feminist radicals understood, since although sexual dissent continued and in some quarters even deepened, its relation to the larger culture and to politics had come into question.

Psychology

Complain though men in the left and the counterculture might about the scrutiny their behavior now received from feminists, women's liberation activists often felt they had better things to do than criticize men. Although feminist radicalism was a response to a male-dominated tradition in the left, the new feminists made clear their view that if they were to challenge that tradition and create a new kind of left, they had work to do on themselves. They were deeply concerned over female psychology, which they were convinced operated to keep women down. This was not because the feminists were conditioned to blame women for their own problems; rather, it was an outgrowth of their roots in the new left. They could not help but agree with Paul Potter's statement, "The experience of growing up is the experience of having the society plant something deep down inside of you, almost at the very bottom, that is not your own. Those incredible things we call our minds do not really belong to us."[71]

Just as new left radicals asserted that the culture of capitalism distorted people's personalities, new left feminists argued that social forces shaped women's and men's psyches and socialized the sexes into rigid gender roles that relegated women to a subservient position in society and led men to assume a birthright of power. "Women's liberation," they explained, "means liberation from the role of woman that we have had built inside us by our society. In effect, we must free ourselves from ourselves."[72] Although new left radicals generally felt that they had overcome the problem of inner alienation through their radical activities, the feminist left insisted that even radicals had a remaining frontier of inner alienation to conquer.

This emphasis on psychology and gender roles—feminists called them "sex roles"—was what these activists thought distinguished them from earlier feminists, much as Robert Pardun had seen "social radicalism" separating the new left from the old. In both cases, the radicals were determined to alter their own minds, their own values and personal ideals, as well as to change institutional and social structures. The feminists of the nineteenth century, Judy Smith wrote, "worked for economic and political equality for women," but "they never challenged the psychological basis of male supremacy. They . . . never denied the traditional definitions of women as inherently different than men." Those earlier feminists, she said, had believed that women were morally superior and that men were more sexual than women. "We in Women's Liberation," she said, "deny any inherent differences between men and women and regard everyone as human beings with the same potential."[73] Another Austin feminist agreed that women needed to reject "the traditional concept of 'femininity'" that, she said, perpetuated a "stereotype of women as being essentially passive, emotional, dependent and somehow inferior to men." Clarice Clark was incensed in 1970 at Benjamin Spock's latest book, *Decent and Indecent*, which asserted that boys and girls were in fact inherently different and that girls would and should be "fascinated" by the child-rearing role. "Keep this book out of the hands of parents with young children," she advised.[74]

The language of individual choice and human potential, indebted to the humanist liberalism of Friedan and many others, carried a strong relativist message, no matter what preferences and prejudices the radicals may have harbored with regard to women's life choices. "Liberation is about free choice, not new dogmas," said one, and perhaps none of her fellow activists would have disagreed.[75] "We believe women must come to see themselves as individual human beings with individual and valid interests of their own," said Judy Smith. "They must come to value their own time and spend it as they [choose]. They must come to understand their own sexuality and their own desires." Women were "unique human beings," but together they encompassed the same range of desires and capacities as men did. The open-ended search for fulfillment tied the radicals not only to liberal thinkers like Friedan but also to those like Paul Tillich, whose therapeutic psychology was rooted in a Christian progressive tradition. What feminists termed *autonomy*, *fulfillment*, or *potential*, Tillich called the achievement of "personality."[76]

Although feminist radicals rejected the notion that any specific gender roles could be natural or inevitable, they did not reject outright the idea of a natural personality. Here again, the new left quality of their thought was clear. In the new left view, people were unhappy because they were alienated from their true human nature. To women's liberationists, people were unhappy because they were alienated from some part of their own true selves, straitjacketed into a sex role that sealed off some part of their full spectrum of feelings and experiences. This implied that a more androgynous identity was the most natural vision of human nature. Whatever the degree of their attachment to notions of a true human nature and an authentic way of life, they asserted that the right approach was "for women and men together to save the best, discard the shit, and set up new forms for which there are no models."[77] Nonetheless, their behavior sometimes belied this relativist sentiment. As the disputes described earlier indicate, the feminists had definite ideas about what roles women ought to choose and about the perceived demands of a radical political movement, and these convictions sometimes led to expressions of disapproval over the choices that some women made. Some thought that at least in the immediate future, a relativist attitude toward women's lifestyles would be insufficient to rectify years of sexist socialization.

The women's liberationists made it plain that to them, the achievement of personality did not mean becoming the opposite of the "traditional" woman. They did not want simply to exchange female roles for male ones. Psychologically, this would be just as confining as the current situation. "Rejecting the old stereotype of women means rejecting the stereotype of men, too," observed one activist. It was "no good for the woman to embrace the male sexual role. . . . The aura of emotional strength and independence, the plastic definition of virility, the power-tripping—all of these are as repressive and unreal as the passive muddle-headed homemaker image."[78] Plastic, unreal: authenticity mattered as much as empowerment. As soon as women came together in Austin to talk about their experiences as women, Judy Smith reported, "We knew we didn't want to become more like men because men have just as restrictive a role as we do. They also are highly manipulated objects in our society. We realized we had to learn to value ourselves and men as human beings."[79]

The rhetoric of humanism suggests that the feminists were trying to forge a newfound feminist unity in a left whose cohesiveness was threatening to dissolve. Far from being separatists, they continually urged men to join them in their project. They echoed Friedan in their ceaseless refrain that women's liberation would benefit men as well as women. According to Bea Vogel, "Women's Liberation is not 'hate men' or 'compete with men' or 'be as good as men.'" Linda Swartz asked, "Sure, it's very satisfying to be secure in your womanhood or your manhood. But isn't it more satisfying to feel that above all you are a human being, that your worth depends on more than your successful incarnation of a sex role?" Smith defined their ultimate goals most clearly: "What we're really working for is human liberation."[80] Like earlier new left radicals, the feminists, while seeking to level the inequalities in power between different social groups, also mooted those differences, in a sense, by asserting a universal experience of alienation or unhappiness rooted in psychology.

Some accounts of the women's liberation movement give short shrift to the psychological emphasis that was so central to the feminists considered here. Some activists around the country viewed this kind of analysis as victim blaming and favored a strict focus on women's oppression by more direct social forces, primarily by men as a class. One important group in New York, the Redstockings, cleverly called this the "pro-woman line."[81] But it is clear that the feminists in Austin did not think they were blaming themselves or other women. Instead, they thought that the sex roles of which they wished to divest themselves had been planted in their psyches, that the fault was not their own. Like the new left, the feminists related social problems to personal issues, which would have been difficult to do if they had denied the reality of the issues.

Feminism and Capitalism

Like the new left overall, the feminist left viewed consumer culture as the epitome of inauthenticity, the agent and site of alienation, perhaps the main enemy agent planting foreign identities in young minds. Haunted by the specter of a "soft totalitarianism," they feared the erasure of personality amid the culture of advanced capitalism. The contemporary advertising industry, they noted, echoing the analysis of Dohrn and Jaffe, forced women into the role of items for sale, leading men and even women themselves to view women as commodities. Through the use of women's bodies to sell innumerable products, "our body becomes a symbol of gratification and conquest. . . . Our sex is a commodity that men seek to buy." Austin Women's Liberation, like feminists elsewhere, criticized the Miss America pageant in particular for parading white women with hourglass figures as the female "ideal" toward which all women should aspire and that men should desire. Miss America "is herself a product," they said, and they scored "the artificiality of the Miss America symbol."[82]

Austin Women's Liberation traced this process of commodification to the larger economic system. "Our society is based on competition and maximization of profit," said Smith. "We are raised to be always in competition with each other" rather than to "build true human relationships." The ethos of competition infected personal life and led women to behave as if they were wares on display for men's consumption, each trying to outshine the other. Furthermore, women were "programmed" to behave as products and also as reliable consumers, playing a key role in propping up capitalism. Smith quoted a document from a "motivations research agency" that asserted, "Properly manipulated, American housewives can be given the sense of identity, purpose, creativity, the self realization, even the sexual joy they lack—by the buying of things." She did not make it clear whether she thought the advertising industry was successful in this effort, but it was a possibility she found plausible and alarming. Another feminist expressed the same fear. "The economic system of capitalism has only a very limited room for individual autonomy. For example: Women must consume make-up for the cosmetic industry to thrive. And our system will psychologically rape you into believing that you are less of a woman if you don't." As either objects or consumers, women might lose their own independent sense of value, becoming the "unfree plastic zombies" that the new left feared. The feminists sealed the link between the oppression of women and other leftist concerns with the coup de grâce: "The system that produced the Miss America pageant also produced the Vietnam War. That system thrives on obedient, docile people with no opinion of their own."[83]

Probably the first political action conducted by Austin Women's Liberation was a bit of guerrilla theater directed at a May 1969 fashion show. The UT home economics department and the Niemann-Marcus department store collaborated to stage this evening event, attended by expensively dressed women. They "got a much freakier crowd than they expected." About fifteen feminists arrived on the scene "to point out how the fashion and advertising industries help build and then exploit the role women are forced into in our society." The feminists wore theater makeup, their faces painted white. They dressed as various feminine hygiene and "beauty" products, adorning themselves with magazine advertisements for hair conditioner and the like (Judy Smith came dressed as a Toni hair-permanent box). The police on hand told the demonstrators not to disrupt the show, and they agreed. Afterward they stood and talked in the lobby with those in attendance about the ideas behind the action. Apparently they intended to offer some good-humored consciousness raising rather than disrupting the event. Their whimsical tone was typical of Austin radicals, rather different from corresponding actions in New York. Perhaps this was a way of disarming the potentially antagonistic attendees; the feminists' apparent joy in their guerrilla action also reflected the therapeutic value they derived from taking their views public. "It was a fine evening," Smith felt.[84]

As their thinking on the issue of consumerism suggests, the most committed Austin women's liberationists maintained an anticapitalist bent in the early 1970s. They viewed their radical feminism as the fulfillment of their leftist politics, marking the end of the "counterfeit Left." Like radical feminists elsewhere, in the late 1960s they began to read leftist literature that focused on gender issues. In 1969 local radicals distributed the recommended reading list of Lyn Wells, a left-wing SSOC activist who was well known in Texas and across the South. In addition to classics of liberal feminism like Eleanor Flexner's *Century of Struggle* and Friedan's *Feminine Mystique*, she suggested left-wing works like Friedrich Engels's *Origins of the Family, Private Property and the State*, Mirra Komarovsky's *Blue Collar Marriage*, and Elizabeth Gurley Flynn's autobiography, *I Speak My Own Piece*. Women's liberationists all over the country gave special scrutiny to Engels's book, which hypothesized a matriarchal society preceding the rise of property relations. Simone de Beauvoir's *The Second Sex* also became a familiar title on the bookshelves of radical feminists.[85]

As noted earlier, Judy Smith had taken courses with Marcuse as an undergraduate; feminists on the left, despite their emerging critique of libidinal radicalism, still found Marcuse's combination of revolution and "liberation" bracing. Barbara Hines and her friends looked for renegade

Marxist writings. In addition to Marcuse, they read Wilhelm Reich and leafed through the pages of *Monthly Review* magazine, and they perused Rosa Luxemburg's works. In the early 1970s, *Women: A Journal of Liberation*, a left-wing journal that published many landmark radical feminist articles, also was regular reading.[86] Unquestionably, into the 1970s this women's liberation circle looked toward some synthesis of feminism and socialism.

The feminists' continuing anti-imperialist involvement made this ambition quite clear, as anti-imperialist activity evinced an explicit hostility to U.S. capitalism by the early 1970s. As the fight against the Vietnam War took on a paradoxical tinge of frustration mixed with a sense of inevitable U.S. defeat, North American leftists expanded the scope of their internationalism, many of them returning to the focus on Latin America that the Cuban revolution had prompted earlier. Given their proximity to the Mexican border, Austin radicals naturally fixed on inter-American affairs. Barbara Hines and Vic Foe both came from internationalist backgrounds, and both developed a strong interest in U.S. relations with Latin America in step with their feminist involvement.

Hines grew up in Brownsville, Texas, on the U.S.–Mexican border, and in 1965 her parents, liberal German Jewish refugees, sent her after high school to study at the University of the Americas in Mexico City, to broaden her horizons, which she did. One semester later, she enrolled at UT, but she did not become politically active until she went abroad again for one and a half years, living in Spain during the senescence of the Franco regime, returning to Austin in early 1969. Her contact with foreign students far more radical than she had pushed her to think hard about the United States' role in the world. Living with her Peruvian boyfriend, an "armchair radical," Hines began participating in the Mexican American movement at UT, picketing with the Latina strikers at the local Economy Furniture factory and organizing a visit to town by Cesar Chavez. She encountered quite a bit of sexism in this political environment, and after she met other radical women in Caroline's philosophy class, she quickly got involved in feminist activity. Although her relationship with her boyfriend ended, her involvement in anti-imperialist and Latino activism did not. Hines and other feminists in Austin, looking for some combination of their feminist and anti-imperialist concerns, were interested in the writings of Margaret Randall, the poet, socialist, and feminist who moved to Cuba in 1969 and published regularly on the role of women in Latin American revolutionary movements.[87]

Anti-imperialist work ultimately seemed like the "completely revolutionary transforming issue" to Vic Foe, although she became involved with feminism first. From a peripatetic "poor intellectual" family, having lived

324 | PART TWO

until she was ten on a Wyoming farm, fluent in Spanish from her three years spent as a child in Mexico, Foe's upbringing was less explicitly political than cosmopolitan and somewhat bohemian (although her grandfather had been a socialist mayor in Red Cloud, Nebraska). Starting college at UT in 1963 after some time in England (her parents had moved to Corpus Christi for the sake of her father's health), she experienced an "enormous culture shock." Foe finished her undergraduate work in three years and received a NASA fellowship for graduate work in zoology. She was not politically involved at that time, even though she was "troubled" by the war, and she married a more conservative Texas man. The marriage did not last two years, and after her divorce in late 1967, Foe moved toward radical politics. Judy Smith, a fellow biologist, invited her to a meeting of perhaps thirty women at Smith's home, initiating consciousness-raising sessions that quickly issued in "task-oriented" caucuses.[88]

Foe's primary political activities were feminist until 1972, when she got deeply involved in the Latin American Policy Alternatives Group (LAPAG), begun by Phil Russell, Connie Lanham, and others. It was funded as one of several projects around the country by the Congregational Church, which hoped to glean insights into Latin American life from a research base independent of the U.S. government–corporation–university nexus. A "radical caucus" basically took over the operation, which had an office with a library in the Austin church and which broadcast a weekly radio show from the UT radio station, mainly summarizing editorials from newspapers around Latin America. In the three years that LAPAG's funding lasted (the national church declined to renew its grant in 1975), Foe moved from a liberal stance of opposition to the Vietnam War, viewing it as a "terrible mistake," to a socialist viewpoint focused on the exploitative economic relations between the United States and the Third World. Although she enjoyed the countercultural effervescence of the Austin environment and considers the more communal lifestyle of that time and place to be superior to the more individualistic culture of subsequent decades, Foe, strongly analytic and proudly rational, always doubted that the counterculture "had a truly revolutionary role to play." The main concession she made to the competing view on the left, the view that cultural politics was revolutionary, was her agreement with other feminists that the nuclear family was a foundation stone of capitalism and that to damage the former posed a threat to the latter. Increasingly, she evaluated issues in terms of their contribution to an anticapitalist politics.[89]

Given the rising prominence of explicitly socialist politics in the radical milieu of this time, feminist radicals worried that some of their ideas might be co-opted by a procapitalist liberal feminism. In February 1970 one radical attended an Austin Women's Club dinner, along with dignitaries such as the mayor, at which a representative of the Women's Bureau in Richard Nixon's Department of Labor spoke, praising the women's liberation movement. The speaker called for a day care system and for equal educational and employment opportunities for American women. At first amazed, the women's liberationist soon realized the import of these comments. Capitalists, the activist concluded, wanted women's liberation to free women from home and family so that they could become the skilled technicians that a changing economic system needed—probably at a cheaper rate than men would bring. She observed that "to utilize the female work force one must have Women's Liberation in some form. Our movement is merely a necessary means to their ends." Although liberal feminists might have welcomed the far-seeing capitalists who favored women's paid labor as allies, this interloper saw a difference between the liberal agenda and her own. To her, women's liberation was based on "a concept of self-determination" that implied "a kind of existential freedom," and capitalism was opposed to that kind of freedom. "Liberation is about realizing human potential for the sake of ourselves, our sex, and our species," said this writer. "Capitalism must be concerned with translating human development into dollars and cents." Nixon and the capitalist leadership thought that "the time has come to sacrifice female blood to the American free enterprise system. If Women's Liberation cannot prevent this from happening, and redirect the energy flow into life affirming patterns, then we will be an unwilling accomplice in that crime."[90] How to prevent this, she did not say. Her alarm indicates both the difficulty of maintaining an independent radical feminist movement with goals separate from those of liberal feminists, in economic as well as cultural terms, and the continuing desire among women's liberation activists to do so.

Like the new left in general, the women's liberation movement cultivated islands of a new society in the old, prefiguring a different way of life and sometimes expressing the hope that in this way they might hasten the decay of the larger social system. Notably, in the Red River Women's Press, which started as Fly by Night Printers, local women attempted to live out a feminist–anarchist politics. A lot of women worked at Fly by Night, and in the early 1970s they voted to make it a women's press. The women who took charge of the press changed its name and continued to run it for several years as an IWW local, doing most of the local "movement printing," including feminist songbooks. Located at the corner of Sixth Street and Lamar, Red River survived a bad flood, although it maintained a "marginal" existence during the 1970s, as Alice Embree, who worked there as an offset printer between 1974 and 1979, puts it. The workers took as their slogan

"The Rising of the Women Is the Rising of Us All" from the IWW's famed Lawrence, Massachusetts, textile strike in 1912. They seemed to recognize they were in no position to conquer capitalism, but they hoped to maintain a spirited dissent from it.[91]

Faced with the difficulty of effecting changes that were radical in leftist terms, radical feminists proved willing to fuse their agenda with that of the liberals, working for goals that would immediately improve the lot of women because like the new left overall, they found avenues toward more fundamental social change blocked. The radicals worked to help secure equal opportunity in the public sphere, a goal that these generally high-achieving women could embrace warmly. By the summer of 1971, feminists at UT were using federal Title VII civil rights regulations prohibiting sex discrimination to change the university. A group on the fringes of the core women's liberation group, led by Bobbie Nelson, who had just received her degree from the UT Law School, formed the Women's Legal Center and the Women's Law Caucus and filed complaints against UT with HEW. They charged UT with discriminatory practices in administrative, staff, and faculty hiring, in student employment and placement, and in extracurricular activities. They also explained how the absence of day care and inadequate maternal leave worked to the disadvantage of women. The group did succeed in getting the university to the bargaining table, and despite UT's obstructionist tactics, the complainants eventually won the legal battle.[92]

Working for the immediate interests of workers (particularly workers who were not white males) was by this time nothing new for the new left. Local new left radicals offered their consistent support to the striking, mainly Latina employees at Economy Furniture through the early 1970s, and the *Rag* provided cheerleading reports on a variety of labor disputes, in central Texas and nationwide. In the 1970s, Embree joined Austin Women Workers, determined to support her own interests in the way she supported those of disadvantaged groups like racial minorities.[93] Legal battles seemed characteristic of the National Organization for Women, but the feminist radicals enthusiastically viewed the Legal Center's activities as part of a larger effort for economic equity. They were aware that regardless of their desires, American capitalism was the framework in which they operated, and they wished to make it fairer and more livable for women in the present.

The Origins of Roe

As the denouement of the Austin women's liberation movement showed, such reform activism, even if it spelled a chastening of radical feminists' ambition, was far from inconsequential in the lives of American women. Radical and liberal feminists teamed up to work for the legalization of abortion, and in 1973 they summoned a legal and social thunderbolt known as *Roe v. Wade.*

Among radical feminists, abortion activism emerged from an initial concern over birth control. Looking for practical, issue-oriented work they could do, by the end of summer 1969 the Austin women fixed on birth control as a matter that addressed both the unique disadvantages women faced in American society and the distinctive inequalities of hip culture. They thought women had as much right to sexual pleasure as men did, but women could not pursue this right on an equal basis unless they had access to birth control information and paraphernalia. Unfortunately, these were difficult for unmarried women to obtain, certainly for female students who used the university health center. As the feminists complained, "Women in this society are punished for their sexuality" by being forced to bear unwanted children. To many radical feminists, uncontrolled childbearing was a central mechanism that men used to keep women down, across cultures and down the centuries, so much so that one prominent radical thinker, Shulamith Firestone, concluded, not without reason, that the replacement of men's role in reproduction with manipulable technologies would be the pivotal event in women's liberation.[94] Their call for reproductive control emerged logically from the desire for personality or self-determination; it also touched on the ecological concern over population growth. Furthermore, it seemed sure to be an issue with much popular resonance, a good organizing tool. In October, Vic Foe, Bea Vogel, and perhaps ten others began staffing the Women's Liberation Birth Control Information Center in a tiny space next to the *Rag* office in the University Y on Guadalupe, using a pay phone to advise women where they might best seek the materials they wanted.[95]

Abortion—which feminists ultimately viewed as a birth control technique and justified on the same grounds of self-determination—had already become a political issue in the 1960s. But it had not penetrated public consciousness very far and remained mainly the province of liberal activists, not all of them feminists. Self-styled women activists, unconnected to a larger feminist movement, had been working on the issue in California and New York since the late 1950s. More commonly, activist physicians as well as population control advocates pushed for the liberalization (rather than the outright repeal) of abortion restrictions in several states, including Texas, where the state-level medical association voted strongly for liberalization in 1968 but where the Roman Catholic Church successfully scotched any chance of statutory changes the next year.[96]

Betty Friedan raised the issue of abortion in NOW starting in 1967, one year after the organization's formation, and in 1969 helped organize the National Association for the Repeal of Abortion Laws (NARAL), prompting the New York state legislature to hold public hearings on a reform bill in February of that year. Then radical feminists got involved. Redstockings members, seated in the audience at the New York hearings, stood up and protested that the only woman on the official witness list was a Catholic nun and demanded that they be allowed to testify as well. Their slogan was "Women Are the Experts." (The *Daily News* headline read "Gals Squeal for Repeal.") The group then organized its own public session of testimony, by women, about abortion. Women in consciousness-raising groups elsewhere, including Austin, discussed abortion early on, with the participants offering their own stories of unsafe and humiliating abortions.[97]

Women's liberation activists in Austin began to work on the issue by writing detailed articles in the *Rag* that gave information about safe and unsafe methods of abortion (including self-abortion techniques). But it was the desperate inquiries of women at the Birth Control Information Center that pressed them into deep involvement in the issue. The feminists sought and received help in getting information from Bob Breihan at the Methodist Student Center. Since 1968 he and two other Methodist ministers in Dallas had been involved in the Clergy Consultation Service on Abortion (CCS), begun a year earlier in New York. Those in the CCS thought that women who wanted abortions would pursue them in any case and that by helping them obtain safe abortions, they, the clergy, would help protect the women's health and well-being. They also provided follow-up counseling to women who wanted it. Judy Smith approached Breihan, and together they gathered information about reliable abortion providers in San Antonio and near Dallas. Texas women who could afford it went south to Mexico, where abortions were legal. Smith and Foe drove to Piedras Negras, across the border from Eagle Pass, to investigate the facilities of a physician who had contacted them to offer his services. They found a clean, courteous, and seemingly professional clinic and started discreetly informing women desiring abortions of the location and the cost ($350). On at least one occasion, they publicized their negative evaluation of a professional abortion referral agent, warning women away from him.[98]

This seemed like only a stopgap, however, and not a very effective one. Instead, the women's liberation activists wanted to make abortion available in Texas; currently it was legal there only if the mother's life was in danger. (They also wondered about their legal liability in giving the referrals.) Putting any hesitations aside, the activists approached the levers of popular participation in the formal political system. Foe attended the state Democratic Party convention and gave an "impassioned" speech in support of her Austin precinct's abortion repeal and gay rights resolutions, and the convention adopted them by large margins. She then went to work full time for two state representatives backing a repeal bill, dropping out of school for one and a half years, and rounded up a wide range of witnesses for hearings on the issue held in the state capitol. The Catholic Church's opposition proved less formidable than Foe had feared, since the church was in fact less unified in its hostility to repeal than to reform. Reform meant to the church that the state would actually approve of specified abortions and implied that some unborn children were superior to others. Since the debate in Austin was shaping up as one between the feminist repeal position and the medical association's reform stance, the church hesitated to enter the fray forcefully.[99] In late 1970, the Austin Women's Liberation Committee to Repeal Abortion Laws participated in statewide meetings of abortion rights activists in Dallas and Houston.[100]

Judy Smith and her companion Jim Wheelis, who was attending the UT Law School, had begun to wonder whether a campaign of reform aimed at the state government was worth the effort. The federal courts recently had ruled in favor of the *Rag*, which had sought to keep the UT administration from banning it on campus, and local radicals thought they might do best to go over the heads of the state legislature. Others working for abortion law reform also had set their sights on the Fifth Circuit of the federal bench, in part because they hoped—correctly as it turned out— that Judge Sarah Hughes, a member of this circuit and a pioneering woman lawyer in Texas, would be sympathetic to their case. Smith and Wheelis knew only one woman lawyer, Sarah Weddington, a recent UT Law School graduate whose husband was a classmate of Wheelis, and they approached her. Weddington was, at most, a liberal feminist and perhaps not even that at the time. One of five women in her law school class of 120, she had been able to find a job upon graduation, despite performing well in school, only in the offices of a former professor who sympathized with her difficulties as a woman. Unbeknownst to her radical acquaintances, however, Weddington had a personal interest in this issue: two years earlier she had traveled to Piedras Negras for an abortion. She and her colleague Linda Coffee decided they would indeed challenge the constitutionality of the Texas law in the federal courts.[101]

Weddington found her test cases in Dallas and filed their suit in March 1970. Norma McCorvey, perhaps five months pregnant and having no wish for a third child, became "Jane Roe." The two lawyers secured her permission, making it clear that any victory in court would come far too late to save her from carrying her pregnancy to term. A victory would benefit other women, in the future. (They needed a pregnant woman for a plaintiff. Neither they nor the radicals who had approached them offered McCorvey, a working-class woman who later felt used by the activists, assistance in pursuing the alternatives of an illegal or Mexican abortion. In fact, the lawyers were relieved that she seemed resigned to the unavailability of the procedure.)[102] Sarah Hughes and the other federal judges in Texas handed down their favorable ruling in June. The original plaintiffs, with the assistance of many hours of research help from radical feminists in Austin, won the final argument in the U.S. Supreme Court on 22 January 1973, rendering irrelevant the abortion laws in Texas and the other states.[103]

Before this decision, the radicals had been working in Texas and around the country for repeal, meeting with success in some states and facing intractable opposition elsewhere. Some, including liberal jurist Ruth Bader Ginsburg and left-wing feminist Barbara Ehrenreich, later concluded ruefully that the *Roe* decision "cut off what might have been a grassroots prochoice movement." Others regret that the high court resolved the debate in favor of reform, because continued political agitation at the state level might have secured repeal, at least in some places. These regrets may exaggerate the sunniness of the outlook for repeal activists around the country in 1973.[104] But it is true that *Roe v. Wade* left radical feminists, as political victories often leave activists, searching for an issue around which to organize, hoping to keep their movement from disbanding.

The radical activists had a perhaps unexpectedly profound impact on American law and life, particularly on American women. Ironically, the radicals contributed crucially to the legal change whose protection became a cornerstone of political liberalism in the years afterward. Liberals and radicals had been able to work together not only because they both favored the interests of women but also because of the mingled provenance and the continued cultural intimacy of post–World War II liberalism and the existentialist search for authenticity. David King, who with his wife Marsha had served as McCorvey's coplaintiffs, "John and Jane Doe," bundled these motivations when explaining his participation in the suit: "We stand for everybody—for woman's right to freedom of choice." He also remarked, further indicating he was a man of his time, "I realized a long time ago the abortion laws were anachronistic and unnatural."[105] The radicals looked for a completely new, authentic society, but their contribution to American life was to advance the liberal hope that individuals would enjoy the liberty to seek authentic lives for themselves.

Blowing in the Wind

Uncannily, the two issues that had done the most in the later years of the new left to sustain radical cohesion both seemed to die in the same month. The Paris Peace Accords and the *Roe* decision, both announced in January 1973, one a bitter and unsatisfying "victory" and the other a largely unexpected breakthrough, dealt fatal blows to a left whose political relevance and whose very stability as a political fact were already widely doubted. The feminist radicals proved unable either to maintain their presence at the forefront of the feminist movement or to reconstitute a left on feminist grounds.

By 1975, cultural feminism, always an important aspect of the women's liberation movement, achieved dominance among those who considered themselves radical feminists. The cultivation of "women's space," even the construction of a separate female society based on cooperative values defined as distinctively female, came to overshadow agitation aimed at directly altering the existing male-dominated society. At least in theory, the exaltation of the "feminine" displaced the rejection of "sex roles." Meanwhile, liberal feminists continued their activism around their established issues, including reproductive rights. But the combination of left-wing radicalism with searching cultural and psychological gender analysis that the radical feminists of the pre-1973 period had forged declined in prominence.

To a large extent, this decline was a function of continuing generational change. Left-wing politics was an exciting new frontier to radical women in the heyday of the new left, and the idea of a left was familiar and congenial to those who began the women's liberation movement in the late 1960s. But the new left had become a relic, seemingly irrelevant, to many women who reached college age in the early or middle 1970s. An atmosphere of antiracist, antiwar, and anti-imperialist activism did not envelop these younger women as it had the cohort that preceded them. The new generation was not preoccupied with such issues. Seeing little heroism in the left, instead only another variety of male domination, they felt no need to salvage leftist principles from a "counterfeit Left," and so they did not seek the synthesis that the early radical feminists had. Judy Smith, for one, thinks that some of the younger women were simply looking for "fun" and were little interested in the hard and often unrewarding work required for radical political organizing, political work to which those who reached adulthood in the 1960s were accustomed.[106]

Many of the feminist leftists, like others on the left, drifted away geographically or politically. Judy Smith and Jim Wheelis left in 1974 for Montana in search of a yet more unspoiled environment, and Linda Smith joined them soon afterward. By 1973 Barbara Hines was in law school in

Boston. Vic Foe continued her research in cell biology, for which she ultimately received a MacArthur "genius" grant. She moved deeper into antiimperialist work and experienced tensions with other feminists, like Judy Smith, who had soured on the strategic move into the state apparatus that had resulted in the *Roe* victory. Smith took a more anarchist turn. (Foe also found that the feminist movement had become "quite intellectually mushy" with the ascendence of cultural feminism.) Barbara Merritt went to divinity school in Berkeley, becoming a Congregationalist minister.[107]

Like the new left overall, the feminist left of the early 1970s made its most lasting political contribution to political liberalism, finding no way to press its more radical vision of social change. However, neither this reformist turn nor the insistence of activists and historians that the feminist radicals had "broken with the left" early in their feminist careers should obscure the underappreciated leftist character of their politics.

In the 1970s, the category of socialist feminism quickly became a term of abuse, referring to women who clearly subordinated the specific interests of women as a group to a Marxist agenda. No doubt the opportunistic entry of Trotskyist operatives—who indeed fit this description—into feminist groups in the early 1970s makes the distinction between socialist and radical feminists seem necessary to many when describing those times. Those in the mainstream of the women's liberation movement became known as radical feminists, meaning that conceptually and politically, they put gender first. Judy Smith, looking back with twenty years' hindsight, endorses this distinction, stating that she and her comrades in Austin were radical feminists, not socialist feminists. The "fundamental" issue they addressed was "power," she says, and power relations flow fundamentally from gender. Their concerns over economic discrimination, for example, stemmed from a gender, not a class, analysis.[108]

Yet Smith's contention that the Trotskyist preoccupation with the question of which form of oppression was paramount—class, gender, or race— was widespread among the radicals in her milieu, and her emphasis on the Austin circle's remoteness from socialist politics hardly reflect her and her comrades' writings and activities in the late 1960s and early 1970s. To some degree, the perceived polarization between socialist and radical feminists— and, for that matter, between both of these groups and cultural feminists— is an overly neat scheme imposed retrospectively on a more complex historical experience. The feminists considered here, whether they were "socialist feminists" or "feminist socialists" or "radical feminists," were both feminists and left-wing radicals.[109] Their ultimate inability to sustain that political synthesis should not make us forget that this is what they tried to do.

During its years of prominence, the feminist left affirmed some aspects of the preexisting left-wing search for authenticity while altering others. The feminists reiterated the new left thesis that a morally corrupt and unnatural culture produced inner alienation and affirmed that venues and methods were required through which individuals could be cleansed of the havoc that society had wreaked in their minds and souls. For the feminist left, culture was the decisive terrain of battle, and an authentic society was defined as a "natural" culture.

The feminist left also agreed that the development of an authentic culture required the existence of autonomous communities that could cultivate authenticity. Since 1966, the new left had identified communities of authenticity not as the universal, purely voluntary "beloved community" of the civil rights movement but as communities defined by given social identities. Until feminism emerged in the left, race and class identities had formed the legitimate bases of authenticity-generating community. The feminist assertion that gender also was such a basis, far from contradicting the new left's understanding of how authenticity could be sustained, strengthened this understanding.

The feminist left's great challenge to the new left quest for authenticity was, of course, to reject the search for an authentic masculinity, to deny that virility equaled true citizenship. On this score, the feminists achieved a partial victory in the American culture of dissent. The legitimacy of the equation of masculinity, authenticity, and citizenship on the left sustained critical damage in the 1970s. In subsequent years, reiterations of Goodman's or Mills's political celebration of manhood were likely to meet with a mixed reception, at best, among radicals. However, the yearning for an authentic masculinity lingered among some men on the left, even if they were more careful in expressing it. Most important, the feminist revision of the search for authenticity and democracy never formed the basis for a regrouping of the American left. In these precincts, feminism became a more effective vehicle of criticism than of mobilization. The feminist left dethroned the quest for an authentic masculinity from its earlier place of honor in the culture of dissent, but the victory was bittersweet. Caught between criticism of and desire for the heroic aspirations of the past, that culture proved resistant to wholesale reformation.

From the Politics of Authenticity
to the Politics of Identity

Everything we thought was wrong is still wrong, and more besides, and we are without the institutions, influence, or understanding to help change it.

ELINOR LANGER, 1973

The most important factor in understanding the history of radicalism in the United States over the last twenty years or so . . . is the defeat of the left in the mid-seventies.

BARBARA EPSTEIN, 1991

BY THE SEASON of defeat and victory, winter 1973, new left radicals had been lamenting their movement's demise for several years.[1] We may conclude, echoing Samuel Clemens, that the earliest obituaries were exaggerated. At least as great, however, is the error of those who, since the official end of the United States–Vietnam War, have insisted on the new left's continued existence. These include leftists hostile to the suggestion that history has passed them by and rightists who wish to preserve the bogeys that proved to be so useful through the ages of Nixon and Reagan.[2] Sympathy may be in order for those who cling to the past, but we ought not endorse their illusions. Things come to an end.

The era of 1960s radicalism ended with anything but a bang. The apocalypse did not come, and leftists did not recognize the rightist victory of 1968 as their own defeat (they ceded that honor to the liberals). There was, after all, plenty of leftist activism in the immediate post-1968 period. In these years a new generation of radicals maintained a coherent leftist community in Austin, centered in the *Rag*, agitating on a broad range of issues. The demise of SDS liberated the left in certain ways, especially in terms of addressing gender issues. The radicals now paid more attention to local politics as well, helping elect Jeff Jones to the presidency of the UT student government in 1970, where he became a spokesperson for a left-wing viewpoint (and intermittently an irritant to John Silber). Leftists forged an electoral coalition with the city's African American and Latino voters, bringing a newly liberal (but still, to them, a disappointingly conservative) city council into power by 1973.

The post-SDS Texas left also embarked on a new program of support work for striking wage laborers during a period of escalating labor conflict, partly because of the influence of Jones, whose father had organized a local of school bus drivers in his hometown of Brentwood, New York, and that of Pat Cuney, who started a group called "Student for Strikers" in 1969.[3] By walking pickets and raising money and awareness, young white Austinites supported agricultural laborers, bus drivers, machine workers, and, most of all, the mainly Latina furniture workers participating in the protracted dispute at the Economy Furniture factory in Austin, who provided "an example to all who would struggle," in the view of one Austin new leftist.[4] Fitting this newfound concern into their familiar humanist framework, the leftists announced, "The struggle of working people for better wages and conditions is only part of a much deeper demand—the demand to be treated like human beings." Reiterating the new working-class analysis, they reasoned, "Most of us will be workers when we get out of UT . . . our basic situations will be the same as that of the strikers."[5] On this basis, ironically, they forged far more of a worker–student alliance than PL ever did.

In the 1970s, young leftists were more likely to call themselves socialists than at any time since the lonely twilight of Stalinism in the 1950s, yet their socialism was distinctly evolutionary, not revolutionary. In the absence of revolutionary expectations, the last cohort of the new left refashioned their movement into a new liberalism, a liberalism that emphasized cultural change. The term *revolution* did not vanish from sight, but, like the German Social Democratic Party of the early twentieth century, many new left radicals in these years "continued to preach revolution and to practice reform."[6] The early 1970s witnessed refurbished cooperation between leftists and insurgent liberals on issues such as the war and abortion rights, indicating in its waning days the new left's tropism toward liberalism.

One Austin leftist complained in 1972 that the local left's politics had become "the same as that of the Texas *Observer*—liberal eclecticism!"[7] He correctly perceived the incrementalism of this multi-issue politics, its tendency to work to abate the various manifestations of a system that leftists still perceived as fundamentally rotten, rather than trying to overturn that system with one central attack. This was formally similar to the multi-issue politics that had attracted the original group of local new left radicals in the early 1960s, but experience and experiment had expunged the radical movement's sense that such a politics would lead to a change in the underlying structure of political life. The most serious bid for a new left politics that would be radical in a literal sense—working to identify and get at the society's political roots rather than clipping back its branches—was the feminist left of this late phase. Several factors undermined this effort, however. The need to agitate around concrete issues tended toward reformism; the pervasive cultural politics of the new left leaned toward reformism of a new kind, a cultural reformism; and too few men found a feminist left politics attractive.

In 1972 some Austin leftists who still thought a national organization was a good idea met with others in Davenport, Iowa, to plot the course of the New American Movement (NAM), a democratic socialist group that emphasized feminism and looked to a revitalized union movement as a potential political ally.[8] Its concern with participatory democracy in both the planned movement and the larger society appealed to those whom the factionalism in SDS had offended and harked back to the original vision of the *Port Huron Statement*.[9] Left-wing publicists and activists around the country in the early 1970s, such as Staughton Lynd and James Weinstein, hoped to build a popular radical movement based on such an agenda.[10] The vision of a democratic socialism lingered throughout the 1970s and 1980s, nursed by leaders like Michael Harrington, but it proved politically inert, unable to point the way to a new society or to attract large numbers of activist followers.[11] Not many had the stomach to travel this long and not very promising road.

Political and economic conditions were inestimably less propitious than those that had given birth to the new left's expansive optimism a decade earlier. The breakneck economic growth of the 1960s, which led stock market enthusiasts to label it the "go-go" decade, had stalled, and the projections of a future society with too much wealth and leisure for its own good evaporated. The political context was set by Nixon's race-tinged "wedge" tactics, his bunkered escalation of the air war against Indochina, and his administration's crackdown on radicals. This crackdown, featuring the liberal use of agents provocateurs in groups such as the Black Panther Party, the American Indian Movement, and various new left splinter organizations in the post-SDS period, was administered largely through the FBI's COINTELPRO. All these aggressive moves by the Nixon administration, both at home and abroad, blunted criticism on Nixon's right flank concerning his pursuit of d<ea>tente with the Soviet Union and the People's Republic of China and his accommodation to increased social welfare spending and environmental regulation. By the early 1970s, a time when strong and confusing political crosscurrents blew across a hardening economic landscape, the American left had become a mere pawn in a larger political game, a useful diversion to those in power rather than a truly important force in the nation's political life.

In addition, cultural conditions had changed in ways fatal to a revitalized new left. The African American movement, faced with problems of its own, was not about to play the catalytic role for white people that it had around 1960, and the union movement, despite its stirrings of democratic activism, was not really an adequate substitute. The attraction that white youth had developed for African American culture in the mid-twentieth century and that had underpinned the black movement's galvanic political effect on idealistic young whites had no parallel in the relations among youth of different classes in the 1970s. Participatory democracy itself had lost much of its allure, the victim of incessant criticism from within the left itself for both its inattention to economic issues and the "tyranny of structurelessness." Efforts to revive a national new left represented the chastened vision of survivors, and as with previous incarnations of this type, its fate was perhaps to be respected but not followed.

In the twenty-five years since the new left unraveled, the United States has not seen a cohesive, organized left regroup. If an organized left were to appear before the millennium, it would end an interregnum double the length of the hiatus between the old and new lefts, which lasted perhaps twelve years, from 1948 to 1960. Many Americans continue to hold leftist views, and there has been plenty of leftist activism between the mid-1970s and the late 1990s, but leftists generally have carried on their politics as individuals, mainly in issue-specific organizations in which they have collaborated with liberals.

Without compelling paths of insurgency to follow, the new left and its existential politics settled back into the larger politics, culture, and society that gave birth to them. This process of partial reconciliation illuminates the developments of the 1970s and 1980s and also reinforces the understanding that the rebellions of the 1960s were in no sense alien to the United States but, rather, were representative products of national and global culture in the cold war era. Temporary economic luxury allowed the flowering of a post-scarcity radicalism. Superpower competition and economic obsolescence impelled the process of racial decolonization, domestically and worldwide (though that "liberation" proved largely formal in both settings). In neither case did fortuitous circumstances produce momentous political change. Circumstance opened the path for people to make history (if not exactly as they pleased) by pursuing long-developing ideals: in one case, the industrial-era yearning for authenticity and, in the other, the broken promises of eighteenth-century democratic revolution and nineteenth-century civil war.

In the 1960s, romantic dreams, religious impulses, and Enlightenment ideals all refreshed the American vision of citizenship, a citizenship of equality and vitality. The racial changes wrought by the civil rights movement quickened the desire of young, white, middle-class Americans to transcend alienation and achieve authenticity, to throw off the weight of weightlessness. The new left's vision of racial equality, participatory democracy, a restored manhood, and an end to the "age of anxiety" seemed as clear then as it seems poignant and time bound now. In place of the Marxist vision of communism, this was the new Prometheanism, the new utopia. By the 1970s, however, few American radicals really thought they would reach utopia.

In the quarter century since the new left's end, leftist politics in the United States has formed along two axes, each of which has been polarized. The first such split is the division between utopianism and reformism; the second results from the breakdown of the new left synthesis of the quests for authenticity and social justice.

In 1950 the sociologist David Riesman, no leftist, nonetheless called for utopian thinking, for he thought it appropriate to a postscarcity age.[12] The young leftists and counterculturalists of the 1960s, agreeing that this was a new age beyond scarcity, furnished all the utopianism anyone could have asked for. By the late 1960s, on the left, this was codified as "libertarian socialism," a society in which everyone had the wherewithal to pursue her or his own project of self-liberation, whether homely or visionary, and in which no "puritanical" restrictions would stand in the way.

The vision of a libertarian socialism, contradictory as it may appear to many, has lingered in the American left. Yet in practical terms, few radicals have advanced either a detailed outline for such a society or political strategies for making the great leap forward to it. Instead, like liberals sympathetic to cultural modernism, leftists have worked on a variety of fronts to preserve existing liberties, such as abortion rights, and to expand, bit by bit, the frontiers of cultural liberty, for example, by establishing legal protections for gay and lesbian citizens.

On material issues, leftists have taken a similar approach, working either to extend—or, more commonly, to guard against severe retrenchments of— protections for workers and consumers, progressive taxation, affirmative action programs designed to redistribute opportunities in racial and gender terms, and environmental regulation. Leftists also have continued to dissent from post-Vietnam imperial projections into the Third World. Overall, circumstances and the lack of any coherent political alternative have led most of those with radical sympathies toward the very liberal eclecticism of which the disappointed leftist cited earlier accused his comrades in 1972. Utopianism has survived but is detached from the wide-ranging activism of American leftists.

The search for authenticity also lives on, but in a less politically charged way than in the period between 1955 and 1975. Critics always claimed that existentialism was apolitical, but during that span of years, they were wrong. The politics of authenticity has changed, however, and the charge is more accurate now. Americans—left, right, and middle—now look for authenticity, for reconnection to the divine and to communities that seem ancient and organic. The search for authenticity has become, in fact, politically promiscuous; the once-strong association between this quest and left-wing politics remains undamaged only in the minds of a few. The search for authenticity has become so pervasive a yearning in the United States, its open expressions so chockablock in our popular culture and so evident across the political spectrum, as to render it less clearly a dissident, much less a specifically leftist, resource.[13] This further demonstrates the close links between the leftist existential politics of the 1960s and the larger culture that produced it. Yet radical movements require both a rootedness in the dominant culture—in its hopes and values—and a compelling claim that only in the path of radicalism can individuals achieve those hopes.

Surprisingly, authenticity has remained a salient term of discussion in the United States even as its opposite, alienation, has dropped from sight. One of the ironies of the new left is the extent to which it apparently succeeded in banishing talk of anxiety and alienation from the political vocabulary of the United States. In the political culture of dissent, nothing in the 1970s changed more certainly than this. The young white radicals of this era were disinclined to keep their complaints to themselves, so we might infer that the problem of anxiety ceased to vex them. The glint of triumph peeks through the rubble of defeat. Perhaps the relevance of authenticity, as an ideal, lingers after it is widely achieved.

But even if the cultural problems that the new left's existential politics addressed remain, political shifts have made less legitimate any discussion of inner alienation. In the 1950s and 1960s, this discussion linked personal unhappiness to defects allegedly at the root of the social, political, or cultural systems in which Americans lived. Since the victory of the right in the late 1960s and the eclipse of the new left, public discourse in the United States has been increasingly dominated by conservative criticism of the national state. In a sense, the government has come to stand in for the malign social, economic, and cultural forces that leftists targeted for criticism in the 1960s. Of course, the new left did its share to delegitimize the American state, unwittingly contributing to perhaps the most powerful strategy of the post-

1960s right.[14] This channeling of political complaint is less conducive to discussion of personal alienation. Certainly one can be alienated from the state, from the formal political system, and new left radicals placed no small emphasis on this phenomenon. Yet they tended to view that kind of alienation as positive, a resource for insurgency, and not as the subject of a political and cultural critique. It is the problem of inner alienation that has almost vanished from public discourse.

Perhaps the new left and the counterculture together simply exhausted existentialism as a path of dissent, demonstrating to all who looked that it led to a cul-de-sac. The American left's principal problem since the 1960s has been less to decide what kind of society it wants than to discover how to make that dream a reality. The problem of social change has proved intractable. Only over the course of decades have middle-class American radicals, the descendants of the "new radicals," gradually admitted the truth, especially painful to people of their social background, that forces much larger than they have directed the course of change. One important element in the eclipse of existential politics was the increased respectability of economic analysis in the left of the 1970s.

After Mariann Wizard left the Communist Party, she established a foundation in Austin dedicated to "the pursuit of happiness." Many of her (non-Communist) comrades responded with incredulity, even outrage. This was frivolous, they said. Scarcity had returned, as any wage earner could relate; the pressing need was to build bridges across class lines. If you want to advocate social change, Wizard retorted in vintage 1960s style, "you gotta have an alternative." The existing society was one of unhappiness, so she advocated happiness.[15] Postscarcity politics lost some of its luster as leftists recognized changing material realities and the class character of their revolt. If existentialist hopes lingered, their expression became less legitimate even for the left.

In the 1960s, radicals felt certain they at least knew how to pose the question of social change. The question was, Who will create change? They offered several different answers. As only James Weinstein, among all historians of radicalism, has noted, leftists in the industrial United States have consistently posed the problem in this way, their perspectives clearly shaped by the tradition of political pluralism against which the new left directed no shortage of polemics.[16] This is as clear an indication as any that the new left's roots lay buried in the substratum of American political culture. The affluence of the first score years of the cold war and the emergence of race as the fulcrum of American politics also applied pressure in the direction of a pluralist understanding of political change. Visions of structural crisis and transformation faded, replaced by a picture of politics in the United States as a complex web of interactions among a set of distinct groups, any of which might apply pressure to the "system" in which they all operated.

Political pluralism was not all there was to 1960s radicalism, however. Both the religious–romantic search for authenticity and the Enlightenment desire for inclusion and equality had strong universalist pedigrees. These visions respectively asserted a uniform relation to the cosmos and demanded a uniform relation to the polis. These individualist values came together, perhaps paradoxically, in the vision of a beloved community. In that community, 1960s radicals expected to find individuals who shared universal experiences and needs, not least the need for community itself. The beloved community promised, as well, to meld the differences among the groups that previously had merely negotiated the terms of their interaction, to make a new, redemptive community of all. One can view this as a characteristically American utopia—the universal nation, the transnational identity—that accompanies the pluralist workaday understanding of society.[17] For all the practical pluralism of the new left, these radicals yearned for some transcendent point above the interactive fray from which they might issue prophetic criticism of their society. An old vision of personal transformation and transcendence, a Protestant heritage to which all Americans could lay claim, even if unknowingly, echoed, as Gitlin suggests, in the new left's "rhetoric of total transfiguration."[18]

With the benefit of time, we can see the universalist vision of rebirth, community, and ultimately revolution tugging at the pluralist understanding of political change, giving the new left's story a measure of pathos. These young white radicals desired a breakthrough to solidarity with "others" that has remained, from the acme of the interracial civil rights movement until the present, an ineradicable aspect of the vision of breakthrough to new, authentic life. Gitlin views the investment of hope in "external agencies" of revolution in the late 1960s, whether the Third World or the poor, as a new left "search for surrogate universals" to fill the role that the proletariat played in the forsaken Marxist scenario. In the 1980s, especially in the "sanctuary" movement against the Reagan administration's policies toward Central America, the politics of "solidarity," aiming for connections between the privileged and "others," remained strong on the American left. Here, as in the days of the civil rights movement, white Americans felt they might achieve meaning and authenticity by making a moral connection with those of a different station and background, even as many of their contemporaries searched for authenticity among their "own kinds." From the 1960s to the

1990s, these universalist impulses betrayed a deep-rooted uneasiness with the fragmented quality of the pluralist search for social change.[19]

If the new left struck an uncertain balance between universalism and pluralism and if the universalist element in new left politics suffered a severe blow from the declining salience of the existentialism to which it was attached, perhaps this explains the laments heard in the 1990s over the declension of dissent into "identity politics."[20] That such a politics ascended between the 1970s and the 1990s, both on the left and more generally in the United States, surely is true. The explanations offered for this development are familiar.

In the early and middle 1960s, a grand alliance for progress made great strides, especially concerning civil rights. Depending on who tells the story, either African Americans, under the influence of black power doctrine, first abandoned the coalition, or else they were pushed out by white liberals who wanted black votes but whose payoff was disappointing. Then women, infected with the separatist virus, departed as well. "On the model of black demands came those of feminists, Chicanos, American Indians, gays, lesbians."[21] Soon the right began its easy domination of a divided opposition. At this time, the heightened pluralism of the left dovetailed with the craze for "symbolic ethnicity" among the distinctly unradical masses of white Americans.[22] By the 1980s, issues of social identity, mainly sexual and racial, dominated radical discussion.

There is truth, as well as exaggeration and diversion from the real issues, in such narratives. In identity politics, individuals define their politics along lines of race, gender, ethnicity, and sexual identity, in part to make themselves feel rooted, real, solid. This political trend thus expresses a quest for authenticity. Sometimes the traditional left-wing search for social justice coincides with identity politics, especially for those who count themselves members of subordinate groups. Considered from the left, however, the shortcomings of identity politics are also evident. Here the search for authenticity lives on, but in fixed, given channels of fellowship. Conservatives sometimes associate identity politics with the recent discussion, in academic circles, of utopian "postmodernist" liberation from fixed conceptual frameworks, of joyous fluidity and multiplicity, but this link is questionable. In fact, this association merely obscures the strongly antiutopian character of identity politics, the bias of this politics against thinking outside an interest-group approach to change. Identity politics is subject to the same criticisms as is the old political pluralism, militant rhetoric notwithstanding. The levers of fundamental social change remain untouched, even unseen. Indeed, identity politics is quite congenial to many who desire no such change, including many of those in the business world, and one should not dismiss that constituency out of hand.[23]

Despite the criticisms expressed by some 1960s radicals toward identity politics, however, the continuity between the new left and identity politics is notable. Identity politics seeks to clear a space for the fulfillment of a particular group's authenticity and for its political organization. These actions may lead to political change, but even if they do not, this space clearing is still considered desirable, for it can alleviate individuals' estrangement from their genuine identity. By the late 1960s, this kind of politics is where the new left's path led. Throughout the 1960s, new left radicals debated whether to attach themselves to the political potential and authenticity of social groups outside themselves or to embrace white, college-educated young people as a site of both radical agency and authenticity. Ultimately, the mainstream of the new left chose the latter course, as the popularity of the new working-class analysis, the movement's countercultural turn, and the rise of radical feminism all, in different ways, attest.

New left activists cultivated islands of authenticity, of a new society freed from alienation, in and around college and university campuses across the United States, and in the 1990s, some of these garden plots were still visible, some of them thriving. But islands are what they remained. Carl Oglesby anticipated this outcome when he asserted that although the new left's prefigurative politics was "morally cosmopolitan . . . its values are *practical* only within the Western (imperialist) cities, and are far from being universally practical even there."[24] Despite campus radicals' protestations in recent years that victories won on campuses themselves are politically significant in the wider world, the historian and socialist Barbara Epstein acknowledges that "on a deeper level, for those of us who were students in the sixties and either took part in or identified with the movements of that time, the experience of being incorporated into academia has involved a profound defeat."[25] The hope that campus agitation might lead to a leftist insurgency faded long ago, but the strategy has remained alive, for it has claimed other merits. This project has offered a balm to the alienation, inner and outer, about which existentialists, liberals, and leftists in the middle class have complained for decades. This was the new left's identity politics.

And what of democracy? The problem that Arthur Schlesinger posed in 1949 was not simply the problem of anxiety, and it was not that of social change. Instead, his powerful question was, How can we salve anxiety while maintaining democracy? He feared that the pressures of anxiety would push us away from the challenge of freedom. The new left resolved the problem that Schlesinger posed by rejecting his association of democracy with anxiety, instead asserting that true (by which it meant radical) democracy and an authentic culture were inseparable. In the view of new left radicals, democracy was not the casualty of authenticity but, rather, a necessary condition of authenticity.

Like countless Americans before them and like those who came after them, new left radicals sought to shift the balance of power in their society by constituting new centers of power in their selves, in individuals and communities. This strategy was clear throughout the new left's career, in the vision of participatory democracy as a supplement to the institutions of electoral politics, in the attempts to build community unions in cities around the country, and in the energy later spent on "counterinstitutions." Power would be redistributed through accretion, not expropriation. Although the new left spoke of democratizing the whole society, its synthesis of democracy and authenticity always took shape in particular communities, often locally. In this way, the linked goals of democracy and authenticity were quietly unhitched from demands for broad social change. Over time, the radicals' focus shifted away from identifying and demanding the conditions that would qualify the United States as a social democracy and toward attempts at creating democratic and authentic experiences in their own lives. The fading of a broad social perspective evidently led to the decline of the ideal of democracy altogether. In the 1970s and 1980s, the search for authenticity continued, but demands for more democracy, like talk of alienation, ebbed.[26]

Some continue to wait for the second coming of the new left. Their wait may not end soon. The new left was less an outgrowth of a continuous history of radical politics in the United States than the evanescent leftist branch of a search for authenticity in industrial American life. This movement's radicalism was sincere, and it spoke many truths about the country where it appeared. Its synthesis of hopes for personal and social regeneration was not new and likely will suffuse future insurgent movements, on both the left and the right. Nonetheless, there may be little reason to think that the precise social and cultural elements that converged in this radical movement will do so again. Undoubtedly, further movements for social change will arise, but as happened in the 1960s, the sources and content of those movements may surprise those who implore the past to reappear.

Introduction

1. Between 1962 and 1964, the dominant forces in SDS, in its Economic Research and Action Projects (ERAP), moved to an emphasis on urban neighborhood organizing among the American poor. This proved to be a temporary (though important) deviation from the new left's initial emphasis on agitation among the American student and youth population, which it had enunciated in the *Port Huron Statement* and to which it returned for good at mid-decade.

2. John Kenneth Galbraith, *The Affluent Society* (Boston: Houghton Mifflin, 1958). Godfrey Hodgson, *America in Our Time: From World War II to Nixon—What Happened and Why* (Garden City, NY: Doubleday, 1976), pp. 75–98, highlights the broad province of the assumption of affluence in this period, calling it the cornerstone of a "liberal consensus" (which was not really very liberal in the contemporary political sense).

David Farber implies, with considerable merit, that the new left simply acted out what Daniel Bell calls the "cultural contradictions of capitalism," its consciousness incubated in a hedonistic consumerism that was integral to, if destructive of, the social system against which it rebelled. David Farber, *The Age of Great Dreams: America in the 1960s* (New York: Hill & Wang, 1994), pp. 16–17; Daniel Bell, *The Cultural Contradictions of Capitalism* (New York: Basic Books, 1978). Also see Warren Susman (with the assistance of Edward Griffin), "Did Success Spoil the United States? Dual Representations in Postwar America," in Lary May, ed., *Recasting America: Culture and Politics in the Age of Cold War* (Chicago: University of Chicago Press, 1989), pp. 19–37.

Peter Clecak, *Radical Paradoxes: Dilemmas of the American Left, 1945–1970* (New York: Harper & Row, 1973), argues that new left radicals simply confused exploitation with alienation. Doubtless some did, but more important, I think, was the conscious new left preference for alienation over exploitation as the basis of left-wing mobilization.

3. For able surveys of the concept's adventures, see Joachim Israel, *Alienation: From Marx to Modern Sociology* (Boston: Allyn & Bacon, 1971); and Richard Schacht, *Alienation* (Garden City, NY: Doubleday, 1970). For clarity's sake, also see Dennis Wrong's piercing discussion, "Myths of Alienation," *Partisan Review* 52 (1985): 223–235.

4. Robert Westbrook, "Politics as Consumption: Managing the Modern American Election," in Richard W. Fox and T. J. Jackson Lears, eds., *The Culture of Consumption: Critical Essays in American History, 1880–1920* (New York: Pantheon, 1981), pp. 146–162; Kenneth Keniston, *The Uncommitted: Alienated Youth in American Society* (New York: Harcourt, Brace & World, 1964); Arthur M. Schlesinger Jr., *The Vital Center: The Politics of Freedom*, rev. ed. (1949; reprint, Boston: Houghton Mifflin, 1962).

5. Schlesinger, *The Vital Center*, pp. 6, 246; Les K. Adler and Thomas G. Paterson, "Red Fascism: The Merger of Nazi Germany and Soviet Russia in the American Image of Totalitarianism, 1930's–1950's," *American Historical Review* 75 (April 1970): 1046–1064; Kennan is discussed in Wilfred McClay, *The Masterless: Self and Society in Modern America* (Chapel Hill: University of North Carolina Press, 1994), pp. 223–224. Though an architect of cold war liberal foreign policy, Kennan was personally conservative.

W. H. Auden coined the phrase "age of anxiety" in his 1947 book of that title. W. H. Auden, *The Age of Anxiety* (London: Faber & Faber, 1947). On the term's circulation, see William Graebner, *The Age of Doubt: American Thought and Culture in the 1940s* (Boston: Twayne, 1991), p. 102.

6. T. J. Jackson Lears, *No Place of Grace: Antimodernism and the Transformation of American Culture, 1880–1920* (New York: Pantheon, 1981); Christopher Lasch, *The New Radicalism in America: The Intellectual as a Social Type, 1889–1963* (1965; reprint, New York: Norton, 1986).

7. The search for authenticity underwent significant changes since it first appeared in industrializing America, changes that I scarcely touch on here. I thank Jon Zimmerman for his advice on this point.

8. James Miller, in his outstanding study of the new left, contrasts the existentialist strain of the new left with the rational tendency, which Miller associates with John Dewey's political philosophy and which he clearly prefers. He explains that over time, this Deweyan tendency lost out to existentialism. Although Miller suggests that from the start, existentialism was an important dimension of the new left's vision of participatory democracy, his portrait of the early new left emphasizes the other elements in their politics. For all the subtlety and intelligence of his narrative, his confinement of existentialism to the later years of the story is insupportable. James

Miller, *"Democracy Is in the Streets": From Port Huron to the Siege of Chicago* (New York: Simon & Schuster, 1987), pp. 141–154, 317. Miller's chapter on participatory democracy (pp. 141–154) is the best brief analysis of the ambiguities of the concept.

The *Port Huron Statement* is reprinted in *"Democracy Is in the Streets,"* and the line cited is on p. 332. The question of whether we should view the new left's politics as simply a means to a personal end is a complex one and requires careful handling. To some, this notion seems to delegitimize the new left as a political movement; others take license to engage in questionable psychological speculation. Perhaps the most notorious example of both tendencies is Lewis Feuer, *The Conflict of Generations: The Character and Significance of Student Movements* (New York: Basic Books, 1969), which interprets the new left as a displacement of young people's oedipal energies onto their teachers. Since Kenneth Keniston revealed in his study *Young Radicals* (New York: Harcourt, Brace & World, 1971) that young activists in the antiwar movement often had rather positive, sympathetic relations with their parents, oedipal explanations have been rather implausible. Keniston's conclusion is confirmed elsewhere, for example, in Doug McAdam, *Freedom Summer* (New York: Oxford University Press, 1988), p. 49. Cyril Levitt, *Children of Privilege: Student Revolt in the Sixties* (Toronto: University of Toronto Press, 1984), argues that a frustrated desire for power motivated new left activism. As my study indicates, one thing for which most new left activists in the United States had little desire was the exercise of power.

Others treat the matter more thoughtfully. Alan Brinkley, "Dreams of the Sixties," *New York Review of Books*, 22 October 1987, pp. 10, 12–16, concludes that new left activists sought the satisfaction of personal yearnings in political activism. Peter Clecak, *America's Quest for the Ideal Self: Dissent and Fulfillment in the 60s and 70s* (New York: Oxford University Press, 1982), emphasizes the persistent entanglement of personal fulfillment and social justice in this era's activism. My main caveat here is that neither personal nor political issues should be isolated as the cause of the new left. From the start, the new left's perspective questioned the very division between personal and political concerns, in part because both kinds of concern had combined to create this movement.

9. Walter Kaufmann, ed., *Existentialism from Dostoyevsky to Sartre* (Cleveland: Meridian Books, 1966); and William Barrett, *Irrational Man: A Study in Existential Philosophy* (Garden City, NY: Doubleday, 1958), also were widely read. Todd Gitlin notes the impact of such paperback nonfiction volumes in the 1950s. Todd Gitlin, *The Sixties: Years of Hope, Days of Rage* (New York: Bantam, 1987), p. 30.

Since World War II, much commentary on existentialism has missed the significance of Christian existentialism, which is ironic, since this is where existentialism began. The atheistic understanding of existentialism, associated with Sartre and Camus, emphasizes the ontological priority of the individual and the need for individuals to create meaning out of an absurd world through acts of personal rebellion. See Kaufmann, *Existentialism*, pp. 11–12. Some refer to individual political efforts as existentialist that seem particularly defiant or that embody a vague heroism amid uncertainty and danger. This is the meaning Norman Mailer attaches to the term, for example, in his essay on John F. Kennedy, "Superman Comes to the Supermarket," in Harold Hayes, ed., *Smiling through the Apocalypse: Esquire's History of the Sixties* (New York: Crown Books, 1987), p. 17. Miller associates existentialist politics with an experimental search for "breakaway experiences," an individualistic quest for feelings of authenticity, which he says corroded both the discipline and the sense of community he admires in the new left of the 1960–1965 period. Miller, *"Democracy Is in the Streets,"* p. 317.

These meanings of existentialism are different in important respects from the historically grounded understanding of existentialism that I excavate in this book. Much of the difference stems from the strong presence of Christian and communitarian impulses in the setting I examine, in contrast to the atheistic and radically individualist Sartrean variety of existentialism. The search for values that would assist the movement from alienation to authenticity, as the people I consider imagined it, would occur only in a community, not as an individual enterprise. Furthermore, that community and those values would not emerge out of nothingness. The people in this story were well aware that they drew on the cultural resources of their locality, their region, and their country in their political and cultural efforts.

10. Some readers will be bothered by my use of the term *therapeutic*. Cultural conservatives tend to view therapeutic culture as a solipsistic search for intense personal experience—similar to the most dismissive definition of existentialism. Similarly, Bell, *Cultural Contradictions of Capitalism*, pp. 120–164, argues that 1960s radicalism was simply a decadent phase in the culture of "modernism," which in Bell's definition is, once again, a search for intense individual experience. The literature on the rise of therapeutic culture in the United States goes back to Philip Rieff, *The Triumph of the Therapeutic: Uses of Faith after Freud* (New York: Harper & Row, 1966); and Christopher Lasch, *The Culture of Narcissism: American Life in an Age of Declining Expectations* (New York: Norton, 1978)—a book that, incidentally, applauds the new left for calling attention to the social sources of personal unhappiness.

Both critics and defenders of therapeutic culture associate it with the modern search for authenticity. The philosophical critique of authenticity is available in Theodor Adorno, *The Jargon of Authenticity*, trans. Knut Tarnowski and Frederic Will (Evanston, IL: Northwestern University Press, 1973); and Lionel Trilling, *Sincerity and Authenticity* (Cambridge, MA: Harvard University Press, 1972); also see James Clifford, *The Predicament of Culture* (Cambridge, MA: Harvard University Press, 1988). These works argue that the experience of authenticity that lies at the center of therapeutic culture is basically a myth, always out of reach and, moreover, that this myth is the distinctive product of an advanced industrial culture. Lears, *No Place of Grace*—a polemic against the 1960s counterculture projected backward in time—combines a maverick cultural conservatism with a neo-Marxist interpretation of therapeutic culture as the handmaiden of advanced capitalism.

These critics make many telling points, but to define the search for authenticity merely as a search for intense experience is too restrictive. And historically, it is not accurate to argue that therapeutic culture is incompatible with political concern or that a search for authenticity automatically leads people out of political concerns. The activists I examine here were deeply involved in a therapeutic culture, but this did not exclude other concerns. Charles Taylor, *The Ethics of Authenticity* (Cambridge, MA: Harvard University Press, 1991), deserves attention as an ethical philosopher's defense of authenticity as a moral ideal. Taylor cites Trilling's concept of authenticity in explaining what he means by the term, which he equates with individual self-fulfillment (pp. 15–16).

11. Van Gosse, *Where the Boys Are: Cuba, Cold War America, and the Making of a New Left* (London: Verso, 1994), p. 9.

12. Karl Marx, "From Economico-Philosophical Manuscripts of 1844," in Eugene Kamenka, ed., *The Portable Karl Marx* (New York: Penguin, 1983), pp. 131–152. Also see Bertell Ollman, *Alienation: Marx's Conception of Man in Capitalist Society* (Cambridge: Cambridge University Press, 1971); and Fritz Pappenheim, *The Alienation of Modern Man* (New York: Monthly Review Press, 1959). For a sampling of the international discussion, see the essays collected in Erich Fromm, ed., *Socialist Humanism: An International Symposium* (Garden City, NY: Doubleday/Anchor, 1966).

Albert Camus quoted in John A. Russell, letter, in *Letter to Laymen* (a publication of the Christian Faith-and-Life Community), May 1961. Camus, an atheist whose atheism nonetheless existed in a productive tension with Christianity, was issuing a call for "true Christians" who would join in this existentialist refusal; Russell was a Methodist minister. For one recent discussion of Camus's politics see Jeffrey C. Isaac, *Arendt, Camus, and Modern Rebellion* (New Haven, CT: Yale University Press, 1992). Sartre (who plays hardly any role at all in the story I trace of existentialism's influence on young people in Texas) made the argument himself that existentialism was a form of humanism, in his own well-known effort to bring his ideas to the attention of a broader audience in the United States. Jean-Paul Sartre, "Existentialism Is a Humanism," trans. Philip Mairet, in Nino Langiulli, ed., *The Existentialist Tradition: Selected Writings* (Garden City, NY: Doubleday/Anchor, 1971), pp. 391–416.

13. Abraham Maslow, *Toward a Psychology of Being* (New York: Van Nostrand, 1968); and Betty Friedan, *The Feminine Mystique* (New York: Dell, 1963). Also see Carl Rogers, *On Becoming a Person: A Therapist's View of Psychotherapy* (Boston: Houghton Mifflin, 1961). On Maslow's politics, see Marty Jezer, *Abbie Hoffman: American Rebel* (New Brunswick, NJ: Rutgers University Press, 1992), pp. 21–25. Friedan's case is complicated; on her obscure leftist background, see Daniel Horowitz, "Rethinking Betty Friedan and *The Feminine Mystique*: Labor Union Radicalism and Feminism in Cold War America," *American Quarterly* 48 (March 1996): 1–42. Existential psychology and humanistic psychology were very closely allied, perhaps indistinguishable; for a signal work in this field, see Rollo May, *The Meaning of Anxiety* (New York: Ronald Press, 1950). The best summaries of all this work can be found in Rollo May, ed., *Existential Psychology* (New York: McGraw-

Hill, 1969); Friedan, *Feminine Mystique*, pp. 299–325; and Ellen Herman, *The Romance of American Psychology: Political Culture in the Age of Experts* (Berkeley and Los Angeles: University of California Press, 1995), pp. 265–273.

See Richard S. Ellwood, *The Sixties Spiritual Awakening: American Religion Moving from Modern to Postmodern* (New Brunswick, NJ: Rutgers University Press, 1994), for an account of this and other aspects of experimental religion in the period that remains mired in new age rhetoric. Also see Harvey Cox, *Turning East: Why Americans Look to the Orient for Spirituality, and What That Search Can Mean to the West* (New York: Simon & Schuster, 1977), for a contemporary account.

14. Such national overviews include Kirkpatrick Sale, *SDS* (New York: Random House, 1973); Irwin Unger, *The Movement: A History of the American New Left* (New York: Harper & Row, 1974); Todd Gitlin, *The Whole World Is Watching: The Mass Media in the Making and Unmaking of the New Left* (Berkeley and Los Angeles: University of California Press, 1980); Gitlin, *The Sixties*; Wini Breines, *Community and Organization in the New Left, 1962–1968: The Great Refusal* (1982; reprint, New Brunswick, NJ: Rutgers University Press, 1989); Miller, *"Democracy Is in the Streets"*; Maurice Isserman and Michael Kazin, "The Failure and Success of the New Radicalism," in Steve Fraser and Gary Gerstle, eds., *The Rise and Fall of the New Deal Order, 1930–1980* (Princeton, NJ: Princeton University Press, 1989); and Peter B. Levy, *The New Left and Labor in the 1960s* (Urbana: University of Illinois Press, 1994). Gregory N. Calvert, *Democracy from the Heart: Spiritual Values, Decentralism, and Democratic Idealism in the Movement of the 1960s* (Novato, CA: Communitas Press, 1991), is partly a national overview and partly a memoir (which is also true, to a lesser extent, of Gitlin's *The Sixties*).

Recent works that have begun to tell local stories of the new left are Kenneth Heineman, *Campus Wars: The Peace Movement at American State Universities* (New York: New York University Press, 1993), which is more about the antiwar movement than the new left per se; William J. Rorabaugh, *Berkeley at War: The 1960s* (New York: Oxford University Press, 1989), which has a diffuse focus; Jack Whalen and Richard Flacks, *Beyond the Barricades: The Sixties Generation Grows Up* (Philadelphia: Temple University Press, 1989), a sociological study following a group of students at the University of California at Santa Barbara in their experiences after college; and Paul Buhle, ed., *History and the New Left: Madison, Wisconsin, 1950–1970* (Philadelphia: Temple University Press, 1990), a collection of personal reminiscences that also includes a good introductory essay by the editor. William Billingsley's forthcoming study of North Carolina will also contribute to this growing literature. Nonetheless, there still is no full-fledged local history focusing specifically on the new left.

Many primary sources and documentary anthologies from the era in question examine new left and antiwar activity at numerous campuses. For samples of this work, see part 3 of Julian Foster and Durward Long, eds., *Protest!: Student Activism in America* (New York: Morrow, 1970); and David Riesman and Verne A. Stadtman, eds., *Academic Transformation: Seventeen Institutions under Pressure* (Berkeley, CA: Carnegie Foundation for the Advancement for Teaching, 1973).

International perspectives are offered in Paul Berman, *A Tale of Two Utopias: The Political Journey of the Generation of 1968* (New York: Norton, 1996); Seymour Martin Lipset, ed., *Student Politics* (New York: Basic Books, 1967); Ronald Fraser et al., *1968: A Student Generation in Revolt* (New York: Pantheon, 1988); and David Caute, *Sixty-Eight: The Year of the Barricades* (London: Paladin Books, 1988).

For examples of the new left "history from the bottom up" tendency, see the essays in Alfred F. Young, ed., *Dissent: Explorations in the History of American Radicalism* (DeKalb: Northern Illinois University Press, 1968); and see the discussion in Ian Tyrrell, *The Absent Marx: Class Analysis and Liberal History in Twentieth-Century America* (Westport, CT: Greenwood Press, 1986), pp. 123–164.

The vast body of work on the civil rights movement provides numerous examples of the value of local and state-level studies. Model local studies include William H. Chafe, *Civilities and Civil Rights: Greensboro, North Carolina, and the Black Struggle for Freedom* (New York: Oxford University Press, 1980); and Robert J. Norrell, *Reaping the Whirlwind: The Civil Rights Movement in Tuskegee* (New York: Knopf, 1985). State-level analysis, a more recent innovation, is pioneered in John Dittmer, *Local People: The Struggle for Civil Rights in Mississippi* (Urbana: University of Illinois Press, 1994); Adam Fairclough, *Race and Democracy: The Civil Rights Struggle in Louisiana, 1915–1972* (Athens: University of Georgia Press, 1995); and Charles M. Payne, *I've Got the Light of Freedom: The Organizing Tradition and the Mississippi Freedom Struggle* (Berkeley and Los Angeles: University of California Press, 1995).

15. For a graphic discussion of the mechanisms and politics of this expansion, see Rebecca S. Lowen, *Creating the Cold War University: The Transformation of Stanford* (Berkeley and Los Angeles: University of California Press, 1997).

16. Sale, *SDS*, p. 206; Miller, *"Democracy Is in the Streets,"* pp. 224–226, 240–242, 244–254. Miller paints this experiment in "office democracy" as a failure.

17. Richard Hamilton, *Restraining Myths: Critical Studies of U.S. Social Structure and Politics* (New York: Wiley, 1975), p. 281; cited in Chandler Davidson, *Race and Class in Texas Politics* (Princeton, NJ: Princeton University Press, 1990), p. xviii.

18. The story of the early leadership of SDS and its break with the social democrats is told most evocatively in Miller, *"Democracy Is in the Streets,"* pp. 110–121, 126–140; Maurice Isserman, *If I Had a Hammer . . . : The Death of the Old Left and the Birth of the New Left* (New York: Basic Books, 1987), pp. 202–219; and Berman, *A Tale of Two Utopias*, pp. 63–77 (which, on pp. 44–45, emphasizes the overrepresentation of Jews in SDS). Gregory D. Sumner uses the term *cosmopolitan democracy* to describe the ideals of an international group of intellectuals in the 1940s in whose outlook he sees a foreshadowing of the new left; he follows James Miller's characterization of the new left's political ideas. Gregory Sumner, *Dwight Macdonald and the* politics *Circle: The Challenge of Cosmopolitan Democracy* (Ithaca, NY: Cornell University Press, 1996).

19. The best recent work in this vein on twentieth-century radicalism is Isserman, *If I Had a Hammer.*

For an example of older work that seeks to establish an American "radical tradition," see Staughton Lynd, *Intellectual Origins of American Radicalism* (New York: Pantheon, 1968), a book that hasn't worn very well. The radical tradition that Lynd and others construct features prominent libertarian or anarchist tendencies and is kin to a politically ambiguous belief in a fundamentally liberal American "national character"; work of this kind seeks to ground left-wing politics in liberal traditions. This is an intriguing political project, and one that is not entirely alien to this study. Such work is problematic, however, in the same way that any history is that relies on "national character," even implicitly, as a historical force. For an extreme example, see David DeLeon, *The American as Anarchist* (Baltimore: Johns Hopkins University Press, 1978). For a more careful but undeveloped effort along these lines, see James Gilbert, "New Left: Old America," in Sohnya Sayres et al., eds., *The 60s without Apology* (Minneapolis: University of Minnesota Press, 1984), pp. 244–247.

20. Ronnie Dugger, *Our Invaded Universities: Form, Reform, and New Starts* (New York: Norton, 1974), pp. 51–52; Alice Carol Cox, "The Rainey Affair: A History of the Academic Freedom Controversy at the University of Texas, 1938–1946" (Ph.D. diss., University of Denver, 1970), pp. 104–106, 111.

Jose E. Limon offers a critical assessment of Dobie in Jose E. Limon, *Dancing with the Devil: Society and Cultural Poetics in Mexican-American South Texas* (Madison: University of Wisconsin Press, 1994), pp. 43–59.

21. On this tradition (which, to some extent, the liberals of the cold war provinces constructed), see Lawrence R. Goodwyn, *Democratic Promise: The Populist Moment in America* (New York: Oxford University Press, 1976); James R. Green, *Grass-Roots Socialism: Radical Movements in the Southwest, 1895–1943* (Baton Rouge: Louisiana State University Press, 1978); Anthony P. Dunbar, *Against the Grain: Southern Radicals and Prophets, 1929–1959* (Charlottesville: University Press of Virginia, 1981), which leans more toward religious leftists; Davidson, *Race and Class in Texas Politics*; and John Egerton, *Speak Now against the Day: The Generation before the Civil Rights Movement in the South* (New York: Knopf, 1994). The tradition was updated and its exploration continued in *Southern Exposure*, a political journal founded in 1974 in Chapel Hill, North Carolina, by southern civil rights and new left activists.

22. Historians of democratic and left-wing movements in more remote periods of the North American past have long appreciated the significance of religion in this context. Recent overviews of radicalism in the United States that pay ample attention to religion and spirituality include Paul Buhle, *Marxism in the United States: Remapping the History of the American Left* (London: Verso, 1987); and Robert H. Craig, *Religion and Radical Politics: An Alternative Tradition in the United States* (Philadelphia: Temple University Press, 1992). Historians of twentieth-century liberalism and radicalism are beginning to catch on. For recent work, see Barbara Epstein, *Political Protest and Cultural Revolution: Nonviolent Direct Action in the 1970s and 1980s* (Berkeley and Los Angeles: University of California Press, 1988); James T. Fisher, *The Catholic Counterculture in America, 1933–1962* (Chapel Hill: University of North Carolina Press, 1989), a work especially compatible with this

one because of its concern with the search for authenticity in American culture; and James F. Findlay, *Church People in the Struggle: The National Council of Churches and the Black Freedom Movement* (New York: Oxford University Press, 1993). William G. McLoughlin, *Revivals, Awakenings, and Reform: An Essay on Religion and Social Change in America, 1607–1977* (Chicago: University of Chicago Press, 1978), pp. 179–216, argues that the cultural upheavals of the 1960s and 1970s represented a "fourth great awakening," but he relates religion mainly to the counterculture of that period, not to political radicalism.

23. See Michael Lerner, *The Politics of Meaning: Restoring Hope and Possibility in an Age of Cynicism* (Reading, MA: Addison-Wesley, 1996). Since 1986 Lerner, a former new left activist in Seattle, has used his magazine, *Tikkun*, as a platform for his religious and political viewpoint. Lerner and *Tikkun* advance this outlook in a Jewish idiom, but they are notably open to other religious traditions (as long as they agree on the major questions).

24. Works that give adequate weight to the role of the civil rights movement in the new left's origins include James O'Brien, "The Development of a New Left in the United States, 1960–1965" (Ph.D. diss., University of Wisconsin, 1971); Sara Evans, *Personal Politics: The Roots of Women's Liberation in the Civil Rights Movement and the New Left* (New York: Vintage Books, 1980); and Clayborne Carson, *In Struggle: SNCC and the Black Awakening of the 1960s* (Cambridge, MA: Harvard University Press, 1980). Interestingly, the well-known overviews of the new left listed above in note 14 underplay the formative role of the civil rights movement, partly because of their emphasis on northern locales, but surely not entirely, since the civil rights movement's impact in this respect was nationwide.

On the need for more work on whites in the civil rights movement, see Julian Bond, "The Politics of Civil Rights History," in Armstead L. Robinson and Patricia Williams, eds., *New Directions in Civil Rights Studies* (Charlottesville: University Press of Virginia, 1991), pp. 13–14. One recent book answering this call, a study of a white northerner, is Charles W. Eagles, *Outside Agitator: Jon Daniels and the Civil Rights Movement in Alabama* (Chapel Hill: University of North Carolina Press, 1993). A wider-ranging study is David Chappell, *Inside Agitators: White Southerners in the Civil Rights Movement* (Baltimore: Johns Hopkins University Press, 1994).

25. Particularly with regard to race, there were variations within this camp, which was epitomized by Americans for Democratic Action (ADA), of which *The Vital Center* was a sort of manifesto. Certainly in its early years, though, ADA's politics was dominated by its anticommunism. See Mary Sperling McAuliffe, *Crisis on the Left: Cold War Politics and American Liberals, 1947–1954* (Amherst: University of Massachusetts Press, 1978); and Steven M. Gillon, *Politics and Vision: The ADA and American Liberalism, 1947–1985* (New York: Oxford University Press, 1987).

26. For statistics, see figures 6 and 7 in Terry G. Jordan, "A Century and a Half of Ethnic Change in Texas, 1836–1986," *Southwestern Historical Quarterly* 89 (1986): 406, 407. The term *Tejano* sometimes refers only to descendants of the Mexican provincial population of Tejas. Over the last century, African Americans have

accounted for a declining share of the Texas population, down from 20 percent in 1887 to 12 percent in 1980 (holding steady in recent decades), while the Mexican American share of the state population has risen dramatically, from 4 percent to 21 percent in the same period. Jordan argues that at some point after the U.S. Civil War, Anglo Texans (the first of whom migrated from the American Southeast) exchanged a southern identity for a western one (p. 388). The deep engagement of the people studied here with the southeastern civil rights movement in the 1950s and 1960s casts at least a small doubt on this thesis.

Davidson, *Race and Class in Texas Politics*, focuses on white–black relations, emphasizing white racial attitudes and their political consequences. On Latino–Anglo relations, see David Montejano, *Anglos and Mexicans in the Making of Texas, 1836–1986* (Austin: University of Texas Press, 1987); and Mario Barrera, *Race and Class in the Southwest: A Theory of Racial Inequality* (Notre Dame, IN: University of Notre Dame Press, 1979).

On the Mexican American movement, see Charles Ray Chandler, "The Mexican-American Protest Movement in Texas" (Ph.D. diss., Tulane University, 1968); Jose E. Limon, "The Expressive Culture of a Chicano Student Group at the University of Texas at Austin, 1967–1975" (Ph.D. diss., University of Texas at Austin, 1978); Jacques E. Levy, *Cesar Chavez: Autobiography of La Causa* (New York: Norton, 1975); Ronald B. Taylor, *Chavez and the Farm Workers* (Boston: Beacon Press, 1975); Carlos Munoz Jr., *Youth, Identity, Power: The Chicano Movement* (London: Verso, 1989); Ignacio M. Garcia, *United We Win: The Rise and Fall of La Raza Unida Party* (Tucson: Mexican American Studies & Research Center, 1989).

27. D. W. Meinig, *Imperial Texas: An Interpretative Essay in Cultural Geography* (Austin: University of Texas Press, 1969), pp. 89, 35. Meinig's book is a superlative introduction to its subject.

Joel Williamson describes a "Volksgeistian Conservatism" among postbellum white southerners that is somewhat similar to what I mean by volk populism. I do not mean, however, to freight the latter term with the spiritualism that Williamson discerns. Joel Williamson, *A Rage for Order: Black/White Relations in the American South Since Emancipation* (New York: Oxford University Press, 1986), pp. 206–232.

Jordan advocates "discard[ing] the myth of the typical Texan," noting that this "myth" cannot accommodate the social diversity of Texas (Jordan, "A Century and a Half," p. 385). I am interested in this Texan identity not as an accurate description of social reality but precisely for its mythic power.

28. Miller, *"Democracy Is in the Streets,"* pp. 141–143, discusses the desire among new leftists to "speak American." For a discussion of these different kinds of culture, see Raymond Williams, *Marxism and Literature* (New York: Oxford University Press, 1977), pp. 121–127. For a discussion of "subcultures" marked by a high estimate of their oppositional character, see Dick Hebdige, *Subculture: The Meaning of Style* (London: Methuen, 1979).

29. Paul Buhle comments that the spontaneous white "sympathy towards Black culture," ranging "from sports to music to sexual fantasy," stretched "further among millions of ordinary teenagers than any previously Left-orchestrated

effort could have envisioned" (Buhle, *Marxism in the United States*, p. 224). Also see Wini Breines, *Young, White, and Miserable: Growing up Female in the Fifties* (Boston: Beacon Press, 1992). The most full-throated expression of this tendency, stressing the supposedly unrepressed sexuality of black males, is Norman Mailer, *The White Negro* (San Francisco: City Lights Books, 1957). Many in the new left and the counterculture were attracted to this notion, albeit in less extreme forms, and this attraction received affirmation in Eldridge Cleaver, *Soul on Ice* (New York: McGraw-Hill, 1968), which argues that young white radicals were trying to reclaim their lost physicality in political protest ("putting their bodies on the line").

30. See Casey N. Blake, *Beloved Community: The Cultural Commentary of Randolph Bourne, Van Wyck Brooks, Waldo Frank and Lewis Mumford* (Chapel Hill: University of North Carolina Press, 1990), as well as Lasch, *New Radicalism*, pp. 62, 79–90, 130–133. Also see Robin D. G. Kelley, "Notes on Deconstructing 'The Folk,'" *American Historical Review* 97 (December 1992): 1400–1408. The association of children with authenticity received new emphasis in the 1960s counterculture.

31. Greg Calvert, national secretary of SDS in 1966/1967, was the main publicist of the new working-class analysis, and he posed the choice between that analysis and a dependence on "external agencies" in a 1967 speech at Princeton University, reprinted as "In White America: Radical Consciousness and Social Change," in Massimo Teodori, ed., *The New Left: A Documentary History* (Indianapolis: Bobbs-Merrill, 1969), pp. 412–418. The only secondary works to pay substantial attention to the new working-class analysis are James Weinstein, *Ambiguous Legacy: The Left in American Politics* (New York: New Viewpoints, 1975), pp. 116–117, 127–132, 140–144; Breines, *Community and Organization in the New Left*, pp. 96–114; Calvert, *Democracy from the Heart*; and Alice Echols, *Daring to Be Bad: Radical Feminism in America, 1967–1975* (Minneapolis: University of Minnesota Press, 1989), pp. 38–41. Because they focus exclusively on the national elites of SDS, these accounts conclude erroneously that this analysis went out of style on the left after a brief vogue in 1966/1967. I discuss the new working-class analysis in more detail in chapter 5.

32. Most accounts of the new left that narrate a process of decline in the new left's development (for example, works such as those by Miller and Gitlin) tend to express strong reservations about the new left's "cultural politics." For a fuller discussion, see Doug Rossinow, "The New Left in the Counterculture: Hypotheses and Evidence," *Radical History Review* 67 (Winter 1997): 79–120. Terry H. Anderson, *The Movement and the Sixties: Protest in America from Greensboro to Wounded Knee* (New York: Oxford University Press, 1995), is notable for its sympathetic view of the counterculture, as is Berman, *A Tale of Two Utopias*, which agrees with the narrative of political decline found in Miller's and Gitlin's books.

33. Schlesinger, *Vital Center*, p. 46; Lasch, *New Radicalism*, pp. 308–310.

For mention of Schlesinger's comments, see Lawrence S. Wittner, *Cold War America: From Hiroshima to Watergate* (New York: Praeger, 1974), p. 64; Stephen J. Whitfield, *The Culture of the Cold War* (Baltimore: Johns Hopkins University Press,

1991), p. 43; and James T. Patterson, *Grand Expectations: The United States, 1945–1974* (New York: Oxford University Press, 1996), p. 181.

Similarly, the Kennedy administration in which Schlesinger served sought to create a "hard," masculine mystique that could rival the allure of communism in winning the hearts and minds of what the American leaders imagined was an essentially passive Third World. See Gosse, *Where the Boys Are.* The Kennedy administration's intention to provide masculine leadership in this global contest indicates the broad province of this way of thinking about power in the cold war United States.

34. A serious gender analysis of the new left has picked up steam in recent years, in Alice Echols, " 'We Gotta Get out of This Place': Notes toward a Remapping of the Sixties," *Socialist Review* 22:2 (1982): 9–33; and Gosse, *Where the Boys Are.* All this work is indebted to Evans, *Personal Politics.* In chapter 8 I discuss further the equation of citizenship with masculinity in cold war America.

35. Robin Morgan, "Goodbye to All That," in Leslie B. Tanner, ed., *Voices from Women's Liberation* (New York: Signet Books, 1970), p. 275. This is not to say that women on the left generally agreed with Morgan's conclusion, "Women are the real Left." This suggestion of separatism was a preview of "cultural feminism" from Morgan, who gradually gave up the recognizable leftist dimension of her politics. Notwithstanding accusations of separatism, feminists in the new left, no matter how far-reaching their criticism of their male comrades, wished to work with them politically, at least until 1973.

36. For a guide to these incidents, see Louis A. Foleno, *A Critical Review of Selected Literature on College Student Unrest in the United States, 1968–1970* (San Francisco: Mellen Research University Press, 1992).

37. Some sympathetic scholars are reluctant to acknowledge the limits of the new left's political success. For example, Wini Breines, "Whose New Left?" *Journal of American History* 75 (1988): 528–545, gives the new left as much credit as possible by conflating the categories of "new left," "the movement," and "the sixties." The accomplishments she chalks up to the efforts of these movements include the advance of multiculturalism and feminism (p. 542), changes for which, to the extent that they have actually occurred, the new left is scarcely responsible. George Katsiaficas, *The Imagination of the New Left: A Global Analysis of 1968* (Boston: South End Press, 1987), depicts a new left that did not end in the 1970s but that instead continued to exist as a political force two decades after 1968. This is a mirror image of the right-wing portrait of new left continuity and influence, which can be found in books such as David Kimball, *Tenured Radicals: How Politics Has Corrupted Our Higher Education* (New York: Harper & Row, 1990). For a highly critical but thought-provoking discussion of the new left's legacy in higher education, see John Paul Diggins, *The Rise and Fall of the American Left* (New York: Norton, 1992).

Chapter 1

1. For inventories of concerns, see "Ideas: An Issue on the Issues," *Texas Observer*, 16 January 1959; and MFC, "Here's What Liberals Want," *Observer*, 9

May 1955. The fight between liberals and conservatives in the Democratic Party, mentioned later, raised the significance of procedural issues; thus "MFC" placed free and fair elections high on the list of his priorities.

2. Chandler Davidson, *Race and Class in Texas Politics* (Princeton, NJ: Princeton University Press, 1991). Also see George Norris Green, *The Establishment in Texas Politics: The Primitive Years, 1938–1957* (Westport, CT: Greenwood Press, 1979).

In the late 1930s, Fath had been president of the University Progressive Democrats at UT, an organization that split from the Young Democrats when the larger group declined to support a second term in the White House for Franklin Roosevelt in 1936. Connally and others who later became close to Lyndon Johnson also were Roosevelt loyalists. While Fath maintained his liberal politics, Connally and Johnson moved right in subsequent years, blowing with the prevailing winds. "Early Years of Creekmore Fath," *Observer*, 21 March 1958. Later I discuss Randolph, who became the main initial benefactor to the *Texas Observer*.

3. See Ronnie Dugger, *Our Invaded Universities: Form, Reform, and New Starts* (New York: Norton, 1974), pp. 51–52; Anthony M. Orum, *Power, Money & the People: The Making of Modern Austin* (Austin: Texas Monthly Press, 1987), pp. 162–163.

4. The House Un-American Activities Committee (HUAC), the archetypal cold war institution, was formed in 1938, and some historians term the ensuing investigations of left-wing subversion the "little red scare." Ellen Schrecker, *The Age of McCarthyism: A Brief History with Documents* (New York: St. Martin's Press, 1994), pp. 12–13. Robin D. G. Kelley, *Hammer and Hoe: Alabama Communists during the Great Depression* (Chapel Hill: University of North Carolina Press, 1990), pp. 186–190, discusses matters in another provincial locale. According to the standard tale, this scare ended with the wartime alliance between the United States and the Soviet Union between 1941 and 1945, and the domestic cold war resumed in full flower in the late 1940s. It seems doubtful, however, that the wartime romance with the Russians extended to the provinces.

5. Allred was an economic liberal, seeking to bring a moderate degree of regulation to the oil and insurance industries of Texas as attorney general between 1931 and 1935 and inaugurating old-age insurance and unemployment compensation as governor during the next four years. Ronnie Dugger, "Allred Revisited," *Observer*, 27 June 1955; Ronnie Dugger, "Death of State's New Deal Governor," *Observer*, 2 October 1959. Allred sought no change in the racial regime of his state, affirming when he ran for the governor's office that the Democratic Party's primary would remain closed to blacks—a central mechanism of political exclusion in a one-party state. Darlene Clark Hine, *Black Victory: The Rise and Fall of the White Primary in Texas* (Millwood, NY: KTO Press, 1979), pp. 156–161. As I discuss later, racial egalitarianism was the most important innovation of the secular political liberalism that emerged from the post–World War II period of right-wing dominance in the United States.

6. Homer P. Rainey, *The Tower and the Dome: A Free University versus Political Control* (Boulder, CO: Pruett Publishing, 1971).

7. Dugger, *Our Invaded Universities*, pp. 42–43; Alice Carol Cox, "The Rainey

Affair: A History of the Academic Freedom Controversy at the University of Texas, 1938–1946" (Ph.D. diss., University of Denver, 1970), pp. 51–52, 60–67. (The four professors were Robert Montgomery, Clarence Ayres, Edward Hale, and Clarence Wiley.) Cox's dissertation provides the most reliable account of these events.

8. Cox, "The Rainey Affair," pp. 42–54; Dugger, *Our Invaded Universities*, p. 43.

9. Dugger, *Our Invaded Universities*, pp. 44–45; Cox, "The Rainey Affair," pp. 67–69.

10. Cox, "The Rainey Affair," p. 88.

11. Dugger, *Our Invaded Universities*, p. 46.

12. Ibid., pp. 51–52; Cox, "The Rainey Affair," pp. 104–106, 111.

13. Mody Boatright, "A Mustang in the Groves of Academe," *Observer*, 24 July 1964. A complicated set of circumstances allowed for Dobie's dismissal. He had been on leave for two years and wished to remain away longer because of an allergic condition that he said the Austin flora would aggravate. The regents cited a rule limiting faculty to a maximum of two years' consecutive leave, "except in very unusual circumstances, such as military service or prolonged illness." Since Coke Stevenson, the former rightist governor, and others of like ilk had identified Dobie—"a highly vocal enemy of reactionary demagogues and a defender of labor unions and of many unpopular causes"—as a bad apple, the firing was widely perceived as political in nature. Henry Nash Smith, "An Enemy of Reactionary Demagogues," *Observer*, 24 July 1964. Jose E. Limon offers another view of Dobie, focusing on his attitudes toward Mexican Americans, in *Dancing with the Devil: Society and Cultural Poetics in Mexican-American South Texas* (Madison: University of Wisconsin Press, 1994), pp. 43–59.

14. Willie Morris, *North toward Home* (Boston: Houghton Mifflin, 1967), p. 168.

15. C. Wright Mills, *The Power Elite* (New York: Oxford University Press, 1956). Mills transferred from Texas A&M to UT in 1935 and stayed at UT until 1939, by which time he had earned a B.A. in sociology and an M.A. in philosophy. He studied economics with Clarence Ayres and devoted most of his attention to pragmatism. See Rick Tilman, *C. Wright Mills: A Native Radical and His American Intellectual Roots* (University Park: Pennsylvania State University Press, 1984), pp. 1–9; Irving Louis Horowitz, *C. Wright Mills: An American Utopian* (New York: Free Press, 1983), pp. 1–37; and Cornel West, *The American Evasion of Philosophy: A Genealogy of Pragmatism* (Madison: University of Wisconsin Press, 1989), pp. 124–138.

16. Orum, *Power, Money & the People*, pp. 205–225 ; Davidson, *Race and Class in Texas Politics*, p. 180; John Henry Faulk, *Fear on Trial* (Austin: University of Texas Press, 1966); Dugger, *Our Invaded Universities*, p. 50.

17. Dugger, *Our Invaded Universities*, p. 64.

18. Ronnie Dugger, "U.T. Regents Veto Mrs. FDR, Stevenson as Speakers," *Observer*, 16 May 1955.

19. C. Wright Mills, "The Decline of the Left," in Irving Horowitz, ed., *Power, Politics and People: The Collected Essays of C. Wright Mills* (New York: Ballantine,

1963), p. 233. This essay originated as a 1959 speech on the British Broadcasting Company. The male construction of Mills's free citizens was no accident, as I discuss in chapter 8.

20. Larry Goodwyn, "The Texas Observer: A Journal of Free Voices," *Southern Exposure* 2 (Winter 1975): 23–28; Ronnie Dugger, "East Texas Justice," *Observer*, 30 April 1957; Ronnie Dugger, "Editor Accused," *Observer*, 1 February 1956.

21. Ronnie Dugger, "The Word Liberal and Its Detractors," *Observer*, 2 May 1955. The magazine he quoted was the British *Reporter*.

22. Smith, "An Enemy of Reactionary Demagogues."

23. Dugger, "The Word Liberal and Its Detractors."

24. Ibid., p. 65; Claudetta Young, "Daily Texan's History Shows 58 Years of Color, Change," *Daily Texan*, 5 December 1958.

25. Ronnie Dugger, "Report of the Regents' Ire over 'Politics,'" *Observer*, 15 February 1956; Ronnie Dugger, "Willie and the College Yell," *Observer*, 22 February 1956; Ronnie Dugger, "Regents Told Texan Free," *Observer*, 29 February 1956; Morris, *North toward Home*, pp. 185–192.

26. Editorial, "Vote for Editors," *Summer Texan*, 20 June 1958.

27. Chandler Davidson, interview with author, 2 February 1992; Lawrence Goodwyn, *Democratic Promise: The Populist Moment in America* (New York: Oxford University Press, 1976).

28. " 'Dido' Incident Arouses University," *Observer*, 14 May 1957.

29. Bud Mims, interview with author, 8 February 1993; Editorial, "On the Policy of No Policy," *Summer Texan*, 7 June 1957; Bud Mims, editorial, "Desegregation Is Not Enough," *Daily Texan*, 16 May 1958.

30. Sara Burroughs, "Senator Says Demos Must Organize, Fight," *Daily Texan*, 13 November 1958 (the quotation is Burroughs's paraphrase of Yarborough's comment).

31. Orum, *Power, Money & the People*, p. 148.

32. Celia Morris, interview with author, 3 February 1993; Clarence Ayres, *The Divine Right of Capital* (Boston: Houghton Mifflin, 1946); Orum, *Power, Money & the People*, p. 148; Dugger, *Our Invaded Universities*, p. 62; "Liberal Demos Choose Ayres for Project," *Daily Texan*, 27 April 1960.

33. Dugger, *Our Invaded Universities*, p. 41; Robb Burlage, interview with author, 1 June 1992; "Demos to Hear Dr. Montgomery," *Daily Texan*, 13 January 1959; Morris, *North toward Home*, p. 175.

34. Robb Burlage interview.

35. Morris interview.

36. Bud Mims, "President's Decision Upheld," *Summer Texan*, 7 June 1957; "Silber Fires Questions at Meeting," *Summer Texan*, 7 June 1957; Dugger, *Our Invaded Universities*, p. 66.

37. "UT Was Child of Politics, Grew Rich through Use of Land," *Daily Texan*, 5 April 1960.

38. Ronnie Dugger, "The Politics of Knowledge," *Change* 6 (February 1974): 31; Dugger, *Our Invaded Universities*, pp. 74–84, 186–196.

39. Allen Lingo, interview with author, 18 June 1992; Morris interview; "Silber against Death Penalty," *Daily Texan*, 19 March 1959.

40. Dorothy Dawson Burlage, interview with author, 9 December 1992; Casey Hayden to author, 17 March 1997.

41. Morris, *North toward Home*, p. 158.

42. Dorothy Burlage interview; Morris interview.
Celia Morris, who attended Bob Montgomery's atomic bomb lecture three times, married Willie Morris. (They later divorced.)

43. Dorothy Burlage interview.

44. "Sixteen Will Leave Thursday for Texas Seminar in Chile," *Summer Texan*, 14 July 1959; Hal Simmons, "'Capitalism Is Doomed,'" *Daily Texan*, 22 September 1959.

45. "Week in Cuba Offered," *Summer Texan*, 7 August 1959; G. W. Ayer, "Students Favor Castro," *Daily Texan*, 27 September 1959.

46. "Socialism on Way, but How?" *Daily Texan*, 7 April 1960.

47. "Communism Parody of Christian Belief—Dr. Geren," *Daily Texan*, 20 February 1959.

48. Jim Hyatt, "Professors to Discuss Reds," *Daily Texan*, 25 October 1960; Jim Hyatt, "To Combat Soviets, Use Reason—Ayres," *Daily Texan*, 26 October 1960.

49. "US World Role Discussed at 'Y,'" *Daily Texan*, 3 December 1959; "Mathis Emphasized International Policies," *Daily Texan*, 2 October 1959.

50. Larry Hurwitz, "SA Decides to Remain in National Association," *Daily Texan*, 27 February 1959; Ralph Johnson, "SA Committee Places NSA on Probation," *Daily Texan*, 24 February 1959; "NSA 'Off-Hook' after SA Group Offers New Bill," *Daily Texan*, 10 March 1959; Leon Graham, "14 Appointments Put NSA 'Back in' at UT," *Daily Texan*, 30 June 1959; Dorothy Burlage interview.

51. Anthony Henry, "NSA Congress Delegate Opposes a Withdrawal," *Daily Texan*, 17 February 1959.

52. Christopher Lasch, "The Cultural Cold War: A Short History of the Congress for Cultural Freedom," in Christopher Lasch, *The Agony of the American Left* (New York: Knopf, 1969), pp. 98–110; Sol Stern, "A Short Account of International Student Politics and the Cold War," *Ramparts*, March 1967, pp. 29–38.

53. Editorial, "A Good Example," *Daily Texan*, 9 January 1959.

54. Editorial, "The Rotten Apple," *Daily Texan*, 16 January 1959; Editorial, "Oath-Taking," *Summer Texan*, 7 July 1959; Bob Moore, "SA Favors Removal of Disclaimer Oath," *Daily Texan*, 25 March 1960; Leon Graham, "Faculty Joins Affidavit Foes," *Daily Texan*, 11 May 1960; "NSA Leaders Urge Repeal of the Oath," *Daily Texan*, 28 April 1959; "Senate Votes 'Nay' on Disclaimer Oath," *Summer Texan*, 17 June 1960; Editorial, "Anti-Oath Stand 'Daily Worker' Line?" *Daily Texan*, 4 February 1959.

55. "Legislators Accuse UT of Teaching Atheism," *Daily Texan*, 24 February 1959; "Solons Modify Atheism Charge," *Daily Texan*, 26 February 1959.

56. Nina McCain, "Charge of Atheism Denounced by Clergy," *Daily Texan*, 25 February 1959.

57. Robb Burlage, "Coming: A 'Silent Generation' Faculty?" *Daily Texan*, 20 March 1959; Nina McCain, "Cures for Tied Tongues," *Daily Texan*, 25 March 1959.

58. Robb Burlage, " 'Might-Have-Been' Factors Tell Story of Little Rock Crisis," *Summer Texan*, 28 July 1959; "Mansfield Mob Thwarts Court Edict," *Observer*, 5 September 1956.

59. Barry Shank, *Dissonant Identities: The Rock 'n' Roll Scene in Austin, Texas* (Hanover, NH: Wesleyan University Press/University Press of New England, 1994), pp. 11–12. In 1928 the Austin City Council drew up a plan to segregate the local black population in East Austin, a plan three-quarters successful by 1940. Previously, most Austin blacks had lived closer to the university and the state capitol, near the center of town. On the development of black Austin until 1950, and especially on civil rights activism in the 1940s, see Orum, *Power, Money & the People*, pp. 169–203.

60. Almetris M. Duren, with Louise Iscoe, *Overcoming: A History of Black Integration at the University of Texas at Austin* (Austin: University of Texas at Austin, 1979). The figure is cited in Dugger, "Willie and the College Yell."

61. "Kinsolving Looks Like Luxury Hotel," *Summer Texan*, 13 June 1958.

62. Jerry Conn, "No 'Firm' Housing Plans," *Daily Texan*, 15 October 1959; "Negro Housing Report Okayed," *Daily Texan*, 25 October 1959; Carl Howard, "Negroes to Get Suitable Housing," *Daily Texan*, 15 November 1959.

63. Joe Carroll Rust, "Commission Asks Strong SA Backing," *Daily Texan*, 2 December 1958.

64. Robb Burlage, "Austin and Little Rock So Alike, yet Different," *Summer Texan*, 21 July 1959.

65. Kay Voetmann, "Atmosphere Separates Austin and Little Rock," *Summer Texan*, 4 August 1959; Key quoted in Davidson, *Race and Class in Texas Politics*, p. 11; Ronnie Dugger, "Who Was Guilty?" *Observer*, 30 April 1957.

66. Alan Brinkley, *The End of Reform: New Deal Liberalism in Recession and War* (New York: Knopf, 1995), pp. 164–167, is forthright on this point. John B. Kirby, "The Roosevelt Administration and Blacks: An Ambivalent Legacy," pp. 265–288, and Barton J. Bernstein, "The New Deal: The Conservative Achievements of Liberal Reform," pp. 260–261, both in Barton J. Bernstein and Allen J. Matusow, eds., *Twentieth-Century America: Recent Interpretations*, 2d ed. (New York: Harcourt Brace Jovanovich, 1972), are critical. Harvard Sitkoff, *A New Deal for Blacks: The Emergence of Civil Rights as a National Issue*, vol. 2, *The Depression Decade* (New York: Oxford University Press, 1978); and Patricia Sullivan, *Days of Hope: Race and Democracy in the New Deal Era* (Chapel Hill: University of North Carolina Press, 1996), are more whiggish, discerning the roots of later changes in race relations under the New Deal regime. John Egerton, *Speak Now against the Day: The Generation before the Civil Rights Movement in the South* (New York: Knopf, 1994), wavers between an honest accounting of how few white southerners dissented from the reign of Jim Crow in these years and a desire to see progress. For a discussion of those few dissenters, who hardly can be called liberals, see Anthony F. Dunbar, *Against the*

Grain: Southern Dissenters and Prophets, 1937–1954 (Charlottesville: University Press of Virginia, 1981); and Robert H. Craig, *Religion and Radical Politics: An Alternative Christian Tradition in the United States* (Philadelphia: Temple University Press, 1992).

67. Larry Goodwyn, "The Negro Issue and Southern Liberalism," *Observer*, 21 November 1958.

68. Ronnie Dugger, "Where People Are Different Colors," *Observer*, 6 June 1959; "Reproach, Reform Program May Solve Racial Problem," *Daily Texan*, 24 November 1959.

69. On the business language of individualism and free enterprise, see Elizabeth A. Fones-Wolf, *Selling Free Enterprise: The Business Assault on Labor and Liberalism, 1945–60* (Urbana: University of Illinois Press, 1994).

70. David Riesman, with Nathan Glazer and Reuel Denney, *The Lonely Crowd: A Study of the Changing American Character* (New Haven, CT: Yale University Press, 1950); William H. Whyte, *The Organization Man* (New York: Simon & Schuster, 1956); Vance O. Packard, *The Hidden Persuaders* (New York: McKay, 1957); Vance O. Packard, *The Status Seekers* (New York: McKay, 1959).

See Daniel Horowitz, *Vance Packard and American Social Criticism* (Chapel Hill: University of North Carolina Press, 1994), for a convincing portrait of Packard as a man confronting the changing present with the tenacious "producerist" values of the past.

71. "Ransom Asserts Import of Students' Individuality," *Daily Texan*, 16 March 1961; Jo Eickmann, "a word from the silent generation," *Daily Texan*, 7 April 1961; Clark Kerr, *The Uses of the University*, rev. ed. (Cambridge, MA: Harvard University Press, 1994).

72. Lee Smith, " 'Power Elite': C. W. Mills Challenges Intellectuals," *Daily Texan*, 4 November 1958; Christopher Shannon, *Conspicuous Criticism: Tradition, the Individual, and Culture in American Social Thought, from Veblen to Mills* (Baltimore: Johns Hopkins University Press, 1996), p. 154. Shannon notes that this "pastoral" was common to twentieth-century American social criticism.

James Miller, *"Democracy Is in the Streets": From Port Huron to the Siege of Chicago* (New York: Simon & Schuster, 1987), pp. 78–91, discusses Mills's influence on the early new left. The writings by Mills that probably influenced the new left the most are *The Power Elite; The Causes of World War III* (New York: Simon & Schuster, 1958); *Listen, Yankee!: The Revolution in Cuba* (New York: McGraw-Hill, 1960); and "Letter to the New Left," *New Left Review* 5 (1960), reprinted as "The New Left," in Horowitz, ed., *Power, Politics and People*, pp. 247–259. In chapters 5 and 8, I have more to say about Mills's significance for the new left.

West, *Evasion of American Philosophy*, pp. 124, 131–138, discusses Mills's individualism and his preoccupation with personal style. Shannon, *Conspicuous Criticism*, notes sharply that Mills's ethics was rooted "not in any particular kind of morality but in a particular kind of self" (p. 166).

73. Horowitz, *Vance Packard and American Social Criticism*, pp. 10–23, emphasizes Packard's stringent Methodist upbringing; Chandler Davidson, "The Jabberwock,"

Daily Texan, 18 November 1959; Tommy Stuckey, "Author Calls Students Conservative, Selfish," *Daily Texan*, 2 December 1960.

Chapter 2

1. On the "religious revival," see Robert Wuthnow, *The Restructuring of American Religion: Society and Faith Since World War II* (Princeton, NJ: Princeton University Press, 1988); and James D. Hudnut-Beumler, *Looking for God in the Suburbs: The Religion of the American Dream and Its Critics, 1945–1965* (New Brunswick, NJ: Rutgers University Press, 1994). David Harrington Watt, *A Transforming Faith: Explorations in Twentieth-Century American Evangelicalism* (New Brunswick, NJ: Rutgers University Press, 1991), pp. 17–21, discusses the Campus Crusade for Christ, which is also mentioned by Bob Breihan, interview with author, 10 November 1991.

2. Ronnie Dugger, *Our Invaded Universities: Form, Reform, and New Starts* (New York: Norton, 1974), p. 76.

3. Frank Wright, interview with author, 30 June 1992. Chapters 3 and 4 discuss the University YMCA–YWCA at length.

4. Willie Morris, *North toward Home* (Boston: Houghton Mifflin, 1967), p. 171; Dick Simpson, *The Politics of Compassion and Transformation* (Athens: Swallow Press/Ohio University Press, 1989), p. 253; Tom Hayden, *Reunion: A Memoir* (New York: Random House, 1988), p. 40.

5. Ronnie Dugger, "A Dogmatic View of Religious Dogmatism," *Observer*, 21 April 1962.

6. Dugger, *Our Invaded Universities*, p. 76.

7. B. S., "Split Develops in the 'Community,'" *Texas Observer*, 28 April 1962.

8. Marcel quoted in Robert C. Solomon, ed., *Existentialism* (New York: Modern Library, 1974), p. ix, possibly the best anthology of writings in this tradition.

9. Q. in B. S., "Split Develops in 'Community.'"

10. Dietrich Bonhoeffer, *Letters and Papers from Prison*, ed. Eberhard Bethge (New York: Macmillan, 1953; rev. ed., 1967), p. 172.

11. "The College House of the Christian Faith and Life Community at Austin, Texas" (a study commissioned by the Hogg Foundation at the University of Texas) (Austin, TX, and Pelham, NY: Millard Research Associates, August 1964), p. 5 (hereafter "The College House"); James I. McCord, "The New Man in the New Age," *Letter to Laymen*, May 1961, p. 8; Richard VanSteenkiste, "College House Seeks to Resolve Basic Issues for Texas Students," *Daily Texan*, 23 April 1961; B. S., "Split Develops in the 'Community.'"

12. "The College House," p. ii; Robb Burlage, interview with author, 1 June 1992; Judy Schleyer Blanton, interview with author, 17 May 1993.

13. Claire Johnson Breihan/O. R. Schmidt, interview with author, 29 June 1992.

14. "The New Man," in *Breakthrough* (promotional publication of the CFLC, n.d. [ca. 1960]), emphasis in original; "The Austin Experiment," in *Breakthrough*; "behind every breakthrough: The Financial Support of Alert New Men," in *Breakthrough*.

15. Paul Tillich, "The Idea and the Ideal of Personality," in Paul Tillich, *The Protestant Era*, trans. and ed. James Luther Adams (Chicago: University of Chicago Press, 1948). Later I discuss further Tillich's relation of community and personality to spiritual reconnection.

The emergence of "personality" as a cultural norm in the United States, as against a supposedly older ideal of "character," is a chestnut of cultural history. This picture of cultural change is on display in David Riesman, with Nathan Glazer and Reuel Denney, *The Lonely Crowd: A Study of the Changing American Character* (New Haven, CT: Yale University Press, 1950); also see Warren Susman, *Culture as History: The Transformation of American Society in the Twentieth Century* (New York: Pantheon, 1984). Richard W. Fox effectively questions this historical sequence in "The Culture of Liberal Protestant Progressivism, 1875–1925," *Journal of Interdisciplinary History* 23 (Winter 1993): 639–660.

16. "The Moral Covenant and Corporate Discipline of the Christian Faith-and-Life Community," CFLC document, p. 3; "The College House," p. 131.

17. "The College House," p. 5.

18. Breihan/Schmidt interview; Allen Lingo, interview with author, 18 June 1992 (hereafter "Lingo interview"); "The College House," p. 35.

19. "The College House," p. 35; B. S., "Split Develops in the 'Community' "; Breihan/Schmidt interview; Robert Bell, interview with author, 11 March 1993; Rasjidah Franklin-Alley, interview with author, 18 March 1993.

20. "The College House," p. 5; Allen Lingo, phone interview with author, 26 November 1991 (hereafter "Lingo phone interview").

21. James Mathews, interview with author, 23 June 1993; Lingo interview; Brad Blanton, interview with author, 14 April 1993. James Mathews, Joe's brother, stayed on the straight and narrow path, eventually becoming a Methodist bishop. For a good discussion of Richard Niebuhr's intellectual and political development, see Richard W. Fox, "H. Richard Niebuhr's Divided Kingdom," *American Quarterly* 42 (March 1990): 93–101.

22. Slicker quoted in B. S., "Split Develops in the 'Community.' "

23. Walter Kaufmann, ed., *Existentialism from Dostoyevsky to Sartre* (Cleveland: World Publishing, 1956; Meridian Books edition, 1966), pp. 11–12. These themes in themselves do not distinguish existentialism from philosophical pragmatism; see James T. Kloppenberg, *Uncertain Victory: Social Democracy and Progressivism in American and European Thought, 1870–1920* (New York: Oxford University Press, 1986); and Morton G. White, *Social Thought in America: The Revolt against Formalism* (New York: Oxford University Press, 1949).

24. This is not true of the other widely read study of the time, that is, William Barrett, *Irrational Man: A Study in Existential Philosophy* (New York: Doubleday, 1958); or of the later Solomon, ed., *Existentialism*.

25. See Paul Tillich, *The Courage to Be* (New Haven, CT: Yale University Press, 1952), pp. 35, 39.

Rollo May, *The Meaning of Anxiety* (New York: Ronald Press, 1950), offers a secular discussion of the same problem, one with which members of the Faith-and-Life Community also were familiar.

26. May, *The Meaning of Anxiety*, p. 60. For differing views of these intellectual developments, see William Hutchison, *The Modernist Impulse in American Protestantism* (Cambridge, MA: Harvard University Press, 1976); and Steven Turner, *Without God, Without Creed: The Origins of Unbelief in America* (Baltimore: Johns Hopkins University Press, 1986).

27. Tillich, *Protestant Era*, pp. 192, 262; Tillich, *Courage to Be*, pp. 136–140, 96–103.

28. See Ernst Troeltsch, *Christian Thought: Its History and Application*, ed. Baron F. von Hugel (New York: Meridian Books, 1957), for a classic expression of liberal thinking on these issues; also see Hutchison, *Modernist Impulse*.

29. Bonhoeffer, *Letters and Papers*. See Eberhard Bethge, *Dietrich Bonhoeffer: Man of Vision, Man of Courage*, trans. Eric Mosbacher et al. (New York: Harper & Row, 1970).

30. John A. T. Robinson, *Honest to God* (Philadelphia: Westminster Press, 1963); Harvey Cox, *The Secular City: Secularization and Urbanization in Theological Perspective* (New York: Collier, 1965; rev. ed., 1990).

31. Bonhoeffer, *Ethics*, ed. Eberhard Bethge (New York: Macmillan, 1955), p. 194; Bonhoeffer, *Letters and Papers*, pp. 178, 180.

32. "The New World," in *Breakthrough*; "Prominent Church Board Aids Experiment," *Letter to Laymen*, February 1962.

33. "The New Man," in *Breakthrough*.

34. Carl Michalson, "Christian Faith and Existential Freedom," CFLC reprint, pp. 6, 7; Jean-Paul Sartre, *Nausea*, trans. Lloyd Alexander (New York: New Directions, 1964); Albert Camus, *The Myth of Sisyphus and Other Essays*, trans. Justin O'Brien (New York: Knopf, 1955).

35. Paul Tillich, *Systematic Theology*, 3 vols. (Chicago: University of Chicago Press, 1951–1963); Tillich, *The Shaking of the Foundations* (New York: Scribner, 1948). Will Herberg characterizes Tillich as a neoorthodox thinker in Will Herberg, ed., *Four Existentialist Theologians: A Reader from the Works of Jacques Maritain, Nicolas Berdyaev, Martin Buber, and Paul Tillich* (Garden City, NY: Doubleday/Anchor, 1958); as does William Lee Miller in "The Rise of Neo-Orthodoxy," in Arthur M. Schlesinger Jr. and Morton White, eds., *Paths of American Thought* (Boston: Houghton Mifflin, 1963), pp. 326–344.

Richard Fox, in his brief discussion of Tillich in *Reinhold Niebuhr: A Biography* (New York: Pantheon, 1985), pp. 257–259, presents Tillich as a therapeutic, amoral thinker who ignored the tragic dimension of human existence as well as political matters. Fox also suggests a connection between Tillich's predatory personal behavior—he was habitually unfaithful to his wife and was known to sexually harass younger women—and his theology. In his later work, for which he became most popular, Tillich avoided explicit discussion of political and moral matters, and he did indeed offer a therapeutic theology. However, his theology had moral and political dimensions, which he downplayed in his later writings, and his therapeutic perspective was both firmly grounded in Christian tradition and compatible with moral and political concerns.

As for his personal behavior, it is entirely appropriate to look to his writings to see if they support such behavior, but I see no such support there. In Tillichian terms, the exploitation of others disrespects their equal status as children of God and hinders their achievement of personality. Far from fulfilling his theology, Tillich's personal behavior violated it. And as I point out, *agape* and *eros* were the varieties of love that Tillich championed in his writing, not *libido*.

36. These quotations are from James Luther Adams's essay, "Tillich's Concept of the Protestant Era," in Tillich, *Protestant Era*, pp. 288, 299; Ved Mehta, *The New Theologian* (New York: Harper & Row, 1966), p. 6.

37. Tillich, *Protestant Era*, p. 281; Tillich, *Courage to Be*, pp. 169–170, 90.

38. See Reinhold Niebuhr, *Moral Man and Immoral Society: A Study in Ethics and Politics* (New York: Scribner, 1932); Reinhold Niebuhr, *The Children of Light and the Children of Darkness: A Vindication of Democracy and a Critique of Its Traditional Defense* (New York: Scribner, 1945); and Fox, *Reinhold Niebuhr*.

39. Fox, *Reinhold Niebuhr*, p. 4.

40. "The College House," pp. 59, 104; Michalson, "Christian Faith and Existential Freedom," p. 5; Dietrich Bonhoeffer, *Ethics*, p. 217.

41. Tillich, *Protestant Era*, pp. 130, 262; Tillich, *Courage to Be*, p. 22; Erich Fromm, *The Sane Society* (New York: Rinehart, 1955); and Erich Fromm, *The Art of Loving* (New York: Harper & Row, 1962).

42. Tillich, quoted in Mehta, *New Theologian*, p. 7. See Paul Tillich, *Morality and Beyond* (New York: Harper & Row, 1963), pp. 38–43; and Paul Tillich, "Being and Love," in Herberg, ed., *Four Existentialist Theologians*, pp. 332–346, for brief discussions.

King's dissertation compared the theologies of Tillich and Henry Nelson Wieman. See Keith Miller, *Voice of Deliverance: The Language of Martin Luther King, Jr. and Its Sources* (New York: Free Press, 1991), pp. 61–62. For King's views, see Martin Luther King Jr., *Strength to Love* (New York: Harper & Row, 1963). Miller makes it clear that King rejected Tillich's concept of God as insufficiently personal, although King did embrace other aspects of Tillich's thought, like the concept of *agape*.

For an extensive exposition of the distinctively Christian quality of *agape*, see Anders Nygren, *Eros and Agape*, trans. Philip S. Watson (Philadelphia: Westminster Press, 1953). (Miller is at pains to note that King did not take his concept of Christian love from Nygren.) According to Nygren, *eros* is fundamentally selfish and egocentric, expressing the human desire for fulfillment in the possession of beautiful things, whereas *agape* is selfless and is "indifferent to value"; that is, it attaches indiscriminately to all humans simply by virtue of their humanity. *Eros* flows from women and men to God, and *agape* is a love freely given by God to us, which we can then return to God and transfer to our fellow humans.

43. Tillich, *Protestant Era*, p. 197.

44. Ibid., p. 155; also see Tillich, *Morality and Beyond*, pp. 38–40, 94.

45. Tillich, *Morality and Beyond*, pp. 268, 115.

46. Tillich quoted in Adams, "Tillich's Concept," p. 290 (emphasis added); Michalson, "Christian Faith and Existential Freedom," p. 9. Also see Tillich, *Protestant Era*, pp. 202–205; and Tillich, *The New Being* (New York: Scribner, 1955).

47. Cover, *Letter to Laymen*, February 1962.

48. Carol Darrell, "The Paralyzed Man," *Letter to Laymen*, February 1962; Keith Stanford, "The Contemporary Dilemma," *Letter to Laymen*, February 1962.

49. Meg Godbold, "The New Possibility," *Letter to Laymen*, February 1962.

50. Edward C. Hobbs, "The Gospel through So-Called Secular Drama" (CFLC reprint), pp. 5, 4; Emil Brunner, "Justification by Grace Alone" (CFLC reprint), p. 6.

51. Dietrich Bonhoeffer, *Life Together*, trans. John W. Doberstein (New York: Harper Bros., 1954), pp. 112, 105–106, 114, 115; also see William Blair Gould, *The Worldly Christian: Bonhoeffer and Discipleship* (Philadelphia: Fortress Press, 1967), p. 6.

52. "The Moral Covenant," p. 3; Lingo phone interview; cover, *Letter to Laymen*, February 1962.

53. Casey Hayden, interview with author, 2 March 1993; W. Jack Lewis, "Dear Everybody," *Letter to Laymen*, November 1959; Rosalie Oakes, interview with author, 23 February 1993.

54. "The College House," pp. 29, 30, 31, emphasis in original.
J. Gordon Melton and Robert L. Moore, *The Cult Experience: Responding to the New Religious Pluralism* (New York: Pilgrim Press, 1982), rejects the widespread fear of new religions or "cults." Rosabeth Moss Kanter, *Commitment and Community: Communes and Utopias in Sociological Perspective* (Cambridge, MA: Harvard University Press, 1972), concludes that a measure of authoritarianism is necessary for the survival of intentional communities.

55. "The College House," p. 29; Hayden interview; Casey Hayden to author, 17 March 1997; Dorothy Burlage, interview with author, 9 December 1992.

56. Bonhoeffer, *Letters and Papers*, pp. 108, 26, 40.

57. Lois Boyd, "A Strange Forty-Four Hours," *Letter to Laymen*, February 1962, emphasis in original.

58. B. S., "Split Develops in the 'Community.'"

59. Cover, *Breakthrough*.

60. Bonhoeffer, *Life Together*, p. 38.

61. Dietrich Bonhoeffer, *The Cost of Discipleship* (New York: Macmillan, 1949; rev. ed., 1959), p. 67.

62. Bonhoeffer, *Letters and Papers*, p. 34; Bonhoeffer, *Ethics*, pp. 22, 327. For criticism of Bonhoeffer for his assent to using violence as a tool of resistance, see John M. Swomley Jr., *Liberation Ethics* (New York: Macmillan, 1972), pp. 144–165.

63. See Gustavo Gutierrez, "The Limitations of Modern Theology: On a Letter of Dietrich Bonhoeffer," in Gustavo Gutierrez, *The Power of the Poor in History*, trans. Robert R. Barr (Maryknoll, NY: Orbis, 1983), pp. 222–234; and Geffrey B.

Kelly, *Liberating Faith: Bonhoeffer's Message for Today* (Minneapolis: Augsburg Press, 1984), pp. 153–171.

Bonhoeffer's writings and example have been used in many instances to justify resistance to political authority. For a discussion of parallels between the thought of Bonhoeffer and Daniel Berrigan, a left-wing Catholic, see Larry Rasmussen, with Renate Bethge, *Dietrich Bonhoeffer—His Significance for North Americans* (Minneapolis: Fortress Press, 1990), pp. 43–56.

64. Bonhoeffer, *Letters and Papers*, p. 211.

65. Cox, *Secular City*, p. 110.

66. Cover, *Letter to Laymen*, February 1962.

67. Stanford, "The Contemporary Dilemma"; Don Warren, "The Summer Letter: No. 1," 16 June 1961.

68. "Our Common Rule (Tentative Outline)" (CFLC reprint), p. 1 (emphasis added).

69. In addition to the works by Fromm and May cited earlier, Rollo May, *Man's Search for Himself* (New York: Norton, 1953); and Viktor F. Frankl, *From Death-Camp to Existentialism: A Psychiatrist's Path to a New Therapy*, trans. Ilse Lasch (Boston: Beacon Press, 1959), figured in the curriculum.

70. Dottie Adams, "The Activist Man," *Letter to Laymen*, February 1962; Darrell, "The Paralyzed Man" (emphasis added).

71. Darrell, "The Paralyzed Man."

72. Warren, "The Summer Letter: No. 1."

73. "Mid-Year Retreat," February 4–5, 1961 (CFLC College House reprint), p. 1.

74. Cover, *Letter to Laymen*, February 1962.

75. "Mid-Year Retreat," p. 6; "The Moral Covenant," pp. 1, 2; "The College House," p. 59.

76. "Mid-Year Retreat," p. 6.

77. Dorothy Burlage interview; Hayden interview.

78. John A. Russell, letter, *Letter to Laymen*, May 1961.

79. "Parish Laymen's Weekend Seminar, Advanced Course CS I-C, Our Rule of Prayer."

80. "The New Image," in *Breakthrough*.

81. Lingo interview.

82. Godbold, "The New Possibility"; Hayden interview.

83. Examples of reports on events in the Third World read by Community participants are Alhaji Muhammad Mgileruma, "Africa in World Affairs: The Policy of Neutralism" (CLFC reprint, from *Vital Speeches of the Day*, 15 September 1961); and "The Message of the Third Assembly, World Council of Churches," adopted at New Delhi, India, the First Sunday in Advent, 1961 (CFLC reprint).

84. Wesley Poorman, "The Church on Today's Campus," *Letter to Laymen*, May 1961; Lingo interview.

85. Lingo interview.

86. Dick Simpson, interview with author, 8 March 1993.

87. "The New Man," in *Breakthrough*.

88. "Choreography for the Daily Office, 1960–1961" (CFLC reprint); "A New Experiment," in *Breakthrough*.

89. Erich Fromm, "The Nature of Symbolic Language," CFLC reprint from *The Forgotten Language: An Introduction to the Understanding of Dreams, Fairy Tales, and Myths* (New York: Rinehart, 1951).

90. Hayden interview.

91. Dugger, *Our Invaded Universities*, p. 76; Hayden to author; Clifford Geertz, "Religion as a Cultural System," in Clifford Geertz, *The Interpretation of Cultures: Selected Essays* (New York: Basic Books, 1973), p. 112. Geertz distinguishes the religious perspective sharply from the aesthetic, arguing that aesthetics focuses on the surface realities of the world around us, on the real, not the really real (pp. 111–112). Perhaps as "ideal types" these categorical differences have merit; if so, one sees in the Faith-and-Life Community a merging of aesthetic and religious perspectives. For a contemporary account of mysticism perused at the Community, see Colin Wilson, *The Outsider* (Boston: Houghton Mifflin, 1956).

92. Bob Breihan interview; Oakes interview. Casey Hayden thinks the debate took place during the 1956/1957 school year; Hayden to author.

Samuel Beckett, *Waiting for Godot: A Tragicomedy in Two Acts* (London: S. French, 1957).

93. Hayden interview; Hayden to author; Kirkpatrick Sale, *SDS* (New York: Random House, 1973), p. 40; Dorothy Burlage interview.

94. Breihan/Schmidt interview; Robb Burlage interview; Lingo interview; Simpson, *Politics of Compassion and Transformation*, pp. 255–263.

95. Judy Schleyer Blanton interview; B. S., "Split Develops in the 'Community'"; Hoyt Purvis, "Question of Goals Causes Staff Split," *Daily Texan*, 17 April 1962; Bob Bryant, interview with author, 8 July 1992; Lingo interview.

96. See Laurence Veysey, *The Communal Experience: Anarchist and Mystical Communities in Twentieth-Century America* (Chicago: University of Chicago Press, 1978).

97. *Port Huron Statement*, in James Miller, *"Democracy Is in the Streets": From Port Huron to the Siege of Chicago* (New York: Simon & Schuster, 1987), p. 332.

98. For a Jewish existentialism, highly compatible with Christian existentialism (as its promotion by King indicates), see Martin Buber, *I and Thou*, trans. Walter Kaufmann (New York: Scribner, 1970). Yet Buber's version is notable in this connection for the absence of a strong concept of love as that which binds people in I–Thou relationships. According to Buber, we should treat others as Thous simply because of our common humanity—the same justification given for the "indifference" of God's love, *agape*, in Christian thought. Nygren, *Eros and Agape*, asserts that the controlling idea of Judaism, the concept that binds humanity to God in that tradition, is *nomos*, indicating the imperative to obey God's law; thus he sets

Judaism radically apart from both Hellenic and Christian thinking on the human–divine relation.

99. Jo Eickmann, " 'The Community' Seeks a Life of Meaning," *Daily Texan*, 12 November 1959; Geertz, "Religion as a Cultural System," p. 112; *Port Huron Statement*, in Miller, *"Democracy Is in the Streets,"* p. 330.

Chapter 3

1. On the social gospel, see Charles Howard Hopkins, *The Rise of the Social Gospel in American Protestantism* (New Haven, CT: Yale University Press, 1940); Henry F. May, *Protestant Churches in Industrial America* (New York: Octagon Press, 1949); Paul Carter, *The Decline and Revival of the Social Gospel* (Ithaca, NY: Cornell University Press, 1954); Robert T. Handy, ed., *The Social Gospel in America, 1870–1920* (New York: Oxford University Press, 1966); Christopher Lasch, "Religious Contributions to Social Movements: Walter Rauschenbusch, the Social Gospel, and Its Critics," *Journal of Religious Ethics* 18 (Spring 1990): 7–25; Ralph Luker, *The Social Gospel in Black and White: American Racial Reform, 1885–1912* (Chapel Hill: University of North Carolina Press, 1991); and Susan Curtis, *A Consuming Faith: The Social Gospel and Modern American Culture* (Baltimore: Johns Hopkins University Press, 1991).

2. Quoted in Jimmy Banks, "YM(?)A—1: Open Door, Big Issues Stir Critics," *Dallas Morning News*, 18 March 1962.

3. Bob Breihan, interview with author, 10 November 1991.

4. Chandler Davidson, interview with author, 2 February 1993.

5. Bob Breihan interview.

6. "Panorama Focuses On: The University 'Y,' " *Daily Texan*, 15 May 1960.

7. Rosalie Oakes, interview with author, 23 February 1993.

8. Celia Morris, "Learning the Hard Way," *Change* 6 (July–August 1974): 45; Willie Morris, "Living Theology: Smith and the 'Y,' " *Texas Observer*, 23 March 1962; "Former 'Y' Exec Dies in Chapel Hill," *Daily Texan*, 29 January 1963.

9. Willie Morris, "Living Theology: Smith and the 'Y.' "

10. Casey Hayden to author, 17 March 1997. On the pacifist element in the early twentieth-century social gospel tradition, see C. Roland Marchand, *The American Peace Movement and Social Reform, 1898–1918* (Princeton, NJ: Princeton University Press, 1972), pp. 323–380; and Charles Chatfield, *For Peace and Justice: Pacifism in America, 1914–1941* (Knoxville: University of Tennessee Press, 1971). On the student peace movement of the 1930s, wracked by its involvement with the Communist Party apparatus, see Robert Cohen, *When the Old Left Was Young: Student Radicals and America's First Mass Student Movement, 1929–1941* (New York: Oxford University Press, 1993).

11. Frank Wright, interview with author, 30 June 1992; Frank L. Wright, *Out of Sight, Out of Mind: A Graphic Picture of Present Day Institutional Care of the Mentally Ill in America* (Philadelphia: National Mental Health Association, 1947).

12. Oakes interview.

13. On the distinctly mixed record of Christian liberals on racial issues in earlier decades, see Luker, *Social Gospel in Black and White*. The social gospel did not stand apart from the racist consensus in white America during the ironically named (in this connection) Progressive Era. Yolanda B. Wilkerson, *Interracial Programs of the YWCA's: An Inquiry under Auspices of the National Young Women's Christian Association* (New York: Woman's Press, 1948), details the Y movement's record and status on racial matters and urges a greater racial egalitarianism. I thank Nancy M. Robertson for alerting me to this report.

As an intriguing note on the links among the social gospel, the American left, and African American politics in this period, Yolanda Wilkerson was married to Doxey Wilkerson, a prominent black Communist in the 1930s and 1940s who later became a faculty member at historically black Bishop College in Marshall, Texas. Doxey A. Wilkerson, "Marxists and Academic Freedom," in Loren Baritz, ed., *The American Left: Radical Political Thought in the Twentieth Century* (New York: Basic Books, 1971), pp. 336–343, is a document of the McCarthy period (1953), a civil libertarian, Popular Front–style defense of people like himself, Marxists in academic life. It evokes a "progressive" politics, rather unusual in Texas, that accommodated elements as diverse as Christian liberalism and communism. Doxey Wilkerson reportedly advised the students at Bishop in their civil rights protests in 1960, which spurred students at the University Y in Austin to undertake their own protests, as I detail in chapter 4.

14. Oakes interview.

15. Dorothy Dawson Burlage, interview with author, 9 December 1992. Burlage warns against inferring a direct and simple causal connection between religion and political activism in this context, insisting instead that activism emerged from an environment of overlapping political and intellectual forces.

16. T. J. Jackson Lears, in *No Place of Grace: Antimodernism and the Transformation of American Culture, 1880–1920* (New York: Pantheon, 1981), asserts that by the late nineteenth century, "liberal Protestantism lost much of its power as an independent source of moral authority and became a handmaiden of the positivist world view" (p. 23) and that "a liberalized Protestant theology softened convictions and promoted ethical confusion" (p. 56). When the character of liberal Protestantism is considered in strictly philosophical and theological terms, the political history of liberal Protestantism in the twentieth-century United States is entirely effaced. If liberal Protestantism was philosophically "positivist," this does not mean that it was necessarily a conservative force. If liberal Protestantism sometimes seemed morally toothless and if it sometimes was put in the service of a ruling-class ideology, this did not have to be so; the rejection of Edwardsian hellfire and damnation did not imply a sunny optimism. Perhaps especially in conservative environments, liberal Protestantism served as a source of oppositional, politically liberal values through much of the twentieth century.

17. "Faith and Decision," "*Y*" *Notes* (University of Texas Y publication), spring 1962. The YWCA and YMCA chairs during the 1961/1962 school year were Susan Reed and Jim Neyland.

18. Ibid.

19. "Miller Recalls 'Y' History," *Daily Illini*, n.d. (December 1958, courtesy of Jim Neyland).

20. Robert Wuthnow, *The Restructuring of American Religion: Society and Faith Since World War II* (Princeton, NJ: Princeton University Press, 1988), details these signs of vitality. James D. Hudnut-Beumler, *Looking for God in the Suburbs: The Religion of the American Dream and Its Critics, 1945–1965* (New Brunswick, NJ: Rutgers University Press, 1994), stands virtually alone as an investigation into the content of this "revival."

21. A. L. Kershaw, *the new frontier for the student YMCA and YWCA* (New York: National Student Council of the YMCA and YWCA, 1955).

22. Ibid. Viktor Frankl, *From Death-Camp to Existentialism: A Psychiatrist's Path to a New Therapy*, trans. Ilse Lasch (Boston: Beacon Press, 1959), asserts that a universal "will to meaning," rather than a "will to power" or a "death-wish," was the fundamental human inclination.

23. Jim Neyland to author, 13 February 1993; Harvey Cox, *Radical Renewal: The Response of the Student YMCA and YWCA in a "World-Come-of-Age"* (New York: National Student Councils of the YMCA and YWCA, n.d. (1959); Harvey Cox, *The Secular City: Secularization and Urbanization in Theological Perspective* (New York: Collier, 1965; rev. ed., 1990).

24. Cox, *Radical Renewal*; Susan Reed, "Cox Advocates Critical Participation in the World," *Word of the Y's* (University of Texas Y publication), 11 January 1961.

25. Brochure for UT YMCA–YWCA, n.d. (1959/1960); Laura McNeil, "Day's Activities Cover Subjects Interesting University Students," *Daily Texan*, 10 December 1961; Larry Lee, " 'Y' Not Retreat," *Daily Texan*, 21 February 1961; James Neyland, "University 'Y' Criticisms Stem from Policy of Freedom to All," *Daily Texan*, 10 December 1961.

26. Neyland, "University 'Y' Criticisms"; "Plans for Cabinet Meeting, April 17, 1961" (from UT-Y).

27. Neyland, "University 'Y' Criticisms"; "What Is the Assembly?" in *Assembly Paper No. 2, Sixth National Student Assembly of the YMCA and YWCA, 27 Dec. 1958–2 Jan. 1959* (hereafter *Assembly Paper No. 2, Sixth NSAY*); Brochure for UT YMCA-YWCA, n.d. (1959/1960); "Phrases to Stimulate Thinking on the Nature of the Student YMCA and YWCA Movements," *Thirty-twelve* (Southwest Regional Student Y publication) 1, no. 4 (April 1961); Richard VanSteenkiste, " 'Y' Directors Express Purpose," *Daily Texan*, 17 February 1961.

28. "Conscience on Campus: An Interpretation of Christian Ethics for College Life, by Waldo Beach" (a summary and discussion), *Assembly Paper No. 2, Sixth NSAY*; "The Assembly Context," *Assembly Paper No. 2, Sixth NSAY*.

29. "The Assembly Context"; "Dialogue between the Biblical Faith and Your Campus," *Assembly Paper No. 2, Sixth NSAY*, emphasis in original.

30. "Dialogue between the Biblical Faith and Your Campus."

31. "Installation Banquet" (from UT-Y), 8 May 1962.

32. "Report of Section on Men and Women in the 20th Century," *Report on National Student Assembly of the YMCA and YWCA, December 1958–January 1959, University of Illinois, Urbana, Illinois* (hereafter *1958–1959 NSAY Report*); Jim Neyland, "The Changing Roles of Men and Women," *Thirty-twelve* 3, no. 2 (November 1962).

At one point Frank Wright and Anne Appenzellar asked Neyland if he knew anything about another male student, who was living at the Y and with whom Neyland had briefly shared an apartment and who apparently had made a pass at another man who lived in the Y (the student who was the object of the pass had told the staffers about it). Neyland informed Wright and Appenzellar that there were a lot of gay students on campus and that they experienced serious difficulties. The staffers reacted somewhat awkwardly at first but afterward suggested that Neyland chair a discussion group at the Y on "Changing Roles of Men and Women." Neyland to author.

33. "Study Material Announced for Regional Conference," *Word of the Y's*, 23 November 1960; "Report of Section on Work and Vocation," *Assembly Paper No. 2, Sixth NSAY*; Jim Neyland, "Our Response to Mass Culture," *Thirty-twelve* 3, no. 1 (October 1962).

34. Myra Nicol, "Issues Facing Higher Education," *Thirty-twelve* 3, no. 1 (October 1962).

35. Reed, "Cox Advocates Critical Participation in the World."

36. *"Who, Me? Involved?"* (brochure for Southwest Regional Conference of Student YMCA and YWCA, at Mt. Wesley, in Kerrville, Texas, 27 December 1959–2 January 1960); *Me in Reality* (brochure for Southwest Regional Conference, Student YMCA–YWCA, Camp Classen, Davis, Oklahoma, 31 May–6 June 1959); "Theme of 'Y' Play Understanding Needed for Man," *Daily Texan*, n.d. (courtesy of Jim Neyland); " 'Y' to Hold Auditions for Play by Student," *Daily Texan*, 23 February 1961.

37. " 'Ikthus' to Open Wednesday In Methodist Student Center," *Daily Texan*, 27 September 1960; " 'Godot' to Be Given by Methodists Friday," *Daily Texan*, 24 February 1961; Gary Mayer, "Ichthus Espouses Art," *Daily Texan*, 9 May 1961.

38. "The Seventh National Student Assembly of the YMCA and YWCA," *Thirty-twelve* 3, no. 1 (October 1962).

39. Jim Neyland and Myra Nicol, "Revolution and Response," *Thirty-twelve* 3, no. 1 (October 1962).

40. Neyland, "University 'Y' Criticisms."

41. Neyland and Wright—as well as Dorothy Burlage, Rasjidah Franklin-Alley, Brad Blanton, and Chandler Davidson—remembered her this way. Neyland to author; Wright interview; Dorothy Burlage interview; Rasjidah Franklin-Alley, interview with author, 18 March 1993; Brad Blanton, interview with author, 14 April 1993; Davidson interview. Reports of students' summer 1960 activities in *Word of the Y's*, August 1960.

42. Casey Hayden, interview with author, 2 March 1993.

43. Hayden interview; Hayden to author; Tom Hayden, *Reunion: A Memoir* (New York: Random House, 1988), p. 48. Casey Hayden disputes Tom Hayden's rendition of her childhood.

44. Hayden, *Reunion*, p. 108; Hayden interview. Ronnie Dugger, *Our Invaded Universities: Form, Reform, and New Starts* (New York: Norton, 1974), p. 76, waxes rhapsodic on the effect Hayden had on him and other men, indicating that some portion of political motivation in this circle derived from young men's competition to impress young women with their "commitment."

45. Hayden interview.

46. Hayden to author; text of Hayden's speech courtesy of Angus Johnston and Casey Hayden. In slightly different form, these sections of her speech are reproduced in Hayden, *Reunion*, pp. 41–42. Mary King also recounts the incident and the positive audience reaction. Mary King, *Freedom Song: A Personal Story of the 1960s Civil Rights Movement* (New York: Morrow, 1986), pp. 74–75.

47. Franklin-Alley interview; Neyland to author.

48. Franklin-Alley interview.

49. On the nonaligned movement and its relation to peace activism in the context of the cold war, see Lawrence S. Wittner, *One World or None*, vol. 1 of *The Struggle against the Bomb* (Stanford, CA: Stanford University Press, 1994).

50. Neyland to author; Franklin-Alley interview.

51. "National Student Assembly YMCA–YWCA, 1958–1959, Leadership Teams"; "In Search of World Community," *Assembly Paper No. 2, Sixth NSAY*; "Report of Section on In Search of World Community," *Report on NSAY, 1958/1959*.

52. "Study Material Announced for Regional Conference," *Word of the Y's*, 23 November 1960; *World Crisis Confronts College Students* (brochure for Southwest Regional Conference of Student YMCA–YWCA, held at Mt. Wesley, Kerrville, Texas, 27 December 1961–1 January 1962).

53. Cruce Stark, "A World in Revolution," *Thirty-twelve* 3, no. 2 (November 1962).

54. "Resolution regarding the People's Republic of China," in "Actions of the 1961 Southwest Regional Assembly of the Student YMCA & YWCA," *Thirty-twelve* 1, no. 4 (April 1961); "Resolution regarding the Peace Corps," *Thirty-twelve* 1, no. 4 (April 1961).

55. Bill Fielder, " 'Y' Relations with UN Prove of Mutual Value," *Summer Texan*, 29 July 1960; Fielder, "Sit-ins Viewed in World Conference," *Daily Texan*, 15 September 1960; Ree Strange, "YMCA's 'Building for Brotherhood' Program Takes Two University Students to West Africa," *Daily Texan*, 1 October 1961. Fielder also noted that the World Student Christian Federation, meeting that summer in Strasbourg, France, voted to support the sit-in movement and that NSCF members in the United States had circulated to student Christian groups around the United States "Information Letters" concerning the sit-ins in an attempt to counteract hostile coverage by the commercial media.

56. " 'Y' Tours Offer Varied Vacation," *Daily Texan*, 15 January 1963; "Reed to Discuss Russia at 'Y,' " *Daily Texan*, 7 November 1961; Jimmy Banks, "University YM(?)A—5: Leaders Say Their Views Have Hurt," *Dallas Morning News*, 22 March 1962; Banks, "University YM(?)A—3: Coed Draws Criticism on Disarmament Views," *Dallas Morning News*, 20 March 1962.

57. *Word of the Y's*, 23 November 1960.

58. Carolyn Coker, "Travelers Tell Views of World Problems," *Daily Texan*, 22 September 1961; James Terry, "Makula Tells of Resistance to Whites among Africans," *Daily Texan*, 1 December 1961.

59. "Cuban–US Situation 'Y' Topic Tonight," *Daily Texan*, 21 March 1961. The NCSF representative was James Monsonis, the organization's president, who later became a prominent early member of SDS.

60. Jo Eickmann, "Integration at UT Due Check Friday," *Daily Texan*, 12 May 1961.

61. Vivien Franklin, "Abolition of HUAC," *Word of the Y's*, 11 January 1961; Jim Hyatt, editorial, "Emotions Aside," *Daily Texan*, 15 December 1960 (Hyatt noted that Franklin planned to send the collected signatures to U.S. Representative James Roosevelt, who was to introduce a bill in the House to abolish HUAC); " 'Y' to Present HUAC's Move," *Daily Texan*, 16 February 1961; Harvey Little, " 'Y' Study Group Criticizes HUAC Anti-Communist Film," *Daily Texan*, 17 February 1961; "Resolutions on the House Un-American Activities Committee," in "Actions of the 1961 Southwest Regional Assembly of the Student YMCA & YWCA," *Thirty-twelve* 1, no. 4 (April 1961).

62. Ronnie Dugger, "We Are the Murderers," *Observer*, 10 June 1961; Jimmy Banks, "University YM(?)A—4: The 'C' Causes Disagreement," *Dallas Morning News*, 21 March 1962; "Students Protest Williams Sentence," *Daily Texan*, 18 May 1961 (the prisoner's name was Charles Elbert Williams).

63. "Resolution on Race Relations," *Report on NSAY, 1958/1959*. Jim Neyland noted that the strongly worded resolution concerning racial discrimination in the Y and in fraternities and sororities printed in this report actually went down to defeat but that an amended version, similar in substance, was passed.

64. Neyland to author.

65. "Peaceful Efforts for Integration Continued," *Word of the Y's*, April 1959.

66. University of Texas YMCA–YWCA Cabinet Agenda, Monday, 29 February 1960; Neyland to author; Franklin-Alley interview. Franklin-Alley recalls getting arrested on this trip, but she is not sure, and Neyland's account is far more detailed, so I accept it as authoritative. If they all had been arrested on this occasion, I think it doubtful any of them would have forgotten it.

67. Neyland to author.

68. " 'Y' Group to Work in Race Relations," *Daily Texan*, 14 September 1960.

69. See Sara M. Evans and Harry C. Boyte, *Free Spaces: The Sources of Democratic Change in America* (New York: Harper & Row, 1986).

Chapter 4

1. Jose E. Limon, "The Expressive Culture of a Chicano Student Group at the University of Texas at Austin, 1967–1975" (Ph.D. diss., University of Texas at Austin, 1978), fig. 2, p. 67. In these years, respectively, 17,762 and 27,345 students enrolled overall. Limon speculates that the loans and grants made available to college students through the 1958 National Defense Education Act (NDEA) changed the composition of the Mexican American student contingent at UT, making it easier for Chicano students from working-class and lower-middle-class families to attend.

2. "18 Years Pass . . . Long Fight Ends," *Daily Texan*, 17 May 1964; Almetris M. Duren with Louise Iscoe, *Overcoming: A History of Black Integration at the University of Texas at Austin* (Austin: University of Texas at Austin, 1974).

3. Pat Rusch, "One Big 'Cannot'—a Negro Student's Life," *Daily Texan*, 6 December 1960; Willie Morris, "Integration at U.T.," *Texas Observer*, 21 October 1960; "Race Relations Research Finds 135 Negro Students," *Daily Texan*, 12 December 1962.

4. Rusch, "One Big 'Cannot' "; Joanne Williams, "Whitis Dorm—Improved Negro Housing," *Daily Texan*, 8 December 1960; Sandra Cason and Mary Simpson, letter, *Daily Texan*, 9 December 1960; John Henry Faulk, letter, *Daily Texan*, 13 December 1960.

5. "Integration Activities Accelerated When Negro Arrives on Campus," *Daily Texan*, 13 December 1962; Robert Bell, interview with author, 11 March 1993.

6. Aldon Morris established that student sit-ins began before the famous Greensboro events of 1960 but that those protests sparked an explosion of sit-in activity around the Southeast. Aldon D. Morris, *The Origins of the Civil Rights Movement: Black Communities Organizing for Change* (New York: Free Press, 1984), pp. 188–213.

7. "Protest at UT," *Observer*, 11 March 1960; Jerry Conn, "Integration Policies Protested," *Daily Texan*, 13 March 1960.

8. Ronnie Dugger, "The Chilled Sunlight," *Observer*, 11 March 1960; "Panorama Focuses on UT's Protesting Pickets," *Daily Texan*, 13 March 1960; Carlos D. Conde, "The Fuse Is Lighted," *Daily Texan*, 18 March 1960.

9. Jerry Conn, "Race Protesters Call Talks with Wilson 'Unsatisfactory,' " *Daily Texan*, 16 March 1960; " 'The Group' Calls Protest Truce," *Daily Texan*, 17 March 1960.

10. "Segregated Cafes Denied Approval," *Daily Texan*, 7 January 1960; " 'Steer' Sign," *Daily Texan*, 14 January 1960; Editorial, "New Step in Steer Here," *Daily Texan*, 8 January 1960.

11. "Fire Hoses Scatter Negroes in Lunch Counter Incident," *Daily Texan*, 31 March 1960; "Bold Sit-Ins in Marshall," *Observer*, 1 April 1960; "From Chapel to Dousings," *Observer*, 8 April 1960; "Eleven Rules," *Observer*, 8 April 1960; "Professor Fired in Racial Strife," *Daily Texan*, 1 April 1960; "An Ex-Red Prof," *Observer*, 8 April 1960; "Probers Say Reds Instigated Sit-Ins," *Observer*, 18 August 1961.

12. "KKK Symbol Cut on Negro," *Daily Texan*, 9 March 1960; "T.S.U. Students' 'Sit-Ins,' " *Observer*, 11 March 1960; "Lunch Counters Serve Negroes," *Daily Texan*, 17 March 1960; "Negro Hit by White; Joske's Closes Cafes," *Daily Texan*, 4 May 1960.

13. Pat Rusch, "Not Another Marshall Here," *Daily Texan*, 22 April 1960.

14. Bettye Swales, "Local Cafe Integration Demanded in 7 Days," *Daily Texan*, 2 April 1960; Julia Salter and Bob Moore, "Students Promise Sit-Ins; Ask LBJ to Support Move," *Daily Texan*, 27 April 1960.

15. Bob Moore and Julia Salter, "Bi-Racial Student Group Picketing for Integration," *Daily Texan*, 28 April 1960; Bob Moore, "Counters Refuse Service in 'Sit-In Strike' by 150," *Daily Texan*, 1 May 1960; "Students 'Sit-In' at Bus Stations," *Daily Texan*, 6 May 1960; Robbie Downing, "SA Endorses Cause of Racial Protestors," *Daily Texan*, 5 May 1960.

16. Editorial, "The Sit-Ins' Fate," *Daily Texan*, 18 May 1960; "Two More Cities' Stores Integrate; Prof Says Fired," *Observer*, 20 May 1960.

17. Lenice Larkin and Oliver Smith (Regional Y staff), "Marshall Bulletin no. 2," 12 April 1960.

18. Students of Bishop College to their supporters, 18 April 1960; Casey Hayden, interview with author, 2 March 1993.

19. Hayden interview; Robert Stone, interview with author, 28 May 1993. Dorothy Burlage, for one, later went to work on NSA's Southern Project, heading up a local organizing project in the South, on a grant from the Marshall Field Foundation that Paul Potter, the NSA National Affairs vice president, had secured. Potter later became president of SDS. Dorothy Dawson and Paul Potter to students, 19 April 1962 (courtesy of Jim Neyland).

20. "Pro-Integration Group Organized," *Daily Texan*, 30 November 1960; the quotation is from Chandler Davidson.

21. Chandler Davidson, interview with author, 2 February 1993; Chandler Davidson, "The Jabberwock," *Daily Texan*, 12 October 1960.

22. Davidson interview; Chandler Davidson, "The Jabberwock," *Daily Texan*, 3 May 1961.

23. Davidson interview.

24. Bell interview; Bert Campbell, "Bomb Try Brings Arrest of Students," *Daily Texan*, 1 December 1960. Two UT students apparently had planted the pipe bomb.

25. "Minister to Speak on Social Change," *Daily Texan*, 16 November 1960; Bob Sherrill, "Sit-Ins' Teacher," *Observer*, 25 November 1960. Smiley was a kind of one-man road show, spreading Gandhian ideas throughout the South. He spent much of 1956 in Montgomery, Alabama, during the famous bus boycott led by Martin Luther King Jr., running "nonviolent workshops" with Bayard Rustin, and according to Aldon Morris, it was in the course of long discussions with Smiley that King became a committed Gandhian. Morris, *Origins of the Civil Rights Movement*, pp. 157–161.

26. Students for Direct Action, "Statement of Purpose," letter, *Daily Texan*, 20 December 1960; Leon Graham, "Integration Groups Work at One Project at a Time," *Daily Texan*, 7 December 1960.

27. "Resolution" (SDA petition stating that after 1 April 1961, the undersigned would attend only integrated theaters that were independent theaters or owned by fully integrated chains, n.d., courtesy of Jim Neyland); Students for Direct Action, "Statement of Purpose."

28. Bob Savage, "Bill Controls Race Sit-Ins," *Daily Texan*, 25 April 1961; Students for Direct Action, "Statement of Purpose."

29. Sandra Cason, "Moral Issue Examined," *Daily Texan*, 11 January 1961.

30. Ronnie Dugger, "Doing Something Real," *Observer*, 30 December 1960, emphasis in original; Graham, "Integration Groups Work at One Project at a Time."

31. Graham, "Integration Groups Work at One Project at a Time"; Dick Simpson, interview with author, 8 March 1993; Dick Simpson, *The Politics of Compassion and Transformation* (Athens: Swallow Press/Ohio University Press, 1989), p. 253; Charles Erickson, interview with author, 30 June 1993.

32. Chandler Davidson, "The Jabberwock," *Daily Texan*, 17 May 1961.

33. Ronnie Dugger, "Doing Something Real."

34. Ibid.

35. Davidson interview; Rasjidah Franklin-Alley, interview with author, 18 March 1993.

36. "Young Demos Form Committee on Civil Rights," *Daily Texan*, 15 November 1960; Graham, "Integration Groups Work at One Project at a Time"; Ed Horn, " 'Ticket Buyers' on Drag Again," *Daily Texan*, 7 December 1960.

37. " 'Action' Group to Pass Cards," *Daily Texan*, 29 November 1960; " 'Y' Integrationists Pass 3,800 Cards," *Daily Texan*, 20 December 1960; "Freshman Poll Results," *Daily Texan*, 18 December 1960.

38. Brad Blanton, interview with author, 14 April 1992; "One Man's Protest," *Observer*, 18 March 1961; Judy Schleyer Blanton, interview with author, 17 May 1993.

39. Don Myers, "2 Youths Arrested in Picket Assault," *Daily Texan*, 11 January 1961; "Austin Man Jailed in Picketer Assault," *Daily Texan*, 12 January 1961; Brad Blanton interview.

40. Ronnie Dugger, "UT Stand-Ins Will Continue," *Observer*, 30 December 1960.

41. *Daily Texan*, 9 December 1960; "English Department," *Daily Texan*, 12 January 1961. Letters pledging faculty support came from the departments of anthropology, chemistry, Germanic languages, history, Romance languages, and social work and a more qualified approval from the economics department, among others. "Faculty Approves," *Daily Texan*, 20 December 1960; "Firing Line," *Daily Texan*, 11 January 1961; "Dislike Exclusion," *Daily Texan*, 31 January 1961; "Pro-Integration," *Daily Texan*, 21 February 1961.

42. "Faculty Ad Asks Movie Integration," *Daily Texan*, 18 May 1961.

43. Dugger, "UT Stand-Ins Continue"; "Stand-In Leaders Plan to Continue Demonstrations," *Daily Texan*, 5 January 1961. Casey Hayden had gotten in touch with Roosevelt during Christmas vacation and told her about the stand-ins. The students wanted to get into the New York media market because the parent company of one of the theaters they were targeting was ABC–Paramount, based in New York. The theater management swore that only the corporate brass could decide to integrate the establishment.

44. "New Republic Story Relates UT Integration Moves," *Daily Texan*, 16 April 1961.

45. "Stand-In Leaders Plan to Continue Demonstrations"; Dugger, "UT Stand-Ins Will Continue"; "SDA Organizes National Pickets," *Daily Texan*, 3 February 1961; "SDA Promised Nationwide Aid," *Daily Texan*, 8 February 1961.

46. Dave Crossley, "Numbers Grow as Groups Join to Protest Segregation," *Daily Texan*, 15 January 1961; "Stand-Ins in Austin Reach Peak," *Observer*, 18 February 1961; "Texas Cities Witness Protests," *Observer*, 18 February 1961.

47. Don Myers, "Schools to Organize Stand-In Efforts," *Daily Texan*, 28 February 1961.

48. "SDA Members 'Visit' Cafes," *Daily Texan*, 5 March 1961; "Aid Drive to Begin for 400 Negroes," *Daily Texan*, 2 February 1961; Hayden interview; Guadalupe Duarte, "Bonner Plans Third 'Strike,'" *Daily Texan*, 17 March 1961.

49. Ronnie Cohen, letter, *Daily Texan*, 15 February 1961; Dugger, "Doing Something Real"; Judy Schleyer Blanton interview; Ed Horn, "'Ticket Buyers' on Drag Again."

50. Dugger, "Doing Something Real"; "Stand-Ins in Austin Reach Peak."

51. Chandler Davidson, "The Jabberwock," *Daily Texan*, 8 February 1961 (the other students were Lewis Woods and Don Hill); Bell interview; Davidson interview.

52. Martha Spencer, "Ticketers Continue Drag Demonstrations," *Daily Texan*, 18 December 1960.

53. Dugger, "Doing Something Real"; Ed Horn, "'Ticket Buyers' on Drag Again"; Ronnie Cohen, letter, *Daily Texan*, 15 February 1961; Don Myers, "SDA's Efforts Await Results"; "Stand-Ins in Austin Reach Peak." The *Texan* editors noted that the Cuban newspaper *Revolution* had run a picture of a black female UT student in line at a stand-in on the Drag; Editorial, "To See Ourselves," *Daily Texan*, 11 January 1961.

54. Peter Gessner, "The Search for a Way thru the Wasteland," *Village Voice*, 24 August 1961; "Appy" (Anne Appenzellar) to Jim Neyland, 16 August 1961.

55. Ronnie Dugger, "Austin Theaters Give In," *Observer*, 9 September 1961.

56. Ibid.; "Drag Theaters Adopt Policy of Integration," *Daily Texan*, 12 September 1961.

57. This development is consistent with Aldon Morris's analysis of the more dramatic events in Birmingham in 1963. According to Morris, in that case the disruption of business by boycotts and demonstrations caused the white economic elite of the city to break ranks with the political elite and to negotiate with civil rights

leaders over questions of integration. Morris, *Origins of the Civil Rights Movement*, pp. 266–274.

58. Wade quoted in Hoyt Purvis, " 'tween the horns," *Daily Texan*, 19 December 1961.

59. Ronnie Dugger, *Our Invaded Universities: Form, Reform, and New Starts* (New York: Norton, 1974), p. 76; Robb Burlage, interview with author, 1 June 1992; Dorothy Dawson Burlage, interview with author, 9 December 1992; Claude Allen, interview with author, 21 January 1993; Davidson interview.

60. Hayden interview; Tom Hayden, *Reunion: A Memoir* (New York: Random House, 1988), p. 52; Casey Hayden to author, 17 March 1997. Tom Hayden writes that they indeed left out the vow of fidelity, not mentioning Mathews's ploy. Possibly Casey Hayden had reason to concoct this part of the story, just as Tom Hayden had reason to leave it out, but omitting it would be a far less elaborate fib than devising it out of whole cloth, which makes me inclined to believe it.

I thank Casey Hayden for giving me a copy of her wedding program, which begins with the line quoted from Ecclesiastes.

61. Neyland to author.

62. Hayden interview; Brad Blanton interview.

63. "Human Relations Conference for 4 States Opens Friday," *Daily Texan*, 13 December 1961; "Timmons to Visit Anti-Violence Talk," *Daily Texan*, 27 April 1962; memo, from SSACC to Platform Speakers and Panel Members for Conference on Social Action and Concern, n.d. (courtesy of Jim Neyland); "Integrationists Continue Action," *Daily Texan*, 17 March 1963.

64. Jim Davis and Lee McFadden, "3 Students Face Trial," *Daily Texan*, 14 May 1963; George Goss, letter, *Daily Texan*, 17 May 1963.

65. Jim Neyland to author, 13 February 1993; Jim Hyatt, "Regents Will Discuss Variety of Subjects," *Daily Texan*, 29 September 1961.

66. Ann Apel, "Student Party," *Daily Texan*, 16 October 1961; "Student Party Set Meeting," *Daily Texan*, 5 February 1961.

67. "From Student Apathy to Student Concern through Student Party" (Student Party platform, spring 1961, courtesy of Jim Neyland); Susan Allen, "Student Party," *Daily Texan*, 5 October 1961.

68. Willie Morris, " 'Mo' Holds His Ground," *Observer*, 25 August 1961. Olian was not an SP member but had the SP's endorsement.

69. Pat Rusch and Richard VanSteenkiste, "Student Party Gains on Reps," *Daily Texan*, 26 October 1961; Bill Hamilton, "New Assemblyman Jordan Breaks Political Race Barrier," *Daily Texan*, 26 October 1961; Neyland to author.

70. Debbie Howell, "Sports Integration OK'd by Assembly," *Daily Texan*, 12 May 1961; Jim Hyatt, "Integration Poll Wins in Record Voting," *Daily Texan*, 26 October 1961; Morris, " 'Mo' Holds His Ground"; Debbie Howell, "Tempers Flare Openly in Fiery SA Debates," *Daily Texan*, 4 October 1961; Howell, "Demonstrators Delay SA; Olian's Resolutions Argued," *Daily Texan*, 13 October 1961; Lou Ann Walker, "Rep Party Victory Sweeps Ten Seats," *Daily Texan*, 1 November 1962.

71. See Lawrence Wittner, *Rebels against War: The American Peace Movement, 1933–1983* (Philadelphia: Temple University Press, 1984), pp. 240–275.

72. Vicke Caldwell, "UT Student 'Peace' Demonstrators Picket, Debate," *Daily Texan*, 18 February 1962; Laura McNeil, " 'Turn' Move Has Friends," *Daily Texan*, 16 February 1962; Caldwell, "Pacifists Protest US Nuclear Tests," *Daily Texan*, 26 April 1962; Martha Tipps, "Austin Minister Files Complaint on Use of Zilker," *Daily Texan*, 23 March 1962.

73. "Socialist Candidate to Speak for Peace," *Daily Texan*, 25 March 1962; leaflet for "Picnic for Peace," n.d. (courtesy of Jim Neyland); Laura McNeil, "Peace Picnickers Hear Thomas Talk," *Daily Texan*, 27 March 1962.

74. Brad Blanton interview. According to a press account of a faculty panel discussion held after the crisis had passed, "that Kennedy made the right move in his actions concerning Cuba was one of the few points of agreement." Lynne McDonald, "Radkey, Shattuck, Schmitt Tell Pros, Cons of Cuban Situation," *Daily Texan*, 30 October 1962.

75. " 'Brains—Not Bombs,' " *Daily Texan*, 28 October 1962; Robert Miller, "Pacifist Author Calls US 'Warfare State,' " *Daily Texan*, 30 November 1962.

Maurice Isserman, *If I Had A Hammer . . . : The Death of the Old Left and the Birth of the New Left* (New York: Basic Books, 1987), pp. 127–128, 151–155, and Wittner, *Rebels against War*, pp. 247–250, discuss Bigelow's journey on the "Golden Rule" and its significance.

76. "Student Pacifists Oppose Shelters," *Daily Texan*, 6 November 1962; Desta Brown, "Fallout Shelters: Adequate or Necessary?" *Daily Texan*, 14 December 1962; "300 Sign Petition for End of Draft," *Daily Texan*, 22 February 1963; Charles D. Laughlin, Jr., "Drive Initiated to Stop Draft," *Daily Texan*, 1 February 1963.

77. Pat Rusch, "Dorm Coeds Hear UT Housing Segregation Restrictions," *Daily Texan*, 27 September 1961—the offending article; one wonders whether the reporter's use of the phrases "Negro boys" and "Negro girls" to describe university students added to the sting that the report delivered. Rusch, "Negroes Stage Sit-In at Kinsolving Dorm," *Daily Texan*, 20 October 1961.

78. Hugh Lowe, "Negro Demonstrators Face Probationary Punishment," *Daily Texan*, 22 October 1961; Stephen B. Oates et al., letter, *Daily Texan*, 29 September 1961; "Erstwhile Protestors Agree to Ceasefire," *Daily Texan*, 24 October 1961.

79. Willie Morris, "Integration Dispute at UT," *Observer*, 27 October 1961; Jeanne Reinert, "Olian Tells Dormitory Ruling at Student Gathering in 'Y,' " *Daily Texan*, 1 November 1961.

At the end of the cooling-off week, the administration told Olian that those students who admitted taking part in the sit-in would stay on probation for the rest of the semester and that those who simply refused to cooperate with the administration's interrogators would remain on probation indefinitely.

80. Ronnie Dugger, "A Drawn Conflict at the University," *Observer*, 3 December 1961; E. Ernest Goldstein, "Goldstein Clarifies Goals of Faculty Resolution," *Daily Texan*, 31 October 1961.

81. Goldstein, "Goldstein Clarifies Goals of Faculty Resolution"; David T. Lopez, "University Officials Named in Dorm Desegregation Suit," *Daily Texan*, 9 November 1961.

82. Robb Burlage, letter, *Daily Texan*, 9 November 1961.

83. "Desegregation at Tech," *Observer*, 29 July 1961; "Rice Voting Favors Discrimination Ban," *Daily Texan*, 19 December 1961; "Baylor Congress OK's Integration," *Daily Texan*, 6 April 1962; "End of Race Ban Asked in Sports," *Daily Texan*, 4 January 1962; "TCU Integrates Most Facilities," *Daily Texan*, 28 January 1964.

84. "New 'Y' Resolution Asks Integration," *Daily Texan*, 27 October 1963; "UT Negroes Set 'Rights' Stand," *Daily Texan*, 7 November 1963; Laura Burns, "Regents Approve Activity Integration," *Daily Texan*, 10 November 1963.

85. Dave McNeely, "Regents Drop Dormitory Segregation; University Becomes Totally Integrated," *Daily Texan*, 17 May 1964; Dave Wilson, "Law Suit Barred Action by Regents," *Daily Texan*, 17 May 1964.

86. "Proposal to Limit Use of 'Y' Heard," *Daily Texan*, 16 February 1961; Hoyt Purvis, "'Y' May Leave SDA Homeless," *Daily Texan*, 17 February 1961; "'Y' Policy Defined," *Daily Texan*, 17 March 1961.

87. James Neyland, "University 'Y' Criticisms Stem from Policy of Freedom to All," *Daily Texan*, 10 December 1961.

88. Jimmy Banks, "University YM(?)A—2: Short Film on Pacifism Causes Row," 19 March 1962; Banks, "University YM(?)A—3: Coed Draws Criticism on Disarmament Views," 20 March 1962; Banks, "University YM(?)A—4: The 'C' Causes Disagreement," 21 March 1962; Banks, "University YM(?)A—5: Leaders Say Their Views Have Hurt," 22 March 1962; and Banks, "University YM(?)A—6: Wright Exerts Influence on Thinking of Students," 23 March 1962, all in *Dallas Morning News*; "Downtown Y's Disclaim Link with Campus Units," *Dallas Morning News* 23 March 1962; "Regional Council Asks Study of 'Y' Programs," *Austin American-Statesman*, n.d. (March 1962).

89. Casey (Hayden) to Jim (Neyland) and Susan (Reed), 5 April 1962, courtesy of Jim Neyland.

90. "Group Criticizes Article by Banks," *Dallas Morning News*, n.d. (March 1962, courtesy of Jim Neyland); Southern Methodist University YMCA/YWCA cabinet to University of Texas, 29 March 1962; James B. Havens, president, SMU-Y, to Frank Wright, 1 April 1962; John Rinehart, Regional Council cochair of YMCA, to UT-Y cabinet, 28 March 1962; Bruce B. Maguire, National Student Committee of the YMCA, to Edwin Price, James Neyland, and Frank Wright, 31 May 1962.

91. Debbie Howell and David Lopez, "'Y' Cabinet Talks about DMN Series," *Daily Texan*, n.d. (April 1962, courtesy of Jim Neyland).

92. Neyland to author; Dale T. Griffee, chairman, Texas Student Ecumenical Council, to George Cogswell, 14 July 1962; Franklin-Alley interview.

93. Jim Hyatt, "'Y' Staff May Shrink from Lack of Funds," *Daily Texan*, 10

October 1961; Susan Ford, " 'Y's Inclusiveness Merits Confidence," *Daily Texan*, 23 October 1962.

94. "Silber Opposes Rump YD Group," *Daily Texan*, 11 May 1962 (Silber was the faculty sponsor of the UT Young Democrats and urged the conservatives to accept the membership's election returns); Jane Paganini, "Yarborough Promises Control of Lobbyists," *Daily Texan*, 17 May 1962; Brad Blanton interview.

95. Larry Lee, "Campus Chest Committee Cuts 'Y' off Annual Drive," *Daily Texan*, 18 October 1962; Ford, " 'Y's Inclusiveness Merits Confidence"; "Independent Income for 'Y'?" *Daily Texan*, 24 October 1962; Editorial, "Charity for . . . (Almost) All," *Daily Texan*, 19 October 1962; " . . . Poor Start," *Daily Texan*, 9 December 1962.

96. Dave Crossley, "2 Reporters Ask for Help after Beating," *Daily Texan*, 13 October 1961; Pat McClure, "NSA Congress Opposes HUAC, Cuban Policies," *Daily Texan*, 4 October 1961.

97. McClure, "NSA Congress Opposes HUAC, Cuban Policies"; Lee McFadden, "NSA—Its Structure, Effectiveness Reviewed," *Daily Texan*, 5 February 1963; Martha Tipps, "Six of Nine Urge UT to Stay in NSA," *Daily Texan*, 6 March 1963.

98. Debbie Howell, "Garvey Defends NSA," *Daily Texan*, 2 February 1962; Carolyn Coe, "Election Rivals Slam, Laud NSA," *Daily Texan*, 13 March 1963.

99. McFadden, "NSA—Its Structure, Effectiveness Reviewed"; Editorial, "NSA: An Available Structure," *Daily Texan*, 7 March 1963.

100. Martha Tipps, "59 Per Cent Say, 'Down with NSA,' " *Daily Texan*, 14 March 1963; Charmayne Marsh, "Sports, Band, Others Suspended from Blanket Tax; UT Quits NSA," *Daily Texan*, 29 March 1963.

101. Carol Darrell et al., letter, *Daily Texan*, 20 March 1963.

102. Houston Wade, "Behind Scenes at Circus," *Daily Texan*, 3 April 1962.

103. Stone interview.

104. Burlage made this comment at a panel on the new left at a conference, "Toward a History of the 1960s," organized by the State Historical Society of Wisconsin, in Madison, 30 April 1993.

105. Susan Lynn, *Progressive Women in Conservative Times: Racial Justice, Peace, and Feminism, 1945 to the 1960s* (New Brunswick, NJ: Rutgers University Press, 1992), makes this quite clear in general. On Hayden and King, see Sara Evans, *Personal Politics: The Roots of Women's Liberation in the Civil Rights Movement and the New Left* (New York: Vintage Books, 1980), pp. 98–100. In chapter 8 I discuss Hayden's later role as well.

106. Student activists from UT were among those who made the long walk from the Rio Grande Valley, hotbed of the United Farm Workers' (UFW) organizing drive, to Austin in August 1966 to press their case before Governor Connally, only to have Connally and other state officials intercept them on the highway, creating a dramatic tableau involving the governor and two clergymen representing the farmworkers. "The Confrontation," *Observer*, 16 September 1966. Under Cesar Chavez's direction, in California, the UFW undertook a more widely known orga-

nizing and consumer boycott drive in the 1960s and afterward. Ronnie Dugger, "Cesar Chavez' Plan," *Observer*, 16 September 1966.

This labor and civil rights movement was an important historical development and deserves scholarly attention in its own right. But it is not part of the story I am tracing in this book, which is the emergence of a white youth left. Students involved in support work for the farmworkers tended to distance themselves from the student left, at a time when in fact there was a prominent student left. Frances Barton, interview with author, 25 June 1992; Lonn Taylor, interview with author, 22 May 1992.

107. Bruce Maxwell, "Cries Bitter Tears," *Daily Texan*, 4 October 1963.

108. Franklin-Alley interview.

109. All this information on Neyland is from Neyland to author.

Chapter 5

1. Kirkpatrick Sale, *SDS* (New York: Random House, 1973), p. 113.

2. Todd Gitlin, *The Sixties: Years of Hope, Days of Rage* (New York: Bantam, 1987), p. 186.

3. Ibid.

4. James Miller, *"Democracy Is in the Streets": From Port Huron to the Siege of Chicago* (New York: Simon & Schuster, 1987), pp. 241–254, 256, terms the experiment a failure and argues that SDS could have used more, not less, central organization. Sale, *SDS*, pp. 223–235, first covered these events, with greater evenhandedness. The key internal document that states the Texas viewpoint in these organizational disputes is Jeffrey Shero, "The S.D.S. National Office: Bureaucracy, Democracy and Decentralization," SDS Papers, reel 20, 3:3, prepared for a national SDS conference held in December 1965, in which Jeff Shero Nightbyrd (he took the name Nightbyrd only in the 1970s) argued for a regionalized restructuring of SDS in which the national office would serve as a clearinghouse for information and a coordinating center among rather autonomous chapters, not as a policy-setting organ.

Tensions burst into the open in 1965 with regard to SDS policy on the Vietnam War and the military draft. Focusing on this controversy, Todd Gitlin also sides with the camp of central coordination and policy planning, against the advocates of decentralization, in *The Whole World Is Watching: Mass Media in the Making and Unmaking of the New Left* (Berkeley and Los Angeles: University of California Press, 1980).

Following these debates, SDS held a national membership referendum on the question of whether the organization even should have national officers with authority to speak for the membership. Nightbyrd, who was the national vice president, played an important role in urging this referendum. Yet his comrades in Austin thought the whole matter was silly, and they didn't follow the national office's lead anyway. The letter from Texas to the *SDS Bulletin*, cited in note 5, was the SDS-UT chapter's response to this referendum.

5. Brethren of the Pineywoods, "Damnation from Texas," *SDS Bulletin*, 27 October 1965.

6. Miller, *"Democracy Is in the Streets,"* pp. 141–143.

7. Quoted in Gitlin, *The Sixties*, p. 115.

8. Miller, *"Democracy Is in the Streets,"* p. 79. The activist was Steve Max.

9. Mills is commonly mistaken for a Marxist, as he was in his lifetime. For a corrective, which stresses his early immersion in American pragmatist thought, see Rick C. Tilman, *C. Wright Mills: A Native Radical and His American Intellectual Roots* (University Park: Pennsylvania State University Press, 1984).

10. On Mills's attractiveness to the new left, see Miller, *"Democracy Is in the Streets,"* pp. 78–91, which casts Mills as a theorist of participatory democracy; and Van Gosse, *Where the Boys Are: Cuba, Cold War America, and the Making of a New Left* (London: Verso, 1994), pp. 176–183, which focuses on Mills's late efforts in behalf of the Cuban revolution.

11. Robert Pardun, interview with author, 27 August 1993. According to Pardun, sometime in 1963 Smith rode to Birmingham—1963 was the summer of the fire hoses in that city—and then to New York for an SDS meeting and brought back the idea of starting an SDS chapter in Austin. Kirkpatrick Sale, in *SDS*, does not mention Smith with regard to any meeting before the 1964 Pine Hill convention.

12. *Port Huron Statement*, in Miller, *"Democracy Is in the Streets,"* p. 332.

13. Werner Sombart argued that the dream of socialism suffered defeat at the hands of such victuals in the United States—thwarted by material abundance. Werner Sombart, *Why Is There No Socialism in the United States?* trans. Patricia M. Hockings and C. T. Husbands (1906; reprint, London: Macmillan, 1976). Echoing the Marxist view, Van Gosse contends that new left radicals were animated by a "desire to overcome the consumption-driven alienation characteristic of late capitalism" (Gosse, *Where the Boys Are*, p. 9). My view on this matter is close to Gosse's, though I don't share his confidence that we are "late" in capitalism's day. Although it seems to me that this is an important factor in the story Gosse tells, he does not dwell on it, preferring to focus on the overt politics of what he aptly calls the search for "solidarity" rather than probing deeply into its cultural origins.

14. The standard titles include John Kenneth Galbraith, *The Affluent Society* (Boston: Houghton Mifflin, 1958); David Riesman, with Nathan Glazer and Reuel Denney, *The Lonely Crowd: A Study of the Changing American Character* (New Haven, CT: Yale University Press, 1950); David Riesman, ed., *Abundance for What?* (Glencoe, IL: Free Press, 1964); Vance O. Packard, *The Hidden Persuaders* (New York: McKay, 1957); and Vance O. Packard, *The Waste Makers* (New York: McKay, 1959). See Robert M. Collins, "Growth Liberalism in the Sixties: Great Societies at Home and Grand Designs Abroad," in David Farber, ed., *The Sixties: From Memory to History* (Chapel Hill: University of North Carolina Press, 1994), pp. 11–44. Galbraith wanted the benefits of economic growth to be channeled into "public goods," not abandoned. Far from being a scourge of consumer culture, Riesman suggested that Americans might recover in the realm of consumption the meaning that had been drained from the realm of work, and he advocated training citizens from childhood to be connoisseurs of consumption. Neither of these critics regret-

ted the economic changes that spelled the rise of consumerism and the transition away from a producerist culture or the political priority given to economic growth.

15. Norman Mailer, *The White Negro* (San Francisco: City Lights Books, 1957); Albert Camus, *The Rebel: An Essay on Man in Revolt*, trans. Anthony Bower (New York: Knopf, 1961).

16. The only historian who has appreciated the parallels among the new left, the old left, and American pluralism in this regard is James Weinstein, in *Ambiguous Legacy: The Left in American Politics* (New York: New Directions, 1975), pp. viii, 116, 148.

17. Jeff Shero Nightbyrd, interview with author, 3 July 1992.

18. On the Student Peace Union (SPU) and the role of its disarmament politics in the early new left, see George R. Vickers, *The Formation of the New Left: The Early Years* (Lexington, MA: Lexington Books, 1974), pp. 51–61. On solidarity with Cuba in the late 1950s and early 1960s, see Gosse, *Where the Boys Are*. On both topics, from the vantage point of a Harvard undergraduate activist, see Gitlin, *The Sixties*, pp. 85–104. On the importance of radical pacifism as a bridge joining both antinuclear activism and the civil rights movement to the new left, see Maurice Isserman, *If I Had a Hammer . . . : The Death of the Old Left and the Birth of the New Left* (New York: Basic Books, 1987), pp. 125–169.

19. This argument is the main burden of Miller, *"Democracy Is in the Streets."*

Since I engage in a running argument with Miller's interpretation of the new left in this chapter, I should note that I have great respect for what he accomplishes in his book. In the political climate of the 1980s, Miller set out to rehabilitate the new left by retrieving the 1960s vision of participatory democracy. In this project he was joined by other academic figures, such as the political scientists Benjamin Barber and Harry Boyte. Benjamin R. Barber, *Strong Democracy: Participatory Politics for a New Age* (Berkeley and Los Angeles: University of California Press, 1984); Harry C. Boyte, *CommonWealth: A Return to Citizen Politics* (New York: Free Press, 1989); and Harry C. Boyte and Sara M. Evans, *Free Spaces: The Sources of Democratic Change in America* (New York: Harper & Row, 1986). Also see generally the journal *democracy*.

Miller succeeded, as his book's positive reception indicated. As part of his reclamation project, he downplayed those elements in the new left that might have proved less popular. In his book he paints a picture in which specific political issues of the time, such as civil rights and the Vietnam War, recede into the background, although he likely does this in part simply to make the new left's political vision less historically bounded. I feel that Miller de-emphasizes the existentialist dimension of the new left—a factor whose importance he acknowledges but that he then proceeds largely to ignore—more because he sees a close relation between existentialism, with its emphasis on action and intensity of feeling, and the violent tendency of the later new left, which became an albatross around this movement's historical neck. (Miller also takes care to disparage any suggestion that the early new left harbored an anarchist tendency; this may result from Miller's desire to exorcise his own anarchist past.) I do not see existentialism leading logically to violence, and furthermore, I think the violence of the new left, even at its very end, has been greatly exaggerated, and saying so is the best way to deflate the movement's violent image. In any event, the 1980s campaign to revive participatory democracy as an active political vision came to naught, so little is risked by revealing that this was not all there was to the new left, even in its early years.

20. Gitlin, *The Sixties*, p. 129.

21. Tom Hayden, *Reunion: A Memoir* (New York: Random House, 1988), p. 73.

22. Philip Sutin, "Hayden Hits Student Failure," *Michigan Daily*, 22 November 1961, quoted in Miller, *"Democracy Is in the Streets,"* p. 72.

For a harrowing account of the Freedom Rides, which evokes both the courage of the riders and the monstrous violence of their opponents, see Taylor Branch, *Parting the Waters: America in the King Years, 1954–1963* (New York: Simon & Schuster, 1989), pp. 412–491.

23. In 1965, Howe wrote, "A generation is missing in the life of American radicalism, the generation that would now be in its late thirties, the generation that did not show up." Irving Howe, "New Styles in 'Leftism,'" in Irving Howe, ed., *Beyond the New Left* (New York: McCall, 1970), p. 23. Given the civil rights protest of the late 1950s and early 1960s, there can be little doubt that Howe spoke of a missing generation of white radicals in particular (though he might have found the civil rights movement insufficiently tuned to his own Marxian socialist tradition).

24. Nightbyrd interview.

25. It is worth noting that most books specifically on the new left underestimate the importance of the civil rights movement in the formation of the new left, presenting this as simply one of several important issues. In contrast, books that touch on the new left but focus elsewhere emphasize the formative role of the civil rights movement on the new left. See, for example, Sara Evans, *Personal Politics: The Roots of Women's Liberation in the Civil Rights Movement and the New Left* (New York: Vintage Books, 1980); and Clayborne Carson, *In Struggle: SNCC and the Black Awakening of the 1960s* (Cambridge, MA: Harvard University Press, 1980). Notable for the attention it pays to civil rights activism is the work of James O'Brien, "The Development of a New Left in the United States, 1960–65" (Ph.D. diss., University of Wisconsin, 1971), and "Beyond Reminiscence: The New Left in History," *Radical America* 6 (July–August 1972): 11–48.

26. Jeremy Brecher, another early SDS activist, called the Swarthmore contingent "fantastically influential," noting that they tended to be "more radical" than the typical early SDS member. Jeremy Brecher, interviewed by Kirkpatrick Sale, 31 March 1970 (tape in the Oral History of the American Left collection, Tamiment Labor Library, New York University).

27. The Cambridge civil rights movement, indigenously organized, also involved students, black and white, from several universities. Peter B. Levy, "Civil War on Race Street: The Black Freedom Struggle and White Resistance in Cambridge, Maryland, 1960–1964," *Maryland Historical Magazine* 89 (Fall 1994): 291–318, chron-

icles this local protest movement; O'Brien, "The Development of a New Left," pp. 110–111, discusses student involvement.

28. The best-known SPAC recruit to SDS was Paul Booth, who became vice president and then national secretary. Becky Adams of SPAC, a former Swarthmore student body president, chaired the session at the Port Huron Conference at which conflict broke out over the question of whether to exclude Communists from the conference and the organization. Gitlin, *The Sixties*, pp. 114–115. Vernon Grizzard later became vice president of SDS, and Nick Egleson became president (although his election was something of a fluke).

Carl Wittman was another highly influential SDS member from Swarthmore, drawing on his experiences in Chester to coauthor, with Tom Hayden, the basic statement of the new left's vision of social change in the 1963–1965 period. Carl Wittman and Thomas Hayden, "An Interracial Movement of the Poor?" in Mitchell Cohen and Dennis Hale, eds., *The New Student Left: An Anthology* (Boston: Beacon Press, 1966), pp. 180–219. On the Chester activity, see O'Brien, "The Development of a New Left," pp. 266–268.

29. In October 1964, the Austin chapter of SDS received the second biggest shipment (53 copies) of the *SDS Bulletin*, the organization's newsletter at the time, outstripped only by Ann Arbor (145). SDS Papers, 2A:38, national office ephemera, 25 November 1964.

30. Alice Embree, quoted in Lauren Kessler, *After All These Years: Sixties Ideals in a Different World* (New York: Thunder's Mouth Press, 1990), p. 44. Such "bumping around," of course, played a major role in the early history of SDS.

31. Gregory Calvert calls the Texas group "anarchistic" as well as "libertarian and decentralist." Gregory N. Calvert, "Democracy and Rebirth: The New Left and Its Legacy" (Ph.D. diss., University of California at Santa Cruz, 1989), p. 497. Sale, *SDS*, p. 113. Gitlin states that as late as 1967, "I doubt whether a single one of the Old Guard had sampled the mystery drug LSD. Most were leery even of marijuana." Gitlin, *The Sixties*, p. 225. On the criminalization of LSD in 1966, see Jay Stevens, *Storming Heaven: LSD and the American Dream* (New York: Perennial Library, 1988), pp. 272–273.

32. Nightbyrd interview.

33. Alice Embree, interview with author, 9 November 1991; Alice Embree, reminiscence (in author's possession). Both Scott Pittman and Judy Perez, early SDS recruits at UT, found that the Young Democrats (YDs) were not eager to get involved in desegregation protests. Scott Pittman, interview with author, 4 May 1993; Judy Schiffer Perez, interview with author, 27 August 1993.

34. Embree interview.

35. Kessler, *After All These Years*, p. 44 (Embree quoted on p. 44); Nightbyrd interview.

36. Carl Oglesby, "The Revolted," in Loren Baritz, ed., *The American Left: Radical Political Thought in the Twentieth Century* (New York: Basic Books, 1971), p. 437; quoted in Edward E. Ericson Jr., *Radicals in the University* (Stanford, CA: Hoover Institution Press, 1975), p. 201.

37. Perez interview. Perez used the term *moralism*, the same word Gitlin uses to describe the atmosphere in households in which the parents had old left backgrounds. "This sense affected even the children of parents who had long since dropped out of left-wing politics," he notes accurately. Gitlin, *The Sixties*, p. 73.

38. Pardun interview. Pardun's family occupied an elevated social niche in a generally modest environment: both his parents had college degrees; his father, whom Pardun describes as conservative, worked for Pueblo Junior College, and his mother held a degree in home economics and worked as a substitute teacher when he was a teenager.

39. Pittman interview.

40. Mariann Garner-Wizard, "The Lie," in Daryl Janes, ed., *No Apologies: Texas Radicals Celebrate the '60s* (Austin, TX: Eakin Press, 1992), pp. 75–93; Mariann Wizard, interview with author, 8 July 1992; Paul Pipkin, Linda Pipkin, and Joe Ebbecke interview, 4 July 1992.

41. Pardun interview. Paul Pipkin notes that SDS members were "very critical of organized religion in general" yet many were looking for alternative forms of spirituality that they could believe in. He cites a widespread interest in Reform Judaism among people on the left in the early 1960s, fueled by an appreciation for the historical role of Jews in the left and by an admiration for the socialist aspect of the nation of Israel. (This, even though, according to Pipkin, most UT students had never met a single Jew before attending college. Attitudes toward Israel changed on the left after the 1967 war in the Middle East.) Pipkin et al. interview.

42. Wizard interview.

43. Garner-Wizard, "The Lie," pp. 92–93.

44. Nightbyrd interview.

45. Robert Pardun, "SDS Members Seek Greater Democracy," *Daily Texan*, 21 February 1964. On the importance of the "multi-issue" perspective, also see Robert Pardun, "It Wasn't Hard to Be a Communist in Texas," in Janes, ed., *No Apologies*, p. 54.

46. Jeffrey Shero, "U of Texas," *SDS Bulletin*, May 1964; Jeffrey Shero, "U of Texas," *SDS Bulletin*, March 1964.

47. Embree interview; Pardun interview.

48. Christopher Lasch, *The New Radicalism in America, 1889–1963: The Intellectual as a Social Type* (New York: Norton, 1986), p. 286. In the early years of the century, both liberals and radicals, according to Lasch, shared a kind of cultural and political modernism. The "countercultural" aspect of this politics also bears an intriguing resemblance to the new left.

49. Pipkin et al. interview; Nightbyrd interview.

50. Willie Morris relates his discovery of a John Birch Society "cell" at the UT campus in 1961, in Willie Morris, *North toward Home* (Boston: Houghton Mifflin, 1967), pp. 265–290.

51. "Lawyer Discusses Oswald's Defense," *Daily Texan*, 24 April 1964; Hal Womack, "Oswald Lawyer Attacks Distorted Facts," *Daily Texan*, 28 April 1964; Embree interview. Interestingly, Charlie Smith's father apparently was one of Jack

Ruby's initial lawyers, immediately after Ruby killed Lee Harvey Oswald. I don't know what role this played in bringing Lane to Texas. Paul Pipkin, in Pipkin et al. interview.

52. Sale, *SDS*, p. 206. This quotation is reproduced in Miller, *"Democracy Is in the Streets,"* pp. 224–225. Nightbyrd repeated it to me, almost verbatim, in the interview I conducted with him.

53. Embree interview.

54. Ibid.; on Wizard's warm relationship with her parents, more conservative than Embree's, see Garner-Wizard, "The Lie," pp. 77–78, 97–98.

Richard Flacks, in his *Youth and Social Change* (Chicago: Markham, 1971), and his "Revolt of the Young Intelligentsia: Revolutionary Class-Consciousness in a Post-Scarcity America," in Roderick Aya and Norman Miller, eds., *The New American Revolution* (New York: Free Press, 1971), pp. 223–263, argues for such a continuity in values. Flacks's findings confirmed those of Kenneth Keniston, in *Young Radicals: Notes on Committed Youth* (New York: Harcourt, Brace & World, 1968), which focuses on antiwar activists who probably were not as far left as the SDS mainstream. The oedipal interpretation of the new left is offered in Lewis Feuer, *The Conflict of Generations: The Character and Significance of Student Movements* (New York: Basic Books, 1969), a book whose argument is notable for the poverty of its empirical basis. Flacks takes this argument one big step further, trying to enlist the parents of new left activists into the anticapitalist legions by asserting that their values were intrinsically subversive of the social order, a contention effectively rebutted by the lucid discussion in Vickers, *Formation of the New Left*.

55. Robert Pardun to Clark Kissinger, 15 March 1965, SDS Papers, Chapter File—Texas, reel 8, 2A:92.

56. Pardun, "It Wasn't Hard to Be a Communist," p. 51.

57. Shero, "U of Texas," *SDS Bulletin*, March 1964.

58. "SDS Members Picket Capitol," *Daily Texan*, 16 February 1964; Shero, "U of Texas," *SDS Bulletin*, March 1964.

59. Robert Pardun, "acting chairman," letter, *Daily Texan*, 7 February 1964. Notably, this is the earliest usage I have documented in this local environment of the term *racist*. Formerly, those agitating for civil rights or against racism used more euphemistic terms.

60. "Rights Bill Lacking, YAF, SDS Agree," *Daily Texan*, 7 May 1964; Shero, "U of Texas," *SDS Bulletin*, May 1964.

61. Jeff Shero to Clark (Kissinger), 9 May 1965, SDS Papers, Chapter File—Texas, reel 8, 2A:92.

62. "UT Students to Spend Summer in Mississippi," *Daily Texan*, 23 April 1964; Shero, "U of Texas," *SDS Bulletin*, May 1964; Perez interview; Pardun interview; Robert Stone, interview with author, 28 May 1993.

63. Pardun, "It Wasn't Hard to Be a Communist," p. 53.

64. For a reliable account of the famous events at Berkeley, see William J. Rorabaugh, *Berkeley at War: The 1960s* (New York: Oxford University Press, 1989),

pp. 18–47. Also see Terry H. Anderson, *The Movement and the Sixties: Protest in America from Greensboro to Wounded Knee* (New York: Oxford University Press, 1995), pp. 87–89, 101–108; and the contemporary compilations, Hal Draper, ed., *FSM: The "New Left" Uprising in Berkeley* (New York: Grove Press, 1965); and Seymour M. Lipset and Sheldon Wolin, eds., *The Berkeley Student Revolt: Facts and Interpretation* (Garden City, NY: Doubleday/Anchor, 1965). It has been charged that the UC regents banned political activity at the behest of right-wing pressure, but Rorabaugh reports finding no evidence of this (*Berkeley at War*, p. 18).

65. Paul Pipkin, in Pipkin et al. interview. On the Deacons for Defense and Justice, see Adam Fairclough, *Race and Democracy: The Civil Rights Struggle in Louisiana, 1915–1972* (Athens: University of Georgia Press, 1995), pp. 342–343, 345, 357–360, 385.

66. Wizard interview.

67. Paul Pipkin, in Pipkin et al. interview.

68. Wizard interview.

69. Related in Garner-Wizard, "The Lie," p. 93.

70. Paul Pipkin, in Pipkin et al. interview; "Hi Kids, Remember . . . ," *Rag*, 13 October 1969.

71. Paul Spencer to author; Susan Torian Olan, "Blood Debts," in Janes, ed., *No Apologies*, p. 19; Ronnie Dugger, "Who Was Charles Whitman?" *Texas Observer*, 19 August 1966; David A. Pratt, letter, "Whitman Hostile to negroes," *Texas Observer*, 16 September 1966; Dick Reavis to author, 28 October 1991; Ray Reece, "Almost No Apologies," in Janes, ed., *No Apologies*, p. 254.

72. Articles on their case appeared in the *Rag* on 3 May 1971 and 9 August 1971. The first trial ended in a hung jury, which voted seven to five for acquittal. The white radical on trial was Bartee Haile, mentioned later.

73. Kaye Northcott, "Vigilantes Still Ride in Houston," *Texas Observer* 29 August 1969; gavan (Duffy), "Space City News Bombed," *Rag*, 31 July 1969; Abe Peck, *Uncovering the Sixties: The Life and Times of the Underground Press* (New York: Pantheon, 1985), pp. 135–146, 231.

74. Gary Thiher and Dick Reavis, "Three Texas Arrests Have Political Notes," *Rag*, 4 November 1968; Judy Smith, "A Trying Experience," *Rag*, n.d. (1 or 2 December 1968).

75. In 1968, Ernest McMillan and Matthew Johnson were convicted and sentenced to ten years each for supposedly destroying property in a grocery store. Although at least thirty people participated in the activity, no one else was arrested. Only one witness, the store owner's son, identified the two men, who were well known as black militants in Dallas. And although the defendants technically were held responsible for only $50 damage apiece and therefore could have been charged with misdemeanors, they were charged with felonies instead, leading to the jail time. P. K. Brown, "SNCC Leaders Convicted," *Dallas Notes*, October 1968.

76. Kaye Northcott, "Troubles on the Left," *Texas Observer*, 29 November 1968; "Stoney!" *Dallas News*, 14–27 October 1970; Jeff Nightbyrd, "Stoney Burns Talks

about Prison," *Austin Sun*, 22 January 1975. *Dallas Notes* started as *Notes from the Underground* in 1967, edited by Nancy Lynne Brown, Doug Baker, and Bartee Haile, students at Southern Methodist University; Burns soon took over. Northcott also reported that the Hailes and eight others were arrested in 1968 in Denton, home to North Texas State University, for selling pornography, after they started passing out an election issue of *Dallas Notes* at a football game. Burns wrote that "the only possibly offensive word in the newspaper was 'shit.'"

77. Judy Smith, "Texas Courts Say: We Try Harder!" *Rag*, 7 October 1968; "Black Leaders to Address Rally for Lee Otis Johnson," *Daily Texan*, 12 October 1969.

78. Really the only clear example of guerrilla fantasies in Texas was Bartee Haile's John Brown Revolutionary League (JBRL), a white Leninist group that worked with militant black activists in Houston. (Bartee Haile and his wife, Margie Haile, were nationally known SDS activists from Dallas; whether she moved with him from Dallas to Houston and whether she also was involved in the JBRL, I don't know.) Also sympathetic to this kind of politics were Genie and Pun Plamondon, leaders of the Fort Worth White Panthers. As I discuss later, Haile and other Houston radicals provided the only support that the Weatherman faction of SDS found in Texas when it took shape in 1969.

For more on the theme of violence versus peace in the countercultural vision of the new left, see chapter 7.

79. Garner-Wizard, "The Lie," p. 94; Wizard interview.

80. Bobby Minkoff, interview with author, 4 and 9 March 1992.

81. In fact, this countercultural sympathy was so strong as to make at least one important member of the campus SDS group, Judy Perez, doubt George Vizard's political seriousness. She recalls his drug experimentation more than any "deep thinking" he did politically. She left Austin (and Robert Pardun) in 1966, however, at just the time when Vizard was assuming a very prominent role in the SDS chapter. Perez interview.

82. Wizard interview.

83. This account comes from Olan, "Blood Debts," pp. 22–25, who relates Vizard's remark as "You goddamn cops! Are we going to have to have guns to protect ourselves?" Leftist Dallas students reported his phrasing in a subtly more aggressive way, as "God Damn cops, some day we'll have guns and be able to protect ourselves." The Dallas paper also reported that the activist who was hit with her own sign was Sandra Wilson. *Notes from the Underground: S.M.U. Off-Campus Free Press*, 1 May 1967. The description of Vizard's physical condition is from a leaflet produced and distributed immediately afterward by Student Religious Liberals and the University Freedom Movement on the UT campus, excerpted in Olan, "Blood Debts," p. 24.

84. Becky Brenner, interview with author, 25 March 1994.

85. Dick J. Reavis to author, 9 November 1995; Brenner interview; Dick J. Reavis, "SDS: From Students to Seniors," in Janes, ed., *No Apologies*, p. 102; Dick J. Reavis to author, 6 January 1992.

86. Paul Pipkin, in Paul Pipkin et al. interview. Some SDS members joined the May Second Movement (M2M) at this time for the same reason. M2M was a front organization of the Progressive Labor Party (PL), which came to play a pivotal role in the collapse of SDS in 1969—leading some analysts to conclude that SDS cut its own throat when it removed the exclusion clause. See, for example, Paul Berman, "Don't Follow Leaders," *New Republic*, 10 and 17 August 1987.

87. Brenner interview.

88. Reavis to author, 9 November 1995; Reavis to author, 6 January 1992; Wizard interview.

89. Brenner interview.

90. Reavis to author, 6 January 1992; Reavis, "SDS: From Students to Seniors," pp. 103–105 (quotation on p. 103); Reavis to author, 9 November 1995. His perception of failure, circa 1967, was sharply at odds with the analysis of many others in SDS, as I point out later.

91. Sale, *SDS*, pp. 121–122, 263–264. In February 1966, M2M voted to disband, declaring that its anti-imperialist perspective had made headway in SDS and other groups, and its members started joining SDS. Presumably all this was done under the direction of PL, M2M's parent group, which had decided both to "bore within" SDS and to establish a tighter cadre organization, in contrast to the relatively loose structure and style of M2M.

92. Olan, "Blood Debts," pp. 26–28.

93. Wizard interview; Garner-Wizard, "The Lie," p. 95.

94. Wizard interview; Embree interview. On the pervasive character of these arrangements in the new left, see generally Evans, *Personal Politics*, pp. 102–192; also see Alice Echols, *Daring to Be Bad: Radical Feminism in America, 1967–1975* (Minneapolis: University of Minnesota Press, 1989), pp. 23–45.

95. Pardun interview.

96. Perez interview. A kind of coda to the different memories that she and Robert Pardun have of gender relations in SDS at that time: Their marriage ended in early 1967, and she left Texas for California in the company of Mike Davis, another SDS activist, whom she then married.

97. The Forty Acres Club, a privately built and operated faculty club, opened as a whites-only facility at UT in spring 1962, even though the businessman who received the contract to operate the club had pledged that it would be integrated. It became the target of protests from the student group, Students for Direct Action, that had organized the effective protests against local movie theaters during the 1960/1961 school year, and liberal faculty members like Irwin Spear declined to join the club. Over Christmas break during the 1963/1964 school year, Johnson brought his entourage, which included one black man, Andrew T. Hatcher, the White House associate press secretary, to the club. Word immediately spread around town that the club was now integrated, which it was, and according to Spear, many local businesses that had been holding out against integration took this as a cue that they should capitulate. C. D., "Jim Crow Haven for UT 'Friends,'" *Texas Observer*, 10

August 1962; Charmayne Marsh, "40 Acres Club Serves Negro Newspaperman," *Daily Texan*, 7 January 1964; Irwin Spear, interview with author, 30 June 1992.

On Johnson and civil rights in general, see David Chappell, *Inside Agitators: White Southerners in the Civil Rights Movement* (Baltimore: Johns Hopkins University Press, 1994), pp. 147–211; Hugh Davis Graham, *The Civil Rights Era: Origins and Development of National Policy, 1960–1972* (New York: Oxford University Press, 1990), pp. 125–297; and John Morton Blum, *Years of Discord: American Politics and Society, 1961–1974* (New York: Norton, 1991), pp. 145–148, 164–170.

98. Clark Kerr, *The Uses of the University* (Cambridge, MA: Harvard University Press, 1963; rev. ed., 1995); Rorabaugh, *Berkeley at War*, p. 31.

99. *Freedom Platform!* n.d. (April 1967), President's Papers, Eugene C. Barker History Center, University of Texas at Austin; *What Is to Be Done?: Thiher's Platform*, n.d., SDS Papers, Chapter File—Texas, reel 8, 2A:92; "SDS Runs Slate at U.T.," *Dallas Notes*, 17–31 March 1968.

100. David Farber, *The Age of Great Dreams: America in the 1960s* (New York: Hill & Wang, 1994), p. 158.

101. Ronnie Dugger, *Our Invaded Universities: Form, Reform, and New Starts* (New York: Norton, 1974), pp. 88–95.

102. C. Wright Mills, *The Power Elite* (New York: Oxford University Press, 1956). Miller stresses Mills's influence on the new left, but curiously, he does not emphasize the idea of the power elite. Miller, *"Democracy Is in the Streets,"* pp. 78–91.

Dugger, *Our Invaded Universities*, furnishes detailed information on the links of UT regents, administrators, and many professors to industrial and financial corporations. What became known as "power structure analysis" was not applied only to UT. In 1970, Houston leftists published extensive documentation of the ties between individual trustees and alumni governors of Rice University and the worlds of "finance," "national corp[orations]," and "the defense–research nexus." "Top 33: Rice's Ruling Elite," *Space City!* 9–22 May 1970.

103. Morris, *North toward Home*, p. 167; Dugger, *Our Invaded Universities*, p. 333. Connally first appointed Erwin to the board of regents in 1963. Joyce Jane Weedman, "Attorney Frank C. Erwin Chosen Regent Friday," *Daily Texan*, 24 March 1963.

104. Dugger, *Our Invaded Universities*, p. 125. Erwin tried to deflect criticism by asserting that all the protesters were SDS members, but this was far from the truth.

105. Morris, *North toward Home*, p. 226.

To say that the true nature of Lyndon Johnson is a hotly debated subject does not convey the ferocity of feeling on all sides. For a sympathetic view, see Robert Dallek, *Lone Star Rising: Lyndon Johnson and His Times, 1908–1960* (New York: Oxford University Press, 1991). For the devil theory of LBJ, see Robert Caro, *The Years of Lyndon Johnson: The Path to Power* (New York: Knopf, 1982); and Robert Caro, *The Years of Lyndon Johnson: Means of Ascent* (New York: Knopf, 1990). Also see Paul K. Conkin, *Big Daddy from the Pedernales: Lyndon Baines Johnson* (Boston: Twayne, 1986); and the perhaps too close but still insightful portrait in Doris Kearns, *Lyndon Johnson and the American Dream* (New York: Harper & Row, 1976).

The second volume of Caro's biography is notable for its odd view of Texas politics in the cold war era. It pits Johnson, the villain, against Caro's hero, Coke Stevenson, a rock-ribbed conservative who opposed "the power of the federal bureaucracy and of federal money" during the New Deal as speaker of the Texas house (*Means of Ascent*, p. 163) and who then led the Texas Democratic Party "Regulars" in holding the line against desegregation in the late 1940s. The issue of race is almost invisible in Caro's presentation of state politics at that time, when in reality it was becoming the central issue of controversy in the wake of the U.S. Supreme Court's 1944 decision ruling the Texas Democratic "white primary" unconstitutional. Chandler Davidson terms the Regulars "part of a South-wide movement among the upper classes to reassert [their] strength within the [Democratic] party." Chandler Davidson, *Race and Class in Texas Politics* (Princeton, NJ: Princeton University Press, 1990), p. 159; Darlene Clark Hine, *Black Victory: The Rise and Fall of the White Primary in Texas* (Millwood, NY: TKO Press, 1979). Caro does note, though, by way of establishing "Calculatin' " Coke's Texan authenticity, that he was "named after Governor Richard Coke, a Confederate veteran who in 1873 wrested the government of Texas from the Carpetbaggers and freed the state from the injustices of Reconstruction" (*Means of Ascent*, p. 146). On racial issues, Johnson carefully staked out a moderate position.

106. Dugger, *Our Invaded Universities*, p. 105.

107. Richard Flacks explores this process of disillusionment in *Making History: The American Left and the American Mind* (New York: Columbia University Press, 1988), pp. 54, 60–62. Also see the comments in Weinstein, *Ambiguous Legacy*, pp. 126–127; and Joel H. Spring, *The Sorting Machine Revisited: National Educational Policy Since 1945* (New York: Longman, 1989).

108. Harry Ransom, statement, released by *UT News* (UT's "news and information service"), 22 April 1967, President's Papers, Barker History Center. One day earlier, Edwin Price, another campus administrator, directly relayed Ransom's warning to David Mahler, an SDS member. Ed. B. Price (Office of the Student Life Staff) to David Mahler, 21 April 1967, President's Papers, Barker History Center.

109. Paul Pipkin et al. interview.

110. Greg Olds, "Freedom and Order at UT," *Texas Observer*, 12 May 1967.

111. Embree interview.

112. Rorabaugh, *Berkeley at War*, pp. 30–37.

113. The two-hundred estimate comes from Paul Pipkin, and the five-hundred number from Dick Reavis. Paul Pipkin et al. interview; Reavis to author, 6 January 1992. Apparently its banning on campus did not keep SDS from meeting; it also had a newly registered shadow group—whose name, University Socialists, was notable—working on campus.

114. James Hollas, "Officials OK SDS Return," *Daily Texan*, 19 November 1967.

115. See Kwame Ture (Stokely Carmichael) and Charles V. Hamilton, *Black Power: The Politics of Liberation in America* (New York: Vintage Books, 1967; rev. ed.,

1992), a book whose avowed existentialist humanism, which helped solidify the white left's support for its program, is rarely recalled. Also see Carson, *In Struggle*, pp. 191–228.

116. Carson, *In Struggle*, pp. 236–242.

117. Hayden interview.

118. Larry Freudiger, "SNCC & Black Power Defended," *Rag*, 7 November 1966.

119. Paul Pipkin, "ERAP Dialogue," *sds Conference Daily*, 30 December 1965 (from a national SDS conference held at the University of Illinois), SDS Papers, reel 20, 3:3.

120. Andrew Kopkind, "They'd Rather Be Left," *New York Review of Books*, 28 September 1967. Todd Gitlin calls this perhaps unintentionally revealing pronouncement "thumpingly accurate." Gitlin, *The Sixties*, p. 246. No doubt, some in the new left still clung to the interracialist vision. Yet I think Gitlin overstates the attachment of the new left to these sentiments at that time, as I explain later.

121. This conference was intended to nominate an independent presidential ticket of Martin Luther King Jr. and Benjamin Spock, but the meeting, held in Chicago over Labor Day weekend, instead turned toward a ritualized incantation of black nationalism, with the African American delegates demanding, and receiving, half the votes on all issues. King and other interracialist figures appeared only briefly and distanced themselves from the effort thereafter. See Gitlin, *The Sixties*, p. 245. Ronnie Dugger found the NCNP distressing. "A coalition is possible only among people who respect each other," he wrote, and he felt that the terms on which the interracial coalition was formed at the gathering entailed a denial of respect for the white participants. Ronnie Dugger, "A Time of Wounds," *Texas Observer*, 15 September 1967. Evans, *Personal Politics*, pp. 196–199, and Echols, *Daring to Be Bad*, pp. 45–50, also criticize the NCNP for its suppression of the concern over sexism that was surfacing in the left at that time.

122. Larry Freudiger, "Grassroots Sociology: A Weekly Discussion of the American Social Revolution and the Reactions against It—The White Revolution," *Rag*, 30 January 1967.

123. C. Wright Mills, "Letter to the New Left," *New Left Review* 5 (1960); reprinted as "The New Left," in Irving Louis Horowitz, ed., *Power, Politics and People: The Collected Essays of C. Wright Mills* (New York: Ballantine, 1963), p. 257. Ericson, *Radicals in the University*, p. 32; and Cornel West, *The Evasion of American Philosophy: A Genealogy of Pragmatism* (Madison: University of Wisconsin Press, 1989), p. 131, are politically disparate accounts that both emphasize Mills's influence on this point.

124. Sale, *SDS*, pp. 110–111; Miller, *"Democracy Is in the Streets,"* p. 190. On the achievements and shortcomings of the ERAPs, see Wini Breines, *Community and Organization in the New Left, 1962–68: The Great Refusal* (South Hadley, MA: J. F. Bergin, 1981), pp. 125–132.

125. Sale, *SDS*, p. 209, note; Miller, *"Democracy Is in the Streets,"* p. 241; Nightbyrd interview.

126. Gitlin, *The Sixties*, p. 192.

127. (Robert Pardun), "Prospectus for a Texas Student Program," n.d. (December 1964), SDS Papers, Chapter File—Texas, reel 8, 2A:92.

128. "Hester Will Host at Coffee House," *Daily Texan*, 3 April 1964.

129. Shero, "Chapter Reports: U. of Texas," *SDS Bulletin*, April 1964.

130. George Goss, "Hazard—The Hidden Becomes Visible," *SDS Bulletin*, January 1964. Goss was a former associate of Vivien Franklin.

131. The only solid white recruit that the project won was a young man with neo-Nazi leanings who ended up as a delegate at the Mississippi Freedom Democratic Party convention. Pardun interview; Perez interview; Pipkin, "ERAP Dialogue."

132. "Prospectus for a Texas Student Program."

133. Goodwyn, who later became well known for his history of the southern Populist movement of the late nineteenth century, founded the Texas Democratic Coalition (TDC) after his participation in the 1962 gubernatorial campaign of Democrat Don Yarborough (the loser to John Connally in a very close race) and served as its executive director. Another liberal Democratic organization, Democrats of Texas (DoT), was active in the late 1950s but collapsed when Lyndon Johnson's election to the vice presidency threw it into a crisis of purpose. The goals of the TDC were to register black and Chicano voters and to bring together liberal activists of all races, from labor unions and other sources, into a group that could exert pressure on the state Democratic Party to take a stronger stance in favor of civil rights, as well as on economic issues. In the spring of 1964, Goodwyn proposed that the coalition organize a student wing, leading to the discussions with SDS leaders in Texas. He also hired Martin Wiginton, a graduate of the UT Law School, who moved left in the late 1960s. The discussions with SDS representatives, who included Nightbyrd, Pardun, and Thorne Dreyer—local "heavies"—took place at Goodwyn's home. In 1965 the coalition was reorganized as the Texas Liberal Democrats (TLD). Lawrence Goodwyn, interview with author, 27 September 1994.

134. "Prospectus for a Texas Student Program," emphasis added.

135. The realignment strategy, which focused on prompting right-wing Democrats to join the Republican Party and pushing the Democrats to the left, was laid out in the *Port Huron Statement* but rapidly lost favor over the next two years. The realignment faction's most visible spokesperson after 1963 probably was Steve Max, a red-diaper baby from New York City who maintained an attachment to the old left's popular front approach. Sale notes that Nightbyrd, running for election as SDS vice president at his first national meeting, at Pine Hill in June 1964, was "being pushed by the realignment group." Sale, *SDS*, p. 113.

136. Gary Thiher, "U of Texas," *SDS Bulletin*, November–December 1964.

137. Greg Olds, "The Texas Left," *Texas Observer*, 22 December 1967.

138. "The Conference," *Texas Observer*, 1 March 1968; Thorne Dreyer, "We Failed to Communicate," *Texas Observer*, 29 March 1968; Greg Olds, "Still Confused," *Texas Observer*, 29 March 1968; Sue Horn Estes, "Where Were the Liberals?" *Texas Observer*, 29 March 1968.

139. Buck Ramsey, "Radicals Organize Defense," *Texas Observer*, 10 January 1969; Gregory Calvert, interview with author, 20 March 1995; Calvert, "Democracy and Rebirth," pp. 498–501.

140. Calvert interview.

141. Goodwyn was left with the impression that SDS had "agendas that didn't get surfaced" during his discussions with the local chapter leaders; he "was being 'handled,' " if not very consequentially, and he knew it. Still, despite these hints of manipulation, he feels that the new left activists "hadn't thought through" exactly what they wanted to do in Texas at that time. The discussions continued for about three months, and then the SDS representatives broke them off without explanation. Goodwyn interview.

142. Ed Hamlett, "Southern Student Organizing Committee: Students in the South," *SDS Bulletin*, January 1965. Hamlett, who was the leader of the "white folks' project" and was elected to the SDS National Council in June 1965 along with Robert Pardun, was a founder of SSOC. Sale, *SDS*, p. 210, note.

143. Jeffrey Shero, "Civil Rights Moderation: How Long?" *Daily Texan*, 22 April 1964; Robert Pardun to Clark Kissinger and Helen Garvy, 30 March 1965, SDS Papers, Chapter File—Texas, reel 8, 2A:92; Shero, "U of Texas," *SDS Bulletin*, May 1964; Jeff Shero to Helen (Garvy), n.d. (late 1964), SDS Papers, Chapter File— Texas, reel 8, 2A:92.

144. Sale reports that Archie Allen, the SDS traveler in "the South" (by which, I infer, he means the Southeast) worked with SSOC in the 1964/1965 school year. Sale, *SDS*, p. 151, note.

145. Ibid., pp. 537–538. One Austin SDS member, probably Paul Pipkin, reporting in June 1969 on his visit to a SSOC meeting, expressed sympathy for the difficult position of the SSOC activists, working in a conservative environment and finding themselves under attack from their left. He passed along a rumor that Mike Klonsky, the SDS national secretary who was a key participant in the cannibalism practiced on SSOC, had written off SDS-UT, just as he had SSOC, for its deviationism. Paul, "A Visit with SSOC: Brothers under the Schism," *Rag*, 19 June 1969.

146. See Carl Davidson, "The New Radicals and the Multiversity," in Massimo Teodori, ed., *The New Left: A Documentary History* (Indianapolis: Bobbs-Merrill, 1969), pp. 323–335; Kenneth Heineman, *Campus Wars: The Peace Movement at American State Universities in the Vietnam Era* (New York: New York University Press, 1993), pp. 97–98, 154; and Sale, *SDS*, pp. 283–284, 290–297. Heineman reports that Davidson, who attended college at Penn State in the early 1960s before going to Nebraska for graduate study, came from a working-class background in Aliquippa. Heineman sees Davidson's viewpoint as genuinely proletarian, as opposed to the "middle-class Marxists who could not relate to home-grown, blue-collar populism" and who did not take Davidson seriously as a thinker (p. 98). Historians, too, are tempted to look for "the real thing."

147. Calvert, "Democracy and Rebirth," pp. 488, 497–503. On homophobia in the new left, see pp. 557–563, the only discussion I know of on this matter.

148. Calvert had studied in Paris before becoming involved in left-wing politics in the United States and undoubtedly was influenced by the ideas he encountered there. Serge Mallet, Andre Gorz, and Alain Touraine are the names prominently associated with the ideas of the new working class and "postindustrial" society in France. Andre Gorz, *Strategy for Labor: A Radical Proposal*, trans. Martin A. Nicolaus and Victoria Ortiz (Boston: Beacon Press, 1967); Serge Mallet, *Essays on the New Working Class*, ed. and trans. Dick Howard and Dean Savage (St. Louis: Telos Press, 1975); and Alain Touraine, *The Post-Industrial Society; Tomorrow's Social History: Classes, Conflicts and Culture in the Programmed Society*, trans. Leonard F. X. Mayhew (New York: Random House, 1971). Mark Poster, *Existential Marxism in Postwar France: From Sartre to Althusser* (Princeton, NJ: Princeton University Press, 1975), pays respectful attention to the concept of the new working class in its brief (and rather dated) consideration of the events in France in May 1968 (pp. 361–369). For a discussion by an Austin SDS activist, see Dick Howard, "Gorz, Mallet, and French Theories of the New Working Class," *Radical America* 3 (April–May 1969): 1–19.

149. A full statement of the theory is available in Greg Calvert and Carol Neiman, *A Disrupted History: The New Left and the New Capitalism* (New York: Random House, 1971); see esp. chap. 2, "The Myth of the Middle Class," pp. 41–68. Calvert and Neiman wrote this book in Austin. Carl Davidson was supposed to collaborate with them on the project, but he took a turn to the hard left, becoming a Leninist and precipitating a falling-out with Calvert. On Calvert's differences with the Leninists, see note 151, below.

Aside from Calvert's own writings, the only serious historical discussions of this idea's American impact are Weinstein, *Ambiguous Legacy*, pp. 141–144; Breines, *Community and Organization in the New Left*, pp. 96–114; and Echols, *Daring to Be Bad*, pp. 37–42. Also see Sale, *SDS*, pp. 338–340, 361, 462–463. However, Weinstein, Breines, and Echols confine the scope of their discussion to debates in the national leadership, providing a synopsis of several sociological accounts of the new working class, and conclude, mistakenly, that the appeal of this idea was ephemeral, lasting scarcely a year. As I state later, the national office collective of SDS quickly turned away from this idea, but it remained popular with new left activists around the country. In addition, Breines emphasizes the French writings on the topic, not their American reception.

150. Harvey Stone, "The University: Final Exam," *Rag*, 27 January 1969.

151. The Marxist character of Calvert's idea belies the unremitting hostility toward "Marxism" that he expresses in his dissertation, as well as his book, *Democracy from the Heart: Spiritual Values, Decentralism, and Democratic Idealism in the Movement of the 1960s* (Novato, CA: Communitas Press, 1991), which is based on the early chapters of his dissertation. Evidently, his pejorative use of *Marxism* refers to two things: first, a strictly materialist view of social reality and social change, which contrasts sharply with Calvert's spiritual bent, and, second, the "puritanical" attitude toward matters of lifestyle that is more properly associated with the Leninist groupings that cropped up on the American left in the late

1960s. Calvert feels that his sexuality was both a real source of animus toward him—especially from those on the left who thought that a "proletarian" politics required a strict heterosexuality and a conservatism regarding gender relations— and something that was used against him by those opposed to his politics on other points, for instance, his emphasis on campus organizing or his pacifist tendencies. By the time he and Neiman wrote *A Disrupted History*, he had become a spokesperson for "libertarian socialism," an idea, like that of the new working class, with substantial support among the new left's rank and file but less among its national "leadership."

152. "SDS Adopts Plans for Year," *Daily Texan*, 21 October 1966.

153. Quoted in Tom Wells, *The War Within: America's Battle over Vietnam* (Berkeley and Los Angeles: University of California Press, 1994), p. 125.

154. Pardun interview.

155. Dreyer, "We Failed to Communicate."

156. Pittman interview; Paul Pipkin, in Paul Pipkin et al. interview; Dickie Magidoff interview, 19 March 1997; Calvert interview. The description is Magidoff's.

157. (Bob) Speck, "The Mechanics of Social Change," SDS-UT retreat working papers, n.d. (1965), SDS Papers, Locality File—Texas, reel 25, 3:62.

158. Quoted in Heineman, *Campus Wars*, p. 154.

159. Judy Pardun, "Alienation and the N.O.," *SDS Bulletin* (vol. 4, no. 2), n.d.

160. Robert Pardun, "Statement by Bob Pardun," SDS-UT retreat working papers, emphasis added.

161. Speck, "The Mechanics of Social Change."

162. Gregory Calvert, "In White America: Radical Consciousness and Social Change," in Teodori, ed., *The New Left*, pp. 414, 413. As I explained earlier, Calvert argued that student liberals were not truly middle class but, rather, members of a new working class who possessed a false consciousness.

163. Ibid., pp. 413, 415, emphasis added.

164. Ibid., pp. 414, 415, emphasis in original. Calvert explains that he stated his views in a fairly polemical way as a response to an equally strident expression of the materialist position at the Princeton conference and that his speech should be viewed in this context. Calvert interview.

165. Caroline quoted in Kaye Northcott, "UT and Larry Caroline," *Texas Observer*, 24 May 1968, and in Jerry Rudes, "Peace Marks Capitol March," *Daily Texan*, 22 October 1967. The *Observer* reported that Caroline said "whole bloody thing," and the *Texan* reported the more evocative "whole bloody mess."

Caroline coauthored a series of articles in the *Rag* entitled "Corruptor of Youth."

166. Larry Caroline, interview with author, 16 December 1992; Embree interview. For a sampling of work in the existentialist Marxist vein, see the essays collected in Erich Fromm, ed., *Socialist Humanism: An International Symposium* (Garden City, NY: Doubleday/Anchor, 1966).

167. For a contemporary account, see John Sullivan, "A Valedictory—II: L'Affaire Caroline," *Texas Observer*, 24 October 1969.

After the philosophy department's budget committee reversed its initial decision and voted to extend Caroline's contract, Silber, in his capacity as dean, intervened to overrule them. Silber made it clear that in his judgment, Caroline's revolutionary statements revealed the younger man as an inferior thinker and rhetorician, disqualifying him as a teacher and scholar. In Silber's view, the doctrine of academic freedom afforded no protection for such inferiority. He dismissed out of hand the suggestion, which came even from great friends of his like Ronnie Dugger, that Caroline's dismissal bore a discomfiting resemblance to the fate of the junior economics instructors at UT who (as related in chapter 1), twenty-five years earlier, had gotten into hot water for speaking at a public gathering in defense of the Fair Labor Standards Act.

The two philosophers' relations became further strained when, at a memorial service at the state capitol in 1968 after the murder of Martin Luther King Jr., speakers called UT a racist institution, which Silber took as a personal comment on him, as a university administrator. Also on this occasion, Larry Jackson, who had been enrolled as a university student on the condition that Caroline tutor him, delivered to Silber a note beginning "Dear Massah," which informed Silber that Jackson was withdrawing from school. Caroline neither defended Silber against the charge of racism (not thinking that Silber had been so accused) nor criticized Jackson, which Silber found unforgivable. Caroline interview.

Silber's political development could serve as the subject of a historical study in its own right. He never had displayed much attraction to leftist arguments, and as radical thinking made inroads among American liberals in the late 1960s, he found himself out of step. The two issues that estranged him were the Vietnam War and black power. Like most internationalist liberals during the cold war, he always had been a "hawk" on foreign policy issues, says Irwin Spear, a liberal antiwar activist on the UT faculty, and Silber expressed sharp disdain toward those who did not take seriously the threat of world communism. Spear interview. Celia Morris, once a protégé and friend of Silber's, reasoned that his acquisition of power also may have changed him politically. Celia Morris, interview with author, 3 February 1993.

168. Magidoff interview; Charlotte Pittman Dethloff, interview with author, 24 March 1997; Scott Pittman, interview with author, 24 March 1997 (hereafter Pittman interview II).

169. Pittman interview II; Magidoff interview; Carolyn Craven, interview with author, 6 December 1995. Sale says that knives flashed, but Craven says this is incorrect. She also disputes Sale's assertion that this incident convinced her that SDS, which she left about a year later, was "irrevocably racist," noting that Sale did not interview her. Sale, *SDS*, p. 250.

In a curious coda to the incident, Scott Pittman accompanied Magidoff and Ellis on the car ride from Champaign–Urbana to Cleveland, where Ellis went to escape contact with the police.

170. Nightbyrd interview. Nightbyrd, incidentally, was one of the few Texas activists that Craven took seriously.

171. Nightbyrd interview; Ture and Hamilton, *Black Power*, pp. 58–77. Ture and Hamilton powerfully attack the "myth" that "political coalitions are or can be sustained on a moral, friendly, sentimental basis" (p. 60). They call on the authority of pluralist thought in American political science to bolster their case, a connection not often noted in discussions of black power thought. The sobering political experience they point to is that of the Mississippi Freedom Democratic Party in 1964 (pp. 86–97).

172. Mariann Vizard, "United Front against Fascism," *Rag*, 7 August 1969; Sale, *SDS*, p. 284. The same convention elected Craven to the national council. One wonders what she and Speck talked about (if they talked at all).

I am interested here in the historical development of this trope of "white guilt." The accuracy of the perceptions on which this trope and the critique implied in it were based is a separate matter. This critique of "guilt"-based politics is quite close to the liberal criticism of the NCNP (National Conference for New Politics), discussed earlier, and it is the same as the criticism of the NCNP in Evans, *Personal Politics*.

173. See the essays collected in Harold Jacobs, ed., *Weatherman* (Berkeley, CA: Ramparts, 1970).

174. Calvert, "Democracy and Rebirth," pp. 472, 588–593; Sale, *SDS*, pp. 420–421. Kathy Archibald and Les Coleman were the national office personnel allied with Forman, with Archibald providing the personal connection. (Coleman, incidentally, was from Texas, a former Harvard student apparently from a wealthy oil family in Houston.) They subsequently formed an alliance with Michael Klonsky, who was an elected leader of national SDS.

175. Bill Helmer, "Nightmare in Houston," *Texas Observer*, 9–23 June 1967. A police officer was shot and killed in the TSU incident, and the police pointed afterward to this as the justification for their own nighttime fusillade against a university building. But Helmer reports that the officer was killed when the incident was almost over and suggests it likely was a stray police bullet that felled him.

176. Hal Wylie, "Larry Jackson: a biographical sketch," *Austin Gar*, March 1972; " 'Blacks Need Identity,' " *Daily Texan*, 19 December 1967; "Community United Front Child Care Center," *Gar*, March 1972. Jackson recently returned to his roots, becoming a political organizer for the Texas Republican Party.

177. Carol Calvert (Carol Neiman at that time was using Greg Calvert's name) and Sandy Carmichael, "Law N Order," *Rag*, 8 December 1968.

178. Reavis to author, 6 January 1992. Reavis reports that Charlie Saulsberry, who was around UT until early in 1969, actually did what Jackson was convicted for; he also says that FPL and Jackson together got the SDS chapter to take part in the protests.

179. Calvert interview.

180. Larry Jackson, letter, *Rag*, 27 January 1969; Larry Jackson, "I Feel Castrated," *Rag*, 17 July 1969.

181. "black activists run for Precinct Chairman," *Gar*, March–April 1972.

182. "Black Group Enumerates 11 Demands," *Daily Texan*, 2 March 1969; Rick Scott, "Silber Attacks Afro Demands as 'Unrealistic, Vague, Racist,'" *Daily Texan*, 28 February 1969; Editorial, "Silber's Talk: What Purpose?" *Daily Texan*, 2 March 1969; Lynne Flocke, "A&S Faculty Supports Black Studies Program," *Daily Texan*, 2 March 1969; Andy Yemma, "Action Taken on Report by Ethnic Group," *Daily Texan*, 3 June 1969.

In the spring of 1970, AABL reorganized itself as "The Blacks," and the new group was avowedly less radical. Lisa Schwertner, "AABL Becomes 'The Blacks,'" *Daily Texan*, 12 April 1970.

At almost exactly the same time that AABL submitted its demands, the Mexican-American Student Organization (MASO), which had formed in 1967, delivered a similar list to the UT administration, without the militant rhetoric: MASO called its items "proposals," not demands. This contrast and the clever timing ensured a positive response from many Anglos on campus. "Mexican-American Students' Ten Proposals," *Daily Texan*, 15 April 1969; Editorial, "MASO 'Ten' Commendable," *Daily Texan*, 13 April 1969. Although SDS members doubtless supported such demands, the relationship between the organized Anglo left and the Chicano movement on campus never became important to either.

On the Chicano student movement, see Carlos Munoz Jr., *Youth, Identity, Power: The Chicano Movement* (London: Verso, 1989); and Jose E. Limon, "The Expressive Culture of a Chicano Student Group at the University of Texas at Austin, 1967–1975" (Ph.D. diss., University of Texas at Austin, 1978).

183. This analogy came from Walter Adams, who in June 1969 was acting president of Michigan State University. Austin Scott, "Black, White Revolutions Separate," *Summer Texan*, 27 June 1969. Students of the labor movement's history will understand that the analogy was far from perfect; still, it contained a grain of serious insight.

W. E. Perkins and J. E. Higginson, "Black Students: Reformists or Revolutionaries?" in Aya and Miller, eds., *New American Revolution*, pp. 195–222, takes a similar view of militant black student demands. For an unusually discriminating discussion of the different varieties of black power politics at that time, see Robert Allen, *Black Awakening in Capitalist America* (New York: Doubleday, 1969).

184. Gitlin, *The Sixties*, p. 388.

See the account in Sale, *SDS*, pp. 557–574. The anti-PL forces dubbed themselves the "Revolutionary Youth Movement" (RYM), which split into RYM I and RYM II, the first of which became Weatherman. The BPP representative, Rufus ("Chaka") Walls, argued, in response to recent discussions of sexism among radicals, that women did indeed have a role to play in the revolution: they should withhold sexual favors from men who did not display revolutionary courage. As I will discuss in chapter 8, by this time feminist arguments had started to make headway on the left around the country, and for all the new left's worship of the black movement's machismo, this was too much.

185. Sale, *SDS*, p. 575, note; Brenner interview; Reavis to author, 6 January 1992.

186. Gitlin, *The Sixties*, p. 387, note.

187. The line was recalled by Robert Pardun, quoted in Sale, *SDS*, p. 225.

188. As early as 1968 Bartee Haile celebrated the movement of SDS away from the "semi-coherent humanist approach" of its early years. Bartee Haile Jr., "SDS Offers Alternative," *Dallas Notes*, 15 August–3 September 1968. Likewise, Victoria Smith of Houston asserted that SDS started out as "a tiny group of liberal and alienated students" but thankfully had evolved toward Weatherman's politics, which she and the Houston group that produced *Space City News* embraced after the RYM–PL split. She called Bernardine Dohrn and Mike Klonsky of RYM "the first real leadership that SDS . . . ever experienced." Smith admitted that "the rank-and-file of SDS is more united in its stand against PL than for the politics of [RYM]." She also acknowledged that "In Texas, SDS doesn't mean very much, except in Austin, that radical oasis." Victoria Smith, "SDS Expels PL: The First Big Split," *Space City News*, 17 July 1969. (Was she expecting others?)

As noted earlier, in 1969 Thorne Dreyer, who previously had been the *Rag*'s impresario, founded *Space City News* (later *Space City!*) after he moved to Houston; there were substantial Austin–Houston connections. Mariann Wizard recalls Dreyer as perhaps the most "hippy-dippy" of the SDS-UT chapter's early leaders, leading one to suspect that his leadership was displaced in Houston by others who favored a "harder" politics. Wizard interview.

189. Harvey Stone, "Action Factions," *Rag*, 30 September 1968; Calvert interview; Jackson, letter to *Rag*. Given the destructiveness of the FPL group in the chapter, it is worth noting that one of the small group was a police informer. Perhaps the aggravation of this kind of factionalism and the off-putting rhetoric, more than incitements to violence, were the most damaging tactics used against radicals at this time by agents provocateurs.

190. Pardun quoted in Sale, *SDS*, p. 461, emphasis in original. Pardun says he considered joining Weatherman, but nothing in his activities during the late 1960s that I know of indicates that his politics resembled theirs, though undoubtedly he knew many of those involved in RYM. Pardun interview.

191. Wizard interview.

192. Paul Pipkin notes that for the first several years of its existence, votes were taken in SDS-UT meetings. Paul Pipkin et al. interview.

193. Jeff Jones, interview with author, 16 and 23 February 1993. He is not to be confused with the Jeff Jones who was a prominent leader of Weatherman (this confusion was a source of humor in Austin).

194. Sale, *SDS*, p. 451; Calvert, "Democracy and Rebirth," p. 614.

In what some considered a breakthrough for the cause of women on the left, Dohrn and Naomi Jaffe coauthored a 1968 article in the newspaper produced by the SDS national office, offering a Marxist–feminist analysis arguing that "women suffer only a particular form of the general social oppression . . . an economy based on domination." They hoped for "an end to sexual objectification and exploitation." Naomi Jaffe and Bernardine Dohrn, "The Look Is You," *New Left Notes*, 18 March

1968, reprinted in Teodori, ed., *The New Left*, pp. 356, 358. Let us be generous and say that the depth of Dohrn's opposition to sexual objectification is a matter on which reasonable people may disagree. For more on the development of different strands of feminism on the left, see chapter 8.

195. Sale, *SDS*, p. 500; Calvert interview. Dohrn subsequently criticized the conference. Bernardine Dohrn, "Calvert's Conference: Legal Defense for Political Dissidents," *New Left Notes*, 18 December 1968.

196. Bill Meachem, interview with author, 29 June 1992.

197. Judy Smith, interview with author, 1 and 8 February 1993; Sale, *SDS*, p. 537; Meachem interview.

198. Scott Pittman, "On Leaving SDS," *Texas Observer*, 18 July 1969.

199. Fayetteville SDS, letter, *Rag*, 21 August 1969.

200. "Stormy Weather," *San Francisco Good Times*, 8 January 1970, excerpted in Jacobs, ed., *Weatherman*; Michele Clark, "wargasm," *Rag*, 17 November 1969.

201. Jeff, Connie, Doyle, Bill, "Something is happening, but you don't know what it is . . . ," *Rag*, 3 July 1969; "Movement," *Rag*, August–September 1969.

Chapter 6

1. Charles DeBenedetti, with Charles Chatfield, assisting author, *An American Ordeal: The Antiwar Movement of the Vietnam Era* (Syracuse, NY: Syracuse University Press, 1990), p. 112.

The quotation at the top of the chapter is from William Appleman Williams, *The Tragedy of American Diplomacy* (New York: Delta, 1959; rev. ed., 1962), p. 307.

2. The central U.S. war aim remained unchanged until the Americans admitted defeat in 1973. Outstanding accounts of the Vietnam War include William S. Turley, *The Second Indochina War: A Short Political and Military History, 1954–1975* (Boulder, CO: Westview Press, 1986), which views events from a Southeast Asian vantage point; Marilyn B. Young, *The Vietnam Wars, 1945–1990* (New York: HarperPerennial, 1991); George C. Herring, *America's Longest War: The United States and Vietnam, 1950–1975*, 3d ed. (New York: McGraw-Hill, 1996); and Christian G. Appy, *Working-Class War: American Combat Soldiers and Vietnam* (Chapel Hill: University of North Carolina Press, 1993), a fine social history.

3. Larry Waterhouse, interview with author, 10 July 1992.

4. Young, *Vietnam Wars*, pp. 136, 139.

5. Kirkpatrick Sale, *SDS* (New York: Random House, 1973), p. 173.

6. Young, *Vietnam Wars*, p. 152.

7. Quoted in Sale, *SDS*, p. 250.

8. Stanley Aronowitz, "When the New Left Was New," in Sohnya Sayres et al., eds., *The 60s without Apology* (Minneapolis: University of Minnesota Press, 1984), p. 21. Some on the left may take exception to this view, hearing in it an echo of conservative indictments of the new left for "giving aid and comfort to the enemy." But the criticism to which I refer speaks to strategy, not morals. One might also consider that those Aronowitz numbers among the partisans of this view included C.

Wright Mills and William Appleman Williams, as well as James Weinstein and others associated with the journal *Studies on the Left*. Mills, of course, came around to the "solidarity" camp, as Van Gosse recounts vividly. Van Gosse, *Where the Boys Are: Cuba, Cold War America, and the Making of a New Left* (London: Verso, 1993), pp. 176–183.

9. Larry Caroline, interview with author, 16 December 1992.

10. Tom Wells, *The War Within: America's Battle over Vietnam* (Berkeley and Los Angeles: University of California Press, 1994), pp. 44–45; DeBenedetti, *American Ordeal*, p. 167.

11. DeBenedetti, *American Ordeal*, pp. 124–125.

Even at the national level, SDS did not abandon the war issue after the April 1965 rally. Soon afterward, the organization held a meeting at Swarthmore College (led by Patch Dellinger, son of the pacifist David Dellinger, who emerged as one of the national leaders of the antiwar movement), where plans were laid for antiwar committees that would spend the summer of 1965 in various cities educating citizens about the war—presaging the 1967 "Vietnam Summer" project. Sale, *SDS*, pp. 197–198. The national leadership simply chose not to give the war issue priority over its other concerns.

The story of the 1965 rally has been told many times; one concise account of the political infighting surrounding the march, especially the hostility directed by older, anticommunist peace groups against SDS and its policy of "nonexclusionism," is James Weinstein, *Ambiguous Legacy: The Left in American Politics* (New York: New Viewpoints, 1975), pp. 134–141. Todd Gitlin, in *The Whole World Is Watching: Mass Media in the Making and Unmaking of the New Left* (Berkeley and Los Angeles: University of California Press, 1980), focuses on the rally and its aftermath—particularly on the controversy in SDS over the attempt by some members of the old guard to stake out a position for the organization on the issue of the draft—as a turning point in the new left's history. He also portrays the turn of events as a failure by SDS to take the lead in the antiwar movement at that time, and he chalks up that failure to internal squabbling.

12. Wells, *War Within*, pp. 47, 48 (Communists and Trotskyists); DeBenedetti, *American Ordeal*, p. 112 (liberals).

13. Robert Pardun, interview with author, 27 August 1993.

14. Wells, *War Within*, p. 47.

15. DeBenedetti, *American Ordeal*, pp. 204–205, 231–232; Wells, *War Within*, pp. 204–211; Johnson quoted in Wells, *War Within*, p. 208. Richard Nixon later experienced a similar frustration when the CIA once again failed to confirm presidential suspicions of Communist Party (CP) control in the antiwar movement (pp. 312–315). The Federal Bureau of Intelligence (FBI) was somewhat more accommodating, given Director J. Edgar Hoover's long-standing belief that all dissidence in American life was traceable to the CP; yet in 1968 Hoover finally caught up with the times, launching a "counterintelligence" program (COINTELPRO) that recognized new left radicals and other dissidents as political nuisances in their own right.

16. Sale, *SDS*, p. 170.

17. This was also shortly before Diem's murder in a coup that the U.S. government encouraged. "SPU Wants Names, Gets Stump Debate," *Daily Texan*, 23 October 1963; Laura Burns, "Student Peace Union Members Hold Peace for Madame Nhu," *Daily Texan*, 25 October 1963. DeBenedetti notes that SDS and SPU chapters organized protests against Nhu elsewhere on her tour (*American Ordeal*, p. 87). On the importance of SPU in the formation of SDS, see George R. Vickers, *The Formation of the New Left: The Early Years* (Lexington, MA: Lexington Books, 1975), pp. 51–61.

18. Carl Oglesby,"Trapped in a System," in Massimo Teodori, ed., *The New Left: A Documentary History* (Indianapolis: Bobbs-Merrill, 1969), pp. 182–188. Oglesby's emphasis on moral will was, of course, only one side of new left thought. This "moralistic" emphasis always competed with the new left's structural analysis, which militated against the capacity of individuals to choose their politics. The tension only became more severe over time.

19. Wells, *War Within*, p. 26; Tom Smith, "Meanwhile . . . Back at the Ranch," *Rag*, 10 April 1967. Nightbyrd recalled that some UT students who became involved in SDS participated in such a vigil as early as Easter 1963, but I have not been able to confirm this. Nightbyrd interview. SDS-UT jointly organized some of the vigils with Houston antiwar activists. By 1966, Chett Briggs was helping plan for the vigils. "Holiday Caravan & Vigil," *Rag*, 12 December 1966; "Vigil for Peace in Vietnam" (advertisement), *Rag*, 20 March 1967.

20. Alice Embree, interview with author, 9 November 1991; John Pope, "Moratorium Caps War Protest," *Daily Texan*, 15 October 1969.

21. Alice Embree, letter, *Rag*, 1 May 1972.

22. Nightbyrd interview; Ed Barrera, "Student Protesters Want to Be 'Involved,'" *Summer Texan*, 4 August 1967; Thorne Dreyer, "Flipped-out Week," *Rag*, 10 April 1967. The term *motherist* to describe antiwar efforts made by women explicitly as women comes from Amy Swerdlow, *Women Strike for Peace: Traditional Motherhood and Radical Politics in the 1960s* (Chicago: University of Chicago Press, 1993). Embree's memory of a "saving remnant" attitude among the early new left has validity, yet as I point out later, as time passed, this stance became even stronger in the radical movement, eclipsing all hope of influencing the political mainstream. Judy Kendall was an assistant professor of drama; her husband, Arnie Kendall, was chairman of the UT drama department. The Kendalls were good friends with many of the central figures in the Austin left, but they were more involved personally in the counterculture than in the left. Caroline interview.

23. Bonnie Barnhart, "CEWV to Sponsor Pro-Peace March," *Summer Texan*, 4 August 1967.

24. For example, at one antiwar rally in 1969, Pat Cuney spoke on the General Electric workers' strike then ongoing, and Jeff Jones spoke on the trial of the Chicago Eight (Linda Davis, "Outcome Viewed on Vietnam Vote," *Daily Texan*, 3 November 1967); at a spring 1970 antiwar rally, the speakers included Judy Smith

from Women's Liberation and Velma Roberts from the Austin branch of the National Welfare Rights Organization (Katie Fegan, "Police Arrest 13 Marchers," *Daily Texan*, 19 April 1970); and as part of the protest activity after the invasion of Cambodia and the shootings at Kent State University in early May 1970, campus leftists organized teach-ins on topics that included the trial of some Black Panther Party members in New Haven, Connecticut; the university's relations with the "war machine"; and university–"community" relations ("2-Day Teach-Ins Focus on 4 Topics," *Daily Texan*, 10 May 1970).

25. University of Texas Committee to End the War in Vietnam to "Faculty and Students," June 1967, flyer, in President's Office Papers, Eugene C. Barker Texas History Center, University of Texas at Austin.

26. Sandy Stuart, "SMC Speakers Connect Chicago, Chuck Wagon," *Daily Texan*, 14 December 1969.

27. University of Texas Committee to End the War in Vietnam (UTCEWV), *Newsletter 3*, 6 June (1967), p. 1, in President's Papers, Barker Texas History Center.

28. Peter Steinfels, "Lives of Children Test the Theories of Men," *National Catholic Reporter*, 28 June 1967; quoted in University of Texas Committee to End the War in Vietnam, *Newsletter 4*, July (1967), p. 6, in President's Papers, Barker Texas History Center, emphasis in original.

29. "Easter Day on Ranch Road One," *Texas Observer*, 14 April 1967.

30. David Gray, "Words and Deeds," UTCEWV, *Newsletter 4*, pp. 4, 3. On the "analogue of Nazi Germany" and "the Nuremberg doctrine of personal responsibility to resist evil" in the antiwar movement, see DeBenedetti, *American Ordeal*, p. 127. DeBenedetti related the Nazi analogy to larger "motifs" of "moral numbness" and "personal morality" in the peace movement (pp. 71–78).

31. David Halberstam, *The Making of a Quagmire* (New York: Random House, 1965).

32. Oglesby, "Trapped in a System."

33. Jerry Rudes, "Peace Marks Capitol March," *Daily Texan*, 22 October 1967; SDS and UTCEWV, *HKJ 1*, n.d., President's Papers, Barker Texas History Center, filed on 27 November 1967. The author of these newsletters was reportedly SDS member Howard Hertz. Linda David, "Speech Draws New Protests," *Daily Texan*, 1 December 1967.

34. SDS and UTCEWV, *HKJ 2*, n.d., President's Papers, Barker Texas History Center, filed on 28 November 1967.

35. " 'We Can Prevail,' " *Texas Observer*, 7 November 1969 (a reprint of Dugger's speech).

36. SDS and UTCEWV, *HKJ 3*, n.d., President's Papers, Barker Texas History Center, emphasis in original.

37. Clark Kerr, *The Uses of the University* (Cambridge, MA: Harvard University Pres, 1963; rev. ed., 1995).

38. In 1967 UT stood at number 109 on the list of nonprofit Defense contractors. It was a healthier thirteenth, though, in terms of overall federal obligations in

1966 among colleges and universities, due in part to large payments from the Department of Health, Education and Welfare. James Ridgway, *The Closed Corporation: American Universities in Crisis* (New York: Random House, 1968), pp. 238, 226, 236. Perhaps because of UT's middling status as a Defense contractor, military research specifically never became a major focus of antiwar agitation at UT. In March 1969, 150 faculty and graduate students quietly participated in a national antiwar strike to protest the role of the military in scientific research. "UT Researchers Halt in Protest," *Daily Texan*, 5 March 1969.

39. *An Appeal to Our Fellow Students and Fellow Teachers*, n.d., President's Papers, Barker Texas History Center, filed on 14 November 1967. This leaflet concerned recruitment on campus by the U.S. Marines. It is not signed by any group; it probably was distributed by a group of antiwar students who protested this recruitment activity on 14 November by sitting down on the floor of the student union around the recruiting table. The protest was not officially undertaken by any campus organization, but it involved SDS activists such as Gary Thiher. Mary Ann Teat, "Recruiters' Presence Sparks War Debate," *Daily Texan*, 15 November 1967. At that time, SDS was banned from campus, so members of the group may have been engaging in activism without using the group's name.

40. The *Port Huron Statement* held out the hope that the university could be "a community of controversy," in which leftists would find a haven. But at the same time, it conceded that "defense contracts make the universities engineers of the arms race." The ambivalence was present at the creation. Nonetheless, early on, the balance was on the side of optimism about the university's political role. *Port Huron Statement*, in James Miller, *"Democracy Is in the Streets": From Port Huron to the Siege of Chicago* (New York: Simon & Schuster, 1987), pp. 374, 373.

41. Carl Oglesby and Richard Shaull, *Containment and Change: Two Dissenting Views of American Foreign Policy* (London: Macmillan, 1967); Lucy Horton, "Peace Marchers Hike to Capitol for Rally," *Summer Texan*, 8 August 1967.

42. SDS, *Fact Sheet on Imperialism and Racism 1*, n.d., spring 1968, President's Papers, Barker Texas History Center. This document offered the orthodox Marxist definition of imperialism as "one of the last stages of fully developed capitalism," reflecting the influence by this time of the Progressive Labor (PL) contingent in SDS. Although many new left activists found persuasive the economic analysis of U.S. foreign policy, they generally were not concerned with what that foreign policy indicated about the advancing stages of capitalism. In contrast to Marxist thought, they tended to think that cultural, not economic, contradictions would precipitate a crisis in U.S. society.

43. As explained in chapter 5, PL at this time condemned all forms of nationalism as reactionary, tarring the Vietnamese and African American movements with the same brush. (It was not clear whether Chinese nationalism was included in this pronouncement.)

44. See Gosse, *Where the Boys Are*, generally, for a full, and highly stimulating, discussion of this process.

45. Caroline interview; "YAF, SDS Groups Debate over Cuba," *Daily Texan*, 23 April 1964.

46. C. Wright Mills, *Listen, Yankee!: The Revolution in Cuba* (New York: McGraw-Hill, 1960); C. Wright Mills, "Letter to the New Left," *New Left Review* 5 (1960): 18–23. In *Listen, Yankee!*, Mills assumes the voice of a Cuban revolutionary and concludes by proposing to *norteamericanos* that they take to the mountains, as Castro had, to prepare for an insurrection. Gosse recounts that in 1960, Mills provoked his Columbia University students thus: " 'I don't know what you guys are waiting for. . . . You've got a beautiful set of mountains in those Rockies. I'll show you how to use those pistols' " (Gosse, *Where the Boys Are*, pp. 179, 182).

47. Caroline interview.

48. Carl Jordan, "Venceremos!" *Rag*, 12 January 1970. In the fall of 1972, a call for those wishing to participate in the fifth Venceremos Brigade were told to contact either "Connie" or "Alice at Sattva"—probably Connie Lanham and Alice Embree. "Cuba," *Rag*, 18 October 1971.

49. See, for example, Mario Savio, "An End to History," *Humanity*, December 1964, reprinted in Loren Baritz, ed., *The American Left: Radical Political Thought in the Twentieth Century* (New York: Basic Books, 1971), pp. 449–452.

50. Philip Russell, interview with author, 28 June 1993.

51. Philip Russell, *Cuba in Transition* (Austin, TX: Armadillo Press, 1971), p. 22.

52. Ibid., p. 21.

53. The most famous statement of the thesis is in David Riesman, with Nathan Glazer and Reuel Denney, *The Lonely Crowd: A Study in the Changing American Character* (New Haven, CT: Yale University Press, 1950). William H. Whyte Jr., *The Organization Man* (New York: Simon & Schuster, 1956), is an ambivalent lament for the passing of the older type.

Vickers, *The Formation of the New Left*, advances the arresting argument that despite its best intentions, the new left actually served to "rationalize" American society by helping spread a "self-directed" personality that was well suited to the roles of college-educated workers in the world of bureaucratic capitalism. See the conclusion of chapter 7.

54. On the concept of "soft totalitarianism" in American social thought of the period, see Wilfred M. McClay, *The Masterless: Self and Society in Modern America* (Chapel Hill: University of North Carolina Press, 1994), pp. 221–268.

Van Gosse contends that *fidelismo* stood in opposition to the normative identity of "team-playing organization men" offered to young (male) Americans in this period (Gosse, *Where the Boys Are*, p. 2). This is true. But the heroic individualism represented in the figure of "Fidel" soon became amalgamated in the imagination of the North American left with the figure of the collective. For leftists in the United States, Cuban socialism embodied their ambivalence about individualism and group life.

55. Gosse, *Where the Boys Are*, p. 180; Paul Goodman, *Growing up Absurd: Problems of Youth in the Organized Society* (New York: Vintage Books, 1960). Mills was referring to those liberals who refused to support the Cuban revolution. Gosse's

book is replete with evidence of Castro's strongly masculine appeal in the United States (evidence whose implications Gosse is somewhat hesitant in following to their logical conclusion).

56. Michele Clark, letters from Cuba, *Rag*, 13 January 1969.

57. Garry Wills, *The Kennedy Imprisonment: A Meditation on Power* (Boston: Little, Brown, 1982); Abbie Hoffman quoted in Gitlin, *The Whole World Is Watching*, p. 197.

58. "Cuba Persecutes Gays," *Rag*, 21 June 1971.

59. Austin Gay Liberation, "Cuba, Gays & You," *Rag*, Summer 1971 (6 September 1971).

60. Susan Duncan, "july 26," *Rag*, 24 July 1972, emphasis added.

61. Williams, *Tragedy of American Diplomacy*, pp. 296–309. On the Kennedy administration's portrayal of the United States as a force for nonsocialist revolutionary change in the Third World, and the wider cultural meaning of this attempt to develop a revolutionary anticommunism, see Arthur M. Schlesinger Jr., *A Thousand Days: John F. Kennedy in the White House* (Boston: Houghton Mifflin, 1965), pp. 165–205; and Gosse, *Where the Boys Are*, pp. 192–199.

62. Paul Pipkin, Linda Pipkin, and Joe Ebbecke, interview with author, 4 July 1992; Oglesby, "Trapped in a System."

63. Nightbyrd interview. Potter later defended his speech, writing that he did not decline to "name the system" because "I was a coward or an opportunist," and Gitlin defends Potter's explanation in *The Sixties*, pp. 184–186, arguing that Potter's elaborate reticence stemmed from a sincere desire to transcend the conceptual baggage of the old left. This rendition of the feelings of the early SDS leadership is plausible. They were not afraid to take unpopular positions. Nonetheless, there also was more than a touch of practiced naïveté in the political demeanor of this leadership circle, an important part of their calculated "all-American" appeal. Furthermore, one has to pay some heed to James Weinstein's contention that Potter's analysis of U.S. foreign policy was limited at that time by "the prevalence of liberal ideology," at the limits of which Potter visibly chafed. Weinstein, *Ambiguous Legacy*, pp. 139–140.

64. See Appy, *Working-Class War*, pp. 218–219, on the currency of this argument among U.S. servicemen.

65. Merry Clark, "Debaters Argue Vietnam Question," *Daily Texan*, 20 September 1967. Larry Caroline made this antidomino argument explicitly in an interview conducted with him and several other CEWV members. Bettye Gormley, "CEWV Demands 'Senseless Killing, Maiming . . . to Stop Now!'" *Daily Texan Panorama*, 19 November 1967.

66. Nightbyrd interview.

67. Irwin Spear, interview with author, 30 June 1992.

68. Nightbyrd interview.

69. "Tupamaros!" *Rag*, 14 September 1970; Ken Steenland, "Death of a Revolutionary," *Rag*, 3 April 1972; Rafael Tinoco, "the chilean lie," *Rag*, 2 November

1970; "Socialist Jews in Israel Say Anti-Zionism Is Not Anti-Jew," *Rag*, 19 October 1970; Vivian Price (Palestine Solidarity Committee), "Kahane," *Rag*, 20 March 1972; Jude, "Quebec," *Rag*, 16 November 1970; "A Look at the IRA," *Rag*, 20 March 1972; P. G. Duffy (American Irish Republican army), letter, *Rag*, 5 June 1972; Phil Prim, letter, *Rag*, 5 June 1972; "Southern Africa," *Rag*, 7 December 1970; Gitlin, *The Sixties*, p. 317.

The central figures in starting CORA were Steve Russell and Betty White. This group urged boycotting products made by corporations, like Polaroid, that were heavily invested in South Africa and (along with the local Vietnam Veterans Against the War chapter) disrupted the UT Business School appearance of a representative from Gulf Oil. "Boycott Polaroid," *Rag*, 19 April 1971; Judy, "Big Business . . . ," *Rag*, 4 October 1971.

Among those arrested in March 1965 were Todd Gitlin and Tom Hayden, both of whom soon afterward expressed strong reservations about SDS's focusing on the Vietnam War. Perhaps the clear racial dimension of the South Africa issue made it more attractive to them; perhaps they liked the emphasis on U.S. banks, indicating a kind of economic analysis that was not then visible in the peace-oriented protest against the war.

70. Dick Howard, "Czechs Bounce—No Credit," *Rag*, 16 September 1968 (a Marxist analysis that nonetheless sided with the Czechs); Phil Russell, "Alliance for Progress," *Rag*, 16 September 1968; Philip Russell, "Mexico . . . Two Eye Witnesses," *Rag*, 21 October 1968; Phil Russell, "movement postmortem," *Rag*, 13 January 1969.

71. William A. Williams, *Empire as a Way of Life: An Essay on the Causes and Character of America's Present Predicament, Along with a Few Thoughts about an Alternative* (New York: Oxford University Press, 1980).

72. Gitlin, *The Sixties*, p. 261.

73. Susan Wagner, "Draft Cards Mailed by Antidraft Group," *Daily Texan*, 17 October 1967; "Committee to End War Disavows Responsibility," *Daily Texan*, 18 October 1967.

74. John Watkins, "Austin Draft Information Centers Supply Students with Alternatives," *Daily Texan*, 26 October 1969; Gregory N. Calvert, "Democracy and Rebirth: The New Left and Its Legacy" (Ph.D. diss., University of California at Santa Cruz, 1989), pp. 521–529; Michael Ferber and Staughton Lynd, *The Resistance* (Boston: Beacon Press, 1971); Sara Evans, *Personal Politics: The Roots of Women's Liberation in the Civil Rights Movement and the New Left* (New York: Vintage Books, 1980), pp. 180–182.

75. Harvey Stone, "GI Coffee Houses Push Peace," *Dallas Notes*, 1–15 August 1968.

76. "Richard Chase Gets 2 Year Sentence," *Dallas Notes*, 7–20 January 1970.

77. "At Fort Hood," *Texas Observer*, 20 September 1968.

78. Greg Olds, "A Crisis of Conscience," *Texas Observer*, 4 August 1967; "Army Dissenters Refused Hearing," *Daily Texan*, 7 November 1967; DeBenedetti,

American Ordeal, p. 155. The GIs themselves initiated the civilian court proceedings in an attempt to prove the war was illegal, since it was undeclared. The U.S. Supreme Court refused to hear their appeal from the federal district court that had rejected their arguments.

79. Waterhouse interview; Larry Waterhouse and Mariann G. Wizard, *Turning the Guns Around: Notes on the GI Movement* (New York: Praeger, 1971); Calvert, "Democracy and Rebirth," p. 502.

80. After speaking at an antiwar rally in Austin in April 1969 and at the 15 October 1969 Moratorium rally there, Pfc. Robert Bower got off with only thirty days at hard labor and a reduction in rank. Michael Simpson, "1,000 March in Peace Parade through Downtown Sunday," *Daily Texan*, 15 April 1969; "g.i. catches it," *Rag*, 24 November 1969; "Court Martials," *Texas Observer*, 2 January 1970. Pfc. Howard Petrick, a Trotskyist, spoke at both local and national Student Mobilization Committee gatherings; the army chose simply to get rid of him, concluding that he would continue to sow dissent even in the stockade. Arthur Yarborough, "The Case of Pfc Howard Petrick," *Texas Observer*, 4 August 1967.

81. Richard Chase was the soldier who was beaten while in the stockade. He had worked on the *Fatigue Press*. After thirty minutes' deliberation, a court-martial found him guilty of disobeying orders and sentenced him to two years at hard labor and a dishonorable discharge. "Army 'Justice,' " *Rag*, 12 January 1970; Mike Love, "Richard Chase Ripped Off," *Space City!* 17–30 January 1970.

In a more spectacular case, forty-three black Fort Hood soldiers refused to go to Chicago for riot control duty before the 1968 Democratic National Convention. "At Fort Hood"; "Law and Orders," *Rag*, 23 September 1968; Wells, *War Within*, p. 282.

82. "At Fort Hood"; Mike Love, "Richard Chase Ripped Off"; Tom Cleaver, "When in the Coarseness—Of Human Events," *Rag*, 18 November 1968; "Court Martials."

83. "Killeen!!" *Rag*, 20 September 1971; "Rally in Killeen December 4," *Fatigue Press* 35 (November 1971), p. 2.

84. "Rally in Killeen December 4," p. 7.

85. Terry DuBose, interview with author, 23 June 1992; Mike Lewis, "FT AF Bergstrom," *Rag*, 21 June 1971; VVAW Texas Regional Office, "We, the winter soldiers, have come home to speak to our parents," *Rag*, 30 August 1971.

86. *Nonviolence*, VVAW flyer, n.d. (courtesy of Terry DuBose), emphasis added.

87. Lori Hansel, interview with author, 2 July 1992.

88. Certainly by the 1960s, the category of "Trotskyism" in the United States had lost much of its earlier ideological content. To take this label meant that one adhered to Marxist-Leninist ideas of a proletarian socialist revolution against capitalism, led by a "vanguard" political party, but that one did not pay fealty to the government of the Soviet Union or any other foreign government (not that one based one's activities on the ideas of Leon Trotsky). By the 1960s, the Trotskyists clearly had abandoned all Leninist notions of a revolutionary seizure of power, instead hoping to build a legal mass movement that could support independent

SWP candidacies in the existing electoral system. The American Trotskyist movement, always very small, did enjoy some notable successes in the area of labor
union organizing in the 1930s, particularly in Minneapolis. The SWP's antiwar
activism in the 1960s was its first significant political activity since that time. How
it survived the interim with cadres who could intervene effectively on the issue of
the war is a question that historians of the American left have not answered, or
even asked.

Historians of the antiwar movement have not treated the SWP in a satisfactory
manner. Charles DeBenedetti and Charles Chatfield, in *An American Ordeal*, favor
the same moderation that the Trotskyists championed, but the authors seem to have
no place for these "moderate radicals," as one might best call them, in their typology of "radicals" versus "liberals." Tom Wells, in *The War Within*, replicates the new
left derogation of the SWP, insisting on their obstructionism and their elevation of
party building over coalition building. These criticisms are justified, yet Wells simplifies matters when he assigns the Trotskyists the lion's share of the blame for factionalism in the antiwar movement and when he slights their constructive work.
Others acted just as divisively, and the SWP deserves a share of the credit for developing broad-ranging activist coalitions against the war. Fred Halstead, chief representative of the SWP in these coalitions (and the party's presidential candidate in
1968), tells his side of this story in *Out Now!: A Participant's Account of the American
Movement against the Vietnam War* (New York: Monad, 1978).

89. Fred Halstead made the remark about "plate-glass revolutionaries"; quoted
in DeBenedetti, *American Ordeal*, p. 397.

90. Steve Russell, "More Trots," *Rag*, 13 March 1972.

91. Paul Pipkin relates that Howard Scoggins, a former merchant marine sailor,
was the key person in Austin who engineered the importation of the Trotskyist
operatives, reportedly from New Jersey, along with adequate organizing funds.
Scoggins and Pipkin lived in the same house during the summer of 1969. Pipkin
says that Scoggins was relatively free of the sectarian maneuverings that marked the
YSA personnel who came to town in the following year. Pipkin et al. interview.

92. Judy (Smith), "More Trots," *Rag*, 13 March 1972.

93. "SMC! Report from Cleveland," *Rag*, 24 February 1970; Jim Denney, interview with author, 8 April 1993; Wells, *War Within*, p. 405.

94. Russell, "More Trots." At an Austin SMC meeting in February 1970,
Singler's YSA faction and its proposal to emphasize a mass demonstration in the
coming spring antiwar activity prevailed over proposals by Jeff Jones and Doyle
Niemann for, respectively, working class–oriented protests in poor areas of Austin
and a combination of film festival and workplace teach-ins. Anne Hagy, "SMC
Adopts Slogan," *Daily Texan*, 26 February 1970.

95. "Trots Reply to Rag," *Rag*, 9 October 1972; "Trot Fronts; a guide," *Rag*, 2
October 1972.

96. Eric Sell, "YSA Replies to the Rag Article," *Rag*, 13 March 1972; Judy
(Smith) et al., "e-liminate the revisionists: Student Elections," *Rag*, 28 February

1972. John Edgar Hoover, *Masters of Deceit: The Story of Communism in America and How to Fight It* (New York: Holt, 1958).

97. J. L., Jack, Toni, Jeff, Nancy, Silly, Chris, Ilda, Blanche, Steve, Kris, Mike, Trey, Gail, Jack, Ellen, Becky, Kenny, et al., "Rimbaud's Birthday: Sattva on Trots," *Rag*, 23 October 1972.

98. Ibid.

99. Ibid.; Hansel interview.

100. Pat Cuney, interview with author, 5 July 1992.

101. Denney interview.

102. Ruth Doyle, "Moratorium Day Activity Encompasses UT, Capitol," *Daily Texan*, 16 October 1969.

103. The SMC called for a march on the sidewalks, since the permit was technically only for use of the street. A small number of participants were arrested for defying the council and walking in the street. Edwin Shrake, "Marching for peace—again," *Texas Observer*, 1 May 1970. The civil liberties angle was uppermost in the *Texan*'s endorsement of the march. "Editorial: The sidewalk or the street?" *Daily Texan*, 17 April 1970.

104. A concise account of events in Austin can be found in Kaye Northcott, "Austin's Last March?" *Texas Observer*, 29 May 1970. Once again, the Austin City Council denied a parade permit, and the protesters prepared once again to march on the sidewalk, but after the march had begun, a federal district court judge ruled that the denial of the permit was an infringement of the marchers' right of free speech and allowed the march to take place in the street. (The local police abided by the judgment.) Unlike hundreds of other schools around the country, UT declined to shut down for the brief remainder of the school year, or even for the remainder of the week of the shootings, when the student body was on strike—decisions made by the regents and engineered by Frank Erwin, in the face of the faculty's large majority vote in favor of shutting down for the week. Even more overwhelmingly, the faculty adopted a resolution condemning the invasion of Cambodia and the renewed campaign of bombing against North Vietnam and called on President Nixon "to take immediate action to demonstrate unequivocally [his] determination to end the war." Quoted in Northcott, "Austin's Last March?"

105. Dave, "Picking up the Pieces no. 9," *Rag*, 31 May 1971. Before the dedication ceremonies at the LBJ School were held, the local police issued preemptive injunctions to several prominent local activists, forbidding them to come near the protest site. Hansel interview. Nonetheless, twenty-nine ultimately were arrested in connection with the protests.

The first violence of any kind at an Austin antiwar demonstration did not come from the demonstrators. It occurred when the police teargassed and maced a crowd of perhaps three thousand who had marched from UT to the state capitol on 5 May 1970, the day after the Kent State shootings. Lyke Thompson, "Demonstrators Tear Gassed," *Daily Texan*, 6 May 1970. This contrasted with the peaceful, even happy mood that prevailed on the day of the biggest march, three days later.

106. Hansel interview. An unaffiliated group of antiwar radicals blew up the Army Mathematics Research Center (AMRC); they did so in the middle of the night and issued a warning to evacuate the building, but nonetheless a young physicist working inside, Robert Fassnacht, died in the explosion. The radicals targeted the AMRC because it conducted weapons-related research for the Department of Defense, contributing to the development of napalm, among other instruments of warfare. The story is told in great detail in Tom Bates, *Rads: The 1970 Bombing of the Army Math Research Center at the University of Wisconsin and Its Aftermath* (New York: HarperCollins, 1992).

107. Maurice Isserman, daringly but suggestively, depicts the violence of the Weatherman terrorists as a form of "witness," political activity with no instrumental goal—though this term usually refers to the activities of radical pacifists. Maurice Isserman, *If I Had a Hammer . . . : The Death of the Old Left and the Birth of the New Left* (New York: Basic Books, 1987), pp. 168–169.

108. Martin Wiginton, "Why We Must Take Action on Mayday," *Rag*, 1 May 1972.

109. Ibid.

110. Tom Hayden argued in early 1968 that the antiwar left's task was to provoke the "sleeping dogs on the right" in the hope that the power elite would favor a settlement of the war to quell political polarization and social disorder. This was the logic behind the antiwar mobilization at the 1968 Democratic National Convention, which Hayden and Rennie Davis, his old SDS comrade, promoted against the wishes of cooler heads. Gitlin, *The Sixties*, pp. 288–291. To get his way, Hayden used an underhanded tactic: keeping a meeting going long enough so that its size dwindles and then reversing an earlier vote when enough of one's opponents leave. In this case, a meeting of the New Mobilization Committee had voted against the Chicago confrontation plan, and Hayden managed to negate that decision. Wells, *War Within*, pp. 238–239. For a vivid account of the events in Chicago generally, see David R. Farber, *Chicago '68* (Chicago: University of Chicago Press, 1988). As the 1968 election results and the subsequent behavior of the Nixon administration demonstrated, this polarization analysis, reflecting the new left's view of reform as a tool of the ruling elite, vastly overrated the investment of that elite in maintaining political consensus and failed to see the usefulness of social disorder to the political right.

111. These protests may well have played a role in the Nixon administration's decision not to move forward with Operation Duck Hook, a multipronged and massive escalation of the war against North Vietnam, though this point is disputed. Still, one certainly can argue that at particular moments, militance restrained the war effort as well. Wells contends that the highly militant 1971 Mayday protests (discussed later) may have influenced the administration's softening of its position on Hanoi's retention of its troops in South Vietnam after the conclusion of a peace agreement. Wells, *War Within*, pp. 377–379, 512–513.

The relative effectiveness of militance and mass mobilizations was the subject of incessant debate in the antiwar movement, as every account of that movement relates, and the question can be debated endlessly. One balanced retrospective on this tactical debate, which concludes that protesters should try a bit of everything, since it's hard to know what works and what doesn't, is Melvin Small, "Influencing the Decisionmakers: The Vietnam Experience," *Journal of Peace Research* 24 (1987): 185–198. Interviews with former government officials, such as those that Wells conducted for his book, shed rather limited light on the matter: Richard Helms or Harry McPherson averring the deep impression that the antiwar movement made on them does not constitute proof that the protesters actually changed any of the key decisions concerning the war.

112. This, too, is debatable. Opposition to the war increased steadily in the campaign's later years, even as vilification of antiwar protesters continued unabated. As all sound studies of public opinion during the war indicate, a large section of the U.S. public both opposed the war and loathed the antiwar protesters. See, for example, Howard Schuman, "Two Sources of Antiwar Opinion in America," *American Journal of Sociology* 78 (November 1972): 513–536; and Howard Schuman, " 'Silent Majorities' and the Vietnam War," *Scientific American*, June 1970, pp. 17–25.

113. Martin J. Murray, "Building Fires on the Prairie," in Martin Oppenheimer, Martin J. Murray, and Rhonda F. Levine, eds., *Radical Sociologists and the Movement: Experiences, Lessons, and Legacies* (Philadelphia: Temple University Press, 1991), p. 103; "Mayday!" *Rag*, 19 April 1971; "Austin Maydays," *Rag*, 26 April 1971; Hansel interview.

114. In 1975 these monetary costs increased greatly when a federal court ordered damages totaling $12 million to individuals who were arrested illegally on 5 May 1971. George W. Hopkins, " 'May Day' 1971: Civil Disobedience and the Antiwar Movement," in Melvin Small and William D. Hoover, eds., *Give Peace a Chance: Exploring the Vietnam Antiwar Movement* (Syracuse, NY: Syracuse University Press, 1992), pp. 85–86.

Hopkins comes to a more generous conclusion than I concerning the effectiveness of these protests, arguing reasonably that militant protests and pacific mass gatherings against the war were complementary, not contradictory, tactics. Hopkins, " 'May Day' 1971," pp. 87–88.

115. On the People's Peace Treaty, see DeBenedetti, *American Ordeal*, pp. 295–296, 316; and Hopkins, " 'May Day' 1971," pp. 74–76. The National Coalition Against War, Racism, and Repression (NCAWRR) actually developed the proposal for the treaty and took it to the NSA for approval, and the NCAWRR subsequently reorganized itself as the PCPJ. The NSA sent a delegation to Vietnam to negotiate for the United States. In February 1971, an NSA conference of two thousand approved the treaty in Ann Arbor, and more than two hundred college and university student governments also endorsed it. It called for an immediate withdrawal of U.S. forces from Vietnam, with a specific date set for the completion of the withdrawal. Hopkins, " 'May Day' 1971," pp. 75–76.

The large rally on 24 April was organized by the Trotskyist-led National Peace Action Coalition (NPAC); it was perhaps the single most successful application of the Trotskyist approach to antiwar protest. NPAC also, unfortunately, played sectarian mischief by purposely scheduling its demonstration so as to steal PCPJ's thunder, hoping that many protesters who came to Washington on 24 April would leave before the Mayday actions began. The result was that with the NPAC rally victimized by a partial news blackout and with the Mayday protests receiving overwhelmingly negative coverage, the public perceptions of all the protests from this two-week period blended together, with the Mayday Tribe's unsympathetic image prevailing. Wells, *War Within*, pp. 479–480, 511–512; Melvin Small, *Covering Dissent: The Media and the Anti-Vietnam War Movement* (New Brunswick, NJ: Rutgers University Press, 1994), pp. 140–160.

The VVAW action was called "Dewey Canyon III," echoing the names of illegal U.S. Army interventions in Laos. Antiwar veterans lobbied members of Congress and asked the Supreme Court why it had not ruled on the constitutionality of the war. And in a highly emotional ceremony, three thousand of them gave back the medals they had received in the war, throwing them toward the Capitol, over the fence that the government had erected to prevent their approach. William F. Crandell, "They Moved the Town: Organizing Vietnam Veterans against the War," in Small and Hoover, eds., *Give Peace a Chance*, pp. 148–151; Wells, *War Within*, pp. 492–496.

116. Stroud, "Opinion," *Rag*, 24 April 1972. I don't know whom Stroud was quoting.

117. Steve Russell, "Thursday Night," *Rag*, 24 April 1972.

118. "Doing It," *Rag*, 31 May 1971.

119. "What Is Direct Action?" *Rag*, 30 August 1971.

120. Ed Hedemann to author, 19 January 1993; Ed Hedemann, "I.R.S . . . .War Tax Resistance," *Rag*, 4 September 1972.

121. Ed Hedemann, "On wars and taxes," *Texas Observer*, 11 December 1970.

122. In the later years of the war, one variety of religious antiwar protest that received increasing attention was the heavily symbolic action of Roman Catholic activists such as Daniel and Philip Berrigan. This activity seemed to be most important in areas with heavy concentrations of white Catholics, mainly in the North. See Francine du Plessix Gray, "The Ultra-Resistance," in *New York Review of Books*, ed., *Trials of the Resistance* (New York: New York Review Press, 1970); Kenneth Heineman, *Campus Wars: The Peace Movement on American Campuses in the Vietnam Era* (New York: New York University Press, 1992), pp. 273–274; and the analysis of Daniel Berrigan's writings in J. Justin Gustainis, *American Rhetoric and the Vietnam War* (Westport, CT: Praeger, 1993), pp. 67–78.

123. Harvey Stone, "Vote for What?" *Rag*, 4 November 1968.

124. Calvert summarizes his views of New Deal liberalism and its obsolescence in Greg Calvert and Carol Neiman, *A Disrupted History: The New Left and the New Capitalism* (New York: Random House, 1971), pp. 163–170.

125. Rick Scott and Chris Shively, "Humphrey Faces Noisy Onlookers," *Daily Texan*, 23 October 1968.

126. Harvey Stone, "Conventional Warfare," *Rag*, 22 August 1968.

Oglesby met in early 1968 with a group of businessmen and pledged to do what he could to bring the new left behind Kennedy's candidacy. Despite the radicalism of his analysis, Oglesby was a pragmatist, and perhaps his "American heart" was not quite beyond repair. He was not in step with the dominant trend of thought in the new left, however, and was soon marginalized. Wells, *War Within*, pp. 226–227.

127. Steve Russell, writing for the *Rag* staff, "Only 3 More Election Days 'til 1984," *Rag*, 30 October 1972.

128. Ibid.

129. "Electoral Politics: Jim Simons, 'nay,' " *Rag*, 6 March 1972.

130. "Electoral Politics: Gavan Duffy, M. Wizard, 'yea,' " *Rag*, 6 March 1972.

131. Judy (Smith), "so you wanna relate . . . ," *Rag*, 1 May 1972.

132. Victoria Foe, interview with author, 4 May 1995.

133. For example, DeBenedetti, *America Ordeal*, pp. 312–347 (the chapter entitled "Normalizing Dissent").

134. Terry H. Anderson, *The Movement and the Sixties: Protest in America from Greensboro to Wounded Knee* (New York: Oxford University Press, 1995), pp. 355–410.

135. Murray, "Building Fires on the Prairie," p. 104.

136. Ronnie Dugger, "The Peace Movement Can No Longer Be Ignored," *Texas Observer*, 10 November 1967.

137. Murray Bookchin, "From the '30s to the '60s," in Sayres et al., eds., *The 60s without Apology*, p. 251. To the best of my knowledge, Bookchin is the only writer who clearly takes the unorthodox position that the antiwar movement badly damaged the new left. Alice Echols cites Bookchin's view in her essay " 'Woman Power' and Women's Liberation: Exploring the Relationship between the Antiwar Movement and the Women's Liberation Movement," in Small and Hoover, eds., *Give Peace a Chance*, p. 181, suggesting that she is sympathetic to his interpretation, but she stops short of making explicit her own view of the matter.

138. The emphasis on militance marked the new left from its beginnings (the favored term in its early years was "direct action"), and the changes that occurred in the movement's tactical thinking were to a large extent changes in the variety of militance that was favored. James Weinstein notes that the "confusion of the form of an action with its political content runs through the history of the left in the United States," forming a hidden connection between the old and new lefts. He contends that in the absence of a socialist perspective, the "form of [the new left's] activity, rather than a comprehensive political perspective or a positive program, became a mark of how 'radical' it conceived itself to be" (Weinstein, *Ambiguous Legacy*, pp. 148, 139). Maurice Isserman argues that the turn away from nonviolent militance in the new left was a response to the lead of the African American movement. Maurice Isserman, "You Don't Need a Weatherman but a Postman Can Be Helpful: Thoughts on the History of SDS and the Antiwar Movement," in Small and Hoover, eds., *Give Peace a Chance*, pp. 32–34.

Chapter 7

1. The currency of this turn of phrase is noted in Paul Buhle, "The Eclipse of the New Left: Some Notes," pp. 4–5, and James O'Brien, "Beyond Reminiscence: The New Left in History," p. 29, both in *Radical America* 6 (July–August 1972).

2. The relation between the categories of "new class" and "new working class" is close but problematic. Both terms connote the view that the college-educated young of the twentieth-century United States constituted the germ of the new society developing inside the shell of the old. But the two analyses in which the terms are embedded differ concerning the genuine class identity of this stratum. New class analysts locate a college-educated "professional–managerial class" (PMC) of "symbol manipulators" who work with words instead of things, in a distinct social niche "between labor and capital." In other words, in this view, the middle-class identity of the college-educated technicians, managers, and professionals is not simply a false consciousness, as the new working-class analysts assert. This view, that the PMC really is a class unto itself, wreaks havoc with the new class analysts' exhortation to the PMC to join forces with the working class in a revolutionary alliance. If the PMC is not to go it alone, there is little reason to think an alliance with capital would not offer an easier path toward the PMC's fulfillment of its historical mission. The signal statement of the new class analysis is by Barbara and John Ehrenreich, "The Professional–Managerial Class," in Pat Walker, ed., *Between Labor and Capital* (Boston: South End Press, 1979), pp. 5–48; and Barbara Ehrenreich updates the analysis in *Fear of Falling: The Inner Life of the Middle Class* (New York: Pantheon, 1989). The concept is discussed tortuously by a variety of authors in Walker, ed., *Between Labor and Capital*; elegantly in Jean-Christophe Agnew, "A Touch of Class," *democracy* 3 (September 1983): 59–72; and polemically in Christopher Lasch, *The True and Only Heaven: Progress and Its Critics* (New York: Norton, 1991), pp. 509–529.

3. Lawrence Goodwyn, *The Populist Moment* (New York: Oxford University Press, 1978), p. 165. Although this is speculation, I find it plausible that Goodwyn was influenced by his sympathetic exposure to a milieu in which the dream of an authentic, anticapitalist movement culture was so widespread.

4. Christopher Lasch, *The New Radicalism in America, 1889–1963: The Intellectual as a Social Type* (New York: Norton, 1986), p. 286.

5. "Malvina Reynolds," *Rag*, 11 November 1968. Reynolds wrote the famous song "Little Boxes," ridiculing the conformism of upper-middle-class culture in 1950s America.

6. Richard Flacks, "Some Problems, Issues, Proposals," in Paul Jacobs and Saul Landau, eds., *The New Radicals: A Report with Documents* (New York: Vintage Books, 1966), p. 163; quotation in Edward E. Ericson Jr., *Radicals in the University* (Stanford, CA: Hoover Institution Press, 1975), p. 4.

Wini Breines is the scholar most closely associated with the idea that the new left's politics was strongly "prefigurative," as opposed to "instrumental." An instrumental politics is committed above all to achieving certain social goals and chooses efficacious means to those ends; a prefigurative politics seeks means that embody the goals in mind. Wini Breines, *Community and Organization in the New Left, 1962–1968: The Great Refusal* (South Hadley, MA: J. F. Bergin, 1982).

7. Kesey advised young people to "turn your backs [on the war] and say . . . Fuck it." Tom Wolfe, *The Electric Kool-Aid Acid Test* (New York: Bantam, 1968), p. 200.

My point here is not to express hostility to the new left's outlook but, for purposes of analysis, merely to gain some critical distance from it. Some historians of 1960s radicalism have evinced a rather unproblematic identification with their subject matter, and this has led to considerable confusion concerning the true relations between the new left and the freak counterculture. Other analysts in their hostility have confused the issue in curiously symmetrical ways. For detailed coverage of the literature, see Doug Rossinow, "The New Left in the Counterculture: Hypotheses and Evidence," *Radical History Review* 67 (Winter 1997): 79–120.

8. Lasch, *True and Only Heaven*, pp. 476–532; David Farber, "The Silent Majority and Talk about Revolution," in David Farber, ed., *The Sixties: From Memory to History* (Chapel Hill: University of North Carolina Press, 1994), pp. 291–316.

9. The following books offer a variety of perspectives on the white youth counterculture of the era: Theodore Rozsak, *The Making of a Counter-Culture: Reflections on the Technocratic Society and Its Youthful Opposition* (New York: Doubleday, 1969); Rosabeth Moss Kanter, *Commitment and Community: Communes and Utopias in Sociological Perspective* (Cambridge, MA: Harvard University Press, 1972); John Case and Rosemary C. R. Taylor, eds., *Co-ops, Communes & Collectives: Experiments in Social Change in the 1960s and 1970s* (New York: Pantheon, 1979); Steven M. Tipton, *Getting Saved from the Sixties: Moral Meaning in Conversion and Cultural Change* (Berkeley and Los Angeles: University of California Press, 1982); Charles Perry, *The Haight-Ashbury: A History* (New York: Random House, 1984); Abe Peck, *Uncovering the Sixties: The Life and Times of the Underground Press* (New York: Pantheon, 1985); Jay Stevens, *Storming Heaven: LSD and the American Dream* (New York: Harper & Row, 1987); Nicholas von Hoffman, *We Are the People Our Parents Warned Us Against* (Chicago: Ivan R. Dee, 1989); Timothy Miller, *The Hippies and American Values* (Knoxville: University of Tennessee Press, 1991); Marty Jezer, *Abbie Hoffman: American Rebel* (New Brunswick, NJ: Rutgers University Press, 1992).

10. Herbert Marcuse, *One-Dimensional Man: Studies in the Ideology of Advanced Industrial Society* (Boston: Beacon Press, 1964). See Paul Robinson, *The Freudian Left: Wilhelm Reich, Geza Roheim, Herbert Marcuse* (New York: Harper & Row, 1969), pp. 202–208; and Richard King, *The Party of Eros: Radical Social Thought and the Realm of Freedom* (Chapel Hill: University of North Carolina Press, 1972), pp. 128–131.

11. Mariann Wizard, interview with author, 8 July 1992; "The King of May Comes to Austin: The Rag Interviews Allen Ginsberg," *Rag*, 24 April 1967.

12. "The King of May Comes to Austin."

13. Jeff Shero Nightbyrd, interview with author, 3 July 1992; Bobby Minkoff, interview with author, 4 and 9 March 1993; *Port Huron Statement*, in James Miller,

"Democracy Is in the Streets": From Port Huron to the Siege of Chicago (New York: Simon & Schuster, 1987), p. 332.

14. Miller, *"Democracy Is in the Streets,"* p. 333; "Statement by Bob Pardun," SDS-UT retreat working papers, n.d., SDS Papers Locality File, 1964–68—Texas, reel 25, 3:62.

15. "Teen Queen—The American Dream," *Rag*, 14 November 1966.

16. Larry Freudiger, "Grassroots Sociology: A Weekly Discussion of the American Social Revolution and the Reactions against It: The White Revolution," *Rag*, 30 January 1967.

17. Ibid.

18. Nightbyrd interview; Nightbyrd quoted in Barry Shank, *Dissonant Identities: The Rock 'n' Roll Scene in Austin, Texas* (Hanover, NH: Wesleyan University Press/University Press of New England, 1994), p. 44.

19. See Robbie Lieberman, *"My Song Is My Weapon": People's Songs, American Communism, and the Politics of Culture, 1930–1950* (Urbana: University of Illinois Press, 1989), one of innumerable books shaped by the political and theoretical concerns descended from the new left's cultural politics; and also the older, hostile account in R. Serge Denisoff, *Great Day Coming!: Folk Music and the American Left* (Urbana: University of Illinois Press, 1971).

20. Todd Gitlin, *The Sixties: Years of Hope, Days of Rage* (New York: Bantam, 1987), p. 75.

21. Shank, *Dissonant Identities*, pp. 40, 41; also see Robin D. G. Kelley, "Notes on Deconstructing 'The Folk,'" *American Historical Review* 97 (December 1992): 1400–1408.

22. Shank, *Dissonant Identities*, pp. 44–45.

23. Roger Abrahams to author, 18 May 1993; "Demonstrations Seek Anti-Discrimination Law; Baez Appears Aiding Protest," *Daily Texan*, 3 April 1964; Jeffrey Shero, "Chapter Reports: U. of Texas . . . ," *SDS Bulletin*, April 1964; Jeff Shero, "the sds phenomenon," *New Left Notes*, 29 July 1966.

24. Terry H. Anderson, *The Movement and the Sixties: Protest in America from Greensboro to Wounded Knee* (New York: Oxford University Press, 1995), p. 95; Clark Kerr, *The Uses of the University*, rev. ed. (Cambridge, MA: Harvard University Press, 1995), p. 143.

25. The term *consumption communities* comes from Daniel J. Boorstin, *The Americans: The Democratic Experience* (New York: Random House, 1973), pp. 89–164. Boorstin refers to far-flung "communities" united by their consumption patterns rather than, as in earlier times, by geography. My point is that these particular consumption communities, reversing the long-term trend Boorstin describes, were formed in part by a geographically based sense of their own cultural distinctiveness.

26. Anderson, *Movement and the Sixties*, p. 95; Paul Sorell, "UT: A Campus of 34,000 Individuals," *Summer Texan*, 15 August 1969; Ronnie Dugger, *Our Invaded Universities: Form, Reform, and New Starts* (New York: Norton, 1974), p. 352.

Anderson says the UT student population grew to "almost 27,000" by 1970 (without citing documentation), yet the *Texan* reported the higher number for the beginning of the 1969/1970 school year.

27. Wizard interview.

28. Shank, *Dissonant Identities*, pp. 46–52.

29. Glenn W. Jones, "Gentle Thursday: Revolutionary Pastoralism in Austin, Texas, 1966–1969" (M.A. thesis, University of Texas at Austin, 1988), pp. 24–41; Shank, *Dissonant Identities*, pp. 46–52; quotation on p. 52.

30. Wizard interview.

31. Barbara Wuensch Merritt, interview with author, 27 April 1993; Lori Hansel, interview with author, 2 July 1992. Merritt transferred from Mary Washington College in Virginia, Hansel from the University of Wisconsin.

32. Gitlin, *The Sixties*, p. 225; Robert Pardun, interview with author, 27 August 1993; Dreyer quoted in Peck, *Uncovering the Sixties*, p. 59; Wizard interview; Dick M/F, "Giving up Needles for Lent . . . ," *Rag*, 10 February 1970.

In 1971 a coalition of hippies and leftists came together in what they called "the Austin Plan," an attempt to deal with the local heroin problem after an ex-philosophy student turned drug addict, Frank Carrasco (known as "Paco"), was shot and killed in a dispute. Although the plan fell apart in acrimony, hostility to heroin remained widespread, with Vietnam Veterans Against the War (VVAW) taking a particular interest in the problem, which seemed especially bad among returned GIs. Many leftists thought that the authorities were not interested in eliminating heroin and cocaine use because these drugs helped erode the potential bases of political resistance. Steve Russell reported that Governor Preston Smith was trying to drop cocaine use from a felony to a misdemeanor: "Speed and smack are pig drugs—good only for controlling people (those who live)," he declared. "Smack Program," *Rag*, 13 September 1971; alan pogue, "Austin Plan (again)," *Rag*, 10 October 1971; Steve Russell, "new drug law," *Rag*, 5 July 1971.

33. Quoted in Peck, *Uncovering the Sixties*, p. 59.

34. Pardun interview; Anthony Howe, "I would suggest that the situation of Texas hippies vis-a-vis their physical well-being could rightly be termed very dangerous, or Paranoia," *Rag*, 2 January 1967; Jeff Shero, "Dallas Police Jail Banana Users," *Rag*, 27 March 1967.

35. Sandy Carmichael, "Mother's Grits Texas Traveling Troupe," *Rag*, 22 August 1968.

36. See Raymond Williams, *Marxism and Literature* (Oxford: Oxford University Press, 1977), pp. 108–114. Also see Stuart Hall and Tony Jefferson, eds., *Resistance through Rituals: Youth Subcultures in Post-War Britain* (London: Hutchinson, 1976); and Dick Hebdige, *Subculture: The Meaning of Style* (London: Methuen, 1979), works that exaggerate the oppositional content of youth culture in the 1970s. (Since all these works are rooted in British cultural studies, their translation into the context of the United States is a complicated matter in any case.) As the later discussion indicates, in practice it was not always easy to distinguish alternative from

oppositional subcultures, but this distinction corresponds roughly to the difference that new left radicals saw between the freak counterculture and their own.

37. On the need for a black cultural revolution in America, see Kwame Ture (Stokely Carmichael) and Charles V. Hamilton, *Black Power: The Politics of Liberation in America*, rev. ed. (New York: Vintage Books, 1992), pp. 30–32, 34–41, 140–145; Harold Cruse, *The Crisis of the Negro Intellectual* (New York: Morrow, 1967); Christopher Lasch, "Black Power: Cultural Nationalism as Politics," in Christopher Lasch, *The Agony of the American Left* (New York: Vintage Books, 1969), pp. 115–168; and William L. Van Deburg, *New Day in Babylon: The Black Power Movement and American Culture, 1965–1975* (Chicago: University of Chicago Press, 1992).

38. "SDS statement on SNCC," *New Left Notes*, 17 June 1966. This statement was adopted by the SDS National Council. It is worth wondering how the radicals thought they would change an "essential" aspect of national culture. Perhaps this should be viewed merely as a rhetorical flourish (with "essentially" a synonym for "really"). Yet if one takes this language seriously, it provides a preview of the frustration that culminated in the politics of Weatherman, in which the only solution to an insoluble problem, like the only explanation for an impossible white antiracist politics, was an exercise of transcendent moral will.

39. Susan T. Olan, "The Rag: A Study in Underground Journalism" (M.A. thesis, University of Texas at Austin, 1981), pp. 1–10, 48–49; Dave Mahler, "Rag Day," *Rag*, 27 January 1969; "subterranean homesick blues," *Rag*, 16 September 1968; letter from staff, *Rag*, March 1969; "Rag Causes Lung Cancer?" *Rag*, 17 July 1969; "Rag Banned," *Rag*, 3 March 1970. The local ACLU and civil liberties lawyer Dave Richards represented the *Rag* in court.

40. Peck, *Uncovering the Sixties*, p. 58; minutes of general meeting, Bowling Green State University SDS, 11 December 1966, SDS Papers, Locality File—Ohio, reel 25, 3:57.

41. Linda Smith, interview with author, 15 March 1993. The trio probably included Dreyer and Thiher and perhaps Nightbyrd.

42. Alice Embree, interview with author, 9 November 1991; Peck, *Uncovering the Sixties*, p. 214; "Rag History," *Rag*, 10 October 1971. Generally, see Olan, "The Rag," pp. 51–52, 81, 93–94, 104–105, 115; and dave, "Rag History," *Rag*, 12 October 1970. In 1970 a "political" faction including David Pratt and Paul Spencer left the *Rag* to start another paper, *Lone Star Dispatch*, with Stoney Burns of *Dallas Notes* (the new venture quickly folded); yet "political" and "cultural" camps continued to coexist at the *Rag*.

43. Judy Smith, interview with author, 1 and 8 February 1993; Steve Russell, interview with author, 1 July 1992. Rochelle Gatlin, *American Women since 1945* (Jackson: University Press of Mississippi, 1987), p. 105, states that the *Rag* simply did not accept sexist advertisements, but this was not the paper's initial policy.

44. Peck, *Uncovering the Sixties*, pp. 21–40.

45. Larry Freudiger, "Grassroots Sociology: A Weekly Discussion of the American Social Revolution and the Reactions against It—The Great Headline Fiasco," *Rag*, 28 November 1966.

46. Jones, "Gentle Thursday," pp. 46–47. This was named after the character in A. A. Milne's *Winnie the Pooh* books, of which some campus coeds who were dating members of the fraternity that initiated the event were enamored. In 1966, Lady Bird Johnson and her daughter Lynda Bird attended Eeyore's.

47. Announcement, *Rag*, 31 October 1966. There was perhaps a note of English inspiration here, characteristic of 1960s youth culture in the United States.

48. Bob Pardun, "Gentle Thursday," *New Left Notes*, 3 February 1967; cited in Sara Evans, *Personal Politics: The Roots of Women's Liberation in the Civil Rights Movement and the New Left* (New York: Vintage Books, 1980), p. 178. Later I explore the gendered aspect of the new left's cultural politics.

49. Jeff Nightbyrd, quoted in Jones, "Gentle Thursday," p. 52.

50. Ibid., p. 47; Susan Jankovsky, "A Challenge for the New Left—'Our Little Crusader' at U.T.," *Observer*, 17 March 1967; Susan T. Olan, "Blood Debts," in Daryl Janes, ed., *No Apologies: Texas Radicals Celebrate the '60s* (Austin, TX: Eakin Press, 1993), p. 20.

51. Kirkpatrick Sale, *SDS* (New York: Random House, 1973), p. 327.

52. Jones, "Gentle Thursday," pp. 54–69; also see Glenn W. Jones, "Gentle Thursday: An SDS Circus in Austin, Texas, 1966–1969," in Barbara L. Tischler, ed., *Sights on the Sixties* (New Brunswick, NJ: Rutgers University Press, 1992), pp. 75–85.

53. Jones, "Gentle Thursday: Revolutionary Pastoralism," *Rag*, 24 April 1967; Thorne Dreyer, "Flipped-out Week," *Rag*, 10 April 1967.

54. See Lasch, *New Radicalism in America*, pp. 69–103; and Casey N. Blake, *Beloved Community: The Cultural Criticism of Randolph Bourne, Van Wyck Brooks, Waldo Frank, and Lewis Mumford* (Chapel Hill: University of North Carolina Press, 1990).

55. For perspectives on the development of this consumer culture, see, among many other works: T. J. Jackson Lears, "From Salvation to Self-Realization: Advertising and the Therapeutic Roots of the Consumer Culture, 1880–1930," in T. J. Jackson Lears and Richard W. Fox, eds., *The Culture of Consumption: Critical Essays in American History, 1880–1980* (New York: Pantheon, 1983), pp. 3–38; Roland Marchand, *Advertising the American Dream: Making Way for Modernity, 1920–1940* (Berkeley and Los Angeles: University of California Press, 1985); Lizabeth Cohen, "The Class Experience of Mass Consumption: Workers as Consumers in Interwar America," in Richard W. Fox and T. J. Jackson Lears, eds., *The Power of Culture: Critical Essays in American History* (Chicago: University of Chicago Press, 1993); Stanley Lebergott, *Pursuing Happiness: American Consumers in the Twentieth Century* (Princeton, NJ: Princeton University Press, 1993); and T. J. Jackson Lears, *Fables of Abundance: A Cultural History of American Advertising* (New York: Basic Books, 1995). On the coming to consciousness of postscarcity and "postindustrial" attitudes, see Daniel Horowitz, *The Morality of Spending: Attitudes toward the Consumer*

Society, 1875–1940 (Baltimore: Johns Hopkins University Press, 1985); Howard Brick, "Optimism of the Mind: Imagining Postindustrial Society in the 1960s and 1970s," *American Quarterly* 44 (September 1992); and Alan Brinkley, *The End of Reform: New Deal Liberalism in Recession and War* (New York: Knopf, 1995), pp. 65–75.

56. Barbara Ehrenreich, *The Hearts of Men: American Dreams and the Flight from Commitment* (Garden City, NY: Doubleday/Anchor, 1983), pp. 42–51; and, generally, Helen Gurley Brown, *Sex and the Single Girl* (New York: Pocket Books, 1963).

57. Carl Rogers, *On Becoming a Person: A Therapist's View of Psychotherapy* (Boston: Houghton Mifflin, 1961); Betty Friedan, *The Feminine Mystique* (New York: Dell, 1963), esp. pp. 299–325; Ehrenreich, *Hearts of Men*, pp. 88–98; and Ellen Herman, *The Romance of American Psychology: Political Culture in the Age of Experts* (Berkeley and Los Angeles: University of California Press, 1995), pp. 290–292. Friedan, of course, argued that women should look beyond a sexual role or a purely sexual definition of feminine identity. But she suggested that precisely by growing beyond that role, women would achieve sexual fulfillment.

58. Beth Bailey, "Sexual Revolution(s)," in Farber, ed., *The Sixties*, pp. 235–262; Beth Bailey, *From Front Porch to Back Seat: Courtship in Twentieth-Century American* (Baltimore: Johns Hopkins University Press, 1988); Paula Fass, *The Damned and the Beautiful: American Youth in the 1920's* (New York: Oxford University Press, 1977); Elaine T. May, *Homeward Bound: American Families in the Cold War Era* (New York: Basic Books, 1988).

59. Jeff Shero, "Changing Sex Mores Pose Questions," *Daily Texan*, 5 December 1963; Marty Heym, "Student Senate," *Oberlin Other*, 12 November 1966; position paper for unnamed candidate for student government at University of Missouri, n.d., SDS Papers, Chapter File—Missouri, reel 7, SA:82; John Garlinghouse, "In Loco Deus," *KU-SDS Journal*, December 1965; Jim Masters, "Agents WASP entis Kansensis," *KU-SDS Journal*, December 1965.

60. "Intellectual Emancipation," *Texan Panorama*, 23 February 1964. The matter of Friedan's politics has been complicated considerably by Daniel Horowitz, "Rethinking Betty Friedan and *The Feminine Mystique*: Labor Union Radicalism and Feminism in Cold War America," *American Quarterly* 48 (March 1996), which reveals her early leftist involvements. Nonetheless, by the time she wrote *The Feminine Mystique*, Friedan had clearly joined the liberal camp.

61. Daniel Bell, *The Cultural Contradictions of Capitalism* (New York: Basic Books, 1976), p. 73.

62. Hansel interview; Nightbyrd interview; Greg Calvert, interview with author, 20 March 1995; Paul Pipkin, Linda Pipkin, and Joe Ebbècke, interview with author, 4 July 1992; Judy Smith interview; Judy Schiffer Perez, interview with author, 27 August 1993; Jeff Jones, interview with author, 16 and 23 February 1993.

63. Marcuse, *One-Dimensional Man*, pp. 56–83. See Robinson, *Freudian Left*, pp. 239–242; and King, *Party of Eros*, pp. 140–141.

64. Gary Thiher, "Desolation Row," *Rag*, 16 April 1969.

65. Ehrenreich, *Hearts of Men*, p. 113; Jeff Shero, "Playboy's Tinseled Seductress," *Rag*, October 1966, emphasis added.

66. Shero, "Playboy's Tinseled Seductress"; Michael Beaudette, "the bent spokesman," *Rag*, October 1966. In fact, a great many underground newspapers from the era displayed vastly more pornography than the *Rag* ever did.

67. Hansel interview. Ehrenreich contends that "the hippies discarded masculinity as a useful category for expression" and sees an emphasis on androgyny in the freak counterculture. Ehrenreich, *Hearts of Men*, p. 107. This is clearly incorrect; unisex hair styles do not androgyny make.

68. Norman O. Brown, *Life against Death: The Psychoanalytic Meaning of History* (Middletown, CT: Wesleyan University Press, 1959). Brown's vision was not the same as that of the new left. He urged an acceptance, even an embrace, of death as a part of life, holding that this would represent the most profound rebellion against Western culture, whereas the new left spoke for a "life culture" that would be the antithesis of the dominant "death culture." In Brown's terms, the new left were not cultural revolutionaries at all.

69. Larry Freudiger, "Grassroots Sociology—A Weekly Discussion of the American Social Revolution and the Reactions against It: Death & Ritual," *Rag*, 28 November 1966; Dreyer, "Flipped-out Week." Freudiger criticized the U.S. funeral industry, drawing on the authority of Jessica Mitford, *The American Way of Death* (New York: Simon & Schuster, 1963).

70. Doran Williams, letter, *Rag*, 24 April 1967.

71. See Michael Sherry, *In the Shadow of War: American Society Since the 1930s* (New Haven, CT: Yale University Press, 1995), pp. 286, 297–299. On the domestic debate over the war generally, see David W. Levy, *The Debate over Vietnam* (Baltimore: Johns Hopkins University Press, 1991), pp. 46–123.

72. Norman Mailer, *Why Are We in Vietnam?* (New York: Putnam, 1967). Possibly I ascribe too much coherence to Mailer's musings.

73. Lawrence is cited at the start of Richard Slotkin, *Regeneration through Violence: The Mythology of the American Frontier, 1600–1860* (Middletown, CT: Wesleyan University Press, 1973), a particularly learned example of this trend of thought and a book whose relation to the Vietnam War the author makes explicit. D. H. Lawrence, *Studies in Classic American Literature* (New York: Viking, 1961).

74. Richard Hofstadter's change of heart on this matter was the most dramatic. Richard Hofstadter, *The Progressive Historians: Turner, Beard, Parrington* (New York: Knopf, 1968), pp. 437–466; Richard Hofstadter, with Michael Wallace, *American Violence: A Documentary History* (New York: Knopf, 1970). Arthur M. Schlesinger Jr. also joined the chorus. Arthur M. Schlesinger Jr., *The Crisis of Confidence: Ideas, Power, and Violence in America* (Boston: Houghton Mifflin, 1969). Further work in this vein can be sampled in Hugh Davis Graham, ed., *The History of Violence in America: Historical and Comparative Perspectives* (New York: Praeger, 1970).

Warren Susman comments that "in the 1950s Americans discovered violence," meaning violence in American society and history. Yet his only citations are to

Hofstadter and Wallace, and Graham, both 1970 publications. I am not convinced this discussion began nearly so early as Susman asserts. Warren Susman, with the assistance of Edward Griffin, "Did Success Spoil America?: Dual Representations in Postwar America," in Lary May, ed., *Recasting America: Culture and Politics in the Age of Cold War* (Chicago: University of Chicago Press, 1989), pp. 24, 35n11.

75. On the perception and reality of a general loss of restraint in American culture in these years and on what is frequently termed a "coarsening" of American culture, see Kenneth Cmiel, "The Politics of Civility," in Farber, ed., *The Sixties*, pp. 263–290.

76. On crime rates and the perception of them, see Michael Barone, *Our Country: The Shaping of America from Roosevelt to Reagan* (New York: Free Press, 1990), pp. 622–623; and Lawrence M. Friedman, *Crime and Punishment in American History* (New York: Basic Books, 1993), pp. 449–451. In 1969, 85 percent of Americans in one poll responded positively to the statement "black militants are treated too leniently," the pith of the silent majority's complaint about the liberal elites of the Great Society years. Farber, "The Silent Majority and Talk about Revolution," p. 298. The conflation of political militance and criminality was essential to the victory of the center-right political coalition that coalesced in the United States in the late 1960s. On the conservative reaction against unrest generally, see Farber, "The Silent Majority and Talk about Revolution," pp. 291–316.

77. David Farber, *Chicago '68* (Chicago: University of Chicago Press, 1988), pp. 203–207, 246–258.

78. The Kerner Commission, chaired by Illinois Governor Otto Kerner, issued a report officially entitled *Report of the National Advisory Commission on Civil Disorders* (New York: Bantam, 1968). On this and similar government commissions of these years, see Anthony M. Platt, ed., *The Politics of Riot Commissions, 1917–1970* (New York: Macmillan, 1971); and Herman, *Romance of American Psychology*, pp. 208–237. Other social scientific studies of violence in the United States from this time include Ted Robert Gurr, *Why Men Rebel* (Princeton, NJ: Princeton University Press, 1970), which focuses on the tensions generated by "rising expectations"; and Jerome Skolnik, *The Politics of Protest* (New York: Ballantine, 1969).

79. William Meachem, "My Plastic Fantastic Lover," *Rag*, 19 June 1969.

80. Wilfred McClay, *The Masterless: Self and Society in Modern America* (Chapel Hill: University of North Carolina Press, 1994), pp. 189–234.

81. William Meachem, "On Revolutionary Violence," *Rag*, 10 July 1969; "Forum on Self Defense"—Pat Cuney, "Fore-warned Is Fore-armed," *Rag*, 14 September 1970. Meachem himself gave up this line of thought before long. After an arrest, he was beaten badly in jail and medically neglected; subsequently he sued the city of Austin. Bill Meachem, "Who Could Imagine That They Would Freak out in Austin, Texas?" *Rag*, 8 December 1969; Bill Meachem, interview with author, 29 June 1992.

82. Reinhold Niebuhr, *Moral Man and Immoral Society* (New York: Scribner, 1932); Donald Meyer, *The Protestant Search for Political Realism, 1919–1941* (Berkeley and Los Angeles: University of California Press, 1960); Richard W. Fox, *Reinhold Niebuhr: A Biography* (New York: Pantheon, 1985).

83. "Forum on Self-Defense"—Judy Smith, " . . . We Are Not the Tupamaros," *Rag*, 14 September 1970.

84. SP-4 Louis DiEugenio, "A GI Speaks Out," *Rag*, 7 August 1969; Judy Baker, letter, *Rag*, 16 September 1968.

85. John Kenneth Galbraith, *The Affluent Society* (Boston: Houghton Mifflin, 1958); Samuel P. Hays, *Beauty, Health, Permanence: Environmental Politics in the United States, 1955–1985* (Cambridge: Cambridge University Press, 1987); Rachel Carson, *Silent Spring* (Boston: Houghton Mifflin, 1962); Thomas R. Dunlap, *DDT: Scientists, Citizens, and Public Policy* (Princeton, NJ: Princeton University Press, 1981). Hays's interpretation of environmentalism plays havoc with the anticonsumptionist stance professed by many ecological activists, especially those influenced by 1960s radicalism.

86. Casey Hayden to author, 17 March 1997.

87. Mark Morrison et al., "What Trees Do They Plant?" *Rag*, 28 October 1969 (this article's title ironically echoed Mayor Richard Daley's question concerning the antiwar protesters at the 1968 Democratic National Convention, who slept in the parks of his beloved Chicago); "Judy" (Smith), *Rag*, 21 October 1969.

88. Morrison et al., "What Trees Do They Plant?"; Victoria Smith, "Trees Fall at UH," *Space City!*, 2–9 May 1970.

89. Nancy Folbre to author, 12 November 1995.

90. Steve (Russell), "Up Shit Creek," *Rag*, 10 November 1969.

91. Paul Spencer, "Analysis of the Water Plan: water, water everywhere and it does is stink [*sic*]," *Rag*, 24 July 1969; "Texas, Our Texas: Big Thicket," *Rag*, August–September 1969; Dave, "Teratogenicide," *Rag*, 15 December 1969; "Malformation," *Rag*, 12 January 1970.

92. Ray Reece, "Almost No Apologies," in Janes, ed., *No Apologies*, pp. 265–269. The political establishment of Austin backed the nuclear power plan, but they lost a referendum on participation in 1972, so they tried again in 1973 and won. Jeff Friedman, who became mayor of Austin in 1975, first gained public notice when as a law student at UT in 1970, he helped secure court orders granting antiwar demonstrators use of the city streets (see chapter 6). In 1973, Friedman, who had won election to the city council with the active support of the local left, earned the enmity of many of these supporters by siding with the nuclear power lobby and mending fences with the city fathers as a prelude to his mayoral campaign. In 1981, city voters resolved to withdraw from the project, but by then the slow-growthers had lost, and suburban subdivisions and strip malls had begun to replace the country outside the city limits. In the early 1990s, when I visited Austin, the city's downtown was marked by tall, glossy, empty office buildings, artifacts of the southwestern savings and loan–financed development bubble, which by then had burst.

93. "Ecology Action," *Rag*, 3 February 1970; "Earth Eat-Out," *Rag*, 27 January 1970; "Ecology Action," *Rag*, 10 February 1970; "Ecology Action," *Rag*, 30 August 1971; Jones interview; Judy Smith interview; Linda Smith interview.

94. Dwight Macdonald, "The Root Is Man," *politics* 3 (April, July 1946); Theodore Rozsak, "The Human Whole and Justly Proportioned," in Theodore

Rozsak, ed., *Sources: An Anthology of Contemporary Materials Useful for Preserving Personal Sanity While Braving the Great Technological Wilderness* (New York: Harper Colophon, 1972), pp. ix–xi. Also see Gregory Sumner, *Dwight Macdonald and the* politics *Circle: The Challenge of Cosmopolitan Democracy* (Ithaca, NY: Cornell University Press, 1996).

95. (Bea Vogel), "radical conservation—part I: technology and environment," *Rag*, 26 June 1969.

96. Bea (Vogel), "Dying—The End of a Myth: Radical Conservation: Part II. One Population," *Rag*, 3 July 1969; "The Unanimous Declaration of Interdependence," *Rag*, 3 November 1969.

97. Vogel, "radical conservation—part I."

98. "Ecology and Waller Creek," *Rag*, 10 November 1969; Johannah, "Up on Waller Creek," *Rag*, 28 October 1969.

99. Gary Snyder, *Earth House Hold: Technical Notes & Queries to Fellow Dharma Revolutionaries* (New York: New Directions, 1969).

100. Vogel, "radical conservation—part I," emphasis added.

101. E. F. Schumacher, *Small Is Beautiful: Economics As If People Mattered* (New York: Harper & Row, 1973). Schumacher, a British economist, was influenced by what he called Buddhist economics.

102. See Paul Goodman, *The State of Nature* (New York: Vanguard, 1946); and Percival and Paul Goodman, *Communitas: Means of Livelihood and Ways of Life* (Chicago: University of Chicago Press, 1947). Also see the book by Kirkpatrick Sale, the first historian of SDS, *Human Scale* (New York: Coward, McCann & Geoghegan, 1980).

103. The fullest portrait of the hip zones in one urban area is the discussion of the Minneapolis–St. Paul food cooperatives in Craig Cox, *Storefront Revolution: Food Co-ops and the Counterculture* (New Brunswick, NJ: Rutgers University Press, 1994).

104. Gitlin, *The Sixties*, p. 429; Jon Wiener, "The New Left as History," *Radical History Review* 42 (Fall 1988): 186.

105. See the nice discussion in Peck, *Uncovering the Sixties*, pp. 165–180; the advertisement is reproduced on p. 164.

106. Meachem interview; "Serve the People: Build Co-ops," *Rag*, 24 November 1969; Embree interview; "Sattva Returns!" *Rag*, 20 September 1971; "join the revival," *Rag*, 15 December 1969.

107. "The Armadillo Press Political Statement Prospectus," *Rag*, 14 August 1969; Embree interview; Hansel interview.

Lasch, ever contrarian, argues that the new left interpretation of the IWW is mistaken. He views the "One Big Union" that the Wobblies preached as a scheme for a centralized labor movement and economy. He suggests that radicals seeking to defend participatory democracy and local ways of life against the centralizing forces of bureaucracy would do better to look for inspiration to the Populist movement and the culturally conservative craft union tradition (Lasch, *True and Only Heaven*, pp. 206–225, 329–340).

108. Dick Howard, memo, n.d. (fall 1965), SDS Papers, Locality File, 1964–1968—Texas, reel 25, 3:62; Dick Howard, "SDS: Present and Future," n.d. (December 1965), SDS Papers, reel 20, 3:3, pp. 5, 8.

109. Dick Howard to author, 25 October 1995.

110. Jerry Farber, "The Student as Nigger: A Course in How to Be Slaves," *Notes from the Underground*, 27 May 1967. The article first appeared in the *Los Angeles Free Press*, but one could find it in the back issues of virtually any underground newspaper of the period. Of course, asserting an identity between "student" and "nigger" was one way to navigate the difficulty of a white collegiate movement, discussed in chapter 5. Nothing dates Farber's article so much as his discussion of slave identity, which resembles the "Sambo" figure that historians of this time viewed as quite real. For the most influential rendering, see Stanley Elkins, *Slavery: A Problem in American Institutional and Intellectual Life* (Chicago: University of Chicago Press, 1958). The main reason for the new left's hesitation in embracing this formulation, one suspects, was simply the shock and controversy attached to the word *nigger*, irony (of which little is evident in Farber's essay) notwithstanding.

111. "Your Mistake," *Rag*, 15 September 1969; "Critical University," *Rag*, 21 October 1969; Free University of Florida pamphlet, 1965–1966 school year, SDS Papers, Free University—Correspondence, reel 5, 2A:42; Dave George and Tom Shelley to Bowling Green State University students, 16 January 1967, SDS Papers, Locality File—OH, reel 24, 3:56.

112. Gitlin, *The Sixties*, p. 429; A. S. Neill, *Summerhill: A Radical Approach to Child Rearing* (New York: Hart, 1960) (this edition features a foreword by Erich Fromm); "Living on the Home Front," *Rag*, 3 May 1971; B. F. Skinner, *Walden Two* (New York: Macmillan, 1948); Aldous Huxley, *Island: A Novel* (London: Chatto & Windus, 1962); Harvey Stone, "Survival," *Rag*, 12 June 1969.

113. Caroline interview (Caroline thinks the parent of the child in question was Walt W. Rostow, who landed on a high perch in the economics and history departments at UT after leaving Washington when Richard Nixon entered the White House); "Education: The Experience of Freedom," *Rag*, 30 August 1971; "Greenbriar School . . . ," *Rag*, 9 March 1970; untitled, *Rag*, 7 June 1971.

114. Mike Rush, "Greenbriar and the Super Bowl," *Rag*, 24 January 1972.

115. "sputter," *Rag*, 24 July 1969; Hermes Trismegistus, "Aquarian Kitchen," *Rag*, 2 November 1970; Editorial, *Rag*, 7 December 1970.

On Hermes Trismegistus, see Jon Butler, *Awash in a Sea of Faith: Christianizing the American People* (Cambridge, MA: Harvard University Press, 1990), p. 24.

116. "19th and University Co-op," *Rag*, 27 January 1970.

117. Alice Embree, letter, *Rag*, 1 May 1972; Wayne Clark, "For Sale: Gas Co-op—Cheap! Cheap!" *Rag*, 23 October 1972.

118. Robert B., "more on community," *Rag*, 9 November 1970.

119. suzi and mike, "Revolution for the Life of It!" *Rag*, 26 October 1970.

120. Alice Embree, "People's Music," *Rag*, 9 August 1971. On emergent and residual cultures, see Williams, *Marxism and Literature*, pp. 122–123.

121. "Texas Troupe Trip," *Rag*, 8 August 1968; Sandy Carmichael, "Mother's Grits Texas Traveling Troupe," *Rag*, 22 August 1968.

122. Caroline interview.

123. Carmichael, "Mother's Grits."

124. Embree, "People's Music."

125. Ibid.

126. Archie Green, "Austin's Cosmic Cowboys: Words in Collision," in Richard Bauman and Roger D. Abrahams, eds., *"And Other Neighborly Names": Social Process and Cultural Image in Texas Folklore* (Austin: University of Texas Press, 1981), pp. 152–194, offers an excellent summary of the changing fortunes of the cowboy figure, including an extensive discussion of the cosmic cowboy vogue. I thank Lonn Taylor for giving me a copy of this essay.

127. Jones interview.

128. Shank, *Dissonant Identities*, pp. 53–54, 77.

129. Bobby Nelson, interview with author, 22 June 1992. Nelson and Martin Wiginton ran Emma Joe's.

130. Jeff Nightbyrd, "Cosmo Cowboys: Too Much Cowboy and Not Enough Cosmic," *Austin Sun*, 3 April 1973; quotation in Shank, *Dissonant Identities*, p. 67.

131. Shank, *Dissonant Identities*, pp. 16, 58, 244–245.

132. Dave, "one comment . . . ," *Rag*, 21 February 1972.

133. Ehrenreich, *Hearts of Men*, p. 114; Ralph Larkin and Daniel Foss, "Lexicon of Folk-Etymology," in Sohnya Sayres et al., eds., *The 60s without Apology* (Minneapolis: University of Minnesota Press, 1984), p. 360, emphasis in original. Ehrenreich attributes this judgment to Marcuse, but clearly she is thinking of the Marcuse of *One-Dimensional Man*, not he of *An Essay on Liberation* (Boston: Beacon Press, 1969), in which Marcuse came around to the hippie camp. He and Ehrenreich share an ambivalence about the counterculture: she never fully integrates her evident sympathy with the beat and hippie men in revolt against "commitment" with her effective feminist critique of the male revolt.

134. Cam Cunningham, Cris Cunningham, Kathy DuBose, Chet Cage, Martin Wiginton, Terry DuBose, Martin Murray, Phyllis Krantzman, Carole Jones, Nicholas Dykema, Gini Coleman, Lotha Piltz, and John Kniffin, "Community Center," *Rag*, 6 March 1972, emphasis added. This group included some of those who looked to the New American Movement (NAM) as a successor to SDS. This indicates the wide influence of this countercultural formulation of radical politics, since the NAM group would have been more likely than others in the new left to criticize the solipsistic tendency of that vision.

135. Doyle Niemann, "I Am Curious (real)," *Rag*, 19 October 1970. This was a review of a volume compiled by the editors of the journal *Socialist Revolution*, and Niemann criticized it for its attachment to old left politics.

136. Niemann, "I Am Curious (real)."

137. George R. Vickers, *The Formation of the New Left: The Early Years* (Lexington, MA: Lexington Books, 1975), pp. 107–125. Despite its limitations,

Vickers's critique is sophisticated, even brilliant, clearing away common misconceptions not only about the new left but also about the society that the new left protested. Regrettably, Vickers's monograph is all but forgotten.

138. John Mackey, "Beyond Unions," *Utne Reader*, March–April 1992, p. 76. Mackey is the CEO of Whole Foods Market. L. A. Kauffman, "Tofu politics," *Utne Reader*, March–April 1992, pp. 72–75, offers a leftist critique of the "personal politics" that led some "progressives" to cross a labor picket in front of a Whole Foods Market in Berkeley. She concludes that regrettably, the personal has come to overshadow the political. However, in addition to this development, the problem may be more specific to the cultural politics of the new left, that is, the libertarian element in 1960s radicalism.

139. Williams, *Marxism and Literature*, p. 114.

140. Jackson Lears, "A Matter of Taste: Corporate Cultural Hegemony in a Mass-Consumption Society," in May, ed., *Recasting America*, p. 54.

In the 1970s and 1980s, Antonio Gramsci, from whose work the concept of cultural hegemony derives, was one theorist to whom leftist intellectuals in the United States turned for guidance and for intellectual legitimation of the politics that the new left already had pioneered and that remained, one might say, hegemonic on the left. According to Gramsci, the sway of one class's values and vision of reality and possibility was as important to class rule as were the tools of coercion. If this outlook is correct, then the mere fact that a social vision emerges from the distinct experience of a particular social class in no way implies that the potential power of this vision is confined to that class. Indeed, in theory, the new left might have assisted in successfully foisting its class outlook on society as a whole. But a basic problem in the American leftists' appropriation of Gramscian strategy was their faith in the marketplace of ideas, discussed earlier. Gramsci belonged to a different political tradition. He envisioned a Leninist party organization directing the effort at cultural change, and the new left's rank and file decisively rejected that political model, as the Leninist groupings of the 1970s discovered. In fact, the Gramscian strategy resembles the cultural apparatus of the old left more than it does the new left's cultural politics. See Antonio Gramsci, *Selections from the Prison Notebooks*, ed. and trans. Quintin Hoare and Geoffrey Nowell Smith (New York: International Publishers, 1971), pp. 123–205. For a sense of the intellectual excitement that Gramscian ideas generated among leftists in the United States in these years, see T. J. Jackson Lears, "The Concept of Cultural Hegemony: Problems and Possibilities," *American Historical Review* 90 (June 1985): 567–593.

141. See Daniel J. Singal, "Towards a Definition of American Modernism," in Daniel J. Singal, ed., *Modernist Culture in America* (Belmont, CA: Wadsworth, 1991), esp. pp. 15–19; and Lynn Dumenil, *The Modern Temper: American Culture and Society in the 1920s* (New York: Hill & Wang, 1995), which is concerned with both "modernity" (a stage in social development) and modernism (a cultural orientation). Most definitions of cultural modernism describe a set of aesthetic ideas and ideals. I am describing a far broader cultural attitude, which gained increasing ground among affluent and college-educated Americans starting in the 1920s. This cultural

orientation might also be described as a kind of tame cosmopolitanism. The basic point is that it is defined by means of a self-conscious contrast with the cultural traditionalism that the new left abhorred, regardless of its intermittent reverence for the traditional.

Chapter 8

1. Paul Goodman, "The Revolution in Berkeley," in Irving Howe, ed., *The Radical Imagination* (New York: New American Library, 1967), p. 217. The essay originally appeared in *Dissent*.

2. Howard Brick, *Daniel Bell and the Decline of Intellectual Radicalism: Social Theory and Political Reconciliation in the 1940s* (Madison: University of Wisconsin Press, 1986), p. 100. Franz Neumann's metaphor of "behemoth," used to describe the fascist political economy of Nazi Germany, preceded that of leviathan (ibid., pp. 80–95); see Franz Neumann, *Behemoth: The Structure and Practice of National Socialism* (New York: Oxford University Press, 1942). Under the influence of Neumann's writing, Mills and Daniel Bell (for a time) became convinced that during World War II the U.S. political economy was developing along similarly fascist lines. Mills, reviewing Neumann's book, wrote that it "helps us locate the enemy all over the world." C. Wright Mills, "The Nazi Behemoth," in Irving Louis Horowitz, ed., *Power, Politics and People: The Collected Essays of C. Wright Mills* (New York: Ballantine, 1963), pp. 177–178.

3. Goodman, "Revolution in Berkeley," p. 206.

Cornel West, *The American Evasion of Philosophy: A Genealogy of Pragmatism* (Madison: University of Wisconsin Press, 1989), pp. 124–138; and Christopher Shannon, *Conspicuous Criticism: Tradition, the Individual, and Culture in American Social Thought, from Veblen to Mills* (Baltimore: Johns Hopkins University Press, 1996), pp. 133–174, are insightful discussions of Mills's thought. Both accounts recognize the importance of personal attitude and style in Mills's thought and influence, yet neither acknowledges the gendered quality of this personal dimension.

4. Staughton Lynd, "The Movement: A New Beginning," *Liberation* 14 (May 1969); quoted in Alice Echols, *Daring to Be Bad: Radical Feminism in America, 1967–1975* (Minneapolis: University of Minnesota Press, 1989), p. 38. As I mentioned in chapter 6, the gender politics of draft resistance has occasioned pointed debate.

5. From the new left's beginning, many women were, in fact if not in title, leaders in the movement. As I discuss later, the position of women in the new left deteriorated in the later years of SDS and then improved greatly. Nonetheless, women occupied a subordinate position even in the early years of the new left, which the very denial of their leadership in the movement, notably in the Economic Research and Action Projects (ERAPs), underlines. See Sara Evans, *Personal Politics: The Roots of Women's Liberation in the Civil Rights Movement and the New Left* (New York: Vintage Books, 1980), pp. 140–142, 151. The premium placed on verbal aggressiveness in internal discussion also frequently seemed to favor men, as my discussion of Austin SDS in chapter 5 indicates.

6. C. Wright Mills, *Listen, Yankee!: The Revolution in Cuba* (New York: Ballantine, 1960), p. 150; quoted in Van Gosse, *Where the Boys Are: Cuba, Cold War America and the Making of a New Left* (London: Verso, 1993), p. 180. Gosse's book is by far the most probing discussion to date of the gender dynamics at work in the new left's early years. In my view, he resists the implications of his own analysis, trying to salvage *fidelismo* from the damage he does it.

7. Norman Mailer, *The White Negro* (San Francisco: City Lights Books, 1957). Alice Echols makes this point as well in her article " 'We Gotta Get out of This Place': Notes toward a Remapping of the Sixties," *Socialist Review* 22 (April–June 1992): 17, 26–27. I share her view that in general, the new left has a (potentially) gendered history that begins before the emergence of the women's liberation movement, and I intend my discussion here as a contribution to that history.

8. In chapter 5 I noted Andrew Kopkind's remark on impotence; Todd Gitlin and Arthur Waskow both described as castrated those white activists who merely functioned as auxiliaries to the Black Panther Party (BPP). Echols, *Daring to Be Bad*, p. 313, note.

9. Echols, *Daring to Be Bad*, pp. 45–50, gives a detailed account. According to Echols, the machinations against the feminists who participated in the NCNP led directly to the organization of the first independent women's liberation group, in Chicago.

10. Eldridge Cleaver, *Soul on Ice* (New York: McGraw-Hill, 1968).

11. Echols, " 'We Gotta Get out of This Place,' " pp. 16, 21. William H. Whyte Jr., *The Organization Man* (New York: Simon & Schuster, 1956). One should note that as with *The Lonely Crowd* and other examples of this genre of cultural criticism, young people may have taken from *The Organization Man* a different message than Whyte intended. Whyte expressed no clear preference for the kind of individualistic, heroic masculinity that, Echols implies, he may have helped underwrite; his viewpoint was more complex than that. Whyte and Mills were up to somewhat different things. I thank Barry Schwartz for his insightful remark to me on the "anti-heroic" character of Whyte's book.

12. Martin Jay, *The Dialectical Imagination: A History of the Frankfurt School and the Institute of Social Research, 1923–1950* (Boston: Little, Brown, 1973); John Higham, "The Reorientation of American Culture in the 1890's," in John Weiss, ed., *The Origins of Modern Consciousness* (Detroit: Wayne State University Press, 1965), pp. 25–30.

13. C. Wright Mills, *White Collar: The American Middle Classes* (New York: Oxford University Press, 1951).

14. Paul Leinberger and Bruce Tucker, *The New Individualists: The Generation after* The Organization Man (New York: HarperCollins, 1991), pp. 132–134. Thoughtfully (and, for sociologists, showing an admirable eye for historical change), they argue that in the 1930s, domestic labor had greater economic and social importance, making a homemaker role far less distasteful to girls then growing up than to their own daughters in the 1950s.

15. Betty Friedan, *The Feminine Mystique* (New York: Dell, 1963); Philip Wylie, *Nest of Vipers* (New York: Holt, Rinehart and Winston, 1942), coined the term "Momism." For intriguing comments on the actual character of gender roles in American courtship in the 1950s, see Jonathan Zimmerman, "The Flight from Cool: American Men and Romantic Love in the 1950s," *History of the Family* 2 (1997): 31–47; and on home life in the 1950s, see Peter G. Filene, *Him/Her/Self: Sex Roles in Modern America*, 2d ed. (Baltimore: Johns Hopkins University Press, 1986), pp. 169–175. Zimmerman indicates the difficulty in generalizing about gender roles in 1950s America, focusing on the alleged "formalization" of male roles. Filene calls the college students of the 1960s the "children of domesticity," and although he endorses the thesis that they rebelled against the cold war cult of domesticity, his account brings into question the ostensible rigidity of 1950s gender roles, in the end leading to the unorthodox notion (one he does not champion) that to the extent the youth of the 1960s truly were reacting against 1950s domesticity, they might have been trying to stave off the erosion of gender role distinctions.

16. Joanne Meyerowitz argues that Friedan flattened out the complexity of the messages sent to American women in the mass media in the years after World War II but still concedes that the attack on career women was real. Joanne Meyerowitz, "Beyond the Feminine Mystique: A Reassessment of Postwar Mass Culture, 1946–1958," *Journal of American History* 79 (March 1993): 1455–1482.

Marynia Farnham and Ferdinand Lundberg, *Modern Woman: The Lost Sex* (New York: Harper Bros., 1947); and Wylie, *Nest of Vipers*, are the standard, strongly misogynist works cited in discussions of the feminine mystique. See Evans, *Personal Politics*, pp. 3–4. *Personal Politics*, pp. 3–23; and Rochelle Gatlin, *American Women since 1945* (Jackson: University Press of Mississippi, 1987), pp. 7–23, provide good discussions of the new domesticity. Echols, " 'We Gotta Get out of This Place,' " p. 22, notes how evanescent this domesticity was, vanishing amid two-income families by the time the radical feminist revolt got under way. For a discussion of the historical anomaly of this period and of the distortions in media representations of 1950s family life, see Stephanie Coontz, *The Way We Never Were: American Families and the Nostalgia Trap* (New York: Basic Books, 1992).

17. Barbara Ehrenreich, *The Hearts of Men: American Dreams and the Flight from Commitment* (New York: Doubleday/Anchor, 1983), pp. 14–98. Ehrenreich's ambivalence about male rebellion mirrors the mixed messages heard about domesticity in the 1950s.

18. Evans and Echols see in works like *Modern Woman* and *Nest of Vipers* simply an attempt to get women into the home and keep them there. This view actually underestimates the misogyny of these writings, which suggest that women will be a toxic presence no matter where they are or what their role. Farnham and Lundberg prescribe therapy to adjust women to the role of homemaker and reduce their destructiveness, but this only indicates that even in their supposedly natural role, women form a fundamentally destabilizing force that needs to be continually

managed and controlled. The apostles of domesticity were themselves uncertain about the adequacy of the arrangement.

19. Evans, *Personal Politics*, p. 116.

Echols is more qualified on this score, contending that the counterculture and the "sexual revolution," by "opening up new sexual vistas . . . made it possible for women to demand genuine sexual self-determination." To her, it is important to point out that women in the new left did not always suffer unsatisfying sexual experiences and that in fact they may have enjoyed more sexual satisfaction in the late 1960s than they or other women did previously (Echols, *Daring to Be Bad*, p. 43). Her viewpoint reflects the debate over pornography and "sexual danger" that animated feminism in the 1980s. She is clearly on the "prosex" side of that debate; see Echols, *Daring to be Bad*, pp. 288–291; Alice Echols, "The Taming of the Id," in Carole Vance, ed., *Pleasure and Danger* (New York: Routledge & Kegan Paul, 1984); and Alice Echols, "The New Feminism of Yin and Yang," in Ann Snitow, Christine Stansell, and Sharon Thompson, eds., *Powers of Desire* (New York: Monthly Review Press, 1983).

The issue is complicated. The feminist critique of the 1980s antipornography movement makes some powerful points, but there is a risk of ahistoricism in projecting that critique backward into the sexual politics of the 1960s. The question here is how rebellious or counterhegemonic the sexual politics of the new left was with respect to its contemporary culture, and on this question, in my view, Evans's interpretation is sounder.

20. "Sex and Caste: A Kind of Memo from Casey Hayden and Mary King to a Number of Other Women in the Peace and Freedom Movements," 18 November 1965, reprinted in Evans, *Personal Politics*, pp. 235–238.

21. A group of women aired their discontent with sexism in SNCC in a November 1964 memo, precipitating Stokely Carmichael's notorious comment that the "only position for women in SNCC is prone." Although Mary King later argued that the response was more complex than Evans, for one, contends, enthusiasm for a feminist viewpoint in SNCC, among black women as well as men, was tepid at best. The history of sexual rivalry between black and white women in SNCC (as many African American women saw it), as well as cultural and social differences over the value of autonomy, played important roles in the absence of interracial sisterhood and presaged stubborn problems in feminist organization in subsequent decades. Evans, *Personal Politics*, pp. 77–82, 84–89, 98–101; Echols, *Daring to Be Bad*, pp. 29–33; Mary King, *Freedom Song: A Personal Story of the 1960s Civil Rights Movement* (New York: Morrow, 1987), pp. 450–460.

Casey Hayden typed this first document, but she harbored reservations about its content and timing and does not view it as leading logically to the "Sex and Caste" memo. Casey Hayden to author, 17 March 1997.

22. Casey Hayden, "A Nurturing Movement: Nonviolence, SNCC, and Feminism," *Southern Exposure* 16 (Summer 1988): 53. Gregory Calvert endorses Hayden's own interpretation of her and King's intent. Gregory N. Calvert,

"Democracy and Rebirth: The New Left and Its Legacy" (Ph.D. diss., University of California at Santa Cruz, 1989), p. 533.

23. Rasjidah Franklin-Alley, interview with author, 18 March 1993.

24. Hayden to author.

25. Evans, *Personal Politics*, pp. 169–185. A rather big series of "ifs."

26. Echols notes that Todd Gitlin, in particular, welcomed the women's workshop and recommended more such discussions (Echols, *Daring to Be Bad*, pp. 35–36).

27. Evans, *Personal Politics*, pp. 161–163.

28. The first was Helen Garvy, a stalwart of the national office at a time when most of the old guard had left for the ERAPs; she became assistant national secretary in the summer of 1964.

Evans incorrectly states that Garvy did not assume this post until 1966, citing this as evidence of sexism in SDS. Greg Calvert makes as much as possible of this error and another similar one (Evans says that Adams became national secretary in 1968, not in 1966), arguing that women occupied a less debased position in SDS at mid-decade than Evans allows. He also says that others in SDS wanted Garvy to run for national secretary in 1965, but she declined, and that he urged Adams, with whom he lately had been romantically involved, to run for election as SDS president at the August 1966 national convention but that she also declined, preferring to leave the national office after only three months. Furthermore, he contends that Evans's failure to assign Jane Adams her true importance in SDS by 1966 caused Evans to understate the significance of Adams's criticism of sexism in the new left in 1967, mentioned later. Evans, *Personal Politics*, p. 112; Calvert, "Democracy and Rebirth," pp. 519–520, 530.

Calvert has a point in saying that these factual errors help tip the scales toward the conclusion that sexism was a serious problem in SDS. Yet the most important point is how uneven the scales were anyway; Calvert doth protest too much. For Calvert's defense of the draft resistance movement, which escalated around this time, against Evans's criticism, see chapter 6.

29. Jane Adams, "People's Power: On Equality for Women," *New Left Notes*, 20 January 1967; Evans, *Personal Politics*, p. 187.

30. Evans, *Personal Politics*, pp. 187–192; Echols, *Daring to Be Bad*, pp. 44–45.

31. Echols notes this theoretical convergence acutely (Echols, *Daring to Be Bad*, pp. 37–42). However, like others who look only to the debates occurring in and around the SDS national office, she concludes erroneously that by late 1967, this line of thought had lost its hold on the new left's imagination. As I describe later, I think the growing strength of feminism from this time forward was due in part to the continuing strength of this strain in the new left at the local level.

32. Calvert, "Democracy and Rebirth," pp. 519–520.

33. Evans, *Personal Politics*, pp. 200–211.

34. Todd Gitlin evokes this state of mind, especially among white men in the left, well and at length (even though he seems to have had more distance from this sensibility than did some of his contemporaries from the SDS old guard, like Tom

Hayden and Rennie Davis). Todd Gitlin, *The Sixties: Years of Hope, Days of Rage* (New York: Bantam, 1987), pp. 285–361, 377–408.

Winifred Breines criticizes these sections of *The Sixties* in which, she argues correctly, Gitlin expresses a disapproval for "the development of militance" and "the romance with the Third World" as well as the counterculture, a disapproval that fails to reflect the positive view that many on the left took of these elements in late 1960s radicalism (a positive view that Breines shares). The title of Gitlin's book is misleading and unfortunate. But if one understands that Gitlin really is telling not the whole story of "the Sixties" but instead his own story, relating the evolution of his particular viewpoint, one can appreciate his narrative as a truthful rendition of one sector of that era's politics. (Breines simplifies matters, incidentally, in saying that Gitlin "reproduces the early SDS leadership's hostility" to the developments of the later 1960s, as the examples of Hayden and Davis—surely sexist, but just as surely apostles of polarization—indicate.) Winifred Breines, "Whose New Left?" *Journal of American History* 75 (September 1988): 534.

35. Marilyn Salzman Webb was the object of the hecklers. Audience members shouted "Take it off!" and "Take her off the stage and fuck her!" Presiding over the fracas was the prominent pacifist and titular head of national antiwar mobilizations David Dellinger, awfully courageous when it came to defying the state. Echols, *Daring to Be Bad*, pp. 114–120, and Gitlin, *The Sixties*, pp. 362–364, give detailed versions of this sorry tale; also see Evans, *Personal Politics*, p. 224.

Gitlin writes that subsequently, Marilyn Webb received a threatening phone call from (Webb thought) Cathy Wilkerson in response to Webb's continued feminist agitation, a call that unsettled Webb deeply and helped drive a wedge between the vocal feminists in national SDS and those who, like Wilkerson, put antiwar and antiracist work first and moved toward Weatherman. In their detailed account of the FBI's machinations against radicals in the 1960s and 1970s, Ward Churchill and Jim Vander Wall contend that neither Wilkerson nor any other woman in SDS made the phone call to Webb and conclude that it was the skillful work of a government agent provocateur. Gitlin, *The Sixties*, pp. 363–364; Ward Churchill and Jim Vander Wall, *The COINTELPRO Papers: Documents from the FBI's Secret Wars against Dissent in the United States* (Boston: South End Press, 1990), p. xv.

36. Dohrn, a Wisconsin native, earned a law degree from the University of Chicago and was involved in Martin Luther King Jr.'s Chicago campaign in 1966 and 1967, moving to the National Lawyers' Guild. In 1967 she made contact with SDS members who were doing neighborhood organizing work in Chicago, yet she remained "only at the fringes of the radical movement." During the 1967/1968 school year she lived in New York City, working for the guild, and became close enough to leading figures in New York SDS that she found herself nominated and elected as interorganizational secretary at the June 1968 national convention. Irwin Unger and Debi Unger, *Turning Point: 1968* (New York: Scribner, 1988), pp. 216–217, quotation on 216. As was not unusual at these conventions, Dohrn ran unopposed. In effect, the national elite of the organization often decided who would take the

offices, and it was not uncommon for the group to have difficulty convincing anyone to run for election.

37. While not giving details of the apparent deterioration of their relationship,
Calvert reports that as early as January 1967, Adams "denounced" his sexuality to him
in a personal letter and claims that Adams and Dohrn together joined in "a malicious
gay-baiting campaign" against him during that year. Although there surely are twists
and turns to the personal relations in the SDS national office that remain hidden, it
seems plausible that others in Chicago viewed Calvert's sexuality as part and parcel
of the "libertarian socialism" he advocated, which the Leninists of the national office
viewed simply as anarchism—a political tendency unrivaled in the derision it elicited
from those on the "hard" left. Calvert, "Democracy and Rebirth," pp. 571, 474, 477.
For a reasoned if unsurprising Communist Party critique from the time, see Gil
Green, *The New Radicalism: Anarchist or Marxist?* (New York: International
Publishers, 1971).

38. Naomi Jaffe and Bernardine Dohrn, "The Look Is You," *New Left Notes*, 18
March 1968, reprinted in Massimo Teodori, ed., *The New Left: A Documentary
History* (Indianapolis: Bobbs-Merrill, 1969), pp. 355–358. This article assimilated the
problem of sexism to a general critique of commodification, providing theoretical
validation for the national office's argument that sexism, though worthy of denun-
ciation, would most efficiently be destroyed by eliminating capitalism. Despite the
limitations of this formulation, which women's liberation groups pointed out, it
would have been nice if they had meant it.

In 1969 the national office group gave birth to Weatherman, which pursued a
more varied program of sexual activity.

39. The phrase "men of steel" comes from Marge Piercy, "The Grand Coolie
Damn," in Robin Morgan, ed., *Sisterhood Is Powerful: An Anthology of Writings from
the Women's Liberation Movement* (New York: Random House, 1970), pp. 421–438.

40. Pat Cuney, interview with author, 5 July 1992; Bobby Minkoff, interview
with author, 4 and 9 March 1993; Rebecca Brenner, interview with author, 25 March
1994; Paul Spencer to author.

41. Alice Embree, interview with author, 9 November 1991; Alice Embree,
"Media Images 1: Madison Avenue Brainwashing—The Facts," in Morgan, ed.,
Sisterhood Is Powerful, pp. 175–191; Abe Peck, *Uncovering the Sixties: The Life and
Times of the Underground Press* (New York: Pantheon, 1985), p. 93.

42. Peck, *Uncovering the Sixties*, pp. 212–215; Robin Morgan, "Goodbye to All
That," in Leslie B. Tanner, ed., *Voices from Women's Liberation* (New York: Signet
Books, 1970), p. 275.

43. Judy Smith, interview with author, 1 and 8 February 1993; Linda Smith,
interview with author, 15 March 1993; David J. Garrow, *Liberty and Sexuality: The
Right to Privacy and the Making of* Roe *v.* Wade (New York: Macmillan, 1994), pp.
389–390. According to Linda Smith, the others present included Connie Lanham,
Helen Mayfield, and Rita Starpattern.

44. Linda Smith interview; Judy Smith interview.

45. Linda (Smith), "Peace Corpse," *Rag*, 24 November 1969; Linda Smith interview; Judy (Smith), "Biafra," *Rag*, 3 February 1970; Judy Smith interview.

46. Judy Smith interview.

47. Judy Smith, "integration negation," *Rag*, 13 January 1969; Judy Smith, "times they aren't a-changin'," *Rag*, 26 June 1969; Judy (Smith), "off the hook," *Rag*, 3 July 1969.

48. Judy Smith, "Urban Renewal: The Home You Save May Be Your Own," *Rag*, 14 October 1968; Judy Smith, "Rats, Roaches, and Rubbish," *Rag*, 11 November 1968.

49. Linda Smith interview; Jeff Jones, interview with author, 16 and 23 February 1993; Nancy Folbre to author, 11 November 1995; Jim Denney, interview with author, 8 April 1993. These remarks, one might say, carry a whiff of sexist resentment of strong women. Only with the demise of SDS were women in the new left able to attain positions that might actually elicit such feelings. Furthermore, these comments reflect real inequalities of power and position in the feminist left.

The "tyranny of structurelessness" became a topic of public discussion in the context of the women's liberation movement. Joreen (Jo Freeman), "The Tyranny of Structurelessness," in Anne Koedt, Ellen Levine, and Anita Rapone, eds., *Radical Feminism* (Chicago: Quadrangle, 1973), pp. 285–299.

50. Mariann Wizard, interview with author, 8 July 1992; Barbara Hines, interview with author, 13 May 1993.

51. Barbara Wuensch, "Women's Liberation," *Rag*, 15 September 1969; Judy Smith, "Women's Conference," *Rag*, 5 October 1970; Hines interview.

52. Judy Smith, "Women's Conference"; "Every Woman's Center," *Rag*, 26 April 1971; Frieda Werden, "Adventures of a Texas Feminist," in Daryl Janes, ed., *No Apologies: Texas Radicals Celebrate the '60s* (Austin, TX: Eakin Press, 1992), p. 201; "Women's Festival," *Rag*, 20 September 1971.

53. Echols, *Daring to Be Bad*, makes sharp distinctions among what she calls "radical," "socialist," and "cultural" varieties of feminism. Both *Daring to Be Bad* and Ellen Willis, "Radical Feminism and Feminist Radicalism," in Ellen Willis, *No More Nice Girls: Countercultural Essays* (Middletown, CT: Wesleyan University Press, 1992)—also found in Sohnya Sayres et al., eds., *The 60s without Apology* (Minneapolis: University of Minnesota Press, 1984)—view cultural feminism as a degenerative force in the feminist movement's later years. They charge that the "cultural" orientation turned feminists inward, away from political engagement. For the period after 1973, this is true. But the stages of radical feminism's development in this period, like the differences among feminist tendencies overall, are portrayed too schematically in these accounts. For all its considerable virtues, *Daring to Be Bad* employs a framework of analysis whose distinctions are too sharp to accommodate the politics of those examined here. See notes 57 and 108, below, for further discussion.

54. Embree interview.

55. Here I basically endorse Evans's view that SDS tossed away its "chance" to embrace feminism, although the cultural forces at work in that organization and its

orbit were strong enough to make the SDS leadership seem as much unable as unwilling to help build a feminist left. I cannot agree with Maurice Isserman's contention that the national leadership of SDS did in fact respond rather quickly and sympathetically to feminist criticism or with Calvert's strenuous argument that Evans understates the "chance" for a feminist left in the framework of SDS. Maurice Isserman, "The Not-So-Dark and Bloody Ground: New Works on the 1960s," *American Historical Review* 94 (October 1989): 1001–1003; Calvert, "Democracy and Rebirth," pp. 521–533.

56. Werden, "Adventures of a Texas Feminist," p. 202.

57. "Breaking Away from the Left" is the title of chapter 3 of Echols, *Daring to Be Bad*, a chapter that covers a period of time ending roughly in 1973. In my view, it was only around this time that "radical feminism" started to become detached from a self-consciously leftist perspective. Echols's typology and her evident sympathy for those she calls radical feminists seem to make a decisive break with "the left" a criterion of genuine feminism. My own preference is for a "big tent" definition of feminism.

Chief among the reasons for Echols's view is, I think, her focus on New York City, where factionalism has historically been more extreme on the left than elsewhere, because of the unusually large number of leftists concentrated there and the consequent absence of the feeling, more prominent elsewhere in the United States, that leftists ought to hang together lest they hang separately. This factionalism may have carried over into debates concerning the relations between the left and feminism in New York before it cropped up among feminists elsewhere. The experience and viewpoint of the Redstockings, a radical feminist group in New York City, of which Ellen Willis (author of the foreword to Echols's book) was a leading member, heavily influence Echols's account. New York-ocentrism rears its head once again.

58. Judy Smith interview.

59. Lori Hansel, interview with author, 2 July 1992; William Hinton, *Fanshen: A Documentary of Revolution in a Chinese Village* (New York: Vintage Books, 1966).

60. Hines interview.

61. Hansel interview; Embree interview; Bill Meachem, interview with author, 29 June 1992.

62. Linda Smith interview; Judy Smith interview; Michele Clark, "wargasm," *Rag*, 17 November 1969.

63. Sue Hester, "A (Woman) Is Not a (Chick)," with a reply by Steve Russell, *Rag*, 5 July 1971; Bill to funnel, *Rag*, 10 October 1971, emphasis in original.

64. "Pippin" to funnel (with reply), *Rag*, 10 October 1971.

65. Jayne Loader to funnel, *Rag*, 4 October 1971; Peck, *Uncovering the Sixties*, p. 47; "Rape," *Rag*, 20 September 1971. It is not easy to say how common rape was in the counterculture, but it was far from extraordinary.

66. Nick and Pat, "Sexual Freedom," *Rag*, 26 April 1971.

67. Judy Smith, "Women's Psyches," *Rag*, 31 July 1969.

68. Merritt interview.

69. Ehrenreich, *Hearts of Men*, pp. 29–67; Helen to funnel, *Rag*, 24 July 1969; Carol to funnel, *Rag*, 18 October 1971.

70. Barbara, "love is the liberator," *Rag*, 27 January 1970; "The Gay Woman," *Rag*, 30 August 1971.

71. Paul Potter, *A Name for Ourselves: Feelings about Authentic Identity, Love, Intuitive Politics, Us* (Boston: Little, Brown, 1971), p. 45.

72. Judy Smith, "women," *Rag*, 12 May 1969.

73. Smith, "Women's Psyches."
There is much truth to her characterization of nineteenth-century feminists, though it is not quite so simple. For interpretations that corroborate Smith's view, see Barbara Epstein, *The Politics of Domesticity: Women, Evangelism, and Temperance in Nineteenth-Century America* (Middletown, CT: Wesleyan University Press, 1981); and, at least in part, Mari Jo Buhle, *Women and American Socialism, 1870–1920* (Urbana: University of Illinois Press, 1981). For a different view, see Ellen C. DuBois, *Feminism and Suffrage: The Emergence of an Independent Women's Movement in America, 1848–1869* (Ithaca, NY: Cornell University Press, 1978).

74. Barbara, "love is the liberator"; Clarice Clark, "The Sexual Revolution Is Yet to Come," *Rag*, 9 March 1970.

75. Barbara, "love is the liberator."

76. Smith, "women"; Barbara, "love is the liberator"; Paul Tillich, "The Idea and the Ideal of the Personality," in Paul Tillich, *The Protestant Era*, trans. and ed. James Luther Adams (Chicago: University of Chicago Press, 1948), pp. 115–135.

77. Barbara, "love is the liberator."

78. Ibid.

79. Smith, "women."

80. Bea (Vogel), "Women's Liberation in Austin," *Rag*, 26 June 1969; Linda Swartz, "It's for Fake," *Rag*, 13 October 1969; Smith, "women."

81. Both Willis, "Radical Feminism and Feminist Radicalism," and Echols, *Daring to Be Bad* (following Willis), tell their stories once again, largely from the Redstockings' viewpoint. The "pro-woman line" held that human psychology was entirely rational, that women understood their predicament, and that women remained in a subordinate social position because they calculated that rebellion was a bad bet. In these writings, Willis and Echols qualify their endorsement of this perspective, making it clear they think both social–institutional forces and psychological factors are involved in the structure of male supremacy. Nonetheless, the "pro-woman line" retains a privileged place in their narratives of the women's liberation movement. They associate psychological explanations of women's oppression with groups, like the New York Radical Feminists, that remain rather marginal in their stories and whose analysis they criticize severely. Echols, *Daring to Be Bad*, pp. 186–197.

82. Smith, "women"; "Miss . . . Who??" *Rag*, 3 November 1969.

83. Smith, "Women's Psyches"; Smith, "women"; Barb, "Women for Fun & Profit?" *Rag*, 3 February 1970; "Miss . . . Who??"

84. Judy Smith, "fashion scene," *Rag*, 12 May 1969.

85. lyn wells, "Woman," *Rag*, 17 July 1969; Evans, *Personal Politics*, p. 173. Kirkpatrick Sale spells Wells's first name "Lynn." Kirkpatrick Sale, *SDS* (New York: Random House, 1973), p. 576.

Eleanor Flexner, *Century of Struggle: The Woman's Rights Movement in the United States* (Cambridge, MA: Belknap Press of Harvard University Press, 1959); Friedrich Engels, *The Origin of the Family, Private Property, and the State* (New York: International Publishers, 1972); Mirra Komarovsky, with Jane Philips, *Blue Collar Marriage* (New York: Random House, 1962); Elizabeth Gurley Flynn, *I Speak My Own Piece* (New York: Masses & Mainstream, 1955); Simone de Beauvoir, *The Second Sex*, trans. and ed. H. M. Parshley (New York: Modern Library, 1968).

Here we do well to locate Flexner's and Friedan's liberal feminist writings against the backdrop of these authors' backgrounds in left-wing, labor union–based political journalism. Both of them obscured these backgrounds when they achieved fame, perhaps fearing the anticommunist repercussions that would discredit their feminism (and Friedan has continued to this day to deny the extent of her leftist past). As Daniel Horowitz indicates, after uncovering Friedan's true political history, *The Feminine Mystique* paired a psychological argument urging women simply to will themselves into the public sphere with a quasi-Marxist analysis of U.S. capitalists' campaign to get women to bolster the economic system by urging consumption as an outlet for women's energies. The resonance of this argument with the cultural critique of the feminist leftists, discussed earlier, is notable. Daniel Horowitz, "Rethinking Betty Friedan and *The Feminine Mystique*: Labor Union Radicalism and Feminism in Cold War America," *American Quarterly* 48 (March 1996): 24–25. Horowitz's article should change the way that historians think about Friedan and about the relation between liberal and radical feminism in this period. Ellen Dubois revaluates Flexner from a left-feminist perspective in Ellen C. Dubois, "Eleanor Flexner and the History of American Feminism," *Gender and History* 3 (Spring 1991): 81–90.

86. Judy Smith interview; Hines interview.

Dick Howard, ed., *Selected Political Writings of Rosa Luxemburg* (New York: Monthly Review Press, 1971).

87. Hines interview.

The trajectory of Margaret Randall's work can be gleaned from her *Part of the Solution: Portrait of a Revolutionary* (New York: New Directions, 1973), *Sandino's Daughters: Conversations with Nicaraguan Women in Struggle* (Vancouver: New Star Books, 1981), and *Gathering Rage: The Failure of Twentieth Century Revolutions to Develop a Feminist Agenda* (New York: Monthly Review Press, 1992).

88. Victoria Foe, interview with author, 4 May 1995.

89. Ibid.

90. Barb, "Women for Fun & Profit?"

91. Embree interview.

92. "Sex and unemployment," *Rag*, March 1969; untitled, *Rag*, 28 June 1971; "Sexual Discrimination at UT no. 2," *Rag*, 19 July 1971. At the behest of HEW, UT

agreed to negotiate with the Women's Negotiating Team (WNT) representing those filing the complaints, although the administration soon proposed the abolition of the WNT, to be replaced by a university-appointed committee, staffed primarily with women employees who had no history of involvement with any women's groups.

93. Embree interview.

94. Shulamith Firestone, *The Dialectic of Sex: The Case for Feminist Revolution* (New York: Morrow, 1970). This is not to say that Firestone's views were widely shared; her technological utopianism, perhaps no less than her separatism, was at odds with mainstream opinion among radical feminists.

95. "Now!" *Rag*, 14 December 1969; Foe interview; Hines interview; Garrow, *Liberty and Sexuality*, pp. 390–391.

96. Ninia Baehr, *Abortion without Apology: A Radical History for the 1990s* (Boston: South End Press, 1990), pp. 7–20; Garrow, *Liberty and Sexuality*, p. 369.

97. Betty Friedan, *"It Changed My Life": Writings on the Women's Movement* (New York: Dell, 1991), pp. 152–155; Echols, *Daring to Be Bad*, pp. 140–142; Baehr, *Abortion without Apology*, p. 40; Garrow, *Liberty and Sexuality*, pp. 167–168; Sarah R. Weddington, *A Question of Choice* (New York: Putnam, 1991), pp. 26–27.

After *Roe v. Wade*, NARAL kept its acronym but changed its name to the National Abortion Rights Action League.

98. Weddington, *A Question of Choice*, pp. 27–29, 31–33; "Birth Control," *Rag*, 3 November 1969; Judy Smith interview; Hines interview; Bob Breihan, interview with author, 10 November 1991; Garrow, *Liberty and Sexuality*, pp. 333, 392–393, 438.

99. Foe interview. Robert F. Drinan, a leftist Catholic priest who entered the U.S. Congress as a representative from Massachusetts, argued vigorously in the 1960s that Catholics should support repeal, and he garnered more support than some have noticed. Garrow, *Liberty and Sexuality*, pp. 342–343, 412–413, 421–422.

100. "Now!"

101. Weddington, *A Question of Choice*, pp. 44–45; Garrow, *Liberty and Sexuality*, pp. 393–396.

102. Weddington, *A Question of Choice*, pp. 50–57, 146–148; Garrow, *Liberty and Sexuality*, pp. 402–404, 439–440, 600; Norma McCorvey with Andy Meisler, *I Am Roe: My Life, Roe v. Wade, and Freedom of Choice* (New York: HarperCollins, 1994). McCorvey had given up her first two children for adoption.

It is possible that McCorvey, whose bisexuality put her far along the path that some radical feminists were just beginning to travel, would have evoked more sympathy from the radicals as an individual had they had personal contact with her. McCorvey's later exploitation by right-wing antiabortion activists, who embraced her as a "victim of abortion" and under whose auspices she experienced a religious conversion in the 1990s, makes her complaints about the abortion rights activists of the 1970s easy for some to dismiss as politically manipulated. Yet the suspicion lingers that class differences prevented the feminists from identifying with McCorvey closely enough to do for her what they did for women who came to the

UT Birth Control Information Center and made her appear, if unconsciously, as a likely means to an end.

103. Garrow, *Liberty and Sexuality*, pp. 451–454, 587–599.

104. Ruth Bader Ginsburg, "A Moderate View on *Roe*," *Constitution*, Spring–Summer 1992; quotation from Barbara Ehrenreich, "Mothers United," *New Republic*, 10 July 1989. Both cited in Garrow, *Liberty and Sexuality*, p. 616. Garrow argues vigorously against such mixed feminist views of *Roe*, arguing that there was no tide rolling on in favor of repeal in 1973 and that *Roe* marked a great advance for feminists and American women. He also defends the integrity of the jurisprudential reasoning in *Roe* (Garrow, *Liberty and Sexuality*, pp. 616–617). Garrow's viewpoint is well taken, although as I indicate, feminist activists were concerned not only with winning this specific fight but also with continuing to build a movement, and Ehrenreich, along with others, evaluates the decision partly in that light.

105. Garrow, *Liberty and Sexuality*, p. 407.

106. Judy Smith interview.

107. Judy Smith interview; Linda Smith interview; Hines interview; Foe interview; Merritt interview.

108. Echols, in *Daring to Be Bad*, pp. 134–137, takes a few shots at socialist feminists, who receive rather little attention in her book overall.

In fairness, I should note that Echols remarks that "radical feminists were anticapitalist—if only implicitly," but this element in radical feminism remains quite subdued in her treatment (Echols, *Daring to Be Bad*, pp. 6–7). Furthermore, as I explain, frequently the radical feminists' leftist politics was quite explicit.

109. Judy Smith interview.

Epilogue

1. Elinor Langer, "Notes for Next Time: A Memoir of the 1960s," *Working Papers for a New Society* 1 (Fall 1973), reprinted in R. David Myers, ed., *Toward a History of the New Left: Essays from within the Movement* (Brooklyn, NY: Carlson, 1989), pp. 65–66, is quoted at the beginning of the epilogue. For other early eulogies, see Carl Oglesby, "Notes on a Decade Ready for the Dustbin," *Liberation* 14 (August–September 1969), reprinted in Myers, ed., *Toward a History of the New Left*; Paul Buhle, "The Eclipse of the New Left: Some Notes," *Radical America* 6 (July–August 1972): 1–9; James O'Brien, "Beyond Reminiscence: The New Left in History," *Radical America* 6 (July–August 1972): 11–48.

2. On the left, see George Katsiaficas, *The Imagination of the New Left: A Global Analysis of 1968* (Boston: South End Press, 1987); on the right, see Roger Kimball, *Tenured Radicals: How Politics Has Corrupted Our Higher Education* (New York: Harper & Row, 1990).

3. Jeff Jones, interview with author, 16 and 23 February 1993; "economy furniture workers," *Rag*, 7 August 1969. Cuney and Nancy Sweeney started the group, which at first they had thought to call "the New Patriots, A 'New' Left Organization." "New Patriots," *Rag*, 7 August 1969.

In general, on the new left's support for labor unions in its later years, see Peter B. Levy, *The New Left and Labor in the 1960s* (Urbana: University of Illinois Press, 1993), pp. 108–127, 147–166.

4. "United Farm Workers," *Rag*, 2 October 1972; "Three Strikes," *Rag*, 18 September 1972; Judy Smith, "Which Side Are You On?" *Rag*, 8 December 1968; quotation from "With Love—Pat," *Rag*, 9 November 1970. The owner of the low-wage furniture factory, Milton Smith, was a member of the Austin Human Relations Commission and, along with his wife, Helen, a recipient of the B'nai B'rith National Humanitarian Award in 1969. "Enough to Make You Gag," *Rag*, 3 June 1969.

5. "Go Strikers!" *Rag*, 15 September 1969.

6. Peter J. Gay, *The Dilemma of Democratic Socialism: Eduard Bernstein's Challenge to Marx* (New York: Columbia University Press, 1952), p. 266.

7. Colin, "Political Independence," *Rag*, 6 November 1972.

8. Elizabeth Alexander, Martin Murray, David Allen, John Houghton, Martin Wiginton, Nancy Allen, Gary Fitzgerald, letter, *Rag*, 31 January 1972; Mike R., "New American Movement," *Rag*, 14 February 1972.

9. J. William More, "The New American Movement," *Space City!* 17–23 February 1972, remarked on the resemblance of NAM to the early SDS.

10. Staughton Lynd, "Prospects for the New Left," *Liberation* 15 (January 1971): 13–28, is a lengthy analysis of the twentieth-century American left's failings that called for "a kind of mass organization in which the qualities most important to the New Left will not be lost" (p. 13). James Weinstein, "Reply to REP," in Harold Jacobs, ed., *Weatherman* (Berkeley, CA: Ramparts, 1970), p. 399, called for "a mass, democratic organization encompassing and at the same time unifying the diverse needs of the *entire proletariat*" (emphasis added), by which he meant college-educated workers as well as others. Weinstein founded the journal *Socialist Revolution*, a theoretical organ in search of a party, which by 1978 made its peace with political reality by renaming itself *Socialist Review*.

11. Harrington, who had a destructive falling-out with SDS at the Port Huron Conference of 1962, tried to pick up the pieces of a shattered left in later years. He helped found the Democratic Socialist Organizing Committee (DSOC) in 1972, after leaving the Socialist Party (SP). This moved his politics somewhat to the left of the SP's cold warrior stance, but DSOC was still mainly a group of older social democrats, of Irving Howe's "missing generation," and it still aimed to work within the councils of the Democratic Party. As I indicate, however, new left radicals were doing this as well, often on a local basis. DSOC was not an activist organization, and Harrington in 1982 negotiated its merger with NAM, creating the Democratic Socialists of America (DSA), effecting a generational entente. But this was a peace between fragments of past left-wing movements, not the beginning of a new one. Robert Gorman reports that NAM had attracted a maximum of fifteen hundred members. Robert A. Gorman, *Michael Harrington: Speaking American* (New York: Routledge, 1995), pp. 144–145.

12. David Riesman, with Nathan Glazer and Reuel Denney, *The Lonely Crowd: A Study of the Changing American Character* (New Haven, CT: Yale University Press, 1950; rev. ed., 1989), pp. 304–307.

13. Peter Clecak, *America's Quest for the Ideal Self: Dissent and Fulfillment in the 60s and 70s* (New York: Oxford University Press, 1983), makes a convincing case for the left's lost monopoly on the search for authenticity.

14. See E. J. Dionne, *Why Americans Hate Politics* (New York: Simon & Schuster, 1991), pp. 31–54, for a blunt argument along these lines. The new left's loathing of the state clearly antedated the escalation of the Vietnam War, as Stanley Aronowitz, "Towards Radicalism: The Death and Rebirth of the American Left," in David Trend, ed., *Radical Democracy: Identity, Citizenship, and the State* (New York: Routledge, 1996), pp. 81–101, indicates.

15. Mariann Garner Wizard, interview with author, 8 July 1992.

16. James Weinstein, *Ambiguous Legacy: The Left in American Politics* (New York: New Viewpoints, 1975), pp. viii, 140.

The pluralism that raised the new left's hackles was exemplified in Robert A. Dahl, *Who Governs?: Democracy and Power in an American City* (New Haven, CT: Yale University Press, 1961), which asserted a dispersal of political power among organized interest groups. Leftists attacked this view of things for its complacency, for its apparent denial of disempowerment and political inequality. For critiques from the left, see Grant McConnell, *The Decline of Agrarian Democracy* (Berkeley and Los Angeles: University of California Press, 1959); and Grant McConnell, *Private Power and American Democracy* (New York: Knopf, 1966), which lament the demise of popularly based political party structures and the ascendance of elitist interest-group pluralism. On a theoretical plane, see R. Jeffrey Lustig, *Corporate Liberalism: The Origins of Modern American Political Theory, 1880–1920* (Berkeley and Los Angeles: University of California Press, 1982); and for a powerful combination of theoretical and empirical argument, see Michael P. Rogin, *The Intellectuals and McCarthy: The Radical Specter* (Cambridge, MA: MIT Press, 1967), pp. 9–31, 261–282.

David Hollinger notes with insight that "pluralism" got such a bad name among leftists in the 1960s that in later years when many of them embraced pluralism, cultural and political, they had to invent a new word for it. Hence "multiculturalism." David A. Hollinger, *Postethnic America: Beyond Multiculturalism* (New York: Basic Books, 1995), pp. 99–100.

17. Randolph Bourne held out the cosmopolitan hope of "trans-national America," which Hollinger updates in *Postethnic America*. Randolph Bourne, "Trans-National America," in David Hollinger and Charles A. Capper, eds., *The American Intellectual Tradition: A Sourcebook*, vol. 2, *1865 to the Present* (New York: Oxford University Press, 1993), pp. 179–188.

18. Todd Gitlin, *The Twilight of Common Dreams: Why America Is Wracked by Culture Wars* (New York: Metropolitan Books, 1995), p. 97.

19. Ibid., pp. 96–104.

20. Arthur M. Schlesinger Jr., *The Disuniting of America: Reflections on a Multicultural Society* (New York: Norton, 1992); Robert Hughes, *Culture of Complaint: The Fraying of America* (New York: Oxford University Press, 1993); Gitlin, *Twilight of Common Dreams*. None of these is quite the revanchist text one might think from criticism on the left (I say more about Gitlin's book later). Still, the rather obvious similarity of identity politics to interest-group pluralism makes these liberal critiques, all with a keen eye for the shocking example, ring a bit hollow. Dinesh D'Souza, *Illiberal Education: The Politics of Race and Sex on Campus* (New York: Free Press, 1991), is both more honest and downright dishonest; the first because its author cares not a lick for pluralism and the second because he is a rightist posing as a liberal (and because his reporting is typically, let us say, embellished).

21. Gitlin, *Twilight of Common Dreams*, p. 100. It would be less than fair to characterize Gitlin's book as merely the plaint of a white male leftist who wishes to reverse the tide of "difference," as I have heard some do. There is truth in Gitlin's narration of the left's collapse. As I explain, I think there are hidden resonances between the new left's politics and the identity politics of latter days. Gitlin himself concedes that "there is no golden past to recover" (p. 103), but his book evokes such a past nonetheless.

22. Herbert Gans, "Symbolic Ethnicity in America," *Ethnic and Racial Studies* 2 (1979): 1–20, is the classic exposition.

23. For an unusually frank discussion, see two essays by Barbara Epstein: " 'Political Correctness' and Collective Powerlessness" (quoted at the beginning of the epilogue), in Marcy Darnovsky, Barbara Epstein, and Richard Flacks, ed., *Cultural Politics and Social Movements* (Philadelphia: Temple University Press, 1995); and "Radical Democracy and Cultural Politics: What about Class? What about Political Power?" in Trend, ed., *Radical Democracy*, pp. 127–139. Others disagree. One approving view, from a former Trotskyist, of identity politics as a postmodernist successor to Marxism is Carl Boggs, *The Socialist Tradition: From Crisis to Decline* (New York: Routledge, 1995), pp. 181–220. His account is notable for its emphasis, contrary to Gitlin, on the continuity between the post-1960s "new social movements" and 1960s radicalism.

24. Oglesby, "Notes on a Decade," p. 37, emphasis in original. In 1969 he called this politics the "new anarchism." Only his insistence on an urban anarchism was off base.

25. Epstein, " 'Political Correctness' and Collective Powerlessness," p. 18. Also see Gitlin, *Twilight of Common Dreams*, pp. 151–165.

26. Trend, ed., *Radical Democracy*, is one attempt to reverse this tide on the left.

Manuscript and Documents Collections

Oral History of the American Left. Tapes. Tamiment Library,
New York University.
President of the University of Texas at Austin. Papers. Eugene C. Barker History
Center, University of Texas at Austin.
Students for a Democratic Society (SDS). Papers (microfilm). Library of
Congress, Washington, D.C.

Interviews (conducted by the author) and Personal Correspondence

Allen, Claude, 21 January 1993.
Barton, Frances, 25 June 1992.
Bell, Robert, 11 March 1993.
Blanton, Brad, 14 April 1993.
Blanton, Judy Schleyer, 17 May 1993.
Breihan, Bob, 10 November 1991.
Breihan, Claire Johnson, and O. R. Schmidt, 29 June 1992.
Brenner, Becky, 25 March 1994.
Briggs, Chett, 27 April 1995.
Burlage, Dorothy Dawson, 9 December 1992.
Burlage, Robb, 1 June 1992.
Calvert, Greg, 20 March 1995.
Caroline, Larry, 16 December 1992.

Craven, Carolyn, 6 December 1995.

Cuney, Pat, 5 July 1992.

Davidson, Chandler, 2 February 1993.

Denney, Jim, 8 April 1993.

Dethloff, Charlotte Pittman, 24 March 1997.

DuBose, Terry, 23 June 1992.

Embree, Alice, 9 November 1991.

Erickson, Charles, 30 June 1993.

Foe, Victoria, 4 May 1995.

Franklin-Alley, Rasjidah, 18 March 1993.

Friedman, Jeff, 24 June 1992.

Goodwyn, Lawrence, 27 September 1994.

Hansel, Lori, 2 July 1992.

Hayden, Casey, 2 March 1993.

Henry, Tony, 3 March 1994.

Hines, Barbara, 13 May 1993.

Jones, Jeff, 16 and 23 February 1993.

Lingo, Allen, 26 November 1991 (cited as Lingo phone interview); 18 June 1992
    (cited as Lingo interview).

Liveoak, Val, 1 July 1992.

Magidoff, Dickie, 19 March 1997.

Mathews, James, 23 June 1993.

Meachem, Bill, 29 June 1992.

Merritt, Barbara Wuensch, 27 April 1993.

Mims, Bud (Robert), 8 February 1993.

Minkoff, Bobby, 4 and 9 March 1993.

Morris, Celia, 3 February 1993.

Nelson, Bobby, 22 June 1992.

Nightbyrd, Jeff Shero, 3 July 1992.

Oakes, Rosalie, 23 February 1993.

Oates, Stephen, 25 August 1993.

Pardun, Robert, 27 August 1993.

Perez, Judy Schiffer, 27 August 1993.

Pipkin, Paul, Linda Pipkin, and Joe Ebbecke, 4 July 1992.

Pittman, Scott, 4 May 1993; 24 March 1997 (cited as Pittman interview II).

Pogue, Alan, 29 June 1992.

Russell, Philip, 28 June 1993.

Russell, Steve, 1 July 1992.

Silverstein, Vivian, 18 May 1993.

Simons, Jim, 26 June 1992.

Smith, Gary, 14 June 1993.

Smith, Judy, 1 and 8 February 1993.

Smith, Linda, 15 March 1993.
Simpson, Dick, 8 March 1993.
Spear, Irwin, 30 June 1992.
Stone, Robert, 28 May 1993.
Taylor, Lonn, 22 May 1992.
Waterhouse, Larry, 10 July 1992.
Wizard, Mariann Garner, 8 July 1992.
Wright, Frank, 30 June 1992.
Zuck, Mel, 4 May 1994.

Abrahams, Roger, to author, 18 May 1993.
Embree, Alice, reminiscence, n.d.
Folbre, Nancy, to author, 12 November 1995.
Greenwood, Bill, to author, 9 March 1993.
Hayden, Casey, to author, 17 March 1997.
Hedemann, Ed, to author, 19 January 1993.
Howard, Dick, to author, 25 October 1995.
Neyland, Jim, to author, 13 February 1993.
Reavis, Dick J., to author, 6 January 1992.
Reavis, Dick J., to author, 9 November 1995.
Spencer, Paul, to author, n.d.
Wilson, Kirk D., to author, 21 January 1993.

Newspapers and Periodicals

Daily Texan (Austin)
Dallas Morning News
Fatigue Press (Killeen, TX)
Gar (Austin)
KU–SDS Journal (Lawrence, KS)
Letter to Laymen (Austin)
New Left Notes (Chicago)
Notes from the Underground/Dallas Notes
Oberlin Other
Rag (Austin)
SDS Bulletin (New York)
Second Coming (Austin)
Space City News/Space City! (Houston)
Summer Texan (Austin)
Texas Observer (Austin)
Thirty-twelve (Dallas)
Word of the Y's (Austin)
"Y" Notes (Austin)

Published Sources

Adams, James L. "Tillich's Concept of the Protestant Era." In Paul Tillich, *The Protestant Era*. Trans. James A. Luther. Chicago: University of Chicago Press, 1948.

Adler, Les K., and Thomas G. Paterson. "Red Fascism: The Merger of Nazi Germany and Soviet Russia in the American Image of Totalitarianism, 1930's–1950's." *American Historical Review* 75 (April 1970):1046–1064.

Adorno, Theodor. *The Jargon of Authenticity*. Trans. Knut Tarnowski and Frederic Will. Evanston, IL: Northwestern University Press, 1973.

Agnew, Jean-Christophe. "A Touch of Class." *democracy* 3 (September 1983):59–72.

Allen, Robert. *Black Awakening in Capitalist America*. New York: Doubleday, 1969.

Anderson, Terry H. *The Movement and the Sixties: Protest in America from Greensboro to Wounded Knee*. New York: Oxford University Press, 1995.

Appy, Christian G. *Working-Class War: American Combat Soldiers and Vietnam*. Chapel Hill: University of North Carolina Press, 1993.

Aronowitz, Stanley. "When the New Left Was New." In *The 60s without Apology*, ed. Sohnya Sayres, Anders Stephanson, Stanley Aronowitz, and Frederic Jameson. Minneapolis: University of Minnesota Press, 1984.

Auden, W. H. *The Age of Anxiety*. London: Faber & Faber, 1947.

Aya, Roderick, and Norman Miller, eds. *The New American Revolution*. New York: Free Press, 1971.

Ayres, Clarence. *The Divine Right of Capital*. Boston: Houghton Mifflin, 1946.

Baehr, Ninia. *Abortion without Apology: A Radical History for the 1990s*. Boston: South End Press, 1990.

Bailey, Beth. *From Front Porch to Back Seat: Courtship in Twentieth-Century America*. Baltimore: Johns Hopkins University Press, 1988.

——. "Sexual Revolution(s)." In *The Sixties: From Memory to History*, ed. David Farber. Chapel Hill: University of North Carolina Press, 1994.

Barber, Benjamin R. *Strong Democracy: Participatory Politics for a New Age*. Berkeley and Los Angeles: University of California Press, 1984.

Baritz, Loren, ed. *The American Left: Radical Political Thought in the Twentieth Century*. New York: Basic Books, 1971.

Barone, Michael. *Our Country: The Shaping of America from Roosevelt to Reagan*. New York: Free Press, 1990.

Barrera, Mario. *Race and Class in the Southwest: A Theory of Racial Inequality*. Notre Dame, IN: University of Notre Dame Press, 1979.

Barrett, William. *Irrational Man: A Study in Existential Philosophy*. Garden City, NY: Doubleday, 1958.

Bates, Tom. *Rads: The 1970 Bombing of the Army Math Research Center at the University of Wisconsin and Its Aftermath*. New York: HarperCollins, 1992.

Beauvoir, Simone de. *The Second Sex*. Trans. and ed. H. M. Parshley. New York: Modern Library, 1968.

Beckett, Samuel. *Waiting for Godot: A Tragicomedy in Two Acts*. London: S. French, 1957.

Bell, Daniel. *The Cultural Contradictions of Capitalism*. New York: Basic Books, 1976.

Berman, Paul. "Don't Follow Leaders." *New Republic*, 17 August 1987, 28–35.

———. *A Tale of Two Utopias: The Political Journey of the Generation of 1968*. New York: Norton, 1996.

Bernstein, Barton J., and Allen J. Matusow, eds. *Twentieth-Century America: Recent Interpretations*. 2d ed. New York: Harcourt Brace Jovanovich, 1972.

Bethge, Eberhard. *Dietrich Bonhoeffer: Man of Vision, Man of Courage*. Trans. Eric Mosbacher et al. New York: Harper & Row, 1970.

Blake, Casey N. *Beloved Community: The Cultural Criticism of Randolph Bourne, Van Wyck Brooks, Waldo Frank, and Lewis Mumford*. Chapel Hill: University of North Carolina Press, 1990.

Bloom, Allan. *The Closing of the American Mind: How Higher Education Has Failed Democracy and Impoverished the Souls of Today's Students*. New York: Simon & Schuster, 1987.

Blum, John M. *Years of Discord: American Politics and Society, 1961–1974*. New York: Norton, 1991.

Boggs, Carl. *The Socialist Tradition: From Crisis to Decline*. New York: Routledge, 1995.

Bond, Julian. "The Politics of Civil Rights History." In *New Directions in Civil Rights Studies*, ed. Armstead L. Robinson and Patricia Williams. Charlottesville: University Press of Virginia, 1991.

Bonhoeffer, Dietrich. *The Cost of Discipleship*. Rev. ed. New York: Macmillan, 1959.

———. *Ethics*. Ed. Eberhard Bethge. New York: Macmillan, 1955.

———. *Letters and Papers from Prison*. Rev. ed. Ed. Eberhard Bethge. New York: Macmillan, 1967.

———. *Life Together*. Trans. John W. Doberstein. New York: Harper Bros., 1954.

Bookchin, Murray. "From the '30s to the '60s." In *The 60s without Apology*, ed. Sohnya Sayres, Anders Stephanson, Stanley Aronowitz, and Frederic Jameson. Minneapolis: University of Minnesota Press, 1984.

Boorstin, Daniel J. *The Americans: The Democratic Experience*. New York: Random House, 1973.

Bourne, Randolph. "Trans-National America." In *The American Intellectual Tradition: A Sourcebook*. vol. 2, *1865 to the Present*. Ed. David Hollinger and Charles A. Capper. 2d ed. New York: Oxford University Press, 1993.

Boyte, Harry C. *CommonWealth: A Return to Citizen Politics*. New York: Free Press, 1989.

Branch, Taylor. *Parting the Waters: America in the King Years, 1954–63*. New York: Simon & Schuster, 1989.

Breines, Wini (Winifred). *Community and Organization in the New Left, 1962–1968: The Great Refusal*. South Hadley, MA: J. F. Bergin, 1982.

———. "Whose New Left?" *Journal of American History* 75 (September 1988):528–545.

———. *Young, White, and Miserable: Growing up Female in the Fifties.* Boston: Beacon Press, 1992.

Brick, Howard. *Daniel Bell and the Decline of Intellectual Radicalism: Social Theory and Political Reconciliation in the 1940s.* Madison: University of Wisconsin Press, 1986.

———. "Optimism of the Mind: Imagining Postindustrial Society in the 1960s and 1970s." *American Quarterly* 44 (September 1992):348–380.

Brinkley, Alan. "Dreams of the Sixties." *New York Review of Books*, 22 October 1987, 10, 12–16.

———. *The End of Reform: New Deal Liberalism in Recession and War.* New York: Knopf, 1995.

Brischetto, Robert, David R. Richards, Chandler Davidson, and Bernard Grofman. "Texas." In *Quiet Revolution in the South: The Impact of the Voting Rights Act, 1965–1990*, ed. Chandler Davidson and Bernard Grofman. Princeton, NJ: Princeton University Press, 1994.

Brown, Helen Gurley. *Sex and the Single Girl.* New York: Pocket Books, 1963.

Brown, Norman O. *Life against Death: The Psychoanalytic Meaning of History.* Middletown, CT: Wesleyan University Press, 1959.

Buber, Martin. *I and Thou.* Trans. Walter Kaufmann. New York: Scribner, 1970.

Buhle, Mari Jo. *Women and American Socialism, 1870–1920.* Urbana: University of Illinois Press, 1981.

Buhle, Paul. "The Eclipse of the New Left: Some Notes." *Radical America* 6 (July–August 1972):1–9.

———. *Marxism in the United States: Remapping the History of the American Left.* London: Verso, 1987.

———, ed. *History and the New Left: Madison, Wisconsin, 1950–1970.* Philadelphia: Temple University Press, 1990.

Butler, Jon. *Awash in a Sea of Faith: Christianizing the American People.* Cambridge, MA: Harvard University Press, 1990.

Calvert, Greg (Gregory N). *Democracy from the Heart: Spiritual Values, Decentralism, and Democratic Idealism in the Movement of the 1960s.* Eugene, OR: Communitas Press, 1991.

———. "In White America: Revolutionary Consciousness and Social Change." In *The New Left: A Documentary History*, ed. Massimo Teodori. Indianapolis: Bobbs-Merrill, 1969.

Calvert, Greg, and Carol Neiman. *A Disrupted History: The New Left and the New Capitalism.* New York: Random House, 1971.

Camus, Albert. *The Myth of Sisyphus and Other Essays.* Trans. Justin O'Brien. New York: Knopf, 1955.

———. *The Rebel: An Essay on Man in Revolt.* Trans. Anthony Bower. New York: Knopf, 1961.

Carmichael, Stokely. See Ture, Kwame.

Caro, Robert. *The Years of Lyndon Johnson: Means of Ascent.* New York: Knopf, 1990.

——. *The Years of Lyndon Johnson: The Path to Power.* New York: Knopf, 1982.

Carson, Clayborne. *In Struggle: SNCC and the Black Awakening of the 1960s.* Cambridge, MA: Harvard University Press, 1980.

Carson, Rachel. *Silent Spring.* Boston: Houghton Mifflin, 1962.

Carter, Paul. *The Decline and Revival of the Social Gospel.* Ithaca, NY: Cornell University Press, 1954.

Case, John, and Rosemary C. R. Taylor, eds. *Co-ops, Communes & Collectives: Experiments in Social Change in the 1960s and 1970s.* New York: Pantheon, 1979.

Caute, David. *Sixty-Eight: The Year of the Barricades.* London: Paladin Books, 1988.

Chafe, William H. *Civilities and Civil Rights: Greensboro, North Carolina, and the Black Struggle for Freedom.* New York: Oxford University Press, 1980.

Chappell, David. *Inside Agitators: White Southerners in the Civil Rights Movement.* Baltimore: Johns Hopkins University Press, 1994.

Chatfield, Charles. *For Peace and Justice: Pacifism in America, 1914–1941.* Knoxville: University of Tennessee Press, 1971.

Churchill, Ward, and Jim Vander Wall. *The COINTELPRO Papers: Documents from the FBI's Secret Wars against Dissent in the United States.* Boston: South End Press, 1990.

Cleaver, Eldridge. *Soul on Ice.* New York: McGraw-Hill, 1968.

Clecak, Peter. *America's Quest for the Ideal Self: Dissent and Fulfillment in the 60s and 70s.* New York: Oxford University Press, 1983.

——. *Radical Paradoxes: Dilemmas of the American Left, 1945–1970.* New York: Harper & Row, 1973.

Clifford, James. *The Predicament of Culture.* Cambridge, MA: Harvard University Press, 1988.

Cmiel, Kenneth. "The Politics of Civility." In *The Sixties: From Memory to History*, ed. David Farber. Chapel Hill: University of North Carolina Press, 1994.

Cohen, Lizabeth. "The Class Experience of Mass Consumption: Workers as Consumers in Interwar America." In *The Power of Culture: Critical Essays in American History*, ed. Richard W. Fox and T. J. Jackson Lears. Chicago: University of Chicago Press, 1993.

Cohen, Mitchell, and Dennis Hale, eds. *The New Student Left: An Anthology.* Boston: Beacon Press, 1966.

Cohen, Robert. *When the Old Left Was Young: Student Radicals and America's First Mass Student Movement, 1929–1941.* New York: Oxford University Press, 1993.

Collins, Robert M. "Growth Liberalism in the Sixties: Great Societies at Home and Abroad." In *The Sixties: From Memory to History*, ed. David Farber. Chapel Hill: University of North Carolina Press, 1994.

Conkin, Paul K. *Big Daddy from the Pedernales: Lyndon Baines Johnson.* Boston: Twayne, 1986.

Coontz, Stephanie. *The Way We Never Were: American Families and the Nostalgia Trap.* New York: Basic Books, 1992.

Cox, Craig. *Storefront Revolution: Food Co-ops and the Counterculture*. New Brunswick, NJ: Rutgers University Press, 1994.

Cox, Harvey. *Radical Renewal: The Response of the Student YMCA and YWCA in a "World-Come-of-Age."* New York: National Student Councils of the YMCA and YWCA, n.d. (1959).

——. *The Secular City: Secularization and Urbanization in Theological Perspective*. Rev. ed. New York: Collier, 1990.

——. *Turning East: Why Americans Look to the Orient for Spirituality, and What That Search Can Mean to the West*. New York: Simon & Schuster, 1977.

Craig, Robert H. *Religion and Radical Politics: An Alternative Tradition in the United States*. Philadelphia: Temple University Press, 1992.

Crandell, William F. "They Moved the Town: Organizing Vietnam Veterans against the War." In *Give Peace a Chance: Exploring the Vietnam Antiwar Movement*, ed. Melvin Small and William D. Hoover. Syracuse, NY: Syracuse University Press, 1992.

Cruse, Harold. *The Crisis of the Negro Intellectual*. New York: Morrow, 1967.

Curtis, Susan. *A Consuming Faith: The Social Gospel and Modern American Culture*. Baltimore: Johns Hopkins University Press, 1991.

Dahl, Robert. *Who Governs?: Democracy and Power in an American City*. New Haven, CT: Yale University Press, 1961.

Dallek, Robert. *Lone Star Rising: Lyndon Johnson and His Times, 1908–1960*. New York: Oxford University Press, 1991.

Darnovsky, Marcy, Barbara Epstein, and Richard Flacks, eds. *Cultural Politics and Social Movements*. Philadelphia: Temple University Press, 1995.

Davidson, Carl. "The New Radicals and the Multiversity." In *The New Left: A Documentary History*, ed. Massimo Teodori. Indianapolis: Bobbs-Merrill, 1969.

Davidson, Chandler. *Race and Class in Texas Politics*. Princeton, NJ: Princeton University Press, 1990.

DeBenedetti, Charles, with Charles Chatfield, assisting author. *An American Ordeal: The Antiwar Movement of the Vietnam Era*. Syracuse, NY: Syracuse University Press, 1990.

DeLeon, David. *The American as Anarchist*. Baltimore: Johns Hopkins University Press, 1978.

Denisoff, R. Serge. *Great Day Coming!: Folk Music and the American Left*. Urbana: University of Illinois Press, 1971.

Diggins, John P. *The Rise and Fall of the American Left*. New York: Norton, 1992.

Dionne, E. J. *Why Americans Hate Politics*. New York: Simon & Schuster, 1991.

Dittmer, John. *Local People: The Struggle for Civil Rights in Mississippi*. Urbana: University of Illinois Press, 1994.

Draper, Hal, ed. *FSM: The "New Left" Uprising in Berkeley*. New York: Grove Press, 1965.

D'Souza, Dinesh. *Illiberal Education: The Politics of Race and Sex on Campus*. New York: Free Press, 1991.

DuBois, Ellen C. "Eleanor Flexner and the History of American Feminism." *Gender and History* 3 (Spring 1991):81–91.

——. *Feminism and Suffrage: The Emergence of an Independent Women's Movement in America, 1848–1869*. Ithaca, NY: Cornell University Press, 1978.

Dugger, Ronnie. *Our Invaded Universities: Form, Reform, and New Starts*. New York: Norton, 1974.

——. "The Politics of Knowledge." *Change* 6 (February 1974):30–39, 60–61.

Dumenil, Lynn. *The Modern Temper: American Culture and Society in the 1920s*. New York: Hill & Wang, 1995.

Dunbar, Anthony P. *Against the Grain: Southern Radicals and Prophets, 1929–1959*. Charlottesville: University Press of Virginia, 1981.

Dunlap, Thomas R. *DDT: Scientists, Citizens, and Public Policy*. Princeton, NJ: Princeton University Press, 1981.

Duren, Almetris M., with Louise Iscoe. *Overcoming: A History of Black Integration at the University of Texas at Austin*. Austin: University of Texas at Austin, 1979.

Eagles, Charles W. *Outside Agitator: Jon Daniels and the Civil Rights Movement in Alabama*. Chapel Hill: University of North Carolina Press, 1993.

Echols, Alice. *Daring to Be Bad: Radical Feminism in America, 1967–1975*. Minneapolis: University of Minnesota Press, 1989.

——. "The New Feminism of Yin and Yang." In *Powers of Desire*, ed. Ann Snitow, Christine Stansell, and Sharon Thompson. New York: Monthly Review Press, 1983.

——. "The Taming of the Id." In *Pleasure and Danger*, ed. Carole Vance. New York: Routledge & Kegan Paul, 1984.

——. " 'We Gotta Get out of This Place': Notes toward a Remapping of the Sixties." *Socialist Review* 22 (April–June 1992):9–33.

——. " 'Woman Power' and Women's Liberation: Exploring the Relationship between the Antiwar Movement and the Women's Liberation Movement." In *Give Peace a Chance: Exploring the Vietnam Antiwar Movement*, ed. Melvin Small and William D. Hoover. Syracuse, NY: Syracuse University Press, 1992.

Egerton, John. *Speak Now against the Day: The Generation before the Civil Rights Movement in the South*. New York: Knopf, 1994.

Ehrenreich, Barbara. *Fear of Falling: The Inner Life of the Middle Class*. New York: Pantheon, 1989.

——. *The Hearts of Men: American Dreams and the Flight from Commitment*. New York: Doubleday/Anchor, 1983.

——. "Mothers United." *New Republic*, 10 July 1989, 30–33.

Ehrenreich, Barbara, and John Ehrenreich. "The Professional–Managerial Class." In *Between Labor and Capital*, ed. Pat Walker. Boston: South End Press, 1979.

Elkins, Stanley. *Slavery: A Problem in American Institutional and Intellectual Life*. Chicago: University of Chicago Press, 1958.

Ellwood, Richard S. *The Sixties Spiritual Awakening: American Religion Moving from Modern to Postmodern*. New Brunswick, NJ: Rutgers University Press, 1994.

Embree, Alice. "Media Images I: Madison Avenue Brainwashing—The Facts." In *Sisterhood Is Powerful: Writings from the Women's Liberation Movement*, ed. Robin Morgan. New York: Random House, 1970.

Engels, Friedrich. *The Origin of the Family, Private Property, and the State*. New York: International Publishers, 1972.

Epstein, Barbara. " 'Political Correctness' and Collective Powerlessness." In *Cultural Politics and Social Movements*, ed. Marcy Darnovsky, Barbara Epstein, and Richard Flacks. Philadelphia: Temple University Press, 1995.

——. *Political Protest and Cultural Revolution: Nonviolent Direct Action in the 1970s and 1980s*. Berkeley and Los Angeles: University of California Press, 1991.

——. *The Politics of Domesticity: Women, Evangelism, and Temperance in Nineteenth-Century America*. Middletown, CT: Wesleyan University Press, 1981.

——. "Radical Democracy and Cultural Politics: What about Class? What about Political Power?" In *Radical Democracy: Identity, Citizenship, and the State*, ed. David Trend. New York: Routledge, 1996.

Ericson, Edward E. Jr. *Radicals in the University*. Stanford, CA: Hoover Institution Press, 1975.

Evans, Sara. *Personal Politics: The Roots of Women's Liberation in the Civil Rights Movement and the New Left*. New York: Knopf, 1979; New York: Vintage Books, 1980.

Evans, Sara M., and Harry C. Boyte. *Free Spaces: The Sources of Democratic Change in America*. New York: Harper & Row, 1986.

Fairclough, Adam. *Race and Democracy: The Civil Rights Struggle in Louisiana, 1915–1972*. Athens: University of Georgia Press, 1995.

Farber, David. *The Age of Great Dreams: America in the 1960s*. New York: Hill & Wang, 1994.

——. *Chicago '68*. Chicago: University of Chicago Press, 1988.

——, ed. *The Sixties: From Memory to History*. Chapel Hill: University of North Carolina Press, 1994.

Farnham, Marynia, and Ferdinand Lundberg. *Modern Woman: The Lost Sex*. New York: Harper Bros., 1947.

Fass, Paula. *The Damned and the Beautiful: American Youth in the 1920's*. New York: Oxford University Press, 1977.

Faulk, John H. *Fear on Trial*. Austin: University of Texas Press, 1966.

Ferber, Michael, and Staughton Lynd. *The Resistance*. Boston: Beacon Press, 1971.

Feuer, Lewis S. *The Conflict of Generations: The Character and Significance of Student Movements*. New York: Basic Books, 1969.

Filene, Peter G. *Him/Her/Self: Sex Roles in Modern America*. 2d ed. Baltimore: Johns Hopkins University Press, 1986.

Findlay, James F. *Church People in the Struggle: The National Council of Churches and the Black Freedom Movement*. New York: Oxford University Press, 1993.

Firestone, Shulamith. *The Dialectic of Sex: The Case for Feminist Revolution*. New York: Morrow, 1970.

Fisher, James T. *The Catholic Counterculture in America, 1933–1962.* Chapel Hill: University of North Carolina Press, 1989.

Flacks, Richard. *Making History: The American Left and the American Mind.* New York: Columbia University Press, 1988.

———. "Revolt of the Young Intelligentsia: Revolutionary Class-Consciousness in a Post-Scarcity America." In *The New American Revolution,* ed. Roderick Aya and Norman Miller. New York: Free Press, 1971.

———. "Some Problems, Issues, Proposals." In *The New Radicals: A Report with Documents,* ed. Paul Jacobs and Saul Landau. New York: Vintage Books, 1996.

———. *Youth and Social Change.* Chicago: Markham, 1971.

Flexner, Eleanor. *Century of Struggle: The Woman's Rights Movement in the United States.* Cambridge, MA: Harvard University Press, 1959.

Flynn, Elizabeth Gurley. *I Speak My Own Piece.* New York: Masses & Mainstream, 1955.

Foleno, Louis A. *A Critical Review of Selected Literature on College Student Unrest in the United States, 1968–1970.* San Francisco: Mellen Research University Press, 1992.

Fones-Wolf, Elizabeth. *Selling Free Enterprise: The Business Assault on Labor and Liberalism, 1945–60.* Urbana: University of Illinois Press, 1994.

Foster, Julian, and Durward Long, eds. *Protest!: Student Activism in America.* New York: Morrow, 1970.

Fox, Richard W. "The Culture of Liberal Protestant Progressivism, 1875–1925." *Journal of Interdisciplinary History* 23 (Winter 1993):639–660.

———. "H. Richard Niebuhr's Divided Kingdom." *American Quarterly* 42 (March 1990):93–101.

———. *Reinhold Niebuhr: A Biography.* New York: Pantheon, 1985.

Fox, Richard W., and T. J. Jackson Lears, eds. *The Power of Culture: Critical Essays in American History.* Chicago: University of Chicago Press, 1993.

Frankl, Viktor F. *From Death-Camp to Existentialism: A Psychiatrist's Path to a New Therapy.* Trans. Ilse Lasch. Boston: Beacon Press, 1959.

Fraser, Ronald, et al., eds. *1968: A Student Generation in Revolt.* New York: Pantheon, 1988.

Freeman, Jo. See Joreen.

Friedan, Betty. *The Feminine Mystique.* New York: Dell, 1963.

———. *"It Changed My Life": Writings on the Women's Movement.* New York: Dell, 1991.

Fromm, Erich. *The Art of Loving.* New York: Harper & Row, 1962.

———. *The Forgotten Language: An Introduction to the Understanding of Dreams, Fairy Tales, and Myths.* New York: Rinehart, 1951.

———. *The Sane Society.* New York: Rinehart, 1955.

———, ed. *Socialist Humanism: An International Symposium.* Garden City, NY: Doubleday/Anchor, 1966.

Galbraith, John K. *The Affluent Society.* Boston: Houghton Mifflin, 1958.

Gans, Herbert. "Symbolic Ethnicity in America." *Ethnic and Racial Studies* 2 (1979):1–20.

Garcia, Ignacio M. *United We Win: The Rise and Fall of La Raza Unida Party.* Tucson: Mexican American Studies & Research Center, 1989.

Garner-Wizard, Mariann. "The Lie." In *No Apologies: Texas Radicals Celebrate the '60s*, ed. Daryl Janes. Austin, TX: Eakin Press, 1992.

Garrow, David J. *Liberty and Sexuality: The Right to Privacy and the Making of* Roe *v.* Wade. New York: Macmillan, 1994.

Gatlin, Rochelle. *American Women since 1945.* Jackson: University Press of Mississippi, 1987.

Gay, Peter J. *The Dilemma of Democratic Socialism: Eduard Bernstein's Challenge to Marx.* New York: Columbia University Press, 1952.

Geertz, Clifford. *The Interpretation of Cultures: Selected Essays.* New York: Basic Books, 1973.

Gilbert, James B. *A Cycle of Outrage: America's Reaction to the Juvenile Delinquent in the 1950s.* New York: Oxford University Press, 1986.

———. "New Left: Old America." In *The 60s without Apology*, ed. Sohnya Sayres, Anders Stephanson, Stanley Aronowitz, and Frederic Jameson. Minneapolis: University of Minnesota Press, 1984.

Gillon, Steven M. *Politics and Vision: The ADA and American Liberalism, 1947–1985.* New York: Oxford University Press, 1987.

Ginsburg, Ruth Bader. "A Moderate View on *Roe.*" *Constitution*, Spring–Summer 1992:17.

Gitlin, Todd. *The Sixties: Years of Hope, Days of Rage.* New York: Bantam, 1987.

———. *The Twilight of Common Dreams: Why America Is Wracked with Culture Wars.* New York: Metropolitan Books, 1995.

———. *The Whole World Is Watching: Mass Media in the Making and Unmaking of the New Left.* Berkeley and Los Angeles: University of California Press, 1980.

Goodman, Paul. *Growing up Absurd: Problems of Youth in the Organized Society.* New York: Vintage Books, 1960.

———. "The Revolution in Berkeley." In *The Radical Imagination*, ed. Irving Howe. New York: New American Library, 1967.

———. *The State of Nature.* New York: Vanguard, 1946.

Goodman, Percival, and Paul Goodman. *Communitas: Means of Livelihood and Ways of Life.* Chicago: University of Chicago Press, 1947.

Goodwyn, Larry (Lawrence R.). *Democratic Promise: The Populist Moment in America.* New York: Oxford University Press, 1976.

———. *The Populist Moment.* New York: Oxford University Press, 1978.

———. "The Texas Observer: A Journal of Free Voices." *Southern Exposure* 2 (Winter 1975):23–28.

Gorman, Robert A. *Michael Harrington: Speaking American.* New York: Routledge, 1995.

Gorz, Andre. *Strategy for Labor: A Radical Proposal.* Trans. Martin A. Nicolaus and Victoria Ortiz. Boston: Beacon Press, 1967.

Gosse, Van. *Where the Boys Are: Cuba, Cold War America, and the Making of a New Left.* London: Verso, 1993.

Gould, William B. *The Worldly Christian: Bonhoeffer and Discipleship.* Philadelphia: Fortress Press, 1967.

Graebner, William. *The Age of Doubt: American Thought and Culture in the 1940s.* Boston: Twayne, 1991.

Graham, Hugh D. *The Civil Rights Era: Origins and Development of National Policy, 1960–1972.* New York: Oxford University Press, 1990.

——, ed. *The History of Violence in America: Historical and Comparative Perspectives.* New York: Praeger, 1970.

Gramsci, Antonio. *Selections from the Prison Notebooks.* Ed. and trans. Quintin Hoare and Geoffrey Nowell Smith. New York: International Publishers, 1971.

Gray, Francine du Plessix. "The Ultra-Resistance." In *Trials of the Resistance,* ed. *New York Review of Books.* New York: New York Review Press, 1970.

Green, Archie. "Austin's Cosmic Cowboys: Words in Collision." In *"And Other Neighborly Names": Social Process and Cultural Image in Texas Folklore,* ed. Richard Bauman and Roger D. Abrahams. Austin: University of Texas Press, 1981.

Green, George N. *The Establishment in Texas Politics: The Primitive Years, 1938–1957.* Westport, CT: Greenwood Press, 1979.

Green, Gil. *The New Radicalism: Anarchist or Marxist?* New York: International Publishers, 1971.

Green, James R. *Grass-Roots Socialism: Radical Movements in the Southwest, 1895–1943.* Baton Rouge: Louisiana State University Press, 1978.

Gurr, Ted R. *Why Men Rebel.* Princeton, NJ: Princeton University Press, 1970.

Gustainis, J. Justin. *American Rhetoric and the Vietnam War.* Westport, CT: Praeger, 1993.

Gutierrez, Gustavo. "The Limitations of Modern Theology: On a Letter of Dietrich Bonhoeffer." In *The Power of the Poor in History.* Trans. Robert R. Barr. Maryknoll, NY: Orbis Books, 1983.

Halberstam, David. *The Making of a Quagmire.* New York: Random House, 1965.

Hall, Stuart, and Tony Jefferson, eds., *Resistance Through Rituals: Youth Subcultures in Post-War Britain.* London: Hutchinson, 1976.

Halstead, Fred. *Out Now!: A Participant's Account of the American Movement against the Vietnam War.* New York: Monad, 1978.

Hamilton, Richard. *Restraining Myths: Critical Studies of U.S. Social Structure and Politics.* New York: Wiley, 1975.

Handy, Robert T., ed. *The Social Gospel in America, 1870–1920.* New York: Oxford University Press, 1966.

Hayden, Casey. "A Nurturing Movement: Nonviolence, SNCC, and Feminism." *Southern Exposure* 16 (Summer 1988):48–53.

Hayden, Casey, and Mary King. "Sex and Caste: A Kind of Memo from Casey Hayden and Mary King to a Number of Other Women in the Peace and Freedom Movements." In *Personal Politics: The Roots of Women's Liberation in the Civil Rights Movement and the New Left* by Sara Evans. New York: Knopf, 1979; New York: Vintage Books, 1980.

Hayden, Tom. *Reunion: A Memoir*. New York: Random House, 1988.

Hays, Samuel P. *Beauty, Health, Permanence: Environmental Politics in the United States, 1955–1985*. Cambridge: Cambridge University Press, 1987.

Hebdige, Dick. *Subculture: The Meaning of Style*. London: Methuen, 1979.

Heineman, Kenneth. *Campus Wars: The Peace Movement on American Campuses in the Vietnam Era*. New York: New York University Press, 1992.

Herberg, Will, ed. *Four Existentialist Theologians: A Reader from the Works of Jacques Maritain, Nicolas Berdyaev, Martin Buber, and Paul Tillich*. Garden City, NY: Doubleday/Anchor, 1958.

Herman, Ellen. *The Romance of American Psychology: Political Culture in the Age of Experts*. Berkeley and Los Angeles: University of California Press, 1995.

Higham, John. "The Reorientation of American Culture in the 1890's." In *The Origins of Modern Consciousness*, ed. John Weiss. Detroit: Wayne State University Press, 1965.

Hine, Darlene C. *Black Victory: The Rise and Fall of the White Primary*. Millwood, NY: KTO Press, 1979

Hinton, William. *Fanshen: A Documentary of Revolution in a Chinese Village*. New York: Vintage Books, 1966.

Hodgson, Godfrey. *America in Our Time: From World War II to Nixon—What Happened and Why*. Garden City, NY: Doubleday, 1976.

Hofstadter, Richard. *The Progressive Historians: Turner, Beard, Parrington*. New York: Knopf, 1968.

Hofstadter, Richard, and Michael Wallace. *American Violence: A Documentary History*. New York: Knopf, 1970.

Hollinger, David. *Postethnic America: Beyond Multiculturalism*. New York: Basic Books, 1995.

Hoover, J. Edgar. *Masters of Deceit: The Story of Communism in America and How to Fight It*. New York: Holt, 1958.

Hopkins, Charles H. *The Rise of the Social Gospel in American Protestantism*. New Haven, CT: Yale University Press, 1940.

Hopkins, George W. " 'May Day' 1971: Civil Disobedience and the Antiwar Movement." In *Give Peace a Chance: Exploring the Vietnam Antiwar Movement*, ed. Melvin Small and William D. Hoover. Syracuse, NY: Syracuse University Press, 1992.

Horowitz, Daniel. *The Morality of Spending: Attitudes toward the Consumer Society, 1875–1940*. Baltimore: Johns Hopkins University Press, 1985.

——. "Rethinking Betty Friedan and *The Feminine Mystique*: Labor Union Radicalism and Feminism in Cold War America." *American Quarterly* 48 (March 1996):1–42.

——. *Vance Packard and American Social Criticism.* Chapel Hill: University of North Carolina Press, 1994.

Horowitz, Irving L. *C. Wright Mills: An American Utopian.* New York: Free Press, 1983.

——, ed. *Power, Politics and People: The Collected Essays of C. Wright Mills.* New York: Ballantine, 1963.

Howard, Dick. "Gorz, Mallet, and French Theorists of the New Working Class." *Radical America* 3 (April–May 1969):1–19.

——, ed. *Selected Political Writings of Rosa Luxemburg.* New York: Monthly Press, 1971.

Howe, Irving. "New Styles in 'Leftism.'" In *Beyond the New Left,* ed. Irving Howe. New York: McCall, 1970.

Hudnut-Beumler, James D. *Looking for God in the Suburbs: The Religion of the American Dream and Its Critics, 1945–1965.* New Brunswick, NJ: Rutgers University Press, 1994.

Hughes, Robert. *Culture of Complaint: The Fraying of America.* New York: Oxford University Press, 1993.

Hutchison, William. *The Modernist Impulse in American Protestantism.* Cambridge, MA: Harvard University Press, 1976.

Huxley, Aldous. *Island: A Novel.* London: Chatto & Windus, 1962.

Isaac, Jeffrey C. *Arendt, Camus, and Modern Rebellion.* New Haven, CT: Yale University Press, 1992.

Israel, Joachim. *Alienation: From Marx to Modern Sociology.* Boston: Allyn & Bacon, 1971.

Isserman, Maurice. *If I Had a Hammer . . . : The Death of the Old Left and the Birth of the New Left.* New York: Basic Books, 1987.

——. "The Not-So-Dark and Bloody Ground: New Works on the 1960s." *American Historical Review* 94 (October 1989):990–1010.

——. "You Don't Need a Weatherman but a Postman Can Be Helpful: Thoughts on the History of SDS and the Antiwar Movement." In *Give Peace a Chance: Exploring the Vietnam Antiwar Movement,* ed. Melvin Small and William D. Hoover. Syracuse, NY: Syracuse University Press, 1992.

Isserman, Maurice, and Michael Kazin. "The Failure and Success of the New Radicalism." In *The Rise and Fall of the New Deal Order, 1930–1980,* ed. Steve Fraser and Gary Gerstle. Princeton, NJ: Princeton University Press, 1989.

Jacobs, Harold, ed. *Weatherman.* Berkeley, CA: Ramparts, 1970.

Jacobs, Paul, and Saul Landau, eds. *The New Radicals: A Report with Documents.* New York: Vintage Books, 1966.

Jaffe, Naomi, and Bernardine Dohrn. "The Look Is You." In *The New Left: A Documentary History,* ed. Massimo Teodori. Indianapolis: Bobbs-Merrill, 1969.

Janes, Daryl, ed. *No Apologies: Texas Radicals Celebrate the '60s.* Austin, TX: Eakin Press, 1992.

Jay, Martin. *The Dialectical Imagination: A History of the Frankfurt School and the Institute of Social Research, 1923–1950.* Boston: Little, Brown, 1973.

Jezer, Marty. *Abbie Hoffman: American Rebel*. New Brunswick, NJ: Rutgers University Press, 1992.

Jones, Glenn W. "Gentle Thursday: An SDS Circus in Austin, 1966–1969." In *Sights on the Sixties*, ed. Barbara L. Tischler. New Brunswick, NJ: Rutgers University Press, 1992.

Jordan, Terry G. "A Century and a Half of Ethnic Change in Texas, 1836–1986." *Southwestern Historical Quarterly* 89 (1986):385–422.

Joreen (Jo Freeman). "The Tyranny of Structurelessness." In *Radical Feminism*, ed. Anne Koedt, Ellen Levine, and Anita Rapone. Chicago: Quadrangle, 1973.

Kanter, Rosabeth M. *Commitment and Community: Communes and Utopias in Sociological Perspective*. Cambridge, MA: Harvard University Press, 1972.

Katsiaficas, George. *The Imagination of the New Left: A Global Analysis of 1968*. Boston: South End Press, 1987.

Kauffman, L. A. "Tofu Politics." *Utne Reader*, March–April 1992, 72–75.

Kaufmann, Walter, ed. *Existentialism from Dostoyevsky to Sartre*. Cleveland: Meridian Books, 1966.

Kearns, Doris. *Lyndon Johnson and the American Dream*. New York: Harper & Row, 1976.

Kelley, Robin D. G. *Hammer and Hoe: Alabama Communists during the Great Depression*. Chapel Hill: University of North Carolina Press, 1990.

———. "Notes on Deconstructing 'The Folk.'" *American Historical Review* 97 (December 1992):1400–1408.

Kelly, Geffrey B. *Liberating Faith: Bonhoeffer's Message for Today*. Minneapolis: Augsburg Press, 1984.

Keniston, Kenneth. *Young Radicals: Notes on Committed Youth*. New York: Harcourt, Brace & World, 1968.

Kerner, Otto, et al. *Report of the National Advisory Commission on Civil Disorders*. New York: Bantam, 1968.

Kerr, Clark. *The Uses of the University*. Rev. ed. Cambridge, MA: Harvard University Press, 1995.

Kershaw, A. L. *the new frontier for the student YMCA and YWCA*. New York: National Student Council of the YMCA and YWCA, 1955.

Kessler, Lauren. *After All These Years: Sixties Ideals in a Different World*. New York: Thunder's Mouth Press, 1990.

Kimball, Roger. *Tenured Radicals: How Politics Has Corrupted Our Higher Education*. New York: Harper & Row, 1990.

King, Martin L., Jr. *Strength to Love*. New York: Harper & Row, 1963.

King, Mary. *Freedom Song: A Personal Story of the 1960s Civil Rights Movement*. New York: Morrow, 1987.

King, Richard. *The Party of Eros: Radical Social Thought and the Realm of Freedom*. Chapel Hill: University of North Carolina Press, 1972.

Kirby, John B. "The Roosevelt Administration and Blacks: An Ambivalent Legacy." In *Twentieth-Century America: Recent Interpretations*. 2d ed., ed. Barton J. Bernstein and Allen J. Matusow. New York: Harcourt Brace Jovanovich, 1972.

Klatch, Rebecca E. "The Counterculture, the New Left, and the New Right." In *Cultural Politics and Social Movements*, ed. Marcy Darnovsky, Barbara Epstein, and Richard Flacks. Philadelphia: Temple University Press, 1995.

Kloppenberg, James T. *Uncertain Victory: Social Democracy and Progressivism in American European Thought, 1870–1920*. New York: Oxford University Press, 1986.

Komarovsky, Mirra, with Jane Philips. *Blue Collar Marriage*. New York: Random House, 1962.

Kopkind, Andrew. "They'd Rather Be Left." *New York Review of Books*, 28 September 1967, 3–5.

Langer, Elinor. "Notes for Next Time: A Memoir of the 1960s." In *Toward a History of the New Left: Essays from within the Movement*, ed. David R. Myers. Brooklyn, NY: Carlson, 1989. First published in *Working Papers for a New Society* 1 (Fall 1973).

Larkin, Ralph, and Daniel Foss. "Lexicon of Folk-Etymology." In *The 60s without Apology*, ed. Sohnya Sayres, Anders Stephanson, Stanley Aronowitz, and Frederic Jameson. Minneapolis: University of Minnesota Press, 1984.

Lasch, Christopher. *The Agony of the American Left*. New York: Vintage Books, 1969.

——. *The Culture of Narcissism: American Life in an Age of Declining Expectations*. New York: Norton, 1978.

——. *The New Radicalism in America, 1889–1963: The Intellectual as a Social Type*. Rev. ed. New York: Norton, 1986.

——. "Religious Contributions to Social Movements: Walter Rauschenbusch, the Social Gospel, and Its Critics." *Journal of Religious Ethics* 18 (Spring 1990):7–25.

——. *The True and Only Heaven: Progress and Its Critics*. New York: Norton, 1991.

Lawrence, D. H. *Studies in Classic American Literature*. New York: Viking, 1961.

Lears, T. J. Jackson. "The Concept of Cultural Hegemony: Problems and Possibilities." *American Historical Review* 90 (June 1985):567–593.

——. *Fables of Abundance: A Cultural History of American Advertising*. New York: Basic Books, 1994.

——. "From Salvation to Self-Realization: Advertising and the Therapeutic Roots of the Consumer Culture, 1880–1930." In *The Culture of Consumption: Critical Essays in American History, 1880–1980*, ed. T. J. Jackson Lears and Richard W. Fox. New York: Pantheon, 1983.

——. "A Matter of Taste: Corporate Cultural Hegemony in a Mass-Consumption Society." In *Recasting America: Culture and Politics in the Age of Cold War*, ed. Lary May. Chicago: University of Chicago Press, 1989.

——. *No Place of Grace: Antimodernism and the Transformation of American Culture, 1880–1920*. New York: Pantheon, 1981.

Lears, T. J. Jackson, and Richard W. Fox, eds. *The Culture of Consumption: Critical Essays in American History, 1880–1980*. New York: Pantheon, 1983.

Lebergott, Stanley. *Pursuing Happiness: American Consumers in the Twentieth Century*. Princeton, NJ: Princeton University Press, 1993.

Leinberger, Paul, and Bruce Tucker. *The New Individualists: The Generation after The Organization Man*. New York: HarperCollins, 1991.

Lerner, Michael. *The Politics of Meaning: Restoring Hope and Possibility in an Age of Cynicism*. Reading, MA: Addison-Wesley, 1996.

Levitt, Cyril. *Children of Privilege: Student Revolt in the Sixties; A Study of Student Movements in Canada, the United States, and West Germany*. Toronto: University of Toronto Press, 1984.

Levy, David W. *The Debate over Vietnam*. Baltimore: Johns Hopkins University Press, 1991.

Levy, Jacques E. *Cesar Chavez: Autobiography of La Causa*. New York: Norton, 1975.

Levy, Peter B. "Civil War on Race Street: The Black Freedom Struggle and White Resistance in Cambridge, Maryland,1960–1964." *Maryland Historical Magazine* 89 (Fall 1994):291–318.

———. *The New Left and Labor in the 1960s*. Urbana: University of Illinois Press, 1993.

Lieberman, Robbie. *"My Song Is My Weapon": People's Songs, American Communism, and the Politics of Culture, 1930–1950*. Urbana: University of Illinois Press, 1989.

Limon, Jose E. *Dancing with the Devil: Society and Cultural Poetics in Mexican-American South Texas*. Madison: University of Wisconsin Press, 1994.

Lipset, Seymour M., ed. *Student Politics*. New York: Basic Books, 1967.

Lipset, Seymour M., and Sheldon Wolin, eds. *The Berkeley Student Revolt: Facts and Interpretation*. Garden City, NY: Doubleday/Anchor, 1965.

Long, Priscilla, ed. *The New Left: A Collection of Essays*. Boston: Porter Sargent, 1969.

Lowen, Rebecca S. *Creating the Cold War University: The Transformation of Stanford*. Berkeley and Los Angeles: University of California Press, 1997.

Luker, Ralph. *The Social Gospel in Black and White: American Racial Reform, 1889–1912*. Chapel Hill: University of North Carolina Press, 1991.

Lustig, R. Jeffrey. *Corporate Liberalism: The Origins of Modern American Political Theory, 1880–1920*. Berkeley and Los Angeles: University of California Press, 1982.

Lynd, Staughton. *Intellectual Origins of American Radicalism*. New York: Pantheon, 1968.

———. "The Movement: A New Beginning." *Liberation* 14 (May 1969):6–20.

———. "Prospects for the New Left." *Liberation* 15 (January 1971):13–28.

Lynn, Susan. *Progressive Women in Conservative Times: Racial Justice, Peace, and Feminism, 1945 to the 1960s*. New Brunswick, NJ: Rutgers University Press, 1992.

Macdonald, Dwight. "The Root Is Man." *politics* 3 (April, July 1946).

Mackey, John. "Beyond Unions." *Utne Reader*, March–April 1992, 75–77.

Mailer, Norman. "Superman Comes to the Supermarket." In *Smiling Through the Apocalypse: Esquire's History of the Sixties*, ed. Harold Hayes. New York: Crown Books, 1987.

———. *The White Negro*. San Francisco: City Lights Books, 1957.

———. *Why Are We in Vietnam?* New York: Putnam, 1967.

Mallet, Serge. *Essays on the New Working Class.* Ed. and trans. Dick Howard and Dean Savage. St. Louis: Telos Press, 1975.

Marchand, Roland. *Advertising the American Dream: Making Way for Modernity, 1920–1940.* Berkeley and Los Angeles: University of California Press, 1985.

———. *The American Peace Movement and Social Reform, 1898–1918.* Princeton, NJ: Princeton University Pres, 1972.

Marcuse, Herbert. *An Essay on Liberation.* Boston: Beacon Press, 1969.

———. *One-Dimensional Man: Studies in the Ideology of Advanced Industrial Society.* Boston: Beacon Press, 1964.

Marx, Karl. "From Economico-Philosophical Manuscripts of 1844." In *The Portable Karl Marx,* ed. Eugene Kamenka. New York: Penguin, 1983.

Maslow, Abraham. *Toward a Psychology of Being.* New York: Van Nostrand, 1968.

May, Elaine. *Homeward Bound: American Families in the Cold War Era.* New York: Basic Books, 1988.

May, Henry F. *Protestant Churches in Industrial America.* New York: Octagon Press, 1949.

May, Lary, ed. *Recasting America: Culture and Politics in the Age of Cold War.* Chicago: University of Chicago Press, 1989.

May, Rollo. *Man's Search for Himself.* New York: Norton, 1953.

———. *The Meaning of Anxiety.* New York: Ronald Press, 1950.

———, ed. *Existential Psychology.* New York: McGraw-Hill, 1969.

McAdam, Doug. *Freedom Summer.* New York: Oxford University Press, 1988.

McAuliffe, Mary S. *Crisis on the Left: Cold War Politics and American Liberals, 1947–1954.* Amherst: University of Massachusetts Press, 1978.

McClay, Wilfred M. *The Masterless: Self and Society in Modern America.* Chapel Hill: University of North Carolina Press, 1994.

McCorvey, Norma, with Andy Meisler. *I Am Roe: My Life,* Roe *v.* Wade, *and Freedom of Choice.* New York: HarperCollins, 1994.

McLoughlin, William G. *Revivals, Awakenings, and Reform: An Essay on Religion and Social Change in America, 1607–1977.* Chicago: University of Chicago Press, 1978.

Mehta, Ved. *The New Theologian.* New York: Harper & Row, 1966.

Meinig, D. W. *Imperial Texas: An Interpretive Essay in Cultural Geography.* Austin: University of Texas Press, 1969.

Melton, J. Gordon, and Robert L. Moore. *The Cult Experience: Responding to the New Religious Pluralism.* New York: Pilgrim Press, 1982.

Meyer, Donald. *The Protestant Search for Political Realism, 1919–1941.* Berkeley and Los Angeles: University of California Press, 1960.

Meyerowitz, Joanne. "Beyond the Feminine Mystique: A Reassessment of Postwar Mass Culture, 1946–1958." *Journal of American History* 79 (March 1993):1455–1482.

Mgileruma, Alhaji M. "Africa in World Affairs: The Policy of Neutralism." *Vital Speeches of the Day,* 15 September 1961.

Miller, James. *"Democracy Is in the Streets": From Port Huron to the Siege of Chicago.* New York: Simon & Schuster, 1987.

Miller, Keith. *Voice of Deliverance: The Language of Martin Luther King, Jr. and Its Sources.* New York: Free Press, 1991.

Miller, Timothy. *The Hippies and American Values.* Knoxville: University of Tennessee Press, 1991.

Miller, William L. "The Rise of Neo-Orthodoxy." In *Paths of American Thought,* ed. Arthur M. Schlesinger Jr. and Morton G. White. Boston: Houghton Mifflin, 1963.

Mills, C. Wright. *The Causes of World War III.* New York: Simon & Schuster, 1958.

——. *Listen, Yankee!: The Revolution in Cuba.* New York: Ballantine, 1960.

——. *The Power Elite.* New York: Oxford University Press, 1956.

——. *White Collar: The American Middle Classes.* New York: Oxford University Press, 1951.

Mitford, Jessica. *The American Way of Death.* New York: Simon & Schuster, 1963.

Montejano, David. *Anglos and Mexicans in the Making of Texas, 1836–1936.* Austin: University of Texas Press, 1987.

Morgan, Robin. "Goodbye to All That." In *Voices from Women's Liberation,* ed. Leslie Tanner. New York: Signet Books, 1970.

——, ed. *Sisterhood Is Powerful: Writings from the Women's Liberation Movement.* New York: Random House, 1970.

Morris, Aldon D. *The Origins of the Civil Rights Movement: Black Communities Organizing for Change.* New York: Free Press, 1984.

Morris, Celia. "Learning the Hard Way." *Change* 6 (July–August 1974):42–47.

Morris, Willie. *North toward Home.* Boston: Houghton Mifflin, 1967.

Munoz, Carlos. *Youth, Identity, Power: The Chicano Movement.* London: Verso, 1989.

Murray, Martin J. "Building Fires on the Prairie." In *Radical Sociologists and the Movement: Experiences, Lessons, and Legacies,* ed. Martin Oppenheimer, Martin J. Murray, and Rhonda F. Levine. Philadelphia: Temple University Press, 1991.

Myers, R. David, ed. *Toward a History of the New Left: Essays from within the Movement.* Brooklyn, NY: Carlson, 1989.

Neill, A. S. *Summerhill: A Radical Approach to Child Rearing.* New York: Hart, 1960.

Neumann, Franz. *Behemoth: The Structure and Practice of National Socialism.* New York: Oxford University Press, 1942.

Niebuhr, Reinhold. *The Children of Light and the Children of Darkness: A Vindication of Democracy and a Critique of Its Traditional Defense.* New York: Scribner, 1945.

——. *Moral Man and Immoral Society: A Study in Ethics and Politics.* New York: Scribner, 1932.

Norrell, Robert J. *Reaping the Whirlwind: The Civil Rights Movement in Tuskegee.* New York: Knopf, 1985.

Nygren, Anders. *Eros and Agape.* Trans. Philip S. Watson. Philadelphia: Westminster Press, 1953.

O'Brien, James. "Beyond Reminiscence: The New Left in History." *Radical America* 6 (July–August 1972).

Oglesby, Carl. "Notes on a Decade Ready for the Dustbin." In *Toward a History of the New Left: Essays from within the Movement*, ed. R. David Myers. Brooklyn, NY: Carlson, 1989. First published in *Liberation* 14 (August–September 1969).

——. "The Revolted." In *The American Left: Radical Political Thought in the Twentieth Century*, ed. Loren Baritz. New York: Basic Books, 1971.

——. "Trapped in a System." In *The New Left: A Documentary History*, ed. Massimo Teodori. Indianapolis: Bobbs-Merrill, 1969.

Oglesby, Carl, and Richard Shaull. *Containment and Change: Two Dissenting Views of American Foreign Policy*. London: Macmillan, 1967.

Olan, Susan T. "Blood Debts." In *No Apologies: Texas Radicals Celebrate the '60s*, ed. Daryl Janes. Austin, TX: Eakin Press, 1992.

Ollman, Bertell. *Alienation: Marx's Conception of Man in Capitalist Society*. Cambridge: Cambridge University Press, 1971.

Orum, Anthony M. *Power, Money & the People: The Making of Modern Austin*. Austin: Texas Monthly Press, 1987.

Packard, Vance O. *The Hidden Persuaders*. New York: McKay, 1957.

——. *The Status Seekers*. New York: McKay, 1959.

——. *The Waste Makers*. New York: McKay, 1959.

Pappenheim, Fritz. *The Alienation of Modern Man*. New York: Monthly Review Press, 1959.

Patterson, James T. *Grand Expectations: The United States, 1945–1974*. New York: Oxford University Press, 1996.

Payne, Charles M. *I've Got the Light of Freedom: The Organizing Tradition and the Mississippi Freedom Struggle*. Berkeley and Los Angeles: University of California Press, 1995.

Peck, Abe. *Uncovering the Sixties: The Life and Times of the Underground Press*. New York: Pantheon, 1985.

Perry, Charles. *The Haight-Ashbury: A History*. New York: Random House, 1984.

Piercy, Marge. "The Grand Coolie Damn." In *Sisterhood Is Powerful: Writings from the Women's Liberation Movement*, ed. Robin Morgan. New York: Random House, 1970.

Platt, Anthony M., ed. *The Politics of Riot Commissions, 1917–1970*. New York: Macmillan, 1971.

Poster, Mark. *Existential Marxism in Postwar France: From Sartre to Althusser*. Princeton, NJ: Princeton University Press, 1975.

Potter, Paul. "The Intellectual and Social Change." In *The New Student Left: An Anthology*, ed. Mitchell Cohen and Dennis Hale. Boston: Beacon Press, 1966.

——. *A Name for Ourselves: Feelings about Authentic Identity, Love, Intuitive Politics, Us*. Boston: Little, Brown, 1971.

Rainey, Homer P. *The Tower and the Dome: A Free University versus Political Control*. Boulder, CO: Pruett Publishing, 1971.

Randall, Margaret. *Gathering Rage: The Failure of Twentieth Century Revolutions to Develop a Feminist Agenda*. New York: Monthly Review Press, 1992.

———. *Part of the Solution: Portrait of a Revolutionary*. New York: New Directions, 1973.

———. *Sandino's Daughters: Conversations with Nicaraguan Women in Struggle*. Vancouver: New Star Books, 1981.

Rasmussen, Larry, with Renate Bethge. *Dietrich Bonhoeffer: His Significance for North Americans*. Minneapolis: Fortress Press, 1990.

Reavis, Dick J. "SDS: From Students to Seniors." In *No Apologies: Texas Radicals Celebrate the '60s*, ed. Daryl Janes. Austin, TX: Eakin Press, 1992.

Reece, Ray. "Almost No Apologies." In *No Apologies: Texas Radicals Celebrate the '60s*, ed. Daryl Janes. Austin, TX: Eakin Press, 1992.

Ridgway, James. *The Closed Corporation: American Universities in Crisis*. New York: Random House, 1968.

Rieff, Philip. *The Triumph of the Therapeutic: Uses of Faith after Freud*. New York: Harper & Row, 1966.

Riesman, David. *Abundance for What?* Glencoe, IL: Free Press, 1964.

Riesman, David, with Nathan Glazer and Reuel Denney. *The Lonely Crowd: A Study of the Changing American Character*. Rev. ed. New Haven, CT: Yale University Press, 1989.

Riesman, David, and Verne A. Stadtman, eds. *Academic Transformation: Seventeen Institutions under Pressure*. Berkeley, CA: Carnegie Foundation for the Advancement of Teaching, 1973.

Robinson, John A. T. *Honest to God*. Philadelphia: Westminster Press, 1963.

Robinson, Paul. *The Freudian Left: Wilhelm Reich, Geza Roheim, Herbert Marcuse*. New York: Harper & Row, 1969.

Rogers, Carl. *On Becoming a Person: A Therapist's View of Psychotherapy*. Boston: Houghton Mifflin, 1961.

Rogin, Michael P. *The Intellectuals and McCarthy: The Radical Specter*. Cambridge, MA: MIT Press, 1967.

Rorabaugh, William J. *Berkeley at War: The 1960s*. New York: Oxford University Press, 1989.

Rossinow, Doug. "The New Left in the Counterculture: Hypotheses and Evidence." *Radical History Review* 67 (Winter 1997):79–120.

Rozsak, Theodore. "The Human Whole and Justly Proportioned." In *Sources: An Anthology of Contemporary Materials Useful for Preserving Sanity While Braving the Great Technological Wilderness*, ed. Theodore Rozsak. New York: Harper Colophon, 1972.

———. *The Making of a Counter-Culture: Reflections on the Technocratic Society and Its Youthful Opposition*. New York: Doubleday, 1969.

Russell, Philip. *Cuba in Transition*. Austin, TX: Armadillo Press, 1971.

Sale, Kirkpatrick. *Human Scale*. New York: Coward, McCann & Geoghegan, 1980.

———. *SDS*. New York: Random House, 1973.

Sartre, Jean-Paul. "Existentialism Is a Humanism." Trans. Philip Mairet. In *The Existentialist Tradition: Selected Writings*, ed. Nino Langiulli. Garden City, NY: Doubleday/Anchor, 1971.

——. *Nausea*. Trans. Lloyd Alexander. New York: New Directions, 1964.

Savio, Mario. "An End to History." In *The American Left: Radical Political Thought in the Twentieth Century*, ed. Loren Baritz. New York: Basic Books, 1971. First published in *Humanity*, December 1964.

Sayres, Sohnya, Anders Stephanson, Stanley Aronowitz, and Fredric Jameson, eds. *The 60s without Apology*. Minneapolis: University of Minnesota Press, 1984.

Schacht, Richard. *Alienation*. Garden City, NY: Doubleday, 1970.

Schlesinger, Arthur M. Jr. *The Crisis of Confidence: Ideas, Power, and Violence in America*. Boston: Houghton Mifflin, 1969.

——. *The Disuniting of America: Reflections on a Multicultural Society*. New York: Norton, 1992.

——. *A Thousand Days: John F. Kennedy in the White House*. Boston: Houghton Mifflin, 1965.

——. *The Vital Center: The Politics of Freedom*. Rev. ed. Boston: Houghton Mifflin, 1962.

Schrecker, Ellen. *The Age of McCarthyism: A Brief History with Documents*. New York: St. Martin's Press, 1994.

Schuman, Howard. " 'Silent Majorities' and the Vietnam War." *Scientific American*, June 1970, 17–25.

——. "Two Sources of Antiwar Opinion in America." *American Journal of Sociology* 78 (November 1972):513–536.

Shank, Barry. *Dissonant Identities: The Rock 'n' Roll Scene in Austin, Texas*. Hanover, NH: Wesleyan University Press/University Press of New England, 1994.

Shannon, Christopher. *Conspicuous Criticism: Tradition, the Individual, and Culture in American Social Thought, from Veblen to Mills*. Baltimore: Johns Hopkins University Press, 1996.

Sherry, Michael. *In the Shadow of War: American Society since the 1930s*. New Haven, CT: Yale University Press, 1995.

Simons, Jim. "Barrister at the Barricades." In *No Apologies: Texas Radicals Celebrate the '60s*, ed. Daryl Janes. Austin, TX: Eakin Press, 1992.

Simpson, Dick. *The Politics of Compassion and Transformation*. Athens: Swallow Press/Ohio University Press, 1989.

Singal, Daniel J., ed. *Modernist Culture in America*. Belmont, CA: Wadsworth, 1991.

Sitkoff, Harvard. *A New Deal for Blacks: The Emergence of Civil Rights as a National Issue*. Vol. 1, *The Depression Decade*. New York: Oxford University Press, 1978.

Skinner, B. F. *Walden Two*. New York: Macmillan, 1948.

Skolnik, Jerome. *The Politics of Protest*. New York: Ballantine, 1969.

Slotkin, Richard. *Regeneration Through Violence: The Mythology of the American Frontier, 1600–1860*. Middletown, CT: Wesleyan University Press, 1973.

Small, Melvin. *Covering Dissent: The Media and the Anti-Vietnam War Movement.* New Brunswick, NJ: Rutgers University Press, 1994.

——. "Influencing the Decisionmakers: The Vietnam Experience." *Journal of Peace Research* 24 (1987):185–198.

Small, Melvin, and William D. Hoover, eds. *Give Peace a Chance: Exploring the Vietnam Antiwar Movement.* Syracuse, NY: Syracuse University Press, 1992.

Snyder, Gary. *Earth House Hold: Technical Notes & Queries to Fellow Dharma Revolutionaries.* New York: New Directions, 1969.

Solomon, Robert C., ed. *Existentialism.* New York: Modern Library, 1974.

Sombart, Werner. *Why Is There No Socialism in the United States?* Trans. Patricia M. Hockings and C. T. Husbands. London: Macmillan, 1976.

Spring, Joel H. *The Sorting Machine Revisited: National Educational Policy since 1945.* New York: Longman, 1989.

Stevens, Jay. *Storming Heaven: LSD and the American Dream.* New York: Harper & Row, 1987.

Sumner, Gregory. *Dwight Macdonald and the* politics *Circle: The Challenge of Cosmopolitan Democracy.* Ithaca, NY: Cornell University Press, 1996.

Susman, Warren. *Culture as History: The Transformation of American Society in the Twentieth Century.* New York: Pantheon, 1984.

Susman, Warren, with Edward Griffin. "Did Success Spoil the United States?: Dual Perceptions in Postwar America." In *Recasting America: Culture and Politics in the Age of Cold War*, ed. Lary May. Chicago: University of Chicago Press, 1989.

Swerdlow, Amy. *Women Strike for Peace: Traditional Motherhood and Radical Politics in the 1960s.* Chicago: University of Chicago Press, 1993.

Swomley, John M. Jr. *Liberation Ethics.* New York: Macmillan, 1972.

Tanner, Leslie, ed. *Voices from Women's Liberation.* New York: Signet Books, 1970.

Taylor, Ronald B. *Chavez and the Farm Workers.* Boston: Beacon Press, 1975.

Teodori, Massimo, ed. *The New Left: A Documentary History.* Indianapolis: Bobbs-Merrill, 1969.

Tillich, Paul. "Being and Love." In *Four Existentialist Theologians: A Reader from the Works of Jacques Maritain, Nicolas Berdyaev, Martin Buber, and Paul Tillich*, ed. Will Herberg. Garden City, NY: Doubleday/Anchor, 1958.

——. *The Courage to Be.* New Haven, CT: Yale University Press, 1952.

——. *Morality and Beyond.* New York: Harper & Row, 1963.

——. *The New Being.* New York: Scribner, 1955.

——. *The Protestant Era.* Trans. and ed. James Luther Adams. Chicago: University of Chicago Press, 1948.

——. *The Shaking of the Foundations.* New York: Scribner, 1948.

——. *Systematic Theology.* 3 vols. Chicago: University of Chicago Press, 1951–1963.

Tilman, Rick C. *C. Wright Mills: A Native Radical and His American Intellectual Roots.* University Park: Pennsylvania State University Press, 1984.

Tipton, Steven M. *Getting Saved from the Sixties: Moral Meaning in Conversion and Cultural Change.* Berkeley and Los Angeles: University of California Press, 1982.

Touraine, Alain. *The Post-Industrial Society; Tomorrow's Social History: Classes, Conflicts and Culture in the Programmed Society.* Trans. Leonard F. X. Mayhew. New York: Random House, 1971.

Trend, David, ed. *Radical Democracy: Identity, Citizenship, and the State.* New York: Routledge, 1996.

Trilling, Lionel. *Sincerity and Authenticity.* Cambridge, MA: Harvard University Press, 1972.

Troeltsch, Ernst. *Christian Thought: Its History and Application.* Ed. Baron F. von Hugel. New York: Meridian Books, 1957.

Ture, Kwame (Stokely Carmichael), and Charles V. Hamilton. *Black Power: The Politics of Liberation in America.* Rev. ed. New York: Vintage Books, 1992.

Turley, William S. *The Second Indochina War: A Short Political and Military History, 1954–1975.* Boulder, CO: Westview Press, 1986.

Turner, James. *Without God, without Creed: The Origins of Unbelief in America.* Baltimore: Johns Hopkins University Press, 1985.

Tyrrell, Ian. *The Absent Marx: Class Analysis and Liberal History in Twentieth-Century America.* Westport, CT: Greenwood Press, 1986.

Unger, Irwin. *The Movement: A History of the American New Left.* New York: Harper & Row, 1974.

Unger, Irwin, and Debi Unger. *Turning Point: 1968.* New York: Scribner, 1988.

Van Deburg, William L. *New Day in Babylon: The Black Power Movement and American Culture, 1965–1975.* Chicago: University of Chicago Press, 1992.

Veysey, Laurence. *The Communal Experience: Anarchist and Mystical Communities in Twentieth-Century America.* Chicago: University of Chicago Press, 1978.

Vickers, George R. *The Formation of the New Left: The Early Years.* Lexington, MA: Lexington Books, 1975.

Von Hoffman, Nicholas. *We Are the People Our Parents Warned Us Against.* Chicago: Ivan R. Dee, 1989.

Walker, Pat, ed. *Between Labor and Capital.* Boston: South End Press, 1979.

Waterhouse, Larry, and Mariann G. Wizard. *Turning the Guns Around: Notes on the GI Movement.* New York: Praeger, 1971.

Watt, David H. *A Transforming Faith: Explorations in Twentieth-Century American Evangelicalism.* New Brunswick, NJ: Rutgers University Press, 1991.

Weddington, Sarah R. *A Question of Choice.* New York: Putnam, 1991.

Weinstein, James. *Ambiguous Legacy: The Left in American Politics.* New York: New Viewpoints, 1975.

——. "Reply to REP." In *Weatherman,* ed. Harold Jacobs. Berkeley, CA: Ramparts, 1970.

Wells, Tom. *The War Within: America's Battle over Vietnam.* Berkeley and Los Angeles: University of California Press, 1994.

Werden, Frieda. "Adventures of a Texas Feminist." In *No Apologies: Texas Radicals Celebrate the '60s,* ed. Daryl Janes. Austin, TX: Eakin Press, 1992.

West, Cornel. *The American Evasion of Philosophy: A Genealogy of Pragmatism.* Madison: University of Wisconsin Press, 1989.

Westbrook, Robert B. "Politics as Consumption: Managing the Modern American Election." In *The Culture of Consumption: Critical Essays in American History, 1880–1980*, ed. T. J. Jackson Lears and Richard W. Fox. New York: Pantheon, 1983.

Whalen, Jack, and Richard Flacks. *Beyond the Barricades: The Sixties Generation Grows Up*. Philadelphia: Temple University Press, 1989.

White, Morton G. *Social Thought in America: The Revolt against Formalism*. New York: Oxford University Press, 1949.

Whitfield, Stephen J. *The Culture of the Cold War*. Baltimore: Johns Hopkins University Press, 1991.

Whyte, William H. Jr. *The Organization Man*. New York: Simon & Schuster, 1956.

Wiener, Jon. "The New Left as History." *Radical History Review* 42 (Fall 1988):173–185.

Wilkerson, Doxey A. "Marxists and Academic Freedom." In *The American Left: Radical Political Thought in the Twentieth Century*, ed. Loren Baritz. New York: Basic Books, 1971.

Wilkerson, Yolanda B. *Interracial Programs of the YWCA's: An Inquiry under Auspices of the National Young Women's Christian Association*. New York: Woman's Press, 1948.

Williams, Raymond. *Marxism and Literature*. Oxford: Oxford University Press, 1977.

Williams, William A. *Empire as a Way of Life: An Essay on the Causes and Character of America's Present Predicament, Along with a Few Thoughts about an Alternative*. New York: Oxford University Press, 1980.

———. *The Tragedy of American Diplomacy*. Rev. ed. New York: Delta, 1962.

Williamson, Joel. *A Rage for Order: Black/White Relations in the American South Since Emancipation*. New York: Oxford University Press, 1986.

Willis, Ellen. "Radical Feminism and Feminist Radicalism." In *No More Nice Girls: Countercultural Essays*. Middletown, CT: Wesleyan University Press, 1992. First published in *The 60s without Apology*, ed. Sohnya Sayres, Anders Stephanson, Stanley Aronowitz, and Frederic Jameson. Minneapolis: University of Minnesota Press, 1984.

Wills, Garry. *The Kennedy Imprisonment: A Meditation on Power*. Boston: Little, Brown, 1982.

Wilson, Colin. *The Outsider*. Boston: Houghton Mifflin, 1956.

Wittman, Carl, and Tom Hayden. "An Interracial Movement of the Poor?" In *The New Student Left: An Anthology*, ed. Mitchell Cohen and Dennis Hale. Boston: Beacon Press, 1966.

Wittner, Lawrence S. *Cold War America: From Hiroshima to Watergate*. New York: Praeger, 1974.

———. *Rebels against War: The American Peace Movement, 1933–1983*. Rev. ed. Philadelphia: Temple University Press, 1984.

——. *The Struggle against the Bomb*. Vol. 1, *One World or None*. Stanford, CA: Stanford University Press, 1994.

Wizard, Mariann G. See Garner-Wizard, Mariann.

Wolfe, Tom. *The Electric Kool-Aid Acid Test*. New York: Bantam, 1968.

Wright, Frank L. *Out of Sight, Out of Mind: A Graphic Picture of Present Day Institutional Care of the Mentally Ill in America*. Philadelphia: National Mental Health Association, 1947.

Wrong, Dennis. "Myths of Alienation." *Partisan Review* 52 (1985):223–35.

Wuthnow, Robert. *The Restructuring of American Religion: Society and Faith since World War II*. Princeton, NJ: Princeton University Press, 1988.

Wylie, Philip. *Nest of Vipers*. New York: Holt, Rinehart and Winston, 1942.

Young, Alfred, ed. *Dissent: Explorations in the History of American Radicalism*. DeKalb: Northern Illinois University Press, 1968.

Young, Marilyn B. *The Vietnam Wars, 1945–1990*. New York: HarperPerennial, 1991.

Zimmerman, Jonathan. "The Flight from Cool: American Men and Romantic Love in the 1950s." *The History of the Family* 2 (1997):31–47.

Unpublished Sources

Calvert, Gregory N. "Democracy and Rebirth: The New Left and Its Legacy." Ph.D. diss., University of California at Santa Cruz, 1989.

Chandler, Charles Ray. "The Mexican-American Protest Movement in Texas." Ph.D. diss., Tulane University, 1968.

"The College House of the Christian Faith and Life Community at Austin, Texas." Austin, TX, and Pelham, NY: Millard Research Associates, August 1964.

Cox, Alice C. "The Rainey Affair: A History of the Academic Freedom Controversy at the University of Texas, 1938–1946." Ph.D. diss., University of Denver, 1970.

Jones, Glenn W. "Gentle Thursday: Revolutionary Pastoralism in Austin, Texas, 1966–1969." M.A. thesis, University of Texas at Austin, 1988.

Limon, Jose E. "The Expressive Culture of a Chicano Student Group at the University of Texas at Austin, 1967–1975." Ph.D. diss., University of Texas at Austin, 1978.

O'Brien, James. "The Development of a New Left in the United States, 1960–65." Ph.D. diss., University of Wisconsin at Madison, 1971.

Olan, Susan T. "The Rag: A Study in Underground Journalism." M.A. thesis, University of Texas at Austin, 1981.

AAUP. *See* American Association of
University Professors
Abortion Laws, National Association
for the Repeal of (NARAL), 328
abortion legislation, 326–30
Abrahams, Roger, 140, 255
Adams, Dorothy, 74, 149
Adams, Jane, 304, 305–6
African Americans, 15, 45, 78, 118, 153
Afro Americans for Black Liberation
(AABL), 201
agape (love), 66–67, 367*n*35, 368*n*42,
371*n*98
AHRC. *See* Austin Human Relations
Commission
alienation, concepts of, 2–4, 7, 65, 162,
193, 282, 340–41, 348*n*2, 348*n*3; feel-
ings of, 97, 155, 195, 206, 284, 318,
340
Allen, Claude, 134, 135, 142, 153
Allred, Jimmy, 26, 35
American Association of University
Professors (AAUP), 27, 28

American Friends Service Committee
(AFSC), 108, 140
Americans for Democratic Action
(ADA), 355*n*25
Anderson, Chester, 315
androgyny, 428*n*67
Anti-Defamation League, 134
anti-imperialism, 221, 233, 323, 331
antiwar movement, 183–84, 407*n*11,
410*n*38–39; and coffeehouses,
231–32; early protests of, 214; in
Killeen, Texas, 230–31; and new
left, 209–46;
anxiety, 61, 82, 297–98, 344; age of, 3–4,
19–20, 53, 339, 348*n*5; fear of, 115,
162
Appenzellar, Anne, 95, 133–34
Armadillo Mayday Tribe, 240
Armadillo World Headquarters, 290
Arms, W. S., 140
Army Mathematics Research Center
(AMRC), 417*n*106
Aronowitz, Stanley, 211

Arrowsmith, William, 37
Austin Draft Information Center, 230
Austin for Peaceful Alternatives (APA), 139–40
Austin Gay Liberation, 225
Austin Human Relations Commission (AHRC), 46, 120–21, 134
Austin Women's Liberation, 312, 321–22, 329
authenticity, 53, 65, 68, 79, 97, 251; and alienation, 2–7, 18–19, 161–63, 164; and democracy, 23, 155; and folk music, 253–54; and liberalism, 11–12, 48–49; and masculinity, 16, 298–99, 300; and new left, 53, 160–64, 344; and racism, 115–16; search for, 8, 82–86, 93, 98, 150, 151, 339–40, 342
Ayer, G. W., 40
Ayres, Clarence, 30, 34–35, 41

back-to-the-land movement, 268
Baez, Joan, 255
Baker, Judy, 273
Bandung Conference, 106
Banks, Jimmie, 145
Bash, Lawrence, 87
Bell, Daniel, 265, 347*n*2, 436*n*2
Bell, Robert, 118, 125, 132
"beloved community," 7, 49, 83, 154, 162, 230, 333, 342
Bergman, Ingmar, 100
Berrigan, Daniel, 420*n*122
Berrigan, Philip, 420*n*122
Bigelow, Albert, 140
The Big Money (Dos Passos), 27
birth control activism, 326–30
Birth Control Information Center, 327–28
Black Panther Party (BPP), 176, 179, 200–2, 206
black power movement, 16, 187, 199,

259, 397*n*121. *See also* civil rights movement
Blanton, Brad, 128, 129, 140, 147, 153
Blanton, Judy Schleyer, 57, 81, 129, 153
Boatright, Mody, 129
Bonhoeffer, Dietrich, 62–63, 77, 84, 94, 176, 284; on breakthrough, 69, 71; and CFLC, 54, 55, 61, 66, 75; on community, 72–73
Bonner, Booker T., 128–29, 131, 140, 153
Bonner, Florence, 129, 153
Bookchin, Murray, 246
boundary-situation paradigm, 67, 70
Bower, Robert, 414*n*80
Boyd, Lois, 71–72
Brann, William, 31, 32
breakthrough, 68–70, 72
Breihan, Bob, 87–88, 169, 176, 216, 328
Breihan, Claire Johnson, 57, 81
Brenner, Becky, 178–79, 306
Briggs, Chett, 110, 145, 216
Brown, Dee, 140
Brown, Desta, 140
Brown v. Board of Education, 90, 637
Brunner, Emil, 69
Buck, Louis, 129
Buckley, William F., Jr., 215
Bultmann, Rudolf, 55
Burgeson, Travis, 236
Burlage, Dorothy, 38, 42, 71, 81, 135, 136, 152; and Camus, 36, 75; and civil rights movement, 165, 166; as foreign traveler, 39, 108
Burlage, Robb, 35–36, 43, 45, 135, 143, 152, 188; and civil rights movement, 151, 165, 166
Burns, Stoney, 176
Busby, Horace, 33
Bush, George, 200
Buss, Fred, 58

Cairns, Charles, 215, 218

Calvert, Greg, 192–93, 195–96, 199, 201, 204, 230–31; in SDS National Office, 305–6; and sexual revolution, 266; mentioned, 239, 242

Campus Chest, 89, 147–48

Campus Crusade for Christ, 54, 145, 365n1

Campus Interracial Committee (CIC), 143, 167, 173

campus ministry, 56, 68, 152

Camus, Albert, 7–8, 36, 75–76, 83, 100, 135, 162

capitalism: corporate, 218, 223, 275; culture of, 318

capital punishment issue, 38, 109–10

Carmichael, Stokely (Kwame Ture), 179, 185, 199, 263

Caroline, Larry, 197, 211, 288, 311; and Cuban revolution, 221–22; and Greenbriar School, 285

Carson, Rachel, 274

Carver, George Washington, 88

Cason, Casey. See Hayden, Casey

Castro, Fidel, 40–41, 221–22, 224, 225, 299

The Catcher in the Rye (Salinger), 100

Central High School (Little Rock), 45

Central Intelligence Agency (CIA), 43, 212–13

CEWV. See Committee to End the War in Vietnam

CFLC. See Christian Faith-and-Life Community

Chase, Richard, 415n81

Chicanos, 13, 323, 336, 355n26, 377n1. See also Mexican-American movement

Chilean Communist Party, 40

Chilean students exchange program, 40

Christian activism, 115

Christian Anti-Communist League (Dallas), 145

Christian existentialism, 6, 53–84, 349n9; and authenticity, 65, 68; and CFLC, 80–84

Christian Faith-and-Life Community (CFLC), 54–60, 62–64, 117, 127, 135, 137, 371n91; and avant-gardism, 72–80; and Christian existentialism, 80–82, 84; communal ideals of, 69–72; conventional approach of, 58; and University Y, 91–92, 146

Christianity: and liberalism, 12, 85–89, 92, 109, 113, 152; religionless, 54, 63

civil liberties, 30, 31, 43–44

Civil Rights in the North (Hayden), 103

Civil Rights in the South (Hayden), 103

civil rights legislation, 42, 173

civil rights movement, 6–7, 12–13, 23, 151, 187, 200, 338–39, 355n24; African Americans in, 116, 118–19, 120, 141, 153; and anti-Semitism, 73; and authenticity, 85, 339; beginning of, 49; and Christian movement, 12, 116; and community, 83; and internationalism, 109; and liberalism, 12, 86; and NSAY, 100; and political consciousness, 153; and social identities, 333; and Student Y movement, 6, 92, 100–1, 110–14; and violence, 173–75; and white students, 13, 15, 151, 164–65, 169, 187, 189–190, 299, 302; youth wing of, 6–7, 85, 116, 164. See also sit-in movement; stand-in demonstrations

Clark, Clarice, 318

Clark, Edd C., 36

Clark, Michele, 206, 224, 314

Clark, Sara, 217

Clay, John, 254, 257

Cleaver, Eldridge, 299

Cleaver, Grace, 201

Clebsch, William, 121

Clergy Consultation Service on Abortion (CCS), 328

Clinton, Sam Houston, Jr., 143
coal miner strike, 189
Coffee, Linda, 329
coffeehouses, GIs, 230–31
Coffin, William Sloane, 101
COINTELPRO (counterintelligence program), 337, 408n15
cold war, 44, 53, 57, 60, 106; liberalism in, 11, 12, 25; and Vietnam War, 209, 227
Committee on Racism and Apartheid (CORA), 228
Committee to End the War in Vietnam (CEWV), 215–18, 236, 243
communism, 3, 11, 17, 147, 148; Chinese, 221; and Christianity, 41; and violence, 125, 177
Communist Party, 120, 177
community, 78, 82, 424n25; and authenticity, 72; and CFLC, 69–72; countercultural, 249; and guilt, 69–70
Community United Front (CUF), 200
Communiversity. See Critical University
conformism, 49
Congress of Racial Equality (CORE), 130
Connally, John, 25, 144, 147, 182–83
conscientious objectors (CO), 90, 261
conservatism, 24, 41–42, 44, 49, 54
consumer culture, 98–99, 162, 267, 347n2, 387n14
cooperative movement, 281–87, 293
corporate liberals, 214
cosmic cowboys, 289–91, 434n126
counterculture, 8, 16, 247–95, 305, 315, 357n32, 393n78, 434nn133–34
The Courage to Be (Tillich), 65
Cowboys (UT fraternal organization), 58, 78, 173
Cox, Harvey, 63, 73, 86, 96, 107; at NSAY, 94–95, 101
Craven, Carolyn, 198–99

Critical University, 275, 283–84
Crozer Seminary (Chester, Pennsylvania), 90
Cuba, 40, 109, 140, 148, 213; revolution in, 164, 221–25, 411n46
CUF. See Community United Front (CUF)
cults, 70
cultural activism, 247, 259
cultural dissent, 53
Cuney, Pat, 236, 245, 272, 306, 336
Curry, Connie, 104

Daily Texan, 31, 43, 117, 129, 140, 241; on Cuba, 40; editors of, 33, 36; on integration, 46, 120; on loyalty oaths, 44; on NSA, 149–50; and Student Y, 96, 144–45, 148; and Texas Observer, 33–34, 123
Daily Worker, 124
Dallas Morning News, 145–46
Dallas Notes, 176
Daniel, Price, 47, 120
Darrell, Carol, 74, 149
Das Kapital (Marx), 223
Davidson, Carl, 192, 194
Davidson, Chandler, 87, 123–28, 130, 135, 152; at Daily Texan, 50–51
Days of Rage, 206
Deacons, 58
Deacons for Defense and Justice, 174
death culture, 19, 269–73, 429n68
Death of a Salesman (Miller), 98
death of God, 62
death penalty. See capital punishment
Decent and Indecent (Spock), 318
democracy, 3, 127, 344; participatory, 1, 10, 11, 349n8, 388n9
Democratic Coalition (Texas), 190, 216
Democratic National Convention: 1960, 105; 1968, 196, 243, 271, 418n110

Democratic Party, 47, 245
Denney, Jim, 236, 238, 311
Department of Defense (DoD), 219
desegregation. *See* civil rights movement; integration; segregation
desublimation, 266, 268
Dietz, Paul, 87, 88
DiEugenio, Louis, 273
Direct Action (group), 241–42
direct action (term), 192, 421n138
Dissent (magazine), 23
The Divine Right of Capital (Faulk), 30
Dobie, J. Frank, 11, 28, 254, 274
Dohrn, Bernardine, 204, 305–6, 441n36
domesticity, 437nn14–15, 438nn16–18
domino theory, 226–27
Dos Passos, John, 27
Doughface progressives, 17
draft resistance movement, 212, 229–30
Drag (Guadalupe Avenue, Austin), 46, 86, 125, 216; and integration, 119–20; theaters on, 128–29, 131, 134
Dreyer, Thorne, 176, 192, 194, 257–58, 260, 269
drug use, 179, 256–57, 390n31, 425n32
DuBois Clubs, 178–79
DuBose, Terry, 232
Duffy, Gavan, 244
Dugger, Ronnie, 79, 103, 135, 140, 184; and antiwar protests, 219–20, 246; and authenticity, 128; and capital punishment, 110; and civil rights, 48–49, 119, 142; and ecological activism, 274; and existentialism, 127; on liberalism, 32, 54–55; on Mathews, 54, 55; and stand-in demonstrations, 127, 131, 134; at *Texas Observer*, 12, 31–32, 33

Earth Day, 277
Echols, Alice, 299, 438n19, 443n57, 445n81
Ecology Action (EA), 277

economic growth, 162, 277
Economic Research and Action Projects (ERAP), 189, 303, 347n1
Edwards, Gloria, 201
Ehrenreich, Barbara, 266–67, 301, 330
Eickmann, Jo, 50
Eisenhower, Dwight D., 31, 45
Ellis, Lee, 197–98, 302
Embree, Alice, 167–72, 180, 185, 186, 197, 288–89, 325; and antiwar protests, 214–15; and co-op movement, 282, 286; Cuba visit of, 223; feminist activities of, 307–8, 312; and guerrilla theater, 314; and youth movement, 287
Enlightenment tradition, 278, 339, 342
environmental activism, 273–80
Epstein, Barbara, 344
ERAP. *See* Economic Research and Action Projects (ERAP)
Erickson, Charles, 127, 142
Erwin, Frank, 183–85, 275–76
Evangelical Christian Communion, 57
Evans, Sara, 301, 303, 305
existentialism, 4, 36, 340–41, 343, 348n8; Christian, 53–83; and counterculture, 249; and liberalism, 86, 92; and Mathews, 59; and political activism, 5, 7, 16, 19, 85, 104, 126–27, 388n19; vocabulary of, 5, 350n9
experimentalism, 95, 352n13
exploitation, 194, 348n2

Fair Labor Standards Act, 27
Faith-and-Life Community. *See* Christian Faith-and-Life Community
Fanshen (Hinton), 313
Farabee, Ray, 43
Farber, Jerry, 283
Farenthold, Frances, 244
fascism, 62, 202, 218
Fassnacht, Robert, 417n106

Fath, Creekmore, 25
Fatigue Press, 232
Faubus, Orval, 45, 47
Faulk, John Henry, 30, 118
Fellini, Federico, 100
Fellowship of Reconciliation, 125
fellowship of sitters, 111
The Feminine Mystique (Friedan), 264,
    308, 446n85
feminism, 80, 230, 297–333, 337,
    443n57; and abortion issue, 326–30,
    447n104; in Austin, 306–14, 320,
    321–22, 328, 329; cultural, 331–32,
    443n53; literature of, 322–23; and
    new left, 298–306; radical, 17–18,
    298, 313, 316, 318, 322, 330, 331,
    443n53, 448n108; and self-libera-
    tion, 16; and sexual revolution,
    268. *See also* gender relations;
    women
fidelismo, 224, 299, 412n54, 436n6
Fielder, Bill, 107
Flacks, Richard, 160
Flexner, Eleanor, 445n85
Flipped-out Week, 215, 263
Foe, Victoria, 245, 311, 323–24, 328–29,
    332
Folbre, Nancy, 275, 311
folk music, 253–55
Folksingers for Peace, 152–53
Ford, Susan, 98, 146
Fortas, Abe, 105
Fort Hood Three, 231, 414n80
Forty Acres Club, 395n97
Frankl, Viktor, 94
Franklin, Jennie, 111
Franklin, Jim, 256
Franklin, Vivien, 108, 128, 135, 144, 154,
    303; civil rights activism of, 136–37;
    and HUAC, 109–10; political
    activism of, 104–6; and Student
    Assembly, 149; and University Y,
    145, 146

Franklin-Alley, Rasjidah. *See* Franklin,
    Vivien
freaks, 257–58, 264. *See also* countercul-
    ture
Freedom Riders, 100, 165
freedom songs, 132
Freedom Summer (1964), 136, 153, 165,
    174
Freedom Village, 131
Freeman, Lee, 129
Free Speech Movement, 50, 174, 178,
    185, 297–98
free universities, 283–84, 293
Freudiger, Larry, 252, 258, 261, 269
Friedan, Betty, 8, 264–65, 272, 301, 308,
    319–20, 328
Friedman, Jeff, 431n92
Friends of Progressive Labor (FPL),
    179, 203
Fromm, Erich, 66, 79

Garvey, Ed, 148
Gates, John, 88
gay activism, 224, 238, 316. *See also*
    homosexuality
Gay Women's Liberation (GWL), 317
Geertz, Clifford, 79, 84
gender relations, 102, 437n15; and com-
    munism, 16–17; and leftist politics,
    181, 301, 305, 401n151, 436n6,
    438n19; and roles, 318–19, 331; and
    Student Y movement, 98, 303. *See
    also* feminism
Gentle Thursday, 258, 261–63, 269,
    426n46
Geren, Paul, 41
Ginsberg, Allen, 250, 256
Ginsburg, Ruth Bader, 330
Gitlin, Todd, 35–36, 189, 202, 257, 342,
    440n34; and co-op movement, 281,
    286; and free schools, 284; and
    white leftist students, 165
Godbold, Meg, 68, 76

Goldenson, Leonard, 133–34
Goldstein, Ernie, 130, 142
Goldwater, Barry, 209–10
Goodman, Paul, 224, 280, 297–98
Goodwyn, Lawrence, 33, 48, 190, 191, 248, 398*n*133
Goss, George, 137, 189, 213
Gosse, Van, 299, 436*n*2
Gould, Joshua, 231
Graham, Billy, 53
Gramsci, Antonio, 435*n*140
Gray, David, 218
Greenbriar School, 285
Gruening, Ernest, 214
guerrilla theater, 288, 313–14, 322
Guinn, Ed, 254, 256
Gulf of Tonkin resolution, 210, 214

Haber, Alan, 36, 103, 122, 135–36, 165, 188
Haile, Bartee, 393*n*78
Halberstam, David, 218
Hale, Edward Everett, Jr., 34
Hamilton, Charles, 199
Hamilton, Richard, 10
Hampton, Carl, 176
Hansel, Lori, 233–34, 239, 265; and women's liberation movement, 313–14
Hardie, Thornton, 139
Harrington, Michael, 135, 337, 449*n*11
Harris, David, 230
Hayden, Casey, 75, 102–4, 169, 187; activism of, 9, 76–77, 122–23, 136, 181, 274; on breakthrough, 70; feminist activities of, 302–3; on integration, 117; and Liberal Study Group, 165; marriage of, 103, 135–36, 381*n*60; on Mathews, 71; at NSAY, 106; at SDA, 124; at SNCC, 152; and stand-in demonstrations, 126, 127, 131; and Student Y movement, 80–146; on symbolism, 79; on Wright, 90

Hayden, Tom, 35–36, 122, 131, 148; on Faith-and-Life Community, 54; marriage of, 103, 135–36, 381*n*60; and *Port Huron Statement*, 81; and SDS, 165, 188, 213
Hays, Samuel, 274
Hedemann, Ed, 241–42
Hedemann, Grace, 241–42
Heinsohn, Ed, 87
Henry, Anthony, 43, 119
Hershey, Lewis, 193
Hester, Sue, 315
Highlander Folk School (Tennessee), 190
Hildreth, Laurie, 87
Hines, Barbara, 311, 322–23, 331
Hinton, William, 313
Hiroshima Day (August 1967), 220
Hitler, Adolf, 62
Hochfeld, Julian, 41
Hoffman, Abbie, 224, 287
Hofmann, Margret, 140
homosexuality, 27, 224–25, 238, 316, 317, 374*n*32, 441*n*37
Horton, Myles, 190
House Un-American Activities Committee (HUAC), 109–10, 145, 359*n*4
Howard, Dick, 194, 283
Howe, Irving, 165
HUAC. *See* House Un-American Activities Committee
Hudgins, Mildred, 57
Hughes, Sarah, 329–30
humanism, 7, 68, 94–95, 99, 217, 351*n*12; and Christian existentialism, 61
Humphrey, Hubert, 177, 243
Huston-Tillotson College, 173

identity politics, 343–44, 450*n*20–21
images, 97, 98; and symbolism, 78–79
individualism, 41, 49, 58, 99

Industrial Workers of the World
(IWW), 160, 179, 192–93, 282–83,
325–26, 432n107
Institute for Latin American Studies
(UT), 148
integration, 39, 45; athletic, 139, 143;
dormitory, 118, 137–38, 139, 141–43,
173; and free enterprise, 133; psychological, 96–97. *See also* civil
rights movement
Intercollegian (magazine), 135
internationalism, 40, 41, 43
International Student Peace Seminar,
108
interracial activism, 116, 121, 187, 188
Iona experiment, 56
IWW. *See* Industrial Workers of the
World

Jackson, Larry, 197, 200–1, 203
Jaffe, Naomi, 306
Jaworski, Leon, 105, 144
Jim Crow laws, 34, 45, 48, 91, 132, 166,
168, 181
John Birch Society, 42, 171
John Brown Revolutionary League
(JBRL), 393n78
Johnson, Harold K., 218–19
Johnson, Lee Otis, 176, 200
Johnson, Lynda Bird, 167
Johnson, Lyndon B., 32, 105, 144,
181–84, 243, 395n97, 396n105;
Vietnam policy of, 209–10, 227
Jones, Glenn, 263
Jones, Jeff, 204, 236, 266, 311, 335–36
Jones, Joseph, 108
Joplin, Janis, 254
Jordan, Gwen, 111, 138
justice: and community, 72; racial, 48,
113; social, 163, 339

Kaufmann, Walter, 60–61
Kendall, Arnie, 285

Kendall, Judy, 215
Keniston, Kenneth, 3, 4
Kennan, George, 3, 217
Kennedy, John F., 3, 47, 140, 150, 171,
224, 382n74
Kennedy, Robert, 210
Kerner Commission, 271
Kerr, Clark, 50, 182, 219
Kerrville conference, 98, 100
Kershaw, A. L., 93–94, 96
kerygma ("good news"), 73, 76
Kesey, Ken, 248, 256
Key, V. O., 47
Kierkegaard, Sören, 60, 64, 74
Killeen, Texas, 231–32, 313
King, David, 330
King, Marsha, 330
King, Martin Luther, Jr., 6, 66–67, 90,
293
King, Mary, 152, 302–3
Kinsolving dormitory protest, 141–42
Knights of Labor, 201
Kopkind, Andrew, 187
Kropotkin, Piotr, 36
Ku Klux Klan, 172, 176
Kwame Ture (Stokely Carmichael),
179, 185, 199, 263

labor disputes, 10, 23–24, 201, 326,
385n106
Landrum, Lynn, 88
Lane, Mark, 171
Lanham, Connie, 324
Lasch, Christopher, 4–5, 17
Latin American Policy Alternatives
Group (LAPAG), 324
Laughlin, Charlie, 110, 137, 141, 145,
152–53
Lawrence, D. H., 270
lay renewal movement, 56
Lears, T. J. Jackson, 4
leftism. *See* new left; old left
Lenin, V. I., 223

lesbian feminists, 317. *See also* gay
   activism; homosexuality
Letters and Papers from Prison
   (Bonhoeffer), 62
Lewis, Mike, 232
Lewis, W. Jack, 66, 70, 75; and CFLC,
   56, 58, 81
liberal cosmopolitanism, 42
liberalism, 347*n*2; backlash against,
   150; in civil rights movement, 113,
   141, 150, 170; *versus* conservatism,
   24, 42; cultural, 16, 291–95;
   humanist, 214, 319; and irreverence, 29; political, 86, 252, 295,
   330, 332; and religion, 61, 87, 116,
   373*n*16; secular, 23, 48, 88, 109; and
   social issues, 124; in Texas, 29–30,
   48, 110
Liberal Study Group, 36, 43, 150, 165
liberation theology, 73
Life Together (Bonhoeffer), 69
Lingo, Al, 59, 76, 77, 78, 81; at CFLC,
   58, 79
Littlefield, Ira, 256
Loader, Jayne, 315
Lockett, Sandy, 256
Lomax, John, 254
Long, Emma, 30
love, 151, 293; and authenticity, 67; as
   Christian theme, 83; and community, 72–73; and death, 269–70;
   society of, 153. *See also agape*
loyalty oaths, 43–44
Lubbock, Texas, 172, 178
Lynd, Staughton, 230, 239, 298, 337

Macdonald, Dwight, 278–79
machismo, 224, 230, 299
Magidoff, Dickie, 198
Mahler, Dave, 284–85
Mailer, Norman, 162, 270, 299
male chauvinism. *See* sexism
Manire, Larry, 107

Mansfield, Texas, 45
Mao Zedong, 179, 201
Marcel, Gabriel, 55, 74
Marcuse, Herbert, 250, 267–69, 288,
   309, 322–23
Marshall (Texas), 120, 126
Marx, Karl, 7, 196
Marxism, 7, 32, 170, 176–77, 193, 197,
   223
Marxism-Leninism, 180, 235
masculinity, 16–18, 224, 230, 299,
   358*n*33–34, 412*n*55, 437*n*11
Maslow, Abraham, 8
materialism, 98–99. *See also* consumer
   culture
Mathews, Joseph Wesley, 55, 59–60, 75,
   81, 102, 135–36, 153; and authentic-
   ity, 72; and breakthrough, 70; at
   CFLC, 54, 59; and Silber, 80, 100;
   and symbolism, 79
Mathis, Don, 42
Maverick, Maury, 25
Maxwell, Bruce, 153–54
Maxwell, Mary Gay, 95
Mayday activities (1971), 240, 418*n*111
McCarthy, Joseph, 23, 31
McCord, James I., 56, 59
McCorvey, Norma, 329–30, 447*n*102
McDew, Charles, 122, 165
McGee, Jay, 288
McGovern, George, 243–44
McWilliams, Carey, 101
Meachem, Bill, 204–5, 272, 313–14
Meinig, D. W., 13–14
A Memory of People (Neyland), 100
Merritt, Barbara, 311, 316, 332
Mexican Americans, 13, 116–17, 152,
   356*n*26, 377*n*1, 404*n*82
Mexican-American movement, 13, 152,
   323, 355*n*26, 385*n*106, 404*n*82
Michalson, Carl, 66, 68
military-industrial complex, 182–85,
   218–19

Miller, Arthur, 98
Miller, James, 164, 348*n*8, 388*n*19
Miller, Tom, 120
Mills, C. Wright, 2, 29, 35, 50, 160–61, 214, 360*n*15, 364*n*72, 386*n*9, 436*n*2; on civil liberties, 30–31; and Cuban revolution, 221–22, 224; and machismo, 161, 224, 297–98, 436*n*3; power elite concept of, 182, 396*n*102; writings of, 124
Mims, Bud, 34
Minkoff, Bobby, 177, 250, 285, 306
Minkoff, Trudy, 306
minstrel shows, 78, 173
Mintz, Charles, 134
Minutemen, 171, 175
The Misunderstanding (Camus), 100
The Mobe (National Mobilization Committee Against the War in Vietnam), 215
modernism, 61, 63, 350*n*10, 391*n*48; cultural, 339
Momism, 300–1, 437*n*15. *See also* domesticity
Montgomery, Robert, 35
morality, 49, 82
Moratorium (1969), 219, 234, 238, 239
Morgan, Edward P., 134
Morgan, Robin, 17, 307–8
Morris, Celia, 39
Morris, Willie, 28, 33, 38, 123
Morrison, Robert, 137
Morse, Wayne, 214
Mother's Grits Troupe, 287–88
multiversity, 182, 189
Muniz, Ramsey, 244
Murray, Martin, 245
music industry, 253–55, 256, 288–89

Nader, Ralph, 278
National Conference for New Politics (NCNP), 187, 299, 397*n*121

National Defense Education Act (NDEA), 44, 377*n*1
National Liberation Front (NLF), 213, 227
National Mental Health Association, 90
National Mobilization Committee Against the War in Vietnam, 215
National Organization for Women (NOW), 308, 328
National Peace Action Coalition, 419*n*115
National Student Assembly of the Y (NSAY), 93–101, 106, 111, 116
National Student Association (NSA), 43, 103–4, 104, 106, 122, 130, 148–49; Congresses of, 36, 42; and Cuba visits, 40
National Student Christian Federation, 109
National Student Council of Y, 93, 94
Neill, A. S., 284
Neiman, Carol, 230–31
Nelson, Bobbie, 326
Nelson, Willie, 290
neoorthodoxy, 60–62
Neumann, Franz, 436*n*2
New American Movement (NAM), 337
New Being, 67, 68–69, 94
new class, 247, 421*n*2
new left: activism of, 11, 242, 245, 337; and anti-imperialism, 233; and antiwar activism, 1, 209–46; and authenticity, 53, 160–64, 344; and capitalism, 318; and civil rights movement, 163–64, 389*n*25; and counterculture, 247–52, 253; cultural revolt of, 301; and death culture, 269; demise of, 335–45; and ecological activism, 275–76, 280; emergence of, 1, 86, 115, 159; existential politics of, 8, 388*n*19; and femi-

nism, 298–306, 318; hegemonic aspirations of, 294; and imperialism, 225; interpretations of, 349*n*8; and liberalism, 170, 291–95; and marginal groups, 15; and Progressive Labor, 205; radicalism of, 18–19, 294–95, 341; and sexual revolution, 264; and university reform, 182, 264–65; women in, 180–81, 298, 436*n*5

New Left Notes, 304

New Man concept, 223–25

New Republic, 35, 130

new working class, 16, 184, 193–94, 201, 205, 251, 259, 304–5, 336, 357*n*31, 400*n*148, 401*n*149, 421*n*2

Neyland, Jim, 98–99, 105, 135–36, 138, 154; civil rights activism of, 136–37; and sit-in movement, 111; and Student Y movement, 94, 96, 101, 137, 144, 146; at Urban Life Project, 133–34

Ngo Dinh Diem, 213

Nhu, Madame, 213

Nicol, Myra, 99, 101

Niebuhr, H. Richard, 59, 94

Niebuhr, Reinhold, 64, 65, 272

Nieman, Carol, 192

Niemann, Doyle, 236

Nightbyrd, Jeff Shero, 9, 169, 191, 199, 386*n*4; on cowboy identity, 290; and folk singing, 252–53; and *Port Huron Statement*, 250; and SDS, 159, 164–66, 188–89, 213; and sexual revolution, 264–66; starts *Rat*, 307–8; on Vietnam War, 215, 226–28

Nixon, Richard M., 202, 211, 243

nonviolence, 121, 125, 235, 242, 379*n*25; and antiwar movement, 233; and SDS, 136; and sit-in movement, 111

North American Congress on Latin America (NACLA), 307

NOW (National Organization for Women), 308, 328

Nowotny, Arno, 144

NSA. *See* National Student Association

NSAY (National Student Assembly of the Y), 93–101, 106, 111, 116

Oakes, Rosalie, 90–91, 108

Oates, Stephen, 141

Observer. See Texas Observer

O'Daniel, Pappy, 26–27

Oglesby, Carl, 167, 214, 220, 226, 243, 344

Olan, Susan, 262

old left, 1, 124, 222–23

Olds, Greg, 191

Olian, Mo, 138–39, 142

Operation Abolition (HUAC film), 109

Operation Duck Hook, 418*n*111

Operation Friendship, 40

Operation Rolling Thunder, 210

The Organization Man (Whyte), 99, 299

Out of Sight, Out of Mind (Wright), 90

pacifism, 87, 90, 388*n*18

Packard, Vance, 49, 51

Palter, Robert, 215

pantheism, 98

Parades, Americo, 140

Pardun, Judy, 195. *See also* Perez, Judy

Pardun, Robert, 168–73, 174, 185, 190, 191, 212, 251, 257; on gender relations, 181; on Progressive Labor, 203; on social radicalism, 318; on student exploitation, 194

PCPJ. *See* People's Coalition for Peace and Justice

peace activism, 150, 210

Peace Corps, 107

Peck, Abe, 260

People's Coalition for Peace and Justice (PCPJ), 241, 419*n*115

People's Music festival, 289

Perez, Judy, 168, 174, 190, 195, 266

Permanent Fund, 37

Person, Ralph, 140, 143

Peterson, Bruce, 231

Petrick, Howard, 414*n*80

Pickle, Jake, 310

Picnic for Peace, 140

Piercy, Marge, 307–8

Pine Hill (New York, 1964), 159, 169

Pipkin, Paul, 168, 171, 185, 187, 190, 226, 266

PIRG. *See* Public Interest Research Groups

Pittman, Charlotte, 198

Pittman, Scott, 168, 198, 205

PL. *See* Progressive Labor Party

Plamondon, Genie, 394*n*78

Plamondon, Pun, 394*n*78

pluralism, political, 342, 343, 450*n*16

police hostility, 109, 129, 176, 200

political activism: and anxiety, 19, 53; and CFLC, 76–77; and community, 73; influence of, 20; liberal, 100, 114; militant, 115, 140–41, 149, 241, 421*n*138; and music, 253; and poverty, 2; and Student Y movement, 102, 152

Poorman, Wesley, 77

populism, 23, 35, 356*n*27

Port Huron Conference, 36, 43, 80, 166, 303. *See also* Students for a Democratic Society

Port Huron Statement, 2, 5, 137, 138, 159, 164, 220, 337; and Christian existentialism, 81, 82, 83, 84; and values, 250–51

postmodernism, 343

postscarcity politics, 2, 162, 249, 338, 341

Potter, Paul, 148, 212, 226

power elite, 181–82, 185, 218

The Power Elite (Mills), 29, 124

prairie power, 9, 159–60

Pravda, 124

Price, Ed, 146

professional-managerial class, 421*n*2. *See also* new class

Progressive Labor Party (PL), 179–80, 200, 222, 235

progressive movement, 48, 50

Protestantism, liberal, 61, 116, 373*n*16

Public Interest Research Groups (PIRG), 278

racial issues, 153, 338; Barbara Smith case (1954), 37; and CFLC Women's Branch, 59, 78; and Christian student movement, 6; and new left radicals, 14–15; during 1950s, 46–47, 51; and Student Y movement, 110–14; in Texas, 47. *See also* civil rights movement; integration; segregation

racism, 48, 77–78, 119, 142, 162

radicalism, 8, 15, 48, 95, 150, 151, 244, 354*n*19&22; political, 72, 114, 282; social, 282, 318, 332

Rag, 187, 191, 192, 224, 236, 239, 243, 258, 259–63; and activism, 279, 335; and Greenbriar School, 285; and sexual revolution, 267; and violence, 273; and women's liberation movement, 306, 308–11, 315, 317, 326, 328, 329; mentioned, 326, 328, 329

Rainey, Homer Price, 25, 26–28, 33, 34, 88

Ramparts, 43

Randall, Margaret, 323

Randolph, Frankie, 25, 30, 31

Ranger, 254

Ransom, Harry, 37, 38, 50, 56, 99, 142, 178, 185

Rat, 306, 307–8

read-ins, 137–38

Reavis, Becky, 202
Reavis, Dick, 178–80, 185, 186, 200–2, 306
reconciliation, 69, 151, 338
red-baiting, 89, 127
red-diaper babies, 40, 165, 399*n*135
Redstockings, 444*n*57, 445*n*81
Reed, Susan, 98, 99, 108, 138, 139; and Student Y movement, 144, 145, 146
Reich, Wilhelm, 288, 323
religion: Christianity without, 54, 63; comparative study of, 62; freedom of, 44–45; and liberalism, 61, 87, 116, 373*n*16
Religious Student Liberals (RSL), 216
Religious Workers' Association (RWA), 111, 117, 118
Republican Party, 24, 145
restaurant demonstrations, 119–21, 173
Reynolds, Malvina, 248
Riesman, David, 339
right-wing extremism, 26, 175. *See also* conservatism
Robinson, John A. T., 63
Roe v. Wade, 327–30, 447*n*104
Roosevelt, Eleanor, 130
Roosevelt, Franklin D., 25
Rowan, Carl, 101
Rozsak, Theodore, 278
Rusk, Dean, 177
Russell, Philip, 223–24, 229, 324
Russell, Steve, 235–36, 241, 315
RWA. *See* Religious Workers' Association

SA. *See* Student Assembly
Sanders, Leroy, 143
Saulsberry, Charlie, 179
Savio, Mario, 50, 182
SCEF. *See* Southern Conference Education Fund (SCEF)
Schlesinger, Arthur, Jr., 3, 17, 108, 161; and anxiety, 53, 62, 82, 297, 344

Schleyer, Judy. *See* Blanton, Judy Schleyer
Schmidt, O. R., 57
Scott Circle, 240
Schouvaloff, Andy, 132
Schumacher, E. F., 280
Scoggins, Howard, 416*n*91
SDA. *See* Students for Direct Action
SDS. *See* Students for a Democratic Society
"The Search for Authentic Experience" (1958 Student Y conference), 6, 93
The Secular City (Cox), 63, 94
Seeger, Pete, 137
Seeliger, Wesley, 100
segregation, 6–7, 38, 104, 162; in Texas, 45–46, 118–19, 143, 363*n*59. *See also* civil rights movement; integration
Selective Service System (SSS), 193, 215, 229
sexism, 198, 202, 268, 304, 308, 441*n*35, 442*n*38; in Cuba, 224–25
sexual revolution, 264–68, 316
The Shaking of the Foundations (Tillich), 65
Shank, Barry, 254, 290
Shattuck, Roger, 37, 130
Shelton, Gilbert, 256
Shero, Jeffrey. *See* Nightbyrd, Jeff Shero
Shivers, Allan, 31, 45
shock therapy, 133–34
Silber, John, 37–38, 41, 130, 142, 197, 335, 402*n*167; and capital punishment, 38, 110; and Mathews debate, 79–80, 100; and Vietnam War, 227–28
Silent Spring (Carson), 274
Simons, Jim, 244
Simpson, Dick, 98, 107, 127, 138, 139, 146, 153; and CFLC, 54, 81; on integration, 117
Simpson, Henry, 119

Simpson, Mary, 119, 142
Singler, Melissa, 236
Sisterhood Is Powerful (anthology), 307
sit-in movement, 85, 100, 111, 116, 118, 119–22, 378*n*6, 383*n*79
Slicker, Joe, 60
SLID. *See* Student League for Industrial Democracy
slogans, 133
Small Is Beautiful (Schumacher), 280
Smiley, Glenn, 125, 379*n*25
Smith, Barbara, 34, 37
Smith, Frank, 44–45
Smith, Blake, 87, 88, 129
Smith, Block, 89–90
Smith, Charlie, 10, 159–61, 169, 174, 213
Smith, Henry Nash, 32, 49
Smith, Judy, 205, 237, 245, 261, 324, 328, 331–32; and ecological activism, 274, 277; and feminism, 308–13, 316, 318–22; and sexual revolution, 266; on violence, 272–73
Smith, Linda, 308–10, 331
SNCC. *See* Student Nonviolent Coordinating Committee
Snyder, Gary, 280
social change, 85, 103, 150, 153, 344
social gospel tradition, 11, 85, 87–92, 88, 152, 372*n*13
socialism, 39, 40–41, 109, 278; libertarian, 237–38, 316, 339, 401*n*151
Socialist Workers Party (SWP), 216–17, 234–35, 238
solidarity, 7, 15, 342, 387*n*13
Soul on Ice (Cleaver), 299
Southern Baptist Convention, 147
Southern Christian Leadership Conference (SCLC), 120, 178
Southern Conference Education Fund (SCEF), 192
Southerners, 73; and civil rights movement, 24

Southern Methodist University (SMU), 88, 107
Southern Student Organizing Committee (SSOC), 191–92
South Texas Nuclear Project, 277
Southwest Regional Conference (YMCA-YWCA), 97, 101–2, 106–7, 109–10, 122, 145
Southwest Student Action Coordinating Committee (SSACC), 136–37
SP. *See* Student Party
SPAC. *See* Swarthmore Political Action Committee
Space City News, 176
speaking American, 14, 160, 356*n*28
speaking bitterness, 313
Spear, Irwin, 130, 216, 227
Spearman, William, 143–44
Speck, Bob, 174, 194, 195, 198–99, 302
Spencer, Paul, 306
spirituality, 12, 82
Spock, Benjamin, 318
SPU. *See* Student Peace Union
SSACC. *See* Southwest Student Action Coordinating Committee
SSOC. *See* Southern Student Organizing Committee (SSOC)
St. John, Powell, 254
stand-in demonstrations, 125, 127–31, 137, 152, 379*n*27, 380*n*43, 381*n*53
Stanford, Keith, 68, 74
Steer Here Committee, 46, 119
Stein, Brent, 176
Stone, Harvey, 193, 243, 284
Stone, I. F., 212
Stone, Robert, 122, 140, 150
student activism, 10, 18, 114, 115, 150, 385*n*106; and alienation, 2–3; in Austin, 33, 86; and Christian movement, 6; and NSA, 43; and radicalism, 95; and socialism, 41. *See also* Student Y movement

Student Assembly (SA), 33, 43, 92, 149; and integration, 46, 121; Steer Here Committee of, 46, 119

student bill of rights, 182

Student Christian Movement of Cuba, 109

student exchange programs, 106

Student League for Industrial Democracy (SLID), 115, 150. *See also* Students for a Democratic Society (SDS)

Student Mobilization Committee (SMC), 234–38

Student Nonviolent Coordinating Committee (SNCC), 7, 80, 136, 162, 165, 174, 230; and black power, 16, 259; in Dallas, 176; formation of, 85, 100, 116; races in, 198; and sexism, 152, 198, 302–5; and stand-in demonstrations, 130

Student Party (SP), 138–39, 149

Student Peace Union (SPU), 139, 213

student power, 138, 182, 192

Students for a Democratic Society (SDS), 1–2, 7, 16, 35, 36, 42, 80, 103–4 115, 135–36; and black power, 259; collapse of, 196–207, 233, 335; conference (1965), 185, 197–98, 209–10, 212, 214; conventions of, 159, 160, 192, 200; formation of, 10, 42; National Council resolution, 211; National Office (Chicago), 10, 195, 200, 203, 204; old guard, 159–60, 165–66, 169, 213, 303–4; and postliberal activists, 115; Texas chapter of, 9, 165–66, 171–73, 176, 181, 184, 185, 189, 195, 214; Weatherman contingent of, 202–4, 222, 239, 314; women in, 17, 302–6, 308, 314. *See also* Port Huron Conference; *Port Huron Statement*

Students for Direct Action (SDA), 123, 127–32, 134–35, 138, 144; and

dormitory integration lawsuit, 142–43; Statement of Purpose of, 125–26

Students for Strikers, 336

student syndicalism, 192. *See also* new working class

Student Y movement, 95, 111, 112, 181; committees of, 96, 98, 102, 103, 113; described, 89; and education system, 99; gendered organization of, 98, 303; internationalism of, 106–7; and racial equality in the South, 91; search for authenticity of, 98. *See also* Young Men's Christian Association-Young Women's Christian Association

Summerhill (Neill), 284

Summer of Love, 249

Summer of Support, 230

"summer soldiers," 48

Supreme Court: *Brown v. Board of Education*, 6, 37, 90; *Roe v. Wade*, 327–30, 447n104; on segregation, 45, 117

Swarthmore Political Action Committee (SPAC), 165–66, 389n28

Swartz, Linda, 320

Sweatt, Heman Marion, 46, 116–17

Systematic Theology (Tillich), 65

Taniguchi, Alan, 274

teach-in movement, 210

Tejanos, 13, 323, 336, 355n26, 377n1. *See also* Mexican-American movement

Texan. See Daily Texan

Texas Board of Pardons and Paroles, 110

Texas Democratic Coalition (TDC), 398n133

Texas Observer, 12, 14, 31, 48, 110, 129, 191; and *Daily Texan*, 33–34, 123

Texas Society for the Abolition of Capital Punishment, 38, 110

Texas Southern University, 120
Texas Student Ecumenical Council, 147
Texas Student Publications (TSP), 33
Texas Tech University, 172, 178
theater protests. *See* stand-in demonstrations
therapeutic culture, 8, 350*n*10
Thiher, Gary, 180, 266, 307–8
Third World: nationalism in, 77, 107, 132, 304; revolutionaries in, 222–23, 225, 228, 229
Thomas, Norman, 122, 140, 150
Thompson, Joann, 81
Threadgill, Kenneth, 254
Tillerson, Don, 141
Tillich, Paul, 58, 66, 68, 71, 79, 367*n*35; on alienation, 4; on authenticity, 98; on Being, 4, 67, 84, 93–94; and boundary situation, 69, 84; on existentialism, 61–62; on personality, 319; theological development of, 64–65
totalitarianism, 223, 272, 293, 321
Tougaloo Southern Christian College, 112–13
Tower, John, 310
Trotskyists, 234–38, 241, 332, 415*n*88, 416*n*91
TSP. *See* Texas Student Publications
Ture, Kwame (Stokely Carmichael), 179, 185, 199, 263
Turning the Guns Around (Waterhouse and Wizard, comp.), 231
Turn toward Peace, 139
"The Unbeliever and Christians" (Camus), 75–76

United Farm Workers (UFW), 385*n*106
United Front against Fascism, 202
University Freedom Movement (UFM), 215, 216

University of Texas (Austin): as center of new left activism, 9; Charter of, 26; conservative Protestantism at, 54; foreign students at, 77; Law School of, 37, 46, 116–17, 142, 186; presidents of, 25; regents of, 29, 138–39, 142–43; during 1940s and 1950s, 33; student housing at, 46
University of Texas Committee to End the War in Vietnam (UTCEWV), 215–17, 230
University Religious Council (URC), 111, 128
University Y (Austin), 54, 86, 88, 89, 98, 146; and civil rights movement, 109, 111, 125, 175; function of, 108–9; funding for, 89, 145–47; integration of, 90–91; and liberal activism, 144; Race Relations Committee of, 103, 113. *See also* Student Y movement
"University YM(?)A" (Banks), 145
urban riots, 271
UT. *See* University of Texas (Austin)
UTCEWV. *See* University of Texas Committee to End the War in Vietnam
utopianism, 339–40, 342

Veblen, Thorstein, 34
Venceremos Brigade, 222
Vietnam Summer campaign, 215
Vietnam Veterans Against the War (VVAW), 232–33, 241, 419*n*115, 425*n*32
Vietnam War, 174, 175, 182, 184, 215; analysis of, 220, 226; and death culture, 269–70; and new left, 1, 221; and SDS protests, 177, 209–20. *See also* antiwar movement
violence, 174–80, 270–73, 272
Vizard, George, 169, 174–80, 185, 193
Voetmann, Kay, 43, 47

Vogel, Bea, 278–80, 320
VVAW. *See* Vietnam Veterans Against
    the War

Waco, Texas, 31, 32, 120
Wade, Houston, 124, 127, 130, 134, 135,
    149–50, 152; on democracy, 126; and
    dormitory integration lawsuit,
    142–43; and read-ins, 137–38
Waiting for Godot (Beckett), 80, 100
Walker, Edwin, 146–47, 171
Wallace, George, 271, 288
Waller Creek Massacre, 274–79, 284
Warren, Don, 74
War Resisters League, 241
Waterhouse, Larry, 209–10, 231
Weatherman faction, 202–6, 239, 314,
    417*n*107; and Cuban revolution, 222
Weber, Max, 279
Weddington, Sarah, 329
Weedon, Don, 200
weightlessness, 4–5, 162, 339
Weinstein, James, 337, 341, 407*n*8
Welfare Rights Organization,
    National, 303
Wells, Lyn, 322
Wenner, Jann, 281
Wheelis, Jim, 329–30, 331
White, Betty, 236
White Collar (Mills), 300
The White Negro (Mailer), 299
White Panthers, 176
white supremacy, 24. *See also* racism
Whitman, Charles, 175
Why Are We in Vietnam? (Mailer), 270
Whyte, William, 299
Wiener, Jon, 281
Wiginton, Martin, 216, 239, 288
Wiley College (Marshall, Texas), 121
Wilkerson, Cathy, 304
Wilkerson, Doxey, 120
Williams, Raymond, 293
Williams, William A., 225, 407*n*8

Willis, Ellen, 443*n*53, 443*n*57, 445*n*81
Wilson, Ed, 290
Wilson, Logan, 30, 34, 37, 88, 119
Wimberley legal defense conference,
    204
Winter Soldiers, 233
Wizard, Mariann, 168–72, 174–81,
    199–200, 203, 215, 244, 257, 288, 341;
    and counterculture, 250
Wobblies. *See* Industrial Workers of
    the World
women: and authenticity, 301; in
    CFLC, 57; in new left, 180–81, 298,
    302–6, 436*n*5, 439*n*28; parietal rules
    and, 264–65; psychology of, 317–20,
    447*n*102; and sexual revolution,
    264–66, 438*n*9; at Student Y, 103,
    152; in Texas, 39. *See also* feminism;
    sexism
Women's Liberation Conference
    (1970), 312
women's liberation movement. *See*
    feminism
Women Strike for Peace (WSP), 215
Woodstock Nation, 287, 289
World University Service, 147
Worthington, Leo, 173
Wright, Frank, 86, 90, 102, 109, 139,
    146; at University Y, 54, 95, 145

YAF. *See* Young Americans for
    Freedom
Yarborough, Don, 147
Yarborough, Ralph, 34, 190
Young, Suzy, 113
Young Americans for Freedom (YAF),
    42, 145, 173
Young Democrats, 34, 121, 128, 132, 147,
    359*n*2
Young Lords, 206
Young Men's Christian Association-
    Young Women's Christian
    Association (YMCA-YWCA), 6,

41, 42, 43, 80, 86, 146; committees of, 96, 98, 102, 103, 113. *See also* University Y
Young People's Socialist League (YPSL), 170
Young Republicans, 147, 174

Young Socialist Alliance (YSA), 236
Young Turks, 25

Zilker Park rally, 140
Zuck, Mel, 108, 140

Lawrence S. Wittner, *Rebels Against War: The American Peace Movement, 1941-1960*   1969

Davis R. B. Ross, *Preparing for Ulysses: Politics and Veterans During World War II*   1969

John Lewis Gaddis, *The United States and the Origins of the Cold War, 1941-1947*   1972

George C. Herring, Jr., *Aid to Russia, 1941-1946: Strategy, Diplomacy, the Origins of the Cold War*   1973

Alonzo L. Hamby, *Beyond the New Deal: Harry S. Truman and American Liberalism*   1973

Richard M. Fried, *Men Against McCarthy*   1976

Steven F. Lawson, *Black Ballots: Voting Rights in the South, 1944-1969*   1976

Carl M. Brauer, *John F. Kennedy and the Second Reconstruction*   1977

Maeva Marcus, *Truman and the Steel Seizure Case: The Limits of Presidential Power*   1977

Morton Sosna, *In Search of the Silent South: Southern Liberals and the Race Issue*   1977

Robert M. Collins, *The Business Response to Keynes, 1929-1964*   1981

Robert M. Hathaway, *Ambiguous Partnership: Britain and America, 1944-1947*   1981

Leonard Dinnerstein, *America and the Survivors of the Holocaust*   1982

Lawrence S. Wittner, *American Intervention in Greece, 1943-1949*   1982

Nancy Bernkopf Tucker, *Patterns in the Dust: Chinese-American Relations and the Recognition Controversy, 1949-1950*   1983

Catherine A. Barnes, *Journey from Jim Crow: The Desegregation of Southern Transit* 1983

Steven F. Lawson, *In Pursuit of Power: Southern Blacks and Electoral Politics, 1965–1982* 1985

David R. Colburn, *Racial Change and Community Crisis: St. Augustine, Florida, 1877–1980* 1985

Henry William Brands, *Cold Warriors: Eisenhower's Generation and the Making of American Foreign Policy* 1988

Marc S. Gallicchio, *The Cold War Begins in Asia: American East Asian Policy and the Fall of the Japanese Empire.* 1988

Melanie Billings-Yun, *Decision Against War: Eisenhower and Dien Bien Phu* 1988

Walter L. Hixson, *George F. Kennan: Cold War Iconoclast* 1989

Robert D. Schulzinger, *Henry Kissinger: Doctor of Diplomacy* 1989

Henry William Brands, *The Specter of Neutralism: The United States and the Emergence of the Third World, 1947–1960* 1989

Mitchell K. Hall, *Because of Their Faith: CALCAV and Religious Opposition to the Vietnam War* 1990

David L. Anderson, *Trapped By Success: The Eisenhower Administration and Vietnam, 1953–1961* 1991

Steven M. Gillon, *The Democrats' Dilemma: Walter F. Mondale and the Liberal Legacy* 1992

Wyatt C. Wells, *Economist in an Uncertain World: Arthur F. Burns and the Federal Reserve, 1970–1978* 1994